Real World
Adobe Photoshop CS3

Industrial-Strength Production Techniques

David Blatner
Conrad Chavez
Bruce Fraser

**Peachpit
Press**

Adobe

Real World Adobe Photoshop CS3

David Blatner, Conrad Chavez, and Bruce Fraser

Copyright © 2008 by Angela Reitz, David Blatner, and Conrad Chavez

Peachpit Press

1249 Eighth Street, Berkeley, CA 94710
510/524-2178 Fax: 510/524-2221

Find us on the Web at www.peachpit.com.

Peachpit Press is a division of Pearson Education.

Real World Adobe Photoshop CS3 is published in association with Adobe Press.

Project Editors: Rebecca Freed, Susan Rimerman
Copyeditor: Jennifer Berger
Production Editor: Lisa Brazieal
Cover Designer: Charlene Charles-Will
Cover illustration: Gordon Studer
Indexer: Rebecca Plunkett

ISBN-13   978-0-321-51868–2
ISBN-10   0-321-51868–3
9 8 7 6 5 4 3 2 1

Printed and bound in the United States of America

For Bruce

1954–2006

Longtime co-author, friend, expert, mentor, demystifier
www.brucefraserlegacy.com

&

For Fay, Harry, Ann, Abe, Katie, and Rita,
who laid the foundation in my family. —David

For Vincent Chavez, 1920–2007. —Conrad

To Jamie
happy Photoshoppin' !
Conrad

Contents

What's Inside

Chapter 4: Color Settings

Chapter 5: Building a Digital Workflow

Chapter 6: Essential Photoshop Tips and Tricks

Chapter 7: Image Adjustment Fundamentals

Chapter 8: The Digital Darkroom

Chapter 9: Making Selections

Chapter 10: Sharpness, Detail, and Noise Reduction

Chapter 11: Essential Image Techniques

Chapter 12: Image Storage and Output

Introduction

Photoshop in the Real World

If you're reading this book because you want to produce embossed type, fractalized tree branches, or spherized images in Adobe Photoshop, you're in the wrong place. There are (at least) half a dozen good books on those subjects. But if you're looking to move images through Photoshop—getting good scans or digital captures in, working your will on them, and putting out world-class final output—this is the book for you. Its *raison d'être* is to answer the many questions that people in production environments ask every single day.

▶ How can I quickly and efficiently process the 500 images coming from my digital camera?

▶ How should I set up my computer for Photoshop?

▶ What settings should I use in the Color Settings dialog?

▶ How do I bring out shadow details in my images without blowing away the highlights?

▶ What methods are available to neutralize color casts?

▶ How do I calibrate my monitor? (And should I?)

▶ What's the best way to silhouette an image for catalog work?

Our Goals for This Book

We originally wrote this book for a lot of reasons, but the biggest one was probably our frustration with the knee-jerk advice we kept hearing about desktop prepress: "Ask your printer."

Go ahead. Ask your printer what values you should enter in the Color Settings and Customize Proof Condition dialogs. In our experience, with nine out of ten printers you'll be lucky if you get more than wild guesses. In this new age of desktop prepress, there's simply no single person you can ask (whether you're a designer, a prepress shop… or a printer). *You're in the pilot's seat, with your hand on the stick (and the trigger).* Where do you turn when the bogies are incoming? We're hoping that you'll turn to this book.

Developing Your "Spidey Sense"

Flipping through nine hundred pages isn't exactly practical, though, when you've got a missile on your tail. So we try to do more with this book than tell you which key to press, or what value to enter where. We're trying to help you develop what our friend and colleague Greg Vander Houwen calls your "spidey sense."

When you're in the crunch, you've gotta have an intuitive, almost instinctive feel for what's going on in Photoshop, so you can finesse it to your needs. Canned techniques just don't cut it. So you'll find a fair amount of conceptual discussion here, describing how Photoshop "thinks" about images, and suggesting how you might think about them as well.

The Step-by-Step Stuff

Along with those concepts, we've included just about every step-by-step production technique we know of. From scanning to silhouettes and drop shadows, to tonal correction, sharpening, and color separation, we've tried to explain how to get images into Photoshop—and back out again—with the least pain and the best quality. And yes, in the course of explaining those techniques, we *will* tell you which key to press, and what values to enter in what dialogs.

History Is Important

We hear some of you mumbling under your breath, "We've been doing prepress for 30 years, and we don't need to learn a new way of doing it." We beg to differ. Print manufacturing, of which prepress is the handmaiden, is in the throes of change. For example, direct-to-plate printing has largely replaced the practice of making plates from film. This cuts out the quality loss inherent in a generation of optical duplication, but takes away our old film-based proofs. Digital photography (which is already starting to be called simply "photography") made the drum scanner obsolete, and in today's ultra competitive marketplace, the old industry-standard 3.2 rounds of proofing and correction just doesn't cut it any more.

Our goal is not to detract from the way you've been doing things. It's to show you how those approaches can be incorporated with new tools and pushed to the limit.

Moving Photography Forward

This book isn't just about prepress. It's also about photography and about images. We believe that photographers understand tone and color as well as any other skilled group of professionals, and one of our aims has been to help photographers translate their own understanding of images into the digital world of Photoshop.

Digital imaging has undoubtedly changed the practice of photography, but images still come from an intentional act on the part of the image maker, and that isn't going to change, whether the photons are captured by goo smeared on celluloid or by photoelectric sensors. We believe that digital imaging offers the photographer as many opportunities as it creates pitfalls. To all the photographers out there who are nervous about the digital revolution, we say, "Come on in, the water's fine." And more to the point, we can't *do* this stuff without you.

How the Book is Organized

One of the challenges we face in writing about Photoshop is not just that it's the "deepest" program we've ever used, but that almost every technique and feature relies on other techniques and features. It's impossible to talk about Photoshop without circular reasoning. However, we have tried to impose some structure to the book. In the first four chapters, we lay the foundation, covering "Building a Photoshop System," "Image Essentials," "Color Essentials," and "Color Settings" (all the color management stuff).

We put all this information first because it's impossible to be effective in Photoshop without it.

Once we've laid the groundwork, we jump into really working with images. In the next six chapters, we explore techniques you'll want to employ with almost every image you work with in Photoshop: "Building a Digital Workflow," "Essential Photoshop Tips and Tricks," "Image Adjustment Fundamentals," "The Digital Darkroom," "Making Selections," and "Sharpness, Detail, and Noise Reduction." In "Essential Image Techniques," we throw in a boatload of information that simply didn't fit any single category.

Sometimes it's hard to remember that there is life outside of Photoshop. We show how to save your Photoshop images for real-world online and print jobs and how to print from Photoshop itself in the last chapter of the book: "Image Storage and Output."

You get one more bonus chapter, "Spot Colors and Duotones," for those of you who prepare photographs and artwork for those printing processes. But that chapter isn't actually part of this book. It's available for download after you register your book at this Web site: *www.peachpit.com/realworldphotoshop-cs3*.

Bruce and David were crazy to take on this book and unravel such an insanely complex subject when they started in 1993, and we're no less crazy today. We don't claim to have the ultimate answers, but the answers we do have are tried, tested, and effective. The methods presented in this book may not be the only way to get good results from Photoshop, but they're the product of endless days and nights of research and testing, of badgering anyone we thought might have an answer, then trying to translate and present these rich insights in some coherent form. While our grasp on reality may have occasionally been tenuous during the production of this book, the techniques we present are firmly grounded in the real world—hence the title.

This Edition

Real World Photoshop has grown in size with each subsequent edition. Photoshop CS3 has not only added even more features, but a new and more specialized version: Photoshop CS3 Extended. If we were to cover every feature of Photoshop CS3 and Photoshop CS3 Extended in detail, you'd have to back a truck up to the bookstore to take this book home.

Our solution was to focus the book more tightly on high-quality photographic editing and output for print and online use. The flip side of that is this book does not go into detail about topics that stray too far from our core focus on photography. If you need information about the Photoshop Extended features that enhance medical or engineering workflows, or you want to know about designing Web pages in Photoshop, you'll want to reach for a more specialized book on the subject. (We do cover Photoshop Extended features that help photographers, such as using image stacks for noise reduction.)

Photoshop has changed over the years, and so have we. Many techniques we once thought brilliant have been superseded by the new features in each Photoshop upgrade. This is a good thing—you'll find that some techniques that required arcane, clever combinations of myriad Photoshop features are now condensed into convenient one-step dialogs, and we've tried to tell you whenever that's happened.

Another change in this edition is that while we continue to illustrate the book with screen shots from the Mac version that we all use, as a nod to the many users of Photoshop in Windows we now include keyboard shortcuts for both platforms.

Upgrading to a New Version

Like death and taxes, upgrading your software is inevitable but not necessarily fun. Some people upgrade as soon as the box hits the shelf; others take years, buying a new version only after their printer refuses to take their old files. Sooner or later, though, you'll be faced with new features, new challenges, and a new bottle of aspirin.

Migrating Your Existing Settings to CS3

The joy of discovering new features in an upgraded application is often tempered by the frustration of realizing that none of your meticulously crafted personal customizations are in your freshly-installed virgin upgrade. Do you really have to go in and reconfigure every last preference and preset in Photoshop? The answer is, probably not. You can get your workflow back a lot faster if you proceed with a little patience and preparation, instead of upgrading and instantly throwing out the old version.

Tip: Don't delete your old copy of Photoshop until you've made a copy of your existing settings.

Tip: Adobe maintains a list of what all of the Photoshop preferences and presets files do, and where they are on your disk. The document title is *Functions, Names, and Locations of Preference Files in Photoshop CS3*. As we write this, the list is at *www.adobe.com/go/kb401600*. For CS2, go to *www.adobe.com/cfusion/knowledgebase/index.cfm?id=331483*.

Tip: If you have trouble installing Photoshop CS3 and you had previously installed the public beta of Photoshop CS3, make sure you have completely removed the public beta. Adobe provides a cleanup script at *www.adobe.com/go/kb401056*.

Preferences. There's no way to directly transfer your current preferences to the new version. However, you can make a record of the settings in your Preferences dialog and enter them into the new version. Instead of writing down all of your settings, take a screen shot of each pane and refer to them as you set up the new version of Photoshop. You can use Adobe Bridge CS3 to browse your screen shots so that you can easily cycle through them as you adjust each preference in the new version of Photoshop.

Presets and other customizations. Actions, keyboard shortcuts, and many other user presets are stored in the Adobe Photoshop CS2 Settings folder. In Mac OS X, this folder is at Users\<username>\Library\Preferences\Adobe Photoshop CS2 Settings. In Windows, it's at Documents and Settings\<user profile>\Application Data\Adobe\Photoshop\9.0\Adobe Photoshop CS2 Settings. You can try copying the ones you care about into the Adobe Photoshop CS3 Settings folder. Some presets may not work correctly if the features that they're based on were changed in Photoshop CS3, so pay careful attention to how everything works as you begin using your migrated presets in your daily work. If you notice any serious problems with a particular preset, it's best to delete its preset file from the Adobe Photoshop CS3 Settings folder and re-create the preset in Photoshop CS3.

Plug-ins. Photoshop plug-ins are installed into the Plug-ins folder inside each Photoshop version's application folder. This means that plug-ins don't automatically appear in a newer version of Photoshop—you have to move them manually. Before you delete your old Photoshop folder, locate each non-Adobe plug-in and drag it to the corresponding folder in the Photoshop CS3 Plug-ins folder.

If you move a plug-in to a newer version of Photoshop and it isn't compatible, Photoshop displays an alert telling you that the plug-in wasn't loaded. At that point, you need to get a newer version of that plug-in.

If you upgrade to Photoshop CS3 on an Intel-based Mac and your old plug-ins don't run, you'll likely need to upgrade to Intel-compatible versions of the plug-ins. If you're desperate to run those plug-ins now, try running Photoshop CS3 in the Rosetta compatibility environment: Select the Photoshop application icon in the Finder, choose File > Get Info, and turn on the Run in Rosetta check box. Unfortunately, Photoshop CS3 runs much slower in Rosetta.

What's New in Adobe Photoshop CS3

Here are some of the most important changes in Photoshop CS3. We're not listing every new feature, just the ones you should know about before jumping into the rest of the book.

Updated user interface. Palettes in Photoshop CS3 come with special new powers. When you group Photoshop CS3 palettes, you can dock palette groups to the left or right sides of the main monitor. You can also collapse palettes down to a single row of compact icons and that includes the Tools palette itself. These changes increase the efficiency of using Photoshop on a single monitor. Multiple-monitor support is unchanged compared to Photoshop CS2.

Adobe Bridge CS3. The file browser and organizer for Photoshop (and for the rest of the Adobe Creative Suite, if you own it) includes many significant and welcome changes. In Bridge CS3, you can easily compare multiple images in a browser window and check details using one or more loupes. Find images quickly with powerful filtering and simplify the display of related images by using stacks. Two Bridge windows can now work in sync across multiple monitors. We cover Bridge in depth in Chapter 5, "Building a Digital Workflow."

Adobe Camera Raw 4.1. The Camera Raw plug-in gains new features in its main window, and on top of that, new tabs with whole sets of additional new features. Recovery gives you more control over highlights and Fill Light opens up shadows better than Curves. Camera Raw now includes Spot Healing and Red Eye tools, HSL corrections, a Parametric curve, and more. You can even use Camera Raw with TIFF and JPEG images, and it's all compatible with the adjustments made in Adobe Lightroom. After initially releasing Photoshop CS3 with Camera Raw 4, Adobe later released the Camera Raw 4.1 update, which added sophisticated sharpening controls based in part on Bruce's sharpening philosophy. You may find that more of your well-shot images can be processed using Bridge and Camera Raw without using Photoshop. We cover Camera Raw in more detail in Chapter 5, "Building a Digital Workflow."

Faster, simpler selections. The Quick Selection tool is like a smarter Magic Wand, and the Refine Edge dialog provides advanced, interactive control for adjusting the edge of the current selection. We'll look at it in Chapter 11, "Essential Image Techniques."

Smart Filters. One of the most requested features in Photoshop is non-destructive filtering, where a filter doesn't permanently change the image and can be edited later. Photoshop CS3 delivers this with Smart Filters, which are built on the Smart Objects feature introduced in Photoshop CS2. Smart Filters are extremely powerful, but the power comes at a price. We'll look at Smart Filters in Chapter 11, "Essential Image Techniques."

Curves done right. The Curves dialog includes several new features, including a clipping display and a histogram. If you're one of the many Photoshop CS2 users who correct images using both Levels and Curves, the Curves dialog in Photoshop CS3 may let you give up the Levels dialog for good.

Auto-Align Layers, Auto-Blend Layers, and improved Photomerge. Auto-Align Layers lines up and seamlessly merges images with common edges, such as a panorama. Auto-Blend Layers cleans up the edges of aligned layers. Both are part of a vastly more intelligent Photomerge feature for creating a large image out of several smaller ones.

Better cloning. Cloning and healing get a serious makeover in Photoshop CS3. The new Clone Source palette gives you control and more feedback when using the Clone Stamp and Healing Brush tools. We'll look at this in Chapter 11, "Essential Image Techniques."

Black and white conversion. Using the new Black and White dialog, you can convert a color image to black and white while thinking like a photographer or designer, instead of thinking like a color technician. This feature is covered in Chapter 11, "Essential Image Techniques."

No more ImageReady. If you used ImageReady in previous versions of Photoshop, you won't find it in Photoshop CS3. ImageReady is gone. Instead, Adobe moved the Web and animation features of ImageReady into Photoshop. Due to this edition's increased focus on pure photography, we don't cover most of the Web authoring features, but we do talk about photographic output for the Web in Chapter 12, "Image Storage and Output."

Native Intel performance in Mac OS X. Photoshop CS3 is a Universal application in Mac OS X, so it now runs natively on Macs with either PowerPC or Intel CPUs. If you use an Intel-based Mac, Photoshop CS3 reaches levels of performance significantly higher than in Photoshop CS2.

Photoshop Extended. Adobe addresses vertical markets such as health care and architecture with Photoshop CS3 Extended. However, we've concentrated on what we're familiar with, straight photography, so this book doesn't cover those specialized uses of Photoshop. For photographers, the most useful feature is Image Stacks (don't confuse these with the Stacks feature in Bridge CS3). Image Stacks bring advanced image processing possibilities for multiple exposures, such as noise reduction and removal of unwanted objects. We show you a noise reduction example in Chapter 10, "Sharpness, Detail, and Noise Reduction."

Other new hotness. Photoshop CS3 offers many other small changes, such as the Adobe Photo Downloader for importing images from digital cameras, a revised Print dialog, improved Vanishing Point perspective editing, the Zoomify feature to show large images in a small space on a Web page, and a more photo-friendly Brightness and Contrast dialog.

Thank You!

We'd like to give special thanks to a few of the many people who helped make what you hold in your hands. Rebecca Freed, our editor of this eighth edition, was forever helpful and patient; production heroine extraordinaire Lisa Brazieal, Pamela Pfiffner, Susan Rimerman, Kim Scott, and our other friends at Peachpit who took our work and made it fly.

A huge thank you must go to Thomas and John Knoll. There would be no Photoshop without them. We'd also like to thank John Nack, Bryan O'Neill Hughes, and the Photoshop team who have been generous with their time and knowledge for so many years. We would also like to extend our appreciation to Scott Byer, Marc Pawliger, Chris Cox, Jeff Tranberry, and others for their remarkable openness and generosity, sharing their expertise with the Photoshop community through their public Adobe blogs and their participation in the Adobe user forums.

If we see further than others, it's because we stand on the shoulders of Photoshop giants, including Ben Willmore, Julianne Kost, Katrin Eismann, Jeff Schewe, Martin Evening, Andrew Rodney, Stephen Johnson, Michael Ninness, Greg Gorman, Russell Brown, Scott Kelby, and Deke McClelland, pixel-meisters all.

And most of all, we owe a monumental debt of thanks to Bruce Fraser. We have done our best to preserve and carry forward his research and invaluable insights in this edition. He provided irreplaceable guidance and clarity to the entire digital imaging community.

Conrad. I sincerely thank my family and friends for their support and patience during the long and demanding process of updating this book. In addition, I thank the Photoshop development team and the exceedingly creative user community for continually expanding the boundaries of what Photoshop can do, and in turn expanding the possibilities of photography itself.

David. My deepest appreciation to Debbie Carlson, my friend and partner, and to Conrad Chavez, who stepped into a difficult task with courage and pulled off a great update. My sincere appreciation to my two sons, Gabriel and Daniel, who constantly remind me that life is more than pixels and vectors.

Building a Photoshop System

Putting It All Together

Photoshop is about as rich a program as you'll ever encounter, and much of this book focuses on ways to help you be more efficient in your use of it. But no quantity of tips, tricks, and work-arounds can compensate for hardware that's inadequate for the task or a poorly configured system. So in this chapter, we look at building an environment in which Photoshop —and you—can excel.

Photoshop takes full advantage of fast Macs and PCs—the faster the better. But the speed of the computer is only one part of the equation. Even the fastest computer available will seem sluggish if you don't have enough RAM, and Photoshop refuses to work at all if you don't have enough hard-disk space. How much is enough? It depends entirely on the size of the files you're working with and the kinds of operations you're carrying out on them.

Choosing a Platform

Discussions of Macs versus PCs usually tend to degenerate into "my dad can beat up your dad"—these spats produce a lot of heat, but little light. We're firmly convinced that price and performance are at parity on the two platforms. The Mac has richer support in terms of multiple monitors, color management, plug-ins, and color measurement equipment. The PC has a greater range of hardware options and general business software.

The bottom line: If you're happy with your current hardware platform, there's probably no reason to switch. You may, however, want to think about upgrading machines that are more than three or four years old. If you're still running Mac OS X 10.3 or earlier, or Windows 2000 or NT, you'll need to upgrade your OS to run Photoshop CS3, and the new operating systems make their own heavy demands on hardware.

If you're planning to upgrade to the latest and greatest Windows Vista or Mac OS X 10.5, do yourself a favor—get a machine that was designed with the new OS in mind. You'll save yourself a ton of time and frustration by doing so. It's possible to run Photoshop CS3 on fairly old machines—the minimum Mac OS requirement is Mac OS X 10.4.8, and the minimum Windows requirement is Windows XP with Service Pack 2—but we can tell you from bitter experience that it will be an uphill struggle. If your time is worth anything to you, trying to run an application like Photoshop CS3 on an outdated machine is a false economy.

Mac. Many Photoshop operations involve really large quantities of number crunching, so the speed of your Mac's processor makes a big difference. Photoshop CS3 unequivocally demands at least a G4—it won't run at all on anything less. While Photoshop makes effective use of the AltiVec acceleration in a G4 and G5, the multiple-core, Intel-based Macs now outpace them. If you want Photoshop CS3 to take advantage of more than 2 GB of RAM, which it can do, you will want a current iMac, a MacBook Pro, or at the very least, a Power Mac G5.

Windows. Photoshop CS3 requires a Pentium 4-class machine, but it's distinctly happier on an Intel Core 2 Duo or Intel Xeon. If you have a 64-bit machine and want to take advantage of more than 2 GB of RAM, Windows XP 64 is highly recommended.

If you decide to switch from one platform to the other, you probably won't have to buy Photoshop all over again. Contact Adobe customer service—they should be able to transfer your Photoshop license to the other platform for a minimal fee.

Processors and cores

Photoshop loves a speedy central processing unit (CPU), particularly as you pile on the megapixels, layers, filters, and Smart Objects. CPU makers used to boost performance simply by increasing the CPU speed in gigahertz (GHz), but they started hitting walls in terms of heat and power consumption. In the short period of time since the previous version of this book, CPU design has shifted from speeding up one processor core to including multiple processor cores in a single CPU. Now, it's easier to find a computer with two 2 GHz cores than computers with one 4 GHz core.

Photoshop has been able to take advantage of multiple processors for several versions now. However, it's important to understand that two 2 GHz cores are not exactly as fast as one 4 GHz core. Overhead is involved in splitting the workload across the cores, and it takes time to move data between the cores. Some operations aren't even practical to split across cores. With computers using many cores, such as the Mac Pro towers with eight cores (two CPUs of four cores each), it's possible to hit the bandwidth limit of the memory bus. Eight cores may process data faster than the memory bus can deliver more pixels to be processed, resulting in cores that wait for things to do. Multiple cores are beneficial when you have multiple applications that each require high CPU usage, or multiple processes that don't depend on each other, such as rendering video frames.

Multiple cores are most effective when doing a lot of processing on a relatively small data set. However, editing a Photoshop document usually involves moving high volumes of image data between the CPU, RAM, and disks, so the transfer speed between those components is a common bottleneck. To make the most of a multiple-core computer with Photoshop, you need enough RAM to minimize disk access. When disk access is inevitably required, you want disks that are fast enough to minimize delays in getting data to the RAM and CPU. As we write this, the speed gain of an eight-core computer versus a four-core computer for Photoshop work is not proportional to the price difference between them, but this could quickly change as motherboard designs and operating systems are updated. If you're trying to make a purchase decision, be suspicious of specs that quote CPU speed improvements alone without accounting for the entire system. We advise you to research Photoshop-specific performance benchmarks for a computer you're thinking about buying.

RAM

The old adage that you can never be too thin, too rich, or have too much RAM holds true for Photoshop CS3, just as it did for previous versions. Just how much RAM you need depends on your typical file sizes and work habits—remember that additional layers, channels, and Smart Objects increase the size of a file—but we don't recommend even *trying* to run Photoshop on a system with less than 1 GB of RAM, and more, *much* more, is better. The absolute minimum amount of RAM you can have, according to Adobe, is 512 MB. That may be doable—barely—but you won't enjoy it. If you typically work on Web-resolution images, use layers and Smart Objects sparingly, and don't use filters or raw files, you may be able to run Photoshop at or near the minimum supported amount of RAM. But if you're doing any more than that, you'll need more RAM.

We used to have various rules about how much RAM is enough, but as Photoshop has added more features that use scratch-disk space, they've largely gone out the window. Photoshop uses RAM as a cache for its scratch file: If what it needs at any given moment is in its RAM cache, it can fetch it quicker. But unless you only work on small flat files, at some point the scratch disk will come into play.

32-bit Hardware. Photoshop can use as much as 2 GB of RAM when running on a 32-bit system. However, if you have 2 GB of RAM installed, you won't want Photoshop to use all of it. Otherwise there won't be any RAM left for the system, causing the system to use the virtual memory on disk, which is much slower. For this reason, you can use the Performance pane in the Preferences dialog to set an upper limit on how much RAM Photoshop is allowed to use (see "RAM Allocation" later in this chapter).

64-bit Hardware. When running on 64-bit hardware, Photoshop CS3 can, in theory, use as much as 3.5 GB of RAM (in practice it uses 3072 MB directly). If you're working on huge images, you may see benefits from even more RAM. When more than 4 GB of RAM is installed, Photoshop lets the OS buffer scratch data into RAM instead of writing it directly to disk.

Photoshop doesn't normally use those buffers because it can be slower to use those buffers instead of using a scratch file on disk. That's because of issues related to system overhead, and also because the way operating systems use virtual memory is not optimal for the way Photoshop needs

Tip: Some people ask if setting up a RAM disk as a scratch disk will make Photoshop run faster. There's no reason to do that, because as we explain on this page, Photoshop can work with your OS to use the available RAM above 4 GB as if it was a RAM disk for scratch data.

to use virtual memory. But if you have enough RAM to hold most or all of your scratch data, it then becomes faster to let Windows or Mac OS X use extra RAM above 4 GB as a cache for scratch data. As you add RAM to your computer, you should see corresponding improvements in performance up to about 8 GB, the point of diminishing returns. You have to be working with files large enough to make good use of all that RAM—if you're editing 300-by-200-pixel Web images with no layers, adding another 4 GB of RAM won't make Photoshop run any faster.

A reliable way to figure whether you'll benefit from more RAM is to keep an eye on the Efficiency indicator while you work. To turn on the Efficiency indicator, click the third option from the left in the status bar at the bottom of a document window and choose Efficiency from the Show submenu (see **Figure 1-1**). If the Efficiency reading drops below 100 percent, more RAM would help. (If you've already maxed out your machine with as much RAM as Photoshop can address, and your efficiency is still below 100 percent, see "Scratch disk space," later in this chapter.)

Figure 1-1
The Efficiency indicator in the Status bar, and where to turn it on

64-bit Macs (Power Mac G5s and Mac Pros) and 64-bit Windows machines let you add 16 GB of RAM or more. If your work typically lets you stay at 100 percent efficiency, you won't get any benefit from adding more RAM, but if you want to allocate 100 percent of the available RAM to Photoshop, it's best to install more than 5 GB of RAM.

Virtual Memory Buffering Plug-Ins on Mac OS X. While Mac OS X lets Photoshop use your extra RAM as a fast cache if you have more than 4 GB of RAM installed, there is a catch. In Mac OS X 10.3 or 10.4, the OS caching behavior may cause Photoshop to pause for a few seconds, which can mess you up if you're painting, for example. For this reason, Adobe provides two plug-ins, ForceVMBuffering.plugin and DisableVMBuffering.plugin, that let you control whether OS X uses high RAM for direct caching. How do you decide which one to use? It comes down to whether you're more interested in responsive painting or quickly handling very large files. Use the following guidelines:

- If you have more than 4 GB of RAM and you use the ForceVMBuffering plug-in, Photoshop will be as fast as it can be with very large files, but you may experience pauses when painting.

- If you have more than 4 GB of RAM and you use the DisableVMBuffering plug-in, you shouldn't experience pauses when painting, but you won't see optimal Photoshop performance with very large files.

- If you have 4 GB of RAM or less installed, don't bother installing either plug-in, because you won't have the amount of RAM that brings the extra Mac OS X caching into play.

Here's the last gotcha: The two plug-ins were supposed to be included in the Goodies\Optional Plug-Ins\Optional Extensions folder on the Adobe Photoshop CS3 installation disk, but were accidentally left out. If they aren't on your installation disk, download them from the Adobe Web site. Go to *www.adobe.com/support/downloads*, click Photoshop-Macintosh, and look for "Adobe Photoshop CS3 VM Buffering Optional Extensions." Installation instructions are in the ReadMe document.

RAM Allocation. Both Mac OS X and Windows XP automatically adjust the amount of RAM each application gets. Photoshop takes a certain amount of RAM when you start it, and if it needs more, the system hands it over. However, you *don't* want Photoshop to use all the RAM on your system—that starves the OS of the RAM it needs to run the machine, causing everything to slow down. The system will start using virtual memory on disk out of desperation.

In Mac OS X, use the Performance pane in the Preferences dialog to set an upper limit on how much RAM Photoshop uses (see **Figure 1-2**). The Performance pane suggests an ideal range of RAM for you to let Photoshop use. It also defaults to an amount of RAM that's a good starting point for most users under most conditions. If you have a large amount of RAM—3 GB or more—you can try increasing that percentage, but if you go too far, you'll hear the hard disk start to thrash whenever the OS or another application needs to grab some RAM.

Mac OS X actually gives you an extra clue: When an application is waiting for the computer, you see the all-too-familiar spinning wristwatch

Tip: If you have more than 1 GB of RAM installed, you may be able to enhance performance by installing the Bigger Tiles plug-in, which processes image data in larger chunks. The plug-in is inside the Photoshop application folder, in the Plug-Ins\Extensions\BiggerTiles\ folder. To install, remove the tilde (~) character from the file name and restart Photoshop.

cursor, but when the OS is the one causing the delay, you see a spinning multicolored wheel, sometimes called "The Spinning Beach Ball." If you see the wheel on Mac OS X, or you hear the hard disk thrashing on either platform when you're working on an image that should fit into RAM, you may need to lower the memory allocation a little.

Tip: If you get an "out of memory" alert, try choosing a command from the Edit > Purge submenu: Clipboard, Histories, Pattern, Undo, or All. If a Purge command is dimmed, it means that buffer is already empty, so there's nothing there to purge.

You can fine-tune your settings based upon your own system, installed RAM, and the way you use Photoshop. Depending upon the number of system processes and applications you typically run, you can try increasing the RAM allocation incrementally while checking the available unused RAM with a system utility. On the Mac, you can use Activity Monitor (built into OS X) to watch RAM usage. On Windows you can watch Performance Monitor, which is also built-in. Because a 32-bit system is limited to 2 GB of RAM, you must never allocate 100 percent of RAM to Photoshop on a 32-bit system— always leave a few hundred megabytes free to avoid starving the system. Even on a 64-bit system with well over 4 GB of RAM, Adobe recommends that you allocate just short of 100 percent (remember, on 64-bit systems Photoshop can still use RAM above 4 GB as a fast cache).

Figure 1-2
Allocating RAM to Photoshop using the Memory Usage preference

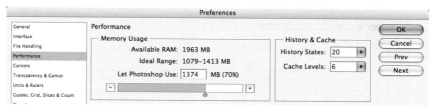

On a computer with 2 GB of RAM, Photoshop sees all available RAM. Because the OS needs part of that 2 GB to run, allocate 70 percent or less of available RAM.

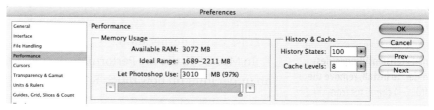

On a computer with 7 GB of RAM, Photoshop sees 3 GB. Because 4 GB of additional RAM is available to the OS, it's OK to set Photoshop to use almost 100 percent of 3 GB.

Note that a few Photoshop filters (Lens Flare, for instance) require that you have enough physical RAM to load the entire image into memory. Even though Photoshop has a virtual-memory scheme, if you don't have enough actual RAM to process the whole image, these effects just won't work.

Image Cache. The Cache Levels setting in the Memory and Image Cache panel of the Preferences dialog (see **Figure 1-3**) also has an impact on RAM usage. Increasing the Image Cache value speeds screen redrawing when you're working with larger files that contain a lot of layers. However, the Image Cache doesn't do too much for small files. The default setting is six levels. If you routinely work with larger, multilayered files, try increasing the cache level to 8. If you work with smaller files, try reducing it.

Figure 1-3

Preferences for Cache Levels, Scratch Disks, and 3D

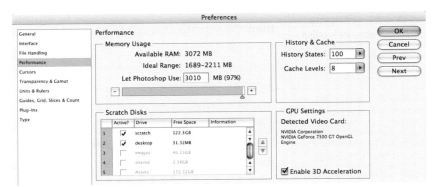

Virtual Memory

Virtual memory is a programming trick that fools the computer into thinking it has more RAM than it really does. It works by reserving a specially marked amount of space on your hard drive that gets treated as RAM. The real, physical RAM is then used as a cache for the virtual memory stored on the disk. If the data that the computer is looking for is cached in RAM, your computer won't slow down, but if the computer has to go searching on the hard disk instead, things can slow down a lot.

Operating systems create one or more virtual memory *swap files* on your hard disk that serve as virtual memory to let multiple applications grab RAM as needed. On top of this, Photoshop has its own virtual memory scheme, which it uses to let you do things that wouldn't fit in physical RAM, such as storing 1000 history states for a 300 MB image (which we don't actually recommend doing). To get optimum performance, you need to configure both the operating system's virtual memory scheme and Photoshop scratch disk space so they play nicely together.

The Photoshop Scratch File and the OS Swap File. Both Windows and Mac OS X use the startup disk for the swap file unless you have told them to do otherwise. On Windows systems, you can change the swap file setting by bringing up Properties for My Computer, selecting the Performance tab, clicking the Virtual Memory button, and selecting the Change option. This lets you specify maximum and minimum swap-file sizes and which drive gets used.

On Mac OS X, the procedure for pointing the swap file at a drive other than the startup disk is way more complex, so much so that it's crazy to try to move it when it's so much easier to move the Photoshop scratch disk instead (see "Scratch Disk Space," on the next page). The only time you may want to move the OS swap file to a different disk is when your startup disk is the fastest, and you'd rather use it for the Photoshop scratch file.

Photoshop performs much better if you assign the Photoshop scratch disk to a different physical mechanism than the OS swap file, so a second hard drive is always desirable. This way, the same set of read-write heads don't have to scurry around like gerbils on espresso while trying to serve the dual demands of the operating system swap file and Photoshop scratch space. If all you have is one single hard disk, you'll have to let Photoshop and the OS fight it out. You can minimize conflicts by being careful with your Memory Usage preference setting.

Setting Up Photoshop Scratch Disks. To tell Photoshop where to store its scratch data, open the Preferences dialog and in the Scratch Disks options, check the Active? check box for any volumes that you want to use for that purpose (see **Figure 1-3**). Photoshop starts with the volume at the top of the list. If the scratch data uses up the first scratch disk, Photoshop extends it into the checked scratch disks from top to bottom. To move a disk up or down in the list, click a disk to highlight it, and then click the arrows to the right of the list's scroll bar.

If you store the Photoshop scratch file on a disk where you want to store other files, it's best for the Photoshop scratch file to be in its own partition that contains no other files ,and does not contain the OS swap file. If the Photoshop scratch file is mixed with other files, that volume may become fragmented and slow down Photoshop. A dedicated partition is much easier to maintain. If you need to defragment it, you can do so very easily by simply reinitializing the partition (erasing everything inside the partition)—you don't need to run a fancy disk optimizer.

Tip: Although the Photoshop scratch file preference is called Scratch Disk, you can assign the scratch file to any volume. A volume can be an entire disk, one partition of a disk, or a number of disks seen as one RAID. For performance reasons, don't set the Scratch Disk preference to a slow disk, removable media, or a volume on the network.

Scratch Disk Space. The space you set aside for a scratch disk should at least equal the amount of RAM you've allocated to Photoshop, as it uses RAM as a cache for the scratch disk space. That means if you've given Photoshop 120 MB of RAM, you must also have 120 MB of free disk space. If you have less, Photoshop will only use an amount of RAM equivalent to the free space on the scratch disk. In practice, you'll likely need more, and if you work with layered, high-bit files or many history states, much more. A good scratch disk is large (many GB) and fast.

Photoshop constantly optimizes the scratch space. If you consider constant disk access (often called *disk thrashing*) to be a warning that things are about to get very slow, you should learn to accept it as normal Photoshop behavior. People are often especially concerned when they see disk access immediately after opening a file. This, too, is normal: Photoshop is simply setting itself up to be more efficient down the line. Photoshop has a couple of ways to tell you how much the scratch disk is involved.

In the lower-left corner of the document window, there's a pop-up menu that shows, among other things, document size, scratch size, and efficiency (see **Figure 1-4**). If you set this to Scratch Sizes, the first number shows the amount of RAM being used by all open documents, and the second number shows the amount of RAM currently allocated to Photoshop. If the first number is bigger than the second, Photoshop is using virtual memory. When the indicator is set to Efficiency, a reading of less than 100 percent indicates that virtual memory is coming into play.

Tip: We often slip into talking about virtual memory as if it always happens on the hard drive, but if you have more than 4 GB of RAM installed, remember that Photoshop may be using your faster unused RAM as a virtual memory buffer before it hits the slower hard drive.

Figure 1-4
Scratch Sizes indicator

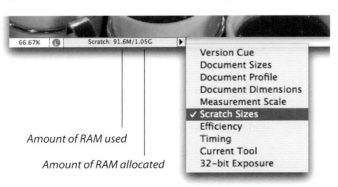

Amount of RAM used

Amount of RAM allocated

RAID Arrays. Using a striped RAID (Redundant Array of Independent Disks) can be a very worthwhile way to set up a scratch disk, particularly if you often edit images too large for your available RAM. Photoshop can write to a RAID much faster than to a single disk, so your performance will improve. The current speed champ is a dual-channel Ultra320 SCSI array with one, two, or three 15,000-RPM drives on each channel, but fast SCSI drives are small and expensive. A software RAID combining two Serial ATA drives is almost as fast, with a much lower cost per megabyte. FireWire 800 arrays also show great potential, but only if you add multiple FireWire 800 channels by adding extra controllers—a single-channel FireWire 800 array is only about 10–15 percent faster than a single FireWire 800 drive. Three channels will get you almost the same speed as Ultra320 SCSI, and four channels (if you have enough PCI slots) will exceed Ultra320 SCSI on a good many operations. Given the high cost and relatively low capacity of SCSI drives, we recommend exploring the alternatives unless you already have a SCSI array—SATA and FireWire 800 drives in the 500 GB range are relatively inexpensive.

Opening and saving large files is also faster with a RAID array. But if you have a choice between buying RAM and buying a fast hard drive, max out the RAM first unless opening and saving large files already constitutes a significant bottleneck in your workflow.

Monitors

The CRT versus LCD debate hasn't completely faded out, even though manufacture of high-end CRTs has essentially ceased. At the same time, LCDs have improved enormously, but the viewing angle is still an issue— the color changes when you move your head vertically or horizontally— and it's still difficult to manufacture a large LCD with uniform brightness. A new generation of LCDs backlit by LEDs shows great promise, with wider color gamuts and more accurate color than today's LCDs, which are backlit by fluorescent light bulbs. However, LED-backlit desktop LCDs are not yet widely available or affordable as we write this.

Many imaging professionals still swear by CRTs, and actively shop the used-monitor market for high-end units that are no longer available new, such as the Sony Artisan and LaCie Electron series with BlueEye. Those monitors offered a USB connection between the monitor and the host CPU that allows the bundled calibration system to automatically adjust the individual R, G, and B gains to achieve the correct white point. Third-party calibrators, such as the ones we discuss later in this chapter, allow you to do the same thing manually with only slightly more effort, as long as your monitor offers separate red, green, and blue gain controls. If you shop for a used CRT, you may want to make sure that it's still bright enough when calibrated and profiled. When a CRT's brightness level drops below 95 cd/m^2 after you set the black level, it doesn't have much useful life left as a color-accurate monitor.

Video Acceleration. There's a widespread but ill-founded belief that accelerated video boards speed up screen redrawing in Photoshop. Adding a faster video card usually won't help very much. The bottleneck in redrawing Photoshop images is almost never the video system—it's getting the image data out of RAM (or even worse, from disk) to the video system.

There is only one area in which the 3D capabilities of a video card matter in Photoshop, and that's if you use Photoshop CS3 Extended to import and work with 3D models. As far as deciding on a 3D card, if you have a 3D card that's sufficient to run the CAD program you used to create the 3D model, it's good enough for Photoshop Extended. If you suspect that your video card isn't working well with 3D layers in Photoshop, try unchecking the Enable 3D Acceleration preference (see Figure 1-3) to render 3D layers using software instead of the video card.

Monitor Calibration and Profiling. If you want to trust what you see on screen (which we certainly do), some kind of monitor calibration and profiling is essential. The free, eyeball-based, software-only monitor calibrators (such as the Apple Display Calibrator Assistant) are better than nothing, but unless you work in a cave, you'll find it's extremely difficult to get consistent results, because your eyes—and hence your "monitor calibration"—adapt to changing lighting conditions.

We believe that every serious Photoshop user would be better served by using a hardware color-calibration puck to measure the behavior of the monitor, along with its accompanying software, which will set the monitor to a known condition and write a monitor profile. There are several good, relatively inexpensive hardware-based monitor calibration packages available. We like the Eye-One Display from GretagMacbeth, BasICColor Display, or the ColorVision Spyder. All of these can calibrate both CRT and LCD monitors, and any of them will do a better job of keeping your displays accurately profiled than any of the eyeball-based tools. We talk more about calibration and profiling in Chapter 4, "Color Settings."

Tip: The Adobe Gamma calibration software that was included with previous versions of Photoshop is no longer included in Photoshop CS3. If you still have an old copy, we don't recommend using it on LCD monitors. Get a hardware calibrator instead.

Multiple-Monitor Support. Any Mac that supports multiple monitors can properly apply the specific color profile for each display. However, some Windows video cards that support multiple monitors report themselves to the operating system as a single device with which only one display profile can be associated. Before buying a video card to use with Photoshop in Windows, it's best to assume nothing and do plenty of research.

We don't have significant experience with multiple-monitor Windows setups, though we know that, aside from the profiling issue, they are nearly as easy to set up in Windows as on the Mac. If your Windows video card doesn't support separate profiles for individual monitors, you can at least display the Photoshop document window on your best, profiled monitor and put the palettes on another monitor.

Notebook Displays. Displays on notebook computers lag behind desktop monitors in quality, because notebook displays need to be thin, light, and low-power. If your only Photoshop computer is a notebook, consider connecting a good external monitor when you're at your desk. An external monitor port is built into many notebooks, and you'll love the extra work area. If you must use the notebook's built-in display to evaluate color—for example, on a photo shoot in the field—it's especially critical that you create a monitor profile for it using a hardware calibrator. That still won't make a notebook display as good as a desktop monitor, but it will be as close as possible.

Image Essentials

It's All Zeroes and Ones

Computers know nothing about images, or tone, color, truth, beauty, or art. They're just very complicated adding machines that crunch numbers. Every piece of data we store on a computer is comprised of numbers. All the commands we send to the computer are translated into numbers. Even this text we wrote is made up of numbers.

Fortunately, you don't have to learn hexadecimal or binary math to use Photoshop—we authors are living math-challenged proof of that. But if you want to put Photoshop under your control, rather than flailing around and occasionally getting good results by happy accident, you do need to understand the basic concepts that Photoshop and other image editors use to represent photographs using numbers.

We'll try to keep it simple—if you want to avoid heavily pixelated output and wildly unpredictable color shifts, you will want to understand the essential lessons in this chapter.

Pixels and Paths

When you get down to the nitty-gritty, there are essentially two ways to make computers display pictures. In Photoshop terminology, the distinction is between pixels and paths. Other terms you may hear are "raster" (rasters are rows or lines, not reggae artists) and "vector." We call the stuff made up of pixels "images" and the stuff made of vectors "artwork."

Pixel-based images. Images are simply collections of dots (we call them *pixels* or *sample points*) laid out in a big grid. The pixels can be different colors, and the number of pixels can vary. No matter what the picture is—whether it's a modernist painting of a giraffe or a photograph of your mother—it's always described using lots of pixels. This is the only way to represent the fine detail and subtle gradations of photorealistic images.

If a graphic came from a capture device (such as a digital camera or scanner), or a painting or image-editing program (such as Photoshop), chances are it's an image.

Vector artwork. Vector artwork, also known as *object-oriented graphics*, describes graphics using instructions instead of dots. Vector graphics just say, "Draw a rectangle this big and put it here." This is a more efficient and space-saving method for describing certain simple types of graphics, such as lines, hard-edged shapes, and text blocks. Vector graphics can have a variety of attributes—line weight, type formatting, fill color, graduated fills, and so on.

To use an analogy, vector graphics are like directions saying, "Go three blocks down the street, turn left at the 7-Eleven, and go another five blocks," while pixel-based images are more saying, "Take a step. Now take another step. And another … " At its core, Photoshop is a tool for working with pixels, but each iteration of the program has offered more support for incorporating vector elements that retain their object-oriented characteristics, such as shapes or type. You can also use vector elements as selections and masks on pixel-based images.

Outside Photoshop, vector graphics come from drawing programs such as Adobe Illustrator, and computer-aided design (CAD) programs. You might also get vector artwork from other programs, such as a program that makes graphs.

Crossing the line. The distinction between images and artwork is blurred when you use software that tries to give you the advantages of both pixel-based and vector graphics. While Photoshop is primarily pixel-based, it includes a pen tool, shape layers, and type layers that let you draw vector graphics and editable text and store them as part of a Photoshop document.

Words, Words, Words

While terminology might not keep you up at night, we in the writin' business have to worry about things as simple as the meaning of the term *bitmap*.

Bruce felt that, strictly speaking, bitmaps are only black-and-white images. This is how Photoshop uses the term. He preferred to describe images made up of colored dots as *raster* images (the word "raster" refers to a group of lines—in this case, lines of pixels—that collectively make up an image). David thinks that only people who wear pocket protectors (some of his best friends do) would use the word "raster." We've settled on calling documents comprised of pixels "images," and calling documents comprised of vectors "artwork."

Another problem we've encountered is what to call all those little dots in an image. As we mentioned earlier, when we talk about points in an image, we like to call them *pixels*, *sample points*, or *samples*.

The term "samples" comes from what a scanner or digital camera does: it samples an image—checking what color it finds—at each photo receptor on the sensor. The term "pixel" is a contraction that specifies the most basic "picture element" in an image.

When we talk about scanning an image (input), or printing an image (output), we talk about "samples" or "pixels per inch" (while "samples" is closer to reality, everyone we know uses the latter, or *ppi*). Many people use "dots per inch" (*dpi*) for resolution on any device, whether it's a printer or a monitor. We reserve the term "dots per inch" for use when speaking of printed output, which actually create dots on paper or film.

We use the term "pixels" for one other thing: screen resolution. But to be clear, we always try to specify "screen pixels" or "image pixels."

Illustrator is primarily a vector-based drawing program, but you can add images from a digital camera to an Illustrator document.

Pixel images and vector artwork are commonly mixed in page-layout programs such as Adobe InDesign. Naturally, a page-layout program should be able to integrate text and graphics from a wide variety of sources. However, if the layout contains an image that you need to edit pixel by pixel, you need to open the image in Photoshop.

Once you've experienced the creative convenience of combining images, artwork, and text in a design, you then start to need a universal format that can store it all. While anything you can create in Photoshop can be stored in the Photoshop file format (PSD), not all programs can read Photoshop files. With the Adobe Portable Document Format (PDF), you can store both images and artwork in one file that can be exchanged easily between programs and platforms. Photoshop can save a Photoshop PDF file, which can store a Photoshop image while preserving vector artwork and text.

Pixels and Images

Photoshop lets you do all kinds of nifty stuff, but at its heart, it pretty much all comes down to pixels. To use Photoshop effectively, you need to understand the basic attributes of pixel-based images: dimension, bit depth, and color model (which Photoshop refers to as *image mode*).

Dimension

Dimension is one attribute that contributes to size. Pixel-based images are always rectangular grids made up of little squares, like a chessboard or bathroom tiles; those little squares are individual pixels (see **Figure 2-1**). The dimensions of the pixel grid refer to the number of pixels along its width and height. A chessboard is always eight squares by eight squares. The grid of pixels that makes up your computer screen might be 1680 by 1050. A 10-megapixel digital camera may produce an image that's 3888 by 2592 pixels.

Figure 2-1
Bitmaps as grids of squares

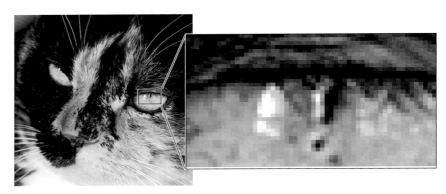

Image dimensions are limited by the capabilities of your capture device, the amount of available storage space, and your patience—the more pixels in the image, the more processing time it takes.

An image's pixel dimensions are only indirectly related to its physical size or resolution: Until you specify how large each pixel is (called *resolution*) the overall image has no specific physical size. That is, the same 100-by-100 pixels can be made as small as a postage stamp or as large as a billboard. We'll discuss resolution and why it's important in more detail later in this chapter.

Tip: A Photoshop document has a maximum size of 300,000-by-300,000-pixels. You may not be able to buy a camera that makes an image that large. It's more likely that you'd hit that limit by using the new Auto-Align feature to stitch very large images out of many small ones.

Bit Depth

Bit depth is the attribute that tells Photoshop how many shades or colors the image can contain. For example, in a 1-bit image (one in which each pixel is represented by one bit of information—either a one or a zero) each pixel is either on or off, which usually means it's black or white. (Of course, if you printed with red ink on blue paper, the pixels would be either red or blue.)

With 2 bits per pixel, there are four possible combinations (00, 01, 10, and 11), hence four possible values, and four possible colors or gray levels (see **Figure 2-2**). Eight bits of information give you 256 possible values; in 8-bit/channel RGB images, each pixel actually has three 8-bit values—one each for red, green, and blue—for a total of 24 bits per pixel. (In 8-bit/channel CMYK [cyan, magenta, yellow, and black] there are four channels rather than three, so a CMYK pixel takes 32 bits to describe.)

Figure 2-2
Bit depth

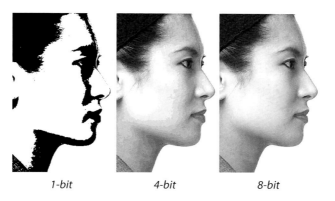

1-bit   4-bit   8-bit

Photoshop lets you work with a variety of bit depths, up to the 32 floating-point bits per channel in HDR (High Dynamic Range) mode. But for most work, the common bit depths are 8 bits per channel (24-bit RGB and 32-bit CMYK) and 16 bits per channel (48-bit RGB).

How many bits are enough? A bit depth of 8 bits per channel provides 16.7 million possible RGB color definitions, which is a much larger number than the number of unique colors the human eye can distinguish, and certainly much larger than the number of unique colors we can print.

Why capture many more colors than we print, or even see? The simple answer is that the larger number of bits gives us more editing flexibility. As you'll see in Chapter 7, "Image Adjustment Fundamentals," every edit opens up gaps between some adjacent pixel values and smooshes others together, reducing the total number of shades.

Image Mode

Bit depth and dimension each tell part of the story, but the third essential attribute of images, the *image mode*, is the one that dictates whether all those numbers represent either shades of gray or colors. As we mentioned earlier, computers know nothing about tone or color; they just crunch numbers. Image mode is the attribute that provides a human meaning for the numbers they crunch.

In general, the numbers that describe pixels relate to *tonal* values, with lower numbers representing darker tones and higher ones representing brighter tones. In an 8 bit/channel grayscale image (256 levels per channel), 0 represents solid black, 255 represents pure white, and the intermediate numbers represent intermediate shades of gray.

In the color image modes, the numbers represent shades of a primary color rather than shades of gray. So an RGB image is actually made up of three grayscale channels: one representing red values, one representing green values, and one representing blue values (see **Figure 2-3**). A CMYK image contains four grayscale channels: one each for cyan, magenta, yellow, and black.

The one exception we mentioned earlier is the Indexed Color mode, in which each value represents an arbitrary color that Photoshop loads from a *lookup table*, a list of colors actually used in the image. Indexed Color images can contain only 256 colors, and since the color values are arbitrary (number 1 could be red, number 2 could be blue, and so on), most of the Photoshop editing tools don't work. In the other modes, we can change tone and color by adjusting the numbers to make a pixel, or one channel of a pixel, lighter or darker, but if we did that on an Indexed Color image, we'd end up with a completely different color! (So Photoshop sensibly prevents us from doing so.)

Resolution

Resolution is one of the most overused and least understood words in desktop publishing. People use it when they talk about scanners and printers, images and screens, halftones, and just about anything else they can

Figure 2-3 How RGB and CMYK color modes combine
Color images (like the one at the top-left corner) can be described with RGB data (top) or CMYK data (bottom). Note that the red, green, and blue channels in this figure had to be simulated using cyan, magenta, and yellow press inks.

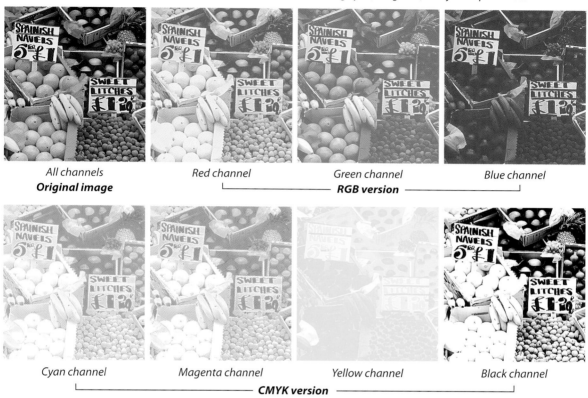

All channels
Original image

Red channel

Green channel

Blue channel

└─────────────── **RGB version** ───────────────┘

Cyan channel

Magenta channel

Yellow channel

Black channel

└─────────────── **CMYK version** ───────────────┘

get their hands on. Then they wonder why they're confused. Fortunately, resolution is easy to get once you get the hang of it.

As we noted earlier, an image in its pure digital state has no physical size—it's just a bunch of pixels, and the pixels can be any size you want. Once you give an image tangible expression, whether on the screen or in print, the number of pixels across the width and height now take up a specific amount of physical space, and that determines the resolution.

The resolution of an image is the number of pixels per unit of measurement—usually the number of pixels per inch (ppi) or pixels per centimeter (ppcm). If your image is 72 pixels wide and you tell it to be 72 pixels per inch, then it's an inch wide. If you print it at half the size, you'll still have the same number of pixels, but they'll be crammed into half the space, so each inch will contain 144 pixels, or 144 ppi (see **Figure 2-4**). Print it at 300 percent of the original size, and the resolution goes down to 24 ppi.

Figure 2-4
Scaling and
resolution

25 percent
(288 ppi)

50 percent
(144 ppi)

Original (72 ppi)

50 percent
(144 ppi)

Original (72 ppi)

300 percent (24 ppi)

You can look at resolution in another way: If you know an image's size
and resolution, you can figure out its dimensions. When you scan a picture
that is 3 inches on each side at 100 pixels per inch, you know that the image
has 300 pixels on each side (100 per inch). If you then scan it at 300 pixels
per inch, the dimensions shoot up to 900 pixels on each side.

The key to making resolution work for you is knowing how many pixels
you need for an image's intended output.

How Much Is Enough?

When it comes to image resolution, bigger isn't necessarily better. The higher the resolution of an image, the longer it takes to open, edit, save, or print. If your output only requires 300 dpi images but you use 1200 dpi photographs in a document just because you can, chances are you're going to wait longer at every step of your workflow and your hard disks will fill up much faster.

But smaller isn't necessarily better either. If your image resolution is too low, your image will look pixelated (see **Figure 2-5**); you'll start seeing the pixels themselves, or adverse effects from excessively large pixels. Loss of detail and mottling are the two worst offenders in this category.

Maybe you thought you could save time by reducing your images to 150 ppi. But if the client rejects the job because the image is too pixelated, any savings are more than wiped out when you have to redo the job. So if bigger isn't better, and too small is even worse, how much is enough? How much image data do you need? The first consideration is image mode: The requirements are very different for line art than for grayscale and color.

Figure 2-5
Pixelation in images when image resolution is too low

Original (200 ppi)   *300 percent (66 ppi)*

Line Art

For bilevel (black-and-white, 1-bit, bitmap-mode) images, the resolution never needs to be higher than that of the printer you're using. This is one situation where image pixels per inch equate to printer dots per inch. If you're printing to a 600-dpi desktop laser printer, there's no reason to have more than 600 pixels per inch in your image (the printer can only output 600 dots per inch, so any extras just get thrown away). However, when you print to a 2,400-dpi platesetter, that 600-ppi image will appear jaggy.

Terms of Resolution

Not everyone talks about resolution in terms of ppi. Depending on the circumstance, your personality, and the time of day, you might discuss a file's resolution in a number of ways, but they're all different ways of talking about the same essential concept: *how much information* the file contains. Here's a quick rundown of your options.

Dimensions. The least ambiguous way of talking about the resolution of images is by their pixel dimensions; that is, the number of pixels on each side of the grid. This doesn't tell you what physical size an image is, but if you understand how much resolution you need for different output methods, it's useful shorthand for expressing how big the image *could be*, depending on what you wanted to do with it. It tells you how much information is in the file. Hard-core Photoshop users like to talk in dimensions because they don't necessarily know (or care) how large the final output will be.

For instance, you could say a capture from a 6-megapixel camera is a 2048-by-3076 image. What does that tell you? With experience, you'd know that your file size is in 8-bit/channel mode is 18 MB, and at 225 ppi you could print a full-bleed letter-size page. Later in this chapter, we discuss ways you can figure all this out for yourself.

Image size. A wordier but equally unambiguous way to discuss resolution is to cite physical dimensions and resolution. For example, you might say a file is 4-by-5 inches at 225 ppi. This makes the most sense to someone doing page layout, because he or she will typically be concerned with how the image is going to look on the printed page. Note, however, that you have to specify both the size and the resolution. Otherwise you're telling only half the story.

File size. A third way to discuss resolution is by the file's size on disk. You can quickly get a sense of the difference in information content of two files when we tell you that the first is 900 K and the second is 12 MB. In fact, a lot of digital imaging gurus *only* think in file size. If you ask them, "What's the resolution of that file?" they will look at you like you're an idiot.

Once you become accustomed to working with a number of different sizes, you'll recognize that the 900 K RGB file is about the size of a 640-by-480 RGB image. At 72 ppi (screen resolution) that's pretty big, but at 300 ppi (typical resolution for a high-quality print job), the image is only about two inches wide.

Megapixels. Digital cameras are often rated in megapixels, which

---

If you're printing line art on press, plan on using an image resolution of *at least* 800 ppi—preferably 1000 ppi or more (see **Figure 2-6**). Lower resolutions often show jaggies and broken lines: On newsprint or very porous paper, you may get away with a lower resolution such as 400 or 600 ppi because the jaggies will disappear with the spreading ink. But unless you have considerable experience with the print process at hand, you can't tell until the job has run, so err on the side of caution.

See Chapter 11, "Essential Image Techniques," for more about the resolution and appearance of line-art images.

is simply the total number of pixels, obtained by multiplying the number of pixels on the short side by the number of pixels on the long side—see **Table 2-1**.

Single-side dimension. People who work with continuous-tone film recorders, such as the Solitaire or the Kodak LVT, frequently talk about a file's resolution in terms of the dimension of one side—typically the width—of the image. For instance, they might ask for "a 4 K file." That means the image should be exactly 4096 pixels across.

K usually means file size (kilobytes). However, in this case, it means 1024 pixels.

The height of the image is relatively unimportant in this case, though if you're imaging to film, it's usually assumed that you know the other dimension of the image because it's dictated by the aspect ratio of the film you're using. High-quality film recorders usually write out to 4-by-5-inch

Table 2-1	Megapixels (MP)
MP	**Dimensions***
1.6	1536 by 1024
2.8	2048 by 1365
3.1	2048 by 1536
4.1	2464 by 1648
6.3	3072 by 2048
8.2	3504 by 2336
11	4604 by 2704
17	5120 by 3413
22	6144 by 4096

Actual pixel dimensions vary by camera model

Table 2-2	Resolution in res
Res	**Pixels per Inch**
1	25.4
2	50.8
3	76.2
4	101.6
5	127
6	152.4
7	177.8
8	203.2
9	228.6
10	254
11	279.4
12	304.8
20	508
40	1016
60	1524
80	2032

chromes (positive transparencies), so if you want to fill the image area, it's usually assumed that the short side of your 8 K image will contain somewhere around 6,550 pixels.

Res. One other method of discussing resolution uses the term *res*. Res is simply the number of pixels per millimeter, and it's a great deal more common in Europe than in the metrically challenged United States. People usually talk about res when they're discussing cap-

ture resolution on drum scanners. For example, a file scanned at res 12 is scanned at 12 sample points (pixels) per millimeter—which is 120 sample points per centimeter, or—in common usage—304.8 sample points per inch (see **Table 2-2**).

Grayscale and Color Halftones

Here's a simple guideline for the proper resolution for printing grayscale and color images to halftoning devices such as platesetters: Image resolution should be no more than twice the screen frequency. For instance, if you're printing a halftone image at 133 lines per inch (*lpi*), the image resolution should be no larger than 266 ppi (see **Figures 2-7** and **2-8**). Any higher resolution is almost certainly wasted information.

We've heard from people who claim to see a difference between 2 times the screen frequency and 2.5 times the screen frequency, but no one has ever shown us a print sample that supported this contention.

Figure 2-6
Resolution of
line art

144 ppi   300 ppi

800 ppi   1200 ppi

It's an absolute certainty that anything higher than 2.5 times the screen frequency is wasted if you're printing to a PostScript output device.

If you print an image whose resolution exceeds that multiplier, Photoshop warns you. You can print the image, but it will take longer to print, and you may even get worse results than you would with a lower-resolution version. In fact, we often use less than twice the screen frequency. With many images, you can use 1.5 times the screen frequency, and you can sometimes get away with less, sometimes even as low as 1.2 times the screen frequency. That means the resolution of the image you're printing at 133 lpi *could* be as low as 160 ppi (but if you want to play it safe, you might use 200 ppi).

So which multiplier should you use? It depends on quality requirements, the quality of your reproduction method, the kind of images you're reproducing, and your output system.

Figure 2-7 Resolution and image reproduction

How much resolution do you need? All of these images are printed using the same 133-lpi halftone screen, but they contain different numbers of pixels. Look for details, such as readability of type.

2:1 sampling ratio, 266 ppi

1.5:1 sampling ratio, 200 ppi

1.2:1 sampling ratio, 160 ppi

1:1 sampling ratio, 133 ppi

Quality requirements. The only reliable way we've found to answer the question of what's "good enough" is whether or not the client's happy. There's no absolute index of quality, and clients have widely differing expectations. The best course of action is to prepare Kodak Approvals, Creo Spectrums, or other high-quality, dot-based proofs of different images using different multipliers to see where the trade-off works for you.

Reproduction method. Images destined for uncoated stock and newsprint can generally withstand a lower multiplier than those printed on coated stock at a high screen frequency, because the more porous stock causes greater dot gain: The halftone dots grow larger because the ink bleeds into the paper. If you're producing a rag or a newspaper and you're still using the two-times frequency rule, you're wasting someone's time and money—and we hope it's not yours.

Image detail. The need for higher resolution also depends on the content of the image itself. Reducing the multiplier reduces the clarity of small

Figure 2-8 Resolution of grayscale images

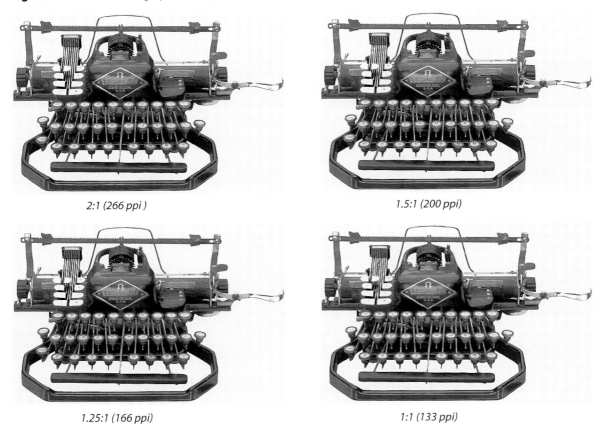

2:1 (266 ppi)

1.5:1 (200 ppi)

1.25:1 (166 ppi)

1:1 (133 ppi)

details, so higher resolution is most important with images that have small (and important) details.

Most pictures of people work fine at 1.25 times the screen frequency, but trees with fine branches and leaves might do best with 1.5 times screen frequency. And if the image has a lot of fine diagonal or curved lines (such as rigging on a sailboat or small text), you may want to use a resolution of 2 times the frequency, particularly if you're paying a premium for a 200-lpi print job on high-quality coated stock. Of course, in those cases, it's probably worth spending a little extra on high-quality proofs to test some of the more difficult images at different resolutions.

If a lot of this halftone talk is going over your head, we recommend a book that David and Conrad coauthored with Steve Roth and Glenn Fleishman called *Real World Scanning and Halftones, 3rd Edition.*

Grayscale and Color Output on Desktop Printers

Many inkjet and laser printers don't use halftone dots. Instead, they use a quite different technique of laying down dots, called *error diffusion*. (See Chapter 12, "Image Storage and Output," for more on the differences between halftone and diffusion dithers.) A common mistake is to take the resolution of the printer in dots per inch, and then send the printer a file with that same resolution in pixels per inch. You do *not* want to send an inkjet printer with a resolution of 1440-by-2880 dpi a 2880 ppi file, or a 1440 ppi file, or even a 720 ppi file! If you do, you'll create an unnecessarily huge file, and you'll drown the printer with data, actually obscuring detail rather than revealing it.

There are all sorts of theories as to the "best" resolution for inkjet printing, some more grounded in reality than others. We'll spare you the esoteric details and simply tell you that we've obtained good results using resolutions between 180 ppi for very large prints and 480 ppi for small prints. Most of the time we print at somewhere between 240 and 360 ppi, depending on the print size and the available resolution in the image. We've yet to find a reason to send a file larger than than 480 ppi to any inkjet printer.

Grayscale and Color Continuous-Tone Output

If you're printing to continuous-tone output devices such as film recorders or dye-sublimation printers, forget all that fancy math. You simply want the resolution of your file to match the resolution of the output device. If you're printing to a 300-dpi dye-sub printer, you want 300 ppi resolution—about 18 MB for a letter-size page. If you're printing to an 8 K film recorder, you really do want 8096 pixels on the short side of the image, or an approximately 240 MB scan.

Sometimes your image may have fewer pixels than you ideally need. Some film recorders and digital printers have excellent built-in upsampling capabilities that rival Photoshop, in which case you can save time, effort, and disk space by letting the output device do the upsampling. But if you're a driven control freak, you may want to control the upsampling process yourself (see "Resampling," on the next page).

Onscreen Output (Multimedia and the Web)

Multimedia is another form of continuous-tone output, but where you often need very high resolution for film recorders, onscreen multimedia projects require very little. It's generally misleading to think in terms of resolution when you prepare images for use on screen. All that really matters are the pixel dimensions.

When people talk about monitor resolution, they almost invariably specify the number of pixels on the screen—800 by 600, 1600 by 1200, and so on. The dots per inch value varies depending on each individual monitor, so you can't rely on dpi when sizing for the screen. For example, you can find a 1280 by 900 pixel display on both 13-inch and 15-inch notebook computers. On a 13-inch notebook, the resolution is around 98 dpi (that's 1280 pixels divided by 13 inches). On the 15-incher, it's around 85 dpi. If you change the 15-inch screen's display settings to 800 by 600 pixels, the resolution becomes 53 dpi. And it works the same way on a Mac or Windows computer. The old advice that Mac monitors are 72 dpi and Windows monitors are 96 dpi became an obsolete myth a long time ago.

Because digital cameras and scanners produce far more pixels than you need on screen, you typically need to downsample an image before using it on a Web page or other video-based output. (See the next section for more info.)

Resampling

One of the most important issues in working with images—and, unfortunately, one which few people seem to understand—is how the resolution can change relative to (or independently of) the size of your image.

There are two ways you can change resolution: scaling and resampling. Scaling doesn't change the number of pixels, just the resolution. Resampling changes the pixel dimensions. If you take a 2-by-2-inch, 300-ppi image and change the size to 1 inch square in InDesign, you're scaling: The pixels get smaller and the resolution increases to 600 ppi.

In Photoshop, you have a choice whether to scale or resample. If you scale that image down without changing the resolution, Photoshop has to throw away a bunch of pixels; that's called *downsampling*. If you double the size to 4 by 4 inches by *upsampling*, the program has to add more pixels by *interpolating* between the other pixels in the image.

Upsampling vs. Downsampling

We used to avoid upsampling when our images mostly came from scanned film, but in the digital age there is no longer a hard-and-fast rule. The lack of film grain in digital captures makes them much more amenable to upsampling than film scans ever were. We often upsample digital camera captures by 200 percent, and sometimes more. Upsampling never adds details that weren't there in the capture, but sometimes it does an uncannily good impersonation! Nevertheless, a 4.1-megapixel capture rarely makes a good magazine cover.

Downsampling is simpler, because it just throws away data in a more or less intelligent manner. In fact, it's a common and necessary practice: Today's digital cameras can record more pixels than you'd need for an image that's less than a full page in size. We downsample to the optimal resolution before printing to save processing time and storage space.

Resampling methods. Photoshop offers five resampling methods: Nearest Neighbor, Bilinear, Bicubic, Bicubic Smoother, and Bicubic Sharper. You choose which you want in the General panel of the Preferences dialog or in the Image Size dialog (see **Figures 2-9** and **2-10**). When you set the resampling method in the Preferences dialog, the settings will apply even when you're not resampling an image using the Image Size dialog, such as when you use the Free Transform tool. Each method has its strengths and weaknesses, and we use each of them in different situations.

▶ **Nearest Neighbor** is the most basic, and it's very fast: To create a new pixel, Photoshop simply looks at the pixel next to it and copies its value. Unfortunately, the results are usually lousy unless the image is made of colored lines or shapes (like an image from Illustrator), but it can be useful for preserving the readability of screen shots.

▶ **Bilinear** is more complex and produces better quality: The program sets the color or gray value of each pixel according to the pixels surrounding it. Some pictures can be upsampled pretty well with bilinear interpolation, but one of the bicubic options often works better.

▶ **Bicubic** interpolation creates better effects than Nearest Neighbor or Bilinear, but takes longer. Like Bilinear, it looks at surrounding pixels, but the equation it uses is much more complex and calculation-intensive, producing smoother tonal gradations.

▶ **Bicubic Smoother** is specifically designed for upsampling. As its name suggests, it gives a smoother result that handles subsequent sharpening better than will the Bicubic sampling method.

▶ **Bicubic Sharper** is designed for downsampling. It does a better job of preserving detail than does the Bicubic method.

The differences between these resampling methods are often subtle, and since we always recommend sharpening after resampling, the resampling itself is only half of the story. Our simple rule: Use Bicubic Smoother for upsampling (but don't expect miracles) and Bicubic Sharper for downsampling.

Figure 2-9

Where to find resampling (interpolation) methods in Photoshop

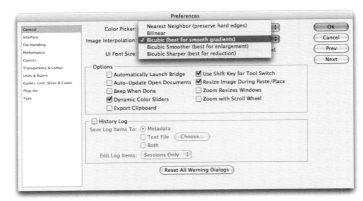

Preferences dialog, General pane

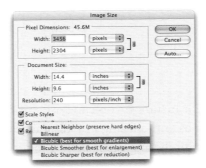

Image Size dialog

Image Mode

As we said earlier, a pixel can have a value of 165, but that doesn't mean anything until you know the image's mode. That 165 could represent a level of gray, a particular color, or it might be only one member of a set of three or four other 8-bit values. Fortunately, Photoshop makes it easy to see what image mode an image is in, as well as to convert it to a different mode if you want.

Ultimately, an image mode is simply a method of organizing the bits to describe a color. In a perfect world, you could say to a printer, "I'd like this box to be navy blue," and they'd know exactly what you were talking about. However, even we can't agree on what navy blue looks like, much less you and your printer. So color scientists created a whole mess of ways for us to describe colors—to each other and to a computer—with some precision.

Photoshop reads and writes only a handful of the many different color modes these scientists came up with. Fortunately, these modes are the most important of the bunch, at least for those in the world of graphic arts. Each of the following image modes appears in the Mode menu in Photoshop.

Bitmap

Tip: Image file formats typically don't support all image modes or bit depths. If you're trying to choose a file format in the Save As dialog and the format isn't listed, you may need to change the image mode. For example, JPEG only supports 8-bit RGB or CMYK images.

David really wishes that Adobe had picked a different word for this image mode. He insists that all images in Photoshop are *bitmapped*, but only "flat" black-and-white images, in which each pixel is defined using one bit of data (a zero or a one), are *bitmaps*.

Pictures that are 1 bit have a particular difference from other images when it comes to PostScript printing: The white areas throughout the image can appear transparent, showing through to whatever the image is printing over. Ordinarily, images are opaque, except for the occasional white silhouetted background made with clipping paths (see "Silhouettes" in Chapter 11, "Essential Image Techniques").

The other major difference between the other image modes and Bitmap mode is that you're much more limited in the sorts of image editing you can do. For instance, you can't use any filters, and because there's no such thing as anti-aliasing in 1-bit images, you just cannot use tools that require anti-aliasing, such as the Smudge tool, the Blur tool, or the Dodge/Burn tool.

Grayscale

Grayscale files in Photoshop are always either 8- or 16-bit images: Anything less than an 8-bit image gets converted to an 8-bit image; anything more than 8 bits gets converted to 16 bits.

In an 8-bit grayscale image, each pixel has a value from 0 (black) to 255 (white), so there are a maximum of 256 levels of gray possible. In a 16-bit

The Image Size Dialog

For those of us who have to teach Photoshop as well as use it, the Image Size dialog is always one of the biggest sources of confusion, because the results you get depend not only on which buttons you click and which fields you type numbers into, but also on the order in which you do so.

The Image Size dialog is split into the two sets of numbers that determine an image's resolution: its pixel dimensions, and its size if it's printed.

▶ **Pixel Dimensions.** The best way to specify an image's size is by its pixel dimensions—these tell you exactly how much data you have to work with. The Pixel Dimensions section shows you both the dimensions and the file's size, in megabytes (or K, if it's under 1 MB).

▶ **Document Size.** A bitmapped image has no inherent size—it's just pixels on a grid. The Document Size section lets you state a size and resolution, so that when you import the file into some other program, it knows what the image's size will be when it's printed.

Resample Image. The most important feature in the Image Size dialog is the Resample Image check box. When this is turned on, Photoshop lets you change the image's pixel dimensions; when it's off, the pixel dimen-

Figure 2-10 Image Size dialog

With Resample Image off, the image's resolution and physical dimension are interdependent, and the pixel dimensions, file size, and details in the image don't change.

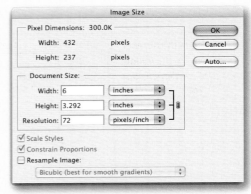

With the units pop-up menu set to Percent, the width and height represent the scaling (200 percent) relative to the original (100 percent) physical dimensions. The resolution drops because the Resample Image check box is off, so each pixel must become larger.

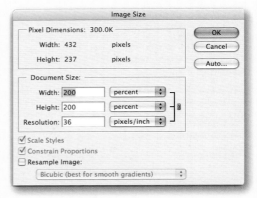

sions are locked. In other words, unless you turn on this check box, you can't increase (upsample) or decrease (downsample) the number of pixels that make up the image (see "Upsampling vs. Downsampling," earlier in this chapter).

When Resample Image is on, you can change the pixel dimensions, the document size, or the resolution. When you change the pixel

dimensions, the file size on disk also changes. Both the new and old size appear at the top of the Image Size dialog, next to the Pixel Dimensions heading.

The Resample Image pop-up menu at the bottom of the dialog becomes available when the Resample Image check box is on.

Changing sizes. Like we said, the Image Size dialog takes some

Figure 2-10 Image Size dialog, continued

Turning on the Resample Image check box lets you change the number of pixels in the image, so the Pixel Dimensions become editable.

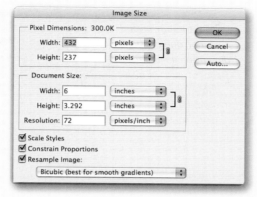

With Resample Image on, changing any attribute alters the pixel dimensions and the file size. The more you increase (or decrease) the pixel dimensions, the more pixels are made up (or discarded), altering the details in the image.

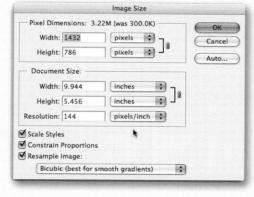

of one another when Resample Image is turned on. Just change one, then the other.

When Resample Image is turned off, the Pixel Dimensions never change, and changing either Document Size or Resolution always affects the other one (see **Figure 2-10**).

The best way to learn how the Image Size dialog works, though, is to open an image, note the starting values, and play around with it. So get going!

Tip: Adjusting by Percent. The word "percent" appears in both the Pixel Dimensions and the Document Size pop-up menus. Percent isn't an absolute size; it's based on the current size of the image you're working on. For example, if you have a 2-by-2-inch image and you type in "200 percent" for Document Size Width and Height, the result will be a 4-by-4-inch image. The resulting number of pixels in the image depends on whether Resample Image is on or off.

We find this especially helpful when we have to re-create an image that was scaled "for position only" in a layout program. First we write down the scaling values on a piece of paper, and then we open the image in Photoshop and type the percentages into the Image Size dialog.

getting used to. One point of potential confusion is that whenever you make a change to one field, some other fields change and others don't. Here's a quick summary of what to watch for.

When Resample Image is turned on and you change the Pixel Dimensions, the Document Size changes, but the Resolution does not. If you change the Document Size, the Pixel Dimensions

change, too, and the Resolution remains unchanged. If you change the Resolution, the Pixel Dimensions change, and the Document Size stays the same. An often overlooked subtlety is that Image Size allows you to change the Document Size and the Resolution in a single operation (which then changes the pixel dimensions). The key is that Document Size and Resolution are independent grayscale image, each pixel has a value from 0 (black) to 32,768 (white), for a theoretical maximum of 32,769 possible gray shades.

Few capture devices can actually deliver all those gray shades, so 16-bit files usually have a lot of redundancy. But that redundancy translates into editing headroom, so if your camera or scanner can capture 12 or more bits per pixel, it's often worthwhile to bring the high-bit data into Photoshop.

Duotone

When you print a grayscale image on a printing press, those 256 levels of gray often get reduced to 100 or so because of the limitations of the press. You can counter this flattening effect considerably by printing the image with more than one color of ink, increasing the tonal range of the printed image. This is called printing a *duotone* (for two inks), a *tritone* (for three inks), or a *quadtone* (for four inks).

The key is that the extra colors aren't typically used to simulate colors in the image; rather, they're used to extend the dynamic range of the underlying grayscale image. Those expensive Ansel Adams books on your coffee table were very likely printed using three or four (or even five or six) *different* black and gray inks.

Tip: As we mentioned in the Preface, you can download the free online chapter from *www.peachpit.com/ realworldphotoshop-cs3*.

Photoshop has a special image mode for duotones, tritones, and quadtones, and even though the file may appear to be in color, each pixel is still saved using only 8 bits of information. The trick is that Photoshop saves a set of contrast curves for each ink along with the 8-bit grayscale image. Creating a good duotone is as much art as science. For more information, see our online chapter, "Spot Colors and Duotones."

Indexed Color

As we said, each pixel in a grayscale image is defined with 8 bits of information, so the file can contain up to 256 different pixel values. But each of those values, from 1 to 256, doesn't have to be a level of gray. The Indexed Color image mode is a method for producing 8-bit, 256-color files. Indexed-color bitmaps use a table of 256 colors, chosen from the full 24-bit palette. A given pixel's color is defined by reference to the table, Essentially, this reference says, "This pixel is color number 123, this pixel is color number 81," and so on.

While Indexed Color can save disk space (it requires only 8 bits per sample point, rather than the full 24 in RGB mode—see below), it gives your image only 256 different colors. That's not a lot of colors when you compare it to the 16.7 million different colors you can get in RGB.

Another major limitation is that most editing tools won't work in Indexed Color mode because almost all of them rely on the numeric values having a relationship to how light or dark the pixel is. Therefore, you should always do your image editing in RGB mode and then convert to Indexed Color mode as a last step: The relatively tiny size of Indexed Color images makes them useful for Web graphics, but not for many other uses.

RGB

Every color computer monitor and television in the world displays color using the RGB image mode, in which every color is produced with varying amounts of red, green, and blue light. (These colors are called *additive primaries* because the more red, green, or blue light you add, the closer to white you get.) In Photoshop, files saved in the RGB mode typically use a set of three 8-bit grayscale files, so we say that RGB files are *24-bit* files.

These files can include up to approximately 16 million colors—more than enough to qualify your image as photographic quality. This is the mode in which we prefer to work when editing color images. Digital cameras and scanners capture images in RGB format. If you have a print or film image scanned by a lab and it comes back as a CMYK scan, it was likely scanned using an RGB sensor and converted to CMYK by the scanning hardware or software. If you're producing images for the Web or digital video, save your files in RGB mode.

CMYK

Tip: A great philosophical debate rages on this issue of whether it's better to work in RGB or in CMYK for prepress work. Here's our advice: If someone gives you a CMYK image, edit that image in CMYK. In all other cases, we recommend staying in RGB for as long as possible.

Traditional full-color printing presses can print only four colors in a run: cyan, magenta, yellow, and black. Every other color in the spectrum is simulated using various combinations of those colors. When you open a file saved in CMYK mode, Photoshop has to convert the CMYK values to RGB values on the fly in order to display the image on your computer screen. It's important to remember that when you look at the screen, you're looking at an RGB version of the data.

If you buy high-end drum scans, they'll probably be CMYK files. Otherwise, to print your images on press or on some desktop color printers, you'll have to convert your RGB images to CMYK. We discuss Photoshop's tools for doing so in Chapter 4, "Color Settings."

Lab

The problem with RGB and CMYK modes is that a given RGB or CMYK specification doesn't really describe a *color*. Rather, it's a set of instructions that a specific output device uses to produce a color. The problem is that different devices produce different colors from the same RGB or CMYK specifications. If you've ever seen a wall full of television screens at a department store, you've seen what we're talking about: The same image—with the same RGB values—looks different on each screen.

And if you've ever sat through a printing-press run, you know that the 50th impression probably isn't exactly the same color as the 5000th or the 50,000th. So, while a pixel in a scanned image may have a particular RGB or CMYK value, you can't tell what that color really looks like. RGB and CMYK are both *device-specific* color modes.

However, a class of *device-independent* or *perceptually based* modes has been developed over the years. All of them are based, more or less, on a color space defined by the Commission Internationale de l'Éclairage (CIE) in 1931. The Lab mode in Photoshop is one such derivative.

Lab doesn't describe a color by the components that make it up (RGB or CMYK, for instance). Instead, it describes *what a color looks like*. Device-independent color spaces are at the heart of the various color management systems now available that improve color correspondence between your screen, color printouts, and final printed output.

A file saved in Lab mode describes what a color looks like under rigidly specified conditions; it's up to you (or Photoshop, or your color management software) to decide what RGB or CMYK values are needed to create that color on your chosen output device.

Photoshop uses Lab mode as a reference when switching between CMYK and RGB modes, taking the values in your RGB Setup and CMYK Setup dialogs into account (see Chapter 4, "Color Settings," for more information on this conversion).

Lab is considerably less intuitive than the other color modes. The Lightness channel is relatively easy to understand, but the a* and b* channels (pronounced "ay-star" and "bee-star") are less so. The a* channel represents how red or green a color is—negative values represent greens, positive ones represent magentas—and the b* channel represents how blue or yellow the color is—negative values represent blue, positive ones represent yellow. Neutrals and near-neutrals always have values close to zero in both channels. Most hard-core Photoshop geeks have a few tricks

Tip: If you're going to work with layers, it's best to do so after you've completed all image mode conversions. Some image mode changes require flattening layered images. If flattening isn't required, a mode change may still change the appearance of the image due to the different nature of channels in the new image mode.

that rely on Lab mode, but many of them can be accomplished more easily by using blend modes instead. Luminosity blending, for example, produces extremely similar results to working on the Lightness channel in Lab mode.

Multichannel

The last image mode that Photoshop offers is Multichannel mode. This mode is the generic mode: Like RGB or CMYK, Multichannel mode has more than one 8-bit channel; however, you can set the color and name of each channel to anything you like.

Today, many scientific and astronomical images are made in "false color"—the channels may be a combination of radar, infrared, and ultra-violet, in addition to various colors of visible light. Some of our gonzo digital photographer friends use Multichannel mode to combine infrared and visible-spectrum photographs into composite images of surreal beauty.

Bitmaps and File Size

As we said at the beginning of this chapter, pixel-based images are rectangles with thousands (or even millions) of pixels. Each of those pixels has to be saved to a disk. If each pixel is defined using 8 bits of color information, then the file is eight times bigger than a black-and-white bitmap. Similarly, a 24-bit file is a full three times bigger than an 8-bit image, and a 48-bit file is twice the size of a 24-bit one.

Big files take a long time to open, edit, print, or save. Many people who complain about how slow editing is in Photoshop are simply working with files much bigger than they need. Instead, you can save yourself the complaining and reduce your file size when you can. Here's a quick rundown of how each attribute of a pixel-based image affects file size.

Dimensions and resolution. When you increase the number of pixels, you increase the file's size by the square of the value. So, if you double the resolution, you quadruple the file size (double the height multiplied by double the width). There can easily be a multimegabyte difference between a 300-ppi image and a 225-ppi image. (And remember that a 225-ppi image is almost always plenty resolution for a 150-lpi halftone screen.)

Bit depth. Increasing bit depth increases file size by a simple multiplier. Therefore, a 24-bit image is three times as large as an 8-bit image, and 24 times as large as a 1-bit image.

Image mode. Changing the image mode can increase file size when the new image mode uses more bits, more channels, or both. For example, going from RGB to CMYK mode adds a fourth 8-bit channel.

Figuring File Size

Now that you know the factors that affect the size of images, it's a simple matter to calculate file size using the following formula:

File size in kilobytes =
Resolution^2 × Width × Height × Bits per sample ÷ 8192

For example, if you have a 4-by-5-inch, 1-bit image at 300 ppi, you know that the file size is 220 K (300^2 × 4 × 5 × 1 ÷ 8192). A 24-bit image of the same size would be 5273 K (just about 5 MB). This formula works because 8192 is the number of bits in a kilobyte.

Of course, all these calculations apply only to flat files. When you start adding layers, layer masks, and alpha channels, it becomes quite difficult to figure file size with any degree of reliability. Each channel or mask adds another 8 or 16 bits to the bit depth (depending on whether the document was in 8-bit/channel or 16-bit/channel mode), but layers are much harder to figure because Photoshop divides each layer into tiles. Empty tiles take up almost no space, but if a tile contains just one pixel, it takes up the same amount of space as a tile that's full of pixels. It's possible, and sometimes useful, to place layered TIFF or Photoshop files in a page-layout application, but we recommend flattening all files before final handoff to keep final files to a manageable size.

Some file formats also offer compression options. It's important to bear in mind that the file size that Photoshop reports in the Info palette or status bar is always the amount of RAM that the uncompressed, flattened image will occupy. We'll discuss compression options and file formats in much greater detail in Chapter 12, "Image Storage and Output."

Tip: Faster File Figuring. There's an even easier way to calculate file sizes than doing the math yourself—let the computer do it for you. The New Document and Image Size dialoges are very handy calculators for figuring dimensions, resolution, and file size. Simply type in the values you want, and the top of the Image Size dialog shows you how big the file would be (see Figure 2-10).

Color Essentials

What Makes a Color

People have many different ways of thinking about, talking about, and working with color, but there's a notion that comes up again and again— that we can create any color by combining three primary colors. Art directors may feel comfortable specifying color changes with the terms *hue*, *lightness*, and *saturation*. Those who came to color through the computer may be more at home with levels of RGB. Scientists think about color in all sorts of strange ways, including CIE Lab, HSB, and LCH. And dyed-in-the-wool prepress folks think in CMYK dot percentages.

Although Photoshop tries to accommodate all these ways of thinking about color, many Photoshop users find themselves locked into seeing color in only one way, such as RGB. This is natural and understandable; we all have one way of thinking about color that matches the kind of work we do or how we learned. If you learn about other three-component ways to see color, you can unlock much more of the power of Photoshop.

"Wait a minute," you say. "CMYK has four constituents, not three!" Well, for now just trust us and set this issue aside for the moment. We promise to deal with it later.

In this chapter, we take a hard look at some fundamental color relationships and how Photoshop presents them. This stuff might seem a little theoretical at times, but we urge you to slog through it; it's essential for our later discussions about tonal and color correction.

Primary Colors

You might have learned the concept of *primary* colors in grade school, and it's still at the heart of much of the color work we do on computers. When we work with primary colors, we're talking about three colors that we can combine to make all the other colors. Ignoring for the moment which specific colors constitute the primaries, there are two fundamental principles of primary colors.

▶ They are the irreducible components of color.

▶ The primary colors, combined in varying proportions, can produce an entire spectrum of color.

The *secondary* colors, by the way, are made by combining two primary colors and excluding the third. What makes the primary colors special—indeed, what makes them primary colors—is human physiology rather than any special property inherent in those wavelengths of light.

Additive and Subtractive Color

Before becoming preoccupied with the behavior of spherical objects like apples, billiard balls, and planets, Sir Isaac Newton performed some experiments with light and prisms. He found that he could break white light down into red, green, and blue components, a fairly trivial phenomenon that had been known for centuries. His breakthrough was the discovery that he could *reconstitute* white light by recombining those red, green, and blue components. Red, green, and blue—the primary colors of light—are known as the *additive primary* colors because as you add color, the result becomes more white (the absence of colored light is black; see **Figure 3-1**). This is how computer monitors and televisions produce color.

But color on the printed page works differently. Unlike a television, the page doesn't emit light; it just reflects whatever light hits it. To print colors, you don't work with the light directly. Instead, you use pigments (like ink, dye, toner, or wax) that *absorb* some colors of light and reflect others.

The primary colors of pigments are cyan, yellow, and magenta. We call these the *subtractive primary* colors because as you add pigments to a white page, they subtract (absorb) more light, and the reflected color becomes darker. (We sometimes find it easier to remember: You *add* additive colors to get white, and you *subtract* subtractive colors to get white.) Cyan absorbs all the red light, magenta absorbs all the green light, and yellow absorbs all the blue light. If you add the maximum intensities of cyan, magenta, and yellow, you get black—in theory (see Figure 3-1).

Figure 3-1
Additive and subtractive primaries

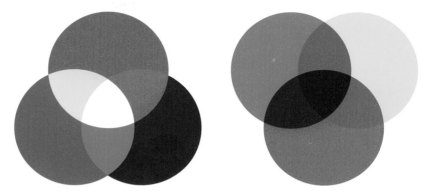

An Imperfect World

A little while ago, we asked you to trust us on the subject of CMYK. Well, we just told you that combining cyan, magenta, and yellow would, *in theory,* produce black. In practice, however, it produces a muddy brown mess. Why? In the words of our friend and colleague Bob Schaffel, "God made RGB…man made CMYK." To that we add: "Who do you trust more?"

Imperfect pigments. If we had perfect CMY pigments, we wouldn't have to add black (K) as a fourth color. But despite our best efforts, cyan pigments always contain a little red, our magentas always contain a little green, and our yellows always contain a trace of blue. Moreover, there's a limit to the amount of ink we can apply to the paper without dissolving it. So when we print in color, we add black to help with the reproduction of dark colors and to achieve acceptable density on press. See Chapter 4, "Color Settings," for more on this.

Imperfect conversions. If we only had to deal with CMY, life would be a lot simpler. However, a large part of the problem of reproducing color images in print is that scanners—since they deal with light—see color in RGB, and we have to translate those values into CMYK to print them. Unfortunately, this conversion is a thorny one (see Chapter 4, "Color Settings," for more on this subject).

The Color Wheel

Before moving on to weightier matters such as gravity, calculus, and his impending thirtieth birthday, Sir Isaac Newton provided the world of color with one more key concept: if you take the colors of the spectrum and arrange them around the circumference of a wheel, the relationships among primaries become much clearer (see **Figure 3-2**).

Figure 3-2
The color wheel

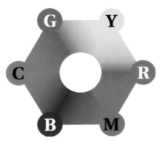

Emitted and reflected (additive and subtractive) colors are complementary to one another. Red is complementary to cyan, green to magenta, and blue to yellow.

The important thing to notice about this color wheel is that the additive and subtractive primary colors are opposite each other, equidistant around the wheel. These relationships are key to understanding how color works. For instance, cyan sits opposite red on the color wheel because it is, in fact, the opposite of red: Cyan pigments appear cyan because they absorb red light and reflect blue and green. Cyan is, in short, the absence of red.

Colors that lie directly opposite each other on the wheel are known as *complementary* colors.

Figuring Saturation and Brightness

So far, we've talked about color in terms of three primary colors. But there are other ways of specifying color in terms of three ingredients. The most familiar one use the terms of *hue* (the property we refer to when we talk about "red" or "orange"), *saturation* (the "purity" of the color), and *brightness.*

Newton's basic two-dimensional color wheel lets us see the relationships between different hues, but to describe colors more fully, we need a more complex, three-dimensional model. We can find one of these in the HSB (Hue, Saturation, Brightness) color cylinder (see **Figure 3-3**).

In the HSB cylinder, you can see that the hues are arranged around the edge of the wheel, and that colors become progressively weaker as

Figure 3-3

The HSB color cylinder

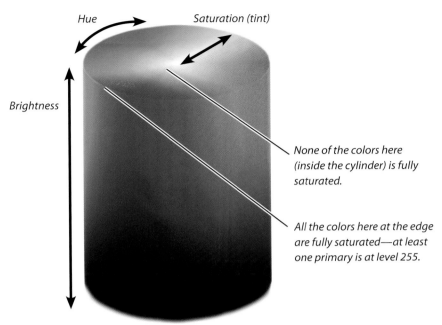

Hue

Saturation (tint)

Brightness

None of the colors here (inside the cylinder) is fully saturated.

All the colors here at the edge are fully saturated—at least one primary is at level 255.

we move into the center—the farther in you go, the less saturated or pure the color is.

Tristimulus Models and Color Spaces

Ignoring the inconvenience of CMYK, all the ways we've discussed of specifying and thinking about color involve three primary ingredients. Color scientists call these *tristimulus* models. (A *color* model is simply a way of thinking about color and representing it numerically: A tristimulus model represents colors by using three numbers.) If you go deep into the physiology of color, you'll find that our perceptual systems are actually wired in terms of three different responses to light that combine to produce the sensation of color. So the tristimulus approach isn't merely a mathematical convenience—it's inherent in how we see.

But tristimulus models have another useful property. Because they specify everything in terms of three ingredients, you can easily view them as three-dimensional objects with *x*, *y*, and *z* axes. Each color has a location in this three-dimensional object, specified by the three values. These three-dimensional models are called *color spaces*. The cylinder in **Figure 3-3** is an example of a color space expressed as a 3D model. However, the simple HSB model can't really describe how you *see* colors. For instance, you know that cyan appears much lighter than blue; but in the HSB cylinder, they both have the same brightness and saturation values. Therefore, while some 3D representations are helpful, we have to go further to understand how to work with color.

How Colors Affect Each Other

There are a lot of times in Photoshop when we find ourselves working with one color space, but thinking about the changes in terms of another color space. As you'll see in Chapter 7, "Image Adjustment Fundamentals," we often recommend that you use curves to adjust RGB values, but that you base your changes on the resulting CMYK percentages as displayed in the Info palette. So, it will speed up your work if you take some time to figure out how color spaces interact; that is, what happens in one space when you work in another.

Here are some ways to think about RGB, CMY, and HSB colors, and how they relate to each other.

Tone. One of the least understood—yet most important—effects of adding colors together is that adding or removing primaries not only affects hue and saturation, it also affects tone. When you increase any RGB component to change the hue—adding light—the color gets lighter. The reverse is true with CMY because you're adding ink, making the color darker.

Hue. Every color, except the primaries, contains opposing primary colors. In RGB mode, red is "pure," but orange contains red alongside a good dose of green (and possibly some blue, too). In CMYK, magenta is pure, and red is not—it contains some amount of yellow in addition to magenta. So to change a color's hue, you add or subtract primary colors.

In the process, you will probably affect the color's tone—adding or removing light (or ink) so the color gets lighter or darker.

Saturation. A saturated RGB color is made up of only one or two primaries; the third primary is always zero. When you add a trace of the third color—in order to change the hue, for instance—you desaturate the color.

Likewise, if you increase the saturation of a color using the Hue/Saturation dialog (or any other), you're removing one of the primaries. If you get out to the edge, where one of the primaries is maxed out and the other two are still changing, you'll change the hue and the tone.

There's another important consideration pertaining to saturated colors. When you saturate a color in an RGB image, detail exists in only one of the three channels. One of the others is always solid white, and the other is always solid black. All the detail is being carried by one channel, which is why saturated colors in images are hard to handle.

Neutrals. A color made up of equal values of red, green, and blue is always a neutral gray (though you may have to do quite a bit of work to make it come out that way onscreen or—once you've converted it to CMYK—on press). The "darkness" of the gray depends on how much red, green, and blue there is; more light makes for a lighter gray. This is useful in a number of situations, including making monitor adjustments and correcting color casts. For a quick summary of relationships among the color spaces, see the sidebar "Color Relationships at a Glance."

Device-Independent Color

Basically, the problem with HSB, RGB, and CMY (and even CMYK) is that they don't describe how a color looks; they only describe the color's ingredients. You've probably walked into a television store and seen about a hundred televisions on the wall, each of them receiving the same color information. But none of them displays the colors in the same way.

In fact, if you send the same RGB values to ten different monitors, or the same CMYK values to ten different presses, you'll end up with ten different colors (see **Figure 3-4**). We call RGB and CMYK *device dependent*, because the color you end up with varies from device to device.

So, Photoshop has a problem in trying to display colors properly on your monitor: It doesn't know what the colors should *look like* to you. It doesn't know what those RGB or CMYK values really mean.

Plus, the program has to take all the little quirks of human vision into account. For instance, our eyes are more sensitive to some colors and brightness levels than to others, and we're more sensitive to small changes in bright colors than we are to small changes in dark ones (if you've had trouble teasing all the subtle shadow details out of your scanned images, this is one reason for that). RGB and CMYK don't give Photoshop the information it needs to know what color is actually being described.

Figure 3-4 Device-dependent color and color gamuts

Because this figure is printed with process inks on paper, it can only simulate the results of sending the same RGB or CMYK values to various devices. It depicts relative appearances, not actual results. Likewise, the color chart just represents the gamuts of different devices, rather than actually showing those gamuts.

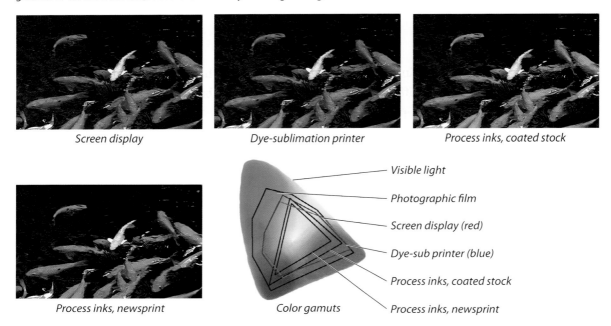

Screen display   *Dye-sublimation printer*   *Process inks, coated stock*

Process inks, newsprint   *Color gamuts*

— *Visible light*
— *Photographic film*
— *Screen display (red)*
— *Dye-sub printer (blue)*
— *Process inks, coated stock*
— *Process inks, newsprint*

Lab Color

Fortunately, there's CIE Lab, which appears on the Mode menu simply as Lab. Lab is designed to describe what colors look like regardless of the device they're displayed on, so we call Lab *device independent*.

Whereas in HSB the hues are represented as lying around a wheel, Lab color uses a more accurate but significantly less intuitive arrangement. In Lab, the third axis (which lies perpendicular to the page and is roughly equivalent to brightness in HSB) is the luminance axis—it represents how bright the color appears to the human eye. But unlike brightness in HSB, it takes into account the fact that we see green as brighter than blue.

Lab color can be an intimidating subject, but for the purposes of color correction, there are really only three things you need to know.

▶   HSB, HSL, and LCH are based on the way we think about color, and RGB and CMYK are based on the ways devices such as monitors and printers produce color, but Lab is based on the way humans actually see color. A Lab specification describes the color that most people will see when they look at an object under specified lighting conditions.

▶ Photoshop uses Lab as a reference when it does mode changes. For instance, when you switch from RGB mode to CMYK mode, Photoshop uses Lab to decide what *color* is being specified by each device-dependent RGB value, and then it comes up with the right device-dependent CMYK equivalent. This idea is critical to the concept of color management.

▶ Finally, don't feel dumb if you find it hard to understand Lab color. It *is* difficult to visualize, because it's an abstract mathematical construct. It uses differing amounts of three primaries to specify colors, but those primaries don't really correspond to anything we can actually experience, as we can with RGB or HSB.

Working with Colors

Some color-correction tasks aren't straightforward. For example, it's difficult to adjust saturation in an image by manipulating RGB or CMYK values directly. But because you have Photoshop, you can use Photoshop tools that let you apply changes in hue, saturation, and brightness to the underlying RGB or CMYK data.

Even with the help of Photoshop, you face two fairly large problems. First, when you change modes, you lose some image information; if your images start with 256 shades of each color, some get lost due to rounding errors during the conversion.

The second problem is that the color spaces in which most of your images are stored, RGB and CMYK, are device dependent: The color you'll get varies depending on the device you send it to. Worse, some devices have a much wider range of colors they can reproduce—called the *color gamut* (see **Figure 3-4** earlier in this chapter). For example, color film can record a wider range of colors than a color monitor can display, and the monitor displays a wider range of colors than you can reproduce with ink on paper; so no matter what you do, some of the colors captured on film simply can't be reproduced in print.

Fortunately, Photoshop lets you specify the gamut of your monitor and your CMYK output devices; we'll show you how to set that up in the next chapter, "Color Settings." In Chapter 7, "Image Adjustment Fundamentals," we'll show you how to use Photoshop to predict the color values and appearance of a color in those other gamuts.

Color Relationships at a Glance

It's worth spending some time to understand the color relationships we're discussing in this chapter. We all have a favorite color space, but if you can learn to view color in more than one way—understanding how to achieve the same results by manipulating CMY, RGB, and HSB—you'll find the world of color correction much less alien, and you'll be much more able to select the right tool for the job.

We suggest memorizing these fundamentals.

► 100 percent cyan = 0 red

► 100 percent magenta = 0 green

► 100 percent yellow = 0 blue

► Increasing RGB values corresponds exactly to reducing CMY values, and vice versa.

► Reducing saturation (making something more gray) means introducing the complementary color; to desaturate red, for example, you add cyan.

► The complement of a primary color is produced by combining equal amounts of the other two primary colors.

► Lightening or darkening a saturated color desaturates that color.

► Changing the hue of a color often changes lightness as well.

► Saturation changes can cause hue changes.

Saturated Primaries—CMY versus RGB

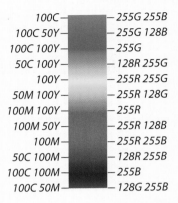

100C	255G 255B
100C 50Y	255G 128B
100C 100Y	255G
50C 100Y	128R 255G
100Y	255R 255G
50M 100Y	255R 128G
100M 100Y	255R
100M 50Y	255R 128B
100M	255R 255B
50C 100M	128R 255B
100C 100M	255B
100C 50M	128G 255B

The colors at left are fully saturated—each contains 100 percent of one or two primaries. The additive and subtractive primaries have an inverse relationship, as you can see by comparing the CMY values along the left side with the RGB values along the right side.

Desaturating Saturated Colors

255R 255G
64R 128G 192B
128R 128G 128B
64R 192G 128B
255R 255B

Desaturating the reds removes red and adds other primaries to the red areas. Adding a third primary "pollutes" the saturated color, causing it to go gray. It may or may not affect lightness.

Lightness and Saturation

Lightening or darkening a saturated color (here, +50 and –50) desaturates it; it pulls the primaries back from 100 percent, it pollutes them with a third primary, or both. Also note the hue shift in the darkened version.

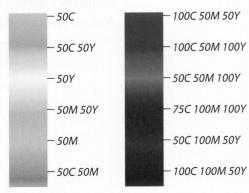

50C	100C 50M 50Y
50C 50Y	100C 50M 100Y
50Y	50C 50M 100Y
50M 50Y	75C 100M 100Y
50M	50C 100M 50Y
50C 50M	100C 100M 50Y

Color Settings

Understanding Color Management in Photoshop

Welcome to the heart of *Real World Photoshop CS3*. We consider every topic in this book to be important, but color management is one of those topics that can quickly make anyone feel stupid. If you're under the delusion that you can use Photoshop *without* using color management, this chapter is a must-read. Without understanding how Photoshop handles color behind the scenes, there's no way to get great color (or black-and-white) images out of this program.

Although behind the scenes, the color management system in Photoshop uses mathematics that approach rocket science, using these tools is much simpler: You just need to understand a few key concepts, learn where the buttons are, and use common sense in deciding when to push them.

In the last chapter, we broke the sad news that RGB and CMYK are very ambiguous ways of specifying color, since the actual color you get will vary from device to device. In this chapter, we'll look at the features Photoshop offers to make what you see on the screen at least resemble, if not actually match, what you get in your printed output.

Color Management Systems Explained

A color management system (CMS) is software that attempts to maintain the appearance of colors when reproduced on different devices. We stress the word "appearance" because it's simply impossible to reproduce many of the colors found in the world in print, or even on a color monitor.

Color management often gets dressed up in much fancier clothing, but it really does only two things.

▶ It lets you assign a specific color appearance to RGB or CMYK numbers that would otherwise be ambiguous.

▶ Within the physical limitations of the devices involved, it lets you keep that specific color appearance as you send your images to different displays and output devices.

No matter how complicated color management options might appear, when you examine them more closely, they always serve those two purposes.

CMS Components

All CMSs employ three basic components:

▶ The *reference color space* (also known as the *profile connection space*, or PCS) is a device-independent, perceptually based color space. Most current CMSs use a CIE-defined color space, such as CIE Lab or CIE XYZ. You never have to worry about the reference color space; it's the theory behind how the software works. Think of it as the common ground for all color devices—a space that can represent any color.

▶ The *color-matching engine* (sometimes known as the *color matching method*, or CMM) is the software that converts color meanings between different device-specific color spaces. Photoshop supports color matching engines other than the Adobe-branded one (ACE) that it shares with the other Adobe Creative Suite applications, but the only reason we can see for using a different engine is if you absolutely must obtain exactly the same conversions from non-Adobe products. In general, the differences between the various CMMs are slight. Think of the CMM as the universal translator between your color devices.

▶ A *profile* can describe the behavior of a device like a scanner, monitor, or printer. For instance, a profile can tell the CMS "This is the reddest red that this device can output." A profile can also define a "virtual color space" that's unrelated to any particular device (the Adobe RGB space is an example of this; we'll see how it's useful later on). Profiles are the key to color management. Without a profile, 100 percent red has no specific meaning; with a profile, the color management system can say "Oh, *that* color of red!" Thanks to the ICC (International Color Consortium) specification, device profiles conform to a standard format that lets them work with all CMSs on all platforms. ColorSync profiles on the Mac and .icm or .icc profiles in Windows both follow the ICC spec and are interchangeable between platforms.

Of the three components, the first two are usually invisible to you. You might change them once in a lifetime, or more likely, you'll never have to think about them at all. But profiles are something you'll probably have to think about on a regular basis, especially if your images come from many sources or go to many different output media.

Conveying Color Meaning

The key concept in using a CMS is conveying color meaning—making those ambiguous RGB and CMYK values unambiguous. If the system is going to keep the color consistent among different devices, it needs to know what color appearance each device in the process represents using RGB or CMYK numbers. If a CMS knows what RGB values a scanner produces when it scans specific colors, and it knows what colors a display produces when we send it specific RGB numbers, it can calculate the new RGB numbers it needs to send to the display to make it reproduce the colors represented by the scanner's RGB numbers.

Tip: *Embedded* and *tagged* mean the same thing: A color profile is included inside the document file. When Photoshop reports that an image is *untagged*, it means no profile is embedded.

Profile embedding. When you embed a profile in an image, you aren't changing the image. You're simply providing a definition of what the numbers in the file mean in terms of actual colors you can see. That is, you're assigning a specific color appearance to the RGB or CMYK numbers. If you don't embed profiles in your images, the numbers in the file are ambiguous and open to many different interpretations. Embedding a profile simply tells color-management-savvy applications which interpretation you want to place on the numbers. Profile embedding is the easiest way to convey the color meaning—the intended color appearance—of the numbers in the digital image.

Source and target profiles. When you ask the color management system to make a conversion—to change the numbers in the file—the CMS needs to know where the RGB or CMYK color values came from and where you want to send them. When you open or create an image, you have to give the CMS this information by specifying a source profile and a target profile.

The source profile (which is sometimes already embedded in the file) says, "This RGB data is from such-and-such a scanner," or "This RGB data is from such-and-such a monitor." This tells the CMS what actual colors RGB or CMYK numbers represent. The target profile tells the CMS where the image is going, so that it can calculate the new RGB or CMYK numbers that will maintain the color in the image on the target device.

For example, imagine that a color management system works with words rather than colors. The purpose of the CMS would be to translate words from one language to another. If you just feed it a bunch of words, it can't do anything. But if you give it the words and tell it that they were written by a French person (the source), it all of a sudden can understand what the words are saying. If you then tell it that you speak German (the target), it can translate the meaning faithfully for you.

Tip: Even the best CMS degrades your image when you convert it from one color space to another. While Photoshop tries to minimize conversion-related data loss by using a device-independent color space, it's best to avoid converting an image between color spaces more than necessary.

The process. Back to pictures: When you scan artwork, you end up with RGB data. But for Photoshop to know what specific colors those RGB values are meant to represent, you have to tell it that the RGB data came from this particular scanner. When you choose your scanner's device profile as the source profile, you're telling Photoshop that this isn't just any old RGB data; it's the RGB data carefully defined by the scanner's device profile.

To make the image on your printer match the original, you choose your printer profile as the target profile. The CMS takes the RGB values in the image and uses the scanner profile as the secret decoder ring that tells it what colors (in the reference color space) the RGB values represent. Then it calculates new RGB or CMYK values based on the printer profile, so it can produce the closest possible colors on your printer.

This is really the only thing CMSs do. They convert color data from one device's color space (one "language") to another. Pretty much everything you do with a CMS involves asking it to make the colors in a source and target profile match each other, and this same two-step is integral to the way Photoshop handles color.

Tip: Here's an easy way to remember the meaning of the source profile, the target profile, and the rendering intent: Think of them as where the color comes from, where the color is going, and how you want the color to get there.

Rendering intents. There's one more wrinkle. Each device has a fixed range of color that it can reproduce, dictated by the laws of physics. Your monitor can't reproduce a more saturated red than the red produced by the color filter or phosphor that a monitor uses to produce red. Your printer can't reproduce a cyan more saturated than the printer's cyan ink, or a white brighter than the white of the paper. The range of color a device can reproduce is called the *color gamut*. Colors present in the source space that aren't reproducible in the destination space are called *out-of-gamut* colors. Since you can't reproduce those colors in the destination space, you have to replace them with some other colors.

The ICC profile specification includes four different methods of handling out-of-gamut colors, called *rendering intents*. (In Photoshop, they're simply called intents.) The four rendering intents act as follows:

Tip: For photographic images, when you aren't sure which rendering intent to use, start with Relative Colorimetric, and then try Perceptual.

- ▶ **Perceptual.** The Perceptual intent attempts to fit the gamut of the source space into the gamut of the target space in such a way that the overall color relationships, and hence the overall image appearance, are preserved, even though all the colors in the image may change somewhat in lightness and saturation. It's a good choice for images that contain significant out-of-gamut colors.

- ▶ **Saturation.** The Saturation intent maps fully saturated colors in the source to fully saturated colors in the target without concerning itself with hue or lightness. It's mostly good for pie charts and such, where you just want vivid colors, but you can also use it as an alternative method of perceptual rendering, so it may be worth previewing the conversion using Saturation rendering to see if it does something useful. For more information on doing that, see "Soft-Proofing Controls," later in this chapter.

- ▶ **Relative Colorimetric.** The Relative Colorimetric intent maps white in the source to white in the target, so that white on your output is the white of the paper rather than the white of the source space, which may be different. It then reproduces all the in-gamut colors exactly, clipping out-of-gamut colors to the closest reproducible hue. For images that don't contain significant out-of-gamut colors, it's often a better choice than Perceptual because it preserves more of the original colors.

- ▶ **Absolute Colorimetric.** The Absolute Colorimetric intent is the same as Relative Colorimetric, except that it doesn't scale source white to target white. If your source space has a bluish white and your output is on a yellowish-white paper, Absolute Colorimetric rendering makes the printer lay down some cyan ink in the white areas to simulate the white of the original. It's generally only used for proofing (see "Soft-Proofing Controls" later in this chapter).

The Conceptual Framework

To achieve the best possible color, Photoshop color management places a different emphasis on some mainstream color management concepts compared to other applications, and it adds some unique and useful concepts of its own. So before we dive into dialogs, let's look at how color management is set up within Photoshop.

Working Spaces and Device Spaces

One of the places where Photoshop goes beyond other applications is in the area of color spaces. Applications that don't pay special attention to color typically support only one color space per color model, and many of those might only support RGB. To prevent color conversions that might give you unwanted color changes, Photoshop can preserve the color spaces of individual documents. You can have multiple RGB and CMYK documents open at the same time, with each one using a different color space. This is great for service bureaus and others who work with images from many different sources, but it also opens several cans of worms. We now have to draw a distinction between the working space and the document space(s), and between working spaces and device spaces.

With per-document color, your chosen working space is just a fall-back position for untagged images (images that don't have embedded profiles). Photoshop offers several different RGB working spaces, and enterprising third parties have created still more. It may seem sensible to edit in the space in which the image was captured—a scanner or digital camera space—or in the final output space, such as an RGB inkjet printer. But working spaces have important properties that make them better suited to image editing than the vast majority of device spaces.

▶ Most device color spaces are not *perceptually uniform*. That means that when you edit your file, the same editing increment in Levels, Curves,

Hue/Saturation, or whatever, may have a much larger effect on some parts of the tonal range and color gamut than on others.

▶ Most device color spaces aren't gray-balanced. One of the key features of the abstract RGB working spaces built into Photoshop (as well as most third-party working spaces) is that when R=G=B, you know you have a neutral gray. This isn't true for most scanner RGB spaces, many digital camera RGB spaces, and pretty much all printer RGB spaces.

▶ Output device spaces typically clip some colors in the image because their gamut is almost always smaller than the original capture. For instance, if you simply apply a monitor or inkjet printer profile to an image you just scanned, you may not get all the colors you deserve.

In contrast, color spaces that are designed to be working spaces tend to be uniform, and are invariably gray-balanced. They do, however, differ widely in their gamuts, so gamut size is one of the key considerations when choosing an RGB working space for a particular job (see "Choosing an RGB Working Space," later in this chapter). So while you're no longer forced to use abstract RGB working spaces, you should do so for any serious image editing. Picking an RGB working space and sticking to it will also make your life easier.

Tagged and Untagged Images

Whenever you open or create an image, Photoshop treats it as a tagged or an untagged image from the moment of opening or creation, depending on how you set the Color Management Policies in the Color Settings dialog in Photoshop. Tagged and untagged images behave differently:

Tagged images. Tagged images are those with an embedded profile, which may be different from the current working space profile. A tagged image keeps its original profile and stays in the "document space" rather than the working space, unless you explicitly assign a new profile, convert to a new profile, or untag the image, which discards the profile. The Color Management Policies let you automatically keep documents in their own space, convert them to the working space, or discard the profile.

Untagged images. Untagged images have no embedded profile. They exist as a bunch of numbers whose actual color meaning is open to interpretation. If you change the working space while an untagged image is open, the image gets reinterpreted to be in the new working space, and the appearance changes. If you move pixels (by copy and paste or drag and drop) to another image in the same color mode, the numerical values are moved to the new document. For operations where Photoshop needs to make an assumption about the actual colors the numbers represent, such as mode changes or displaying on the monitor, Photoshop treats untagged images as being in the current working space for that mode. It also does so when you move pixels to a document in a different color mode, such as pasting from an RGB document to a CMYK one.

You can always convert a tagged image to an untagged one, or vice versa, by using the Assign Profile command (Edit > Assign Profile), or the Embed Profile check box in the Save As dialog, to embed a profile.

Document Profiles at a Glance. You can tell at a glance whether a document is tagged or untagged in the status bar or in the Info palette. Both require a little bit of setup. To display the document profile in the status bar, choose Document Profile from the pop-up menu at the lower left of the document window (see **Figure 4-1**). To display the document profile in the Info palette, choose Options from the Info palette menu and select the Document Profile check box.

Figure 4-1
Watching the
document profile

You can display a document's profile in the Info palette, as well as in the status bar at the bottom of a document window.

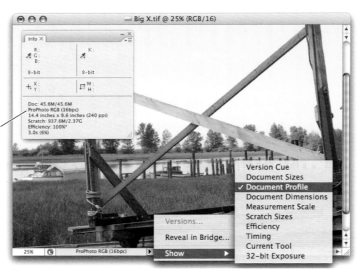

For tagged images, the status bar and Info palette show the profile name. For untagged images, they display "Untagged RGB" (or "Untagged CMYK," or "Untagged Grayscale," depending on the document's mode).

Tip: If you're working in one of the full-screen modes, the status bar is hidden, and in that case the Info palette becomes a better place to keep tabs on document profiles.

A subtler clue can be found in the document window's title bar. The pound sign (#) at the end of the title bar indicates an untagged document. An asterisk (*) at the end of the title bar indicates a document that's tagged with a profile different from the current working space. If neither character appears, the document is tagged with the working space profile.

To tag or not to tag? In the vast majority of cases, untagged documents are a bad thing because they force us to guess the intended appearance portrayed by the numbers in the file, and hence create extra work for everyone. The only situations that justify untagged documents are those where the numbers are unambiguous because of the context, or the appearance generated by the numbers is irrelevant.

For example, we didn't embed profiles in any of the CMYK images we used in this book, because they're all going to the same printing condition, and we set InDesign's CMYK working space to the profile that describes that printing condition. Our CMYK profile is about 2.8 MB, so by not embedding it in every image, we saved a huge amount of disk space and FTP transmission time. The CMYK numbers are unambiguous, because they're governed by the working space profile for the InDesign document.

By the same token, we don't embed profiles in images destined for the Web. The very few Web browsers that pay any attention to embedded profiles assume that untagged RGB is sRGB, so we convert our Web images to sRGB, then export the image without the profile.

When we work with profiling targets, the whole point of the exercise is to find out what colors the device in question produces when we feed it the numbers in the target, so there's no point in making any assumptions about the appearance represented by the numbers.

Last but not least, if you're working in a closed-loop CMYK workflow, where you just don't want the CMYK numbers to change when sent to your printing process, there's no point in embedding a profile.

In all other situations, we strongly recommend embedding profiles in your images. Doing so lets you convey your color intentions clearly to all the devices and all the people in your workflow. Failure to do so forces the people to guess your intentions, causing extra work and frustration for all concerned.

Photoshop Color Management at a Glance

The color architecture in Photoshop is deep but straightforward. Here, in a nutshell, are the controls you need to know about to make Photoshop produce the results you want.

▶ The Color Settings dialog lets you set default working spaces for RGB, CMYK, and grayscale; Color Management Policies, which dictate how Photoshop uses (or ignores) embedded profiles in images; and warnings for documents without profiles or a profile that doesn't match the working space.

▶ The default working spaces are the ones Photoshop always uses when it encounters untagged images (those with no embedded profiles), and are also the ones it uses as the destination when you convert between color modes by choosing RGB, CMYK, or Grayscale from the Image > Mode submenu.

▶ Untagged images use their color mode's current working space. If you change the working space, Photoshop reinterprets the image as being in the new working space. Tagged images stay in the space represented by the embedded profile unless you explicitly ask for a conversion to another space.

▶ Color Management Policies let you control what happens when a document's profile is missing or doesn't match the working space. Preserve Embedded Profiles opens each image in the color space of its embedded profile. Convert to Working RGB/CMYK/Grayscale forces a conversion from the embedded profile space to the working space. Off ignores embedded profiles and treats all images as being in the current working space. Untagged images—those that don't contain an embedded profile—are always treated as being in the current working space.

▶ Photoshop *always* displays images through your monitor profile, which it picks up from the operating system. It performs an on-the-fly conversion on the data sent to the video card from the document's space (either the document's own embedded profile or the current working space) to your monitor space. This conversion is only for display—it doesn't affect the contents of the file.

Proofing Simulations

One of the hardest—and most important—tasks in Photoshop is proofing what your final output will look like on your screen or on a color printer. Photoshop gives you very fine control over both, which we'll talk about in great depth later in this chapter and in Chapter 12, "Image Storage and Output." Here's the quick version, though:

▶ The Proof Setup command (View > Proof Setup) gives you full control over onscreen proofing simulations. Proof Setup's simulations are window-specific, so you can simultaneously view the same file in different simulations.

▶ You can view how different rendering intents will convert an image to a destination space before actually making the conversion.

▶ Choosing Edit > Assign Profile lets you assign a profile to any image. Assigning a profile doesn't change the numbers in the image, it just attaches a new meaning to those numbers, and hence it changes the appearance, sometimes dramatically.

▶ Choosing Edit > Convert to Profile lets you convert images to any profiled space, with a choice of rendering intents. Unlike Assign Profile, Convert to Profile changes the numbers in the image but preserves the appearance. Convert to Profile offers more control over color-space conversions than changing modes from the Mode submenu, because it lets you preview different rendering intents, and it allows you to perform RGB-to-RGB or CMYK-to-CMYK conversions, which are impossible using the Mode commands.

▶ The Proof Colors command offers a live preview of conversions to any RGB, CMYK, or grayscale output space. You can work in a working space while previewing the output space. Proof Colors offers separate control over the rendering from source space to proof space and from proof space to the monitor, providing very accurate previews.

▶ The Color Management panel in the Print dialog lets you perform a conversion on the data that's sent to the printer. The conversion can be a simple one from document space to the output space, or a more complex one from the document space to the Proof Colors space to the output space. The former is handy for printing final art on a composite printer directly from Photoshop. The latter is useful for proofing final press output on a composite printer.

If you learn how to use all these controls effectively, you'll have mastered color management in Photoshop in its entirety. Maybe you should write a book!

On your way to mastering color management in Photoshop, just remember the basic principle that color management only does two things: it assigns a color appearance to the numbers, and it changes the numbers to preserve that appearance in a different scenario. Learn to figure out whether you're assigning an appearance or making a conversion.

▶ You can see how an image prepared for one output process will behave when sent to another output process without adjustment: This is particularly useful when you're faced with the prospect of repurposing CMYK files made for one printing condition to work with another.

▶ You can work inside an accurate output simulation to optimize your image for a particular output process.

But to make this magic work, you *must* calibrate and profile your monitor, and we highly recommend that you take steps to control your viewing environment (see the sidebar "Creating a Consistent Environment," later in this chapter).

Photoshop and the Monitor

In the days of film, when you could find out what the color should look like by looking at the film on a light table, you could argue that monitor profiling and calibration was in the "nice but not essential" category. But with the advent of digital capture, the monitor is the first place the image comes into existence in any meaningful way, so monitor calibration becomes an absolute mission-critical necessity!

When you work in any space except Monitor RGB, Photoshop uses the monitor's profile to transform the data on the fly as it gets sent to the video card so that the monitor displays the color correctly. The great benefit of this approach is that it makes it possible for people using very different monitors on different platforms to view the same image the same way.

Remember: Photoshop displays *everything* through your monitor profile. If the profile doesn't describe the real behavior of your monitor accurately, everything you see, and hence everything you do to your images, will be off by a little or a lot, depending on how inaccurate the profile is.

But to make this magic happen for you, you need an accurate profile for each monitor, and you need to let Photoshop know which profile it should use for the monitor. To display color accurately, Photoshop needs to know how your monitor behaves—what color white it produces, what sort of tonal response it has, and what actual colors it produces when it's fed pure R, G, or B. Photoshop gets all its information about the monitor from the display profile. If you want the color on your monitor to be accurate, you *must* have a customized ICC profile that accurately describes the behavior of your monitor.

You also have to maintain your monitor profile. Monitors drift over time, and though LCDs tend to drift much more slowly than CRTs, a profile that was accurate when it was created may not be accurate a week, a month, or a year later. In theory, there are two distinct ways to compensate for monitor drift.

▶ You can create a new profile regularly—a process technically known as *characterization*.

▶ You can adjust the behavior of the monitor regularly to bring its behavior into agreement with the behavior described by the profile, a process called *calibration*.

Tip: Because Photoshop 6 was the first version of Photoshop to implement color management completely and properly (as far as we're concerned), you must use Photoshop 6 or later to use and benefit from color management as we describe it in this book. (Yes, we do hear about some people who are still using Photoshop 5.)

Tip: To see which monitor profile Photoshop is using, choose Edit > Color Settings, click the RGB pop-up menu, and look at the Monitor RGB command. The name of the monitor profile is appended to Monitor RGB. The monitor profile is the same as the one used by the operating system, such as the Displays system preference in Mac OS X.

In practice, most monitor profiling tools do both, and they make no clear distinction between the two. The practical distinction boils down to the aim points you choose, and the reasons for preferring one approach over the other stem entirely from the features offered by the monitor.

Calibration Parameters

Monitor profiling packages typically ask for the following parameters:

▶ White luminance: The brightness of pure white on the monitor, specified in candelas per square meter (cd/m^2), or foot-lamberts.

▶ White point: The color of the monitor's white, specified either in Kelvins or as a daylight temperature such as D50 or D65 (see the sidebar, "How White Are Your Whites?"). For practical monitor calibration purposes, you can treat 5000 K and D50, or 6500 K and D65, as interchangeable.

▶ The tone response curve, usually specified as a gamma value.

Some packages also let you set a separate black luminance value, but only for CRT displays—LCD displays have a fixed contrast ratio, so the black luminance depends entirely on the white luminance.

Mac OS X and Profiles

Mac OS X offers a bewildering variety of places to store profiles. You'll find them in the System\Library\ColorSync\Profiles folder, in the Library\ColorSync\Profiles folder, in the Library\ColorSync\Profiles\Displays folder, in the Library\Application Support\Adobe\Color\Profiles folder, in the Library\Application Support\Adobe\Color\Profiles\Recommended folder, in the Users\UserName\Library\ColorSync\Profiles folder, and in some cases, buried several levels deep in subfolders in the Library\Printers folder.

As David would say with characteristic understatement, "Oy!"

Here's the deal: There are really only three places where you probably want to store profiles.

If you want to make a profile available to everyone who uses the Mac, save it in the Library\ColorSync\Profiles folder. Don't try to put it in the System\Library\ColorSync\Profiles folder. A good rule of thumb is that the only thing that should mess with the OS X System folder is the OS X installer, or a hard-core UNIX geek who is comfortable driving the Mac from the Terminal window.

If you want to make a profile available only to you (or to someone else logged in as you), save it in the Users\YourUser Name\Library\ColorSync\Profiles folder. (If you're the only user, you may as well save all your profiles there.)

If you want to make a profile available from the Color Settings dialog in Photoshop when the Advanced check box is unchecked, save it in the Library\Application Support\Adobe\Color\Profiles folder.

Display Adjustments

The ability to calibrate a display depends on the controls that can affect its behavior. You can calibrate any display by changing the lookup tables in the video card that drives the display, but the glaring weakness in this approach is that all current video card lookup tables (LUTs) are 8 bits per channel. Whenever you edit an 8 bit/channel image, you end up with fewer levels than you had when you started, and the same holds true for tweaking the video card LUT.

Some displays allow you to make adjustments that change the display's behavior, avoiding the losses inherent in tweaking the 8-bit video card lookup tables. With those displays, it makes sense to calibrate to a specific white point and/or gamma value.

Other displays—including most, but not all, LCD—have no physical adjustments other than the brightness of the backlight. With this type of display, it makes the most sense to profile its native, unadjusted behavior, and let the color management system—which typically uses 20 bits per channel instead of the video card LUT's 8 bits—do the work of correcting the displayed colors.

Basic LCD monitors. Most current LCD monitors, including the Apple Cinema Displays, only allow you to adjust the brightness of the backlight. On these types of displays, it makes sense to set the brightness to a comfortable level (bearing in mind that, as with CRT monitors, the higher you set the white luminance, the faster you'll wear out the display), then just profile the monitor at its native white point and gamma. If the software forces you to choose an explicit gamma value, use gamma 2.2.

High-end LCD monitors. Some high-end LCD monitors—notably the EIZO FlexScan and ColorEdge series—contain their own lookup tables, independent of the video card, with 10, 12, or even 14 bits of precision. The extra bits don't let the monitor display more colors—the operating system pipeline through which applications communicate with the display is only 8 bits per channel wide—but they do let you calibrate the display to a specific white point and gamma without incurring the losses inherent in doing so in the 8-bit video card LUT. For these displays, we recommend a white point of D65, native gamma if it's an option, and gamma 2.2 if it isn't.

LED-backlit monitors. Just to confuse matters, there's a new kid on the block. LED-backlit monitors use arrays of LEDs for the backlight instead of a fluorescent tube. Some LED backlights use white LEDs, but better models use separate arrays of red, green, and blue LEDs. With these RGB-array LED backlights, you can adjust the white point by varying the strength of the red, green, and blue LEDs. RGB-array LEDs are typically found in desktop monitors, while notebooks and other compact displays use white LEDs because they are smaller and lighter, though less adjustable.

LED-backlit monitors typically also have their own internal LUTs, which can be 12 bits (or higher) for desktop displays. We prefer profiling the native tone response of the display when the profiling software lets us do so, but we typically use gamma 2.2 when it doesn't.

This type of display is just starting to appear on the market. As availability goes up and the prices come down, we expect them to replace fluorescent-backlit LCDs for serious imaging work. RGB-array LED backlights are capable of much larger gamuts than fluorescent-backlit displays.

CRT monitors. CRT monitors are pretty much an orphaned technology now. Sadly, the high-end CRTs, such as the Sony Artisan and the Barco Reference Calibrator, have been discontinued. Manufacture of high-end CRT displays has largely ceased.

But there are still a few CRTs in good working order out in the field. Most CRT displays allow separate control over the RGB guns. (Some only let you control two of the three, in which case the master gain control, usually labeled "Contrast," controls the third.)

With CRT displays, we recommend adjusting the RGB gains to achieve the desired white point and target luminance. The gamma value, however, can only be achieved by adjusting the video card LUT. If the profiling package offers native gamma as an option, use it. Otherwise we recommend choosing gamma 2.2 because it's closer to the native gamma of CRT displays than any of the other likely choices, and hence involves smaller tweaks to the video card LUT than other gamma settings do.

Profiling Tools

If you're serious about working visually with Photoshop (rather than just going by the numbers), you'll get the best results if you use a profiling package that includes a hardware measurement device. Various eyeball-based profiling utilities (such as Apple Display Calibrator software) are available, but they have two major drawbacks:

Tip: If a monitor profile you created makes images look like a psychedelic mess, the profile was probably generated incorrectly, or you might have used a bad profile as a starting point—especially if you calibrated by eye instead of using a hardware calibrator. A usable monitor profile should make images look natural, so if an image that you know is properly corrected looks way off, you probably need to profile the monitor again.

▶ Most are designed for CRT displays, and don't do a good job of estimating the tonal response of LCDs.

▶ They use the user's eyeballs as the measurement device. Our eyes are highly adaptable, which is great for a mammal living on planet Earth, but distinctly suboptimal when the goal is to set the monitor to a known state. Because human eyes involuntarily and uncontrollably adapt to the current ambient lighting conditions, they aren't accurate enough for consistent color.

Colorimeters and spectrophotometers have none of the eye's wonderful adaptability, so they always produce the same answer when fed the same stimulus. For monitor calibration and profiling, that's a big advantage! If you must use eyeball-based tools, these guidelines may help improve the results:

▶ Minimize your eyes' adaptability by profiling under the same lighting conditions each time you make a profile. Ideally, the monitor should be the brightest thing in your field of view. (This is always true, but it's particularly critical during profiling—see the sidebar "Creating a Consistent Environment.")

▶ Give the display at least a half an hour of warm-up time before profiling.

Tip: Adobe Gamma was an eyeball-based calibrator included with earlier versions of Photoshop. If you still have it, don't try to use it on LCDs. Adobe Gamma was designed for CRT monitors, and the mechanism it uses for estimating gamma doesn't work well on LCD monitors.

▶ Many eyeball-based profiling tools take an existing profile as their starting point. Often, if you take an existing display profile built with the eyeball-based tool as your starting point, the end result is very bad indeed. Start with a known good profile.

A good many people are still reluctant to spend money on display profiling hardware and software. If you don't care how the image looks on the monitor and you're happy to just go by the numbers, you don't really need a custom monitor profile or the gear to build one. In all other cases, and especially if you're shooting with digital cameras, trying to save money by doing eyeball calibration and profiling is a classic example of being penny-wise and pound (or euro?) foolish. As with most things, with monitor-profiling tools you tend to get what you pay for, but even the least expensive instrumented package will return more accurate and more consistent results than any of the visual tools.

Creating a Consistent Environment

Three factors combine to produce the sensation we describe as color: the object, the light source that illuminates that object, and the observer. You are the observer, and your color vision is subject to subtle changes brought on by things as disparate as age, diet, mood, and how much sleep you've had. There isn't a lot you can do about those, and their effects are relatively minor, but it's good to bear them in mind, because they make the phenomenon of color very subjective. The other factors that affect your color vision are, fortunately, easier to control:

Lighting. Consistent lighting is vital if you want to create a calibrated system. In the United States, color transparencies and print proofs are almost always evaluated using light with a controlled color temperature of 5000 Kelvins (K). In Europe and Asia, 6500 K is the standard—it's a little more blue. (Strictly speaking, the relevant standards—D50 and D65—are daylight curves that aren't absolutely identical to the black-body radiation described by the Kelvin scale, but for most practical purposes they're interchangeable.)

You need to provide a consistent lighting environment for viewing your printed output; otherwise the thing you're trying to match—the original image or the final output—will be constantly changing. You can go whole hog and install D50 lighting everywhere, bricking up any offending windows in the process, but for most of us, that's impractical. Be careful, though—many D50 lamps require a special fixture to avoid overheating, because the unwanted wavelengths are reflected through the back of the lamp into the fixture. You can also situate your monitor so that it's shielded from direct window light, turn off room lights for color-critical evaluations, and use a relatively inexpensive 4700 K Solux desk lamp for evaluating photographs and prints.

Theoretically, the ideal working situation is a low ambient light (almost dark) environment. This maximizes the apparent dynamic range of the monitor and ensures that no stray light is distorting your color perception. However, some shops have noted a significant drop in productivity when they force their employees to work in dark, windowless rooms, so go as far toward approaching that ideal as you feel is reasonable.

Consistency is much more important than the absolute color temperature of the light source; the variations we've measured in the color temperature of viewing booths at various commercial printers are strong evidence of that. If you work in a studio with a skylight and floor-to-ceiling windows, the color of the light will change over the course of the day, and hence, so will your perception of color. In a situation like that, you really need to create an area where you can view prints and transparencies under a light source that's shielded from the ambient light.

A hood to shield the monitor from stray reflections is also very worthwhile—a cardboard box spray-painted matte black may not be elegant, but it's every bit as effective as more expensive solutions, and doesn't distort the color the way most antiglare shields do.

Context. Your color perception is dramatically affected by surrounding colors. Again, you can go to extremes and paint all your walls neutral gray. (Bruce wound up doing this because his office was painted pale pink when he first moved in, and he found that it was introducing a color cast into almost everything—including his dreams.)

It's easier and more important, however, to make your desktop pattern a neutral, 50 percent gray. Pink-marble, green-plaid, or family-snapshot desktop patterns may seem fun and harmless, but they'll seriously interfere with your color judgment. We also recommend not wearing Hawaiian shirts when you're making critical color judgments. Designer black, you'll be happy to know, is just great.

Setting Aim Points

Tip: When is your monitor worn out? One measure is when a monitor no longer reaches the target white luminance value of your profiling package. If you aren't using a hardware calibrator, another less precise way to tell is if the monitor doesn't seem bright enough when you turn up the contrast all the way.

Use the capabilities of your monitor as a guide in setting aim points for calibration. The goal is to change the video card LUT as little as possible so that you get the full 256 shades per channel that the operating system allows you to send to the monitor.

Aim points and the working space. We should make it abundantly clear that the white point and gamma of your display are entirely independent of the white point and gamma of your RGB working space. The color management system translates working space white point and gamma seamlessly to that of your display. The goal in setting white point and gamma for the display is simply to make the display behave as well as it can.

White luminance. The trade-off in setting the white luminance is that you want it high enough to be comfortable, but low enough to avoid wearing out the display prematurely. If a display can't reach 75 cd/m^2 after profiling, it's a candidate for replacement. LCDs are typically much brighter than CRTs, but overdriving them will wear them out just as it will with CRTs. A reasonable rule of thumb is to set the luminance at about 80 percent of

How White Are Your Whites?

For several years, we advocated calibrating monitors to a white point of D50 and a gamma of 1.8 to match the proofing illuminant and dot gain of the commercial printing industry. Hard lessons taught by bitter experience made us back away from that recommendation.

It's very difficult for a CRT monitor to achieve satisfactory brightness when calibrated to a D50 white point because the blue phosphors are the most efficient, and calibrating to D50 invariably involves turning down the blue channel. Often, the result is a monitor that looks dingy and yellow. Our eyes respond to brightness in a nonlinear way, and when the brightness of the monitor is too low (below about 75 cd/m^2), we see yellow instead of white.

But even with LCDs that can produce a blindingly bright D50, a second problem seems to arise when you attempt to compare an image on the monitor side-by-side with a hard copy in a D50 light box. We've been able to achieve close matches, but we've also noted that the highlights on the monitor tend to appear redder than those of the hard copy, even when both monitor and light box are calibrated to D50 and balanced to the same level of illumination.

We haven't yet heard a technical explanation of this phenomenon that completely satisfies us (and we're not sure we'd understand one anyway), but we've experienced it ourselves, and we've heard enough reports from others that we believe it's a real issue. Part of the explanation may be that, while a theoretically ideal D50 illuminant produces a continuous spectrum, both the lamps in light boxes and the phosphors in monitors produce spiky, discontinuous output that's concentrated full power (less if it appears too bright), until that setting becomes too dim. Then you can crank it up while starting to shop for a replacement.

Reasonable starting points are around 80–95 cd/m² for CRT, and around 120 cd/m² for LCDs (though if the display can produce a much higher luminance, you may want to set it higher).

Target white point. On displays with genuinely adjustable white points—which means CRTs and a very few exotic LCDs at this point—we recommend adjusting the display to a D65/6500 K white point. See the sidebar, "How White Are Your Whites?" for our detailed rationales for doing so. Some combinations of profiling package and display let the profiling package control the display's internal controls via a DDC (Display Data Channel) connection, either through a separate USB connection or through the monitor cable itself. Besides being easier than adjusting the display through the front panel, DDC connections often allow the profiling package to make finer adjustments than the front-panel interface allows.

If the white point isn't adjustable in the display itself, as is the case with most LCDs, we recommend profiling with the native white point—it's usually very close to D65 anyway

in fairly narrow bands. There are many different combinations of wavelengths that produce the tristimulus values that add up to a D50 white point.

There may also be a perceptual effect in play. One of the well-known tricks our eyes play on us is called "discounting the illuminant." If we look at a red apple under red light, we still see it as red rather than white, because we know it's red, and we discount the red light. But when we look at a monitor, we can't discount the illuminant because the image *is* the illuminant!

One solution is to separate the monitor and the light box—for example, you can work with the monitor in front of you and the light box behind you, switching from one to the other—which seems to resolve the problem in large part. Interestingly enough, though, others have reported that calibrating the monitor to D65 rather than D50 creates a much better match with a D50 light box.

Another factor that nudges us towards D65 and away from D50 is that, whenever we measure the color temperature of daylight within a thousand meters of sea

level, we invariably find that it's much closer to D65 than to D50. Our eyes seem to adapt easily to a D65 monitor white.

Obviously this subject needs a great deal more research, but we've come to the conclusion that it makes more sense to calibrate the monitor to D65 than to D50. Most LCDs have a native D65 white point anyway, so for LCDs, just use the native white point. If you're happy with a D50 monitor white, don't fix what isn't broken, but if you're running into any of the aforementioned issues, we strongly recommend that you try D65 instead.

Target gamma. With those profiling packages that allow it, we generally prefer to use native gamma as the aim point. Sometimes this is a hidden feature—for example, the Sony Artisan software in Expert mode lets you enter "---" (three dashes) to use the display's native gamma.

If native gamma isn't an option, we use gamma 2.2 for CRT displays. LCDs are a bit more complicated—the tonal response curve of an LCD doesn't really match a gamma curve. With most LCDs and most profiling packages, if forced to choose a gamma value, we'll use gamma 2.2.

Perhaps in recognition of the fact that LCDs don't really follow a gamma curve, some profiling packages now offer more exotic tone-response curves. With "standard" LCDs that don't have their own internal LUTs, we still prefer using native gamma if possible. But if that isn't an option, or if you're using a display with internal LUTs that the profiling software can address, we encourage you to investigate these options. We've obtained good results using the L* curve in Integrated Color Solutions' ColorEyes, and the DICOM curve in NEC's SpectraView II.

If you just want to go by the numbers. It's possible to do good work with Photoshop using an uncalibrated, uncharacterized monitor—you just can't trust what you see on the screen. If you want to simply go by the numbers—reading the RGB levels and the CMYK dot percentages—you can use the Info palette to check your color and simply ignore what you see on the monitor. Even with a calibrated monitor, it's usually a good idea to check those numbers anyway.

If you aren't concerned with the monitor appearance, open Color Settings, select the RGB pop-up menu in the Working Spaces section, and choose Monitor RGB. We don't advocate this—we prefer to work visually—but it is possible, particularly if you're working in a closed-loop environment where you always go to the same output conditions. Of course, if you do this, you may as well ignore the rest of this chapter.

Color Settings

Once you've created a custom monitor profile, it's time to get to the meat of the color controls built into Photoshop. The Color Settings dialog (choose Edit > Color Settings, or press Command-Shift-K in Mac OS X or

Ctrl-Shift-K in Windows; see **Figure 4-2**) functions as Color Central, letting you set up working spaces and color management policies for RGB, CMYK, and grayscale images. It also lets you specify what to do about missing or mismatched profiles. You can choose each of these settings individually or just use one of the presets, which then makes all the choices for you (customizing the settings gives you more control, of course). If you click the More Options button, the dialog expands to let you change the color management module (CMM), and the default rendering intent for conversions, as well as a few more esoteric controls we'll discuss later in this section, and makes the full lists of installed profiles and presets available.

Figure 4-2
The Color Settings
dialog

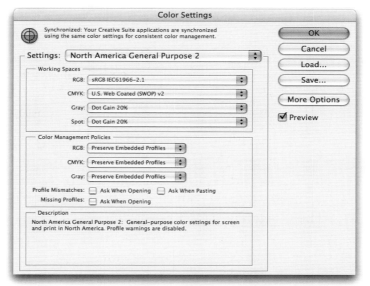

Color Settings Presets

The Settings pop-up menu at the top of the Color Settings dialog lets you load presets to configure Color Settings with a single menu command that sets working spaces, policies, and warnings for you (see Figure 4-2). Presets are a reasonable place to start, but if you've gotten this far into this chapter, you're obviously the kind of person who believes presets are made to be overwritten.

The real power of the Settings pop-up menu isn't in the settings Photoshop provides, but rather in the fact that you can save your own settings to disk and then recall them quickly later. Even better, while you can always load a Color Settings preset from anywhere on your hard drive (using the Load button), if you save your settings in the right place, they become available from the Presets pop-up menu. (On Mac OS X, the "right place" is inside the Library\Application Support\Adobe\Color\Settings folder; in Windows, it's inside Program Files\Common Files\Adobe\Color\Settings.)

Saving presets that appear in the Settings menu offers an easy way to configure Photoshop for an entire workgroup. And if you own the entire Creative Suite, you can even synchronize the color settings to the same preset across all the CS applications: In Bridge, choose Edit > Creative Suite Color Settings, and click Synchronize Color Settings.

The presets that Adobe offers fall into two broad categories: those that ignore color management, and those that use it. As you can probably guess, we fall squarely into the "use it" camp.

General Purpose 2. The three General Purpose 2 presets (North American, Europe, and Japan) set the RGB working space to sRGB; they set the CMYK working space to U.S. Web Coated (SWOP) v.2 (North American), Euroscale Coated v2 (Europe), or Japan Color 2001 Coated (Japan); they set the Gray working space to Dot Gain 20%; and they set all the policies to Preserve Embedded Profiles while disabling the missing profile and profile mismatch warnings.

What's the "2" all about? These presets are an improvement over the General Purpose Default settings that first appeared in Photoshop CS. The version 2 settings preserve embedded profiles for all color modes (which means you see the image displayed the same way it was when it was last saved), and they no longer use a different default rendering intent than all the other presets. The default rendering intent for all Photoshop CS3 presets is Relative Colorimetric with Black Point Compensation.

Prepress 2. The three prepress settings—Europe, Japan, and U.S. Prepress 2—tell Photoshop to use color management wherever possible, and to give you as much feedback as possible about missing and mismatched profiles. They differ only in their choice of CMYK profiles and the dot gain for grayscale and spot colors (20 percent in the United States, and 15 percent in Europe and Japan). If your work is destined for a printing press and you don't have a custom profile for your printing or proofing conditions, one of these choices may be a good starting point.

Tip: If you want any Color Settings preset to appear in the short version of the Settings pop-up menu, move it into the Recommended folder inside the Settings folder (at the location described on the right). If there are presets you don't want to see, remove them from the Settings folder or the Recommended folder.

Tip: If you are working with a printer who provides a Color Settings preset optimized for their prepress workflow, install their preset and choose it in the Color Settings dialog.

The North America and Japan Prepress 2 presets are identical to the prepress defaults that shipped with Photoshop CS. The Europe Prepress 2 preset uses the Europe ISO Coated FOGRA27 CMYK profile as the CMYK working space instead of the older Euroscale Coated v2, which, unlike the new profile, wasn't readily traceable to any standardized printing condition, so we have to consider it an improvement.

Monitor Color. As its name suggests, Monitor Color loads your monitor profile as the RGB working space, and essentially tells Photoshop not to use color management, setting all the policies to Off (we discuss the meaning of policies later in this chapter). It treats all your documents as though they are in the working space for that color mode, ignoring any embedded profiles. For some inexplicable reason, though, it turns on the Profile Mismatch: Ask When Opening warning, which makes no sense since the profile will be ignored anyway.

Web/Internet. If you prepare images *exclusively* for the World Wide Web, the new Web/Internet presets (one each for North America, Europe, and Japan) may be quite useful. The Web is, of course, the same in Japan as it is in North America or Europe: The only difference between the three presets is the CMYK working space, which is U.S. Web Coated (SWOP) v2 for North America, Japan Color 2001 Coated for Japan, and Europe ISO Coated FOGRA27 for Europe.

The dangerous aspect of the Web/Internet presets is that they set the policy for RGB to Convert to Working RGB. That's probably OK if all your work is destined for the Web, but since it automatically converts every RGB file to sRGB, you'll be unhappy when larger-gamut RGB images destined for print get squashed into sRGB with no intervention on your part!

Extra Presets

When you click the More Options button in Color Settings, you gain access to all the presets that ship with Photoshop (see **Figure 4-3**)—not just the ones designed for your region. If you upgraded from a previous version of Photoshop, you'll see all the old presets from the previous version too. Most of the older presets had flaws, but some are downright dangerous.

Color Management Off. As its name suggests, Color Management Off tells Photoshop not to use color management, setting all the policies to Off (again, we discuss the individual policies later in this chapter). It treats

Figure 4-3

The Color Settings dialog with fewer and more options

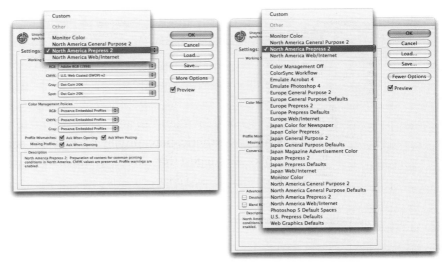

all your documents as though they are in the working space for that color mode, ignoring any embedded profiles. It also loads your display profile as the RGB working space, so it could reasonably be called "Emulate Correctly Configured Photoshop 4," but since hardly anyone ever configured color correctly in Photoshop 4, we won't quibble.

Emulate Photoshop 4. Choosing Emulate Photoshop 4 ignores color management for the most part, setting different working spaces for RGB, CMYK, and grayscale (it uses Apple RGB as the working space on the Mac, and sRGB as the RGB working space in Windows). If you're in a strictly-by-the-numbers all-CMYK print or all-RGB Web workflow, and you're firmly convinced that color management has nothing to offer, this option might make sense. (But then why are you reading this chapter?) Even then, with a decent monitor profile, Color Management Off is a better alternative.

ColorSync Workflow. Macintosh users have one more option: ColorSync Workflow. This sets the ColorSync Default Profiles as the RGB, CMYK, and Gray working spaces. Since Tiger (Mac OS X 10.4) has no mechanism for setting default ColorSync profiles, this option is rendered useless under Tiger, and we tended to avoid it under earlier OS versions because it set the Engine to the Apple CMM rather than Adobe's ACE, which we prefer.

If you've read this far, the odds are that none of the Color Settings presets is ideal for you, so don't be afraid to customize them and create your own settings. The following sections deal with the individual settings in the Color Settings dialog that are likely candidates for customization.

The RGB Working Space

So what are these strange things, the RGB working spaces that you choose in the Color Settings dialog? They're arbitrary, device-independent RGB spaces. Some real techno-geeks will quibble with applying the term "device-independent" to an RGB space, preferring to reserve the term for purely synthetic, perceptually based color spaces like CIE Lab. To those folks, we suggest that while a useful distinction can be made between perceptually based spaces and RGB spaces, that distinction does not revolve around device independence. RGB working spaces in Photoshop don't depend on the vagaries of any given piece of hardware, so we feel it's truthful to call them "device-independent RGB."

Why Use RGB Working Spaces?

Tip: The working space is most important when you open untagged images, because the working space is essentially a default color space for documents that aren't already tagged with a profile. If you usually work with tagged images, the working space may not come into play very often.

The RGB working spaces built into Photoshop are designed to provide a good environment for editing images. As such, they have two important properties that aren't shared by the vast majority of device spaces.

▶ **Gray balance.** The built-in working spaces are gray-balanced, meaning simply that equal amounts of R, G, and B always produce a neutral gray. This is hardly ever the case with device (scanner, camera, display, printer) spaces. Since one of the easiest ways to bring color into line is to find something that should be neutral and make it so, gray balance is an extremely useful property.

▶ **Perceptual uniformity.** The built-in working spaces are approximately perceptually uniform, meaning that changing each channel's numeric values in the image by the same increment results in about the same degree of visual change, no matter whether it's in the highlights, the midtones, the shadows, the pastels, or the saturated colors. Again, device spaces generally don't work that way.

All color-space conversions entail some data loss, but the conversion from capture (camera or scanner) to working space is, in our experience, invariably worthwhile, and when it's done in 16-bit/channel mode, the loss is so trivial it's just about undetectable. Even in 8-bit/channel mode, you're likely to produce much better results editing in a working space rather than a device space.

Why not just use Lab? After all, Lab is, by design, a device-independent, perceptually uniform color space. But Lab has at least two properties that make it less than ideal as a standard editing space.

First, Lab is pretty nonintuitive when it comes to making color corrections—small adjustments to a* and b* values often produce large changes in unexpected directions. A bigger problem, however, is that Lab, by definition, contains all the colors you can see, and as a corollary, it also contains many "colors" you can't see.

When we use 8 bits per channel to represent this whole range of color, the distance from one value to the next becomes large—uncomfortably large, in fact. And since any real image from a scanner or digital camera contains a much smaller range of color than Lab represents, you wind up wasting bits on colors you can't capture, display, print, or even see. If you work with 16 bit/channel images, the gamut problem is much less of an issue, but editing in Lab is still not particularly friendly, and conversions from capture space to Lab generally involve more data loss due to quantization error than the conversion to RGB working spaces.

Choosing an RGB Working Space

The main difference between RGB working spaces is the gamut size—the range of color that they can represent. You may think you should just choose the largest gamut available so that you'll be sure of encompassing the gamuts of all your output processes, but (as is almost always the case in digital imaging) there's a trade-off involved—at least if you're using 8 bit/channel images.

As we explained in Chapter 2, "Image Essentials," RGB images are made up of three grayscale channels, in which each pixel has a value from 0 to 255. This holds true for every 24-bit RGB image, irrespective of the working space it lives in. If you choose a very large-gamut space, the 256 possible data values in each channel are stretched to cover the entire gamut; the larger the gamut, the farther apart each value is from its neighbors.

The practical implication is that you have less editing headroom in a large-gamut space than you do in a small one: When you edit images, you invariably open up gaps in the tonal range as levels that were formerly adjacent get stretched apart. In a small-gamut space, the jump from level 126 to level 129 may be visually insignificant, whereas in a larger space, you'll get obvious banding rather than a smooth transition.

The simplest option is to settle on a single RGB editing space for all your work, but you may wish to use a larger space for 48-bit images than you do for 24-bit ones, or a larger space for digital captures than for film scans. In a service bureau environment, you'll have to support all sorts of RGB spaces—which is easy in Photoshop—in which case the default working space should simply be the one you use most.

If you're working with legacy images that have already been edited in a small-gamut space, or JPEG digital captures, there's no good reason to convert them to a larger space, and if you do, you may encounter some of the aforementioned issues. But if you work with scans from modern scanners, or raw captures from today's digital cameras, large-gamut spaces are not only safe, but may be needed to do full justice to the image.

Gamut Size Revisited

The naive presumption is that since RGB spaces are bigger than CMYK, they can hold all the CMYK colors we can print. That's not really the case. RGB color spaces all have a characteristic three-dimensional shape, where maximum saturation happens at fairly high luminance levels. Print spaces have a different characteristic gamut shape, where maximum saturation is reached at lower luminances. If you bear in mind that you increase RGB saturation by adding light, and you increase print saturation by adding ink, this makes perfect sense.

Two-dimensional gamut plots disguise this fact, which is why they can be seriously misleading. Three-dimensional gamut plots make the relationships between gamuts much clearer. **Figure 4-4** shows three views of Adobe RGB and U.S. Sheetfed Coated v2 CMYK plotted in three dimensions. The differences in size are obvious, but note the difference in shape.

In fact, Adobe RGB (1998) just barely contains the gamut of U.S. Sheetfed Coated v2 except for the saturated CMYK yellow, which lies just outside the gamut of Adobe RGB (1998). So if your primary concern is with press output, Adobe RGB (1998) may be a safe choice of working space.

For inkjet printing however, Adobe RGB (1998) may be on the small side. **Figure 4-5** shows Epson Ultrachrome inks (the inks found in the Epson Stylus Photo 2200, 4000, 7600 and 9600 printers) on Premium Luster paper, plotted as a solid against Adobe RGB as a wireframe. Adobe RGB clips a huge chunk of the yellow-orange range, a significant chunk of saturated darker greens and blues, and a tiny bit of magenta-red. The pigmented

Figure 4-4
3D gamut plots, rotated

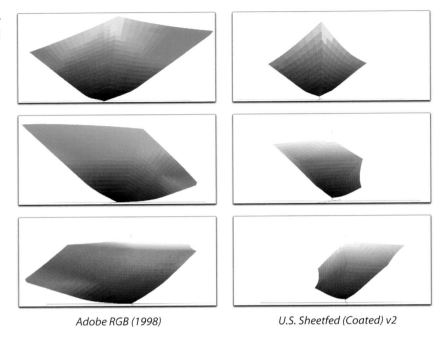

Adobe RGB (1998)   *U.S. Sheetfed (Coated) v2*

Ultrachrome inks have a smaller gamut than the dye-based inks found in many inkjet printers, so this illustration is conservative.

Adobe RGB is the largest of the four "recommended" RGB working spaces that appear, along with Monitor RGB, in the RGB working space menu when Color Settings is opened with More Options turned off. **Figure 4-6** shows Apple RGB, Colormatch RGB, and sRGB plotted against U.S. Sheetfed Coated v2.

All three of the smaller spaces clip U.S. Sheetfed Coated v2 to a significant degree, though Colormatch clips the least. Needless to say (but we'll say it anyway), if the color can't be represented in the source space (in this case, working RGB), it won't be present in the output either. Since CMYK inks give us a fairly small box of crayons to play with anyway, we'd prefer

Figure 4-5
Adobe RGB and
Epson Ultrachrome

 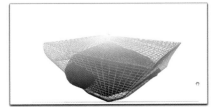

Epson Ultrachrome (solid) and Adobe RGB (wireframe). Note the significant degree to which Adobe RGB clips the yellow-oranges, greens, and blues.

Figure 4-6
Working RGBs and
U.S. Sheetfed Coated v2

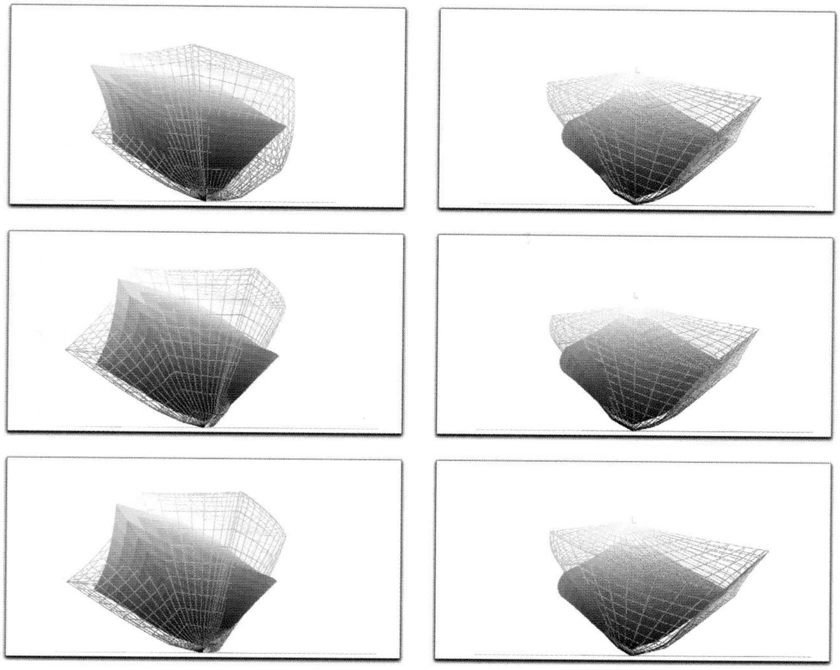

Apple RGB

Colormatch RGB

sRGB

to be able to make full use of them without having any of our printable colors clipped by our choice of working space, so we regard Adobe RGB (1998) as the minimum requirement for RGB destined for print. (David uses it even for preparing Web graphics, and then converts to sRGB before exporting the untagged GIF, JPEG, or PNG file.)

Apple RGB and Colormatch RGB are legacy monitor-based spaces whose time has passed. Apple RGB is based on the original Apple 13-inch color monitor—it's been out of production for more than 15 years—and Colormatch RGB is based on the almost-as-long-gone Radius Pressview. Unless you have to deal with massive amounts of legacy imagery in one of these spaces, there's really no reason to use either as a working space. Essentially, the two rational choices from the four recommended spaces are sRGB for Web or multimedia image, and Adobe RGB for everything else. Then there's Monitor RGB . . .

Monitor RGB. When you choose Monitor RGB, Photoshop uses your monitor profile as the RGB working space: It's listed in the RGB Working Space menu as "Monitor RGB: YourMonitorProfileName."

If you choose Monitor RGB, Photoshop displays RGB images by sending the numerical values in the RGB file directly to the video card. It uses the definition of those RGB values supplied by the monitor profile to convert RGB to other color spaces.

The only reason we can think of to choose Monitor RGB as your working space is if you're working exclusively on Web graphic, and you need the RGB color in Photoshop to match the RGB color in non-color-managed applications like Adobe Dreamweaver. Using your monitor profile as the working space will ensure that RGB in Photoshop looks exactly the same as RGB in all your non-color-managed applications—unfortunately, it will also ensure that RGB looks different on your machine than it does on everyone else's. (That's why Photoshop introduced the idea of an RGB working space in the first place.)

If you're a Windows user, you'll likely find that the differences between Monitor RGB and sRGB are quite small. Mac users, though, will typically see a bigger difference. Web designers who work on the Mac may want to do most of their work using Monitor RGB, and then convert the final result to sRGB. That way, Windows users will see something close to what was intended, while Mac users who use Safari—or Internet Explorer with ColorSync turned on—will also see something close to the intended color. Mac users who use Firefox will see dark images, but they should be used to that . . .

On the other hand, many images destined for the Web also end up in print as repurposing becomes increasingly important. That's why David uses the Adobe RGB working space even when he's creating Web graphics. Then he uses soft-proofing in Photoshop to see what the image will look like on the Web (see "Soft-Proofing Controls," later in this chapter).

Other RGB Working Spaces

If you check the Advanced Mode check box in Color Settings, the RGB menu expands to include every RGB profile installed on your machine. In Advanced mode, Photoshop allows you to use any RGB profile as an RGB working space, or even to create your own. Don't go hog-wild with this! Editing in your SuperHamsterScan 9000 Turbo Z profile's space is possible, but it probably won't be perceptually uniform, and worse, it probably won't be gray-balanced. It's extremely hard to edit images well in a space that isn't gray-balanced, and almost impossible to do so in one where the color balance shifts from dark to light (typical of capture profiles).

However, you may want to consider some working spaces that aren't installed in the Recommended profiles folder. You can also define your own RGB working space, in which case you've definitely earned the title of Advanced User, but having already gone down that road, we recommend that you do so only after identifying very specific problems and exhausting all other available solutions.

David likes to keep things simple, and uses Adobe RGB virtually all of the time. Conrad uses different RGB working spaces for different purposes. It isn't absolutely necessary to load these as working spaces in Color Settings—you can always use the Assign Profile command (see "Assign Profile" later in this chapter) to assign a profile other than the working space to an image—but if you're going to be working with a bunch of images in the same space, it makes life slightly easier to load that space as the working space. The following is by no means an exhaustive list, but we've found each of these spaces useful.

Tip: Images you edit in Photoshop may not look the same in applications that don't support color management. Depending on the color space you use, when sending images to others, you may need to use the Convert to Profile command to convert images to a more common color space. For example, all images published on Web pages should be converted to sRGB.

ProPhoto RGB. Formerly known as rgbMaster, and before that as ROMM (Reference Output Metric Method) RGB, Kodak's ProPhoto RGB is an extremely wide-gamut RGB space. In fact, it's so wide that its primaries are imaginary; there is no light source that could produce these colors, and we couldn't see them if there was. It needs these extreme primaries to accommodate the dark, saturated colors we can readily achieve in print and that get clipped by smaller spaces. It's wide enough that we recommend doing major edits only on high-bit files in ProPhoto RGB; small tweaks to 8 bit/channel files, however, are safe.

ProPhoto RGB has the ability to hold *color difference* that represents detail, rather than the ability to represent ridiculously saturated colors. The fact that it covers the entire gamut of all output spaces is simply a nice bonus.

EktaSpace. Developed by photographer Joseph Holmes, EktaSpace is a large-gamut space that's a little more conservative, and hence a little more manageable, than ProPhoto RGB. There's been some debate over whether EktaSpace really covers the entire E6 gamut. Our experiments suggest that, while it may be possible to capture colors in-camera (without resorting to games like exposing the film with a monochromatic laser) that will be clipped by EktaSpace, it's not likely. EktaSpace will hold any colors you're likely to encounter on E6 film that's shot and processed under normal conditions. It's possible to use 8 bit/channel images in EktaSpace, but you'll get much more editing headroom with 16-bit files.

EktaSpace can be useful for transparency scans when it's important to preserve the characteristics of the individual film stock. You can download the EktaSpace profile from www.josephholmes.com.

BruceRGB. Unlike both ProPhoto RGB and EktaSpace, BruceRGB is a small-gamut space. Bruce designed it to offer the maximum editing headroom on 8 bit/channel images destined for CMYK printing. It's basically a compromise between Adobe RGB (1998), which is a little too big, and ColorMatch RGB, which is too small. It covers most of the gamut of CMYK offset printing and is a reasonable match to most RGB inkjet printers. It clips some cyans and oranges, but not much more so than Adobe RGB.

More recently, Bruce noted that today's scanners and cameras are so much better than those from 1998, when he developed the space, that BruceRGB was no longer necessary for most people to use. In addition, it is now so much easier to work with high-bit images that if you need a color space larger than AdobeRGB, you might as well work in ProPhoto RGB at 16 bits per channel. However, BruceRGB is a good example of a custom RGB space created to handle a specific situation.

Custom RGB Spaces

If you're a hard-core imaging geek who likes to live dangerously, you can define your own RGB working space. It's not that difficult, because an RGB working space is defined by just three primary xy values for red, green, and blue; a white point; and a gamma value. For example, if you use a high-quality scanning-back digital camera that lets you set the gray balance for each image, you may want to define a working space whose primaries are the same as the camera's, thereby (in theory) ensuring that your working space matches your input device.

To define a custom RGB working space, you first need to click the More Options button in Color Settings. This lets you choose Custom RGB from the RGB menu, which in turn opens the Custom RGB dialog (see **Figure 4-7**). Custom RGB allows you to choose a name for your custom space as well as specify the gamma, the white point, and the primaries. If you're not already intimate with these terms, then you should probably just skip to "Choosing a CMYK Working Space."

Gamma. The Gamma field lets you enter a value for the gamma of your working space. This is completely independent of your monitor gamma—there's no reason to match your working space gamma to your monitor

Tip: When you save custom RGB settings, you're actually creating an ICC profile. In Mac OS X, save them in the Library\ColorSync\Profiles folder. In Windows 2000/XP, save profiles in the WinNT\System\Spool\Drivers\Color directory. That way, the profile that describes your RGB working space will be available to other ICC-aware applications.

Figure 4-7
Custom RGB

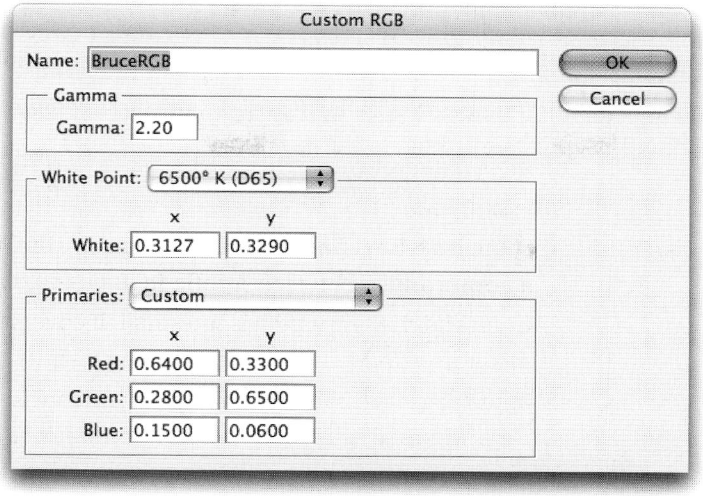

The Custom RGB dialog lets you define custom RGB working spaces by
defining the gamma, white point, and primaries.

gamma, and there may be plenty of good reasons not to do so. To simplify
(the long explanation would be very long and tedious), the gamma of the
editing space controls the distribution of the bits over the tone curve. Our
eyes don't respond in a linear fashion to changes in brightness: A gamma
of 2.2 is generally reckoned to be more or less perceptually uniform, so
we recommend using that value for your working space gamma. It has
the added benefit of devoting more bits to the shadows, which is where
we find we usually need them during editing.

Tip: To find the xy chromaticities
of the primaries for a chosen
built-in space, first load that
space from the RGB menu, and
then choose Custom from the
Primaries menu. The Primaries
dialog appears, showing the xy
chromaticities for the red, green,
and blue primaries. If you wish,
you can even plot them on a
chromaticity chart like the one
in **Figure 4-8.**

White Point. This setting defines the white point of the RGB working space.
You can choose one of the ten built-in white point, or choose Custom to
define a custom white point by entering xy chromaticities (the xy components of a color defined in CIE xyY). As with the gamma setting, the white
point of the working space is independent of the monitor white point. It's
also independent of the output white point. For a variety of reasons, we
suggest using D65 as the white point for most RGB spaces. (For a more
detailed discussion of white points, see the sidebar "How White Are Your
Whites?" earlier in this chapter.) If you use one of the built-in spaces,
Photoshop will select this setting for you.

Primaries. The Primaries setting lets you choose from the Primaries
menu, which contains six sets of phosphor-based primaries for common

monitors and three sets of abstract primaries. Or you can enter custom xy values for R, G, and B to set the boundaries of the color gamut.

For example, here are the settings for BruceRGB:

▶ White point = 6500K

▶ Gamma = 2.2

▶ Red xy = 0.6400 0.3300

▶ Green xy = 0.2800 0.6500

▶ Blue xy = 0.1500 0.0600

Defining custom RGB spaces isn't for the faint of heart, and there are now so many RGB spaces available that relatively few people should need to build their own. But it's always nice to know that you can.

Figure 4-8 shows a chromaticity plot of some of the spaces built in to Photoshop, compared with the chromaticities of SWOP inks. A word of caution: color gamuts are complex three-dimensional objects, and a

Figure 4-8

xy chromaticities

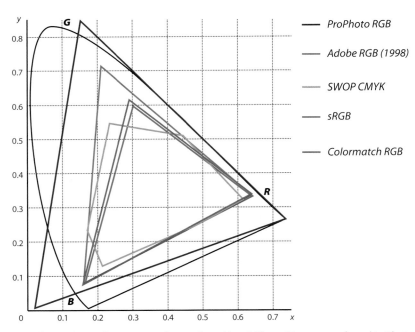

This figure shows the gamuts of several working RGB working spaces found in Photoshop, and the gamut of SWOP CMYK, plotted in CIE xyY space. It illustrates the trade-off inherent in choosing an RGB space between clipping the gamut of CMYK and wasting bits on unprintable colors.

chromaticity plot is very much an abstraction. We include this figure to help you visualize the implications of different RGB primaries, not as an exact comparison of their color gamuts.

RGB Output Profiles as Working Spaces

It's possible to load an RGB output profile as your working space. This may even seem like a good idea if you're one of the many Photoshop users whose final output is a desktop inkjet printer. But even if you only ever print to an RGB printer, using your RGB output profile as your RGB working space is a bad idea. RGB output spaces have two properties that make them very difficult to use as working spaces: They're rarely gray-balanced, and they're far from perceptually uniform.

You may find that you want to make small adjustments to your image after converting it to your RGB printer space, but with a good output profile, you can obtain the same results more easily by keeping your image in the working space and using the soft-proofing controls in Photoshop to provide an accurate simulation of your output on screen (see "Soft-Proofing Controls," later in this chapter).

To make the actual conversion from the working space to your printer's RGB output space, you have several choices as to where to apply your RGB output profile. (See "Print," later in this chapter.) The one place you *don't* want to use your RGB output profile is as an RGB working space!

Choosing a CMYK Working Space

Unlike RGB working spaces, which may be entirely abstract and not based on any real device, CMYK working spaces always reflect some real combination of ink (or toner, or dye) and paper. The ideal situation is to have a custom ICC profile for the specific CMYK process to which you're printing, but in the real world, some shops are ahead of others in achieving this workflow. If you do have a custom ICC profile for your CMYK print process or for an industry-standard proofing system such as Kodak Approval or Creo Spectrum, click the More Options button and load that profile into the CMYK pop-up menu in the Color Settings dialog.

When Color Settings is in its abbreviated form, your choices of CMYK working space are limited to the press profiles that are installed by Photoshop, plus Custom CMYK, which users of older versions of Photoshop

Tip: If you're using an accurate CMYK profile either as a working space or as a profile in tagged CMYK images, you shouldn't have to worry about dot gain, GCR, and so on. Because a properly created profile represents the output conditions, all output characteristics should already be accounted for by the profile.

may recognize as the old "Built-in" panel of Photoshop 5's CMYK Setup. Mac users also get the option to choose ColorSync CMYK, which, with the advent of Tiger (Mac OS X 10.4), is hardwired to "Generic CMYK," a profile that represents no printing condition known to mankind and so is best ignored.

In the absence of a custom profile, Adobe's press profiles are much, much better than the old mechanism in Photoshop 5 and earlier. They typically produce smoother gradations and better saturation than the old CMYK Setups, and the ink colors are more accurate.

If you're still working with a printer who is more comfortable with the old-style Photoshop CMYK setups, they're still available. Choosing Custom CMYK from the CMYK pop-up menu opens the Custom CMYK dialog, as shown in **Figure 4-9**.

Figure 4-9
Two ways to specify
a CMYK color space

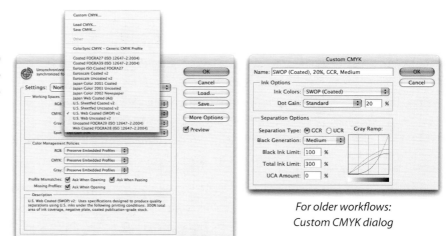

For older workflows:
Custom CMYK dialog

The current standard:
CMYK profiles in Photoshop

Should You Use Custom CMYK?

Before we get into the details of the Custom CMYK dialog, a disclaimer is in order. The Custom CMYK feature was born at the introduction of CMYK capabilities in Photoshop 2.0 (which shipped in June of 1991). The fact that it has persisted in one form or another through all subsequent revisions of Photoshop shows that it's perfectly possible to make great color separations using this mechanism, but nevertheless, terms like "ancient," "weird," and "junk" are more than slightly applicable.

If you're a relatively experienced Photoshop user and you're comfortable with defining CMYK settings this way, we have a few tricks that you may find useful. But if you're relatively new to the world of color and Photoshop, you'd be *much* better off spending your time and ingenuity investigating some of the many packages available for creating and editing ICC profiles (like GretagMacbeth ProfileMaker Pro or Monaco Profiler).

Ultimately, Adobe left Custom CMYK in Photoshop mostly for backward compatibility. ICC profiles are the wave of the future, and if you're at the beginning of your learning curve, you're better off concentrating on those instead. That said, there's still some life in the old dog, and we've even been able to teach it a couple of new tricks!

Editing Custom CMYK

Tip: You can save a Custom CMYK setting as an ICC profile by choosing Save CMYK from the Color Settings CMYK menu. Profiles made this way support only the relative and absolute colorimetric rendering intents, so they're more limited than profiles produced by full-blown profiling packages.

The Custom CMYK dialog has two sections: Ink Options, which lets you define the colors of your inks and the way they behave on your paper stock; and Separation Options, which lets you tell Photoshop how you want the inks to build color when converting to CMYK. Note that the Custom CMYK mechanism is entirely separate from the ICC profiles built in to Photoshop (or anyone else's)—the SWOP definitions in Custom CMYK, for example, bear only a passing resemblance to those in the U.S. Web Coated (SWOP) v2 profile, or to the current SWOP specification. Custom CMYK is *not* a mechanism for editing ICC profiles!

Ink Colors. The Ink Colors setting tells Photoshop about the color of the inks you'll be using. You can create your own custom inkset or use one of the ink sets built in to Photoshop such as SWOP, Eurostandard, or Toyo, each of which has ink definitions for coated, uncoated, and newsprint stock (see **Figure 4-10**). The SWOP ink sets differ substantially from the current SWOP spec; but a great many Photoshop users have been using them for years, so you should talk to your commercial printer about which ink definitions to use.

The built-in ink sets are paper-specific (that is, if you print cyan on a slightly pink paper, it'll look different than if you print it on a slightly blue paper). Unfortunately, no one seems to remember which paper stocks the built-in sets specify. Plus, even though there are rough standards for inks used on web presses, they actually vary widely, and a magenta on the West Coast might be different than one on the East Coast.

Figure 4-10
Preset ink sets

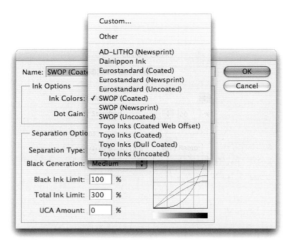

The Ink Colors menu lets you choose one of the definitions built in to Photoshop for ink sets, or choose Custom to define your own.

You can generally produce good results using one of the built-in ink sets. We used to provide directions for measuring inks and plugging the measurements into the Custom Ink Colors dialog, but quite honestly, if you have an instrument that can measure the inks, you almost certainly have accompanying profiling software that will do a far better job than Custom CMYK ever could, so we strongly recommend biting the bullet and building real profiles instead.

The Ink Colors dialog (see **Figure 4-11**) lets you set the CIE xyY or CIE Lab values for the eight progressive colors (cyan, magenta, yellow, black, cyan+magenta, cyan+yellow, magenta+yellow, cyan+magenta+yellow), and the white of the paper stock. The only way to determine these accurately is to measure them from press output with a spectrophotometer, but as noted above, if you have a spectrophotometer, you probably have a profiling package too, so just use it instead.

In truly dire emergencies, you can eyeball the ink colors. This technique isn't particularly accurate—in fact, it's a kludge—and we only recommend using it as a way to improve the color from desktop four-color inkjet and thermal-wax color printers driven by a CMYK RIP (raster image processor), though in a pinch, we might use it for a digital press or direct-to-plate scenario too. It doesn't work with three-color CMY printers, or with inkjets that take RGB data and print through a QuickDraw or GDI (Graphics Device Interface) driver, or on dye-subs; we've tried. But it doesn't require measuring equipment other than your eyeballs.

Figure 4-11
Ink Colors
dialog

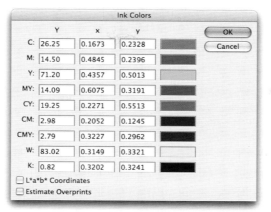

*The Ink Colors dialog lets
you enter custom xyY or Lab
values for your inks, or click
the color swatches to open
the Color Picker and choose
an ink color by eyeball.*

You need to print a set of color bars, which you must specify as CMYK colors (don't make them in RGB and then convert). Then, choose Custom from the Ink Colors pop-up menu to open the Ink Colors dialog. Clicking on each color swatch opens the Color Picker dialog. You can then edit each progressive color to match your printed output. Generally, desktop printers use colorants that are purer and more saturated than press inks, so head in that general direction.

Don't expect miracles from this technique—your results will depend on your monitor calibration, your lighting, and your skill in matching colors by eye. It should get you into the ballpark, but given the amount of work involved and the uncertain quality of the results, we recommend that you investigate obtaining, building, or commissioning an ICC profile instead.

Tuning CMYK Previews. If you find that CMYK images don't look right on your screen (that is, they don't match what you're printing), there's a good chance your monitor profile isn't correct. However, if the problem doesn't lie with the monitor profile, you can try to create a custom CMYK inkset just for viewing your images. You can sometimes improve the accuracy of the CMYK Preview by fine-tuning the ink colors, then saving the result with a name that clearly indicates it's only to be used for viewing CMYK, not for creating it. The easiest way to do this is to open the CMYK image or images you're trying to match, make a duplicate, and use Assign Profile to make it an untagged CMYK image (see "Assign Profile," later in this chapter). Then go to Color Settings, turn on the Preview check box, choose Custom CMYK, choose Custom from the Ink Colors menu, and adjust the ink colors until you see the match you want. You may have to wait a second or two for the changes to show up in your image. Again, this technique is a kludge, and is no substitute for a good ICC profile, but in a pinch it can be better than nothing.

To save this setting, select Save CMYK from the Color Settings CMYK menu. This saves the settings as an ICC profile. Remember to name it something that tells you that it's for viewing only; using this to convert RGB to CMYK could be disastrous. To use this profile for viewing, you'll load it into the Customize Proof Condition dialog (see "Customize Proof Condition dialog," later in this chapter). When you're done making it, hit Cancel so you leave the dialogs without actually using this new setup.

Using Estimate Overprints for spot inks. The Estimate Overprints check box in Custom Ink Colors is primarily useful if you substitute Pantone spot inks (or other inks for which you have known CIE values) for CMYK—you can use Estimate Overprints to see how they'll interact with one another. Be aware that this is a highly experimental procedure, and the strongest possible, closed-track, professional-driver, don't-try-this-at-home caveats apply. But if you're in a situation where you're forced to do a job using spot inks instead of process inks, loading the spot inks into Custom Ink Colors and using Estimate Overprint will give you at least some idea of what'll happen when you overprint them (see our online chapter, "Spot Colors and Duotones"). Using Estimate Overprints to avoid taking four measurements for the various CMY combinations is a very silly idea—the minimal time savings simply aren't worth it.

Dot gain. When ink hits paper, it smooshes some, bleeds some, and generally "heavies up on press" (even if your press is a little desktop printer). That means that your 50-percent cyan halftone spot won't look like 50 percent when it comes off a printing press. It's your responsibility to take this dot gain into account when building your images, and if you don't, your pictures will always appear too dark and muddy. Custom CMYK gives you two methods to compensate for dot gain (see **Figure 4-12**). The simpler method—entering a single percentage value—is also less accurate. Using individual dot gain curves for each ink will generally yield better results, but it takes a little more time and effort.

Figure 4-12

Dot gain compensation

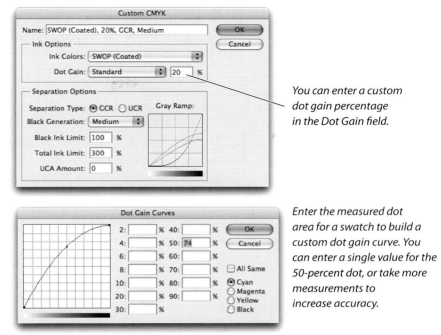

You can enter a custom dot gain percentage in the Dot Gain field.

Enter the measured dot area for a swatch to build a custom dot gain curve. You can enter a single value for the 50-percent dot, or take more measurements to increase accuracy.

Where to adjust dot gain. Photoshop automatically compensates for dot gain when it converts images to CMYK for printing. It's much less work to build the dot-gain compensation into the separation process than to try to compensate for it manually on an image-by-image basis. In a pinch, you can make slight compensations for dot gain in an already-separated CMYK file using Curves, but you'll generally get better results by going back to the original RGB image, adjusting the dot-gain value in Custom CMYK, and generating a new CMYK file using the new settings. In fact, one of the few advantages Custom CMYK has over ICC profiles is the ease with which you can adjust for minor variations in dot gain between different papers.

You'll hear all sorts of numbers bandied about with reference to dot gain, so it's important to be clear about what Photoshop means—and what your service providers mean—by a given dot-gain percentage, as they're often different (see the sidebar "Dot Gain: Coping with Midtone Spread"). All the built-in ink sets contain default dot gain values, but you shouldn't consider them to be much more than a starting point. As we said earlier, the ink sets are paper-specific—the ink colors typically don't vary much from paper stock to paper stock (unless you're printing on puce, lime green, or goldenrod paper), but the dot gain can vary tremendously from one paper to another.

Table 4-1 shows some rough numbers for typical dot gain. If you come up with values that are vastly different from these, double-check your calculations or measurements, reread the sidebar "Dot Gain: Coping with Midtone Spread," and talk to your service providers to make sure that there isn't some misunderstanding. Bear in mind that higher halftone screen frequencies have more dot gain than low ones. The values in the table are based on 133- to 150-line screens with the exception of newsprint, which is based on an 85-line screen.

Table 4-1	**Press and stock**	**Typical dot gain**
Dot gain settings	Web press, coated stock	17–22 percent
	Sheetfed press, coated stock	12–15 percent
	Sheetfed press, uncoated stock	18–22 percent
	Newsprint	30–40 percent
	Positive plates	10–12 percent

Dot Gain Curves. Single-value dot gains work reasonably well if you're using one of the built-in ink sets because the differential gain for each ink has already been factored in, but Photoshop offers an easy, unambiguous way to define the anticipated dot gain in the form of Dot Gain Curves.

The only disadvantage to using Dot Gain Curves is that you need to use a densitometer (or a colorimeter or spectrophotometer that can read dot area) to read printed swatches. (You can often piggyback the swatches onto another job by printing them in the trim area, and if you don't have one of these devices, your printer or service bureau probably does.)

Choosing Curves from the Dot Gain pop-up menu opens the Dot Gain Curves dialog (see Figure 4-12). It allows you to enter the actual dot values measured in 2, 4, 6, 8, 10, 20, 30, 40, 50, 60, 70, 80, and 90 percent patches for each ink. Measuring all the patches is probably overkill. In a pinch, you can simply measure the 50-percent dot and type in the measured value, but we recommend taking measurements of at least the 4, 6, 8, 10, 40, 50, and 80 percent swatches for each ink. Don't be tempted by the All Same check box, because it's very unusual to find exactly the same dot gains on all four inks.

Separation Options. The Separation Options section (see Figure 4-12) is where you tell Photoshop how you want to use the inks you've defined in the Ink Options section. It lets you control the total amount of ink you'll put

Dot Gain: Coping with Midtone Spread

Dot gain is the tendency for half-tone dots to increase in size from film to press. The biggest cause is the ink spreading as it hits the paper—the more absorbent the paper, the greater the dot gain—but some dot gain occurs when the ink is transferred from the ink roller to the blanket roller on press, and some may even creep in when the film is made into plates. Because dot gain makes your images print darker than anticipated, compensating for it is essential.

Dot gain in Photoshop is always measured at the 50-percent value, because that's where its effect is greatest. The larger the circumference of the halftone dot, the more it's subject to dot gain; but above 50 percent, the dots start to run together, so they don't gain as much. For the same reason, high screen frequencies are more prone to dot gain than low screen frequencies, because the dots have larger circumferences.

The subject of dot gain attracts more than its share of confusion because people measure differ-ent things under the name "dot gain." Then, to make matters worse, they have different ways of expressing that measurement.

Dot gain in Photoshop. The Photoshop documentation states that the Photoshop dot gain value is the dot gain from film to press. However, since Photoshop also assumes that it's printing to a lin-earized platesetter—one that will produce a 50-percent dot when asked for one—we think it's less confusing to say that the dot gain Photoshop uses is really the dif-ference between the digital data and the final printed piece.

Dot gain in Photoshop is the absolute additive amount by which a 50-percent dot increases. So if a 50-percent dot appears on the print as 72 percent, Photoshop would call this a 22-percent dot gain.

When you ask your printer about the dot gain anticipated for your job, he or she may give you the gain from color proof to final print. There's a simple way to remove this ambiguity. Ask your printer, "What will happen to the 50-percent dot in my file when it hits the press?" If the response is that it will print as a 78-percent dot, that's 28-percent dot gain as far as Photoshop is concerned, and that's the number you should use for your Dot Gain setting in Custom CMYK.

But Photoshop offers an even simpler way to remove the ambiguity: Just measure the dot area of the 50-percent dot, then simply plug that value into the 50-percent field in Dot Gain Curves—that way, no guesswork or arithmetic is involved.

Who makes the proof? Many service bureaus will sell you a proof such as a Kodak Approval, but it's unlikely that their proof-ing system is set up to match the press and paper stock on which your job will run. If you give this proof to your printer, he or she may tell you he or she can match it, but that'll be just a guess. If the printer makes the proof, there's no guesswork involved, and the responsibility is clear.

on the paper, as well as the black generation—the relationship between black and the other colors. Note that unlike the Ink Options settings, the Separation Options have no effect on the display of CMYK images—these only control how colors will convert to CMYK.

The decisions you make in Separation Options can make or break a print job, and there's no single correct answer or hard-and-fast rules because every combination of press, ink, and paper has its own optimum settings.

When it comes to determining them, there's no substitute for experience. But understanding the way the Separation Options work is key to making sense of your own experience.

Rules, guidelines, and caveats. It's important to remember that these guidelines are useful starting points, nothing more. You'll hear all sorts of recommendations from experts; most are valid, but it's unlikely that any of them will apply perfectly to your particular situation. Just how far it's worth going to optimize your color separations for a specific press depends in part on the economics of the situation, and in part on the degree of process control used by the commercial printer. It's the exception rather than the rule that every impression in a print run will be identical, but the amount of variation within a press run varies widely from shop to shop. Typically, the less variation, the higher the prices.

Creating ideal separations for a given press is often an iterative process—you run press proofs and measure them, go back to original RGB files, reseparate them, and repeat the whole process until you arrive at the optimum conditions. This is both time-consuming and expensive, and for most jobs the economics simply don't justify it. If you're willing to dedicate a print run to testing, you're better off ignoring the whole Custom CMYK mechanism and building a good ICC profile instead.

UCR vs. GCR. The Photoshop Classic separation engine offers two different methods of black generation: UCR (Undercolor Removal) and GCR (Gray Component Replacement). Both reduce the total amount of ink used to compensate for ink-trapping problems that appear when too much ink is applied to the page. (In this context, *trapping* is the propensity for one ink to adhere to others—it has nothing to do with building chokes and spreads to compensate for misregistration on press.)

> ▶ UCR separations replace cyan, magenta, and yellow ink with black only in the neutral areas. This uses much less ink in the shadows.

> ▶ GCR extends into color areas of the image as well—it replaces the proportions of cyan, magenta, and yellow that produce neutral gray with a corresponding percentage of black ink.

GCR separations are generally considered easier to control on press than are UCR separations, at least by the theoreticians. The downside of GCR is that it can make the shadow areas look flat and unsaturated

Tip: Need to test your printing specs on a budget? A printer can sometimes piggyback a test onto someone else's print job, particularly if you show that you can offer them a significant amount of business. Preparing several different versions of an image (and a few color bars, too) and ganging them on a page can help you identify problems early.

Figure 4-13
Black generation

A UCR separation uses black ink only in the neutral areas. It produces rich shadows but can be hard to control on press because it uses a lot of ink compared to GCR separations.

A Light GCR setting replaces slightly more CMY with K than does a UCR separation. In this image, Light GCR puts slightly more black into the sky and the water than does the UCR separation.

Maximum GCR replaces all of the neutral components of the CMY inks with black. It's easy to control on press because the black plate carries most of the image, but it can make shadow areas look flat.

since they're being printed only with black ink, so many commercial printers distrust GCR separations. UCA (Undercolor Addition) allows you to compensate for flat shadows by adding some CMY back into the neutral shadow areas (see "Undercolor Addition (UCA)," later in this chapter).

Some experts contend that UCR separations are better for sheetfed presses and that GCR is better for web presses, but we just don't buy it. We almost always use GCR separations with some UCA. But we've found that UCR sometimes works better than GCR when printing to newsprint with a low total ink limit—say, 220 to 240 percent. We suspect that many printers who profess to hate GCR separations often run them unknowingly, usually with good results, as long as the black generation amount isn't too extreme.

Black generation can be image-specific: If we take the extreme examples represented by two images—one, a pile of silver coins, the other, a city skyline at night—the first is an ideal candidate for a fairly heavy black plate using Medium or Heavy GCR, since there's little color, and carrying most of the image on the black plate improves detail and makes it easier to maintain neutral grays on press. The second image, though, will have significant color and detail in the deep shadows, and too heavy a black will make it flat and lifeless.

Black Generation. The Black Generation pop-up menu is available only when Separation Type is set to GCR. This feature lets you control the areas of the tonal range that Photoshop replaces with black (see **Figure 4-13**). For the vast majority of situations, we prefer a Light black setting, in which Photoshop begins to add black only after the 40-percent mark. Often, however, a Medium black (where black begins to replace colors after only 20 percent) may work better for newsprint. We almost never use the Heavy or Maximum black settings, but Maximum black can do wonders when printing images that were captured from your screen (like the screen shots in this book), and is also useful when printing to color laser printers.

Custom black generation. The Custom option allows you to create your own black-generation curve. This isn't something you should undertake lightly—the black plate has an enormous influence on the tonal reproduction of the image. However, if you want to make slight modifications to one of the built-in black-generation curves, you can—choose the curve you want to view, then choose Custom. The Black Generation dialog appears with the last selected curve loaded (see **Figure 4-14**).

If your printer asks for a "skeleton black," you can use the Custom option to create a skeleton black curve—a very light black setting that still extends high up into the tonal range, typically to 25 or 30 percent. You should attempt to do this only if the printer demands it, and even then, only if you have considerable experience in evaluating images by looking at the individual color plates.

Black Ink Limit. Black Ink Limit does just what it says—it limits the amount of black ink used in the deepest shadows. The Photoshop Classic

Tip: Here's an easy way to check what values you'll actually get from a given setup. Close all open documents, set the foreground and background colors to default, then click the black swatch to open the Color Picker. The CMYK percentages shown in the Color Picker are the ones the current setup will generate for black.

Printing to Desktop Printers

If you're one of the growing number of Photoshop users who print exclusively, or mainly, to desktop printers, rest assured that the bulk of the material contained in this chapter applies as much to you as it does to those whose printing is done on a commercial press. If you're printing to an inkjet printer, you'll have less variation to worry about on output since inkjet printers are stable and inkjet inks are generally consistent from batch to batch. True photographic printers such as the Fuji Pictrography and the Durst Lambda also offer much better consistency than any printing press. So in some ways, your task is easier than printing on a press. But in other ways, it's more complicated.

The main question you have to answer is whether you drive the printer as an RGB or a CMYK device. Photographic printers are true RGB devices—they expose photosensitive paper using red, green, and blue lasers or LEDs— so the CMYK color mode simply doesn't apply. Inkjet printers use cyan, magenta, yellow, and black inks (plus, sometimes, light cyan, light magenta, and even light black, which we used to know as gray), which in theory at least makes them CMYK devices. But in practice, unless you're printing through a PostScript RIP, desktop inkjet printers function as RGB devices because traditionally, the OS-level graphics languages have lacked any facility for passing CMYK to printers. Quartz, the graphics engine in Mac OS X, has the theoretical capability to hand off CMYK, but we've yet to see a printer driver that exploits it. Photoshop will let you send CMYK to these printers, but the printer driver will immediately convert it to RGB before doing anything else with it.

A PostScript RIP may seem to allow more control over the printing process by letting you control the individual inks, but that usually isn't the case. PostScript RIPs that use the printer's native screening algorithms usually send RGB to that part of the print process: Those that truly provide ink-level control use their own screening, which usually looks much worse than the printer's native screening. A PostScript RIP makes sense from a workflow standpoint if you're using a desktop printer as a proofer, but if your desktop print is your final output, we recommend using the RGB driver, or a specialized RIP designed for photo output, such as Colorbyte's ImagePrint.

RGB output. If you're printing RGB, you can skip the entire CMYK section in this chapter. You should, however, read the sections "Choosing an RGB Working Space," "Soft-Proofing Controls," and "Converting Colors When You Print" carefully. We recommend using ICC profiles for your printer. If you print using the printer vendor's inks and papers, the canned profiles that come with the printer can work well. If you're using third-party inks and papers, though, a custom profile will improve your output immensely. Inexpensive scanner-based profiling packages such as Pantone Huey work well with inkjet printers, and can pay for themselves in savings on ink and paper. Don't use your RGB printer profile as an RGB working space, because RGB printer spaces aren't gray-balanced or perceptually uniform, making editing difficult. Instead, use a working space such as ProPhoto RGB, and fine-tune your image for output using Proof Setup to create a simulation of the printed output.

CMYK output. If you're printing CMYK through a PostScript RIP, almost everything we say in this chapter about press CMYK applies equally to desktop printers. Ideally, you should use a custom ICC profile for your inks and papers. If you always print using the same inks and paper, consider building a custom profile or commissioning one from one of the many companies and individuals offering such services. Or use some of the techniques we discuss in "Should You Use Custom CMYK?" to make a custom CMYK space for your printer, especially if you experiment with different inks and paper stocks.

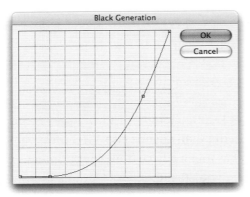

Figure 4-14
Custom Black
Generation dialog

*Choose Custom to
create a custom black-
generation curve.*

mechanism seems to get less happy the further away this is set from 100 percent, so we generally recommend using 95 to 100 percent as a starting point. Below 95 percent, you get progressively less black ink than you requested. How *much* less will depend on the total ink limit.

Total Ink Limit. Total Ink Limit also does what it says—it limits the total amount of ink used in the deepest shadows. The ideal value depends on the combination of press, ink, and paper, but bear in mind that it isn't necessarily desirable to use the maximum amount of ink that the printing process can handle. It's generally true that more ink will yield a better image (within the limits of the press), but it also creates more problems with ink trapping and drying, show-through, and offsetting, and (for printers) it costs more because you're using more ink. Your printer will know, better than anyone else, the trade-offs involved.

For high-quality sheetfed presses with coated stock, a total ink limit of 300 to 340 percent is a good starting point—you may be able to go even higher with some paper stocks. For newsprint, values can range from 220 to 280 percent (see the next section, "Typical Custom CMYK Setups").

Undercolor Addition (UCA). UCA is used with GCR to compensate for loss of ink density in the neutral shadow areas. Using UCA lets you bring back richness to the shadows, yet still retain the benefits of easier color-ink balancing on the press that GCR offers.

The need for UCA is image-dependent. If your shadows look flat, the image can probably benefit from modest amounts of UCA. We rarely use more than 10 percent, and typically use less. (Because David doesn't like to think a whole lot, he usually sets this to 5 percent and forgets about it.)

Tip: You can easily add profiles to the list that appears in the CMYK menu in basic mode (when the More Options button is visible) by storing the profile, or an alias/shortcut to the profile, in the right place. In Mac OS X, that place is inside the Library\Application Support\Adobe\Color\Profiles\Recommended folder. In Windows, it's inside the Program Files\Common Files\Adobe\Color\Profiles\Recommended folder.

Typical Custom CMYK Setups

Table 4-2 (see page 108) gives some general guidelines for different types of print jobs. The dot-gain values are based on 133- to 150-line screens, except for newsprint, which assumes an 85-line screen. If you use these values, you should get acceptable separations; but every combination of press, ink, and paper has its own quirks, and your printer should know them better than anyone else. View these values as useful starting points, and get as much advice from your printer as you can.

When you click the More Options button in Color Settings, you can choose any installed CMYK profile as the CMYK working space. Bear in mind that the Convert to Profile command lets you convert images to any CMYK profile, so it isn't necessary to load a particular CMYK profile as the CMYK working space. It's simply more convenient to load the CMYK profile you're going to use most as the CMYK working space.

Press Profile Families

The main reason that some people continue to use the Photoshop Classic mechanism is that they're stuck with one ICC profile with a single black generation. When you build your own CMYK profiles for a press or proofer, it's always a good idea to build a family of profiles with different

Canned vs. Custom Profiles

Canned profiles—profiles supplied by a third party that are based on something other than measurements of your specific device—have earned a bad reputation, often deservedly so. But under the right circumstances, generic ICC profiles can be very useful. It's true that each combination of printing press, ink, and paper is unique. However, virtually all press operators pride themselves on their ability to match a contract proof such as an Imation Matchprint or Fuji ColorArt.

If they couldn't, color printing would be almost impossible.

Proofer profiles. Proofing systems are generally very consistent from shop to shop. This makes them good candidates for canned profiles—stable, repeatable, consistent output processes like contract proofers simply don't need custom profiles. You need to make sure that the profile you choose has the correct ink limits, black generation, and substrate for your job, but as long as you pay attention to these

variables, you can produce excellent results using generic proofer profiles.

Sheetfed press. While sheetfed presses vary a little more than do proofing systems, we've seen excellent results from generic sheetfed press profiles too, providing the paper stock isn't too weird. Bear in mind that the press operator has a great deal of control over the final result—a profile only has to be a reasonable match to the press.

black generations—some profiling tools will even let you take an existing profile and regenerate it with new black generation settings.

Photoshop Classic is very old technology with more than its fair share of quirks. We debated leaving it out of this edition entirely, but we recognize that some people still rely on it. If you're one of them, we gently suggest that you investigate twenty-first century profiling technology. It has evolved a great deal more in the past 15-odd years than has Photoshop Classic, and will let you produce better results with less work.

Choosing a Gray Working Space

Grayscale is a first-class citizen in Photoshop, with its own profiles independent of RGB or CMYK. However, note that grayscale profiles only contain tone reproduction information; they have no information about the color of the black ink or of the paper.

When Color Settings is displayed with Fewer Options, you can choose among grayscale dot gains of 10, 15, 20, 25, or 30 percent, depending on your printing conditions. You can also choose either gamma 1.8 or 2.2, which are good choices for grayscale images destined for the screen, or for unknown printing conditions. Of course, there's nothing to prevent you from using these gamma values for print images, or the dot-gain curves for onscreen use, but generally speaking, gammas are designed for onscreen and dot-gain curves are designed for print.

Custom Gray

When you click the More Options button in Color Settings, you gain access to all the grayscale profiles installed on your system, as well as the ability to define custom grayscale working spaces (which you can then save as grayscale ICC profiles, if you want).

Custom Dot Gain. If you print a lot of grayscale work on the same sort of paper stock, it may well be worth it to build your own custom dot gain (remember, the more you customize, the better results you'll get). You can define a custom dot gain by choosing Custom Dot Gain from the Gray menu in the Color Settings dialog. The Custom Dot Gain dialog (see **Figure 4-15**) lets you plug in values for the 2, 4, 6, 8, 10, 20, 30, 40, 50, 60, 70, 80, and 90 percent dots. You can enter a single value for the 50-percent field (for example, to define 18-percent dot gain, you'd enter 68 in the 50-percent field), but you'll get much better results if you first print a ramp with patches for all the values in the dialog, then measure the actual dot area for each one, and enter them all in the dialog. This will give you a very accurate grayscale profile.

Figure 4-15
Custom Dot Gain for grayscale

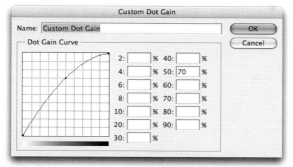

The Custom Dot Gain dialog lets you specify a precise dot-gain compensation for grayscale images.

Of course, it's not absolutely necessary to measure every single patch, but we strongly recommend that you at least measure the highlight (2, 4, 6, 8, and 10 percent) patches plus the 40- and 80-percent patches. Obtaining accurate measurements for the highlights lets you set your all-important highlight detail quickly and easily.

Custom Gamma. Grayscale gamma settings are designed primarily for onscreen images. We can't envisage too many situations where you'd need to define a gamma other than the gamma 1.8 and gamma 2.2 built in to Photoshop, but if for some reason you need to do so, choose Custom Gamma from the Color Settings Gray menu. Permissible values range from 0.75 to 3.0 (see **Figure 4-16**).

CMYK black channel. If you need to mix grayscale and color images in the same job, you might find it useful to simply load the black channel of your CMYK profile as your Gray working space. To do so, choose Load Gray from the Gray pop-up menu, then select the CMYK profile you wish to load from the dialog and click Load. The profile appears in the Gray pop-up menu as Black Ink—ProfileName. Note that the Black Ink Limit in a CMYK profile has no effect on grayscale images (because Black Ink Limit only applies when you convert to CMYK). The grayscale setting uses the dot gain of the black ink, letting you use the entire dynamic range of the black channel.

Figure 4-16
Custom Gamma for
grayscale

*The Custom Gamma
dialog lets you
create a custom
gamma setting for
grayscale images.*

Save Gray. To use a custom grayscale setting elsewhere in Photoshop (for instance, in the Proof Setup, Assign Profile, or Convert to Profile dialogs) and in other ICC-savvy applications, you need to save your grayscale setting as an ICC profile. To do so, choose Save Gray from the Gray pop-up menu, browse to the appropriate folder or directory for your platform, and click Save. Your grayscale profile will now be available for use in any application that understands grayscale ICC profiles.

Spot Spaces

The Spot feature in the Color Settings dialog lets you specify a dot gain for spot colors. As with grayscale settings, spot color settings know nothing about the actual color of the ink and paper, and they contain no information about the way the spot ink interacts with other inks. Spot settings essentially behave identically to grayscale ones.

The Spot pop-up menu in the Color Settings dialog contains dot gain settings for 10, 15, 20, 25, and 30 percent dot gain. When you click the More Options button in Color Settings, you can also define a Custom Dot Gain, choose a custom grayscale profile, or load the black channel of a CMYK profile. The procedure for doing any of these is identical to that for Grayscale mode. But spot inks differ widely in how they behave on paper, and the only way to know what will happen is to print a tint build.

Loading the black channel of a CMYK profile for Spot is primarily useful if you need to use black as a spot color in a CMYK image: Making type, callouts, or drop shadows print with only black ink are good examples. But using tints of spot colors, which spot dot gains seem to invite, is a very uncertain process. The dot-gain curve ensures that the tint you request is the one you'll get, but the only way to find out how the spot color will interact with the process inks is, unfortunately, to print it.

Color Management Policies

While the working space definitions allow you to tell Photoshop what colors the various numbers in your images represent, the Policies and Warnings sections of the Color Settings dialog (see **Figure 4-17**) do something quite different: They let you tell Photoshop how to use the interpretations of the numbers.

Figure 4-17
Color Management
Policies

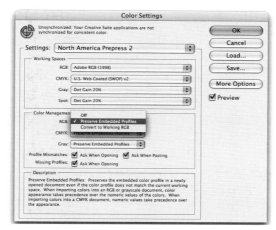

Color Management Policies let you tell Photoshop how to manage color.

The policies control how Photoshop handles several aspects of color management. When you open a document with an embedded profile, the policies tell Photoshop to do one of the following:

► Use the embedded profile instead of the working space, opening the document as a tagged document in its own document space (which may or may not be the same as the current working space).

► Convert the image from the document space represented by the embedded profile to the current working space.

► Ignore the profile and treat the document as untagged (in which case the numbers in the file are interpreted according to the current working space).

► Ignore the profile and treat the document as a Tagged document in the working space.

When you create a new document, the policies tell Photoshop whether to treat it as an untagged document or as a tagged document in the working space.

When you move pixels between documents (by copying and pasting or by dragging), the policies tell Photoshop to move either the numerical values of the pixels or the colors those numerical values represent.

When you save a document, the policies tell Photoshop whether or not to embed the profile currently associated with the document. You can override the policy's setting for profile embedding in the Save As dialog, but the policy dictates whether the Embed Color Profile check box is turned on or off when the dialog appears.

You can set individual policies for RGB, CMYK, and grayscale images, but the policies themselves behave almost identically in each color mode. The most sensible policy to use in a color-managed workflow is Preserve Embedded Profiles.

Off. The Off choice is somewhat misleadingly named, as there's really no way to turn off color management entirely in Photoshop CS3. It does, however, treat your images pretty closely to the way Photoshop did prior to version 5. When you set the policy for a color mode to Off, Photoshop behaves like this:

▶ When you open a file that contains an embedded profile, Photoshop discards the embedded profile and treats the image as untagged, *unless* the embedded profile happens to match the current working space. In that case, the image is treated as a tagged document in its own document space, which in this case happens to be the same as the working space. If you change the working space in the Color Settings dialog, all your untagged images will change, taking on the new working space definition, but the tagged images keep the old working space definition, now acting as a document space. (If you find this confusing and counterintuitive, you're not alone. We think it would be a lot simpler if Off simply treated all your documents as untagged.)

▶ When you save the document, no profile is embedded (unless you turn on Embed Profile in the Save As dialog, in which case the current working space profile is embedded), *unless* Photoshop is handling the document as a Tagged document because its embedded profile matched the working space that was in effect when it was opened. In that case, the profile that was embedded in the file when it was opened is re-embedded when you save, unless you turn off the Embed Color Profile check box in the Save As dialog (see **Figure 4-18**).

▶ When you open a file that has no embedded profile, Photoshop treats it as untagged. When you save the document, no profile is embedded (unless you turn on Embed Color Profile in the Save As dialog, in which case the current working space profile is embedded).

▶ When you create a new document, Photoshop treats it as untagged. When you save the document, no profile is embedded (unless you turn on Embed Color Profile in the Save As dialog, in which case the current working space profile is embedded).

▶ When you transfer pixels between images in the same color mode by copy and paste or by drag and drop, the numerical values get transferred. That means if the two documents are in different color spaces, the colors change even though the numbers are preserved. (If the two images are in different color modes—CMYK and RGB, for instance—the color appearance is always preserved.)

Figure 4-18
The Embed Color Profile check box

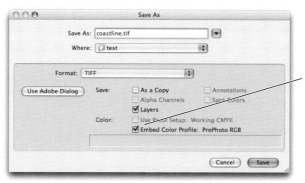

You can control whether or not Photoshop embeds a profile by checking or unchecking the Embed Color Profile check box in the Save As dialog. Photoshop always tells you which profile will be embedded (if you choose to embed a profile).

Off is the policy you want if you're a dyed-in-the-wool, by-the-numbers type who has been cursing at Adobe for years for stuffing color management down your throat. Of course, you don't have to set all the policies to Off. If you're in an all-CMYK, by-the-numbers workflow, you can set the policy to Off just for CMYK, and still get the benefits of color management in the other spaces. Similarly, if your work is mostly for the Web, and you need RGB in Photoshop to behave the same as RGB in the vast majority of Web browsers, you can set the policy to Off for RGB. (Well, actually, as we noted earlier in the chapter, on the Mac you may also want to set your RGB working space to Monitor RGB to ensure that RGB in Photoshop matches RGB in your other, non-color-managed applications.)

However, if you want to use color management in Photoshop, you'll want to choose one of the other policies and simply untag on a case-by-case basis documents that need to be untagged (see "Assign Profile," later in this chapter).

Preserve Embedded Profiles. This is the third-millennium, industrial-strength color management approach. Preserve Embedded Profiles is the safe policy, in that it makes sure Photoshop doesn't do color conversions when you don't want it to. With this policy, the working spaces in Color Settings are there only as a convenience because each image can live in its own document space. On the other hand, it can also be the dangerous policy because if you're not at least a little careful, you can wind up editing images in color spaces that are wildly inappropriate for editing. For instance, if your scanner software embeds its own profile in an image, this policy might mean you're editing the image in the scanner's space, which is significantly less than optimal. Overall, though, it's the policy that we typically use. With this setting selected, here's what happens to your images:

▶ When you open an image that contains an embedded profile, Photoshop preserves the profile and treats the image as tagged, using the embedded profile as the document space (which may or may not be the current working space). When you save the document, the document space profile (the profile the image had when you opened it) is once again embedded in the saved file.

▶ When you open an image with no embedded profile, Photoshop treats the image as an untagged image. (It preserves the lack of an embedded profile, if you will.) When you save the document, no profile is embedded (unless you turn on Embed Color Profile in the Save As dialog, in which case the current working space profile is embedded).

▶ When you create a new document, Photoshop treats it as a tagged document and assigns the current working space profile as the document space. When you save the document, Photoshop embeds the document space profile. (Even if you change the working space in the Color Settings dialog, it has no effect on the image, which stays in the document space.)

▶ When you transfer pixels between two RGB or two grayscale images (by copy and paste or drag and drop), the actual color gets transferred. If the two images are in different color spaces, the numbers change even though the color appearance is preserved.

▶ When you transfer pixels between two CMYK images, the numerical values get transferred. If the two CMYK documents were in different CMYK spaces, the color appearance would change even though the numbers would be preserved. While this routine is the reverse of what happens with RGB and grayscale files, it is actually more logical and useful.

We believe quite strongly that Preserve Embedded Profiles is the best policy for the vast majority of Photoshop users. It keeps track of color for you and rarely performs any conversions that aren't explicitly requested (and *never* does so if you keep the Profile Mismatch: Paste warning turned on). If you have to deal with files from many different sources, this is almost certainly the policy you want to use. It does a good job of keeping color management out of your face, but it also offers tremendous power and flexibility for hard-core color geeks.

Convert to Working Space. Convert to Working Space tells Photoshop to convert everything into your working RGB, CMYK, or grayscale. It tells Photoshop to convert images to the current default working space automatically. We find this method a bit too authoritarian, though if your workflow relies on picking a single RGB, CMYK, or grayscale color space and normalizing all your images into it, you'll almost certainly want to use this policy. But we think it's best thought of as an automation feature: If it does something you wanted done with no intervention, that's great; on the other hand, if it does something unexpected behind your back, it's not so great! Here's what happens to your images with this setting selected:

▶ When you open a file that already has the current working space profile embedded, Photoshop preserves the profile and treats the image as a tagged image, using the embedded profile as the document space. When you save the document, the document space profile (the profile the image had when you opened it) is once again embedded in the saved file, even if you change the working space in the Color Settings dialog when the image is open.

	Press and paper	Inks	Dot gain
Table 4-2	Sheetfed Coated	SWOP (Coated)	12–15%
Suggested separation settings	Sheetfed Uncoated	SWOP (Uncoated)	17–22%
	Web Coated	SWOP (Coated)	17–22%
	Web Uncoated	SWOP (Uncoated)	22–30%
	Newsprint 1	SWOP (Newsprint)	30–40%
	Newsprint 2	SWOP (Newsprint)	30–40%

▶ When you open a file that has an embedded profile different than the current working space, Photoshop converts the image from the embedded profile's space to the current working space. From then on, it treats the image as a tagged image, with the working space profile that was in effect when it was opened as the document space.

▶ When you open an image with no embedded profile, Photoshop treats the image as untagged. If you change the working space, Photoshop keeps the numbers in the file unchanged and reinterprets them as belonging to the new working space (so the appearance changes). When you save the document, profile embedding is turned off by default (though you can turn it on in the Save As dialog).

▶ When you create a new document, Photoshop treats it as a tagged document in the current working space. If you later change the working space, Photoshop preserves the working space profile that was in effect when the document was created. When you save the document, that same profile is also embedded.

▶ When you transfer pixels between two images (whether it's RGB-to-RGB, RGB-to-CMYK, or whatever), the color appearance gets transferred, even if that means Photoshop changes the numbers (which it'll have to do if the files are in different color spaces).

Convert to Working Space is a useful policy when you need all your images to be in the same space, such as when you're compositing RGB images or repurposing CMYK images from several different sources for a single output. It's a handy automation feature when you need to convert a bunch of pictures quickly. But unless you're very sure about what

Black generation	Black limit	Total ink	UCA
GCR, Light	100%	320–340%	0–10%
GCR, Light	100%	270–300%	0–10%
GCR, Light	100%	300–320%	0–10%
GCR, Light	100%	280–300%	0–10%
GCR, Medium	95–100%	260–280%	0–10%
UCR	70–80%	220–240%	

you're doing, it's safer to use Preserve Embedded Profiles instead, and perform the conversions manually whenever you need to change an image's working space (see "Applying Profiles Outside Color Settings," later in this chapter).

Profile Warnings

Although they appear in the Color Management Policies section of the Color Settings dialog, the Missing Profile and Profile Mismatch warnings operate independently from the policies. (You can think of it this way: The policy determines the initial default setting of some of the warnings.) Unless you're adamantly opposed to the use of color management, we suggest you turn all the warning check boxes on and keep them on until you decide you don't need them. They offer choices, letting you override the default behavior of the policy you've chosen for a specific color mode, though we'd find them even more useful if they didn't demand clairvoyance on our part and would let us see the image before making decisions.

Profile Mismatch: Ask When Opening. When Profile Mismatch: Ask When Opening is turned on, Photoshop alerts you when you open a document with an embedded profile that's different from the current working space (see **Figure 4-19**). Even better, the Embedded Profile Mismatch dialog offers you three choices for handling the profile mismatch:

▶ **Use The Embedded Profile (Instead Of The Working Space)** tells Photoshop to keep the embedded profile, treating the document as a tagged image in the embedded profile's space. The embedded profile is then used to display the image, and is also used as the source profile for any subsequent color conversion. This is typically what you'd want.

▶ **Convert Document's Colors To The Working Space** does what it says: It performs a conversion from the embedded profile's space to the current default working space. This makes sense if you need several images in the same working space (for example, to composite them).

▶ **Discard The Embedded Profile (Don't Color Manage)** strips off the embedded profile and opens the document as an untagged image. The numbers in the document are left unchanged and are interpreted according to the current working space definition. You might use this if you know you're going to significantly edit the color and tone of the image and you don't care about any color interpretations that were already assigned. Similarly, this might be appropriate for an image destined for the Web, especially if you'll be saving it in the sRGB space.

Figure 4-19
Embedded Profile
Mismatch dialog

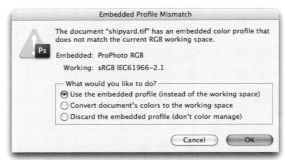

The Embedded Profile Mismatch warning offers three choices for handling images whose embedded profile differs from the working space.

The Embedded Profile Mismatch dialog chooses one of these three as the default (the one that you'll get if you just hit the Enter key). The default it picks depends on the policy you've chosen for that color mode. Of course, the dialog always allows you to override the default behavior for the policy on an image-by-image basis.

Profile Mismatch: Ask When Pasting. The second check box, Ask When Pasting, comes into play when you move pixels between two images that are in the same color mode, but in different color spaces (like sRGB to AdobeRGB, or from one CMYK setup to another). When this is selected, Photoshop asks you whether you want to paste the numerical values or the color appearance (see **Figure 4-20**). Note that when you copy and paste or drag and drop between images that are in different color modes (like RGB to CMYK), this alert doesn't do anything because Photoshop only lets you paste the color appearance.

Figure 4-20

Paste Profile Mismatch
dialog

The Paste Profile Mismatch warning lets you choose whether to paste the numerical values or the perceived color those values represent.

Just to be clear: In this dialog, Convert (Preserve Color Appearance) tells Photoshop to change the numbers in the image so that you get roughly the same color. It's like doing a profile-to-profile conversion. We add the caveat "roughly" just in case a color in one profile simply cannot be represented in the gamut of the target profile. The Don't Convert (Preserve Color Numbers) option simply copies the numbers from the source file into the target file without worrying about color changes. As with Profile Mismatch: Ask When Opening, the default option is set to match the current policy for the color mode.

Missing Profile: Ask When Opening. The third warning, Missing Profile: Ask When Opening, comes into play when you open a document with no embedded profile. When this is turned on, Photoshop lets you choose how you want it to interpret the numbers in documents with no embedded profiles (see **Figure 4-21**).

▶ **Leave As Is (Don't Color Manage)** tells Photoshop to treat the file as an untagged document. The numbers in the file are preserved and interpreted according to the current working space (which means that the appearance may change radically).

▶ **Assign Working Space** tags the document with the current working space profile. As with the previous option, the numbers in the file are preserved and interpreted according to the current working space. The difference is that the document is treated as tagged, so it keeps that profile if you subsequently change the working space.

▶ **Assign Profile** lets you tag the document with a profile other than the working space profile. Again, the numbers in the file are preserved, but in this case they're interpreted according to the profile you choose.

> ▶ **Assign Profile And Then Convert Document To Working Space** lets you assign a source profile to the document and then convert it to the working space. This is the only option of the four that actually changes the numbers in the file.

Figure 4-21
Missing Profile
dialog

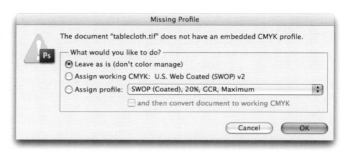

If you're in a workflow in which you know where images are coming from and where they're going, you can probably turn off the warning dialogs off. When you don't need them, they do get kind of annoying after a while.

Color Settings with More Options

When you click the More Options button in the Color Settings dialog, you gain access to the Conversion Options and Advanced Controls, as well as to a wider range of profiles (we've discussed that earlier in this chapter). The Conversion Options can be useful in typical workflows, but the Advanced Controls are a grab-bag of options that may be useful to a very small number of serious players, and are dangerous buttons for almost everyone else.

Conversion Options

Tip: The terms color management module (CMM) and color management engine (CME) mean the same thing.

The Conversion Options section of the dialog lets you control useful things like the default rendering intent in Photoshop and color management module (CMM)—things you probably won't need to change very often, but might want to occasionally (see **Figure 4-22**).

Engine. The Engine pop-up menu lets you select the CMM that Photoshop uses for all its color space calculations. The options that appear on the menu depend on which CMMs are installed on your system. Unless

Figure 4-22
Conversion Options

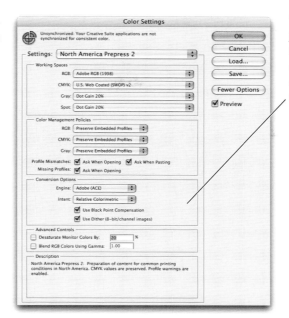

The Conversion Options let you choose the color engine, the default rendering intent, and settings for black point compensation and dithering in 8-bit/channel conversions.

you have really pressing reasons to use a different CMM, we recommend sticking with the Adobe (ACE) engine. When the engines work correctly, there is only a tiny change in pixel values with the different engines; except for the bugs, we've never noticed a visual difference.

Mac users will notice separate entries for the Apple CMM and Apple ColorSync. Apple CMM means that the Apple CMM will always be used.

Intent. The Intent pop-up menu is significantly more useful for the average user. Intent lets you choose the default rendering intent that Photoshop uses in any of the following color space conversions:

▶ Converting documents on opening

▶ Converting documents by choosing a different mode from the Mode menu (like separating RGB to CMYK)

▶ Calculating the numbers that appear on the Info palette for color modes other than the one the document uses

▶ Calculating the numbers that appear in the Color Picker for color modes other than the one the document uses

Every other feature in Photoshop that lets you convert colors from one profile's space to another has its own rendering intent controls. The default rendering intent in Photoshop is relative colorimetric with black point compensation. These defaults are always the subject of some pretty heated debate. We offer three observations:

▶ While some users may prefer perceptual rendering as the default choice, rendering intent is best treated as an image-specific and conversion-specific decision. Relative colorimetric renderings may actually do a better job than perceptual rendering when your images don't have a lot of significant out-of-gamut colors.

▶ Color conversions in Photoshop have always been relative colorimetric in the past.

▶ It's just a default. You can always override it to suit the needs of the image at hand.

Since Photoshop makes it very easy to both preview and apply different rendering intents for each image, the rendering intent setting here is more a matter of convenience than of necessity.

Use Black Point Compensation. The Use Black Point Compensation option, when selected, maps the black of the source profile to the black of the target profile, ensuring that the entire dynamic range of the output device is used. In many cases you'll find no difference whether it's turned on or off, because it depends on the contents of the particular profiles involved. See the sidebar "Black Is Black (or Is It?)" later in this chapter for a detailed look at the Black Point Compensation feature.

In earlier versions of Photoshop we offered a complex set of rules about when to turn this on and off, but we now recommend that you just leave Use Black Point Compensation turned on at all times.

Use Dither (8-bit/Channel Images). The Use Dither feature is somewhat esoteric. All color space conversions in Photoshop are performed in a high-bit space. When Use Dither is turned on, Photoshop adds a small amount of noise when the 8-bit channels are converted into the high-bit space. This makes banding or posterization much less likely to occur (that's a good thing). But if your final output will be JPEG, this tiny dithering is likely to produce a larger file size (because it introduces more discrete colors into the image), and if you're using Photoshop for scientific work, where you need to perform quantitative analysis on colors, you should turn this off, as it will introduce noise in your data. Otherwise, leave it on.

Advanced Controls

The Advanced Controls are aptly named. We recommend leaving them alone unless you have a pressing need to do otherwise, but in the interest of full disclosure, here's what they do.

Desaturate Monitor Colors By. The Desaturate Monitor Colors By feature attempts to solve a problem with large-gamut working spaces: Rendering to the monitor is always relative colorimetric, so colors in the working space that lie outside the monitor gamut get clipped to the nearest equivalent the monitor can display. You can think of desaturating the monitor as the poor man's perceptual rendering. Unless you're working with a very large space like Kodak's ProPhoto RGB, don't even think about messing with this. Even then, we don't use it—we find that the problem is much less severe than theory would lead one to expect.

For those brave (or foolhardy) souls who want to experiment with it, a setting in the 12 to 15 percent range seems somewhat useful for Kodak ProPhoto RGB, and 7 to 10 percent seems good for EktaSpace. If you're working with one of these spaces, try turning the feature on and off to see if it's doing anything useful for you. Whatever you do, don't forget to turn it back off before you try to do any normal work; otherwise you'll find yourself producing excessively colorful imagery!

Blend RGB Colors Using Gamma. The Blend RGB Colors Using Gamma feature controls how RGB colors blend together. To see its effect, try painting a bright green stroke on a red background with the check box turned off, and then again with the check box turned on and the value set to a gamma of 1.0. With the check box turned off, the edges of the stroke have a brownish hue, as they would if you were painting with paint. With it turned on, the edges are yellowish, as they would be if you were painting with light. You can think of the behavior with the check box off as artistically correct, and with it turned on as colorimetrically correct. Permissible values are from 1 to 2.2.

The Color Picker

Why are we talking about the Color Picker in this chapter? Simply put, a great many people overlook the fact that the Color Picker is subject to the choices you make in Color Settings, because the numbers that appear in the Color Picker for all the color modes other than the current document's mode are the product of color space conversions made using the default profiles, engine, and rendering intent.

We've lost count of the number of e-mails we've received from confused puppies who tried to specify black as 0C 0M 0Y 100K in an RGB document and then got bent out of shape because:

▶ The resulting color was dark gray.

▶ It picked up a bunch of C, M, and Y on conversion to CMYK.

Well, 100K isn't black because black ink isn't perfectly black or perfectly opaque—if it were, we'd never need to lay down more than 100 percent total ink. If you specify 0C 0M 0Y 100K in the Color Picker, then look at the RGB values, or the Lightness value in Lab, you'll find that they aren't zero. And unless your CMYK working space uses Maximum GCR, 0C 0M 0Y 100K isn't a "legal" value for a converted RGB 000 black—we almost always want to add some amount of CMY to increase the density.

The Color Picker is governed by two simple rules:

▶ The "real" color being specified is represented by the numbers relevant to the color mode of the current document, which may not be the numbers you're entering. If you enter CMYK numbers while working on an RGB document, the color you're actually specifying is represented by the numbers that appear in the RGB fields and vice versa.

▶ When you specify color in a mode other than the document's, the actual color is calculated by taking the color values you entered, then converting them to the document's mode using the working space profile for the mode you specified as the source profile, the document's profile as the destination profile, and the rendering intent specified in Color Settings.

When you think about it, it's hard to imagine how this could work any other way, but how may of us think that way in the Color Picker?

Applying Profiles Outside Color Settings

The settings in the Color Settings dialog represent the fallback position for performing color conversions. But two commands on the Edit menu offer much more flexibility for applying profiles and performing conversions on an image-by-image basis. In fact, we hardly ever convert colors (from RGB to CMYK, for example) using plain ol' mode changes, because we like to be able to preview and select the rendering intent that does the best job on the image at hand.

Assigning and Converting

We still encounter many users who get confused as to when they should assign and when they should convert. Back at the beginning of this chapter, we told you that color management does only two things:

▶ Associates a specific color appearance with a set of otherwise-ambiguous RGB or CMYK numbers.

▶ Maintains that color appearance in a new context by changing the numbers to make the new device or process produce the desired color appearance.

Assign Profile is the mechanism for associating a color appearance with the RGB or CMYK numbers. Normally, you only have to do this with untagged images. Convert to Profile is one of the mechanisms for calculating a new set of numbers that maintain that color appearance, such as when you convert an RGB image to CMYK.

Assign Profile

Assign Profile lets you tag an image with a specified profile or untag an image by removing its profile. It doesn't do any conversions; it simply attaches a description (an interpretation, as it were) to the numbers in the image, or removes one (see **Figure 4-23**).

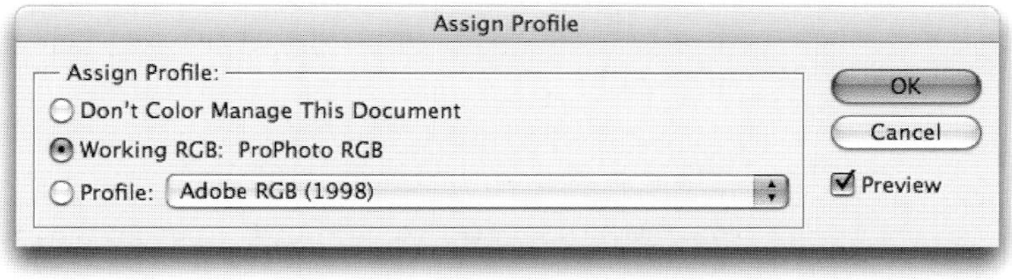

Figure 4-23
Assign Profile
dialog

Assign Profile

Assign Profile:
- ○ Don't Color Manage This Document
- ● Working RGB: ProPhoto RGB
- ○ Profile: Adobe RGB (1998)

OK
Cancel
☑ Preview

We mainly find Assign Profile useful when we're trying to decide what profile should be attached to an untagged document. Unlike the profile assignment in the Missing Profile dialog, Assign Profile lets you preview the results of applying various profiles. This gives you the opportunity to make an educated guess rather than a blind one.

The Assign Profile dialog offers three options, which are identical to the first three options in the Missing Profile warning (see "Color Management Policies," earlier in this chapter).

Don't Color Manage This Document. Don't Color Manage This Document tells Photoshop to treat it as an untagged document. The numbers in the file are preserved and are interpreted according to the current working space, and the embedded profile is stripped out. If you're delivering final CMYK to shops that are scared or confused by color management, if you're delivering images in sRGB for the Web, or if you've inadvertently embedded a profile in a calibration target, you can use this option to strip out the profile.

Working RGB or Working CMYK. Working RGB or Working CMYK (depending on the current color mode of the image) tags the document with the current working space's profile (whatever is set in the Color Settings dialog). As with the previous option, the numbers in the file are preserved but reinterpreted according to the current working space. The difference is that the document is treated as tagged, so it keeps that profile if you later change the working space. If you've opened an untagged document and decided that it really does belong in the working space, use this option to make sure that it stays in the working space.

Profile. Profile lets you tag the document with a profile other than the default working space profile. Again, the numbers in the image are preserved, but in this case they're interpreted according to the profile you assigned. For example, if you scan an image using software that doesn't embed a profile, but you have a profile for your scanner, you can use this option to assign color meaning to the image you've just scanned. You'll then probably want to use Convert to Profile (coming up next) to move the image into a more reasonable editing space, like AdobeRGB.

The Preview check box lets you preview the results of applying or removing a profile (it's rare that we turn this off—the preview is pretty fast, even on a 2.5 GB file).

Convert to Profile

Convert to Profile, as its name suggests, lets you convert a document from its profile space (or, in the case of an untagged document, the current working space) to any other profiled space, with full control over how the conversion is done (see **Figure 4-24**).

Figure 4-24

Convert to Profile dialog

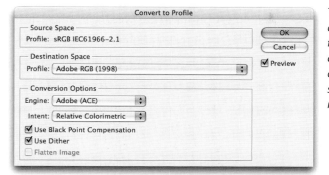

The Convert to Profile dialog gives you full control over color conversions. You can choose the destination space, engine, and rendering intent.

The Convert to Profile dialog displays the source profile and lets you specify a destination profile, engine, and rendering intent. It also allows you to turn black-point compensation on and off, decide whether to use dithering for 8 bit/channel images, and specify whether to flatten the image. Best of all, it lets you preview the results of the conversion correctly while the dialog is still open, so you can see the effects of the various options.

The engine, rendering intent, black-point compensation, and dithering options all work identically to those in the Color Settings dialog (see "Conversion Options," earlier in this chapter).

The Flatten Image option is there as a convenience, for when you want to produce a final flat file for output. When we use Convert to Profile, we usually make a duplicate of the layered file first (choose Image > Duplicate), and then run Convert to Profile on the duplicate, with Flatten Image turned on—that way we keep our layered master files intact.

We use Convert to Profile instead of choosing an Image > Mode command for most conversions (whether converting RGB to CMYK, cross-rendering CMYK to CMYK, or whatever), because it offers more control, and especially because you can preview different rendering intents. Rendering intents only know about the color gamut of the source color space—they don't know anything about how much of that gamut is actually used by the source image—so applying perceptual rendering to an image that contains no significant out-of-gamut colors compresses the gamut unnecessarily. With Convert to Profile, you can see how the different rendering intents will affect a particular image and choose accordingly.

Soft-Proofing Controls

If you're sane, you probably want to get some sense of what your images are going to look like before you commit to $50,000 print run. There are three ways to proof your pictures: traditional (print film negatives and create a laminated proof like a Matchprint), on a color printer (like one of the new breed of inkjet printers), or on screen. On screen? If you've been paying attention during this chapter, you know that you can set up your system to trust what you see on screen. Proofing images on screen is called *soft-proofing*, and Photoshop offers soft-proofing capabilities with accuracy limited only by the accuracy of the profiles involved.

In Photoshop, soft-proofing has its own set of controls separate from the Color Settings dialog. These allow you to preview your output accurately, whether it's RGB or CMYK. This is a huge advantage for those who print to RGB devices like film recorders or to photorealistic inkjet printers that pretend to be RGB devices. Soft-proofing is a big improvement for those who print CMYK too. We can soft-proof different conversions to CMYK while we're still working in RGB and have them accurately depicted on screen. For example, you can quickly see how the same image would look on newsprint and in your glossy brochure.

The View > Proof Colors command lets you turn soft-proofing on and off. Soft-proofing changes only the onscreen display for the current document window, without altering other windows or saved image data. By default, Proof Colors works as follows:

▶ It first simulates the conversion from the document's space to working CMYK, using the rendering intent and black-point compensation settings specified in Color Settings.

▶ It renders that simulation to the monitor using relative colorimetric rendering. If Black Point Compensation is turned on in Color Settings, it's also applied to the rendering from the proof space to the monitor.

Tip: You can open several windows for the same image (by choosing View > New View) and apply different soft-proofing settings to each window. This lets you see how the image will appear under different output scenarios. You can use this feature to adjust the unproofed image while watching the effect on multiple soft-proofed views of the same image.

The default Proof Setup settings probably don't represent the output you're trying to preview, so to really benefit from soft-proofing, you need to be more specific. Your first stop is the Proof Setup submenu (see **Figure 4-25**), which governs exactly what Proof Colors shows you. If your actual output conditions are represented by one of the menu items, choose it so that Proof Setup will use those conditions when it shows you the soft proof.

Figure 4-25
Proof Setup submenu

The Proof Setup submenu lets you choose a wide variety of soft-proofing options, including your own custom settings.

However, chances are that the output conditions listed by default on the Proof Setup submenu aren't specific enough to represent your output conditions. To unleash the power of soft-proofing, you need to use the Customize Proof Condition dialog, which gives you the tools you need to nail your soft-proofs precisely and list them on the Proof Setup submenu.

Customize Proof Condition Dialog

The Customize Proof Condition dialog lets you independently control the rendering from the document's space to the proof space, and from the proof space to the screen. It allows you to preview accurately just about any conceivable kind of output for which you have a profile. You can open the Customize Proof Condition dialog (see **Figure 4-26**) by choosing View > Proof Setup > Custom.

Custom Proof Condition. The Custom Proof Condition pop-up menu lets you recall setups that you've saved in the special Proofing folder. (On Mac OS X, this folder is in harddrive\Library\Application Support\

Figure 4-26

Setting up your soft-proof

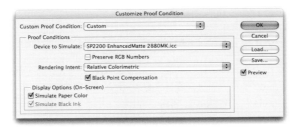

You can control color conversions from the document space to the proofing space, and from the proofing space to the monitor.

Adobe\Color\Proofing. In Windows, it's in the Program Files\Common Files\Adobe\Color\Proofing folder.) You can save proof setups anywhere on your hard disk by clicking Save, and load them by clicking the Load button, but the setups you save in the Proofing folder appear on the list automatically. (Even better, they also appear at the bottom of the Proof Setup submenu, where you can choose them directly.)

Device to Simulate. The Device to Simulate pop-up menu lets you specify the proofing space you want to simulate. You can choose any profile, but if you choose an input profile (for a scanner or digital camera), the Preserve Numbers check box becomes checked and dimmed, and all the other controls become unavailable. (We're not sure why you would choose an input profile, but we suppose it's nice to have the option.) Generally, you'll want to choose an RGB, CMYK, or grayscale output profile.

Preserve RGB/CMYK/Gray Numbers. The Preserve Numbers check box, when selected, tells Photoshop to show you what your file would look like if you sent it to the output device without performing a color-space conversion. It's available only when the image is in the same color mode as the selected profile (as when both are in RGB); when you turn it on, the Rendering Intent pop-up menu becomes unavailable, since no conversion is requested.

We've found that this feature is particularly useful when you have a CMYK file that was prepared for some other printing process. It shows you how the CMYK data will work on your output, which can help you decide whether you need to edit the image, convert it to a different CMYK space, or just send it as is. It's also useful for seeing just how crummy your image will look if you send it to your desktop inkjet printer without converting it to the proper profile (see "Converting Colors When You Print," later in this chapter).

CIE Limitations and Soft-Proofing

All ICC color management is based on the system of mathematical models developed by the Commission Internationale de L'Éclairage (CIE), starting with CIE XYZ (1931), and including later variants such as CIE Lab and CIE xyY. These models were all developed with a very specific purpose in mind, which was to predict the degree to which two solid swatches of reflective material of a specific size on a specific background at a specific distance under a known illuminant would appear to match.

By design, the CIE models ignore many of the contextual effects that modulate our color perception, such as surround color, simultaneous contrast, and the dozens of effects named after the color scientists (Abney, Hunt, Stevens, Bezold-Brücke, and Bartleson-Breneman, to name but a few) who documented them. For solid colors viewed under tightly controlled conditions, these effects don't matter much, but for pixels in images, they almost certainly come into play. Moreover, the CIE models were never designed for cross-media comparisons like that between a monitor and a hard copy.

We know quite a lot about white-point adaptation—the tendency of our eyes to see the brightest thing in the scene as white—but science knows relatively little about black-point adaptation, which is very likely equally important in soft-proofing. It's not that CIE colorimetry is wrong, just that we've taken to applying the CIE models to situations for which they weren't designed. With our current understanding of color perception, it's probably unrealistic to expect an exact match between an image on a monitor and a hard copy of that same image, because we experience them differently. But soft proofing in Photoshop is better than any we've seen, and with a little experience, we believe you'll be able to make useful judgments about how your images will print based on what you see on a calibrated monitor when you turn on the View > Proof Colors command.

Rendering Intent. The Rendering Intent pop-up menu lets you specify the rendering intent you want to use in the conversion from the document's space to the proof space. This is particularly useful for helping you decide whether a given image would be better served by perceptual or relative colorimetric rendering to the output space. It defaults to the Color Settings default rendering intent until you change it, whereupon it remembers what you last used. However, when you save a proof setup, your selected rendering intent is saved with it; so, if you find that you're continually being tripped up by the wrong intent, you can just save a proof setup with your preferred rendering intent.

Black Point Compensation. The Black Point Compensation check box lets you choose whether or not to use black-point compensation in the conversion from the document's space to the proof space. You'll almost invariably want to keep this turned on, but you can always unselect it and see the effect to make sure.

Display Options (On-screen). The check boxes in the Display Options section—Simulate Paper Color and Simulate Black Ink—control the rendering of the image from the proofing space to the monitor. When both Simulate Paper Color and Simulate Black Ink are turned off, Photoshop does a relative colorimetric rendering (with black-point compensation if that option is turned on in Color Settings). This rendering maps paper white to monitor white and ink black to monitor black using the entire dynamic range of the monitor. If you're using a generic monitor profile, this is probably as good as you'll get (of course, with a canned monitor profile, you can't trust anything you see on screen anyway). With a good monitor profile, though, you should check out the alternatives.

▶ When you turn on Simulate Black Ink, Photoshop turns off black-point compensation in the rendering from proof space to the monitor. As a result, the black you see on the monitor is the actual black you'll get on output (within limits). Most monitor profiles have a "black hole" black point. The black ink simulation will be off by the amount that real monitor black differs from the monitor profile's black point. (On a well-calibrated monitor, the inaccuracy is very slight.) If you're printing to a low-dynamic-range process like newsprint or inkjet on uncoated paper Simulate Black Ink will give you a much better idea of the actual blacks you'll get in print.

▶ Turning on the Simulate Paper Color check box makes Photoshop do an absolute colorimetric rendering from the proof space to the display. (Simulate Black Ink becomes checked and dimmed, since black- point compensation is always disabled in absolute colorimetric conversions.) In theory at least, turning on Simulate Paper Color should give you the most accurate soft proof possible.

In practice, the most obvious effect of selecting Simulate Paper Color isn't that it simulates the color of the paper, but rather that you see the compressed dynamic range of print. If you look at the image while turning on Simulate Paper Color, the effect is dramatic—so much so that we look away from the monitor when we turn it on, then wait a few seconds before looking at the image to allow our eyes to adapt to the new white point. More importantly, we also make sure that we hide all white user interface elements, so that our eyes *can* adapt.

Black Is Black (or Is It?)

We usually think of black as being "just black," but black on different devices appears differently. (Solid black on newsprint is much grayer than solid black on glossy sheetfed stock, for instance.) Black-point compensation in Photoshop forces us to think about this fact. The information here is fairly complex, but the basic principle is simple. When you transform an image from one color space to another, there are two ways of transforming the black point: absolute and relative.

Transformations involve first mapping the source gamut to the reference color space (also known as the Profile Connection Space, or PCS), which in most cases is Lab, and then mapping the Lab values to the destination space. In a relative black-point transformation, the source black is mapped to a L* value of 0 in the PCS, but in an absolute black-point transformation, it's mapped to the actual L* value that the source device can produce, which is usually substantially higher than zero. (A zero L* value represents the total absence of any reflected light,

which is blacker than anything other than a black hole can reproduce.) The ICC profiles specify whether the transform should be absolute or relative.

This can lead to undesirable results. For example, Radius ColorMatch RGB profiles map RGB 0,0,0 to L*a*b* 3,0,0 in the PCS. A CMYK profile that uses absolute black transformation may map to a black value in the PCS of L*a*b* 7,0,0. If you convert an RGB image to CMYK using this pair of profiles, your shadow detail will get clobbered because the first few levels in the RGB document will convert to L* values in the PCS between 3 and 7. Since these are all darker than the output device can produce, they'll be clipped to black, and your shadow detail goes bye-bye.

If the same RGB profile is used with a CMYK profile that maps device black to L*a*b* 2,0,0, you'll get very different, equally undesirable results. The RGB black will convert to L*a*b* 3,0,0, which is lighter than the black the output device can produce. The resulting image will appear slightly washed

out because it doesn't contain any true blacks.

To use the entire dynamic range of the output device, you need a relative black transformation both from source to PCS and from PCS to output. Black-point compensation in Photoshop forces this to happen, no matter what the profiles say. It works by estimating the black point for the source and the target.

If they're the same, as they would be if both profiles use relative black encoding, the feature does nothing. But if the black levels are different, it adds an extra processing step: After the source color is converted into the PCS, Black Point Compensation adjusts the PCS to map the source profile's black to the destination profile's black via a straightforward linear transformation of the L* values in the PCS. This ensures that the entire dynamic range of the source is mapped into the entire dynamic range of the target without clipping the shadows or washing out the blacks. For this reason, we leave Black Point Compensation turned on.

Obviously, the quality of the soft-proofing simulation depends on the accuracy of your monitor calibration and on the quality of your profiles. But we believe that the relationship between the image on screen and the final printed output is, like all proofing relationships, one that you must learn. We've never seen a proofing system short of an actual press proof that really matches the final printed piece—laminated film proofs, for example, often show greater contrast than the press sheet, and may have a slight color cast too, but most people in the print industry have learned to discount the slight differences between proof and finished piece.

It's also worth bearing in mind the limitations of the color science on which the whole ICC color management effort is based. We still have a great deal to learn about color perception, and while the science we have works surprisingly well in many situations, it's only a model (see the sidebar "CIE Limitations and Soft-Proofing"). The bottom line is that each of the different soft-proofing renderings to the monitor can tell you something about your printed images. We recommend that you experiment with the settings and learn what works for you and what doesn't.

Proof Setup Submenu

The Proof Setup submenu (under the View menu) contains several other useful commands. For instance, when you're viewing an RGB or grayscale image, you can view the individual CMYK plates (or the CMY progressive) you'd get if you converted to CMYK via the Image > Mode command. You can also use these commands to view the individual plates in CMYK files, but it's much faster and easier to use the keyboard shortcuts to display individual channels or click on the eyeball icon in the Channels palette.

The next set of commands—Macintosh RGB, Windows RGB, and Monitor RGB—is available only for RGB, grayscale, and indexed color images, not for CMYK or Lab. They show you how your image would appear on a "typical" Mac monitor (as defined by the Apple RGB profile), a "typical" Windows monitor (as defined by the sRGB profile), and on your personal monitor (as defined by your monitor profile) if you displayed it on these monitors with no color management. These might be useful when producing Web graphics, for instance. The rest of the menu lists custom proof setups saved in the Proofing folder.

The soft-proofing features in Photoshop let you see how your image will really appear on output, so you can optimize the image to give the best possible rendition in the selected output space. They also help you to be lazy by letting you see if the same master file can produce acceptable results on all the output conditions to which you plan on sending it, relying on color management to handle the various conversions. So whether you're a driven artist seeking perfection or a lowly production grunt doing the impossible on a daily basis, the soft-proofing tools in Photoshop will become an invaluable addition to your toolbox.

Converting Colors When You Print

Photoshop lets you perform color conversions as it sends the data to a printer. You can either convert from the document space to a selected printer profile using a selected rendering intent, or from the document space to a selected Proof Setup space using the rendering intent in Proof Setup, and then to the printer profile. The second method lets you print an RGB file to a composite printer and make the printer simulate the CMYK output you've been soft-proofing—that is, it gives you a hard copy of your soft-proofed image without your having to first convert the image to final output CMYK.

If you're familiar with Print with Preview in previous versions of Photoshop, you'll notice that the Print dialog in Photoshop CS3 is essentially an improved version of Print with Preview.

Print dialog

We cover most of the cool new features in the Print dialog in Chapter 12, "Image Storage and Output;" however, we'll cover the color management aspects of the dialog here.

Tip: You might notice the Match Print Colors check box in the Print dialog. New in Photoshop CS3, Match Print Colors does not affect the color conversions between Photoshop and the printer. All it does it apply your current Proof Setup to the proxy image in the Print dialog, so that the Print dialog can display a more accurate representation of the colors you'll get.

Choose File > Print to open the Print dialog. To use the color management features in the Print dialog, choose Color Management from the unnamed pop-up menu that appears at the top of the options group on the right (see **Figure 4-27**).

The color management options let you control the data that's sent to the printer, choosing whether to let Photoshop do the conversion to the printer space (we invariably let Photoshop do the conversion).

Print. The Print radio buttons let you choose the Document space (to reproduce the image as well as your printer allows) or the Proof space (to produce a hard copy of your soft-proof simulation). If the image window from which you're printing has a custom proof setup, it will appear as the Proof option; otherwise the choice reads Profile N/A. This is slightly misleading, because if you click the Proof radio button, it actually enables the Proof Setup Preset menu in Options, described below.

Options. The Options section lets you choose whether Photoshop sends converted data to the printer, and if it does, how to convert.

Figure 4-27
The Print dialog's Color
Management controls

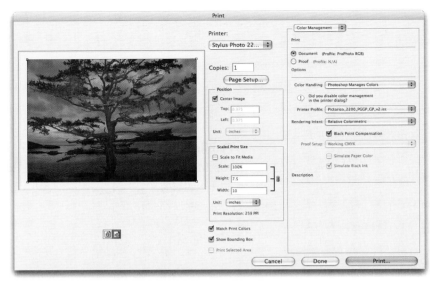

The Print dialog in Photoshop CS3 supports print preview and soft-proofing.

Color Handling. The Color Handling pop-up menu (see **Figure 4-28**) determines what options are available in the rest of the Options section.

▶ **Printer Manages Colors** sends the source data unconverted. Use this option to let the printer driver do the color conversion to the printer space. Color-managing CMYK images on PostScript printers requires PostScript 3—on a PostScript Level 2 printer, choose Lab Color instead. PostScript color management varies enormously. We don't recommend this method because Photoshop can usually do a better color conversion than most printer drivers.

▶ **Photoshop Manages Colors** enables the Printer Profile menu. Photoshop converts the data sent to the printer to the profile space described by the profile chosen from the Printer Profile menu, using the rendering intent specified in the Rendering Intent pop-up menu.

▶ **Separations** is available only for CMYK documents. It sends the individual plates to the printer, unmodified, as four separate pages. If you choose Separations, you may want to choose Options from the pop-up menu at the top right of the Print dialog so you can specify options such as crop and registration marks.

▶ **No Color Management** is almost the same as Printer Manages Colors—it sends the numbers in the document to the printer, but it

Figure 4-28

The Color Handling
pop-up menu

doesn't include the profile that describes them. We use this option for printing profiling targets, and precious little else.

Printer Profile. The Printer Profile menu is enabled only when you choose Photoshop Manages Colors from the Color Handling menu. Choose the profile that describes the printer to which you're printing and the paper and ink the printer is using.

Rendering Intent. The Rendering Intent menu is enabled when you choose either Printer Manages Colors or Photoshop Manages Colors from the Color Handling menu, but in our experience, it behaves reliably only in the former case. Choose the Rendering Intent that works best for the image by previewing the print using Proof Setup. (The Black Point Compensation check box is only enabled when Photoshop Manages Colors is selected in the Color Handling menu. As previously noted, we leave it turned on.)

Proof Setup. The Proof Setup menu is available with all Color Handling pop-up menu choices except Separations, and is enabled when you click the Proof radio button. Photoshop executes the conversion specified in the selected Proof Setup preset before sending the data to the printer using the options controlled by the Color Handling menu.

It also disables the Rendering Intent menu. The rendering of the simulated proof space to printer space is controlled instead by the Simulate Paper Color and Simulate Black Ink check boxes. When both are unselected, Photoshop converts the simulated proof data to the printer space using relative colorimetric rendering with black-point compensation. Checking Simulate Black Ink turns off the black-point compensation, while checking Simulate Paper Color makes Photoshop use absolute colorimetric rendering instead, forcing the printer to reproduce the actual "paper white" and actual "ink black" of the simulated proof.

In our experience, this feature works well when Photoshop Manages Colors is selected in the Color Handling menu, but can produce random results when any of the other alternatives are selected in the Color Handling menu. By all means, experiment, but don't say we didn't warn you!

Print

Photoshop applies all the color management options you set up in the Print dialog to the data that gets sent to the printer driver. You won't see any trace of them in the Print dialog. If you use the Print dialog to convert the image for output, make very sure that you don't have another conversion specified in the Print dialog or you'll get a double correction and a nasty print. Look for color management options like None or No Color Adjustment in the printer driver, and choose them to make sure that the driver doesn't sabotage you by throwing an extra conversion into the mix.

The color management features through the Print dialog allow you to control your printing from a single master RGB source file precisely—whether you're trying to reproduce an original image as exactly as possible or make your printer simulate all sorts of other output conditions. This helps you by saving time and by cutting down on the number of different versions you need to prepare for a given image.

Isolating Variables

All color management operations are dependent on a minimum of two profiles. Simply viewing a document requires the profile that describes the document and the profile that describes the current display. Other operations involve three or even more profiles. If you run into issues that don't appear to be a result of operator error, it's likely that one or more of the profiles involved is a weak link. Use the process-of-elimination method to troubleshoot problems. Test each profile in isolation and change one thing at a time. You're likely to find the culprit much quicker than you will by flailing around and changing multiple parameters willy-nilly.

Color management isn't a panacea, and it doesn't remove the need for intelligent human color correction. It's just a useful tool that provides a solid floor for you to stand on when you make your (hopefully intelligent, certainly human) corrections.

Building a Digital Workflow

Making Quick Work of Digital Camera Images

In the previous edition of this book, we said it was only a matter of when, not if, digital would replace film for most applications. Now we look back on that statement and laugh, because in the short time between these editions, the transition from film to digital has largely become complete. In addition, photographers have latched onto the idea of processing files of raw data straight from the camera's sensor because it provides a level of control and potential quality comparable to developing and printing your own film.

That said, anyone who has made the switch from film to digital can tell you that the time savings of digital photography (compared to film) is often offset by new tasks that photographers didn't have to worry about before. Having total control over the processing of every image means a photographer must now set aside the time and acquire the skills to do it right, instead of sending film to the lab and getting something else done while waiting for the lab to develop or print it. Digital storage is so cheap and capacious that a typical shoot now produces far more frames than it would have using film. But that also means there are that many more frames to cull and process afterward, burdening a photographer further.

The good news is that Adobe Photoshop CS3 benefits from what everyone learned from earlier stages in the transition to serious digital photography. Photoshop CS3, along with the Adobe Bridge and Adobe Camera

Raw software included with it, can fulfill the key tasks of a high-volume digital camera workflow from beginning to end—something that wasn't possible in previous versions. Also, Adobe has added so many useful features to Adobe Camera Raw 4.x that in some cases, you may not even need to open the images in Photoshop.

We assume that you're not interested in spending any more time than you have to on each image, so we've set up this chapter with that idea as the guiding principle. This chapter is about how to get through Adobe Camera Raw in the fewest number of moves, and we'll also talk about processing large numbers of images as quickly as possible. If your photography is more about spending the bulk of your time on a few important images, concentrate on the sections about culling images in Bridge and working in Camera Raw. But before we get into strategies for these workflows, let's look at digital raw capture.

Digital Raw Formats

Camera Raw appears as a file format in the Open dialog in Photoshop, but it isn't actually a single file format. Rather, it's a catchall name for camera files that consist of unprocessed data straight from the camera's sensor. One of the reasons they're called raw files is that they haven't even been processed into the RGB color of more common camera formats such as JPEG. Each camera produces its own flavor of raw data, so Camera Raw and its competitors usually need to be updated for the raw formats of new cameras.

A list of officially supported cameras appears on Adobe's Web site. As we write this, the URL is *www.adobe.com/products/photoshop/cameraraw.html*. Cameras that are not on the list sometimes work anyway; this is called *unofficial* support and it sometimes means the software company is still testing the camera. Adobe wisely doesn't officially support a new camera until it has thoroughly tested a final, shipping version of the camera. If you want to buy a new camera that shoots in raw format, check Adobe's list to see if it's supported yet; if it isn't, have patience. Chances are that the raw format of any significant new camera will be supported in the next release of Camera Raw, which is updated about four times a year.

What Is a Raw Capture?

Digital still cameras use color filters over each sensor in the area array to split the incoming light into its red, green, and blue components. Each sensor captures only one color, depending on which filter that covers it. The actual capture is essentially a file that records the amount of light recorded by each element in the array.

Considerable processing is required to turn this raw capture into an RGB color image—so much in fact, that today's on-the-fly raw processing would not have been practical on the computers available just a few years ago. When your camera is set up to save JPEG files (that's the default for most digital cameras), the conversion is performed by the camera's firmware, using the on-camera settings for white balance, tone, saturation, sharpness, and so on. However, when you tell your camera to save images in its raw format, the processing is deferred until you open the image on the computer using specialized software (like Camera Raw).

Why Shoot Raw?

Shooting raw images is much more flexible than shooting JPEG. When you shoot raw, the only on-camera settings that permanently affect your capture are the shutter speed, aperture value, ISO value, and focus. All other settings—white balance, tone curve, color space, contrast, saturation— are written into the capture as *metadata* (literally, data about data) that accompanies the raw information. Camera Raw may use this metadata as guidance in processing the capture into an RGB image, but the settings have no effect on the actual capture of the image pixels.

Raw captures allow tremendous flexibility in postprocessing, letting you reinterpret white balance and exposure with no degradation to the image. Rather than stretching or squeezing levels, you're simply reinterpreting the way the captured photons get converted into an RGB image.

Raw capture offers other key benefits:

▸ It creates a smaller file on disk than an uncompressed RGB image.

▸ It allows you to capture a high-bit image from a one-shot camera.

▸ It allows you to convert the image into RGB spaces other than the ones supported by the camera.

Digital Raw Workflow Quick Start

Figure 5-1

Start by copying raw images to a new folder (never open images directly from the camera storage media). To do this, from within Bridge you can launch Adobe Photo Downloader. Point Bridge to the image folder using the Folders panel. Bridge will generate thumbnails and previews, and reads the metadata from each image. This not only gives you large previews, but also verifies that the raw images were copied correctly to the computer.

Photo Downloader

Bridge

Folders panel   Preview   Thumbnails

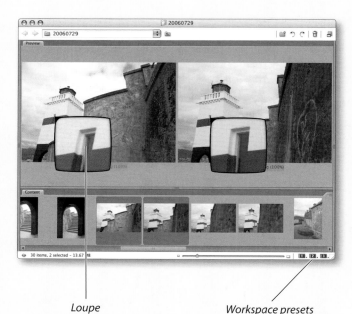

Change the view to make images easier to evaluate. Here, we switched to Horizontal Filmstrip view by clicking the workspace preset button marked "2" at the bottom right corner of the Bridge window. You can save different Bridge configurations by choosing Save Workspace from the Workspace submenu (under the Window menu).

In Bridge CS3, select multiple images in the Content panel to display multiple previews in the Preview panel. In addition, click a preview to display a movable loupe. Both features greatly simplify comparing images in detail. Press + or - to zoom the loupe, or zoom all loupes by also pressing the Command (Mac) or Ctrl (Windows) keys.

Loupe   Workspace presets

Double-click an image's thumbnail to launch the Camera Raw plug-in, which allows you to control the conversion of the raw file into any of four preset RGB working spaces.

The histogram, preview, and RGB readouts all show the results of the conversion from the raw file to the designated working space.

To apply the settings without opening the image, click Done. Camera Raw remembers the settings until you next open the file.

To apply the settings quickly to similar images, choose Edit > Develop Settings > Previous Conversion.

The settings are recorded in the image's metadata, and are used when you open the image.

You can now convert the raw images straight into Photoshop without revisiting the Camera Raw dialog, either by Shift-double-clicking the selected images, or by choosing Batch from the File Browser's Automate menu to process the images automatically using Actions.

There are several disadvantages to using/shooting raw, too. Of course, the primary one is that you need to process the images, which takes time. But raw files are also larger than JPEG images, so it may take longer to save them to your camera's storage medium (which will fill faster, too). However, we've struggled with most of the software that converts raw files, and we're convinced that Camera Raw is one of the fastest available—fast enough to make shooting raw worthwhile for all but the most time-critical applications.

Moreover, Camera Raw starts working for you automatically as soon as you point Bridge at a new folder of raw images, quickly generating thumbnails and previews so you can see the raw images in enough detail to make an initial choice between the "hero" shots you plan to keep and the less successful efforts you plan to discard (or revisit later).

If you want to simply jump in with both feet, take a quick look at **Figure 5-1**, then get to work. But the combination of Bridge and Camera Raw is complex enough that you'll probably want to read the rest of this chapter to get the rest of the juicy details! (There is even an entire book on the subject: *Real World Camera Raw with Adobe Photoshop CS3*—which expands on many of the ideas in this chapter.)

Digital Workflow Phases

We've spent most of this chapter looking at the various tools offered by Bridge and Camera Raw. But knowing what buttons to push to get the desired result just means you know how to do the work. To turn that understanding into a practical *workflow*, you need to understand and optimize each part of the process.

There are four basic stages in a raw workflow. You may revisit some of them—going back and looking at the initial rejects, or processing the images to different kinds of output file—but everything you do will fall into one of four stages.

▶ **Copying files from the camera.** You start by copying the raw images to at least one hard disk.

▶ **Verifying images.** You point Bridge at the newly copied images and let it cache the thumbnails, previews, and metadata.

▶ **Preproduction.** You work with the images in Bridge, selecting, sorting, applying metadata, and editing with Camera Raw.

▶ **Production.** You process the raw images to output files.

In the remainder of this chapter, we'll look at each of these four stages, but our emphasis lies in the preproduction stage—the work you do in Bridge and Camera Raw—because most of the actual work happens in this stage.

Workflow Principles

There are likely as many workflows are there are photographers—maybe more! One of the wonderful things about Bridge, Camera Raw 4.x, and Photoshop CS3 is the incredible workflow flexibility that they offer. The price of this flexibility is, of course, complexity. There are multiple ways to accomplish most tasks, and it may not be obvious at first glance which way is optimal in a given situation. Understanding the different ways of accomplishing the basic tasks is the tactical level. But to make a workflow, you also need a strategy that tells you how and when to employ those tactics.

Even a single photographer may need more than one workflow. On the one hand, there's the workflow you need when you're on a shoot, the client is looking over your shoulder, and you need to agree on the hero shots before you strike the lighting and move on. On the other hand, there's the workflow you'd like to follow when you're reviewing personal work with no deadlines attached. Between these extremes are many points on the continuum.

We can't build your workflow for you, so we'll offer two key principles of workflow efficiency that should always guide you.

▶ Do things *once,* early, and efficiently.

▶ Do things automatically whenever possible.

▶ Be methodical.

Do Things Once

When you apply metadata such as copyright, rights management, and keyword to your raw file, the metadata is automatically carried through to all the TIFFs, JPEGs, or PSDs that you derive from that raw file.

By the same token, if you exploit the power of Camera Raw to its fullest, many of your images may need little or no postconversion work in Photoshop, so applying Camera Raw edits to your images is likewise something that can often be done only once.

A key strategy that helps you do things once is: Start with the general and proceed to the specific. Start with the things that can be done to the greatest number of images, then make increasingly more detailed treatments of ever-decreasing numbers of images, reserving the full treatment—careful hand-editing in Camera Raw and Photoshop, applying image-specific keywords, and so on—to those images that truly deserve the attention.

Do Things Automatically

Automation is a vital survival tool for more easily dealing with the volumes of data a raw workflow entails. Once you've told a computer how to do something, it can do that something over and over again. Photoshop actions are obvious automation features, but metadata templates and Camera Raw presets are important automations, too.

We rarely open a single image from Camera Raw directly in Photoshop unless we're stacking multiple renderings of the raw file into the same Photoshop image.

In the vast majority of cases, we convert our raw images using either Batch or Image Processor commands on the Tools > Photoshop submenu in Bridge. Upon opening any images—raw or otherwise—in Photoshop, we often use actions to create adjustment layers so that the images are immediately ready for editing.

Be Methodical

Once you've found a rhythm that works for you, stick to it. Being methodical in this way makes mistakes less likely and allows you to focus on the important image decisions that only you can make.

For better or worse, computers always do *exactly* what you tell them to, even if that's jumping off a cliff. Established routines (and Actions) help ensure that you're telling the computer to do what you really want it to.

Copying Files from a Camera

The first thing you've got to do is get your images off the camera and into your computer. There are two parts to this: The hardware you use to connect the computer to the camera, and the software you use to transfer the images from the camera to your computer.

Hardware. You can use the cable that came with the camera, but using a card reader is generally faster and more efficient, as we explain below.

Software. After the computer sees the card, you can use any software that transfers the images to your hard disk. The simplest way is to mount the card as a volume on the desktop and drag the images from there to a folder on your hard disk. We recommend using software designed to copy images from a camera, such as the Adobe Photo Downloader, because camera-download utilities provide an opportunity to automate several important tasks as the images are copied. We talk more about this in "Using Adobe Photo Downloader" below.

Best practices. Transferring your images from the camera to the computer is one of the most critical, yet often one of the least examined, stages of your workflow. It's critical because at this stage, your images exist only on the camera media. Compact Flash, Secure Digital, and microdrives aren't dramatically more fragile than other storage media, but at this stage, there's only one copy! Losing previews or camera raw settings is irritating, but you can redo the work. If you make mistakes while you copy images to your computer, you can lose images.

The following ground rules have thus far prevented us from losing even a single image.

▶ **Don't use the camera as a card reader.** Most cameras will let you connect them to the computer and download your images, but that's a bad idea for at least three reasons: Cameras are very slow as card readers, when the camera is acting as card reader, you can't shoot with it, and you're draining the camera's battery.

▶ **Never open images directly from the camera media.** It's been formatted with the expectation that the only thing that will write to it is the

Tip: Image files on a memory card can be corrupted by something as simple as pulling the card out of the reader without first ejecting it in the software. If you think you've lost images on a card, do not format it! Doing so will permanently delete any recoverable data on the card. Cards from major vendors often include data-recovery software such as PhotoRescue—turn to that software first. If that fails, and the data is truly irreplaceable, several companies offer data recovery from memory cards, usually at a fairly hefty price.

camera. If something else writes to it, maybe nothing will happen, but then again, maybe something bad will.

▶ **Don't rely on just one copy of the images.** Always copy them to two separate drives before you start working.

▶ **Don't erase your images from the camera media until you've verified the copies.** See "Verifying Images," later in this chapter.

▶ **Always format the cards in the camera in which they will be shot.** Formatting camera cards with a computer is not reliable.

Following these rules takes a little additional time up front, but much less time than a reshoot would (if reshooting is even a possibility).

Using Adobe Photo Downloader

With Photoshop CS2, you had to copy images to your computer by manually dragging and dropping them from the card to a folder on your computer. If you wanted to automate the process, you had to find a camera-download utility. Fortunately, Photoshop CS3 comes with the Adobe Photo Downloader utility, which simplifies and automates downloading. Among other things, it can:

▶ Set a folder on your hard disk as a destination for images being copied from the card.

▶ Rename images to your standard as you import them.

▶ Make a backup copy of the images in a different folder.

▶ Apply a metadata template to all incoming images (we talk about this later, in "Applying Keywords and Metadata"). For example, you can add a copyright notice to every image as it's imported.

Opening Adobe Photo Downloader. You won't find Adobe Photo Downloader as a stand-alone application—you launch it from Adobe Bridge. To open Adobe Photo Downloader, start Adobe Bridge and then choose File > Get Photos from Camera. If an alert appears asking you if you want Adobe Photo Downloader to launch whenever you connect a camera or card, you can click No until you make a final decision as to whether you prefer Adobe Photo Downloader to other methods. When you do make a

Tip: If the wrong program launches when you plug in a camera or card, make sure that the program you want to use (such as Adobe Photo Downloader) is set as the default downloader, and check other photo downloaders on your machine (such as Adobe Lightroom or Apple Image Capture) and make sure they're not set to be the default downloader. In most cases, download behavior is set in a program's preferences.

final decision, the next time that alert appears, you can click Don't Show Again so it won't come up every time you start the utility.

Dialog Views. You can display the Photo Downloader window as a Standard dialog or Advanced dialog (see **Figure 5-2**). The Standard Dialog contains most of the features, but we prefer the Advanced Dialog because you can do a few more very useful things: See previews of the images you're about to copy, deselect any images you don't want to copy, and apply a metadata template to all incoming images.

Figure 5-2
Adobe Photo Downloader,
Advanced dialog

Setting Photo Downloader Options

Copying images is something you don't want to do more than once, so take a little time to get it right the first time. When you're done setting the following options, click Get Photos to start copying images.

Previews, source, and image selection. In the Advanced Dialog, check the previews to see if you're downloading what you want. If the previews don't look right, make sure the Source pop-up menu is set correctly, in case there are multiple cameras or cards plugged in to the computer.

If you don't want to download an image, deselect its check box. To change this option for multiple images at once, Command-click (Mac) or Ctrl-click (Windows) the images you want to change (they'll become selected, indicated by blue borders), and then change the check box for any selected image. The Check All and UnCheck All buttons at the bottom of the Advanced dialog are shortcuts for changing the check boxes.

Tip: Add your Location folder as a Favorite in Bridge or on your desktop, so that you can always get to it in one click.

Save Options. The location is the folder where the images will be copied; click the Choose button to change the folder. If you want Photo Downloader to automatically create subfolders for your shoots, choose a folder-naming option from the Create Subfolder(s) pop-up menu.

To have Photo Downloader automatically rename images as they're copied, choose a renaming option from the Rename Files pop-up menu. In addition to the date-based naming options, the Same As Subfolder option bases the filenames on the name of their subfolder.

The "Preserve Current Filename in XMP" option only applies if you rename a file. It keeps the original filename in the image's XMP metadata, and you can view this information in Bridge.

Advanced Options. We recommend checking the Open Adobe Bridge check box, because if it's on, as soon as the images are copied, Adobe Bridge opens to that folder, so that you can work with your images right away.

We also like to check the Convert to DNG option, because the DNG (Digital Negative) format packages raw sensor data in one convenient, vendor-independent file, without storing the metadata in separate "sidecar" files that you have to track along with the raw file. For information about the options you find when you click the Settings button, see "The Main Control Buttons" later in this chapter.

The Save Copies To check box creates a second copy of each image in the folder you specify. The best way to use the Save Copies To check box is to set the folder to a completely different hard disk. This may all seem paranoid, but professional photographers require this level of backup in case something goes horribly wrong, often using a small portable drive as their backup. For example, if a photojournalist copies photos from a card to a laptop, then erases the card so that he or she can take more photos, and then the laptop's hard disk dies (and you *know* that happens), the only existing images of a one-time event may be gone forever.

Apply Metadata. If you've set up metadata templates in advance, you can choose one from the Template to Use pop-up menu. We recommend that you create and apply a template that at least adds your name and copyright information to all images you shoot. For more information about setting these up, see "Using Metadata Templates" later in this chapter.

We recommend that you carefully consider your Photo Downloader settings in the context of how you want your overall photo collection to be organized. If you work out folder and file-naming conventions and your standard metadata in advance, your photo collection will automatically build itself in an organized fashion. If you just copy images without taking advantage of the automatic organizational options available in today's downloading utilities, you'll have a growing pile of images to rename, annotate, and organize later, and take it from us, that isn't any fun to deal with.

Verifying Images

Once you've copied the raw files to your hard disk, the next thing to do is to point Adobe Bridge at the folder containing the raw images. (If you checked the Open Adobe Bridge option in Photo Downloader, this should happen automatically.) If you haven't opened Adobe Bridge yet, it's in the Adobe Bridge CS3 folder, inside the Applications folder (Mac) or Program Files folder (Windows).

Bridge is command central for dealing with hundreds of images. You'll use it to make your initial selects, to apply and edit metadata including Camera Raw settings, and to control the processing of the raw images into a deliverable form.

But before you start doing any of these things, give Bridge a few minutes to generate the thumbnails (see **Figure 5-3**) and previews and to read the image metadata. It's a good idea to let it finish building the cache for the folder before starting work.

The reason is simple. While you can identify and open raw images as soon as the thumbnail appears, the thumbnails are generated by the camera and Bridge simply displays them. To build the high-quality previews, though, Camera Raw has to actually read the raw data. A good way to inspect the high-quality previews in detail is with the loupe; see "Evaluating and Comparing" later in this chapter.

If there's a problem reading the images, the problem will only show up on the high-quality thumbnail and preview. The initial thumbnails are the camera-generated ones, and they don't indicate that the raw file has been read successfully. The high-quality ones *do* indicate that the raw file has

Tip: Professional photographers use the term "selects" (as a noun) to describe the best images from a shoot. If you also use Adobe Lightroom, you'll notice that it calls selects Picks.

been read successfully, so wait until you see them before you erase the raw image files from the camera media.

If you see a problem at this stage, check the second copy (if you made one) or go back to the camera media if you haven't erased the card already. It's fairly rare for the data to get corrupted in the camera (though it does sometimes happen, particularly in burst-mode shooting), so the first suspect should be the card reader.

Figure 5-3
Imported raw files
in Adobe Bridge

Camera Raw, Bridge, and Photoshop

When you want to turn raw camera files into usable images, Adobe Camera Raw is your friend. Like the Photo Downloader, Camera Raw isn't stand-alone software; it's plug-in software that you can use only from within Photoshop or Bridge.

Camera Raw can be the first stage of your digital workflow if you use it to prepare images that you intend to send to Photoshop for more precise editing. However, the controls in Camera Raw are quite capable—so much so that many images may not need to be sent to Photoshop. While Camera Raw can't print, it does have the ability to generate DNG, JPEG, TIFF, and Photoshop files on its own. If you use Camera Raw this way, it can be the last stage in your digital workflow.

Tip: If you try to open many images in Camera Raw but your available RAM is limited, Camera Raw may display an alert telling you that you're opening too many images at the same time. If you don't want to open fewer images, first make sure you don't have unnecessary applications running, and then make sure you're launching Camera Raw from Bridge instead of from Photoshop. Bridge needs less RAM to operate than Photoshop, so Camera Raw can open more files at once from Bridge than it can from Photoshop.

There may be times when you want to work in Camera Raw but you don't need to pass the images to Photoshop just yet. That's why you can also open Camera Raw from Bridge. In Bridge, you can run Camera Raw without having to open Photoshop, which can free up RAM on your computer for other things.

The ability to open Camera Raw in either Photoshop or Bridge may seem incidental, but there are practical advantages. For example, if you want to edit the Camera Raw settings for one or more images but don't plan on opening them in Photoshop, you can open Camera Raw in Bridge while Photoshop is busy (such as when it's running a batch process). Or you could edit an image in Camera Raw in Photoshop while Bridge is busy caching a folder full of images. You can even open one Camera Raw window in Bridge and another in Photoshop, though doing so can make you one very confused puppy!

The subtle clue as to which application is currently hosting Camera Raw appears in one button: When Camera Raw is hosted by Bridge, the default button is labeled Done (clicking it closes Camera Raw, applies the settings to the raw file, and returns you to Bridge). When in Photoshop, the button is labeled Open (clicking it closes Camera Raw, applies the settings to the raw file, and opens the converted image in Photoshop).

Refining a Shoot Using Bridge

If you already know which shots you want to open in Camera Raw, you can skip this section and go on to the next one. However, there's another option if you usually shoot more than one frame of each subject to ensure that you get the right shot: After you copy images to your hard disk, use Bridge to narrow down your shoot, selecting only the best images to open and edit in Camera Raw and Photoshop. Doing this has several benefits:

▶ You can rate images to prioritize them. You can also mark images as rejected so that you can delete them, freeing up disk space.

▶ You can compare multiple images and use a loupe to compare images in detail.

▶ You can stack images to keep related images together.

▶ You can filter your images to display only images that contain specific metadata, such as a keyword.

If you need to narrow down your shoot before going into Camera Raw, you should read about the above Bridge features above in detail before you start working in Camera Raw. See "The Preproduction Phase" later in this chapter.

Opening Images with Camera Raw

You can open a supported file with Camera Raw in several ways:

▶ In Photoshop, choose File > Open, select one or more raw files, and click Open.

▶ In Bridge, or on your desktop, select at least one raw file and double-click it.

▶ In Bridge, you can also open a selected, supported file in Camera Raw by pressing Return.

Opening the file from your desktop works as long as Photoshop is the application that is set to open your camera's raw files; if the file icon has an Adobe icon with a "CRW" badge, you should be able to double-click it. A raw file opened in Photoshop automatically opens in Camera Raw.

If you open multiple files in Camera Raw, you'll see the filmstrip which lets you select which images are affected by the settings you change, along the left side of the dialog. You can also use the Synchronize button to spread settings from one image to others inside Camera Raw (see "Filmstrip Mode," later in this chapter).

Turn off default autocorrection. Camera Raw autocorrects images by default. Some people seem to love this feature, while others hate it because it tries to "correct" your manual exposure settings, like bracketing. Fortunately, the behavior is easily changed: Open Camera Raw preferences and turn off the check box for Apply Auto Tone Adjustments and click OK, make sure that White Balance is set to As Shot, then choose Save New Camera Raw Defaults from the Camera Raw menu. Note that the defaults are per

Tip: Camera Raw is now so packed with features that it deserves its own book. Fortunately, such a book does exist. To gain a complete understanding of Camera Raw, pick up a copy of *Real World Camera Raw with Adobe Photoshop CS3* by Bruce Fraser and Jeff Schewe, by the very same Adobe Press that brought you this book.

camera model, so you'll need to do this for each camera model you use. You can still apply autocorrection to an individual image by clicking Auto, or by pressing Command-U in Mac OS X or Ctrl-U in Windows. See "Using Auto Tone Adjustments," later in this chapter, for more details.

It's Not Just for Raw Anymore

One of the biggest changes to Camera Raw in Photoshop CS3 is that you can now open TIFF and JPEG images in Camera Raw and lets you use Camera Raw features on them. This doesn't magically bring the inherent qualities of raw files to TIFF and JPEG files, however; it just makes some tasks easier. For example, it can sometimes be easier to get rid of a color cast using the White Balance control in Camera Raw rather than playing with the various color-correction features in Photoshop. Another powerful advantage is that you can now use Camera Raw and Bridge batch-processing features on TIFF and JPEG files, such as the ability to synchronize nondestructive Camera Raw adjustments instantly across multiple images. This means that even photographers who shoot in JPEG can take advantage of the Camera Raw workflow, even if the images themselves are not as flexible as raw files.

By default, TIFF and JPEG images open in Photoshop. To open a TIFF or JPEG image in Camera Raw, Control-click (Mac) or right-click (Windows) an image and choose Open in Camera Raw from the context menu. In Photoshop, you can choose File > Open, select a TIFF or JPEG image, change the Format pop-up menu to Camera Raw, and then click Open, although you can open only one file at a time this way.

Camera Raw Static Controls

The Camera Raw dialog offers two sets of controls; one static set that is "sticky" (the settings remain unchanged until you change them) and another that is dynamic, and image-specific. The later set changes depending on which tab is currently selected (see **Figure 5-4**).

The static controls fall into several groups: the toolbar, including the preview controls; the histogram; the Camera Raw menu, and the main control buttons. Let's look at each of these.

Figure 5-4
Adobe Camera Raw 4
static controls

Toolbar

Histogram and
RGB readout

Image preview

Camera Raw menu

Main control buttons

The Toolbar

The Camera Raw toolbar (see **Figure 5-5**) contains eleven buttons, including two new tools and a new button that opens the Preferences dialog.

Edits in Camera Raw never change the pixels in the original files. Whether you edit raw, TIFF, or JPEG files, Camera Raw stores its changes as metadata, only applying the changes to files you export from Camera Raw or open in Photoshop. The changes are stored in the file if Camera Raw can write to the file's metadata (DNG, TIFF, and JPEG files). If that's not possible, the changes are stored in an XMP metadata sidecar file with the same base name as the raw file.

Figure 5-5
Camera Raw toolbar

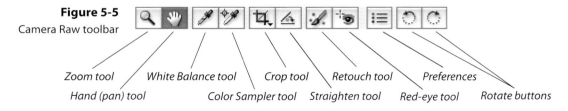

Zoom tool   White Balance tool   Crop tool   Retouch tool   Preferences

Hand (pan) tool   Color Sampler tool   Straighten tool   Red-eye tool   Rotate buttons

Zoom and pan. The zoom (magnifying glass) and pan (grabber hand) tools work just like their Photoshop counterparts.

Tip: The White-balance tool in Camera Raw works best on a light gray that's close to diffuse highlight, but one that still contains detail, rather than on a specular highlight that's pure white. The second-to-lightest gray patch on the old 24-patch Macbeth ColorChecker works well, as do bright (but not blown-out) midday clouds.

White balance. The White Balance tool (press I) lets you set the white balance by clicking on the image. Unlike the white Eyedropper in Levels or Curves, it doesn't allow you to choose a source color, and it doesn't affect the luminance of the image. Instead, it lets you set the white balance—the color temperature and tint—for the capture by clicking on pixels you think should be neutral.

Click-balancing with the white balance tool provides a very quick way to set color temperature and tint simultaneously, especially if you placed a gray card in the image. You can always fine-tune the results using the individual Temperature and Tint controls in the Basic tab, which we'll cover in due course.

Color samplers. The Color Sampler tool (press S) lets you place as many as nine individual color samplers, each of which gets its own readout, in the image (see **Figure 5-6**). Combined with the static RGB readout, the Color Sampler tool lets you monitor the values of up to ten different locations in the image, which should be enough for any reasonable use.

Figure 5-6
The Color Sampler tool

Color sampler readout

Color sampler

Crop. The Crop tool (press C) lets you drag a cropping rectangle, choose one of several common predefined aspect ratios, or define your own custom aspect ratio from the tool's pull-down menu (see **Figure 5-7**). The same menu allows you to clear the crop. The Camera Raw preview always shows the crop in the context of the whole image, but you'll see the crop in filmstrip previews, Bridge previews and thumbnails, and of course in the image itself when you open it in Photoshop.

Straighten. The Straighten tool (press A) is an enormous time-saver for those of us who sometimes fail to keep our horizons horizontal. It should

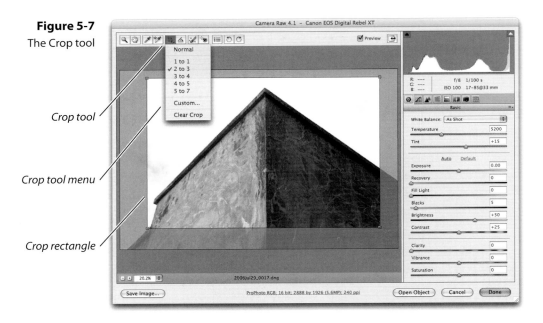

Figure 5-7
The Crop tool

Crop tool

Crop tool menu

Crop rectangle

really be called the Straighten and Crop tool because it also automatically applies the crop that maintains the maximum rectangular image when the Crop tool is set to Normal, or a straightened crop of the specified aspect ratio when the Crop tool is set to something else. If there's an existing crop, it's preserved and rotated. Compared to straightening and cropping an image in Photoshop using the Measure tool, Arbitrary Rotate tool, and the Crop tool, we much prefer the Straighten tool's speed and simplicity (see **Figure 5-8**).

Rotate buttons. The Rotate 90 Degrees Left and Right buttons (press L and R, respectively) aren't really tools—you don't have to do anything inside the image preview—but since they're placed so closely to the toolbar (see **Figure 5-5**), we'll deal with them here. Clicking on them or pressing their keyboard shortcut rotates the image preview. When you finish editing the image in Camera Raw, the rotation is applied to thumbnails and previews in Bridge, and is honored whenever you open the raw image in Photoshop.

Retouch. The new Retouch tool (press B) is a spot touch-up tool, similar to the Spot Healing Brush in Photoshop (see "The Healing Brushes and the Patch Tool" in Chapter 11, "Essential Image Techniques"). To retouch a spot, select the Retouch tool, position it over the center of the spot you want to remove, and drag until the resulting circle is larger than the spot

Tip: All of the keyboard shortcuts for zooming in Photoshop (seen on the View menu in Photoshop) also work in Camera Raw; for example, press Command-Option-0 (Mac) or Ctrl-Alt-0 (Windows) to display actual pixels. For the Pan tool, hold down the spacebar. Press Z to choose the Zoom tool and H for the Hand tool. Double-clicking the hand tool fits the entire image in the preview, and double-clicking the zoom tool zooms to Actual Pixels view.

Figure 5-8
The Straighten tool

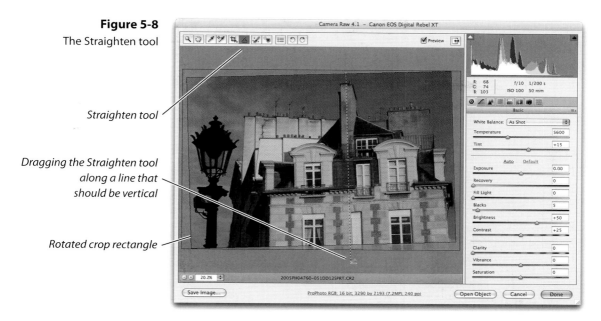

Straighten tool

Dragging the Straighten tool
along a line that
should be vertical

Rotated crop rectangle

(see **Figure 5-9**). Press V to toggle the Show Overlay check box to see if the retouch looks good. If it doesn't, you can drag the green dashed circle to change the retouching source, or drag the red dashed circle to change the retouched spot. You can also change the size of the circles by dragging the edge of either circle, or by changing the Radius value in the options below the toolbar. If you set the Radius when no spots are selected, you'll be setting the default radius. You can tell that a spot is selected when you can see both the source and destination circles. A lone circle is deselected; click inside it to select it.

The Type pop-up menu in the toolbar determines how the Retouch tool works. When the Retouch tool is set to Heal, it tries to smoothly merge the source (the green dashed circle) to the destination (the red dashed circle) by matching texture, lighting, and shading. It's more common to choose Heal from the Type pop-up menu, particularly when removing skin blemishes. To exactly copy one spot to another, choose Clone from the Type pop-up menu.

Though Photoshop has more retouching options, such as the ability to remove long scratches and power lines, there are two good reasons to perform spot retouching in Camera Raw. First, the edits are nondestructive, so you can change them later at any time; in Photoshop, actual pixels are altered in the original image. Second, it follows our recommendation

Figure 5-9
The Retouch tool

Retouch tool

Blemishes

Removed blemish and
deselected retouch circle

Removed blemish and
selected retouch circles

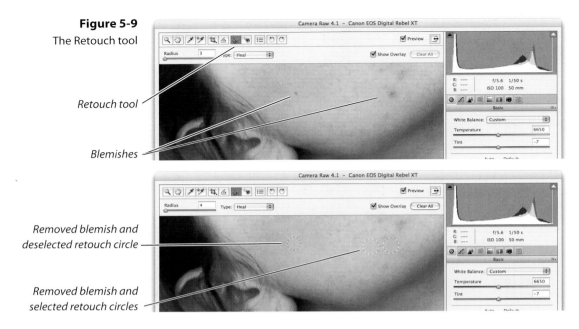

to do any edits you can as early as possible in the digital workflow, so that you only have to do them once.

Tip: With both the Retouch and Red-eye tools, where you click and drag is important. When working with the adjustment shapes each tool leaves behind, click inside a shape to select it, and drag inside a shape to move it. If you drag from the edge of a shape, you change its size.

Red eye removal. The Red-eye Removal tool (press R) is a quick way to get rid of red-eye from on-camera flash. Drag a rectangle around an entire eye (it works better if you surround more eye, not less), and Camera Raw detects red-eye and applies the default correction settings (see **Figure 5-10**). Like the Retouch tool, you can resize a red-eye rectangle by its edges, reposition it by dragging, add multiple rectangles (most people have more than one eye), and select and deselect rectangles. When a rectangle is selected, you can change the Pupil Size and Darken values in the toolbar. Don't make a rectangle much bigger than an eye, or you may have trouble getting the Pupil Size to be small enough.

The Preview Controls

Two sets of controls affect the preview image (**Figure 5-11**). The Zoom buttons and the Zoom level menu control the size of the preview image, while the Preview check box affects its state.

Zoom Level menu. The Zoom Level menu lets you choose a zoom level for the image preview. But if you find yourself using this feature, go back and read the tip about keyboard shortcuts for zooming, on page 150.

Figure 5-10
The Red-eye Removal tool

Red-eye Removal tool

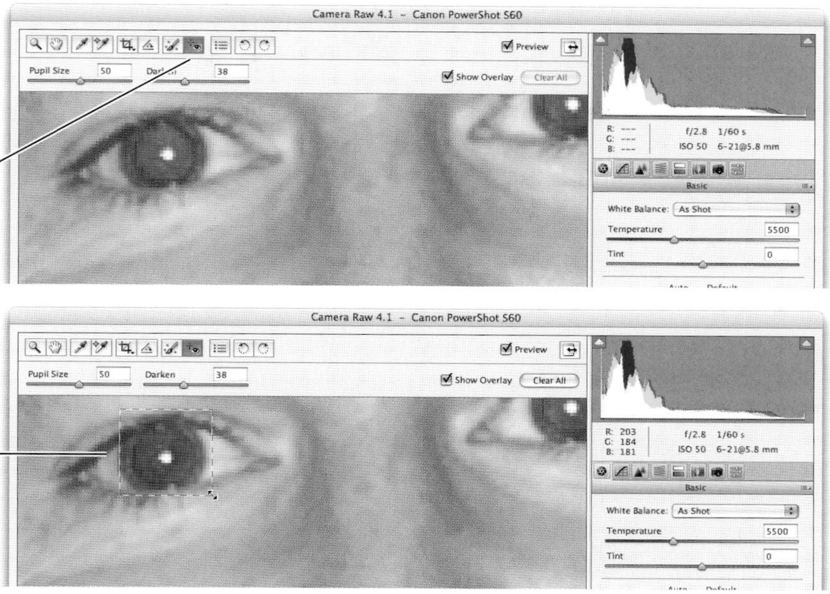

Removed red-eye and selected red-eye removal rectangle

Tip: If you see a yellow warning triangle in the image area of the Camera Raw dialog, Camera Raw isn't finished processing the image. Don't judge image quality until the yellow warning triangle goes away.

Preview check box. The Preview check box (press P to turn this on or off) applies only to the current editing tab, toggling between its current settings and those that were in effect when you opened the image. It has no effect on changes you've made in other tabs. To see the settings that applied before you opened the image—toggle between Image Settings and Custom Settings on the Settings menu (see Figure 5-14).

Figure 5-11
Preview controls

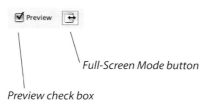

Full-Screen Mode button

Preview check box

Full-screen mode. To make the Camera Raw window fill the entire monitor, click the Full-Screen Mode button next to the Preview check box. Full-screen mode works best if you have a fast machine, because Camera Raw takes longer to refresh the dialog when it's larger. Along those lines, if your machine is on the slow side, you can speed things up by making the Camera Raw dialog smaller.

The Histogram and RGB Readout

The histogram and RGB readout provide information about the current state of the image (see **Figure 5-12**). The histogram displays the histograms of the red, green, and blue channels that will be created by the current conversion settings, *not* the histogram of the raw image (which would look strange since digital cameras capture at linear gamma—all the image data would be scrunched over to the left). The histogram can show you, at a glance, exactly what's happening to your exposure and clipping at the current image settings. If you're unfamiliar with histograms, see "The Histogram Palette" in Chapter 7.

Figure 5-12
The Histogram with the RGB and EXIF readouts

Histogram

RGB and EXIF readouts

Note that if the clipping disappears when you set the Space menu (in the Workflow Settings) to ProPhoto RGB, you can be certain that it's showing gamut clipping from a smaller output space.

Tip: For more information about avoiding clipped highlights and shadows, see "The Basic Tab," later in this chapter.

Shadow and highlight clipping warnings. The Shadow and Highlight Clipping Warning buttons, at the top left and right corners of the histogram (see **Figure 5-13**), provide a quick way to check for shadow and highlight clipping. The shortcuts are U (for underexposed) and O (for overexposed), respectively. These are most useful for a quick check on the state of the image. For a more interactive clipping display that's more useful when you're actually making adjustments, hold down the Option key (Mac) or Alt key (Windows) while dragging the Exposure or Blacks slider.

Figure 5-13
Shadow and highlight clipping warnings

Red indicates highlight clipping

Blue indicates shadow clipping

Shadow Clipping Warning button   Highlight Clipping Warning button

RGB readout. The RGB readout (see Figure 5-12) shows the RGB values for the pixels under the cursor. The values are those that will result from the conversion at the current settings. The RGB readout always reads 5-by-5 *screen* pixels at zoom levels of 100 percent or less, so it may display different values at different zoom levels. When you fit the entire image in the window, you're sampling an average of many pixels. At zoom levels greater than 100 percent, the sample size is always 5-by-5 *image* pixels.

EXIF readout. To the right of the RGB values is a panel that displays information from the image's EXIF data (see Figure 5-12), if present in the image. If the EXIF readout is blank, as it will be in a scanned image, the image doesn't contain EXIF data. EXIF data does, however, exist in images produced by digital cameras, unless the last person who saved an image chose to strip the EXIF data from the file.

Camera Raw and Color

One of the more controversial aspects of Camera Raw is its color handling, specifically the fact that Camera Raw has no facility for applying custom camera profiles. Having tried most camera profiling software and having experienced varying degrees of disappointment, we've concluded that unless you're shooting in the studio with controlled lighting and a custom white balance for that lighting, camera profiling is an exercise in frustration, if not futility. So we've come to view the Camera Raw incompatibility with custom camera profiles as a feature rather than a limitation.

The way Camera Raw handles color is ingenious and, thus far, unique. For each supported camera, Thomas Knoll, the creator of Camera Raw, has created not one but two profiles: one built from a target shot under a D65 (daylight) light source, and the other built from the same target shot under an Illuminant A (tungsten) light source. The correct profiles for each camera are applied automatically in producing the colorimetric interpretation of the raw image. The White Balance (Color Temperature and Tint) sliders in Camera Raw let you interpolate between, or even extrapolate beyond, the two built-in profiles.

For cameras that write a readable white-balance tag, that white balance is used as the "As Shot" setting for the image; for those that don't, Camera Raw makes highly educated guesses. Either way, you can override the initial settings to produce the white balance you desire.

It's true that the built-in profiles are "generic" profiles for the camera model. Some cameras exhibit more unit-to-unit variation than others, and if your camera differs substantially from the unit used to create the profiles for the camera model, the default color in Camera Raw may be a little off. So the Calibrate controls let you tweak the conversion from the built-in profiles to optimize the color for your specific camera. This is a much simpler, and arguably more effective, process in most situations than custom camera-profile creation.

The Settings Menu

The Settings pop-up menu lets you change the settings applied to the image (see **Figure 5-14**). The items that always appear are Image Settings, Camera Raw Default, Previous Conversion, and Custom Settings.

Figure 5-14

Settings menu

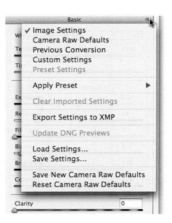

Image Settings. If Image Settings is available, you've previously applied edits to the image. If you're working on an image, choosing Image Settings will show you the settings that were in effect before you started editing. If the image is brand-new and has never been edited, the Image Settings values equal those of the next item, Camera Raw Default.

Camera Raw Defaults. Camera Raw Defaults is what it says—it's the default setting that applies to all images unless and until you override it. It's also the setting used by Bridge to create high-resolution previews when it sees a folder full of new raw images. If you find that the shipping default settings aren't to your liking, you can set your own Camera Raw Defaults for each supported camera model. If you get yourself in a mess by doing so, you can return Camera Raw to the shipping default settings using the appropriate commands from the Camera Raw menu.

Previous Conversion. Choosing Previous Conversion applies the settings from the last image you opened in Camera Raw to the current image.

Custom Settings. Custom Settings denotes the current settings you're applying in Camera Raw. As we mentioned previously, you can toggle between Image Settings and Custom Settings to compare your current edits with the ones that were in effect when you opened the image in Camera Raw.

You can also save your own custom settings as presets, which then become available from this menu. It's easy to overlook the mechanism for doing so, though, because it lives on the Camera Raw menu, which—although it's one of the most important of the static controls—is unfortunately an unlabeled button. Let's take a look at this menu next.

Preset Settings. If you last applied Camera Raw settings to the image by choosing a preset, the name of the preset appears here.

Apply Preset submenu. Presets you've created with Camera Raw appear in this submenu, but it's easier to apply them from the Presets tab.

Clear Imported Settings. Camera Raw and Bridge are no longer the only software that can read and write Camera Raw settings. Adobe Lightroom does it too, since Lightroom and Camera Raw use the same raw-processing engine. However, Lightroom and Camera Raw are not always updated at the same time, so occasionally one of them will add controls that aren't available yet in the other. When you open a raw image using software that's missing options that were available in the last application that edited it, you may find it difficult to control the image because it's influenced by settings you can't change. When that's the case, Clear Imported Settings is a way to set those options to their default values.

Exporting Settings to XMP. The Export Settings to XMP command offers a way to write a sidecar .xmp file when you have the Camera Raw Preferences set to save edits in the Camera Raw cache. This offers a way to produce sidecar files when you want to copy the images to removable media for use on another computer while preserving the edits. If the preference is set to use sidecar files, Export Settings will export a sidecar file only if one doesn't already exist. If there's an existing sidecar file, Export Settings does nothing.

Update DNG Previews. When you edit a DNG file, your changes are written to the DNG metadata, but by default, the DNG preview isn't updated. Update DNG Previews rewrites the preview so that you can see the current state of the file in applications that don't render DNG on the fly. If you want DNG previews to update automatically, check the Update JPEG Previews check box in the DNG File Handling section of the Camera Raw Preferences dialog.

Loading and Saving Settings

The Load Settings and Save Settings commands let you load and save settings or settings you make with any of the image-specific controls—the ones located in the tabs below the histogram. When you choose Save Settings, a dialog appears asking you which settings you want to save. This means you can save a preset for just a few options without changing any others. For example, you could create a setting that only applies color noise reduction (see **Figure 5-15**).

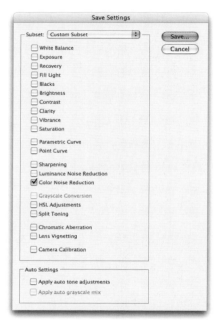

Figure 5-15
Save Settings dialog

When you save settings to the default location, they appear on the Settings menu automatically. That location on a Mac is (username)\Library\Application Support\Adobe\Camera Raw\Settings. In Windows, it's Documents and Settings\(username)\Application Data\Adobe\Camera Raw\Settings. These saved settings also appear in the Presets tab and in the Edit > Develop Settings submenu in Bridge. If you save settings anywhere else, you can load them using the Load Settings command in Camera Raw.

Camera Raw Preferences

The Camera Raw Preferences (see **Figure 5-16**) let you decide whether your raw edits are saved in the Camera Raw database or in sidecar .xmp files, and whether to apply sharpening to the converted image or to the preview only. They also allow you to choose the location and size of the Camera Raw cache and let you purge the Camera Raw cache. Camera Raw 3.1 and later added settings that control the behavior of DNG files—they have no effect on other raw formats.

Figure 5-16

Camera Raw Preferences

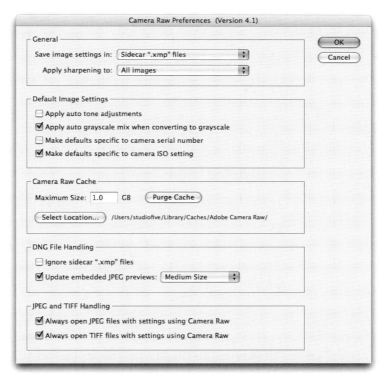

Save Image Settings In. Camera Raw treats the raw images as read-only, so your Camera Raw edits for the image get saved either in a sidecar .xmp file—a small file designed to travel with the image—or in the Camera Raw database. Each approach has strengths and weaknesses, and choose your approach using the Save Image Settings In option in this dialog.

Saving your edits in the Camera Raw database means that you don't have to keep track of sidecar files or worry about making sure that they get renamed along with the image—the Camera Raw database indexes the images by file content rather than name, so if you rename the raw file, the Camera Raw database will still find the correct settings. The major disadvantage is that when you move the images onto a different computer or burn them to a CD or DVD, the edits won't travel with the images.

Saving your edits in sidecar files allows the edits to travel with the images. Adobe gives you a lot of help in handling the .xmp sidecar files. By default, Bridge hides them and automatically keeps them with their respective images when you use Bridge to move or rename them. The only danger is that if you move or rename the images *outside* Bridge, you need to keep track of the sidecars yourself.

A solution to this potentially confusing issue is to convert your raw images to DNG format (see "The Main Control Buttons," later in this chapter for more on this). Camera Raw treats raw files as read-only because all the vendors' proprietary formats—Canon's CRW and CR2, Nikon's NEF, Olympus' ORF, and so on—are undocumented. Rather than taking the risk of messing up the file by writing metadata such as Camera Raw settings into it, Camera Raw uses sidecar files or its own database. But DNG is a completely documented, open format, so when you use DNG, Camera Raw settings and other metadata get written directly into the DNG file itself.

Apply Sharpening To. The Apply Sharpening To option lets you choose whether to apply sharpening to the previews *and* to the converted image, or to the previews only. Setting this option to Preview Images Only lets you enjoy reasonably sharp preview, but apply more nuanced sharpening to the converted images. Note that this preference only affects the Sharpness setting, not either of the noise-reduction settings, which are found on the same Detail tab as the Sharpness control (see "The Detail Tab," later in this chapter).

If you plan to apply sharpening later in your workflow, such as in Photoshop, it's better to set this to Preview Images Only. However, if you're going to export final images from Camera Raw, you probably want to set this option to All Images—otherwise no Camera Raw sharpening will be applied to the exported images.

Default Image Settings. Click the Preferences icon in the toolbar to see the Default Image Settings preferences. Uncheck Apply Auto Tone Adjustments if you don't want Camera Raw to automatically adjust each image that you open in Camera Raw; Apply Auto Grayscale Mix When Converting to Grayscale is a similar preference for the times when you convert color images to black and white using the Convert to Grayscale check box in the HSL/Grayscale tab (see "The HSL/Grayscale Tab" later in this chapter), but we think you should leave that one on. Make Defaults Specific to Camera Serial Number is useful if you own multiple bodies of the same camera and want different defaults for each camera. Conrad likes to check Make Defaults Specific to Camera ISO Setting, because he wants different ISO settings to use different default settings for noise reduction.

Camera Raw cache. The Camera Raw cache holds pre-parsed raw data for the most recently used raw files, which is used to speed up the following operations:

▶ Opening the Camera Raw dialog

▶ Switching between images in the Camera Raw filmstrip

▶ Updating the thumbnails in the Camera Raw filmstrip in response to settings changes

▶ Rebuilding the thumbnails/previews in Bridge in response to settings changes

The cache file sizes average about 5 MB, so at the default size limit of 1 GB, the Camera Raw cache will hold the pre-parsed data for about the 200 most recently accessed images. If you commonly edit folders with more than 200 raw files, you will probably want to increase the Camera Raw cache's size limit. Nothing is stored exclusively in the Camera Raw cache, so purging it never means you will lose data.

DNG File Handling. The two check boxes under DNG File Handling control the behavior of DNG files. They have no effect on other raw formats.

▶ **Ignore Sidecar ".xmp" Files.** This preference addresses a relatively obscure situation that arises only when you have a DNG and a proprietary raw version of the same image in the same folder, and they're identically named except for the extension. If you edit the proprietary raw file, Camera Raw also applies the edits to the DNG, to maintain compatibility with older versions of Photoshop CS and Photoshop Element, which write sidecar files for DNG instead of writing to the DNG file itself. This setting lets you tell Camera Raw to ignore sidecar files and leave the DNG file alone in this situation.

▶ **Update Embedded JPEG Previews.** This setting controls when the embedded JPEG previews in DNG files get updated. When it's turned on, Camera Raw updates the embedded preview as soon as you dismiss Camera Raw after editing a DNG file, thereby incurring a speed penalty since the previews take time to write and save.

You can defer the speed hit by turning this item off. Then, when you want to update the previews, choose Update DNG Previews from the Camera Raw menu, which opens the Update DNG Previews dialog where you can choose the preview size.

When you choose Full Size, Camera Raw embeds both Full Size and Medium Size previews. The downside is that Full Size previews take longer to build, and make a slightly larger file. Bear in mind, though, that you can choose whether Photoshop or Bridge will get tied up generating the previews so you can continue working in the other application while the one hosting Camera Raw builds the previews.

Tip: If you want Camera Raw to use the same JPEG preview size that it applied the last time you chose the Update DNG Previews command, hold Option/Alt while choosing Update DNG Previews to skip the Update DNG Previews dialog and apply the last-used preview size.

JPEG and TIFF Handling. These two options need a little bit of decoding because the way they work isn't obvious. Turning on the check boxes for Always Open JPEG Files with Settings Using Camera Raw and Always Open TIFF Files with Settings using Camera Raw does *not* mean JPEG and TIFF files will always open in Camera Raw. The clues are the words "with settings." If you turn on these check boxes, then files in those formats will open in Camera Raw if they already contain Camera Raw settings—in other words, they will open in Camera Raw if you've previous edited them in Camera Raw. If you haven't edited them in Camera Raw, they'll open in Photoshop even if you've checked these options. And if you uncheck these options, files in those formats always open in Photoshop, even if you've edited them in Camera Raw.

If you want to ensure that a JPEG or TIFF file opens in Camera Raw even if it doesn't contain Camera Raw settings, you must open the file in one of two ways: Either select the file in Bridge and use the File > Open with Camera Raw command (which is also available on the context menu); or in Photoshop choose File > Open, and then change the Format pop-up menu to Camera Raw.

Tip: The Bridge preference Prefer Camera Raw for JPEG and TIFF Files doesn't affect how those file types open. If the images contain Camera Raw settings, it controls whether Bridge uses Camera Raw settings to render JPEG and TIFF thumbnails.

The Main Control Buttons

The main control buttons (see **Figure 5-17**) let you specify the action that Camera Raw will perform on your raw image.

Save Image. Click Save Image (Command-S in Mac OS X or Ctrl-S in Windows) to export a copy of the raw image as a DNG, TIFF, JPEG, or Photoshop file directly from the Camera Raw dialog without opening the image in Photoshop. Clicking Save Image opens the Save Options dialog, which lets you specify the destination, the file format, any format-specific options such as compression, and the name for the saved file or files. When you click Save in the Save Options dialog, you're returned to Camera Raw, and the file gets saved in the background.

Figure 5-17
Main control buttons

It's also worth noting that Camera Raw is in itself a DNG converter. If you've decided that you want to stay with proprietary raw files as your working files, but would prefer to hand off DNG files when you need to submit raw images (to make sure that your metadata gets preserved), you can do it straight from Camera Raw.

If you don't want the Camera Raw dialog to go away after you're done saving, hold down Option (Mac) or Alt (Windows) to change the Save Image button into the Save button. When you click the Save button, the Save Options dialog doesn't appear; the selected images in Camera Raw are saved using the last settings you used in the Save Options dialog.

Tip: The Save button is especially useful when you select multiple images in filmstrip mode, because the conversion happens in the background. That means that you can keep working in Camera Raw while Camera Raw exports image after image.

Open. Click Open (Command-O in Mac OS X or Ctrl-O in Windows) to close the Camera Raw dialog and open the image in Photoshop using the settings you applied in Camera Raw. These settings are written to the raw file's metadata, and Bridge's previews and thumbnails are updated to reflect the new settings. When Camera Raw is hosted by Photoshop, Open is the default button.

If you want to open selected images in Photoshop but you don't want the current Camera Raw settings to be saved with the raw files (maybe you're experimenting), press Option (Mac) or Alt (Windows) to change the Open button to Open Copies. Finally, if you want to open selected images in Photoshop as Smart Objects (see "Smart Objects" in Chapter 11), press Shift to change the Open button to Open Objects.

If this button already says Open Object or Open Objects, the default behavior of the button has been changed. That's set in the Camera Raw Workflow Options, which we will talk about soon.

Cancel. Click the Cancel button (press Esc) to ignore any adjustments you've made since opening Camera Raw, close the Camera Raw dialog, and return you to the host application, leaving the raw file settings unchanged. If you have many images open in Camera Raw, all of those images lose all changes you made to them in the current Camera Raw session.

To return all Camera Raw settings to the state they were in when you launched Camera Raw (either Image Settings, if the image had previously had its own Camera Raw settings applied, or Camera Raw Defaults if it hadn't), press Option (Mac) or Alt (Windows) to change the Cancel button to Reset. The Camera Raw dialog stays open after you click Reset.

Done. Click Done (or press Return or Enter) to close the Camera Raw dialog, write the settings you applied in Camera Raw to the raw file's metadata, and return to the host application. Previews and thumbnails in Bridge are updated to reflect the new settings. When Camera Raw is hosted by Bridge, Done is the default button.

Adjusting with Precision and Speed

While it may be obvious that you adjust settings in Camera Raw by dragging the sliders, you can also take advantage of other adjustment tricks. Some give you more precision and others give you more speed.

▶ You don't have to drag the slider itself. For more precision, position the cursor over the name of an option until the cursor turns into a two-headed arrow, and drag left or right using the entire width of the monitor. This gives you finer control than you get by using the short width of a slider.

▶ When the cursor is blinking a value or a value is highlighted, press the up arrow or down arrow keys to adjust the value. The amount of the adjustment varies depending on the setting. Add the Shift key to adjust the value by a larger amount.

▶ Undo does work. Even though the Undo command is not available on the Edit menu when Camera Raw is open, you can still undo changes in the Camera Raw image controls by pressing the traditional Undo keyboard shortcut, Command-Z (Mac) or Ctrl-Z (Windows). Press the Undo shortcut again to toggle between the current and previous values. In addition, Camera Raw 4 has multiple undo; just add the Option (Mac) or Alt (Windows) key to the Undo shortcut to move back through Undo steps, or add the Shift key to move forward through Undo steps.

Camera Raw Workflow Options

At the bottom of the Camera Raw dialog is blue underlined text that looks like a Web link. You'll notice that the text is a line of image specifications; click the text to open the Workflow Options dialog and change the specs (see **Figure 5-18**). These controls apply to the current image or to all the images being converted in a batch process. The workflow options aren't saved with individual images; the Camera Raw dialog simply continues to use the settings until you change them again.

Figure 5-18
Workflow Options

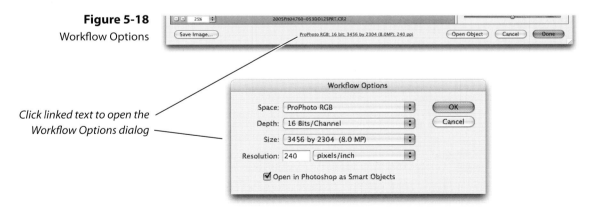

*Click linked text to open the
Workflow Options dialog*

Space. Choose a destination color space for the conversion from one of four preset working spaces: Adobe RGB (1998), Colormatch RGB, ProPhoto RGB, or sRGB IEC61966-2.1 (the last being the "standard" flavor of the sRGB standard). See the sidebar "Camera Raw and Color" for details on how Camera Raw handles the color management aspect of the conversion.

Note that the space you choose here determines the boundaries for the clipping warnings in the Camera Raw dialog.

Depth. Choose whether to produce an 8-bit/channel image or a 16-bit/channel one. A 16-bit/channel file needs twice as much storage space as an 8-bit/channel one, but it provides 128 times the tonal steps between black and white, so it offers much more editing headroom.

Crop Size. Choose the pixel dimensions of the converted image. If you see a minus sign (-) after a set of dimensions, choosing those dimensions will downsample the image. Similarly, if you see a plus sign (+) after a set of dimensions, choosing those dimensions will upsample the image. The dimensions in the middle of the list (with no minus or plus sign) represent the number of pixels saved into the image file by the camera.

Resolution. Choose a resolution for the converted image. Changing Resolution doesn't change the number of pixels in the converted image, only their density.

If you want to set image resolution or pixel dimensions with more control than you have in the Workflow Options dialog, leave the settings at the native values, wait until you've opened the image in Photoshop, and then choose the Image > Image Size command in Photoshop.

Tip: To use Camera Raw to resample an image to pixel dimensions that aren't in the Size pop-up menu, use the Crop tool in Camera Raw instead. The Crop tool lets you specify pixel dimensions up to 10,000-by-10,000 pixels, so you can use it to produce a much larger file than the sizes that appear on the Size menu in Camera Raw. The Crop tool method works for downsampling too.

Camera Raw Image Controls

The image controls—the ones you're likely to change with each image—occupy the rest of the Camera Raw dialog. The tabs are:

▶ Basic, which deals with color balance, essential tone mapping, and overall image quality.

▶ Tone Curve, where you can fine-tune contrast.

▶ Detail, which provides controls for sharpening and noise reduction.

▶ HSL/Grayscale, where you can adjust specific color ranges, or, if you turn on its Convert to Grayscale check box, tonal ranges.

▶ Split Toning, where you can tone highlights and shadows differently, is a technique that adds depth to limited-color images.

▶ Lens Correction, which can correct chromatic aberration, defringing, and vignetting.

▶ Calibration, which lets you fine-tune the built-in color profiles in Camera Raw to better match the behavior of your specific camera body.

▶ Presets, a list of all of the presets available to Camera Raw.

You can switch quickly between tabs by pressing keys 1 through 8 together with the Command and Option keys (Mac) or the Ctrl and Alt keys (Windows). For example, on the Mac, press Command-Option-2 to display the Tone Curve tab.

These image controls are really the meat and potatoes of Camera Raw, offering very precise control over your raw conversions. Some of the controls may seem to offer functionality that also exists in Photoshop, but there's a significant difference between editing the tone mapping in Camera Raw, which tailors the conversion from linear to gamma-corrected space, and editing the tone mapping by stretching and squeezing the bits in a gamma-corrected space in Photoshop.

The more work you do in Camera Raw, the less work you'll need to do afterward in Photoshop. At the same time, if you get your images close to the way you want them in Camera Raw, they'll be able to withstand much more editing in Photoshop—which you may need to do to optimize for a specific output process, or to harmonize the appearance of different images you want to combine into a single one.

Tip: On Mac OS X, Command-Option-8 is the default shortcut for enabling or disabling screen zooming for the visually impaired. If you'd rather use that shortcut for the Presets tab in Camera Raw, open the Keyboard & Mouse system preference, click the Keyboard Shortcuts tab, and change the Turn Zoom On Or Off shortcut to a different shortcut (Conrad changed it to Command-Option-9).

The Basic Tab

The controls in the Basic tab (Command-Option-1 in Mac OS X or Ctrl-Alt-1 in Windows) let you tweak the essential tonal and color qualities of an image, such as white balance and overall contrast (see **Figure 5-19**). It's the default tab in Camera Raw. Three controls in this tab deserve special attention: The Temperature, Tint, Exposure, and Recovery controls. They let you do things to the image that simply cannot be replicated in Photoshop after you convert the image.

Clarity and Vibrance have no direct analogs in Photoshop, although you can replicate their effects with some effort. Fill Light is somewhat like the Shadow portion of the Highlight/Shadow feature in Photoshop.

Figure 5-19
The Basic tab

Tip: There are an awful lot of controls in Camera Raw, but unlike with Photoshop, it's easy to remember what order to use the controls to preserve the best image quality. Adobe intentionally designed the control layout so that you can simply go through the tabs from left to right, and within each tab, adjust the controls from top to bottom.

The Contrast, Brightness, and Blacks controls provide similar functionality to Levels and Curves in Photoshop, with the important difference that they operate on the high-bit linear data in the raw capture, rather than on gamma-encoded data postconversion. If you make major corrections ("major" meaning more than half a stop) with the Exposure slider, you'll certainly want to use the Recovery, Brightness, Contrast, Fill Light, and Blacks controls to shape the raw data the way you want it before converting the raw image. With smaller Exposure corrections, you may still need to shape the tone in Camera Raw rather than in Photoshop, especially if you want to avoid shadow noise in underexposed images.

The Saturation control in Camera Raw offers slightly finer global adjustments than the Hue/Saturation command in Photoshop, though unlike the Photoshop command, it doesn't allow you to address different color ranges selectively. But in Camera Raw 4.1 or later, you can do that in the HSL/Grayscale tab.

White Balance. The two controls that set the white balance, Temperature and Tint, are the main tools for adjusting color in the image. Setting the white balance correctly should make the rest of the color more or less fall into place in terms of hue. Note that the "correct white balance" includes (but isn't limited to) "accurate white balance"—you can use white balance as a creative tool, too.

Tip: If you can't figure out the white balance for an outdoor shot and the White Balance Eyedropper isn't helping, try choosing Daylight from the White Balance pop-up menu as a starting point. Automatic white balance may not work properly with a scene dominated by a color that isn't neutral, such as a green forest.

► **Temperature.** The Temperature control lets you specify the color temperature of the lighting in Kelvins, thereby setting the blue-yellow color balance. Lowering the color temperature makes the image more blue to compensate for the yellower light; raising the color temperature makes the image more yellow to compensate for the bluer light. If this seems counterintuitive—we think of higher color temperatures as bluer and lower ones as yellower—the trick is to remember that the Temperature control *compensates* for the color temperature of the light, so if you tell Camera Raw that the light is bluer, it makes the image yellower.

► **Tint.** The Tint control lets you fine-tune the color balance along the axis that's perpendicular to the one controlled by the Temperature slider—in practice, it's closer to a green-magenta control than anything else. Negative values add green; positive ones add magenta.

Figure 5-20 shows an image as shot, and with some white-balance adjustments that greatly alter the character of the image. Notice that the adjustments involve the use of both the Temperature and Tint sliders.

The white-balance controls let you alter the color balance dramatically with virtually no image degradation, which you simply can't do once the image is converted and opened in Photoshop. The freedom with which you can reinterpret the white balance is one of the main advantages of capturing raw rather than JPEG images.

Tone-mapping controls. Learning how the four tone-mapping controls—Exposure, Blacks, Contrast, and Brightness—interact is essential if you want to exercise control over your images' tonal values. It may not be obvious, but the controls work together to produce a five-point curve adjustment.

Exposure and Blacks set the white and black endpoints, respectively. Brightness adjusts the midpoint. Contrast applies an S-curve around the midpoint set by the Brightness, darkening values below the midpoint and brightening those above. **Figure 5-21** shows Brightness and Contrast adjustments translated approximately into Photoshop point curves.

Let's go into even more depth on each of these controls.

Tip: Because half of the linear data in a raw capture describes the brightest f-stop, many digital photographers use the Expose to the Right (ETTR) technique. With ETTR, you set the camera exposure so that as much data as possible is as far to the right of the camera's histogram as possible, but without clipping the highlights. As a result, you'll probably have to lower the brightness of each image in Camera Raw, but it's worth it: ETTR optimizes the signal-to-noise ratio (translation: image noise becomes less visible).

► **Exposure.** The Exposure slider is first and foremost a white-clipping adjustment, like the white triangle in the Levels dialog in Photoshop. Half of the data in a raw capture is devoted to describing the brightest f-stop, so placing the highlights correctly is your highest priority. First

Figure 5-20
White balance

White Balance as shot

*White Balance adjusted
to cool the image*

*White Balance adjusted
to warm the image*

set the Exposure slider, holding down Option (Mac) or Alt (Windows) to see the clipping display, so that the only clipping is on specular highlights. If this causes the overall image to be too dark, then raise Exposure back up and use the Recovery slider to restore the highlights (see **Figure 5-22**).

Large increases in exposure value (more than about three-quarters of a stop) will increase shadow noise and may even make some posterization visible in the shadows, simply because large positive exposure values stretch the relatively few bits devoted to describing the shadows further up the tone scale. If you deliberately underexpose to hold highlight detail, your shadows won't be as good as they could be. We certainly don't advocate overexposure—perfect exposure is always best—but *slight* overexposure is often better than significant underexposure.

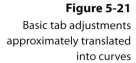

Figure 5-21
Basic tab adjustments
approximately translated
into curves

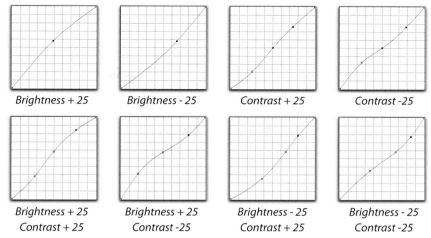

Brightness + 25   Brightness - 25   Contrast + 25   Contrast -25

Brightness + 25 / Contrast + 25   Brightness + 25 / Contrast -25   Brightness - 25 / Contrast + 25   Brightness - 25 / Contrast -25

Tip: Don't forget to use the shadow and highlight clipping warnings (press U and O keys to toggle them); they help you see whether you need to increase or decrease your Blacks and Exposure values. See "The Histogram and RGB Readout" earlier in this chapter.

▶ **Recovery.** The Recovery slider offers the amazing ability to let you recover highlight information from overexposed images. Figure 5-22 shows a fairly typical example of highlight recovery. The actual amount of highlight data you can recover depends primarily on the camera model, and secondarily on the amount of compromise you're prepared to tolerate in setting white balance. But it's not at all unusual to recover two-thirds of a stop, and it's often possible to recover more.

In Camera Raw 3, the only way to recover highlights was to set Exposure to a negative value. That still works, but naturally it often makes the image darker than you want it to be, which often requires additional Tone Curve tweaks. In Camera Raw 4, the addition of Recovery lets you set Exposure to a more reasonable value.

▶ **Fill Light.** The Fill Light slider opens up shadows in a way that isn't easily reproduced by Brightness, Contrast, or the Tone Curves (see **Figure 5-23**). For example, if you open up the shadows with a curve, you might lighten the rest of the image too much. Fill Light gets around this by lightening the shadows as much as it can without affecting the highlights.

You may experience a slight delay the first time you drag the Fill Light slider for each image, because it initially generates a mask, which Fill Light uses to restrict the adjustment to the shadows. On a slower machine, drag Fill Light a little, let go, and wait for it to build the mask before tuning your adjustments. You can't see or adjust this invisible mask, but it works well in most cases.

Figure 5-22
Exposure and
Recovery

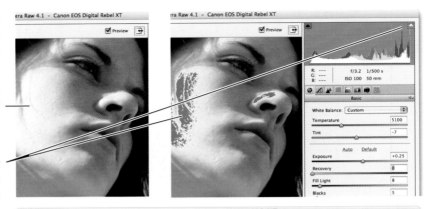

*After raising Exposure to
lighten the image, important
highlights are clipped.*

*Turning on the Highlight
Clipping Warning button
in the histogram marks the
clipped areas in red.*

*Increasing Recovery restores
the blown highlights.*

▶ **Blacks.** The Blacks slider is the black-clipping control, like the black input slider in the Levels dialog in Photoshop. But because the Blacks slider operates on linear-gamma data, small moves make bigger changes than does the black input slider in Levels. If you think the default value of 5 is too aggressive, you may want to set a lower default value.

▶ **Brightness.** The Brightness control is a nonlinear adjustment that works very much like the gray input slider in Levels. It lets you redistribute the midtone values without clipping the highlights or shadows. Note, however, that when you raise Brightness to values greater than 100, you can drive 8-bit highlight values to 255, which looks a lot like highlight clipping. But if you check the 16-bit values after conversion, you'll probably find that they aren't clipped.

▶ **Contrast.** Contrast applies an S-curve to the data, leaving the extreme shadows and highlights alone. Increasing the Contrast value from the default setting of +25 lightens values above the midtones and darkens values below the midtones, while reducing the Contrast value does

Figure 5-23
Fill Light

Reducing Exposure and Brightness to emphasize the sunset makes shadows very dark.

Increasing Fill Light opens up shadows with minimal effect on lighter tones.

the reverse. The midpoint around which Contrast adds the S-curve is determined by the Brightness value, so if Contrast isn't doing what you want, make sure Brightness is set correctly.

Intensity controls. Camera Raw 4 features three controls in this section, where Camera Raw 3 contained only the Saturation command.

▶ **Clarity.** The Clarity slider controls local contrast, and can help produce that quality some photographers call "pop." Instead of adjusting contrast uniformly, Clarity adjusts contrast among adjacent areas of light and dark within an image (see **Figure 5-24**). Most images benefit from applying a moderate amount of Clarity, but as you increase the value, back off if you start to see unsightly halos around edges. Also, go easy when applying Clarity to portraits, because the way Clarity accentuates details and texture is usually not flattering for human faces. Clarity can dramatically improve images that naturally have low local contrast, such as reflections, foliage, and subjects photographed through haze.

Perhaps you've used Photoshop to enhance local contrast by setting the Unsharp Mask filter to a high Radius and low Amount value. The Clarity slider is based on a similar principle, but with additional processing. Clarity can appear to have a sharpening effect, but it's important to note that Clarity is not a substitute for sharpening. For that, there's the Detail tab.

► **Vibrance.** The Vibrance slider is intended as a "safer" version of the Saturation slider. It applies a greater increase in color saturation to colors that are not already saturated (see **Figure 5-25**). For example, if you increase saturation for an image that contains both muted and saturated reds, the muted reds become more saturated but the bright reds are prevented from becoming ridiculously saturated. It's a good way to improve color with less of a chance of colors going out of gamut.

Vibrance has one more key function. The Photoshop team built skin-tone protection into Vibrance, so you can boost image saturation much further before people in your image acquire radioactive tans.

► **Saturation.** The Saturation slider adjusts color intensity evenly for all colors. While every image editor needs a Saturation feature, the fact

Camera Raw + Bridge = Lightroom?

Between Photoshop CS2 and CS3, Adobe released an entirely new software product called Adobe Photoshop Lightroom. Although the name Photoshop is in the official name of the product, Lightroom isn't a cut-down version like Photoshop Elements is, and it isn't a plug-in either. So what is Lightroom, and does it play well with Photoshop CS3?

The simplest way to describe Lightroom is that it's an integrated combination of Adobe Camera Raw 4 and Bridge CS3. There are several reasons why this is not as redundant as it sounds. First, you can't have Camera Raw and Bridge without buying Photoshop, and that's rather expensive. Lightroom is a more affordable alternative for those who don't need access to the complete Photoshop feature set.

The Lightroom user interface is designed with the image at the center of the screen, surrounded by panels, with almost no dialogs to distract you from your image. Controls are presented as five modules that you can move among freely: Library (like the Content panel in Bridge), Develop (containing Camera Raw controls), Slideshow (a bit better than the Bridge slideshow), Web (where you can export Flash and HTML Web sites to disk or upload them to a server), and Print.

In this chapter you can see that Camera Raw has matured into a powerful image-processing program in its own right. If your images are well-lit, focused, and need no retouching, you may be able to produce finished images from Camera Raw without moving them through Photoshop. Because the Develop module in Lightroom includes the Camera Raw engine, it can provide the same level of image processing.

Another nice thing about Lightroom is that it removes many of the artificial walls that exist in the Bridge-Camera Raw workflow. In Photoshop CS3, Camera Raw exists in a modal dialog, which isolates it from Bridge and Photoshop. In Lightroom, you can switch easily between the Develop module and the Library or any of the other modules.

While Bridge is a type of file browser, Lightroom tracks images in a database called a catalog, and you can save multiple catalogs. The database allows Lightroom to do a few things Bridge can't, such as managing images even when their original files are on a volume that isn't currently mounted.

Both Bridge and Lightroom include keyword features. As we write this, keywording in Lightroom is faster, and much more flexible and powerful than Bridge's. Both let you locate and browse photos by keyword and metadata, but because Lightroom uses a database, it's more efficient at searching through images in many different folders on multiple disks.

One point in favor of Lightroom is getting polished final output quickly. Camera Raw and Bridge are incapable of printing; for those programs, the road to printing still goes through Photoshop. Suddenly you find that you're chaining together three programs just to organize, edit, and print your photos. The same goes for building Web galleries. Lightroom can accomplish all of that in one program using its Library, Develop, Web, and Print modules.

On the surface, it appears that Lightroom is aimed at an audience that doesn't need the full power of the Photoshop/Camera Raw/Bridge combo, and that's generally true. However, there are quite a few Photoshop users who find Lightroom a valuable addition to their workflow. For many of these users, the reasons are the smoother integration between the raw controls and the image library and the additional power that a database brings to digital asset management. If you are a pro who processes a high volume of images, the additional integration and more powerful image management features in Lightroom may save enough billable hours of labor to pay for the program, even if you already have Photoshop. If you are a non-professional or low-volume photographer, the improvements to Camera Raw 4 and Bridge CS3 may be all you need to get the job done.

Figure 5-25
Vibrance and Saturation

*Original colors
could use a boost*

*Increasing Saturation
oversaturates bright colors
and skin tones*

*Increasing Vibrance by the
same amount enhances
dull colors effectively, while
protecting skin tones and
already saturated colors*

that Camera Raw now has Vibrance means that you may reach for the Saturation slider less often than you used to.

Improving printed output with the new camera raw controls. The tonal range and color gamut of print is so much narrower than what your camera and monitor can produce that it isn't unusual to spend a lot of time using layers and masks in Photoshop to shoehorn an image into the gamut of your printed output. Now, in Camera Raw 4.x, you can achieve many of the same goals just by using the four new sliders—Recovery, Fill Light, Clarity, and Vibrance. Recovery and Fill Light are quick and reliable ways to move highlight and shadow detail a little closer to the midtones and away from the extreme ends of the tonal scale that are harder to print. Because compressing detail into the midtones usually means you lose a little contrast, you can then use the intelligent Clarity and Vibrance sliders to preserve and enhance contrast in the resulting range of tones and colors without pushing them back out to the extremes, as the Contrast slider would.

It may not be possible for you to use Camera Raw to completely prepare an image for printed output—for one thing, you can't load a printer profile and visually check your adjustments against it—but those four sliders can reduce the amount of work you have to do with layers and masks in Photoshop to compress an image's tonal and color range.

Using Auto Tone Adjustment

When you click Auto (see **Figure 5-26**) in the Basic tab (it's on by default), Camera Raw tries to come up with optimum settings for each image, essentially autocorrecting tone and exposure. While the word "auto" usually makes us squirm, this feature is more sophisticated than it might seem at first glance.

Figure 5-26
Applying auto tone adjustment

Click the underlined Auto text in the Basic tab

Tip: To free up space in the Camera Raw window, Camera Raw 4 lacks the Auto check boxes that were next to each slider in Camera Raw 3.7 and earlier. You can still reset each slider individually—just double-click a slider.

Tip: The difference between Auto and Default is that Auto tries to calculate settings for each image, while Default applies the same set of values to all images.

However, keeping Auto as part of the default setting makes it difficult for you to learn the behavior of a camera because Camera Raw adjusts each image individually, so you don't get to see a consistent baseline interpretation. Beginners will likely find that Use Auto Adjustments provides a quick way to get decent results, but it also makes it much more difficult for them to learn the relationship between shutter speed, aperture setting, and the result. If you don't want Auto to be applied to new images by default, click the Preferences button in the Camera Raw toolbar (Command-K in Mac OS X or Ctrl-K in Windows), and in the Default Image Settings options group, uncheck Apply Auto Tone Adjustments.

In Camera Raw 3, Auto was a toggle; you could turn it on and off with a shortcut. However, its behavior was confusing in the way it interacted with the defaults and any settings you changed. In Camera Raw 4, Auto now works like other options. Once you apply it, you can either undo it or apply a different option or preset.

Using Camera Raw Defaults

Camera Raw contains default settings for images shot by each camera model. They're applied as you download images from a camera. You can create your own defaults, and the image metadata will tell Camera Raw which default to use for each camera model.

If you're editing an image and want to return to the camera defaults, click Default in the Basic tab (see **Figure 5-27**).

Figure 5-27
Applying camera defaults

Click the underlined Default text in the Basic tab

Tip: A common question is how to import images into Camera Raw and Bridge without applying Auto adjustment. Simply click Default (which neutralizes Auto) and then save new Camera Raw defaults.

You can save a new Camera Raw setup. For example, you may find the default Blacks setting of 5 a little too high or you may notice that you consistently find yourself lowering the Color Noise Reduction slider. So set the controls the way you want them, then choose Save New Camera Raw Defaults from the Camera Raw menu.

Getting good default settings ("good default settings" means different things to different people) is generally an iterative process. Don't be afraid to experiment. It won't harm your raw files in any way, and if you get hopelessly messed up, you can easily set everything back to the shipping defaults and start over by choosing Reset Camera Raw Defaults from the Camera Raw menu.

You can fine-tune camera defaults in Camera Raw preferences. See "Camera Raw Preferences" a little later on. No set of defaults will do equal justice to every image, so just try to find default settings that provide a good starting point for your images and hence save you time.

Workflow Guidelines for the Image Controls

With the dramatic expansion of tabs and sliders in Camera Raw 4 (the Basic tab alone is now loaded with eleven, count 'em, eleven sliders), it can be hard to figure out which slider to move to fix a particular problem. Although it's generally a good idea to move through the sliders from top to bottom, there are some interrelationships among the sliders in the Basic tab, and with sliders in other parts of Camera Raw, that you should keep in mind.

▶ Just about all the other controls depend on your setting Exposure and Blacks correctly—the clipping points for white and black. If you don't set both Exposure and Blacks correctly, your image's tonal range will be suboptimal, and you'll probably spend extra time wrestling with the other controls to try and compensate for that basic problem.

▶ Similarly, setting White Balance correctly will make it easier to use all of the other color controls in Camera Raw.

▶ If you find yourself consistently making the exact same selective color corrections on your processed raws, you may want to visit the Camera Calibration tab to tweak the color for your specific camera (see "The Camera Calibration Tab," later in this chapter).

▶ Many people are unclear about the difference between Exposure and Brightness. Exposure is much more important because it affects white-point clipping. Brightness only shifts the tonal midpoint up or down, without clipping. To see the difference, watch the histogram as you adjust each slider.

▶ If you set Brightness and Contrast as well as you can in the Basic tab, you probably won't have to make major moves in the Tone Curve.

▶ Some users ask how they can use the Basic tab in the same way that they use Levels in Photoshop. For the white, black, and gray (middle) slider in Levels, adjust Exposure, Blacks, and Brightness, respectively, in Camera Raw. The controls do not correspond exactly because corrections are applied using Gamma 1.0 in Camera Raw (Photoshop uses the gamma of the working space), but it's as close as you're going to get. Note that in both sets of controls, you can hold down the Option (Mac) or Alt (Windows) key to preview any clipping of highlights or shadows.

We see a distressingly large number of photographers who convert their raw images at Camera Raw default settings, then complain that Camera Raw produces flat, unsaturated results that require a lot of Photoshop work. The defaults in Camera Raw tend to be more conservative than those of proprietary raw converters, which generally aim to match the in-camera JPEG. They often bury shadow detail to hide noise and produce a pleasingly contrasty result. Camera Raw, on the other hand, shows you everything the camera has captured, warts and all, and lets you work with all the bits so that you can create better quality than any automatic converter.

Raw files are always interpreted, as when printing color negative film. There is no definitive way to develop a raw file. The default appearance of images in each raw converter reflects the philosophy of the team that created it, and Camera Raw is no exception to that. We suggest that you refine the look you want by using the Camera Raw controls on a representative sample of images, and then set the Camera Raw defaults (see the earlier section, "Camera Raw Defaults") so that your preferred adjustment apply to all the images you download from your camera.

The Tone Curve Tab

The old Curve tab in Camera Raw 3 is now the Tone Curve tab in Camera Raw 4 (see **Figure 5-28**). The Tone Curve tab (Command-Option-2 in Mac OS X or Ctrl-Alt-2 in Windows) offers a luminosity-based curve control that lets you fine-tune the image's tonality. If you're used to thinking of the Curves command in Photoshop as the best way to edit images, you may be tempted to skip the slider controls in the Basic tab and use the Tone Curve tab for all your tone-mapping adjustments, but that's not a good idea. To understand *why* it isn't a good idea, you need to know a little about how the Tone Curve tab actually works.

Like the sliders on the Basic tab, the Tone Curve tab operates on the linear capture—in fact, the slider adjustments and the curve adjustments get concatenated into a single operation during the raw conversion. But the user interface for the Tone Curve tab makes it appear that the curve is operating on gamma-2.2-encoded data. (If the curve interface corresponded directly to the linear data, the midtone value would be around level 50, and the three-quarter tone would be all the way down at level 10 or so, which would make it pretty hard to edit!)

The key point is that the Tone Curve tab settings are applied in addition to and after the slider adjustments in the Basic tab. You'll find that it's much easier to use the sliders for rough tonal shaping and the Tone Curve tab for fine-tuning than it is to try to do all the heavy lifting in the

Figure 5-28
The Tone Curve tab, with the
Parametric curve shown

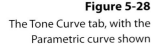

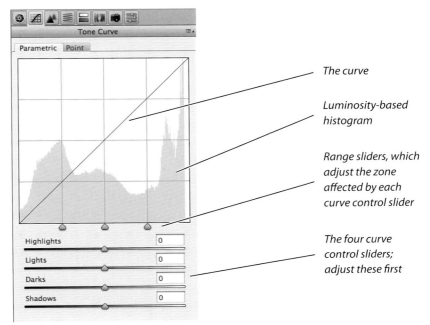

The curve

*Luminosity-based
histogram*

*Range sliders, which
adjust the zone
affected by each
curve control slider*

*The four curve
control sliders;
adjust these first*

Tone Curve tab. In other words, instead of trying to do everything in the Tone Curve tab, use it to refine your Basic tab adjustments.

There's one more significant change from Camera Raw 3: There's a new type of curve-editing interface, Parametric, and it's now the type of curve you see first when you click the Tone Curve tab. The point curve from Camera Raw 3 has literally been pushed into the background. Yes, Parametric is a technical-sounding term, but bear with us—in the end, we think you'll decide that Parametric curve editing is actually much easier than the old Point curve interface.

Using Parametric Curves

If you've ever used an audio equalizer (like the one in iTunes, for example), you already have a head start in understanding the Parametric tab in Camera Raw. As in an audio equalizer, you get a series of sliders, each corresponding to a tonal range. You simply grab the slider representing the range you want to boost or cut, and drag. All right—it isn't quite that simple; for instance, the Camera Raw sliders are horizontal, not vertical like the ones you see in audio equalizers. But the basic idea is the same. We think that the following sequence is the simplest path through the

Parametric tab (see **Figure 5-29**). We'll use the example of an image that needs a little more contrast.

1. Drag the Darks and Lights sliders. To increase contrast (which is usually what you'll need to do), drag the Darks slider to the left and drag the Lights slider to the right.

Tip: You can reset any individual slider by double-clicking it.

2. If you think that the extreme highlights and shadows still need work, drag the Highlights and Shadows sliders. These sliders affect only the ends of the curves, and not every image needs these adjustments. However, the Highlights and Shadows sliders are a good way to control the tones at the ends of the tonal scale.

3. With some images, you may find that a slider isn't giving you enough control in the tonal range you want to adjust. In this case, turn to the three Range sliders along the bottom of the curve graph. Those three sliders define the four ranges affected by the four horizontal sliders. For example, if you wish the Darks slider's effect were a little higher on the tonal scale, drag the first slider under the graph to the right a little. High-key and low-key images are situations in which you may want to shift or expand the tonal range controlled by a particular slider.

Tip: If you've been trained to avoid using the master curve in the Photoshop Curves dialog to edit RGB images, don't worry about that in Camera Raw. In Camera Raw 4.1 (and in Lightroom), the Tone Curve is engineered to minimize the hue shifts that can occur when you use a single curve to edit RGB images, resulting in a clean tonal edit.

If you've done a good job setting Exposure, Blacks, Brightness, and Contrast in the Basic tab, you'll probably find that you don't need to move the Parametric sliders very far.

If you can't remember the above sequence, just think of it as moving from the inside out: Adjust the inner Darks and Lights sliders first, and then if necessary, adjust the outer Highlights and Shadows sliders.

Parametric curves can be easier than point curves because parametric curves work as if the key points are already placed for you, and it's easier to create a curve that avoids posterization. If you need still more control, or you're just too used to placing your own points, you can still use the Point tab.

Using Point Curves

The Point tab is based on the Curves dialog in Photoshop and they share some features. When you click the Point tab, you'll find that by default, Camera Raw 4 applies a Medium Contrast curve preset (it's selected in

Figure 5-29
Adjusting the
Parametric curve

*Set the Darks and Lights
sliders first, to tune the
basic S-curve.*

*If necessary, set the
Highlights and Shadows
sliders to refine the extreme
ends of the tonal scale.*

*If the horizontal sliders
aren't affecting the tonal
ranges you want, adjust
the range sliders under the
graph. Here, the image
is so bright that the far
right slider was moved in
to let the Highlights slider
control a wider range of
the lightest tones.*

the Curve pop-up menu). If you prefer a different default, you can edit the curve points and then save a new Camera Raw Default.

To place a new point on the curve, click the curve. A more efficient way to place a point is to position the mouse over a tone in the image that you want to adjust, and then Command-click (Mac) or Ctrl-click (Windows). This adds a new point on the curve at the tone you clicked. You can preview where on the curve a point will be added if you keep the Command (Mac) or Ctrl (Windows) key pressed as you move the mouse over the image; a small circle appears on the curve, marking the level you're currently mousing over. There are three ways to delete a curve point: Command-click (Mac) or Ctrl-click (Windows) a point, select it, and press the Delete key, or drag it over one of the adjacent curve points.

Control-Tab (on both Mac and Windows) selects the next curve point, and Control-Shift-Tab selects the previous point. To select multiple curve points, Shift-click each one. The up, down, left, and right arrow keys move the selected curve point by one level: add Shift to move in increments of 10 levels. You can also enter numeric values for the selected curve point in the Input and Output entry fields.

To make saved tone curves appear on the Tone Curve menu, save them in Username\Library\Application Support\Adobe\Camera Raw\Curves (Mac), or Documents and Settings\Username\Application Data\Adobe\Camera Raw\Curves (Windows). This is a different folder from the one for all other Camera Raw settings and subsets, but if you save a subset containing only a tone curve, it's saved in this folder automatically. If you save tone curves anywhere else, you can load them using the Load Settings command in Camera Raw (see "Loading and Saving Settings," earlier in this chapter).

Adjustments and previewing. The most practical way to adjust the curve is to place points on it by Command-clicking (Mac) or Ctrl-clicking (Windows), then use the arrow keys to make an adjustment, wait for the preview to update, and continue to fine-tune using the arrow keys. **Figure 5-30** shows a typical Tone Curve tab adjustment.

If you've used the Curves dialog in Photoshop, you might notice that the Tone Curve tab in Camera Raw doesn't preview your curve edits in real time. The Curves dialog in Photoshop adjusts pixel values directly, but the Tone Curve tab in Camera Raw has to do a lot more work. The raw data is in linear form (gamma 1.0) and the Tone Curve interface is in gamma 2.2, so Camera Raw must map your edits between the two. By not providing real-time preview, it's easier for the curve interface to be responsive.

Adjustments to the Parametric and Tone Curve tabs are cumulative, so if a curve isn't doing what you expect it to, check the other tab to see if there's an existing adjustment there that contradicts what you're trying to do.

Figure 5-30
Adjusting the point curve

To add contrast to the grass, first Command-click (Mac) or Ctrl-click (Windows) a dark blade of grass to set a curve point for that tone.

After adding a curve point for a light blade of grass, dragging the points, and adding a third point (the far right point) to keep the highlights from changing, grass contrast is improved. Because all tones in that range are changed, the dark side of the barn and fence are also affected.

The Detail Tab

The sliders in the Detail tab (Command-Option-3 in Mac OS X or Ctrl-Alt-3 in Windows) let you apply overall sharpening and reduce noise in both the Luminance and Color components of an image (see **Figure 5-31**). Camera Raw 4.1 expands sharpening from the old single slider to four surprisingly powerful and intelligent controls. To see the effect of these controls, you need to zoom the preview to at least 100 percent. At other magnifications, the actual results of sharpening can't be represented accurately on a monitor.

Figure 5-31
The Detail tab

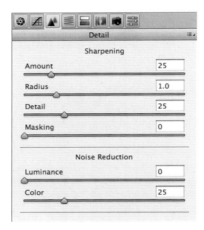

Color noise is often more noticeable than luminance noise. If you see color splotches in areas that should be neutral, try turning up Color noise reduction, but not so far that you lose saturation in color details. Luminance noise reduction is more apparent at very high ISO speeds and with some types of image content.

Sharpening

Sharpening is yet another feature that Adobe has greatly expanded in Camera Raw 4.1. However, the four Sharpening sliders don't resemble either of the two prominent sharpening dialogs in Photoshop (Unsharp Mask and Smart Sharpen). The reason for this is that Camera Raw 4.1 sharpening is based on advanced edge-masking techniques documented by Bruce and others. Edge masking can restrict sharpening to the edges (where you want it), and away from broad areas like skin (where you don't want it).

To preview the effect of only the Sharpening slider you're adjusting, set the magnification to 100 percent and then Option-drag (Mac) or Alt-drag (Windows) a Sharpening slider. You'll see a grayscale preview that nicely isolates the effect for you so you can clearly see what's changing. When previewing the Masking option, your sharpening settings are applied to white areas at full strength, gray areas at partial strength, and are not applied at all to black areas; you may want to turn off the shadow and highlight clipping warnings so that they don't distract you. In most of our examples, we'll show you the grayscale preview because it makes it easier to see what's going on.

Amount. The Amount slider (see **Figure 5-32**) adjusts how much sharpening Camera Raw applies. In most cases, a low to moderate value is appropriate. The Radius, Detail, and Masking sliders use different methods to modify the strength of the Amount value in various parts of the image.

Figure 5-32
Amount

Amount set to values of 0 (left) and 85 (right), with all other Sharpening sliders at default values

Radius. The Radius slider (see **Figure 5-33**) controls the width of the halo around each detail that's sharpened. If the halos become visible or details start to smear or smeared or look like blobs, you've set Radius too high.

Figure 5-33
Radius (grayscale preview)

*Radius set to values of
1.0 (default, narrow halos)
and 2.5 (wide halos)*

Detail. The Detail slider (see **Figure 5-34**) affects how much the Radius halos are visible on high-frequency details, such as skin pores or other fine textures. A low Detail value filters out Radius halos on those details, while letting the Radius value to apply to larger features. Setting Detail to its maximum value lets Radius apply to all details without modification.

Figure 5-34
Detail (grayscale preview)

*Detail set to values of
25 (default, larger details
sharpened only) and 90
(most details sharpened)*

Masking. The Masking slider (see **Figure 5-35**) affects the degree to which sharpening is restricted to edges only. Edges are considered to be the image areas with highest contrast. At zero, no masking is applied—the current Amount, Radius, and Detail values are applied to the entire image at full strength. As you increase the Masking value, less sharpening is applied to non-edge areas, while edges continue receiving full-strength sharpening. Increasing the Masking value can help you sharpen images that are blurrier than average, because when you increase the Masking value, you can use much higher Amount values without accentuating noise, grain, or other unwanted detail in non-edge areas.

Figure 5-35
Masking (grayscale preview)

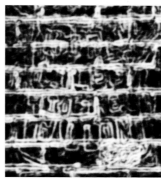

Masking set to values of 25 (almost no areas masked) and 85 (most areas masked except high-contrast edges)

So how much sharpening is enough? That depends on how you use Camera Raw in your workflow.

Tip: For a deeper explanation of the principles behind edge masking, see "Edge Masking" in Chapter 10. Actually, reading all of Chapter 10 will give you insight into all of the Detail tab.

▶ If you use Camera Raw in between your camera and Photoshop, you can apply capture sharpening—just enough sharpening to make up for the softness inherent in all image sensors. Then, in Photoshop, apply the appropriate amount of output sharpening to the versions of the image that you prepare for different output media. If you do this, first open Camera Raw preferences and choose All Images from the Apply Sharpening To pop-up menu.

▶ If you would rather use Photoshop sharpening controls for all sharpening, open Camera Raw preferences and choose Preview Images Only from the Apply Sharpening To pop-up menu. Then, don't use the Camera Raw Sharpening controls at all.

▶ If you intend to use Camera Raw as the final step in your workflow, saving completed images directly from Camera Raw, apply the appropriate amount of sharpening for your final output. If you do this, first open Camera Raw preferences and choose All Images from the Apply Sharpening To pop-up menu.

Reducing Noise

The sensors in today's digital SLR cameras are rather noise-free at low ISO speed settings, but if you shoot at high ISO speed settings or use a digital point-and-shoot camera, noise is likely to be present.

To minimize noise when you shoot digital, never underexpose your images. Noise lives in the shadows, so if you boost shadows in Camera Raw or Photoshop, noise becomes more visible. If you shoot so that an image file is brighter than normal (without clipping highlights), the act of lowering Exposure or Brightness in Camera Raw pushes noise further down into the shadows, hiding it.

Tip: The Color Noise Reduction slider can make a big difference at low values, so you can easily be tempted to turn it up further. Be careful, though—increasing Color Noise Reduction too far can dull bright colors in important details.

It's difficult to show typical noise scenarios in print because noise that looks objectionable on the displayed RGB file is often invisible by the time the image has been converted to CMYK and printed.

While the Luminance slider comes first in the Detail tab, we often try the Color Noise Reduction slider first, so that's how we're covering the options here. Camera Raw defaults agree with us: By default, Luminance is set to 0 and Color is set to 25.

Color Noise Reduction. Color noise appears as random speckles of color rather than gray. In our experience, all cameras need some amount of color-noise reduction (see **Figure 5-36**). While the visibility of color noise varies with ISO speed, the required correction seems to vary less than it does with luminance noise. That means you can generally find a good default value for your camera, and then deviate from it only when you see an obvious problem. Now that Camera Raw reads TIFF and JPEG images, it's worth noting that the Color Noise Reduction slider can also work wonders with the visible color grain in scanned color film.

Figure 5-36
Noise Reduction: Color

This is a detail of a digital SLR image shot at ISO 1600. We set the Color slider to 0 and 25 (default).

Luminance Noise Reduction. The Luminance Noise Reduction slider (see **Figure 5-37**) lets you control grayscale noise that makes the image appear grainy—a typical problem when shooting at high ISO speeds. The default setting is zero, which provides no smoothing; but some cameras benefit from a small amount—say 2 to 4—of luminance noise reduction even at slow speeds, so you may want to experiment to find a good default for your camera. At high ISO speeds—800 and up—you'll typically need to apply luminance smoothing at even higher settings.

At very high settings, the Luminance slider produces images that look like they've been hit with the Median filter, so always check the entire image at 100 percent size or larger before committing to a setting.

Figure 5-37
Noise Reduction: Luminance

With Color set to 25, we set Luminance Noise Reduction to 25 and 50. At 50 we're starting to lose image detail, so a value under 50 is probably correct.

The HSL/Grayscale Tab

The controls in the HSL/Grayscale tab (Command-Option-4 in Mac OS X or Ctrl-Alt-4 in Windows) are new in Camera Raw 4. The controls in this tab have two main purposes: to correct specific ranges of color and to convert an image to grayscale while controlling how colors map to gray tones.

Using the HSL Controls

HSL stands for Hue, Saturation, and Luminance; see Chapter 3, "Color Essentials," to review those color concepts. With these powerful controls, you may not need to move some images on to Photoshop when you can't nail the color balance with the Temperature and Tint sliders in Camera Raw. Hue, Saturation, and Luminance each gets a tab of their own, and each of those tabs contains eight sliders (see **Figure 5-38**). That's a lot of sliders, but don't be intimidated, because each tab is simply a variation on the same idea.

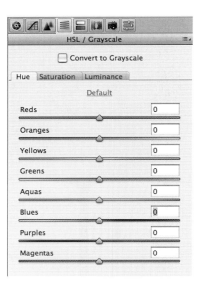

Figure 5-38
The HSL tab

Each tab contains a slider for eight color ranges. These ranges were not chosen strictly mathematically, but because they are colors that typically need correction in photographs. To figure out how to use the controls, first you identify what's wrong with the color you want to correct in the image, in terms of hue, saturation, or luminance (see **Figure 5-39**).

▶   If a color isn't quite the right hue, such as grass that's too yellow, go to the Hue tab and then drag that color's slider to shift it to the correct color.

▶   If a color needs to be less or more vivid, click the Saturation tab and drag that color's slider left to gray down the color, or right to increase saturation. You might use this to make a blue sky more blue.

▶   If you want a color to be lighter or darker, click the Luminance tab and drag that color's slider left to darken it, or right to lighten it.

If you don't see much of a change, you probably aren't dragging the correct color slider. It's also possible for a slider to change a part of the image you weren't expecting; for example, a black object can change if it has a color cast. To adjust skin tones, try the Oranges and Yellows sliders first.

Figure 5-39
Desaturating one color

Figure 5-39
Desaturating one color

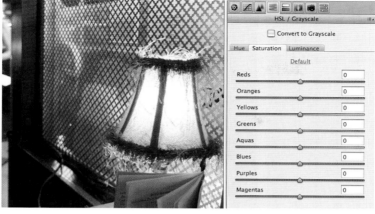

This image was white-balanced for the tungsten lightbulb in the lamp, which caused the daylight coming in from the window to appear distractingly blue.

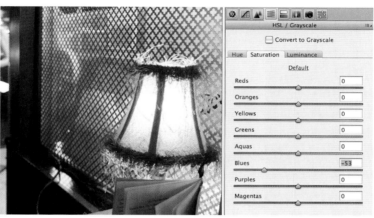

In the HSL/Grayscale tab, we clicked the Saturation tab and lowered the Blues value to make the lighting appear more natural.

Controlling Grayscale Conversions

In Camera Raw 3, it was possible to convert an image to grayscale by setting Saturation to zero in the Basic tab, and you could control the lightness of colors in the grayscale image by playing with the Calibrate tab (something that the Calibrate tab was not designed for). In Camera Raw 4, grayscale conversion is much more straightforward, with controls actually designed for that purpose. And the results are very good.

To convert an image to grayscale, simply turn on the Convert to Grayscale check box at the top of the HSL/Grayscale panel. You'll notice that in addition to the image losing all its color, the Hue, Saturation, and Luminance tabs disappear and are replaced by a single Grayscale Mix tab (see **Figure 5-40**). On top of that, the sliders in the Grayscale Mix tab move around by themselves and take on new values.

Figure 5-40
Grayscale conversion

*This is a color image
before being converted
to grayscale.*

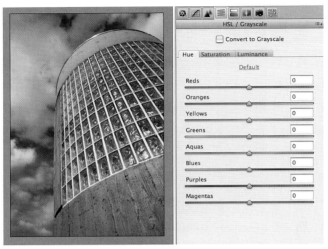

*Clicking the Convert to
Grayscale check box applies
the Auto Grayscale Mix.*

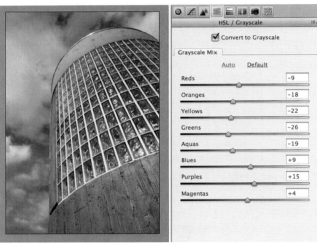

*We manually customized
the grayscale mix by raising
the Yellows and lowering
the Blues to create more
contrast between the
building and the sky.*

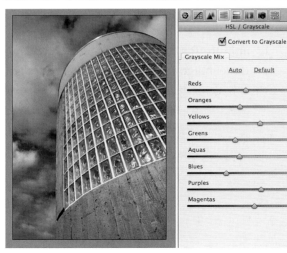

Tip: If you don't want Camera Raw to automatically calculate grayscale mix values, open Camera Raw preferences and uncheck the Apply Auto Grayscale Mix When Converting to Grayscale check box. If you just want to set all of the sliders for the current image to their original values, click Default in the HSL/Grayscale panel.

What happened? When you turn on the Convert to Grayscale check box, by default Camera Raw tries to calculate how to get the best distribution of tones out of that particular image, and that's why the Grayscale Mix sliders adjust themselves. In many cases, the Auto Grayscale Mix is a great starting point, and you may be satisfied with it. If not, you can drag the sliders yourself.

Here's how the Grayscale Mix sliders work: When you convert to grayscale, you take away hue and saturation. What's left is the luminance value of each color. However, as you change the saturation of different colors, they occupy different ranges of tones. For instance, at maximum saturation, pure yellow is lighter than any other color. When you convert to grayscale, the resulting distribution of tones can appear unnatural or just weak. The Grayscale Mix sliders let you make specific color ranges lighter or darker in grayscale, so you can get the tone and contrast relationships that bring out the image qualities you want to emphasize. For example, if you drag the Reds slider to the left to darken reds, red lipstick darkens and stands out more effectively. If you've ever placed a color filter in front of a camera lens when shooting black-and-white film, it's the same idea, but with a lot more control.

The Split Toning Tab

The controls in the Split Toning tab (Command-Option-5 in Mac OS X or Ctrl-Alt-5 in Windows) are new in Camera Raw 4, and let you apply different colors to the lighter and darker parts of an image. This is more of a special effect, not an image-correction feature. Here's how to use Split Toning.

1. Split toning typically starts with a grayscale image (see **Figure 5-41**). If the image in Camera Raw is still in color, you can switch to the HSL/Grayscale tab and turn on the Convert to Grayscale check box, and then return to the Split Toning tab.

2. Drag both Saturation sliders to a value well above zero, or your Hue changes won't be visible. You can leave one of the Saturation sliders at zero if you don't want to apply a color to that tonal range.

3. Set the Hue sliders to the hues you want for highlights and shadows.

Figure 5-41
Split Toning

Corrected grayscale images are good candidates for split toning.

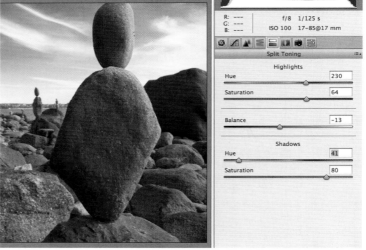

Adjust the hue and saturation of highlights and shadows. Remember that split toning adjustments take effect only when Saturation is higher than zero.

4. Drag the Balance slider to control at what point along the whole tonal scale the Highlights hue changes over to the Shadows hue.

The one time you may not want to use Split Toning in Camera Raw is when you want to produce a true multitone image, such as a duotone, tritone, or quadtone. Those are best produced in Photoshop, where you can use the Image > Mode > Duotone command to create and control separate channels for each ink. The results of the Split Toning tab are suitable for reproduction in most other media, such as printing on RGB or CMYK devices, and of course on-screen media. However, if you do want to create a multitone image from a raw image, you can use the Convert to

Grayscale option and Grayscale Mix in the HSL/Grayscale tab to create a high-quality grayscale, which you can immediately convert to a multitone image in Photoshop.

The Lens Corrections Tab

The controls in the Lens Corrections tab (Command-Option-6 in Mac OS X or Ctrl-Alt-6 in Windows) let you address problems that occasionally show up in digital captures, especially with lower quality sensors and lenses.

Tip: To see the color fringes clearly and to judge the optimum settings for the sliders, set the Sharpness slider in the Detail tab to zero. Color fringes are usually most prominent along high-contrast edges, and sharpening makes it harder to see exactly where the color fringes start and end.

Chromatic aberration. Chromatic aberration is the name given to the phenomenon where the lens fails to focus the red, green, and blue wavelengths of the light to exactly the same spot, causing red and cyan color fringes along high-contrast edges. In severe cases, you may also see some blue and yellow fringing. It typically happens with wide-angle shots, especially with the wide end of zoom lenses, and is typically worse at more open aperture settings.

▶ **Chromatic Aberration R/C.** This slider lets you reduce or eliminate red/cyan fringes by adjusting the size of the red channel relative to the green channel. While the red/cyan fringes are usually the most visually obvious, chromatic aberration usually has a blue/yellow component too.

▶ **Chromatic Aberration B/Y.** This slider lets you reduce or eliminate blue/yellow fringes by adjusting the size of the blue channel relative to the green channel.

Tip: When correcting chromatic aberration, Option/Alt-Drag a slider to hide the other channel. This makes it much easier to apply exactly the right amount of correction to both channels. Red/cyan fringing is usually much easier to see than blue/yellow fringing, but chromatic aberration is almost always a combination of both.

Figure 5-42 shows before-and-after versions of a chromatic aberration correction. As with the controls in the Detail tab, zoom the preview to 100 percent or more when making corrections with the chromatic aberration sliders.

Vignetting. Vignetting, where the corners are darker because the lens fails to illuminate the entire sensor area evenly, is a problem you may encounter when shooting wide open.

▶ **Vignetting Amount.** This slider controls the amount of lightening or darkening (negative amounts darken, positive amounts lighten) applied to the corners of the image.

Figure 5-42
Fixing chromatic aberration

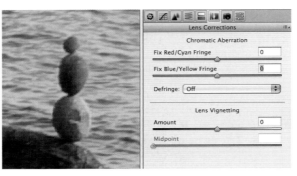

*In this corner detail of
a digital SLR frame,
red and yellow fringes
are visible along edges.*

*Dragging the two
Chromatic Aberration
sliders minimizes
the problem.*

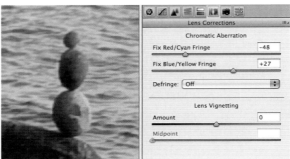

► **Vignetting Midpoint.** This slider controls the area to which the Vignetting Amount adjustment gets applied. Smaller values reduce the area; larger ones increase it.

Defringe. The Defringe option (see **Figure 5-43**) helps minimize color fringing, which can occur when sensors are overloaded by light, and shows up more often in high-contrast scenes. You may see it in specular highlights such as chrome, or at other times when the raw data is clipped to white, such as sunlight sparkling on the ocean, or city lights at night. It's often called purple fringing, because it often appears as a fuzzy purple border around a highlight.

If you see color fringing, choose Highlights or All Edges from the Defringe pop-up menu, depending on the extent of the color fringing. The color fringe should disappear and the affected edge should take on the natural color of the objects around it.

Figure 5-43

Defringing

In this detail of a frame from a digital point-and-shoot camera, the bright on-camera flash and mediocre lens created purple fringing in the metal jewelry.

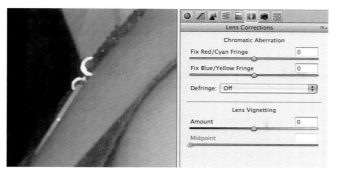

Choosing Highlight Edges from the Defringe pop-up menu reduces the fringing.

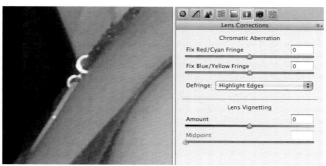

The Camera Calibration Tab

The controls in the Camera Calibration tab (Command-Option-7 in Mac OS X or Ctrl-Alt-7 in Windows) let you fine-tune the default tone and color rendering of raw images. In Photoshop CS2, this was called the Calibrate tab.

As we explained earlier in this chapter (see the sidebar "Camera Raw and Color"), Camera Raw contains two built-in generic profiles for each supported camera. The controls in the Camera Calibration tab let you fine-tune the behavior of the built-in camera profiles to tweak for any variations between *your* camera and the one that was used to build the built-in Camera Raw profiles for the camera model (see **Figure 5-44**).

Camera Profile. For most cameras, there's only one choice on the Camera Profile pop-up menu—the version of Camera Raw (ACR) that was used to produce the profile. Don't be concerned if the version doesn't match the version number of the current Camera Raw, because once Adobe creates a camera profile, there's usually no need to update it. If Adobe has updated the profile of your camera, you may see another choice in the Camera

Figure 5-44
The Camera Calibration tab

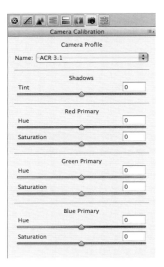

Profile pop-up menu. It's usually a good idea to use the newest profile, but if you have older images that were corrected using an older profile, in some cases you'll need to choose the older profile to see the image as you edited it back then.

You can't add your own camera profiles to the Camera Profile pop-up menu. We explain why in the earlier sidebar "Camera Raw and Color."

Using the Calibrate controls. By far the easiest way to get good Camera Calibration tab settings for your specific camera is to employ the free AcrCalibrator script written by our friend and colleague Thomas Fors. You can download the script, along with the instructions for using it, from this Web site: *www.fors.net/chromoholics/.*

Besides the script, you'll need a GretagMacbeth ColorChecker—the old 24-patch ColorChecker, in either its full-sized or miniature form, is ideal, but you can also use the newer ColorChecker SG, which contains the old target. Tom's site provides good directions for lighting and shooting the target. Simply follow the instructions that accompany the script, and let it do its thing.

If you're a driven control freak who distrusts anything automatic (or you're simply deranged), Bruce documented the manual process on which the script is based in the book *Real World Camera Raw with Adobe Photoshop CS2*, and at *www.creativepro.com/story/feature/21351.html.*

The Presets Tab

You can store your favorite Camera Raw settings in the Presets tab (Command-Option-8 in Mac OS X if you've disabled the Universal Access shortcut for screen zooming in System Preferences; or Ctrl-Alt-8 in Windows). The Presets tab (see **Figure 5-45**) is new in Camera Raw 4, but the presets feature isn't new. Adobe simply gave presets their own tab, making them much easier to manage.

To create a new preset here, first adjust the settings you want to save in any of the other Camera Raw tabs. Then click the New Preset button at the bottom of the Presets tab. In the New Presets dialog, turn on check boxes for the settings you want to save. The Subset pop-up menu can select predefined groups of settings for you; it's also useful to use the Subset pop-up menu when you want to save only a few settings—it's faster to select a subset than to manually uncheck a lot of check boxes. Click OK and it's in the list, ready for you to apply to any image.

While you can also apply a preset by choosing it from the Apply Preset submenu on the Camera Raw Settings menu, it's easier just to click it in

Figure 5-45
The Presets tab and
the New Preset dialog

New Preset button

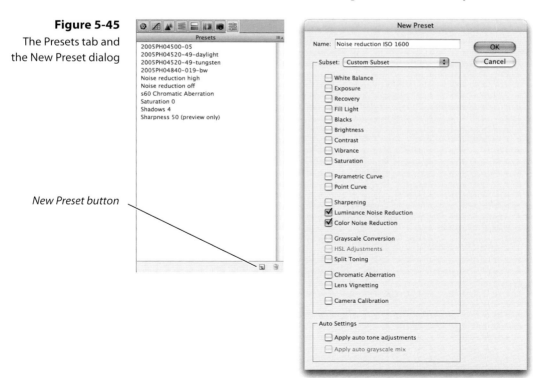

the Presets tab. In addition, the Presets tab is easier than a submenu when it comes to trying a few presets, one after the other.

To delete a preset, select it and then click the trash can icon at the bottom of the Presets tab. If you want to rename or manage your presets, they're stored in UserName\Library\Application Support\Adobe\ CameraRaw\Settings\ (Mac), and Documents and Settings\UserName\ Application Data\Adobe\CameraRaw\Settings\ (Windows).

Filmstrip Mode

If you had to adjust every slider on every image with a lot of images open in Camera Raw, you might conclude that Camera Raw was an instrument of torture rather than a productivity tool. Fortunately, the combination of Camera Raw, Bridge, and Photoshop offers several ways of editing multiple images. One of these is built right into Camera Raw itself: When you select multiple images to open, either by selecting them in Bridge or in the Open dialog in Photoshop, Camera Raw opens them in filmstrip mode (see **Figure 5-46**). In filmstrip mode, changes you make in the image controls apply to all images selected in the filmstrip.

Figure 5-46
Filmstrip mode

Select All and Synchronize buttons

Selected images are highlighted

Current image is highlighted with a border

Filmstrip

The filmstrip mode in Camera Raw offers a great deal of flexibility when it comes to editing multiple images. You can select all the open images using the Select All button, which makes all your edits apply to all the

Tip: To zoom multiple images at once, select the images in the filmstrip before changing the magnification.

selected images. You can also select contiguous ranges of images by Shift-clicking, or discontiguous images by Command-clicking (Mac) or Ctrl-clicking (Windows) images. When the focus is on the filmstrip, you can navigate through the images using the up and down arrow keys, or select them all by pressing Command-A.

You can also click a star rating under each filmstrip, and you can mark images for deletion by pressing the Delete key.

Synchronizing Settings in the Filmstrip

When you select more than one image, the Synchronize button becomes available at the top of the filmstrip (see **Figure 5-46**). The Synchronize button lets you apply all the settings or any subset for the image that's currently being previewed, to any additional images you select. This feature is of most use when you open a series of images that need similar corrections, but within that general mandate, you have a great deal of flexibility in how you choose to work. It's also useful when you've edited one image in Camera Raw and then you realize you want to apply the same edits to other images in the filmstrip.

For example, you can synchronize tonal adjustments, or noise reduction, all the settings, or whichever combination of settings is most applicable. A general rule of thumb is to start out by applying the settings that are applicable to the largest number of images, then whittle them down to smaller groups that can take the same corrections.

Using Adobe Bridge

Thus far, we've largely focused on editing individual images in Camera Raw. But if you tried to edit every image individually in Camera Raw, even in filmstrip mode, you probably wouldn't have much time to have a life. Back in the days of film, you didn't scan every image and edit it in Photoshop. Instead, you looked at the film on a light table, and picked those images that were worthy of further attention.

That's where Bridge comes in. You can make your initial selects from a shoot using Bridge as a digital light table. When you want to convert your images, you can host Camera Raw in Bridge and have it convert images in the background. You can also use Bridge to add and edit metadata—one of the first things we do to a new folder of raw images is to add our copyright notices to each image. And while we admit to being less assiduous than we really should be, we also use Bridge to add keywords to images so that we have some hope of finding them again several years hence. See the sidebar "All About Metadata," later in this chapter.

Bridge is a surprisingly deep application that serves the entire Adobe Creative Suite, not just Photoshop, and a comprehensive guide to its features would require a book in its own right. Nevertheless, we want to guide you through a number of our favorite features and describe how we use this powerful application.

What's New in Bridge CS3

While Bridge CS3 still won't replace digital asset management programs, some of the enhancement in Bridge CS3 make it much more effective within a digital image workflow.

It's faster. Bridge CS2 was maligned for being sluggish. Bridge CS3 fixes many of the performance issues, although you'll still wait for it to build the initial cache for folders containing raw images. There are also new options that help you tune performance.

It's easier to find photos. The new Filter panel organizes the content in the folder you're viewing, potentially saving you from having to make some types of searches. For example, you can quickly see all photos with a certain keyword, date, or rating.

It's easier to organize and compare photos. Several new features make Bridge much more useful when sifting through groups of images. When you select multiple images in the Content panel, the Preview panel can now display all of the images you selected (up to nine). In addition, you can inspect an image in detail by adding a loupe to any image in the Preview panel. You can also group multiple images as a stack, which is similar to the stacks in Lightroom and Apple Aperture.

Also, Bridge workspaces are more accessible, so it's easier to manage your windows; and metadata templates are much easier to create and edit. All in all, Bridge CS3 is a respectable upgrade.

Launching Bridge from Photoshop

On single-monitor systems, we usually keep Bridge hidden or in the background unless we're actually using it. On dual-monitor systems, we keep Bridge open on the second monitor all the time.

The simplest way to launch Bridge is the way you launch any other application on your platform of choice. From Photoshop, you have the following additional options:

▶ Choose File > Browse, or press Command-Option-O (Mac) or Ctrl-Alt-O (Windows).

Figure 5-47

The Go to Bridge button in Photoshop

▶ Click the Go to Bridge button in the Options bar (see **Figure 5-47**).

▶ Turn on the Automatically Launch Bridge option in Photoshop General Preferences—that way, whenever you launch Photoshop, Bridge automatically launches too.

Before we look at any more details of how Bridge and Camera Raw work, or how you can automate your workflow, we want to focus on some theories and philosophies that we think are helpful. First, we'll give you an orientation of the things you'll want to do in a digital workflow, and if you need more details on specific features, see "Bridge Windows" and "Bridge Commands" at the end of this chapter.

Making Key Bridge Workflow Decisions

An efficient workflow requires planning. You can flail around and try everything—it's actually not a bad way to get your feet wet—but at some point, you have to decide what works and stick with it. The issues in this section are, in our experience, important Bridge workflow aspects to think about in advance.

How do you want to store the Bridge cache? Certain changes you make to a folder using Bridge, such as sort order and information that can't be stored in XMP files, are stored in the Bridge cache. By default, Bridge stores the cache in one centralized location on your computer, but you can also have Bridge keep folder information in cache files that are stored inside each folder you've managed with Bridge. Each approach has its strengths and weaknesses, but your life will be simpler, and your workflow more robust, if you pick one approach and stick to it. Bridge provides control over the cache in two places: the Cache panel of the Preferences dialog (see "Cache Preferences" later in this chapter), and in the Tools > Cache submenu (see "Cache Commands" later in this chapter).

Where do you want to store Camera Raw settings for individual images? Raw files are read-only, except for the raw files you store in the DNG format. If you edit read-only raw files, those changes have to be stored somewhere. You can save the Camera Raw settings for each image in the Camera Raw database, in sidecar XMP files, or in the case of DNG format, in the DNG file itself.

The Camera Raw database indexes images by their content, not by their filenames, so you can copy, move, or rename them willy-nilly without losing track of your raw settings—but only as long as the images remain on the same computer as the Camera Raw database. Move the raw files to another computer, and their settings will be left behind on the originating computer. If you always remember to use the Export Settings command in Camera Raw to write out a sidecar .xmp file for the image, and you always remember to include the sidecar file with the image, there's no problem. But that's a lot of "always remembering."

Bridge does its best to keep track of sidecar .xmp files. As long as you copy, move, and rename your raw files only in Bridge, the sidecar files travel with them automatically. But if you copy, move, or rename your raw files *outside* of Bridge, you must keep track of your sidecar files and move them with the images manually. Again, it's not an ideal solution.

A third alternative is to use the DNG format instead. The convenience of having all the metadata, including Camera Raw settings, stored in the file itself outweighs the one-time speed bump entailed in converting the raws to DNG. But if you want to use your camera vendor's converter, and your camera doesn't write DNG, you should stick with proprietary raws for your working files, at least for now.

To control how Bridge handles Camera Raw Settings, see "Camera Raw Preferences" earlier in this chapter.

How do you want to name your files? If you'd like to name your files consistently instead of accepting the rather meaningless default camera file names, we suggest the following two simple rules:

▶   Adopt a naming convention that makes sense to you, and stick to it (in other words, be consistent).

▶ If you want that name to be consistently readable across platforms and operating systems, stick to alphanumeric characters—no spaces (the underscore is a good alternative), and no special characters.

The only place a period should appear is immediately in front of the extension—today's operating systems tend to treat everything following a period as an extension, and promptly hide it, so periods in the middle of filenames often cause those filenames to be truncated. Many special characters are reserved for special uses by one or another operating system. Including them in filenames can produce unpredictable results. For example, in Mac OS X, if a filename starts with a period, the system treats it as an invisible file, and it's a good idea to avoid colons or any type of slash character.

It's worth the time to put a lot of thought into your file naming convention and to test it all the way through your workflow before you use it in production so that you can watch for potential gotchas. For example, how do you distinguish a raw file from its derivative files, such as a layered Photoshop version for print, a mid-resolution version for HDTV, and a low-resolution sRGB JPEG for the Web? Conrad likes to use a unique date-based base filename for an image (such as 20070418-463) and add a consistent set of characters to tell him which variant it is (such as 20070418-463_PRT.psd and 20070418-463_WEB.jpg).

Another question to consider is how you want the images to sort. Do you want images to list in proper order when you sort by name? Then you'll want to number using leading zeros, and if you use the date in the filename, you'll want to use a year-month-day convention. For example, for June 2, 2007, you'll want to write dates as 2007-06-02, not 6-2-07.

Once you settle on a filename convention, you can craft the Adobe Photos Downloader or Tools > Batch Rename dialog to rename your incoming files consistently.

What's your system for rating and labeling images? Bridge and Camera Raw offer two independent mechanisms, labels and ratings, for flagging images. The ratings system mimics the time-honored practice of making selects on a light table by marking the keepers from the first round with a single dot, adding a second dot to the keepers from the second round, and so on. Of course, the primary difference between labels and ratings is that ratings are on a scale, while labels aren't. For that reason, we recommend that you reserve ratings for ranking images. It's entirely up to you what labels mean.

There are different philosophies for rating images. Some photographers always start at one star and use successive passes to narrow down the images by adding additional stars, reserving five stars for only the very best images. Others use three stars as a baseline, with four and five stars marking keepers, and one and two stars marking alternates. Ratings can be read by other software that understands IPTC metadata, so if you hand off images to someone else down the line, you may want to make sure that you use a rating systems that meshes well with theirs.

Labels are available for purposes that aren't easily taken care of using keywords, ratings, and other metadata, and labels are often used only temporarily during the editing process. For example, you might use a label to mark just the images you want to upload to an online gallery, or to mark images with unusual lighting conditions that require special attention. For more information, see "Rating and Labeling" and "The Filter panel" later in this chapter.

Working the flow. These four issues—Bridge cache, Camera Raw settings, naming conventions, and rating/labeling strategies—are things that can't be changed later without considerable pain. By all means, spend some time trying out the options before setting your strategies in stone, but once you've found the approach that works best for you, don't change it arbitrarily. If you do, you risk losing work, whether it's Camera Raw edits, Bridge thumbnails, or ratings, or simply winding up with a bunch of incomprehensibly named files. Any of these violates the first workflow principle—do things once, early, and efficiently. When you don't, you pay for it with that most precious commodity: your time.

The best way to resolve the four issues is to take a workflow view that's both long and wide. Think of every way that you're likely to use your images at every stage of your workflow, and all of the problems you've encountered in your experience. The more you design workflow standards that take into account your entire workflow and the requirements of yourself and your clients, the more easily you can reduce and avoid unwanted complexity, inconsistency, and unintended consequences.

Image Previews and the Cache

It isn't hard to build an image manager for most image formats. File formats such as JPEG are so familiar and computers so fast now that you just read the file and make a little thumbnail if it doesn't already have one.

Sounds simple, but it isn't that simple for raw file formats. By definition, raw images are records of sensor impulses that have not yet been converted into RGB channels, so for you to be able to see a raw image in a file manager such as Adobe Bridge, one of two things needs to happen: Either the file needs to provide a prerendered preview of the contents, or the viewing software needs to generate a preview from the raw data as fast as it can. In practice, both happen. When you shoot in raw format, your camera embeds a preview image in the raw file. That's good, but not necessarily good enough. The preview represents only the default rendering of the camera, and depending on how you set your camera, the preview may not even be at full resolution. Besides, as soon as you use any software to make any adjustment to a raw file, the built-in preview immediately becomes inaccurate.

Fortunately, Bridge can generate its own preview from a raw file. As soon as you point Bridge to a folder of raw files, it uses the Camera Raw engine to generate thumbnails and generously sized previews that allow you to make good judgments about each image without actually converting it, so that you can quickly make your initial selects.

Note that the previews are based on the Camera Raw default settings for your camera. If you find that they're consistently off, it's a sign that you need to change the default develop settings for your camera (see "Using Camera Raw Defaults" earlier in this chapter).

Bridge stores image previews in its cache. Bridge will seem slow when you view images for which a cache hasn't been built yet, so for best performance, try to set aside time to let Bridge build the cache for a folder you need to work on; see "Verifying Images" earlier in this chapter. As you edit raw files, Bridge updates the previews so that they accurately represent all of the adjustments you've made.

Bridge also gives you control over how the cache works in the Cache panel of the Preferences dialog (see "Cache Preferences" later in this chapter) and in the Tools > Cache submenu (see "Cache Commands" later in this chapter).

The Preproduction Phase

Preproduction generally means doing the minimum number of things to the maximum number of images so that you can quickly get to the point where you can pick the "hero" images that are truly deserving of your time, while leaving the rejects ready for revisiting.

Because the order in which you perform preproduction tasks—such as selecting, sorting, renaming, assigning keywords, and so on—isn't critical, the order in which we'll discuss them is arbitrary. In those cases where the result of one task depends on the prior completion of another, we'll point that out.

We do, however, offer one golden rule: Start with the operations required by the largest number of images, and complete these before you start handling individual images on a case-by-case basis. For example, the first thing we always do with a folder full of new raw images is to select all the images and enter our copyright notice by applying a metadata template.

Similarly, if you know that you want to add the same keyword or keywords to all the images in a shoot, do it early (see "Applying Keywords and Metadata," later in this chapter). But if you don't care about copyrighting or keywording your rejects, you can make your initial selects first.

Evaluating and Comparing

One of the most useful improvements to Bridge CS3 is in the area of evaluating and comparing images, which you need to do before you can rate and label images. You can now preview multiple images at the same time and use a loupe to see image details and compare sharpness. Unfortunately, these functions don't appear in the user interface at all, so you can only discover them by accident or learn about them in a book (voilà!).

Tip: If the Preview panel isn't big enough for you, you can do a fair bit of evaluating, rating, and labeling in Slideshow mode. Choose View > Slideshow, press H to view the zoom, rating, and labeling shortcuts, and then do these tasks full-screen.

Evaluating a single image. To evaluate an image, make sure the Preview pane is visible and select an image in the Content panel to make it appear in the Preview panel. When you're purely evaluating images, you may want to create a workspace with a large Preview pane so that the image is easier to see. To inspect an image in detail, click the Preview image to bring up a loupe (see **Figure 5-48**), which you can drag around an image. You can zoom the loupe by pressing the plus (+) or minus (-) keys. When you drag the loupe in a way that would push it off the edge of an image, it automatically flips around so that you can still see it. To put the loupe away, click the loupe again—we find that it sometimes takes a couple of tries.

Comparing multiple images. To compare up to nine images at the same time (see **Figure 5-49**), select more than one image in the Content panel

Figure 5-48
Evaluating an image with the loupe

Click the preview to bring up the loupe

Figure 5-49
Comparing multiple images, each with its own loupe

Tip: To use an entire second monitor for previewing images, choose Window > New Synchronized Window, put the new window on a second monitor, and display only the Preview panel in that window. Because it's synchronized, the second window updates as you change the selection in the Content panel. This is especially useful if you need more space to compare multiple images.

using the standard shortcuts for selecting multiple images (Shift-click or Command/Ctrl-click depending on which images you want to select). You can't zoom images in the Preview panel, but you can click to add a loupe to each image by clicking each one of them. For example, if you want to see which of five images has the eyes in sharpest focus, click and drag a loupe to the eye in each image.

The key (literally) to using multiple loupes is the Command key (Mac) or Ctrl key (Windows). If you have multiple loupes in position in different images and you want to move them all at the same time, Command-drag (Mac) or Ctrl-drag (Windows) any of the loupes. To change the zoom level of all loupes simultaneously, hold down Command (Mac) or Ctrl (Windows) as you press the plus (+) or minus (-) keys.

In Bridge CS2, the only way to inspect images was to go through the slow process of opening them in Camera Raw and zooming in. We think the multiple-image capability and loupe are overdue and very welcome.

Rating and Labeling

Ratings give you a way to separate the keepers from the rejects. Labels let you mark images for any reason. Ratings and labels become part of the image's metadata that you can use to search and to filter which images get displayed.

The fastest way to apply ratings and labels is with the keyboard. Many photographers and photo editors are used to looking at image after image and pressing a key to rate them. All of the ratings and labels shortcuts are listed on the Label menu in Bridge CS3. You can use the same shortcuts in Camera Raw if you've opened multiple images so that the filmstrip is visible in Camera Raw.

You can also apply ratings in the Content pane or Camera Raw by clicking or dragging in the star ratings area under a thumbnail. In the Content pane, you may need to enlarge the thumbnail until you can see the row of stars.

Bridge CS3 and Camera Raw 4 support the new Reject rating. The Reject rating was added because many photographers requested a way to mark images that they didn't even want to rate. At first glance it might seem that you could leave the rating blank, but it was not always clear whether no rating meant "have not rated yet" or "do not want." Some photographers used a label to mark rejects, but this also caused problems because labels aren't defined the same way by different users or programs, while ratings are more consistently used. The Reject rating solves all of these problems.

Bridge makes it easy to rapidly narrow the field by applying ratings and then using the Filter panel to display files by their rating. You'll usually need multiple passes to complete the process.

Choose a rating workspace. Start by choosing a workspace that makes it easy to apply and view images and ratings. We suggest the Horizontal Filmstrip workspace (see Figure 5-49), which you can quickly apply by pressing Command-F5 (Mac) or Ctrl-F5 (Windows). You can also choose it from a numbered workspace button at the bottom right corner of a Bridge window or from the Window > Workspace menu.

Mark the rejects. Select the first image and decide whether you want to keep using it. If you're positive that don't even want to save it, reject it by pressing Option-Delete (Mac) or Alt-Delete (Windows). The word "Reject" will appear in red below the image (see **Figure 5-50**). Your rejects don't have to be definitive at this point, because you're not going to delete them just yet. You can add more rejects later. However, rejects should be images that are just plain unusable—bad compositions, unwanted facial expressions, exposures that can't be saved with any tools, that sort of thing.

Figure 5-50
Marking as a reject

*Rejects are labeled in the
Content panel*

Tip: Having trouble seeing images well enough to rate them? Try enlarging the thumbnails or selecting multiple images so that you can compare them in the Preview panel. Just remember to change the selection before you apply the rating, because applying a rating affects all selected images.

Rate the rest. In the Filter panel, click to check No Rating (see **Figure 5-51**) and make sure no other rating levels are checked. You are now seeing all of the images that haven't been rated. The great thing about the No Rating filter is that as you rate images, they become hidden, so you only see the images that still need to be rated without being distracted by the rest. Of course, if you want to see images that have already been rated, just turn on the Filter panel check boxes for other rating levels.

From here on out, it's pretty easy. Just press the keyboard shortcut for the star rating you want to apply to each image: Press Command (Mac)

Figure 5-51
No Rating filter

Click to check No Rating and display only unrated images.

Tip: You can rate or label a selected image by pressing a number key alone (without the Command or Ctrl modifier) if you open the Metadata pane of the Preferences dialog and turn on the check box Require the Command/Ctrl key to Apply Labels and Ratings. You might prefer to leave that preference off to avoid applying ratings accidentally through stray keypresses. (You must still press Command/Ctrl to rate images in Camera Raw.)

or Ctrl (Windows) together with a number key from 1 to 5. To remove the rating from selected images, press Command-0 (Mac) or Ctrl-0 (Windows). Those shortcuts apply a specific rating, but if you want to bump an image's current rating up or down, press the Command/Ctrl key along with the comma key (,) to lower the rating by one star, or the period key (.) to raise the rating. It may make more sense to remember those two keys by their Shift meanings, the less-than sign (<) and greater-than sign (>), because that's what they do to the rating. Don't press Shift to apply them, though.

After you rate an image, press an arrow key to move to another image in the Content view or Camera Raw filmstrip.

Don't feel that you have to get all your ratings right the first time. You can always go back and adjust them. Some photographers prefer to rate shots all in one pass. Others use a multiple-pass method, applying one star first, then making another pass to add another star to the standouts, and repeating that until they find their four- or five-star images. It's all up to you.

Tip: If thumbnails appear without label and rating information under them, check the View menu to make sure that the Show Thumbnail Only command is not checked.

Labels. While the stars are incremental, labels are not—they're simply arbitrary markers. You can apply any of the first four labels by pressing the Command (Mac) or Ctrl (Windows) key together with a number key from 6 to 9 (see **Figure 5-52**).

Labels are less portable than ratings. Your labels will show up as white on any machine that uses a different label definition than yours, which is almost certain to happen if you use something other than the default label definitions (red, yellow, green, blue, and purple), and reasonably likely to happen even if you do use the default definitions, since the recipient may

Figure 5-52

Labeled images
in the Content
and Filter panels

not. They can always search for your label text, but it's probably simpler just to use ratings.

For more information, see "Rating, Labeling, and the Label Menu" later in this chapter.

Applying Camera Raw Settings Using Bridge

To work efficiently, look for and select images that require approximately the same edit. Once you've done so, you can apply the edits in any of the following three ways (or mix and match the techniques as required). Remember, at this stage in the workflow, you're simply aiming for good, not perfect. (Perfect comes later, when you've whittled the images down to the few you'll actually deliver.)

Edit by example in Bridge. Select the first of the images that need the same edit, then open it in Camera Raw. The choice of host application—Bridge or Photoshop—depends on what else is going on. If Photoshop is busy batch-processing files, host Camera Raw in Bridge. If Bridge is busy building the cache, host Camera Raw in Photoshop. If they're both busy, host Camera Raw in Bridge—Bridge's multithreading lets you work in Camera Raw even while Bridge itself is busy doing other tasks.

Make your edits—white balance, exposure, whatever the image needs—and then dismiss the Camera Raw dialog by clicking Done (it's the default option in Camera Raw hosted by Bridge, but not in Camera Raw hosted by Photoshop).

Now, from the Apply Camera Raw Settings submenu (in Bridge's Edit menu), choose Copy Camera Raw Settings, or press Command-Option-C (Mac) or Ctrl-Alt-C (Windows). Then select all the other images that need the same edit and choose Paste Camera Raw Settings or press Command-Option-V (Mac) or Ctrl-Alt-V (Windows). If necessary, select the combination of subsets or settings you want to apply from the Paste Camera Raw Settings dialog first (see "Select, Find, and Edit with the Edit Menu," later in this chapter).

This approach works well when you need to apply the same settings to a large number of images that are identifiable by relatively small thumbnails, because you can select them quickly. But if you need to make small changes to the settings for each image, the following two approaches are better ideas.

Edit by applying presets. If you've saved presets for Camera Raw in the Settings folder for Camera Raw (see "Loading and Saving Settings" earlier in this chapter) you can apply them to all the selected images by choosing Apply Camera Raw Settings from Bridge's Edit menu, then choosing the settings or settings subsets from the submenu. Saving settings subsets as presets is particularly powerful, because you can simply choose them in succession. Each one affects only the parameters recorded when you saved it, so you can load a preset for White Balance, followed by one for Exposure, Brightness, Contrast, Calibrate settings, and so on.

Edit in Camera Raw. The method that offers the most flexibility is to open multiple images in Camera Raw. The number of images you can open in Camera Raw depends on how much RAM is available. As a result, you can open more images in Camera Raw when you host it from Bridge rather than Photoshop, simply because Bridge doesn't need as much RAM as Photoshop.

That said, it's more practical to work with smaller sets of images. If you open ten or more images, you'll get a dialog asking if you really want to open ten files. We recommend clicking the Don't Show Again check box, and cheerfully opening as many images as your machine can reasonably handle without bogging down (if the hardware is at all recent, it's almost certainly a considerably larger number than 10).

When you open multiple images, Camera Raw works in Filmstrip mode, which contains the Synchronize button so that you can transfer settings from one image to any other images selected in the filmstrip. For all the details about that, see "Filmstrip Mode" earlier in this chapter.

You can mix and match these approaches. Editing in Camera Raw brings you the benefits of zoomable previews and Undo. (And if you simply can't resist the temptation, you can fine-tune individual images too.)

All About Metadata

Metadata (which literally means "data about data") isn't a new thing. The File Info dialog in Photoshop has allowed you to add metadata such as captions, copyright info, and routing or handling instructions for years. But digital capture brings a much richer set of metadata to the table.

Most current cameras adhere to the EXIF (Exchangeable Image File Format) standard, which supplies with each image a great deal of information on how it was captured, including the camera model, the specific camera body, shutter speed, aperture, focal length, flash setting, and, of course, the date and time.

IPTC (International Press Telecommunications Council) metadata has long been supported by the File Info dialog, allowing copyright notices and the like. Other types of metadata supported by Photoshop include GPS information from GPS-enabled cameras (it's immensely cool that our good friend Stephen Johnson's stunning landscape images include GPS metadata that will allow people to identify where they were shot ten or 100 years from now, and note how the landscape has changed). You apply Camera Raw settings as metadata to instruct Photoshop how you want the image to be processed before actually doing the conversion. You can even record every Photoshop operation applied to the image as metadata using the History Log feature.

Adobe has been assiduous in promoting XMP (eXtensible Metadata Platform), an open, extensible, W3C-compliant standard for storing and exchanging metadata. All the Creative Suite applications use XMP, and because XMP is extensible, it's relatively easy to update existing metadata schemes to be XMP-compliant. However, it will probably take some time before all the other applications that use metadata, such as third-party digital raw converters, get updated to handle XMP. But let's be very clear: XMP is not some proprietary Adobe initiative. It's an open, XML-based standard. So if you find that another application is failing to read XMP metadata, contact the publisher and tell them you need them to get with the program!

Right now, metadata is mostly used to help organize and find images, but examples of other innovative uses are starting to appear. For example, Camera Raw 4 can optionally apply different default processing settings depending on the ISO speed setting and even the camera serial number, both found in image metadata. The more information you have about an image, the better your chances of being able to do useful things to it automatically; and the more things you can do automatically, the more time you can spend doing those things that only a human can do, like exercising creative judgment.

Sorting and Renaming

By default, Bridge sorts images by filename, so new images appear in the order in which they were numbered by the camera. However, as we noted earlier, you can vary the sort order by choosing any of the options at the top of the Filter panel (see **Figure 5-53**), or in the View > Sort submenu.

You can also create a custom sort order by dragging the thumbnails around, just as you would with chromes on a light table. When you do so, the Manually item on the Sort menu is checked. Your custom sorting order is stored only in the Bridge cache for the folder. If you move or rename the folder, Bridge will still remember the sort order. But if you combine images

Figure 5-53

Filter panel sorting controls

— *Sort order control; click to reverse current sort order*

Sort criteria pop-up menu

from several folders into a different folder, you have in effect created a new sort order, and it may well not be the one you wanted. So a simple way to preserve that order is to use Batch Rename to rename the images including a numbering scheme that reflects your custom sort order (see "The Tools Menu," later in this chapter).

Applying Keywords and Metadata

The key to being efficient with keywords and metadata is the same as that for being efficient with applying Camera Raw edits: Look for and select images that need the same treatment, and deal with them all at once.

IPTC metadata. The only metadata that is editable in Bridge (or in Photoshop, for that matter) is the IPTC metadata. For recurring metadata such as copyright notices, metadata templates provide a very convenient way to make the edits (see "Using Metadata Templates," later in this chapter).

Alternatively, you can select multiple images and then edit the metadata directly in the Metadata panel (see **Figure 5-54**). Click in the first field you want to edit and type in your entry. Then press Tab to advance to the next field. Continue until you've entered all the metadata shared by the selected images, and then click the check mark icon at the lower right of the panel, or press Enter or Return, to confirm the entries.

Keywords. Keywords show up in the IPTC section of the Metadata panel, but you can't enter or edit them there; you have to use the Keywords panel (see **Figure 5-55**). The Keywords panel contains individual keywords grouped into sets (represented by the folder icons). The default keywords and sets are pretty useless unless you know a lot of people called Julius or Michael, but you can easily replace them with ones that are more useful for your purposes.

To apply a keyword, select one or more images and then click in the column to the left of the keyword. A check mark appears in the column, and Bridge writes the keyword to each file (or its XMP sidecar file, or to the Camera Raw database if the file is read-only). To remove a keyword, select the images and then turn off the check mark.

Figure 5-54
Editing the Metadata panel

Deleting a keyword from the Keywords panel doesn't delete the keyword from any images to which it has been applied; it only deletes it from the panel. So it makes sense to store in the panel only the keywords you know you'll use a lot. For keywords that apply only to the current session, we create them in a set called Temp and delete them when we're done, to keep the panel manageable.

Bridge CS3 replaces the keyword sets of Bridge CS2 with hierarchical keywords. The Keywords panel doesn't look any different in this respect, but it does work differently. You can still create a parent keyword and add child keywords under it, but applying a parent keyword no longer applies all of its child keywords by default. Now you have the option of applying a child keyword or both a child keyword and its parent; Shift-click a keyword check box to accomplish the latter. For more information about applying

Figure 5-55
The Keywords panel

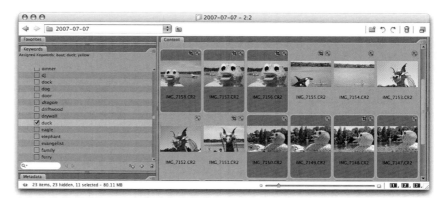

keywords and the additional new features in the Keywords panel, see "The Keywords panel" later in this chapter.

Using Metadata Templates

Let's face it: Using the Metadata panel is like filling out a form (name, contact info, copyright info, keywords, caption, city, state… you get the idea). Filling out forms is no fun, particularly if you have to do it more than once. This fact makes applying metadata seem like a chore to many people. Metadata templates go a long way toward making metadata entry much less of a chore.

A metadata template is simply a preset that contains any prefilled metadata you want. We highly recommend that you get to know metadata templates and use them thoughtfully, because they can save you a lot of time. Not only do they save time in a Bridge window, but you can also apply a metadata template as you import images from a camera (see "Copying Files from a Camera" earlier in this chapter) so that images already have your fundamental metadata before you first view them in Bridge.

Use the Create Metadata Template command to make a new metadata template. As with all metadata commands, you can find this command under the Tools menu (choose Tools > Create Metadata Template), or you may find it easier to click the Metadata panel menu and choose the command there. Now you can begin creating your template.

1. To use an existing template as a starting point, choose it from the pop-up menu at the top right corner of the dialog (see **Figure 5-56**).

2. Enter a Template Name, and fill out any metadata fields that you want to include in the template.

3. Check your spelling. You don't want an error to creep into the hundreds of images that may be edited with a metadata template!

4. Make sure you turn on the check box to the left of any field you want to include in the template. To force a field to be blank, leave it blank and check its check box. Unchecked fields don't affect existing data.

5. Click Save.

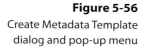

Figure 5-56

Create Metadata Template
dialog and pop-up menu

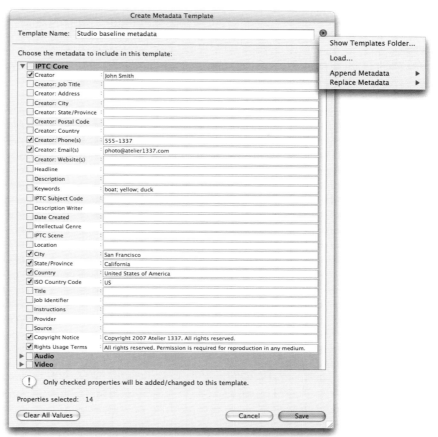

To edit a metadata template, just choose its name from the Edit Metadata Template submenu, which is on the same menu as the Create Metadata Template command.

To edit a metadata template, select the images you want to change. Then, choose the name of the template from the Append Metadata or Replace Metadata submenus, which are on the same menu as the Create Metadata Template command. The difference between Append Metadata and Replace Metadata requires a little explanation.

Append Metadata. The data in a metadata template field (such as City) is applied to the image only if the same field in the image is empty. If there's already data in that field in the image, then the template data for that field isn't applied to the image, which keeps the existing data for that field.

Replace Metadata. The data in a metadata template field always replaces the data in the same field in an image.

Note that Append Metadata and Replace Metadata only change image metadata for the fields where the check box is on. If a field's check box is off in a metadata template, neither Append nor Replace will change that field in an image.

Exchanging Settings with Lightroom

Adobe has worked hard to make sure that you can exchange metadata and Camera Raw settings between Bridge CS3 and Lightroom 1. Version numbers are important—as Adobe updates both products, their feature sets change, and one product may gain features that the other product doesn't know about and can't render or support. So watch your updates and read your ReadMe files to be aware of compatibility changes. As we write this, Camera Raw 4.1, Bridge CS3 2.1, and Lightroom 1.1 settings are completely compatible.

As we mentioned earlier, you can store Camera Raw settings and metadata separately from the images in the Camera Raw database or in XMP sidecar files, or with the image in DNG files. For Bridge and Lightroom to communicate, the one option that won't work is the Camera Raw database, because Lightroom doesn't read it. You must store settings and metadata in either XMP sidecar files or DNG files.

Even when the versions are compatible and the files are present, you've got two programs writing to the same files, and that can lead to synchronization problems. You sometimes have to be a traffic cop to make sure data goes where it's supposed to. Here are the rules of the road:

Tip: You can also keep the Lightroom Library view and file metadata up to date using folder synchronization. In the Lightroom Library module, choose Library > Synchronize Folder, make sure Scan for Metadata Updates is checked, and click Synchronize.

Bridge to Lightroom. If you're using DNG files, you're OK because the settings are inside the files that Lightroom will be opening. If you aren't using DNG files, then read on. In the General pane of the Camera Raw Preferences dialog, the Save Image Settings In pop-up menu should be set to Sidecar .xmp Files. If it isn't, then after you edit images in Camera Raw, you must choose Export Settings to XMP from the Camera Raw settings menu to create the sidecar files.

If you're in Lightroom and for some reason you don't see changes you made in Bridge, select the out-of-date images in the Library module and choose Metadata > Read Metadata From File.

Lightroom to Bridge. In Lightroom, you may want to choose File > Catalog Settings and turn on the Automatically Write Changes into XMP check box so you don't have to do it manually. We say you *may* want to choose it, because having that option on can cause a lot of CPU and disk activity in the background as Lightroom checks and updates every image in your library. If that option is off, then select the images in the Library module in Lightroom and choose Metadata > Save Metadata To File. Now the metadata is updated for Bridge to read.

You may see your Lightroom changes the next time you view that folder in the Content panel in Bridge. If you don't see the changes in Bridge, press F5 (the shortcut for View > Refresh). If that doesn't do it, you may want to purge that folder's cache (choose Tools > Cache > Purge Cache For Folder).

The Production Phase

If you started this digital workflow by bringing raw files in from your camera, no matter how much work you've done with them in Bridge and Camera Raw, if you want to be able to use those files anywhere else, you must convert them to a non-raw file format. The production phase is where you actually produce those versions of your best images, your selects.

Like so many other aspects of the digital workflow that you've seen up to this point, when it comes to the production phase, you've got choices.

▶ If you need to print an image, or you know that an image needs more work than Camera Raw can handle, you can use Camera Raw to open the image in Photoshop as a new Photoshop document. From there, you can save the image in any file format Photoshop supports.

▶ If you've been able to achieve all of the necessary adjustments and edits in Camera Raw and now all you need is a final file (such as a TIFF or JPEG file), you can save the image directly from Camera Raw and call it done.

▶ If you need to run Photoshop automation or actions on one or more images, you can use the Tools > Photoshop submenu in Bridge, which includes the powerful Batch command.

The exercise of your creative judgment is one aspect of the workflow that you can't automate, but automation can and will speed up the execution of that creative judgment. When it comes to efficiency in converting raw images, actions are the key. We generally convert raw images in batches using actions rather than simply opening them in Photoshop.

Opening in Photoshop with Camera Raw

The most basic way to open a raw image in Photoshop from Bridge is to select the image in Bridge and choose File > Open in Camera Raw or press Command-R (Mac) or Ctrl-R (Windows). In the Camera Raw dialog, verify the blue, underlined Workflow Options at the bottom of the dialog (if necessary, click the underlined text to change them), and when everything's ready, click Open Image (see **Figure 5-57**). For more information about the output options, see "Camera Raw Workflow Options" earlier in this chapter.

Figure 5-57
Camera Raw
output buttons

Tip: We like to open raw images in Photoshop as a Smart Object (clicking the Open Object button in the Camera Raw dialog), because it makes it possible to edit the raw file in that Photoshop document without re-importing it.

If you want to convert multiple images, select them in Bridge before opening Camera Raw. After the Camera Raw dialog opens, be sure to click Select All before clicking Open Images.

Keep in mind that if you turned on the Open in Photoshop as Smart Objects check box in Workflow Options dialog, the Open Image button will say Open Object instead. Whatever the button currently says, you can temporarily switch it to the alternate button by holding down the Shift key. For more information about Smart Objects, see "Smart Objects" in Chapter 11.

When you double-click a raw file in Bridge, Camera Raw opens, hosted either by Bridge or Photoshop. This depends on whether you checked or unchecked the Double-Click Opens Camera Raw Settings in Bridge preference in the General panel of the Preferences dialog in Bridge.

Saving Files Directly From Camera Raw

In Photoshop CS2, we only saved files from Camera Raw to convert them to DNGs or occasionally to generate JPEG or TIFF files. More commonly, we ran the images from Bridge through Photoshop using batch actions, because there were too many tasks that Camera Raw could not do.

This has changed. Camera Raw 4.1 has many more tone and color corrections than Camera Raw 3 did, includes spot healing and cloning, and can apply sharpening using options that are in some ways more sophisticated than anything in Photoshop, short of building your own sharpening actions. If you tend to shoot well-exposed, well-focused images, you may find that thanks to Camera Raw 4.1, many more of those images do not need to go on past Camera Raw to Photoshop, except for printing. You can export those images as final files straight from Camera Raw 4.1.

To save files from Camera Raw, select the images you want to save (if you have multiple images open in Camera Raw), and click Save Images (see Figure 5-57). Specify settings in the Save Options dialog and click Save. Most of the settings in the Save Options should look familiar: Choose a location for the saved files and customize filenaming (see "Batch Rename" later in this chapter). In the Format pop-up menu, choose Digital Negative (DNG), TIFF, JPEG, or Photoshop.

Camera Raw saves files in the background, so you can continue to work on other images in the Camera Raw dialog. While Camera Raw is saving in the background, you can close Camera Raw and do more work in Bridge, or select different images to open Camera Raw again, all without interrupting the background save operation. As Camera Raw saves images in the background, it displays a progress indicator at the bottom of the Camera Raw dialog (see **Figure 5-58**); click the underlined status text to open the Camera Raw Save Status dialog. This dialog lists all files remaining to be processed, and you can click Stop to cancel the save.

Figure 5-58
Saving multiple images in the background from Camera Raw

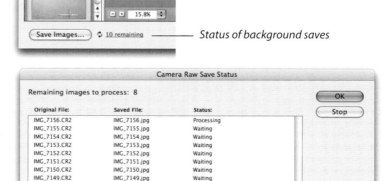

Status of background saves

*Camera Raw
Save Status dialog*

Converting Files Through Automation

Saving directly from Camera Raw is useful when you've done everything the image needs in Camera Raw, but when some images need additional work in Photoshop. The Photoshop submenu offers a variety of useful routines for creating images in a deliverable form, but by far the most powerful and flexible is the Batch command. That's what we'll tackle next.

Automating with the Batch Command

The Batch command is one of the most powerful features in Photoshop. It's conceptually very simple. You point it at a batch of images, it runs an action on them, it (optionally) renames the images, and then it does one of the following:

► Saves new files

► Opens images in Photoshop

► Saves and closes, overwriting the source files

As you'll see shortly, though, the devil is in the details, and some of the details in the Batch dialog are distinctly counterintuitive. To open the Batch dialog from within Photoshop, choose File > Automate > Batch. To batch process files from within Bridge, select the images you want to process and then choose Tools > Photoshop > Batch.

The Batch dialog is split into four different sections, each of which controls a different aspect of the batch process's behavior (see **Figure 5-59**).

► **Play** lets you choose an action from an action set that will be applied to all the images. Note that we discuss actions and how to create them in more detail later in this chapter, as well as in Chapter 11.

► **Source** lets you choose the images on which the batch will be executed, and also lets you pick some very important options we'll explore in a moment. Your choices from this menu are: a folder full of images (click the Choose button to choose the specific folder); the currently open files; images imported through the Photoshop File menu's Import command; or—when running Batch from within Bridge—the images that are currently selected in Bridge. For raw images, the source will invariably be a folder or the selected images in Bridge.

Figure 5-59

Batch dialog

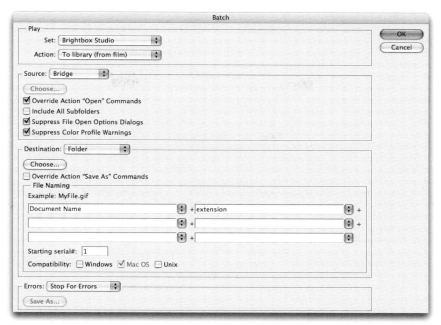

► **Destination** lets you control what happens to the processed images. Choose None to leave them open in Photoshop after processing. To save the changed files and close them, choose Save and Close (more on this soon); Folder lets you designate a folder in which to save the processed images. This section also includes the same renaming features offered by Batch Rename.

When you process raw images, you'll choose None or, much more commonly, Folder. Save and Close often ends up being a "hurt-me" button, because its normal behavior is to overwrite the source image. With raw files, this is usually impossible and always undesirable. Photoshop can't overwrite files in formats it can't write, including most raw image formats; but if you use a camera that records its raw images as .tif, there's a real danger of overwriting your raws if you choose Save and Close—so avoid it!

► **Errors** lets you choose whether to stop the entire batch when an error is encountered or log the errors to a file. We usually stop on errors when we're debugging an action used in Batch and log them to a file when we're actually running a batch in a production situation. However, when processing raw files, the batch typically either works on all files or fails on all files.

Rules for Batching Files

The difficulties that users typically encounter in running the Batch dialog are in the way the selections in the Source and Destination sections interact with the action applied by the batch operation. Here are The Rules. (Note: These are our rules, and we swear by them. They don't represent the only possible approach, but by the time you're sufficiently skilled and knowledgeable to violate them with impunity, you'll have long outgrown the need for a book like this one!)

Rules for opening files. To make sure that the raw files get opened and processed the way you want them in a batch operation, you need to record an Open step in the action. In the case of raw images, you'll want to make sure that the Settings menu in Camera Raw is set to Image Settings so that it applies the custom-tailored Camera Raw settings you've made for each image, and you'll also want to make sure that the Camera Raw workflow settings—Space, Bit Depth, Size, and Resolution—are set to produce the results you want.

Now comes one of the counterintuitive bits. If you record an Open step in the action, you must turn on the Override Action Open Commands option in the Batch dialog. If you don't, the batch will simply keep opening the image you used to record the Open step in the action. Override Action Open Commands doesn't override everything in the recorded Open command; it just overrides the specific choice of file to open, while ensuring that the Selected Image and workflow settings get honored.

Some people find this set of behaviors so frustrating and counterintuitive that they latch onto the fact that you can run Batch using an action that doesn't contain an Open step and hence doesn't require messing around with the check box. The problem with doing so is that you lose control over the Camera Raw workflow settings—the batch will just use the last-used settings. So you may expect a folder full of 6144-by-4096-pixel images and get 1536-by-1024-pixel ones instead, or wind up with 8-bit sRGB instead of 16-bit ProPhoto RGB. If you simply follow The Rules, you will have complete control over the workflow settings.

Rules for saving files. To make sure that the processed files get saved in the format you want, you need to record a Save step in the action that will be applied in Batch. This Save step dictates the file format (such as TIFF,

JPEG, or PSD) and options that go with that format (TIFF compression options, JPEG quality settings, and so on).

Now comes the second counterintuitive bit. You must turn on the option labeled Override Action "Save As" Commands in the Batch dialog, or the files won't get saved where you want them, won't get saved with the names you want, or possibly won't even get saved at all! When you turn on this option, the file format and parameters recorded in the action's Save step will be applied when saving the file, but the name and destination will be overridden by the options you specify in the Batch dialog.

Rules for running a batch operation. Two other settings commonly trip people up. Unless you turn on the Suppress File Open Options Dialogs check box, the Camera Raw dialog pops up whenever the batch opens a file, and waits for you to do something. Turning on this option just opens the image directly, bypassing the Camera Raw dialog. The Camera Raw settings for each image are used, but the batch operation isn't interrupted by the appearance of the dialog.

If the workflow settings recorded in the action result in an image in a color space other than your Photoshop working space, you should also turn on the Suppress Color Profile Warnings check box; otherwise the batch may get interrupted by the Profile Mismatch warning. The day always gets off to a bad start when you find that the batch operation you'd set up to generate 2000 Web-ready JPEGs overnight is stalled on the first image with a warning telling you that the file is sRGB when your working space is ProPhoto RGB! (This feature didn't work in Photoshop CS. Fortunately, it's fixed in Photoshop CS2 and later.)

Playing by The Rules. If you follow this relatively simple set of rules, your batch operations won't fall prey to any of these ills, and they'll execute smoothly with no surprises. If you fail to do so, it's very likely that your computer will labor mightily and then deliver either results that are something other than you desired or, even more frustrating, nothing at all!

So with The Rules in mind, let's look first at creating some actions and then at applying them through the Batch command.

Recording Batch Actions

Writing actions for batch-processing raw images is relatively simple. You don't need to worry about making sure that the action can operate on files that already have layers or alpha channels, or that are in a color space other than RGB. You're always dealing with a known quantity.

Bear in mind that if your actions call other actions, the other actions must be loaded in the Actions palette in Photoshop, or the calling action will fail when it can't find the action being called. An easy way to handle this is to make sure that any actions on which other actions are dependent are saved in the same set as the actions that depend on them.

Simple Action: Save as JPEG

Let's begin with a simple action that opens a raw image at its native resolution and saves it as a maximum-quality JPEG in the sRGB color space.

Creating an action and action set. Start out by creating a new action set called "Batch Processing" in which to save the actions you'll create in the rest of this section (see **Figure 5-60** and "Actions, Automate, and Scripting," in Chapter 11, "Essential Image Techniques.")

Creating a new action. Before creating the action, select a raw image in Bridge that has already had custom Camera Raw settings applied. That way, once you've created the action, you can start recording immediately

Figure 5-60
Creating an action set

To create a new action set, click the Create New Set button.

Enter a name and click OK.

The new set appears in the Actions palette.

without recording any extraneous steps, such as selecting a file, and you can correctly record the Camera Raw Selected Image setting.

Now click the Create New Action icon in the Actions palette in Photoshop, enter a name (such as "Save as JPEG") for the action, and then click Record to dismiss the dialog and start recording the action.

Recording the Open step. Now that you're recording, switch back to Bridge and open the image in Camera Raw by pressing Command-O (Mac) or Ctrl-O (Windows)—you must open the image in Camera Raw hosted by Photoshop. The Camera Raw dialog will appear (see **Figure 5-61**).

When you use the action in Batch, the Camera Raw dialog won't appear, so it's essential to get the settings right when you record this step. You need to record several key settings in the Camera Raw dialog.

▶ Set the Settings menu to Image Settings to ensure that each image gets opened using its own custom settings, rather than the ones you chose for this particular image.

▶ Set the Space pop-up menu to sRGB to produce a converted image that's already in sRGB, the standard color space for the Web.

▶ Set the Depth menu to 8 bits/channel, because you're simply saving JPEGs (which only support 8-bit channels), and this action won't include any operations that could benefit from a higher bit depth.

Figure 5-61
Preparing Camera Raw
for a batch process

*Click the Camera Raw
settings menu and make
sure Image Settings
is checked.*

*If the workflow options
aren't correct, click the blue
link text to change them.*

▶ Set the Size menu to the desired size (in this case, we chose 1536 by 1024).

▶ Set the Resolution field to 72 pixels per inch (to preserve the polite fiction that Web images are 72 ppi; see Chapter 12, "Image Storage and Output").

Then click OK to open the image. (If the Profile Mismatch warning appears, click OK to dismiss it. This doesn't get recorded in the action, and anyway, you'll suppress the warning when you use the action in Batch.) The image opens, and the Open step appears on the Actions palette.

Recording the Save step. To record the Save step, choose Save As from the File menu, or press Command-Shift-S (Mac) or Ctrl-Shift-S (Windows). The Save As dialog appears. The filename and the destination for saving that you enter has no impact on the batch process because you'll use the Batch dialog to specify that, so we tend to use an obvious test name such as "test.jpg" and choose the Desktop or a test folder as a destination, to simplify later cleanup.

In this example, make sure that the format is set to JPEG, and incorporate any other settings in this dialog that you want to include in the action. Then click Save to proceed to the JPEG Options dialog, set the desired quality, set the Format Options to Baseline (Standard) for maximum compatibility with JPEG-reading software, and then click OK. The file is saved on the Desktop as "test.jpg," and the Save step appears in the Actions palette. Then close the open document so that a Close step appears in the Actions palette.

Stop and save the action set. Finally, click the Stop button in the Actions palette to stop recording. Photoshop doesn't allow you to save individual actions to disk—only action sets. So if you want to save an action as soon as you've written it, you need to select the action set that contains it in the Actions palette and then choose Save Actions from the Actions palette menu (see **Figure 5-62**).

Until you save actions explicitly using the Save Actions command, they exist only in Preferences in Photoshop, and those are updated only when you choose File > Quit (Mac) or File > Exit (Windows) to close Photoshop normally. If Photoshop is unexpectedly closed for any other reason, such as a crash or power outage, any unsaved actions will be lost. So if your actions are even slightly complex, it's a very good idea to save them before

Tip: Always, always, always test and debug your actions on expendable copies of images in a test folder before you run them on the real thing. There's nothing worse than watching irreplaceable originals come out of the end of an action completely messed up because of an inadequately tested action. Similarly, we recommend that you set your actions to save processed files to an output folder, not over the original files, so that you can check them, and if necessary, chuck them if something goes horribly wrong.

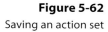

Figure 5-62
Saving an action set

doing anything else. You can save actions anywhere, but if you want them to appear automatically in the Actions palette even if you delete the preferences, save them in the Adobe Photoshop CS3\Presets\Actions folder.

When you expand the steps in the Actions palette by clicking the triangles beside those that have them, you can see exactly what has been recorded for each step (see Figure 5-62 and Figure 5-63). When you use this action in Batch with the appropriate overrides selected (see "Rules for Batching Files," earlier in this chapter) the filenames and folder locations you recorded will be overridden by the settings in the Batch dialog, and all the other settings you've recorded here—the Camera Raw workflow settings and the JPEG Save Options—will be honored.

Variants. You can create variants of this action by recording different Open or Save steps. For example, you can create larger JPEGs by changing the Size setting in the Camera Raw dialog to one of the larger sizes, and you can embed thumbnails or create lower-quality JPEGs by making those settings in the Save As and JPEG Options dialogs, respectively. To save in a different format with different options, just choose the desired format and options when you record the Save step.

Complex Action: Save for Edit

Now let's try a more complex example: an action that produces 16-bit/channel TIFFs with adjustment layers set up for final editing in Photoshop. It's designed for use on "hero" images that merit individual manual edits in Photoshop. It doesn't actually *do* any of the editing, because the required edits will almost certainly be different for each image in a batch. Instead, it simply does a lot of the repetitive grunt work involved in setting up an image for editing, so that when you open the image, all the necessary adjustment layers are already there, waiting for you to tweak them. (Or, if you don't need them, you can throw them away later.)

Create the new action. You can record this action in the same set as the previous one, since it's also designed for raw processing. As before, select a raw image in Bridge that has had custom Camera Raw settings applied before you start recording the new action. Then click the Create New Action icon in the Actions palette, enter a name (such as "Save for Edit") in the New Action dialog, and click Record to start recording.

Recording the Open step. As before, start by launching Camera Raw from Bridge by pressing Command-O (Mac) or Ctrl-O (Windows). In the Camera Raw dialog, again make sure that Settings is set to Selected Image. This time, though, you'll make some different workflow settings.

▶ In the Space menu, choose ProPhoto RGB, our preferred working space.

▶ Set the Depth menu to 16 bits per channel, because you'll want to make the edits in Photoshop in 16-bit/channel mode.

▶ Set the Size menu to the camera's native resolution.

▶ Enter 240 pixels per inch in the Resolution field, because you'll almost certainly check your edits by printing to an inkjet printer at 240 ppi (see Chapter 12, "Image Storage and Output").

Then click OK to open the image. The image opens, and the Open step appears on the Actions palette.

Adding the edits. This action adds three different editing layers to the image before saving and closing; a Levels adjustment layer; a Curves adjustment layer; and a Hue/Saturation adjustment layer, as follows.

▶ Add a Levels adjustment layer by choosing Levels from the New Adjustment Layer submenu (under the Layer menu). Just click OK to create a Levels adjustment layer that does not, as yet, apply any adjustments. Remember, you'll make the adjustments on an image-by-image basis in Photoshop; the action just does the grunt work of creating the layers.

▶ Add two more adjustment layers—a Curves layer, then a Hue/Saturation layer—and click OK when their respective adjustment dialogs appear.

Recording the Save step. As before, choose Save As from the File menu, naming the file "foo" and save it on the Desktop for easy disposal after you're finished making the action. This time, choose TIFF as the format, make sure that the Layers and Embed Color Profile check boxes are turned on (creating untagged ProPhoto RGB files is a very bad idea). Then click Save to advance to the TIFF Options dialog and make your preferred settings. (Again, see Chapter 12, "Image Storage and Output," for advice.)

Finally, close the image (to record that step in the action as well), and click the Stop button in the Actions palette to stop recording. **Figure 5-63** shows the resulting action in the Actions palette with all the steps expanded.

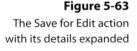

Figure 5-63
The Save for Edit action with its details expanded

As with the earlier, simpler action, when you use this action in a batch process with the necessary overrides applied in the Batch dialog, the filenames and locations will be overridden by the Batch settings, while everything else in the Open and Save steps will be honored.

Running the Batch Dialog

Using the actions we've just shown you in Batch is really very simple—as long as you remember The Rules! (If you need to take another look, refer back to "Rules for Batching Files," earlier in this chapter.) Play by The Rules, and all will go smoothly. Violate them at your peril.

Common errors. Other than choosing incorrect settings in the Batch dialog, there are three common situations that can cause a batch operation to fail.

▶ There isn't sufficient space on the destination volume to hold the processed files.

▶ No source files were selected in Bridge.

▶ Files with the same names as the ones you're creating already exist in the destination folder.

If these points seem blindingly obvious, we only mention them because they've tripped us up more than once. With those caveats in mind, let's look at setting up the Batch dialog to run the Save for Edit action you built in the previous section. As we pointed out earlier, the key settings in Batch are the overrides in both the Source and Destination sections of the panel.

Source settings. Whenever you run a batch operation using an action that includes an Open step, you must check Override Action Open Commands in the Source section. To process raw images, you also need to turn on Suppress File Open Options Dialogs—otherwise the Camera Raw dialog will pop up for every image. And whenever you run an unattended batch operation, it's a good idea to check Suppress Color Profile Warnings so that the batch process doesn't get stuck on a Profile Mismatch warning.

Destination settings. Similarly, whenever you run a batch operation using an action that includes a Save As step, you must turn on Override Action "Save As" Commands in the Destination section; otherwise the files won't get saved. **Figure 5-64** shows the Batch dialog set up to run the Save for Edit action.

Tip: If you get a "Folder Not Found" error during a batch process, check all folder paths used in the action, in actions called by that action (if present) and in the Batch dialog. Also check if you've set the Errors pop-up menu at the bottom of the Batch dialog to Log Errors To File. If you have, click the Save As button and choose that folder again to ensure it's a valid path.

Figure 5-64
Batch dialog with options
specified to run the Save for
Edit action

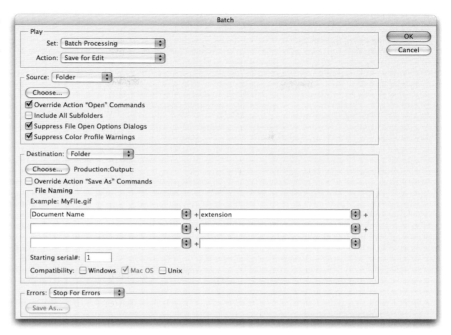

Bridge Windows

In Bridge, you can open as many windows as you like by choosing File > New Window, or pressing Command-N (Mac) or Ctrl-N (Windows). Each window can show the contents of a different folder or volume (subfolders appear as folder icons).

Bridge CS3 has a new type of window: the synchronized window (see **Figure 5-65**). Choose File > New Window, or press Command-Option-N (Mac) or Ctrl-Alt-N (Windows). When you open a new synchronized window, its panels display information with about the same content as the

Figure 5-65
Synchronized windows

Two images selected in the Content panel on the left appear in the Preview panel of the separate synchronized window on the right

Tip: If you see two numbers separated by a colon in a Bridge window title bar, you're looking at a synchronized window. For example, 2:2 means you're looking at the second of two synchronized windows.

window that was active when you created the new synchronized window. When two windows are synchronized, selecting different files in one window changes the displayed content in all windows synchronized to the first window. This gives you more flexibility in the content you can display, but the biggest benefit is that you can spread out your Bridge work area across multiple monitors. For example, you can have a synchronized window on a second monitor that contains only the Preview panel, so that you can preview a selected image at a much bigger size than when the Preview panel had to share space with other panels in just one Bridge window.

Arranging Windows

A few additional tricks can help you manage your Bridge windows. First, you can, of course, minimize windows to the Dock (Mac) or Taskbar (Windows). Also, you can set windows to either Compact mode or Ultra-Compact mode. In these modes, Bridge windows by default "float" above Full-mode windows, so they're easily available (see **Figure 5-66**). The compact modes are useful at times when you're in another application and you need Bridge close by, such as when you're laying out a publication in Adobe InDesign and dragging content into it from Bridge.

Tip: If a Bridge window doesn't respond to a keyboard shortcut, it may not be the foreground window, especially if one of the other windows is in Compact mode. To activate a Full mode window, select one or more thumbnails in that window. (It isn't enough to click the window; you actually have to select a thumbnail in the window.)

You can cycle through all open Full-mode windows by pressing Command-~ (tilde key, Mac) and Alt-Tab (Windows), but the shortcut doesn't apply to Compact or Ultra-Compact windows, so it's just as well that they float by default.

You can toggle between Full and Compact modes by pressing Command-Return (Mac) or Ctrl-Enter (Windows). The shortcut toggles between Full and either Compact or Ultra-Compact modes, depending on which of the compact modes you'd last applied to the window.

Bridge Window Panels and Workspaces

In Full mode, Bridge windows contains several panels (see **Figure 5-67**) that you can arrange into *workspaces*. Bridge provides several default workspaces that you can apply from the Window > Workspaces menu. It's faster to choose them from the three numbered buttons at the bottom right corner of a Full-mode window. Holding the mouse button down on any of the three buttons reveal the same menu of workspaces, and here's why: When you choose a workspace from any of these buttons, that workspace becomes the default for that button, so all you have to do to get that

Figure 5-66
Bridge window modes

Two images selected in the Content panel on the left appear in the Preview panel of the separate, synchronized window on the right

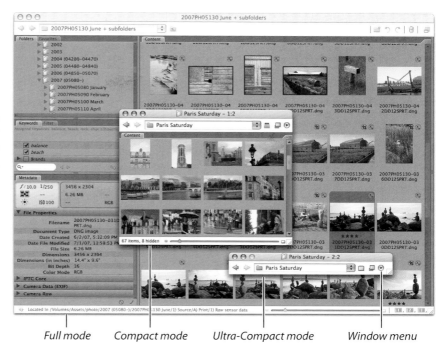

Full mode   Compact mode   Ultra-Compact mode   Window menu

The icons at the top right corner of a window let you switch between modes.

Full to Compact

Compact to Ultra-Compact

Ultra-Compact to Compact

Compact to Full

workspace next time is click that button. That means you can preset three different workspaces into those buttons for one-click access to them.

The default workspace (Window > Workspace > Default) displays all panels except for the Inspector (only useful if you're using the Version Cue file management system). The default workspace is divided into three vertical panes. The center pane contains the Content panel, which lists the files in the folder you're currently viewing. The left-hand pane contains the Favorites, Folders, and Filter panels; in other words, it determines which files you see in the Content panel. The right-hand pane contains the Preview, Metadata, and Keywords panels; in other words, it shows you details about the file you select in the Content panel. By now you may have noticed that as you go from left to right in the default workspace, the information you see about your files goes from general to specific.

We talk about each panel in more detail a little later.

Tip: Compact windows don't have to float. You control this by turning off Compact Windows Always Float on Top from a compact window's menu. But turning off floating can make Compact- and Ultra-Compact-mode windows hard to find.

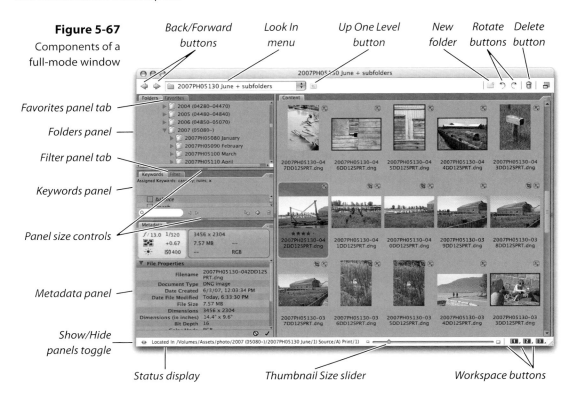

Figure 5-67
Components of a
full-mode window

Back/Forward buttons

Look In menu

Up One Level button

New folder

Rotate buttons

Delete button

Favorites panel tab

Folders panel

Filter panel tab

Keywords panel

Panel size controls

Metadata panel

Show/Hide panels toggle

Status display

Thumbnail Size slider

Workspace buttons

Bridge Tools and Buttons

Bridge's tools and buttons are arranged in three logical groups. The navigation controls are at the upper left of the window, the content controls are at the upper right, and the display controls are at the lower right.

Navigation controls. The Back/Forward buttons work like those in Web browsers, letting you move backward and forward through recently visited folders. The Look In menu shows the current folder and its path, the number of recently visited folders specified in the Preferences in Bridge, and folders or Navigation controls. You can add items to this list by choosing Add Folder to Favorites from the File menu or by dragging a folder into the Favorites panel. The Up One Level button lets you navigate upward through the folder hierarchy.

Content controls. The content controls are in a somewhat loose logical grouping, but they all affect the main window content in some way. The New Folder icon lets you create a new folder inside the folder you're currently browsing. You can do the same by pressing Command-Shift-N (Mac) or Ctrl-Shift-N (Windows). The Rotate Left and Rotate Right buttons (press

Tip: If you frequently receive images from a source other than directly from a digital camera, such as from a scanner, set up a drop folder where new images are deposited and add it to your Favorites in Bridge. Click the folder in the Favorites panel to monitor all new images as they come in.

Command-[and Command-], respectively, on the Mac, or Ctrl-[and Ctrl-] in Windows) rotate the selected thumbnails and previews and instruct Bridge to apply the rotation to the file when it gets opened. The Trash icon (press the Delete key) moves selected items to the Trash/Recycle Bin but doesn't empty it; do that from your desktop.

Display controls. The Thumbnail Size slider at the bottom of a Full mode Bridge window lets you control the size at which thumbnails in Bridge are displayed. You can also change thumbnail size using the same keyboard shortcuts for the Zoom tool in Photoshop and Camera Raw: To zoom in or out, press Command-+ (plus sign) or Command-- (minus sign) (Mac) or Ctrl-+ (plus sign) or Ctrl--(minus sign) (Windows). To the right of the Thumbnail Size slider are the three workspace preset buttons we mentioned earlier.

Bridge Panels

The main window in Bridge—the one that displays thumbnails—lets you do a great deal of your work, but the other panels are very useful for specialized tasks.

Tip: The new Bridge Home item in the Favorites panel is a great way to find information and tutorials about Photoshop and Creative Suite 3 applications if you're connected to the Internet.

The Favorites panel. The Favorites panel (see **Figure 5-68**) is a handy place for storing shortcuts to places that you often want to return to in a Bridge window. In addition to actual volumes and folders, the Favorites panel can hold *Collections*, which are saved search criteria that act as virtual folders. You can configure the preset items from the Preferences in Bridge (see "Bridge Menu Commands," later in this chapter) and you can add items to the Favorites panel by dragging or by choosing File > Add to Favorites. The Bridge Central favorite in Creative Suite 2 is replaced by Bridge Home in CS3. Also, Collections are no longer a Favorites item, because you can store them in any folder, which you can then add to the Favorites panel.

Tip: When a folder is selected in the Folders panel, you can use the right arrow and left arrow keys to expand and collapse that folder.

The Folders panel. The Folders panel (see Figure 5-68) displays the volume and folder hierarchy, allowing you to navigate to different folders. Once you click on one of the folders, you can navigate up and down the folders list using the up and down arrow keys, and you can collapse and expand volumes or folders that contain subfolders using the left and right arrow keys. Command-up arrow (Mac) or Ctrl-up arrow (Windows) moves you up to the next level in the folder hierarchy. The panel menu contains but one command, Refresh.

Figure 5-68

The Favorites
and Folders panels

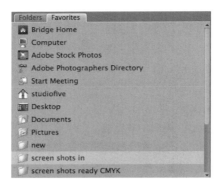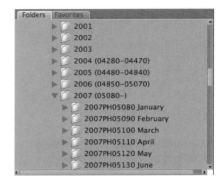

The Filter panel. The Filter panel (see **Figure 5-69**) lists some of the more useful metadata found in images in the Content panel, such as creation dates, file types, ratings, labels, and keywords so you can quickly show subsets of images. For example, if you want to see only the images in the Content panel that have a rating of five stars, just click the five-star listing in the Filter panel. The Filter panel is new in CS3 because it significantly expands on the filtering capabilities of CS2, where only a few filter options were available. The top of the Filter panel includes sort options and an extremely useful folder icon that can display the contents of all subfolders within the current folder.

The Content panel. The Content panel (see Figure 5-69) displays the files you've selected using the Favorites, Folders, or Filter panel. It displays the listed content as thumbnail images, which you can adjust in size using the slider at the bottom of the window. Although Bridge in Photoshop CS3 is primarily used with photographs, Bridge can display any file type supported by the Adobe Creative Suite, such as PDF documents or InDesign documents, so the Content panel can be useful for quickly inspecting files on your hard disks. You can get around in the Content panel using the usual keyboard shortcuts—arrow keys and the Home, End, Page Up, and Page Down keys.

The Metadata panel. The Metadata panel (see **Figure 5-70**) displays the metadata associated with the currently selected image or images (see the sidebar "All About Metadata"). When you have more than one image selected, many of the fields will likely read "Multiple Values Exist."

Metadata fields that are editable appear in the panel with a pencil icon next to the title. To edit these fields, select the images or images whose metadata you wish to edit, and then either click the pencil icon or click directly in

Tip: If you find yourself working through a list of images between Bridge and Photoshop, here's a way to run the round-trip from the keyboard: In the Content panel in Bridge, press an arrow key to go to the next image, then press Enter or Return to open the image in Photoshop. When you're done with that image in Photoshop, press Command-Option-W (Mac) or Ctrl-Alt-W (Windows) to close the image and return to Bridge in one keystroke. That's the Photoshop shortcut for File > Close and Return to Bridge.

Figure 5-69
The Filter
and Content panels

Display Subfolders button

Sort pop-up menu

Sort order icon

Clear Filter button

Keep Filter When Browsing
button

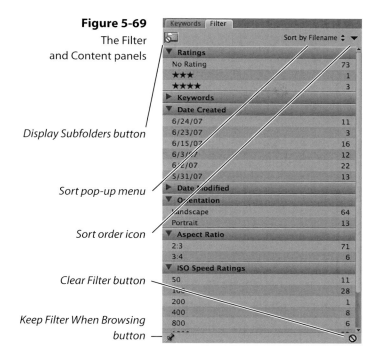

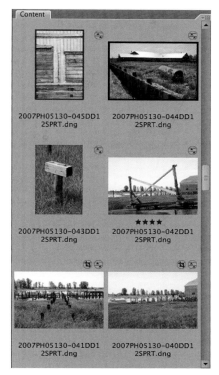

the text area to enter the new metadata. To confirm entries, click the Apply check box at the panel's lower-right corner, or press Enter (Mac) or Alt-Enter (Windows). The only IPTC field that isn't editable here is the Keywords field. To edit keywords, you need to use the Keywords panel.

The Metadata panel's menu lets you launch a search using the Find command (press Command-F in Mac OS X or Ctrl-F in Windows), which is replicated in Bridge's Edit menu; increase or decrease the font size used in the panel; and append or replace metadata from saved templates, which appear in the menu. The Preferences command takes you directly to the Metadata panel of Bridge Preferences. It's definitely worth taking the few minutes needed to decide which fields you want to display—very few Photoshop users need to see them all! There are several new metadata categories you can display (or hide) in Bridge CS3, including Audio, Video, and DICOM (medical) metadata.

The Metadata panel contains two separate sets of IPTC metadata. The older IIM (Information Interchange Model) set is there for compatibility with legacy images—it has been superseded by the new IPTC Core schema for XMP metadata. You can find out more about the IPTC standards at *www.iptc.org.*

The Keywords Panel. The Keywords panel (see Figure 5-70) lets you create keywords and apply them to a selected image or images. The keywords are written into the Keywords field of the IPTC metadata, so they're visible in the Metadata panel—you just can't edit or apply them there. Bridge CS3 contains important keyword enhancements, such as hierarchical keywords, and the ability to enter keywords by typing.

▶ To create a keyword, click the New Keyword button at the bottom of the Keywords panel, type the keyword, and press Return or Enter.

▶ To apply a keyword, turn on the check box to the left of the keyword. You can also start typing a keyword into the search field at the bottom of the Keywords panel; as you type, Bridge highlights matches in the keyword list. If the keyword you want is highlighted in green, press Return or Enter to apply that keyword. If the keyword you want is highlighted in yellow, it's an alternate match that you must select manually, either by turning on its check box with the mouse or pressing the up arrow and down arrow keys to highlight the keyword in gray and then pressing Return or Enter. If nothing's highlighted, the keyword doesn't exist yet, so simply press Return or Enter to apply the keyword and add it to the list of keywords. You can also move among highlighted alternates by clicking the Find Previous Keyword and Find Next Keyword buttons at the bottom of the Keywords panel, next to the search field. Note that the search field in the Keywords panel doesn't search for keywords in images, but in the keyword list.

▶ Bridge CS3 2.1 supports hierarchical keywords, which replace the keyword sets in Bridge CS2. To create a sub-keyword (or child keyword), click the New Sub Keyword button at the bottom of the Keywords panel. A parent keyword appears with a triangle to the left of its name, which you can click to expand and collapse the list of its sub-keywords. It's very important to understand that unlike Bridge CS2, clicking a parent keyword doesn't apply all of the child keywords, and by default, clicking a sub-keyword doesn't apply the parent keyword. If you want a parent keyword to be applied when you apply one of its child keywords, open Bridge Preferences, click the Metadata panel, and turn on the Automatically Apply Parent Keywords option (see Figure 5-74).

Tip: You can use the keyboard to turn off a selected keyword's check box the same way you turn it on: by pressing the Return or Enter key.

Tip: If you miss the keyword sets that were in Bridge CS2, you can still have them. Add a keyword in square brackets (such as [cat]) and it will function as a keyword set name instead of a parent keyword.

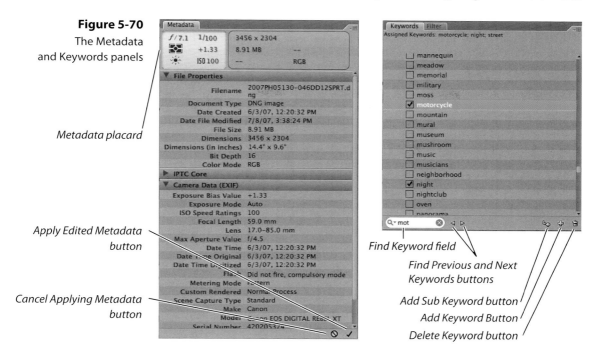

Figure 5-70
The Metadata and Keywords panels

Metadata placard

Apply Edited Metadata button

Cancel Applying Metadata button

Find Keyword field

Find Previous and Next Keywords buttons

Add Sub Keyword button

Add Keyword Button

Delete Keyword button

Bridge CS3 and Lightroom support hierarchical keywords, but as we write this, not many other programs do. If you send images to colleagues such as stock-photo agencies, who use other software, consult with them before using hierarchical keywords. You may be required to modify how your applications write those keywords into image metadata. In the Metadata panel of the Bridge Preferences dialog, the options Write Hierarchical Keywords and Read Hierarchical Keywords determine whether keywords are written to image metadata are written or read as a hierarchy or as a flat list of keywords. Both options let you customize the character Bridge uses to recognize keyword hierarchies when the character appears between keywords. Setting these options may become easier in the future if hierarchical keywords catch on and standards for handling them emerge.

The Preview panel. The Preview panel displays the selected image, always fitting the image to the size of the Preview panel. While you may be using the Preview panel primarily with photos, the Preview panel in Bridge CS3 lets you play back content such as audio, video, and Flash content, and you can turn pages in PDF files. The Preview panel is where you can display the loupe and compare multiple selected images at once, as we discussed in "Evaluating and Comparing," earlier in this chapter.

The Inspector panel. The Inspector panel is only used with the Version Cue file management system, which is outside the scope of this book.

Bridge Menu Commands

Bridge serves not only Photoshop, but the entire Creative Suite, so a good many of its menu commands aren't relevant to a digital raw workflow. Moreover, many of the menu commands offer relatively inefficient ways to accomplish tasks that can be performed more easily by other means, so we'll content ourselves with providing an overview of the menus, along with details about the commands we find particularly useful.

Preferences and the Bridge Menu

The Bridge menu, which is found only in the Mac version of Bridge, contains only one important command: Preferences (Command-K in Mac OS X or Ctrl-K in Windows). You can also open the Preferences dialog from the Camera Raw menu (see "The Camera Raw Menu" earlier in this chapter). In Windows, Preferences is on the Edit menu. The Preferences dialog contains six different panels.

General Preferences. The Appearance preferences (see **Figure 5-71**) let you customize the shade of gray for the overall user interface; the Image Backdrop actually affects the background color of the Content and Preview panels. You might have noticed that the screen shots for this book are set to a lighter gray than the default dark gray that Bridge ships with; that's because Conrad (who made the screen shots) prefers more of a middle gray.

The Behavior preference affects how files open. If you turn off the Double-Click Edits Camera Raw Settings in Bridge option, double-clicking opens Camera Raw in Photoshop instead.

Favorite Items controls what's displayed in the Favorites panel; turning off individual Favorite Items frees up space in the Favorites panel. The Reset button lets Bridge once again display all of the alert dialogs in which you've previously checked Don't Show Again.

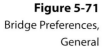

Figure 5-71

Bridge Preferences, General

Thumbnails Preferences. The Performance and File Handling (see **Figure 5-72**) options let you trade off performance and quality. The default settings try to balance the two goals. For best performance, turn off Prefer Adobe Camera Raw for JPEG and TIFF files, select Quick Thumbnails, and lower the Do Not Process Files Larger Than value. For the most accurate Bridge thumbnails in Content view, turn on Prefer Adobe Camera Raw for JPEG and TIFF files, select High Quality Thumbnails, and raise the Do Not Process Files Larger Than value.

If Convert to High Quality When Previewed is selected, by default all thumbnails display a quick preview or a preview already embedded in the file; but when you select a file (causing it to appear in the Preview panel), Bridge takes the time to generate a high-quality preview. It's a good balance between performance and quality, but it also means that you'll see a mix of quick and high-quality thumbnails.

The Details options control how much information you see in the Content panel, and whether you want to see tool tips pop up in front of images as you mouse over them. The more lines of metadata you add, the fewer thumbnails you can display. However, you can toggle between displaying thumbnails with and without metadata by choosing View > Show Thumbnail Only, or pressing Command-Shift-T (Mac) or Ctrl-Shift-T (Windows).

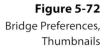

Figure 5-72

Bridge Preferences, Thumbnails

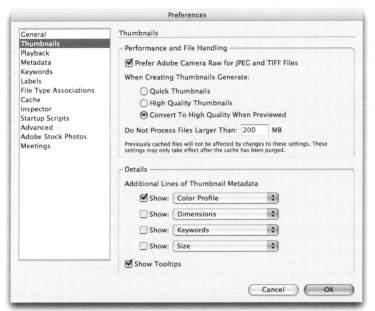

Playback Preferences. The Playback preferences apply to audio and video files, but you may find them useful if you manage audio clips that accompany your photographs, if you use the movie mode on fixed-lens (point-and-shoot) cameras, or if you preview files to use with the Video Layers features in Photoshop CS3 Extended. Most are self-explanatory, but the Stack Playback Frame Rate deserves a description—it sets the playback frame rate for the Play button that appears in a stack when you create a stack of ten or more still images.

Metadata Preferences. The Metadata preferences (see **Figure 5-73**) let you specify which metadata fields are displayed on the Metadata panel. If you don't have a GPS-enabled camera, for example, you may as well hide all the GPS fields. This panel also offers the Hide Empty Fields option, which can save space. The Show Metadata Placard option displays the section at the top of the Metadata panel that contains EXIF information (and resembles a camera LCD), and the section next to it that contains file properties. The Metadata placard duplicates information that is shown in the Camera Data EXIF and File Properties sections of the Metadata panel, but if you find the Metadata placard useful as a quick reference, you can leave the option on.

Figure 5-73
Bridge Preferences,
Metadata

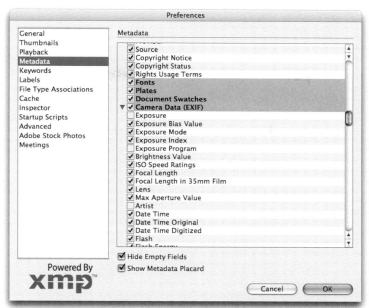

Figure 5-73
Bridge Preferences,
Metadata

Keywords Preferences. We described these options (see **Figure 5-74**) in "The Keywords panel," earlier in this chapter. In Bridge CS3, these preferences are exclusively concerned with handling hierarchical keywords.

Figure 5-74
Bridge Preferences,
Keywords

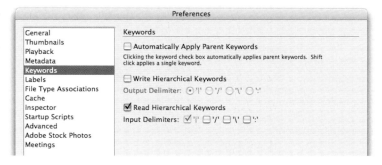

Labels Preferences. These options let you associate text with label colors (you can't change the colors) to something more useful than the color names (see **Figure 5-75**). The label text is searchable in Bridge, and can be displayed both in the Metadata panel and as an additional line of metadata accompanying the thumbnails if you choose that option in the General Preferences tab. If you change the label text in Preferences, images that have previously had labels applied lose the label color—it turns white— but the label text remains part of the image's metadata.

Figure 5-75
Bridge Preferences,
Labels

File Type Associations Preferences. These options let you specify the default application for opening files from Bridge. They apply only to the behavior you get when opening files from Bridge, and have no effect on OS-level behavior (see **Figure 5-76**).

Figure 5-76
Bridge Preferences,
File Type Associations

Cache Preferences. The Bridge cache holds the image thumbnails and previews, custom sort order, and—for file types that can't store metadata either in the file itself or in a sidecar .xmp file—label and rating information. For raw files, only the thumbnails, previews, and custom sort order are stored uniquely in the Bridge cache, but since the thumbnails and previews take some time to generate, they're pretty important.

You can let Bridge keep its cache only in a single, central location, determined by the Cache Location preference (see **Figure 5-77**) or you can have Bridge use decentralized caches, which are stored in each folder you browse with Bridge. The decentralized caches contain only the information about the items in that folder. Turn on the Automatically Export Caches to Folders When Possible check box to enable that option. The only advantage offered by using a centralized cache is simplicity—you know where all your cache files are. The significant disadvantages of the centralized cache are:

▶ If you move or rename a folder outside Bridge, the connection to the cache files is lost.

▶ When you burn a folder full of images to a CD or DVD, you first have to go through the extra step of exporting the cache. If you don't, the recipient of the CD or DVD has to take the time to recache the folder, rebuilding thumbnails and previews, and any custom sort order is lost. By the way, the "When Possible" part of the Automatically Export Caches to Folders When Possible preference refers to the fact that you can't create new cache files on a read-only volume, such as a DVD; cache updates can happen only in the Bridge centralized cache.

Figure 5-77
Bridge Preferences,
Cache

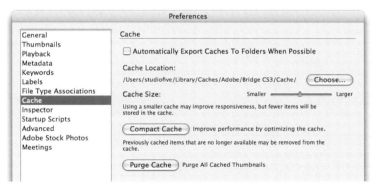

Tip: Using decentralized caches is sometimes referred to as using *distributed* caches.

Using decentralized caches avoids both problems. The cache files are written directly into the folder to which they pertain, and travel with the folder even when it's renamed or moved. But note that if Bridge for some reason can't write a decentralized cache (the volume may be read-only, or mounted on a server) it writes to the central cache instead.

The only real downside to using decentralized caches is that every folder that Bridge has opened ends up with two additional files, named Adobe Bridge Cache.bc and Adobe Bridge Cache.bct. By default, Bridge hides these files, but the Mac OS X Finder does not. In Windows, it depends on whether you've set your Folder Options to display hidden and system files. If all this file management makes you squirrely, by all means, use the centralized cache; otherwise it's well worth suffering the small inconvenience to obtain the benefits of decentralized caching. (And besides, it's often useful to be able to see the cache files so that you can check that they're present and up-to-date.)

For Cache Size, we recommend the default size or larger, unless you are running very low on disk space or have a small hard disk in a computer, such as a notebook. The Compact Cache button optimizes the cache, which can be good to do periodically. The Purge Cache button causes Bridge to rebuild thumbnails from scratch, which can help when thumbnails don't seem to reflect the actual contents of files.

Inspector Preferences. You might find this panel blank if you aren't using the Version Cue file-management system. This preference controls what displays in the Version Cue panel. Version Cue is outside the scope of this book.

Startup Scripts Preferences. Because one of the functions of Bridge is to be a central management application for the Creative Suite, it serves many masters, and the Startup Scripts panel (see **Figure 5-78**) is evidence of that. It lists all of the scripts that load various functions that you may

Figure 5-78
Bridge Preferences,
Startup Scripts

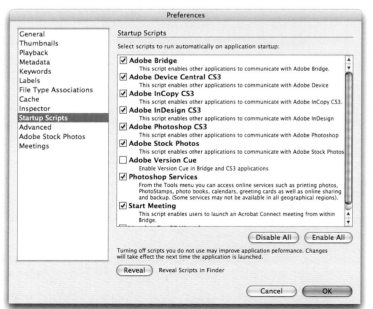

or may not care about. Scripts that you may not care about still take time to load at startup, so if you want to lighten that load and speed up Bridge a little, turn off the check boxes for any functions you don't anticipate using. You'll probably want to leave on any check boxes having to do with Photoshop and Bridge.

Advanced Preferences. This panel contains preferences that don't fit into the other categories (see **Figure 5-79**). Use Software Rendering bypasses your video card when it renders in Bridge; try working with this check box on if you believe your video card is having problems drawing content, particularly when using the loupe. The International preferences let you customize the user interface and keyboard input in case you want to set your operating system to one language but use Bridge in another.

Figure 5-79
Bridge Preferences,
Advanced

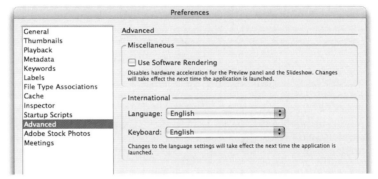

Adobe Stock Photos and Meetings Preferences. The Adobe Stock Photos and Meetings Preferences only matter if you use these features. They're online services that require accounts; we don't cover them in this book.

The File Menu
The bulk of the commands on the File menu let you do things that are better accomplished via keyboard shortcuts—opening images, creating new windows, and so on.

In the case of raw images, the subtle difference between Open (Command-O in Mac OS X or Ctrl-O in Windows) and Open in Camera Raw (Command-R in Mac OS X or Ctrl-R in Windows) is that the former opens the raw image or images in Camera Raw hosted by Photoshop, while the latter opens the raw image or images in Camera Raw hosted by Bridge. There are several easier ways to open images than choosing the menu commands, including context menus and the aforementioned keyboard shortcuts, and the ones listed in **Table 5-1**.

Three submenus on the File menu don't have keyboard shortcuts but are sometimes useful: Copy To, Move To, and Place. Copy To and Move To are quick ways to copy or move selected files to folders on your Recent Folders list. Place sends selected files to the target application; the number of applications you see on the Place menu depend on how many compatible Creative Suite applications you've installed. If you have only Photoshop, that's the only application you'll see, and if you have the entire Creative Suite, you'll see a number of applications on the Place menu. Applications that don't directly open images, such as InDesign, require that you already have a document open in the target application before you can place a file from Bridge. When placing into Photoshop, if you have a document open in Photoshop, Bridge will place an image into that document, and if there is no document open, Photoshop simply opens the file.

Most of the other commands are self-explanatory. However, the File Info command, which opens the File Info panel (see **Figure 5-80**), deserves

	To do this...	...press this.
Table 5-1 Keyboard shortcuts for opening raw images	Open raw images in Camera Raw hosted by Bridge, leaving Photoshop unaffected.	Command/Ctrl-R
	Open raw images in Camera Raw hosted by Photoshop, bringing Photoshop to the foreground and leaving Bridge visible in the background.	Command/Ctrl-O, Return/Enter, or Command/Ctrl-down arrow
	Open raw images in Camera Raw hosted by Photoshop, bringing Photoshop to the foreground and hiding Bridge.	Option-Return/Alt-Enter, or Command-Option-down arrow / Ctrl-Alt-down arrow
	Open raw images directly into Photoshop, bypassing the Camera Raw dialog, bringing Photoshop to the foreground and leaving Bridge visible in the background.	Shift-Return/Enter, or Command-Shift-down arrow / Ctrl-Shift-down arrow
	Open raw images directly into Photoshop, bypassing the Camera Raw dialog, bringing Photoshop to the foreground and hiding Bridge.	Option-Shift-Return / Alt-Shift-Enter, or Command-Option-Shift-down arrow / Ctrl-Alt-Shift-down arrow

Figure 5-80

File Info

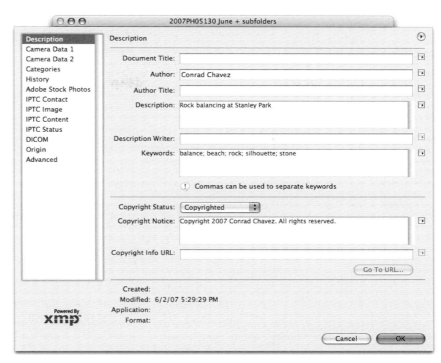

a closer look. While Bridge allows you to open File Info when multiple images are selected, it's a relatively inefficient way to apply keywords and other metadata when compared to the Metadata and Keywords panels. Nevertheless, the File Info panel is still useful for taking image-specific keywords that we don't want to save in a keyword set and adding them to small numbers of images, and for examining metadata in something close to raw form. For example, in File Info you can see exactly how the camera encodes things like shutter speed and aperture value, or the date and time a photo was shot, by looking in the Advanced panel of File Info under EXIF Properties. If you still want to create a metadata template in the File Info dialog, the metadata pop-up menu is still present under the round button at the top right corner of the File Info dialog, as it was in Photoshop CS2.

Select, Find, and Edit with the Edit Menu

In Windows, the Edit menu hosts the Bridge Preferences command. It also hosts the usual Copy, Paste, Cut, and Duplicate commands, as well as the Rotate commands (whose functionality is replicated by the Rotate buttons in Bridge). The important commands for the raw workflow are the various Select commands, the Find command, and the Apply Camera Raw Settings command.

There are a few minor changes to the Edit menu in Bridge CS3. The Select commands for labeled files are gone (you can do that more directly in the new Filter panel), and the Apply Camera Raw Settings submenu is now labeled Develop Settings.

Select commands. The Select commands offer quick ways to manipulate selections. Select All (Command-A in Mac OS X or Ctrl-A in Windows), Deselect All (just add the Shift key to the Select All shortcut) and Invert Selection (Command-Shift-I in Mac OS X or Ctrl-Shift-A in Windows) do exactly what they say—Invert Selection deselects the files that were selected and selects those that weren't. The two remaining commands, Select Labeled (Command-Option-L in Mac OS X or Ctrl-Shift-L in Windows) and Select Unlabeled (Command-Option-Shift-L in Mac OS X or Ctrl-Alt-Shift-L in Windows), work in conjunction with the Label feature in Bridge, which lets you apply one of five labels, or no label, to images. See "Rating, Labeling, and the Label Menu," later in this chapter.

Find command. The Find command lets you perform searches using a wide range of search criteria (see **Figure 5-81**), including a handy selection of metadata fields which are new in Bridge CS3, such as ISO (speed).

In addition to the criteria, the Find dialog has the following important features:

▶ **The Match menu** lets you choose whether to find files if any criterion is met (equivalent to an "or" between the criteria), or to find files only if all criteria are met (equivalent to an "and" between the criteria).

▶ **Include All Subfolders** does what it says—it extends the search to include any subfolders in the folder specified in the Look In menu.

▶ **Include Non-Indexed Files** looks at files that have not yet been added to the Bridge cache. Turning this option on may add time to the search, because non-indexed files need to be indexed.

Save As Collection. When you perform a search, you have the option to save the search criteria as a Collection. When you click the Save As Collection button, you can save the search results in any folder you want, and optionally add it to your Bridge Favorites.

Tip: The CS2 feature Show Find Results In New Browser Window option is not present in Bridge CS3, but you can create a new window before searching. If you don't create a new window, you can easily return to the previous view by clicking the Back button. Search results also appear in the Recent Folders menu, so you can always pull those up again too.

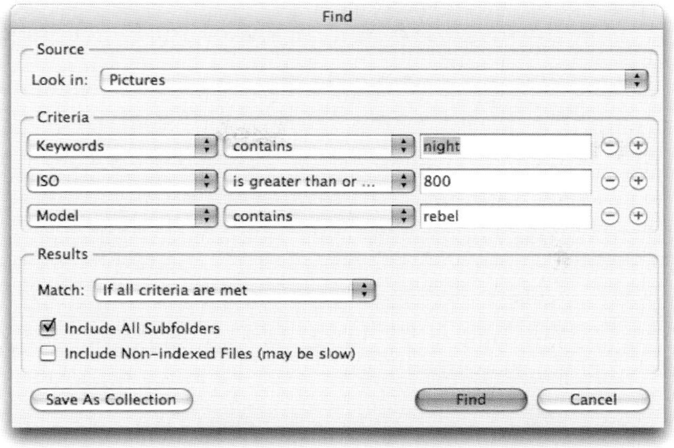

Figure 5-81

Find

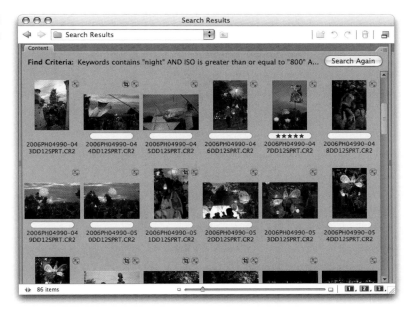

Figure 5-82

Search results

When you open a collection, the saved search runs and the current results appear (see **Figure 5-82**). To refine the search, click Search Again and the Find dialog appears so you can edit the criteria.

Develop Settings. The Develop Settings submenu lets you apply Camera Raw Defaults or Previous Conversion (the last-used Camera Raw settings) to selected images. It also lets you copy settings from an image and apply them to others by pasting, or clear existing settings from an image. Finally, it lets you apply any saved settings that you've saved in the

Settings folder for Camera Raw (see "Loading and Saving Settings" earlier in this chapter).

The difference between applying Camera Raw defaults and clearing Camera Raw settings is rather subtle. The effect on the image is identical in both cases, but Bridge offers a useful piece of feedback that shows whether or not an image has settings applied to it (see **Figure 5-83**). When you apply Camera Raw defaults, Bridge treats the image as having settings applied; when you clear the settings, Bridge treats the image as having no settings applied.

Figure 5-83

Settings icon on a thumbnail

When you choose Camera Raw Defaults or make any other edits to an image, this icon appears. If you don't see this icon, no Camera Raw edits are applied to the image.

The Copy Camera Raw Settings command (Command-Option-C in Mac OS X, or Ctrl-Alt-C in Windows) copies all the Camera Raw settings from the selected image. When you choose Paste Camera Raw Settings (Command-Option-V in Mac OS X, or Ctrl-Alt-V in Windows), the dialog shown in **Figure 5-84** appears, giving you the opportunity to choose all

Figure 5-84

Paste Camera Raw Settings dialog

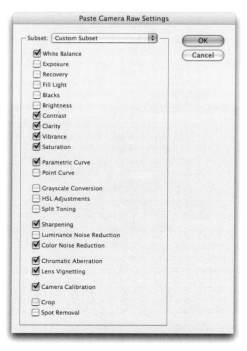

the settings, choose any individual parameter, or choose everything in between and apply your choices to the image or images to which you're pasting the settings.

Pasting Camera Raw Settings to multiple images offers an alternative to working directly in Camera Raw in filmstrip mode.

Bridge Display and the View Menu

The commands on the View menu offer a variety of controls over the way Bridge displays both its windows and their contents. In the former category, several of the commands replicate the functionality of the control buttons in Bridge's windows—Compact Mode, As Thumbnails, As Filmstrip, As Details, and As Versions and Alternates (the last is relevant for Version Cue users only). Others show and hide the individual panels—Favorites, Folders, Preview, Metadata, and Keywords.

Tip: To zoom in the slideshow, press the – or + key. To toggle between the current view and 100 percent (Actual Pixels) magnification, click the image. At magnifications above 100 percent, drag to pan the image.

Slideshow and Slideshow Options. The Slideshow command offers an alternative to Bridge's light table metaphor by presenting selected images as a slideshow; you can also enter the slideshow by pressing Command-L (Mac) or Ctrl-L (Windows). While you're in the slideshow, you can rate, rotate, and zoom the image while enjoying the benefits of a large image preview. Press H (with no modifier) to display all the keyboard shortcuts that apply in the slideshow (see **Figure 5-85**).

Figure 5-85
Slideshow
with Help screen displayed

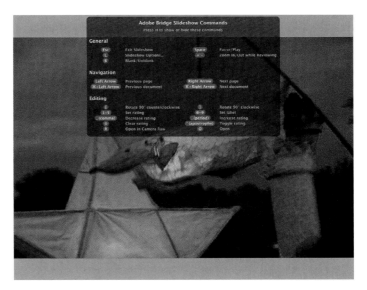

The Slideshow Options command lets you adjust how the slideshow displays, such as how the image fits on screen and whether to display its caption. It's easier to use the Slideshow Options dialog (see **Figure 5-86**) while the slideshow is running (in the slideshow, press L) because you will see the effects of your changes interactively.

Sort. You can sort the contents of the Bridge window based on the file properties listed in the Sort submenu. Or, if you sort images into a custom order by dragging their thumbnails around, you'll see a check mark next to the Manually item. Choosing Manually from the submenu has no effect unless you've previously sorted your images manually, in which case it switches to the last manual sort order you used. If you like to keep the Filter panel open, you may find that the Sort menu at the top of the Filter panel is more accessible.

Show Thumbnail Only. The Show Thumbnail Only command suppresses the display of the filenames and any other optional metadata displayed under the thumbnails in the Content panel only (see **Figure 5-87**). Press Command-T (Mac) or Ctrl-T (Windows) to toggle the metadata display.

Content filtering commands. These commands control the types of content Bridge displays in its windows. There used to be more of these commands under the View menu in Bridge CS2, but in CS3, Adobe sensibly moved most of them over to the new Filter panel, leaving only three here.

Tip: The commands for showing and hiding panels that were under the View menu in Bridge CS2 have moved to the Window menu in Bridge CS3.

Figure 5-87
Show Thumbnail Only

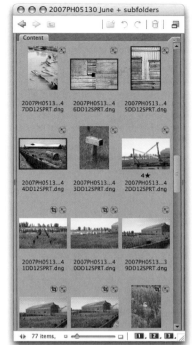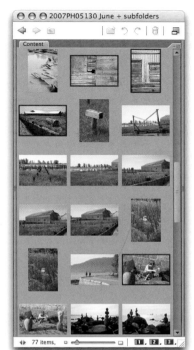

If you don't need to see titles and status icons, choose View > Show Thumbnail Only to display more thumbnails in less space.

▶ **Show Rejects** displays files marked with the Reject rating.

▶ **Show Hidden Files** displays sidecar .xmp files and Bridge cache files, as well as files that are normally hidden by the operating system, in its windows *and* in the Content panel. By default, it's turned off.

▶ **Show Folders** toggles the display of folders in the Content pane. By default, it's turned on. The only time you might want to turn this off is if you are trying to concentrate on the images in a folder and you don't want to be distracted by folders that are also stored there.

Sort. Content panel sorting options are in this menu. If the content doesn't seem to be sorting the way you think it should, check this menu. The Manually command is turned on if you rearranged content by dragging it around in the Content panel.

Refresh. Does what it says. We don't use it often, although it can come in handy if you suspect that the Content pane isn't showing the current state of a folder. If refreshing doesn't improve matters, think about purging that folder's cache (Tools > Cache > Purge Cache For Folder).

The Stack Menu

Stacks are a new feature in Bridge CS3. You can use stacks to simplify the Content panel view by grouping similar images (see **Figure 5-88**). For example, if you bracket the exposure of a scene, you can keep all of the bracketed frames in one stack by selecting the images and choosing Stack > Group As Stack or press Command-G (Mac) or Ctrl-G (Windows). When a stack is selected, you can expand or collapse it by clicking the number in the top left corner of the stack that tells you how many files are in the stack. If you want a particular image to be at the top of a stack, open the stack, select an image, and choose Stack > Promote to Top of Stack.

Bridge stacks are not to be confused with Image Stacks in Photoshop CS3 Extended (see "Reducing Noise in Image Stacks" in Chapter 10, "Sharpness, Detail, and Noise Reduction").

Figure 5-88

Stacks

Similar images can take up a lot of space in the Content panel.

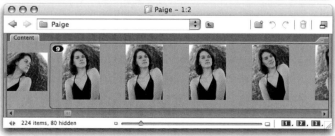

Group any selected images into a stack (Stacks > Group as Stack). The number of images appears in the top left corner of a stack.

Click the number to expand a stack.

Rating, Labeling, and the Label Menu

The Label menu offers a not-very-efficient alternative to the keyboard shortcuts for applying labels or ratings to your images. The only things you can do from this menu that you can't do with keyboard shortcuts are to remove a label and to apply the fifth label, which by default is called Purple (though you can change its name in Bridge's Preferences; see "Labels Preferences," earlier in this chapter).

Tip: To work more efficiently in Camera Raw, apply a label to images you want to process together in Bridge (you can apply a label with a single-key shortcut). Then filter the view to show each labeled group.

Labels and ratings are entirely separate. Labels apply the selected label color to the image thumbnail's label area and write the label text into the image's metadata (in the Label field under File Properties). Ratings apply zero to five stars to the image thumbnail's rating area, and write the rating (from one to five) into the image's metadata (in the Rating field under File Properties).

You can search images by label and by rating and sort images by label *or* by rating. Perhaps most usefully, you can use the Filter panel to specify which images are displayed in the Bridge window based on label, on rating, or both.

Labels and ratings are simply arbitrary flags that you can apply to images. It's entirely up to you to decide what they mean. For some suggestions on how to use these features, see "Rating and Labeling" earlier in this chapter.

Tip: The Reject rating is a good safety valve. Instead of trashing unwanted images right away, mark them with the Reject rating. When you're ready to trim down the number of images, set the Filter panel to show only rejects, review them carefully to make sure you aren't going to delete something you want to keep, and then trash them all at once.

Applying labels and ratings. By far the easiest way to apply labels or ratings is to use the keyboard shortcuts (most of which also work in Camera Raw). Look on the Label menu to see the keyboard shortcuts for each label and rating. Inside Camera Raw, the purple label can be toggled using Command-Shift-0 (Mac) or Ctrl-Shift-0 (Windows). A slower but sometimes convenient alternative is to click and drag in the rating area of the thumbnail—dragging to the right increases the rating, and dragging to the left reduces it. Last but not least, Command-' (apostrophe), toggles one star on or off. New in Bridge CS3 and Camera Raw 4 is the Reject rating.

The Tools Menu

The Tools menu provides access to several useful Photoshop-hosted automation features as well as the Batch Rename feature, allows you to manipulate Bridge's cache files, and provides an alternative means of applying metadata templates if you don't want to use the Metadata panel menu.

Figure 5-89
Batch Rename

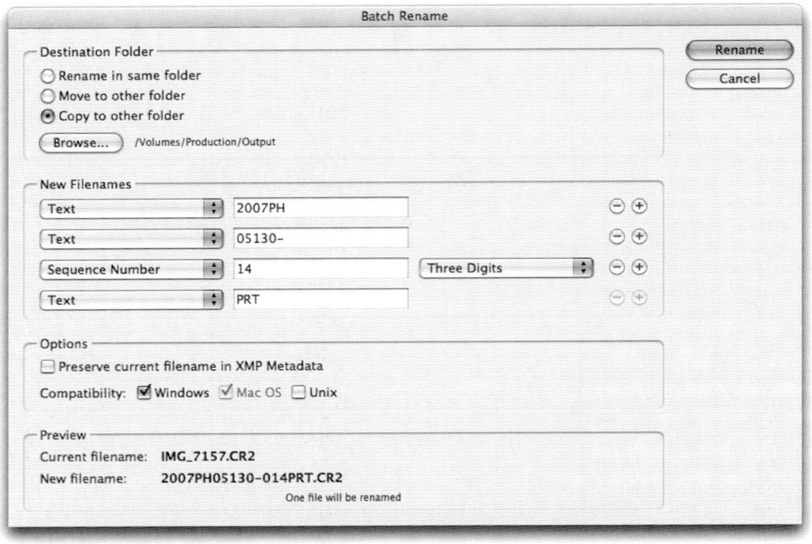

Batch Rename. In the Batch Rename dialog (see **Figure 5-89**), you can rename selected files and their filename extensions. Files are renamed in the order they appear in the Content panel, which means you can change the numbering sequence by manually reordering files before you batch-rename them.

The Preserve Current Filename in XMP Metadata option actually adds a custom metadata tag containing the current filename. If you've already applied Camera Raw settings before renaming, you can skip this option because the Camera Raw settings metadata already contains the original filename. But if you're renaming otherwise-untouched raw files and you want the original filename to be retrievable, it's a good idea to turn on this option.

Metadata Template commands. In Photoshop CS2, the only place to create and manage metadata templates was in the File Info dialog in either Bridge or Photoshop. In Photoshop CS3, Adobe wisely added a section to the Tools menu where you can more easily create, apply, and edit metadata templates. To use these commands, see "Using Metadata Templates" earlier in this chapter.

Cache commands. The Tools menu contains two commands for managing the Bridge cache. Use the Build And Export Cache command to create a cache for the current folder and subfolders and store the cache in the current folder. Use this command to build a folder cache in advance, so

Tip: The Preserve Current Filename in XMP Metadata option gives you your only opportunity to undo a batch rename. Choose File > Batch Rename again, but this time, set just one New Filenames option, and set it to Preserved Filename.

that you can have optimal performance while working with the images in that folder. Use the Purge Cache for Folder command to delete and rebuild the cache for a folder if you suspect that the cache is having problems representing the contents of the folder. When you purge a cache, attributes stored only in the cache may be deleted, such as the folder's sort order; metadata stored inside individual files should not be affected.

Photoshop submenu. The Photoshop submenu (see **Figure 5-90**) provides access to several useful features that also appear on the File > Automate menu in Photoshop. If you have any Photoshop actions that you'd like to run on multiple files selected in Bridge, this is the place to do it. To run any of these automations using images selected in Bridge as the source, you *must* launch them from the Tools menu—if you try to launch them from the File > Automate submenu in Photoshop, you'll find that Bridge is either grayed out or simply unavailable as the source.

Figure 5-90

Photoshop submenu

To invoke any of the Automate features from Bridge, use the Content panel to select the images you want processed through the automation, then choose that automation from the Tools > Photoshop submenu. Photoshop then goes to work, opening the images using the Camera Raw settings you've applied, or the camera-specific default settings (if you haven't applied settings to the image), then processing them using the settings you've specified for the automation. You can keep working in Bridge while Photoshop is processing the images. In Photoshop CS2, if you started automation from Bridge while Photoshop was busy with a previous automation, the second wouldn't start, but Photoshop CS3 can now queue automations, moving on to the next one after the previous one finishes.

Photoshop Services menu. Photoshop Services are online services that support Photoshop. For example, you can select images in Bridge and use Photoshop Services to print, store, sell, or back up your images. These services are generally provided by companies other than Adobe.

The Window Menu and Workspaces

Tip: Press the Tab key to expand the center panel and hide the side panels.

The Window menu in Bridge CS3 is considerably longer than it was in Bridge CS2. As in Bridge CS2, the Window menu contains some of the standard operating system commands such as Minimize and Bring All To Front (Mac). It also contains the Workspace submenu and the Download Status command; you'll use Download Status only if you're downloading content from an online service such as Adobe Stock Photos. Bridge CS3 also adds a list of open windows to the bottom of the Window menu, a glaring omission from Bridge CS2 that we're very happy to see in CS3.

While the Window > Workspace submenu is useful for managing workspaces, as with any submenu, it's a hassle to guide the mouse two levels deep into a menu. We think you'll prefer to control workspaces from the workspace buttons at the bottom left corner of a Full Mode window in Bridge (see **Figure 5-91**).

Figure 5-91
Workspace button menus

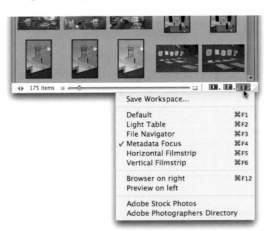

The only command that lives only in the Window > Workspace submenu is the Reset To Default Workspace command. Bridge CS3 adds the Default, Horizontal Filmstrip (see **Figure 5-92**), and Vertical Filmstrip to the list of built-in workspaces on the Workspace menu.

Figure 5-92

Two built-in workspaces: Horizontal Filmstrip and Metadata Focus

Tip: You can apply a workspace by pressing Command (Mac) or Control (Windows) and a function key; refer to the shortcuts on the Window > Workspace submenu. In Mac OS X, the VoiceOver system shortcut (Command-F5) conflicts with the Bridge shortcut for the Horizontal Filmstrip workspace, but you can redefine or turn off that shortcut in the Keyboard Shortcuts tab of the Keyboard & Mouse system preferences.

Bridge windows are eminently configurable. You can dock the panels as you wish by dragging their tabs to other panels, resize them by dragging their borders, and remove panels you don't need using the View menu commands. You can't drag a panel to another Bridge window, however.

Whenever you create a panel arrangement you like, save it as a workspace. To do this, configure a window the way you want the workspace to appear, then choose Save Workspace from the Workspace submenu, or from the menu that appears when you click and hold one of the three numbered workspace buttons at the bottom right corner of a Bridge window. Specify options (see **Figure 5-93**), and then click Save. Turn on the Save Window Location As Part Of Workspace option if you always want the window to appear in the same place (very useful on dual-monitor setups). Your saved workspace is then added to the Workspace menu.

Figure 5-93

Saving a workspace

Tip: The default workspace uses three columns of panels. You can adjust panel widths or hide panels by dragging the dividers.

We highly recommend that you select three of your favorite workspaces for the three workspace buttons at the bottom right of a Bridge window, so that all you have to do to apply one of those three workspaces is to click on the button.

For those of you who have to know where everything gets saved, workspaces are stored in Users\UserName\Library\Application Support\ Adobe\Bridge\Workspaces on Mac the and in Documents and Settings\ Username\Application Data\Adobe\Bridge\Workspaces in Windows.

Essential Photoshop Tips and Tricks

Making Photoshop Fly

The biggest speed boost you can give to Photoshop is to accelerate your own productivity. If you get paid by the hour, rather than by the amount of work accomplished, you may want to skip this chapter. If you want to realize the full potential of Photoshop as a lean, mean, pixel-processing machine, read on! We'll break you of the habit of choosing tools by clicking on their icons, and help you avoid those lengthy mouse voyages up to the menu bar.

Window Tips

As applications pile on the palettes and options, screen space remains a premium even as monitor sizes grow. Space is an even bigger challenge if you need to manage multiple windows. Use these tips to shuffle and stack windows as expertly as a Las Vegas casino dealer.

Screen modes. Click and hold the Screen Mode icon at the bottom of the Tools palette to see four screen modes. We like to cycle through the modes by pressing F. You can also pick a screen mode from the Screen Mode submenu (under the View menu), but the other ways are so much more convenient that you'll probably go to the View menu only if you're recording an action that plays back a screen mode change.

In addition to the Standard Screen Mode (regular windows), Full Screen Mode (black background with no menu bar) and Full Screen Mode with Menu Bar (gray background), Photoshop CS3 adds a new Maximized Screen Mode (see **Figure 6-1**)—a middle ground between Standard Screen Mode and the two full screen modes. As you show and hide palettes, Maximized resizes the document workspace so that it always stays out of the way of the open palettes. Maximized Screen Mode may throw off veteran Mac Photoshop users, because it is unlike either the Standard or Full Screen modes that existed in previous versions. Think of Maximized as Full Screen Mode with scroll bars. Maximized is actually welcomed by many who've switched from Windows to the Mac, because Maximized is a standard feature in Windows. We like to work in Full Screen mode instead of wasting space on title bars, scroll bars, and the like.

Note: In Photoshop CS2, each document window could have its own screen mode. In Photoshop CS3, changing the screen mode affects all document windows.

Figure 6-1
Maximized vs.
Full Screen modes

The new Maximized screen mode keeps the image centered as the palette arrangement changes. You get to keep the status bar and scroll bars.

Click here or press F to switch screen modes.

Full Screen mode takes over all screen space, even the space underneath palettes.

Tip: If you used Photoshop CS2, you may be wondering how to show and hide the menu bar. The old Shift-F shortcut in CS2 no longer works in Photoshop CS3. Instead, switch to Full Screen Mode with or without the menu bar, and change the surrounding color if needed.

Changing the surrounding color. All modes surround the document with gray except for Full Screen mode, which is black. To change this, Control-click (Mac) or right-click (Windows) the surrounding area and choose an option from the context menu that appears. You can also change the surrounding color by Shift-clicking the Paint Bucket tool, but frankly, that's more work because we can never remember where the Paint Bucket is hiding in the Tools palette. (Psst… it's under the Gradient tool.)

Full Screen scroll. Just because your image is in Full Screen mode doesn't mean you can't scroll around: Just hold down the spacebar (to get the Hand tool) and drag. In the Full Screen mode, you can use the Hand tool to slide past the edge of the image into the gray or black area, no matter how far you're zoomed in; going past the edge is something scroll bars can't do (see **Figure 6-2**). Scrolling past the image edge is useful when you're cropping or retouching close to the edge of an image, and it's a big reason Conrad prefers the Full Screen mode over the Maximized mode.

Figure 6-2
Seeing image handles beyond the image edge in Full Screen Mode

Tip: If a document opens at too low of a magnification, try closing palettes. Photoshop wants to show you the whole document when you first open one, and there's less space to show everything when more palettes occupy the workspace.

Tidy up your windows. When you have multiple document windows open, Photoshop will neatly arrange them on your screen if you choose Tile Horizontally, Tile Vertically, or Cascade from the Arrange submenu (under the Window menu). The Tile commands display windows side-by-side, while Cascade stacks the windows with a slight offset.

Flip through the windows. We often find ourselves in Photoshop with five or more windows open at a time—a frustrating situation when we need to move through them all quickly. You can press Control-Tab to switch from one open document to the next. (In this case, it's the Control key on both Mac and Windows.) This way, you can rotate through the windows without taking your hands off the keyboard, even if you're in Full Screen mode with no menus.

Two windows on the same document. Are you often jumping back and forth between two views? For example, between different magnifications, color modes, or preview modes? If so, consider opening a second window by selecting New Window from the Arrange submenu (under the Window menu). Whenever you change something in one window, Photoshop updates the other window almost immediately.

Tip: In Windows, a menu with document commands appears if you right-click a document's title bar.

From window to folder. To open another image in the same folder as a document currently open in Photoshop in Mac OS X, Command-click on the title in the document window's title bar and select the folder from the pop-up menu that appears. This tells Photoshop to switch to the desktop and open that folder. In Windows, you can see a document's folder path by holding the cursor over a document's title bar until a tool tip appears.

Navigation Tips

In this section, we first explore some of the fastest ways to move around your image, including zooming in and out. Then we discuss moving pixels around both within your document and from one document to another. It's funny, but we find that even expert users forget or never learn this basic stuff, so we urge you to read this section even if you think you already know all there is to know about navigating Photoshop.

Magnification

Images have pixels. Computer monitors have pixels. But how does one type of pixel relate to the other type of pixel? When one image pixel is displayed on one monitor pixel, you're seeing every detail of the image. In Photoshop, this happens at 100 percent magnification, or the Actual Pixels command under the View menu. This view doesn't necessarily tell you how big the image will appear in print or even on the Web, because different monitors have different resolutions.

At 400 percent, the image is magnified four times, so each image pixel is displayed using 16 monitor pixels (see **Figure 6-3**). At 50 percent, you're seeing only one-quarter of the pixels in the image, because zooming out

Figure 6-3
How magnification affects
the image detail you see

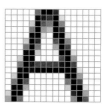
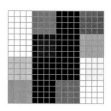
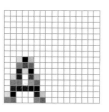

At 100% magnification,
(Actual Pixels view)
one monitor pixel
represents
one image pixel

At 400% magnification,
16 monitor pixels
represent
one image pixel

At 50% magnification,
one monitor pixel
represents
16 image pixels

causes Photoshop to downsample four image pixels to one monitor pixel. At any percentage other than 100, you're not seeing a fully accurate view of your image, because you aren't seeing the exact number of pixels in the image.

When you're viewing at an integral multiple of 100 (25, 50, 200, 400 percent, and so on), Photoshop displays image pixels evenly. At 200 percent, four screen pixels (two horizontal, two vertical) equal one image pixel; at 50 percent, four image pixels equal one screen pixel, and so on. However, when you're at any "odd" percentage, the program has to jimmy the display in order to make things work. Photoshop can't cut a screen pixel or an image pixel in half, so instead it fakes the effect using anti-aliasing. Magnifications lower than 100 percent can give you a distorted view of resolution-dependent effects, such as sharpening.

The moral of the story is that you should always return to the Actual Pixels (100 percent) view to get the most accurate view of your image. You'll be doing this all the time, so learn the shortcuts: Command-Option-0 (zero) (Mac) or Ctrl-Alt-0 (Windows), or double-click the Zoom tool in the Tools palette.

Tip: The maximum zoom percentage has been raised to 3200 percent in Photoshop CS3.

Don't select the zoom tool. We never select the Zoom tool from the Tool palette because it takes too long. You can temporarily switch to the Zoom tool by holding down Command-spacebar to zoom in or Command-Option-spacebar to zoom out (Mac), or Ctrl-spacebar to zoom in or Ctrl-Alt-spacebar to zoom out (Windows). Each click is the same as choosing Zoom In or Zoom Out from the View menu.

Drag to zoom. When you drag a rectangle using the Zoom tool, the area you drag magnifies to fill the window.

Zoom with keyboard shortcuts. If you just want to change the overall magnification of an image, zoom in and out by pressing Command-+ (plus sign) or Command-- (minus sign) in Mac OS X, or by pressing Ctrl-+ (plus sign) or Ctrl-- (minus sign) in Windows. When zooming, the window won't extend under the edges of palettes; if you want this to happen, use one of the Full Screen modes. In Mac OS X, adding the Option key to this mix tells Photoshop to zoom in or out without changing the size of the window. For some reason, it's just the opposite in Windows: The Ctrl key zooms without resizing, and holding down Ctrl and Alt zooms *and* resizes. In any case, if you want the opposite behavior to be the default, disable the Zoom Resizes Windows check box in the General Preferences dialog.

Zoom with the scroll wheel. If your mouse has a scroll wheel, you can use it to scroll or zoom. By default, it's set to scroll, and pressing Option (Mac) or Alt (Windows) makes the scroll wheel zoom instead. To reverse this behavior, check Zoom with Scroll Wheel in General Preferences.

Fit image within screen. Double-clicking on the Hand tool is the same as clicking Fit Screen in the Options bar when the Zoom tool or Hand tool is selected, or pressing Command-0 (zero) (Mac) or Ctrl-0 (Windows)—it makes the image and the document window as large as it can without going outside the screen's boundaries. The image may not zoom to the full width or height of the monitor if palettes are present.

Zoom field in the document window. At the bottom left corner of the window, Photoshop displays the current magnification percentage. This isn't only a display; you can change it. Double-click to select the whole field, type the zoom percentage you want, then press Return or Enter. If you're not sure what percentage you want, press Shift-Return instead of Return and the field will remain selected so you can enter a different value (see **Figure 6-4**).

Figure 6-4
Zoom field

Type the zoom percentage you want here, then press Return or Enter.

Using Print Size magnification. Generations of Photoshop users have been baffled by the View > Print Size command, mostly because when you choose it, it never matches the size of the image when you actually print it! Well, never say never; there is a way to make it work. The only way the Print Size command can know the actual print size is to know the resolution of your monitor, so that the rulers become accurate. To make Print Size work right, do the following:

1. Open the Displays system preference (Mac) or the Displays control panel (Windows), and note your monitor's current resolution setting (for example, 1280×854 pixels).

2. Grab an actual, real-world ruler and measure the width of your monitor image (not the frame in inches). Be careful not to scratch your screen!

3. Divide the horizontal pixel dimension of your monitor by the horizontal real-world dimension of your monitor. For example, my widescreen LCD monitor is set to 1680 pixels across a physical width of 17 inches, and $1680/17 = 98.8$ pixels per inch.

4. Open the Preferences dialog, click the Units and Rulers pane, and enter your pixels per inch value into the Screen Resolution field (see **Figure 6-5**).

Figure 6-5
Setting screen resolution for accurate Print Size

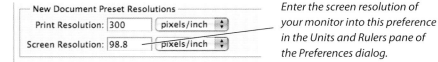

Enter the screen resolution of your monitor into this preference in the Units and Rulers pane of the Preferences dialog.

Now when you choose View > Print Size, Photoshop can take into account both your screen resolution and the resolution of the image in the Image > Image Size dialog, and correctly display the printed size of the image. Another wonderful result of all this is that your rulers now match the real world at Print Size magnification. If the rulers don't match exactly, adjust the Screen Resolution field slightly until they do.

Moving the View

Tip: To use the Zoom or Hand tool on every open image window at the same time, hold down the Shift key as you click the Zoom tool or drag the Hand tool.

If you're like most Photoshop users, you find yourself moving around the image a lot. Do a little here . . . do a little there . . . and so on. But when you're doing this kind of navigation, you should rarely use the scroll bars. There are much better ways.

Use the Hand. The best way to make a small move around your image is to select the Hand tool with your keyboard (by pressing the spacebar) instead of choosing it from the Tool palette. Then just click-and-drag to where you want to go.

End Up Down Home. Many people ignore the very helpful Page Up, Page Down, Home, and End keys when working in Photoshop, but we find them invaluable for perusing an image for dust or scratches.

When you press Page Up or Page Down, Photoshop scrolls the image by one whole window of pixels up or down. While there's no Page Left or Page Right button, you can jump one window of pixels to the left or right by pressing Command-Page Up or Command-Page Down in Mac OS X, or Ctrl-Page Up or Control-Page Down in Windows. You can scroll in 10-pixel increments by adding the Shift key to any of the shortcuts above.

Also note that pressing the Home button jumps you to the top left corner, and the End button jumps you to the bottom right corner of the document. David often uses this technique when using the Crop tool to quickly adjust the top left and bottom right corners.

If you're on a laptop, these keys may be overlaid with the arrow keys. For example, on a Mac laptop, the Up Arrow key also has Page Up printed on it. To use the Page Up function of that key, add the Fn key at the bottom left corner of the keyboard, so that you press Fn-Up Arrow to get Page Up.

Tip: After you match up windows, you can zoom or move them together using the earlier Shift key tip.

Match up your windows. When you're working on multiple images at the same time, it's often helpful to sync up their views. Several commands on the Arrange submenu (under the Window menu) automate this process. The Match Zoom feature sets the magnification percentage for every open image to the zoom level of the current document. Match Location leaves the magnification alone but scrolls each document window to the same part of the image as the current file. For instance, if the current file displays the lower-right corner, then all the images will scroll to the lower-right corner. (Unfortunately, Match Location is only approximate; it won't match to the exact pixel.) The one we use most often is Match Zoom and Location. You can guess what it does.

Context-sensitive menus. When you Control-click (Mac) or right-click (Windows), Photoshop displays a context-sensitive menu that changes depending on what tool you have selected in the Tool palette; it's worth trying out with any tool you use (see **Figure 6-6**).

Figure 6-6
Context menu
for the Move tool,
displaying available layers
under the cursor

For brush or retouching tools, the context menu is a quick way to adjust the brush. The context-sensitive menu for the Move tool lets you select a layer. If you have four layers in an image and three of them overlap in one particular area, you can Control-click (or right-click) on that area and Photoshop asks you which of the three layers you want to jump to. If the Move tool isn't selected, you can almost always get the Move tool's context menu by Command-Control-clicking in Mac OS X, or Ctrl-right-clicking in Windows.

The context-sensitive menu for the Marquee tool contains a mishmash of features, including Delete Layer, Duplicate Layer, Load Selection, Reselect, Color Range, and Group into New Smart Object (we have no idea why Adobe picked these and left others out). Many of these features don't have keyboard shortcuts, so this menu is the fastest way to perform them.

Navigator Palette

You can use the Navigator palette as command central for all scrolling and zooming (see **Figure 6-7**). However, we rarely use this palette because we zoom much faster with the keyboard shortcuts, but if you get along with the Navigator palette, don't let us stop you from using it.

A thumbnail of the image fills most of the palette, with a red frame marking the contents of the active window. (If your image has a lot of red in it, you might want to change the frame color by choosing Palette Options from the Palette menu). Dragging the outline pans the contents of the active window. Command-dragging (Mac) or Ctrl-dragging (Windows) lets you define a new outline, thereby changing the zoom percentage.

Figure 6-7
Navigator palette

The percentage field at the lower left of the palette works exactly like the one at the lower left of the image window. You can click the Zoom In and Zoom Out buttons instead of using the keyboard shortcuts for zooming. David's favorite feature in this palette is the magnification slider, which lets him change the zoom level dynamically, but you can also do that by scrolling a mouse wheel while pressing Option (Mac) or Alt (Windows).

Moving Tips

Before we talk about moving things around, it's useful to understand that in Photoshop, multiple types of moves can be available at any one time. For instance, if you've selected an area on a layer, at that moment you can move the selection boundary or the selected pixels, and the way you want to go dictates which tool or keyboard shortcut you use.

If you simply make a selection and then drag it with one of the selection tools, you move the selection boundary but not the selected pixels. If you want to move the pixels, use the Move tool (press M). No matter what tool is selected, you can always temporarily get the Move tool by holding down the Command (Mac) or Ctrl (Windows) key.

When you move or copy selected pixels with the Move tool, you get a floating selection, which is like a temporary layer that disappears when you deselect. While the selection is still floating, you can use the Fade command (in the Edit menu) to change its opacity or blend mode.

With the Move tool, you don't have to worry about positioning the cursor first—just drag anywhere within the document window. This is a great speedup, especially when you're working with heavily feathered selections. Also, if you want to move an entire layer and the layer is already selected in the Layers palette, you can use the Move tool to drag the entire layer right away, without using a selection tool or the command first.

Our selection tips don't apply only to selected pixels. They'll also work on objects like a selected path, or on the currently selected layer or layer mask in the Layers palette. Most of the tips also work on the selection boundary itself if you choose Edit > Transform Selection first.

Moving precisely. If it's hard to keep your hand steady when working precisely, try the arrow keys and the Options bar instead of the mouse.

With the Move tool selected, each press of an arrow key moves the layer or selection by one pixel. If you add the Shift key, the selection moves 10 pixels. Modifier keys work, too: Hold down the Option key (Mac) or Alt key (Windows) when you first press an arrow key, and the selection is duplicated, floated, and moved one pixel (don't keep holding down the Option/Alt key after that, unless you want a *lot* of duplicates). Remember that you can always get the Move tool temporarily by adding the Command key (Mac) or Ctrl key (Windows) to any of these shortcuts.

To move an object or layer precisely by entering X and Y coordinates, first choose Edit > Free Transform. (If you're moving the selection boundary, choose Select > Transform Selection instead.) Then enter new X and Y coordinates in the Options bar.

Moving multiple layers. Layers are great, but you often can't do the same thing to more than one layer at the same time. Fortunately, moving layers is easy: Simply select more than one layer in the Layers palette. If you've ever selected multiple files in a folder on your desktop, it's the same thing in the Layers palette: Shift-select the first and last layers; to select a discontiguous range, Command-click (Mac) or Ctrl-click (Windows) each layer you want to add to the selection.

Copying pixels. If you select pixels and choose Edit > Copy, you only get the pixels on the currently active layer(s) (the one(s) selected on the Layers palette). To copy selected pixels across all visible layers, select Copy Merged instead (Command-Shift-C in Mac OS X, Ctrl-Shift-C in Windows).

Some people use this technique to make a merged copy of the entire image (not just a selection). It works, but remember that when you can achieve the same result using the clipboard and using layers, layers are usually faster and use less RAM. The fastest and most efficient way to merge all layers into a new document is to choose Layer > Duplicate Layers, and choose New from the Destination pop-up menu to merge all layers and send them to a new document in one step.

Pasting pixels. In the most common color modes, such as RGB and CMYK, pasting pixels into a document automatically creates a new layer. When a selection is active, you'll also see the Edit > Paste Into command (Command-Shift-V in Mac OS X, or Ctrl-Shift-V in Windows), which adds a new layer with a layer mask based on the selection so that the pixels you're pasting appear only inside the selection. If you add the Shift key

Tip: Making a selection and using the Paste Into command (or the Paste Outside feature that you get by adding the Shift key) lets you create both a layer and a layer mask in one step.

to the Paste Into keyboard shortcut, the pixels you're pasting appear only outside the selection, because adding Shift inverts the layer mask that's created.

Drag and Drop Selections and Layers. To move selected pixels (or a layer) from one document to another, drag it from one window into the other (if you've got a selection, remember to use the Move tool, or else you'll just move the selection boundary itself). Again, dragging requires less memory than copying and pasting. If you're trying to copy an entire layer, you can also just click its thumbnail in the Layers palette and drag it to the other document's window. Either way, if you want to drop the selection smack in the exact center of the destination document, Shift-drag instead.

Guides, Grids, and Alignment Tips

Moving pixels is all very well and good, but where are you going to move them? If you need to place pixels with precision, you should use the ruler, guides, grids, and alignment features. The ruler is the simplest: you can hide or show it by pressing Command-R (Mac) or Ctrl-R (Windows). Wherever you move your cursor, you can track the cursor position using the tick marks appear in the rulers (or the coordinates on the Info palette).

Tip: If you can't move a guide, see if the View > Lock Guides command is on. If it's on, turn it off.

Guides. You can add a guide to a page by dragging it out from either the horizontal or vertical ruler. Or, if you care about specific placement, you can watch the ruler tick marks or the Info palette coordinates, or select View > New Guide so you can type in a numerical position. (If you don't think in inches, you can change the default measurement system; see "Switch Units," later in this chapter.) **Table 6-1** lists a number of grids and guides keystrokes that can help you use these features effortlessly.

Snap to ruler marks. We almost always hold down the Shift key when dragging a guide out from a ruler; that way, the guide automatically snaps to the ruler tick marks. If you find that your guides are slightly sticky as you drag them out without the Shift key held down, check to see what layer you're on. When Snap To Guides is turned on, objects snap to the guides *and* guides snap to the edges and centers of objects on layers.

	To do this . . .	Press this . . .
Table 6-1 Grids and guides keystrokes	Hide/Show Extras (grids, guides, etc.)	Command-H (Mac) Ctrl-H (Windows)
	Hide/Show Guides	Command-' (apostrophe) (Mac) Ctrl-' (Windows)
	Hide/Show Grid	Command-Option-' (Mac) Ctrl-Alt-' (Windows)
	Snap To Guides	Command-; (semicolon) (Mac) Ctrl-; (Windows)
	Lock/Unlock Guides	Command-Option-; (Mac) Ctrl-Alt-; (Windows)

Switching guide direction. Dragged out a horizontal guide when you meant to get a vertical one? No problem: Just Option-click (Mac) or Alt-click (Windows) the guide to switch its orientation (or hold down the Option/Alt key while dragging the guide out of the ruler).

Mirroring guides. If you rotate your image by 90 degrees, or flip it horizontally or vertically, your guides will rotate or flip with it. If you don't want this to happen, choose View > Lock Guides, or press Command-Option-; (Mac) or Command-Option-; (Windows).

Guides outside the image. Just because your pixels stop at the edge of the image doesn't mean your guides have to. You can place guides out on the area surrounding the image and they'll still be functional. This is just the ticket if you've got a photo that you need to place so that it bleeds off the edge of your image by 0.25 inch.

Change guides and grids. Guides are, by default, cyan. Grid lines are, by default, set one inch apart. If you don't like these settings, change them in the Guides, Grid & Slices pane of the Preferences dialog, or just double-click any guide with the Move tool.

Alignment and distribution. People often use the alignment features in page-layout applications, but Photoshop has alignment and distribution features, too, and they're a godsend for anyone who really cares about precision in their images. Alignment lines up layers, and distribution spaces layers evenly between the two outermost selected layers. Here's how you can align or distribute layers:

1. Select two or more layers in the Layers palette.

2. If you want the layers to align or distribute to each other, make sure no pixels are selected by choosing Select > Deselect or press its shortcut, Command-D (Mac) or Ctrl-D (Windows).

   If you want layers to align or distribute within a specific area, use the Rectangular Marquee tool to drag a selection boundary. To align or distribute to the canvas size, make sure the Background layer is one of the selected layers, or choose Edit > Select All. When a selection exists, the Layer > Align command changes to Align Layers to Selection.

3. Press V to activate the Move tool, and then click on one of the Align buttons in the Options bar (see **Figure 6-8**). Alternatively, you can also Choose Layer > Align or Layer > Distribute and then choose a command from the Align submenu.

Figure 6-8

Aligning layers using the Options bar with the Move tool selected

Start by selecting the layers to align.

The three layers in their original positions

Clicking the Align Vertical Centers button in the Options bar

The three layers after aligning their centers vertically

Clicking the Distribute Left Edges button in the Options bar

The three layers after evenly distributing their left edges

Aligning or distributing to a specific object. Normally, when you align along the left edges, Photoshop moves all the layers except for the one that has the leftmost data (or the rightmost data when aligning left, and so on). You can force Photoshop to lock one layer and move the others by *linking* the layers: Select the layers, click the Link icon at the bottom of the Layers palette, then click on the layer you want to remain in place. Now when you choose from the Align or Distribute submenu, all the layers move except for the currently selected layer.

When distributing layers vertically, Photoshop "locks" the layers that are closest to the top and the bottom of the image canvas; when distributing horizontally, it locks the leftmost and rightmost layers. All the layers in between get moved. For example, if you choose Vertical Centers from the Distribute Linked submenu, Photoshop moves the layers so that there is an equal amount of space from the vertical center point of one layer to the next.

Dialog Tips

Dialogs seem like simple things, but since you probably spend a good chunk of your time in Photoshop looking at them, wouldn't it be great to be more efficient while you're there? Here are a bunch of tips that will let you fly through those pesky beasts.

Yes, you can. The most important lesson to learn about dialogs in Photoshop is that just because one is open doesn't mean you can't do anything else. For instance, if the Curves dialog is open, you can still scroll and zoom the document. Check the menu bar when a dialog is open—you can use any command that isn't dimmed. For example, because palette commands are available on the Window menu, you can even open and close palettes when a dialog is open. The palette we end up opening most often from inside dialogs is the Info palette, because it gives us readouts of color values.

Scrub-a-dub-dub. You can edit values in dialogs by *scrubbing*, or dragging horizontally over a value. For example, if you're in the Image Size dialog, hold down Command (Mac) or Ctrl (Windows) as you position the mouse over any number field. When the cursor appears as a finger with a two-headed horizontal arrow, you can drag left to lower the value, or drag right

*Command/Ctrl-drag over most
number fields to increase or
decrease the value.*

to raise the value (see **Figure 6-9**). This also works in palettes that have number fields, including the Options bar. For faster scrubbing, hold down the Shift key, which multiplies the normal adjustment by ten.

Save your settings. Many dialogs in Photoshop have Save and Load buttons that let you save to disk all the settings that you've made in a dialog. They're particularly useful when you want to use the same dialog settings on many images.

For instance, let's say you're adjusting the tone of an image with Curves. You increase this and decrease that, and add some points here and there… Finally, when you're finished, you click OK and realize that you'd like to apply the same curve to 50 other images shot under the same conditions. Instead of laboriously reconstructing the same curve 50 times, just click the Save button in the Curves dialog to save the curve settings as a file. Now, from any other image, you can open the Curves dialog, click the Load button, and select the curves setting files you saved. This is especially useful when you build actions that automate your workflow, because you can have your action load a settings file. You can also send settings files to your colleagues so they can load them.

Instant replay. There's one other way to undo and still save any tonal-adjustment settings you've made. If you hold down the Option (Mac) or Alt (Windows) key while selecting a command from the Image > Adjust submenu, the dialog opens with the last-used settings. Similarly, you can add the Option/Alt key to the adjustment's keyboard shortcut. For instance, in Mac OS X, Command-L is the shortcut for Levels, so Command-Option-L opens the Levels dialog with the same settings you last used. This is a great way to specify the same Levels or Curves (or Hue/Saturation, or any other adjustment) for several different images. But as soon as you quit Photoshop, it loses its memory.

Previewing Tips

Most of the tonal- and color-correction features and many filters offer a Preview check box in their dialogs. Plus, all the filters that have a dialog have a proxy window that shows the effect applied to a small section of the image (some dialogs have both). If you're working on a very large file on a relatively slow machine, and the filter you're using has a proxy window, you might want to turn off the Preview check box so that Photoshop doesn't slow down redrawing the screen while you're making adjustments. However, most of the time, unless we're working with a very slow filter like Smart Sharpen, we just leave the Preview feature on.

We use the Preview check box to view "before" and "after" versions of our images, toggling it on and off to see the effect of the changes without leaving the dialog. (Sometimes the changes we make are subtle and gradual, but a before-and-after usually lets us see exactly what we've accomplished.) In Photoshop CS3, we now press the P key to toggle the Preview check box. If you loved this shortcut in Adobe Camera Raw and wished it were in Photoshop (like we did), Photoshop CS3 grants your wish. Pressing P for Preview works in most, but mysteriously not all, Photoshop CS3 dialogs.

The following tips don't apply to the dialogs for the more creative filters, such as Dry Brush and Plastic Wrap. They use a different dialog that provides a large preview image inside the dialog but not in the main window. We don't really cover those filters because they're more about special effects, and we're more about image correction.

Proxies. The proxy in dialogs shows only a small part of the image, but it updates almost instantly. Previewing time-consuming filters such as Smart Sharpen or Reduce Noise on a large file can take a long time. Some very time-consuming filters such as the Distort filters offer a large proxy instead of a preview.

Before and after in proxies. You can always see a before-and-after comparison by clicking in the proxy. Hold down the mouse button to see the image before the filter is applied, and release it to see the image after the filter is applied. This is obviously quicker than redrawing the whole window with the Preview check box.

Change the proxy view. To see a different part of the image, click-and-drag in the proxy (no modifier keys are necessary). Alternatively, you can click in the document itself. The cursor changes to a small rectangle and wherever you click shows up in the Preview window.

Similarly, you can zoom the proxy in and out. The *slow* way is to click on the little (+) and (-) buttons. Much faster is to click the proxy while pressing the Command (Mac) or Ctrl (Windows) key to zoom in, or the Option

(Mac) or Alt (Windows) key to zoom out. However, we rarely zoom in and out because you see the true effect of a filter only at 100 percent view.

Note that proxies only show the layer you're working on at any one time. This makes sense, really; only that layer is going to be affected.

Keyboard Shortcuts in Dialogs

We love keyboard shortcuts. They make everything go much faster, or at least they make it *feel* like we're working faster. Here are a few shortcuts that we use all the time inside dialogs.

Option/Alt. Holding down the Option (Mac) or Alt (Windows) key in a dialog almost always changes the Cancel button to a Reset button, letting you reset the dialog to its original state (the way it was when you first opened it). If you want to go keyboard shortcuts the whole way, press Command-Option-period to do the same thing (there's no equivalent shortcut in Windows).

Command-Z/Ctrl-Z. You already know the shortcut Command-Z (Mac) or Ctrl-Z (Windows) because it's gotten you out of more jams than you care to think about. You can use the same shortcut to undo within most dialogs, too. Inside dialogs, you get only one undo step.

Arrow keys. When a dialog contains a number field, you can change those numbers by pressing the Up or Down arrow key. Press once, and the number increases or decreases by one. If you hold down the Shift key while pressing the arrow key, the number changes by 10. (Note that some dialog values change by a tenth or even a hundredth; when you hold down Shift, they change by 10 times as much.) This is a great way to fine-tune adjustments without cramping your mouse hand.

A few dialogs use the arrow keys in a different way. In the Lens Flare filter, for instance, the arrow keys move the position of the effect.

Tab key. As in most Mac and Windows applications, the Tab key selects the next text field in dialogs with multiple text fields. Shift-Tab to move to the previous field instead.

P for Preview. As we mentioned a little earlier, press P to toggle the Preview check box in any dialog that has one.

New Document Tips

Before we move on to essential tips about tools, we need to take a quick look at the New dialog, which has a few very helpful (and in some cases hidden) features. For instance, note that the New dialog has an Advanced button; when you click this, you're offered two additional settings: Color Profile and Pixel Aspect Ratio. Color Profile lets you specify a profile other than the working space for your image. (You can choose the default working space too, but since that's what you'd get anyway, it's a bit pointless to choose it here.) Note that we cover working spaces in Chapter 4, "Color Settings." Pixel Aspect Ratio lets you use nonsquare pixels, in case your image is destined for video. If video isn't in your game plan, then avoid this pop-up menu entirely.

Preset document sizes. The Preset pop-up menu in the New dialog lets you pick from among many common document sizes, such as A4, 640×480, and 4×6 inches. You may not see very many choices if you click the Preset pop-up menu, but that's because it's a two-stage process: First choose a category from the Preset pop-up menu, and then choose a size from the Size pop-up menu. If you need a preset other than the ones on the list, just set the New dialog the way you want it, then click the Save Preset button (see **Figure 6-10**). You can delete user-created presets using the Delete Preset button, but the built-in ones that ship with Photoshop are there to stay.

Figure 6-10
The dialog
for new documents

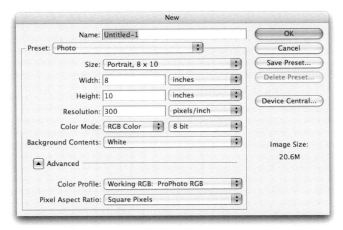

When you save a document preset, Photoshop gives you the choice of which settings to remember: Resolution, Mode, Bit Depth, Content, Profile, and Pixel Aspect Ratio. For example, let's say you turn off the Profile check box; when you later choose your preset from the Preset pop-up menu, Photoshop leaves the image's profile set to the current working space instead of overriding it.

Note that some built-in presets (those having to do with video), can also automatically add guides to the document. Unfortunately, there's currently no way to save presets with guides yourself.

Clairvoyant image size. The New dialog tries to read your mind. If you have something copied to the Clipboard when you create a new document, Photoshop automatically selects Clipboard from the Preset pop-up menu and plugs the pixel dimensions, resolution, and color model of that copied piece into the proper places of the dialog for you. If you'd rather use the values from the last new image you created, hold down Option (Mac) or Alt (Windows) while selecting New from the File menu, or press Command-Option-N (Mac) or Ctrl-Alt-N (Windows).

Break up measurements. Photoshop is just trying to help make your life easier: When you select a measurement system (inches, picas, pixels, or whatever) in the New dialog—or the Image Size or the Canvas Size dialogs—Photoshop changes both the horizontal and vertical settings. If you want vertical to be set to picas and horizontal to be millimeters, then hold down the Shift key while selecting a measurement system. That tells the program not to change the other setting, too.

Copying sizes from other documents. In the New dialog, notice that all open documents are listed at the bottom of the Preset pop-up menu. If you want your new document to match an open document, simply choose the name of that document in this menu.

Keyboard Shortcut Tips

You can change keyboard shortcuts you don't like, and you can add shortcuts where there weren't any before. Of course, the ability to change keyboard shortcuts is great for you, but can wreak havoc for others using your machine. Fortunately, Photoshop lets you save keyboard shortcut sets, and you can include a set as part of a saved workspace that also includes your favorite palette arrangement and menu customizations.

Use your own set. To edit or add a keyboard shortcut, choose Edit > Keyboard Shortcuts or press Command-Option-Shift-K (Mac) or Ctrl-Alt-Shift-K (Windows). If you edit the default set, it's saved as "Photoshop Default (modified)," so you can still get the original default back (just choose Photoshop Defaults from the Set menu). We recommend giving sets useful names; otherwise they can be lost when you choose another set or if you need to reset your preferences while troubleshooting a problem. To save a new set, click the New Set button (see **Figure 6-11**); by default, Photoshop saves the set in the proper location on your hard drive (inside your Photoshop application folder, in Presets > Keyboard Shortcuts).

Figure 6-11
The dialog for editing keyboard shortcuts

Click the Create New Set button to save the current set as a new one.

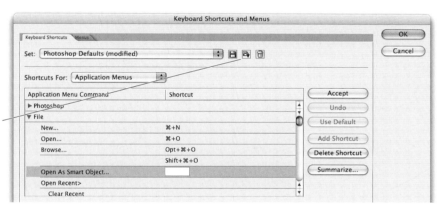

To customize keyboard shortcuts, follow these steps:

1. Pick Application Menus, Palette Menus, or Tools from the Shortcuts For pop-up menu.

2. Click an expansion triangle to reveal menu commands, and then select a command or tool from the list.

3. When the field in the Shortcut column is highlighted, you can type the keyboard shortcut you want to apply to this feature. If the shortcut is already in use, Photoshop alerts you and gives you choices.

4. If you want to create another shortcut for the same feature (there's no reason you can't have more than one shortcut that does the same

thing), click the Add Shortcut button. If you're done with this feature and want to change another, click the Accept button. When you're done applying shortcuts, click OK.

Note that you can edit or add keyboard shortcuts for palette menus and tools in addition to regular menu commands. You can even save shortcuts for third-party features that appear as commands, such as Import and Automate plug-ins, filters, or scripts!

What was that shortcut again? With the advent of editable keyboard shortcuts, the number of different shortcuts for you to keep track of threatens to overwhelm any mortal's brain. Fortunately, you can click the Summarize button in the Keyboard Shortcuts and Menus dialog to export a list of every feature and its shortcuts. Photoshop saves this file in HTML format, so you can open it in any Web browser and you can print it.

Tip: If you don't want to apply a new keyboard shortcut and the Shortcut field is still highlighted, press Cancel to back out of the change. Be careful. If you press Cancel a second time, you'll close the dialog without saving changes.

Conflicts with system shortcut keys (Mac only). In Mac OS X, Apple appropriated two keyboard shortcuts that were crucial for Photoshop users: Command-H and Command-M. Photoshop users know these as the shorcuts for Hide Selection and Open Curves dialog. The Mac OS X folks use these shortcuts for Hide Application and Minimize Application. In Photoshop, the Photoshop keyboard shortcuts always win. However, you can hold down the Control key, too, to get the system shortcuts (press Command-Control-H to get Hide Application, and so on).

Menu Customization Tips

Photoshop is practically overflowing with menu commands. If you have trouble remembering which commands apply to your workflow, you can customize Photoshop menus by colorizing or hiding them. We think menu customization works best when you spend most of your time using Photoshop in a very specialized way, or when you're trying to train yourself or others on a specific workflow.

To edit menu commands, choose Menus from the Edit menu or press Command-Option-Shift-M (Mac) or Ctrl-Alt-Shift-M (Windows) to open the Keyboard Shortcuts and Menus dialog—it's the same dialog used for customizing keyboard shortcuts, but when opened with the Menus command, it opens showing the Menus tab (see **Figure 6-12**). As with

Figure 6-12
The dialog for editing menus

*Click the Create
New Set button to
save the current
set as a new one.*

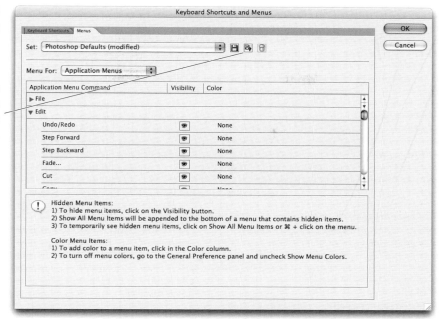

keyboard shortcuts, you can save your customizations as a set, and we recommend that you do so. Note that you can't hide the Quit or Close commands in Photoshop.

Tips for Tools

After you're finished moving around in your image, zooming in and out, and moving pixels hither and yon, it's time to get down to work with the tools in Photoshop. The tools have all sorts of hidden properties that can make life easier and—more importantly—more efficient. While we think it's best to talk about a tool in the chapter where it applies the most (for example, we take a good close look at the Selection tool in Chapter 9, "Making Selections") some tools can be used in more than one area, and those are the tools we'll look at here.

Tool shortcuts. The most important productivity tip we've found in Photoshop has been the ability to select any tool with a keyboard shortcut. Like other programs in the Adobe Creative Suite, Photoshop tool shortcuts do not use any modifier keys. You press the key alone, without pressing Command, Option, Control, or Alt. **Figure 6-13** shows the tool shortcuts.

Figure 6-13
Keyboard shortcuts for the
Tools palette

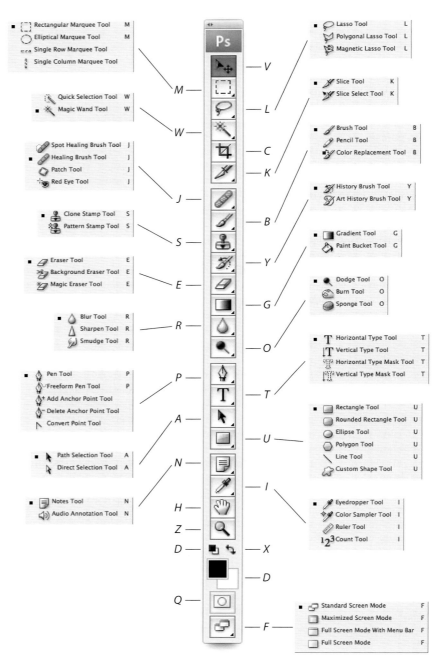

*Of course, these are just
the defaults; you can edit
the shortcuts by selecting
Keyboard Shortcuts in the
Edit menu.*

Some tools in the Tool palette keep multiple related tools undercover. For instance, the Dodge tool also "contains" the Burn and the Sponge tools. The slow way to access the different modes is to press the tool icon to bring up the flyout palette containing the different modes. A faster method is to press the tool's keyboard shortcut once to select it, and then hold down the Shift key while pressing it again to toggle among the choices. Press M once, and you jump to the Marquee tool; then press Shift-M, and it switches to the elliptical Marquee tool; press Shift-M once more, and it switches back to the rectangular Marquee tool. Note that this shortcut doesn't cycle through the single-row marquee or the single-column marquee.

Photoshop lets you change this behavior: If you turn off the Use Shift Key for Tool Switch check box in the General panel of the Preferences dialog—see "Setting Preferences," later in this chapter—then you don't have to hold down the Shift key to rotate through the tools; each time you press M, you'll get a different tool. Conrad prefers to use Shift to cycle through tools, because it ensures that pressing a letter key selects the last tool you used in a tool group. If you cycle without Shift and the Tools palette is hidden, pressing a letter could cycle to another tool in the group that isn't the tool you thought you were using.

Change a tool's blend mode. You can change blend modes (Normal, Screen, Multiply, and so on) by pressing Shift-minus sign and Shift-plus sign. If you have a painting tool selected (like the Brush tool), this changes the mode of the selected tool. If you're using a tool that doesn't use blend modes, the shortcut escalates to change the mode of the layer itself.

Activate the opposite tool. Some tools have an opposite, kind of like an evil twin except that the opposite tool isn't evil (perhaps just misunderstood). When you're using one of these tools, you can get its opposite by pressing Option (Mac) or Alt (Windows). For example, if you're using the Blur tool, pressing Option/Alt temporarily changes it into the Sharpen tool. The same thing happens with the Dodge and Burn tools.

Options bar shortcuts. The tools on the Tool palette only go so far. You often need to modify the tool's default settings on the Options bar. Try this: Select a tool, then press Return. The Options bar, even if hidden, appears at this command. Plus, if there is a number-input field on the Options bar, Photoshop selects it for you. When you press Return with the

Tip: A very efficient way to use Photoshop (or any Adobe Creative Suite software) is the two-handed method: Keep one hand on the mouse or stylus and the other hand over the keyboard, ready to press single-key tool shortcuts. By switching tools using your nonmouse hand on the keyboard, you can keep the mouse over the area you're editing instead of repeatedly pulling the mouse or stylus over to the Tools palette.

Lasso or Marquee tools selected, for example, the Feather field becomes highlighted on the Options bar.

If there is more than one number-input field on the Options bar, you can press Tab to jump from one to the next. Finally, when you're finished with your changes, press Return again to exit from the bar and resume work.

Brush Tips

You can customize the brushes in Photoshop (see **Figure 6-14**). It's important to remember that these brush presets aren't only for painting with the Brush tool—they also work with any tool that paints, such as the Eraser tool, the Clone Stamp tool, the History Brush tool, and so on. While most of the brush options are designed for fine-art work (simulating charcoal, water colors, and so on), every now and again you may find them helpful in a production environment, too—especially for detailed retouching.

Figure 6-14

The Brushes palette

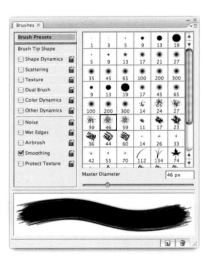

Brush shortcuts. Did you know that the [and] keys (the square brackets) increase and decrease the diameter of a brush? Plus, Shift-[and Shift-] change the brush's hardness. We now keep one hand on the keyboard and one on our mouse (or tablet pen); when we want to change tools, we press the key for that tool. When we want to change brush size, we cycle through the brushes with the [and] keys until we find the size we like. Here's one more shortcut, too: The Command and period keys move up and down through the brush presets.

Fastest brush selection. Actually, one of the best ways to select a brush is probably via the context menu. On the Mac, hold down the Control key when you click with any of the painting tools and Photoshop displays the Brushes menu wherever you click. In Windows, right-click to see the menu. After selecting a brush size, press Enter or Esc to make the palette disappear.

Hovering pseudoselections. Instead of selecting a brush from the Brushes palette, then painting with it to see how it will really look, hover the cursor over the preset for a moment and Photoshop will display a sample of that brush at the bottom of the palette. If you don't like it, hover over another brush. When you find one you like, click on it to select it.

Opacity by the numbers. In between changing brush sizes, we're forever changing brush opacity while painting or retouching. If you're still moving the sliders around on the Options bar, stop it. Instead, just type a number from 0 to 9. Zero gives you 100 percent opacity, 1 gives you 10 percent, 2 gives you 20 percent, and so on. For finer control, press two number keys in quick succession—for example, pressing 45 gets you 45 percent opacity. If you have a non-painting tool selected in the Tool palette, then typing a number changes the opacity of the layer you're working on (unless it's the Background layer, of course). Note that if the Airbrush feature in the Options bar is turned on, then typing numbers affects the Flow percentage rather than the Opacity setting.

Touching up line art. We talk about scanning and converting to line art in Chapter 11, "Essential Image Techniques," but since we're on the topic of painting tools, we should discuss the Pencil tool for just a moment. One of the best techniques for retouching line-art (black-and-white) images is the Auto Erase feature on the Options bar. When Auto Erase is turned on, the Pencil tool works like this: If you click on any color other than the foreground color, that pixel—along with all others you touch before lifting the mouse button—is changed to the foreground color (this is the way it works, even with Auto Erase turned off). If you click on the foreground color, however, that pixel—along with all others you encounter—is changed to the background color. This effectively means you don't have to keep switching the foreground and background colors while you work.

Sampling exactly the right layers. If you're working on a multilayer image, you may find yourself frustrated with tools like the Smudge, Blur, Magic Wand, or the Clone Stamp tools. That's because sometimes you want these tools to "see" more layers than just the one you're working on, and sometimes you do not. Photoshop CS3 expands gives you a choice for each of these tools with the Sample pop-up menu on the Options bar. (Note that in older versions, this was a check box called Use All Layers or Sample Merged.)

When Sample is set to Current Layer, each tool acts as though the other layers weren't even there. If you choose All Layers, Photoshop samples from the other visible layers (both above and below it) and acts as though they were merged together. A third option, Current and Below, does what it says.

So what good are these new options? One common use is when you want to patch or clone onto a new empty layer, leaving the original layers intact. This is called nondestructive cloning, because if you are unhappy with the results, you can simply erase the patches on the new layer and try again. Without the Sample menu options, you would be able to paint only on the same layer you're sampling. With the Sample pop-up menu, you can choose Current and Below or All Layers to paint on a blank layer while sampling from other layers that remain intact (see **Figure 6-15**).

The button next to the Sample pop-up menu is the Ignore Adjustment Layers button, also new to Photoshop CS3 and definitely a worthwhile addition. In previous versions of Photoshop, if you cloned or healed in a document included adjustment layers and you sampled multiple layers, the sample would include the effect of adjustment layers. This was frustrating, because the sample would not match the rest of the layer and the adjustment layer would be applied again to the merged sample. We had to remember to turn off adjustment layers before sampling multiple layers and then turn them back on, and this drove us up the wall. Fortunately, the wonderful new Ignore Adjustment Layers button means that we can now leave adjustment layers on and sample multiple layers perfectly.

If you want your samples or selections to involve only one layer, that's a situation where you'll want to choose Current Layer from the Sample pop-up menu.

Photoshop CS3 goes even further in helping you clone effectively, in the form of the new Clone Source palette. We cover the Clone Source palette in Chapter 11, "Essential Image Techniques."

Figure 6-15
Layer sampling options

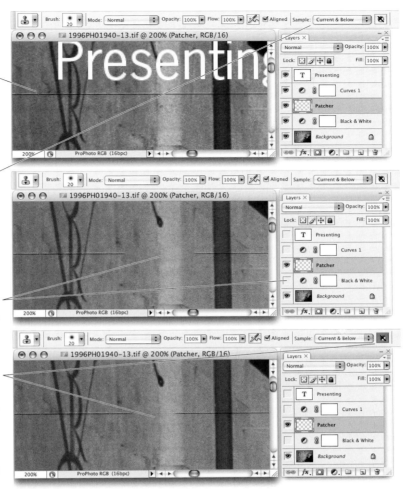

This scan has a long scratch that we'll remove with the Clone Stamp tool, painting the fix on the Patcher layer. We leave all layers visible to edit the image in context, and chose Current & Below from the Sample pop-up menu to avoid cloning the type.

To check our work, we hide all layers except Background and Patcher, but we discover that the tool cloned the effect of the Black & White adjustment layer.

We undo, turn on the new Ignore Adjustment Layers button, show all layers, and clone out the scratch again. Hiding other layers reveals that this time the tool cloned the area without the adjustment layer's influence.

Cropping Tool Tips

We almost always scan a little bigger than we need, just in case. So we end up using the Cropping tool a lot. The nice thing about the Cropping tool (as opposed to the Crop feature on the Image menu) is that you can make fine adjustments before agreeing to go through with the paring. Just drag one of the corners or side handles. Here are a couple more ways you can fine-tune the crop.

See what gets cropped. By default, Photoshop darkens the area outside the cropping rectangle so that you can see what's going to get cropped out before you press Enter. You can adjust this by clicking the Color swatch in the Options bar (when the Cropping tool is selected) and picking a different color from the Color Picker (such as white). You may want to increase the opacity of the color in the Options bar, too. David likes to ghost the cropped-out pixels to near-white, while Conrad likes cropped-out pixels to match the full-screen background color around the image.

Rotating and moving while cropping. You can crop and rotate at the same time with the Crop tool: after dragging out the cropping rectangle with the Crop tool, just place the cursor outside the cropping rectangle and drag to rotate the rectangle. When you press Return or Enter, Photoshop crops and rotates the image to straighten the rectangle. It can be tricky to get exactly the right angle by eye—keep an eye on the Info palette. Also, if the cropping rectangle isn't in the right place, you can always move it—just place the cursor inside the cropping rectangle and drag.

Adjusting for keystone distortion. What do you do about lines in your image that are supposed to be vertical or horizontal, but aren't? For example, if you take a picture of a painting hanging on a wall, you often need to do so from one side to avoid flash reflections, so the subject ends up being skewed rather than rectangular. Fortunately, our faithful Cropping tool offers a cool option: adjusting for perspective. The key is to turn on the Perspective check box in the Options bar after drawing the cropping rectangle; this lets you grab the corner points and move them where you will.

However, positioning the corner points of the cropping "rectangle" can be tricky. You must first find something in the image that is supposed to be a rectangle and set the corner points on the corners of that shape. In the example of a building, you might choose the corners of a window. Then, hold down the Option and Shift keys (Mac) or Alt and Shift keys (Windows) while dragging one of the corner handles; this expands the crop but retains its shape. When you have the cropping shape the size you want it, drag the center point icon to where the camera was pointing (or where you imagine the center of the focus should be). Then press Enter or Return (see **Figure 6-16**).

By the way, we find that when we're using this tool, Photoshop often alerts us that either the center point or the corner points are in the wrong position. This usually happens when you haven't selected the corner points of something that *should* be rectangular. In other words, Photoshop acts as a safety net, stopping you when you choose a distortion that isn't likely to happen in a real photograph. Sometimes simply moving the center point to a different location (by trial and error) does the trick.

Figure 6-16

Correcting keystone distortion with the Cropping tool

This sign is distorted because it was photographed at an angle. We dragged the Cropping tool around it, turned on Perspective in the Options bar, and then dragged each corner of the crop rectangle to fit the distorted shape of the sign.

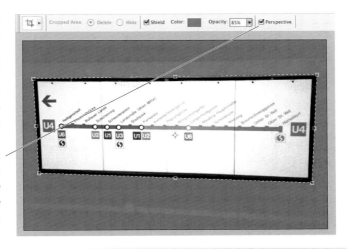

When we pressed Return/ Enter, the Cropping tool converted our perspective polygon into a rectangle, correcting the keystone distortion.

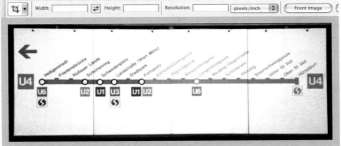

For serious distortion corrections, though, you're better off using the Lens Correction filter, which we discuss in Chapter 10.

Save that layer data. When you crop, you don't have to lose what's beyond the newly cropped edges of the document. After you drag a crop rectangle, you'll see a Hide button on the Options bar. Click that button and after you commit to the crop, the cropped-out pixels will be remembered as *big data*—material that hangs outside the actual visible image rectangle. Then, if you didn't get the crop just right, you can either move the image around with the Move tool or re-crop using a different rectangle (see "Expand the Canvas by Cropping," later in this chapter). Note that this only works on layers other than the Background layer.

Resampling while cropping. Warning: The Cropping tool may be changing your resolution or even resampling your image data without your knowing it! The Height, Width, and Resolution fields in the Options bar (when you have the Cropping tool selected) let you choose a size and resolution for your cropped picture. Basically, these fields save you the step of visiting the Image Size dialog after cropping. But remember that when you use them, they always change your image resolution or resample the image (see Chapter 2, "Image Essentials," for more on the pros and cons of resampling). That means your image resolution can drop or increase without your realizing it. (In this case, Photoshop is *not* resampling the data, just adjusting the size of the pixels.) Instead, see the next tip for how to crop to an aspect ratio without altering any other image specs.

If you type a value into the Resolution field, Photoshop resamples the image to that value. This resampling behavior is handy when you want to resample down, but be careful that you don't ask for more resolution than you really have; resampling up is usually best avoided. (Note that you can only set the Height, Width, and Resolution values *before* you start cropping; once you draw a cropping rectangle, the Options bar changes.)

Cropping to an aspect ratio. Let's say you want to crop your image to a 4-by-6 aspect ratio (height-to-width, or vice versa), but you don't want to resample the image (which adds or removes pixels, causing blurring) or change the image resolution. This is a common requirement in Web design, where pixel-perfect graphics would be ruined by resampling. The Cropping tool can't perform this task, so you'll need a different technique. First, select the Marquee (rectangular selection) tool and choose Fixed Aspect Ratio from the Style pop-up menu in the Options bar. The Options bar then lets you type values in the Height and Width fields (here you'd type *4* and *6*). Next, marquee the area you want cropped, and then select Crop from the Image menu. See Chapter 9, "Making Selections," for tips and tricks for the Marquee tool.

Expand the canvas by cropping. Once you've created a cropping rectangle with the Cropping tool, you can actually expand the crop past the boundaries of the image (assuming you zoom back until you see the gray area around the image in the document window). Then, after you press Enter, the canvas size actually expands to the edge of the cropping rectangle. This is David's favorite way to enlarge the canvas.

Cropping near the border. If you're trying to shave just a sliver of pixels off one side of an image, you'll find it incredibly annoying that Photoshop snaps the cropping rectangle to the edge of the image whenever you drag close to it. Fortunately, you can temporarily turn off this behavior by

Tip: To toggle all snap-to options on or off, choose View > Snap. The shortcut is Command-Shift-; (Mac) or Ctrl-Shift-; (Windows).

unchecking the command View > Snap > Document Bounds. Or, you can hold down the Control key to temporarily disable snapping.

Eraser Tool Tips

The Eraser tool has gotten a bad rap because people assume you have to use a big, blocky eraser. No, you can erase using any brush—one that's soft or hard, like an airbrush, or even with the textured brushes in the Brushes palette. And what's more, you can control the opacity of the Eraser (don't forget you can just type a number on the keyboard to change the tool's opacity). This makes the eraser fully usable, in our opinion. However, just because a tool is usable doesn't mean you have to use it. Whenever possible, we much prefer masking to erasing. The difference? Masks (which we cover in Chapter 8) can "erase" pixels without actually deleting them. Masks just hide the data, and you can always recover it later. Nevertheless, the Eraser tool can, on occasion, get you out of a jam. Here are a few tips:

Erase to History. The Erase to History feature (it's a check box on the Options bar when you have the Eraser tool selected) lets you use the Eraser tool to replace pixels from an earlier state of the image (see "When Things Go Worng," later in this chapter, for more on the History feature). Erase to History more or less turns the Eraser into the History Brush tool. For instance, you can open a file, mess with it until it's a mess, then revert *parts of it* to the original using the Eraser tool with Erase to History turned on.

The important thing to remember is that you can temporarily turn on the Erase to History feature by holding down the Option (Mac) or Alt (Windows) key while using the Eraser tool.

Watch Preserve Transparency when erasing. Note that the Eraser tool (or any other tool, for that matter) won't change a layer's transparency when you have the Preserve Transparency check box turned on in the Layers palette. That means it won't erase pixels away to transparency; rather it just paints in the background color. Don't forget you can turn Preserve Transparency on and off by pressing / (forward slash).

Erasing to transparency. When you use a soft-edged brush to erase pixels from a layer (rather than the Background layer), the pixels that are partially erased—that is, they're still somewhat visible, but they have some transparency in them—cannot be brought back to full opacity. For example, if you set the Eraser to 50 percent opacity and erase a bunch of pixels from a layer, there's no way to get them back to 100 percent again. The reason: You're not changing the pixel's color, only the layer's transparency mask. This isn't really a tip, it's just a warning. What you erase sometimes doesn't really go away.

Gradient Tool Tips

One of the complaints Adobe heard most in times gone by was that blends in Photoshop resulted in banding. The answer they always gave was to "add noise" to the blend. It's true; adding noise reduces banding significantly. Fortunately, Photoshop adds noise for us. Of course, you can stop it by turning off the Dither check box in the Options bar, but there's almost no reason to do so. You *may* want to turn dithering off if you're doing scientific imaging or printing to a continuous-tone device that can actually reproduce the gradient without banding.

Adding more noise. If you're still getting banding even with Dither turned on, you may want to add even more noise to a blend. However, note that you don't always need to apply the Add Noise filter to the entire gradient; use the filter selectively.

Instead, you might find it better to add noise to only one or two channels. View each channel separately (see Chapter 9, "Making Selections") to see where the banding is more prevalent. Then add some noise just to the blend area in that channel.

Blends in CMYK. Eric Reinfeld pounded it into our heads one day: If you're going to make blends in Photoshop images that will end up in CMYK mode, create them in CMYK mode. Sometimes changing modes from RGB to CMYK can give you significant color shifts in blends.

Many custom CMYK profiles produce strange results when you make a blend. In particular, blues tend to have a saturation "hole" and become less saturated when you expect them to become more so. You can often get better results by creating the blend in one of the CMYK working spaces that ship with Photoshop, then assigning your custom profile to the result. The CMYK profiles that come with Photoshop may not represent your exact printing conditions, but they tend to offer much smoother gradients than third-party profiles built with any of the common profiling tools. This is a mildly perverse use of color management, but it works—see Chapter 4, "Color Settings," for more detail about assigning profiles.

Gradients on layers. Some people make hard work of creating a blend that fades away into transparency. They go through endless convolutions of Layer Masks and Channel Options, or they spend hours building custom gradients, and so on. They're making it difficult for themselves by not opening their eyes. When you have the Gradient tool selected, the Options bar offers a pop-up menu with various gradient presets in it (see **Figure 6-17**). By default, these presets include gradients that use transparency. You can create or edit a gradient preset by clicking once on the gradient swatch in the Options bar. You can also select a different set of gradient presets from the pop-out menu to the right of the swatch.

Gradients as a layer. If you harbor even the slightest suspicion that you might need to edit a gradient, and you don't need anything on a layer except a gradient, think about adding it as a gradient layer, which is a kind of adjustment layer that you can edit at any time. To create a gradient layer, choose Layer > New Fill Layer > Gradient, or click the Create New Fill or Adjustment Layer button at the bottom of the Layers palette and choose Gradient Layer. After you create a gradient layer, you can edit its settings by double-clicking it in the Layers palette—much faster and easier than painting it all over again with the Gradient tool! However, if you're creating a gradient on a mask, you'll need to use the Gradient tool.

Figure 6-17
Gradient presets

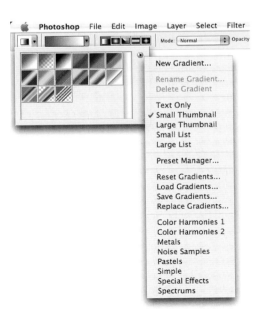

Ruler and Count Tool

In Photoshop CS3, the Ruler tool is the tool formerly known as the Measurement tool. Adobe changed the name to avoid confusion with the new Count tool in Photoshop Extended. We still sometimes hear people complain that Photoshop doesn't have a measuring tool. We think it's because the Ruler tool hides under the Eyedropper tool by default. The Ruler tool is extremely useful for measuring distances and angles. The keyboard shortcut for this tool is I (or Shift-I if it's hiding under the Eyedropper tool). Here's a rundown of how this tool works.

▶ To measure between two pixels, click-and-drag from one point to the other with the Ruler tool.

▶ Once you have a measuring line, you can hide it by selecting any other tool from the Tool palette. To show it again, select the Ruler tool.

▶ You can move the measuring line by dragging the line (not the endpoints). If you drag an endpoint, you just move that end of the line.

▶ You can't really delete a measuring line, but you can move it outside the boundaries of the image window.

▶ You can turn the measuring line into a V-shaped compass in order to measure an angle by Option-clicking (Mac) or Alt-clicking (Windows) one end of the measuring line and dragging (see **Figure 6-18**).

Where do you find the measurement? On the Info palette or the Options bar, of course. The palette displays the angle and the horizontal and vertical distances, along with the total distance in whatever measurement system you've set up in Units Preferences.

Measuring before rotating. We know you always hold the camera perfectly level, but you may occasionally have to level someone else's crooked photo or scan. Again, the Ruler tool can help immensely. If you select Arbitrary from the Rotate Canvas submenu (under the Image menu) immediately after using the Ruler tool, Photoshop automatically grabs the angle and places it in the dialog for you.

There are two things to note here. First, the angle in the Rotate Canvas dialog is usually slightly more accurate than the one on the Info palette (within half a degree). Second, if the angle is more than 45 degrees, Photoshop automatically subtracts it from 90 degrees, assuming that you want

Figure 6-18

Measuring up

When you drag the Ruler tool, the Info palette reports the width (W) and height (H), as well as the X, Y cursor position. In this example, the measurement units are pixels.

Option-drag (Mac) or Alt-drag (Windows) either end of a ruler line segment to extend a second segment. The Info palette displays the angle and the length of both segments (L1 and L2).

to rotate it counterclockwise to align with the vertical axis instead of the horizontal axis.

Count tool. The Count tool is new in Photoshop CS3 Extended. It's grouped with the Ruler, Eyedropper, and Color Sampler tools. It's intended for the common scientific task of counting objects in an image, such as stars or microbes. The Count tool is out of the scope of this book, so we aren't giving it much space, but if you do need to count objects, you can simply click the Count tool on each object you want to count in an image, and the tool leaves behind a label with the current count. The Photoshop Help file also includes a procedure for counting objects automatically, if they can be isolated easily using Photoshop selection tools.

Notes Tools

While the majority of images touched by Photoshop are edited by a single person, people are increasingly working on pictures in teams. Perhaps the team is a retoucher and a client, or perhaps it's four Photoshop users, each with specific skills—whatever the case, it's important for these folks to communicate with each other. Enter the Notes tools (press N). Photoshop has two Notes tools: one for text annotations and one for audio annotations. We suggest using audio annotations to your images only if you've never learned to type or if you're tired of having so much extra space on your hard drive—audio notes can make your files balloon in size (each 10 seconds of audio you add is about 140 K compared to about 1 K for 100 words of text notes).

To add a text annotation, click once on the image with the Notes tool and type what you will. If you type more than can fit in the little box, Photoshop automatically adds a scroll bar on the side. In addition, you can change the note's color, author, font, and size in the Options bar at any time.

Double-clicking on a note opens it (so you can read or listen to it) or closes it (minimizes it to just the Notes icon). Single-clicking on the Notes icon lets you move it or delete it (just press the Delete key). Or, if you want to delete all the notes in an image, press the Clear All button in the Options bar. Clearing all notes can be useful when you're creating a final version of an image.

Not just for Photoshop. If you want to send a Photoshop image with annotations to someone who doesn't have Photoshop, relax. If you choose File > Save As to save the image in Photoshop PDF format, text and audio annotations can be read and heard using Adobe Acrobat or the free Adobe Reader. You can also use Preview in Mac OS X, but you can only read text annotations.

Move the Notes away. By default, Photoshop places your notes windows at the same place in your image as the Notes icon. However, that means the little notes window usually covers up the image so you can't see what the note refers to. We usually drag the Notes icon off to the side or slightly out into the area that surrounds the picture. Conrad likes to keep notes just visible in the corner of an image because he's missed notes that were outside the image area; when he doesn't want to see notes he simply presses Command-H (Mac) or Ctrl-H (Windows), which toggles the View > Extras command. If you can't see notes in your Photoshop file but you suspect that they're there, make sure the Annotations item is turned on in the Show submenu (under the View menu). When this is off, no Notes icons appear.

Tool Preset Tips

Each tool in the Tool palette offers one or more options, such as the size of a brush's diameter, or whether a selection is feathered, or what mode a tool will paint in (Multiply, Screen, and so on). It's a hassle to remember to set all the tool options, especially if you need to change them frequently. Fortunately, Photoshop can remember multiple tool settings for you if you use the Tool Presets feature.

The Tool Presets feature lives in two places: at the far left side of the Options bar, and in the Tool Presets palette (choose Window > Tool Presets). We find that the palette is most useful for fine artists who need to switch among various tool presets, often within the same image (see **Figure 6-19**). Production folks like us tend to keep the palette closed and select tools from the Tool Presets pop-up menu in the Options bar. One of the reasons that tool presets live on the Options bar is that a tool preset includes the settings you've made in the Options bar.

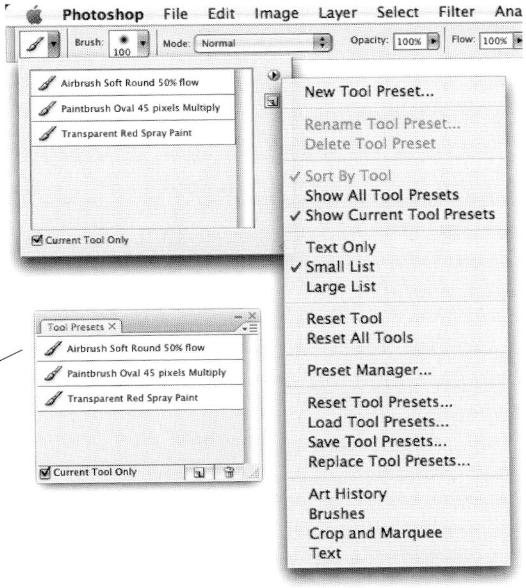

Figure 6-19

Tool presets from the Options bar

The same presets are available in the freestanding Tool Presets palette.

To create a new tool preset, select any tool in the Tool palette, change the Options bar to the way you want it, click on the Tool Presets pop-up menu in the Options bar, then click the New Tool Preset button (it looks like a little page with a dog-eared corner). Or, even faster, after setting up the tool, you can Option-click (Mac) or Alt-click (Windows) the Tool Presets icon in the Options bar. When Photoshop asks you for a name, we suggest giving the tool preset a descriptive name, like "ShapeTool Circle 50c20m."

Photoshop also comes with several premade collections of tool presets, such as Art History and Brushes. The trick to finding these (and doing all sorts of other things with tool presets, like saving your own sets), is to open the Preset Manager dialog (see **Figure 6-20**) by choosing Preset Manager from the Tools palette menu; the same menu is available in the top right corner of the Tool Presets pop-up menu from the Options bar.

Figure 6-20
Preset Manager dialog

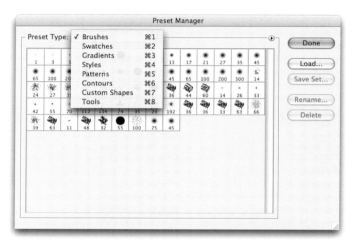

Unfortunately, there's no way to edit a tool preset once you make it— you can only create a new one and delete the old one by choosing Delete Tool Preset from the Tool Preset menu.

To reset the tool options for either a single tool or for all the tools, Control-click (Mac) or right-click (Windows) on the Tool Presets icon on the Options bar.

Palettes and Workspaces

There's little doubt that palettes are both incredibly useful when you need them and incredibly annoying when they're in your way. You don't have to accept how the palettes are arranged by default. The most important tip is that you can regroup palettes by dragging a palette tab to another palette tab, or stack them by dragging a palette tab to the bottom of another palette. Photoshop CS3 extends the traditional grouping and stacking behavior with palette docks that stick to the left and right sides of the monitor.

The new palette docks and workspaces in Photoshop CS3 change the rules a bit. If you think you're pretty familiar with palettes in Photoshop, you may be able to skip most of this section, but you'll still want to read the all-new Workspace tips.

Workspace Tips

Tip: If you or one of your "friends" has hopelessly scrambled your shortcuts, menus, or workspace beyond recognition, just reset your settings. On the Window > Workspace submenu, you'll find the commands Reset Palette Locations, Reset Keyboard Shortcuts, and Reset Default Workspace.

In the past, workspaces were simply a way to save palette arrangements, keyboard shortcuts, and custom menu sets for quick and easy recall. In Photoshop CS3, workspaces gain a new set of features that help you work with large collections of palettes in faster, more space-efficient, and less obtrusive ways.

To save a workspace, set up the palettes the way you want them, option-ally load any custom keyboard shortcut and menu sets, and choose Window > Workspace > Save Workspace. Saved workspaces appear on a Workspace pop-up menu on the Options bar, as well as at the bottom of the Workspace submenu, below the workspaces that come with Photoshop. For even easier recall, use the Keyboard Shortcuts and Menus dialog to assign keyboard shortcuts to your favorite workspace menu commands.

New workspace features. Photoshop CS3 introduces the same turbo-charged workspaces that now appear in the rest of the Adobe Creative Suite 3 applications: You can create vertical stacks of grouped palettes and dock them to the edge of the screen, collapse palettes into labeled or unlabeled icons to save space, and automatically expand and collapse the docked stacks to maximize your screen space.

► If a palette group has a light gray top bar, it's free-floating. If it has a dark gray top bar, it's docked to the side of the monitor or to another palette stack (see **Figure 6-21**). As always, you can drag a palette tab to dock it with others or tear off a palette dock so that it's free-floating.

► To expand or collapse a stack, click the dark gray bar at the top of a stack (see **Figure 6-22**). If the bar is very narrow, you can click the light gray double triangle icon at the right edge of the dark gray bar; it does the same thing.

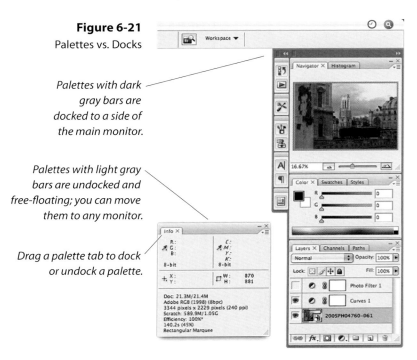

Figure 6-21
Palettes vs. Docks

Palettes with dark gray bars are docked to a side of the main monitor.

Palettes with light gray bars are undocked and free-floating; you can move them to any monitor.

Drag a palette tab to dock or undock a palette.

Figure 6-22
Expanding and collapsing docked palettes

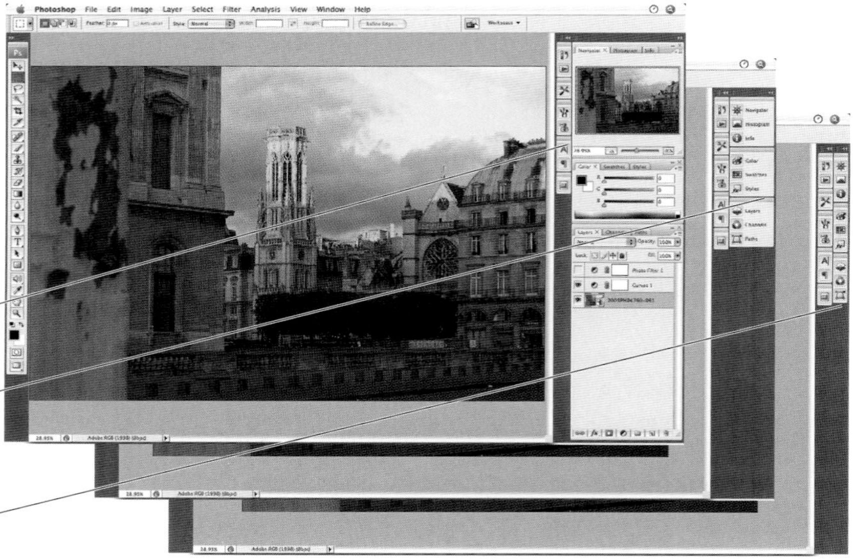

Far right stack expanded

Collapsed to labeled icons

Collapsed to unlabeled icons to maximize space for the image

▶ To make a stack narrower or wider, drag the vertical ribs at the left side of a dark gray top bar. You can set the width of both the collapsed and expanded state of a stack. A collapsed stack can be as narrow as a vertical stack of unlabeled icons (see Figure 6-22), or if you're still learning what the icons represent, you can widen a collapsed stack to reveal the labels. If you need to free up as much space as possible while still keeping a stack visible, we recommend collapsing palettes all the way down to the icons—remember, you can still see an icon title by holding the mouse over an icon until its tool tip appears.

▶ You can dock a palette to either side of the screen or to another palette stack; just drag a palette tab to either side of the screen until a blue line appears at a dockable location (either the screen edge or the edge of already docked palettes). We find that having multiple stacks against the side of the screen starts to make sense on high-resolution, wide-screen monitors, where there's actually room to spread out horizontally. If you have room to leave frequently used palettes open, you don't have to repeatedly expand and collapse palettes.

▶ You can dock palettes only to the sides of your main monitor, not to the top or bottom. You can't dock stacks at all on any other connected monitor. However, you can keep free-floating palettes on another monitor and group them however you like. In other words, if you prefer to keep your palettes on a second monitor, like we do, you can continue to do that in Photoshop CS3.

▶ When you click a collapsed icon to pop open a palette (see **Figure 6-23**), by default the palette stays open until you click its icon again or click another palette. However, when palettes stay open, they tend to intrude upon the image area. If you'd prefer that an expanded palette puts itself away, open the Preferences dialog, click the Interface panel, and then click Auto-Collapse Icon Palettes.

Figure 6-23
Icon expanded into palette

Actions palette expanded

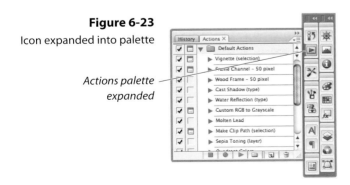

We think workspaces are extremely useful, because there is no one right way to arrange things. When Conrad connects his laptop to a color-calibrated desktop monitor, he likes to use the higher-quality desktop monitor as the main image viewing area and place as many palettes as possible on the laptop monitor. When he uses the laptop by itself, there isn't nearly enough room to replicate the two-monitor desktop arrangement, so he becomes picky about which palettes are visible. To switch instantly between the two palette arrangements, Conrad saved each arrangement as its own workspace.

We recommend that you save your favorite palette arrangement even if you don't need to create any others. Like your customized keyboard shortcuts and menus, if you don't save a palette arrangement in a workspace, it exists only in the Photoshop preferences file, so save your favorite workspace to avoid losing it if something happens to the Preferences file.

General Palette Tips

The flexibility of workspaces in Photoshop CS3 may reduce the amount of manual palette arrangement that was the norm in earlier versions. Still, when you need to maximize the amount of free screen space or create a specific palette arrangement, you need to know all of the ins and outs of palettes in Photoshop.

Make the palettes go away. If you only have one monitor on which to store both your image and the plethora of Photoshop palettes, you should remember two keyboard shortcuts. First, pressing Tab makes the palettes disappear (or reappear, if they're already hidden). We find this absolutely invaluable, and use it daily.

Second, pressing Shift-Tab makes all palettes except the Tool palette disappear (or reappear). We find this only slightly better than completely useless; we would prefer that the shortcut hid all the palettes except the Info palette.

As we mentioned earlier, you can leave docked palettes hidden and reveal them temporarily by moving the mouse to the edge of the screen where they're docked.

Making palettes smaller. Another way to maximize your screen real estate is by collapsing one or more of your open palettes. If you double-click on the palette's name tab, the palette collapses to just the title bar and name

Figure 6-24
Collapsing palettes

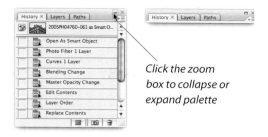

Click the zoom
box to collapse or
expand palette

(see **Figure 6-24**). Or if you click the zoom box of a palette, the palette reduces in size to only a few key elements. For instance, if you click the zoom box of the Layers palette, you can still use the Opacity sliders and Mode pop-up menu (but the Layer thumbnails and icons get hidden).

Mix and match palettes. There's one more way to save space on your computer screen: mix and match your palettes. As in other Adobe software, you can drag one palette on top of another to group them (see **Figure 6-25**). Then if you want, you can drag them apart again by clicking and dragging the palette's tab heading. (In fact, these kinds of palettes are called "tabbed palettes.")

Figure 6-25
Grouping palettes

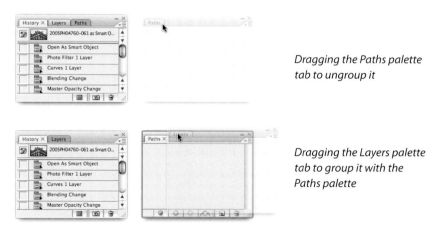

Dragging the Paths palette
tab to ungroup it

Dragging the Layers palette
tab to group it with the
Paths palette

For instance, David always keeps his Layers, Channels, and Paths palettes together on one palette. When he wants to work with one of these, he can click on that palette's tab heading. Or better yet, he uses a shortcut to make it active (see "Actions" in Chapter 11, "Essential Image Techniques," for more on how to define your own keyboard shortcuts).

Conrad, on the other hand, always keeps his Layers and Channels palettes separate, even when he's working on a single-monitor system. He likes to see the different views of a document's structure simultaneously. Neither of us ever mixes the Info palette with another palette, because we want it open all the time.

Photoshop offers one more way to combine palettes: by docking them. Docking a palette means that one palette is attached to the bottom of another one. Docked palettes always move together, and when you hide one, they both disappear. To dock one palette to another, drag it over the other palette's bottom edge; don't let go of the mouse button until you see the bottom edge of the palette become highlighted (see **Figure 6-26**).

Figure 6-26
Docking palettes

Docking the History palette to an existing palette group

Where's the Palette Well? Many users took advantage of the Palette Well, a slot in the Options bar where you could stash palettes as a compact row of tabs in Photoshop CS2. Adobe didn't carry the Palette Well forward into the new docking palette machinery, since you can now collapse docked palettes all the way down to a vertical row of icons. If you simply can't reprogram your muscle memory and must have palette tabs at the right side of the Options bar, you can create a group of palettes and stash them there in collapsed form (see **Figure 6-27**).

Scrubby sliders. We talked about adjusting number fields by scrubbing them—Command-dragging (Mac) or Ctrl-dragging (Windows) over a number field (see "Dialog Tips" earlier in this chapter). You can do the same thing over number fields in most palettes.

Figure 6-27
Simulating the
Photoshop CS2 Palette Well

Palette menus. Most palettes have a pop-up menu at the top right corner of the palette. They've always been there, but in Photoshop CS3 the icon has changed to resemble a tiny menu (see **Figure 6-28**). When clicking a palette menu, take care not to click the Close icon above it by mistake. Get to know your palette menus—sometimes it seems like half of the power of Photoshop is inside palette menus, which are so easy to miss.

Figure 6-28
The Layers palette menu

Reset Palette Locations. Every now and again, your palettes might get really messed up—placed partly or entirely off your screen, and so on. Don't panic; that's what Reset Palette Locations (in the Workspace sub-menu, in the Window menu) is for. Reset Palette Locations is best used when you haven't created your own workspace, because it sets palette positions back to the factory defaults. If you *have* created your own work-space, it's best to choose the workspace instead, of course.

Layers Palette

In every version since Photoshop 3.0 (when the layers feature was intro-duced), the Layers palette has become increasingly important to how people use Photoshop. With such a crucial palette, there have to be at least a few good tips around here…

Displaying and hiding layers. Every click takes another moment or two, and many people click in the display column of the Layers palette (the one with the little eyeballs in it) once for each layer they want to show or hide. Cut out the clicker-chatter, and just click and drag through the column for all the layers you want to make visible. Or Option-click (Mac) or Alt-click (Windows) in the display column of the Layers palette. When you Option/Alt-click an eyeball, Photoshop hides all the layers except the one you clicked on. Then, if you Option/Alt-click again, it redisplays them all again.

Creating a new layer. Layers are the best thing since sliced bread, and we're creating new ones all the time. But if you're still making a new layer by clicking on the New Layer button in the Layers palette, you've got some learning to do: Just press Command-Shift-N (Mac) or Ctrl-Shift-N (Windows). If you want to bypass the New Layer dialog, press Command-Option-Shift-N (Mac) or Ctrl-Alt-Shift-N (Windows).

Renaming layers. It's a very good idea to rename your layers from "Layer 1" or "Layer 2" to something a bit more descriptive. However, don't waste time looking for a "rename layer" feature. Instead, just double-click on the layer name to rename it. Note that this works in the Channels, Paths, and File Browser palettes, too.

Text layers name themselves after the text you've typed. They also rename themselves if you edit the text, so they're fairly low-maintenance. However, if you manually rename a text layer, it will no longer update when you edit its text in the document.

Duplicating layers. Duplicating a layer is a part of our everyday workflow, so it's a good thing that there are various ways to do it.

▶ In the Layers palette, drag the layer's thumbnail on top of the New Layer button.

▶ In the Layers palette, Option-drag (Mac) or Alt-drag (Windows) the layer's thumbnail to a new position in the Layers palette.

▶ Press Command-J (Mac) or Ctrl-J (Windows). If some pixels are selected, then only those pixels will be duplicated to a new layer.

▶ Select Duplicate Layer from the Layers palette menu or by Ctrl-clicking (Mac) or right-clicking (Windows) a layer.

▶ In the document window (not the Layers palette), Control-click (Mac) or right-click (Windows) a layer with the Marquee, Lasso, or Cropping tool and choose Duplicate Layer from the context menu.

The method you use at any given time should be determined by where your hands are. (Keyboard? Mouse? Coffee mug?)

Moving and duplicating layer masks. In the Layers palette, simply drag a layer mask's thumbnail to a new layer. To duplicate a layer mask, Option-drag (Mac) or Alt-drag (Windows) a layer mask thumbnail.

Selecting layers. You can select different layers (without ever touching the Layers palette) by using shortcuts: Press Option-[or Option-] (Mac) or Alt-[or Alt-] (Windows) to select the next visible layer behind or in front of the current layer. Add Shift to extend the selection to multiple layers. To select the top and bottom layers, respectively, press Option-. (period) and Option-, (comma) in Mac OS X, or press Alt-. (period) and Alt-, (comma) in Windows.

Tip: If only one layer is visible when you press the layer arrangement shortcuts, Photoshop hides that layer and shows the next layer. This is great for cycling through a number of layers, though it doesn't always work when you have layer groups.

Rearranging layers. To move the selected layer down or up in the Layers palette, press Command-[or Command-] (Mac) or Ctrl-[or Ctrl-] (Windows). To move the selected layer to the bottom or top of the layer stack, add the Shift key to either shortcut.

Faster layer selection. Perhaps the fastest way to select a layer is to select the Move tool and then turn on the Auto Select Layer check box in the Options bar. Now you can switch to a layer simply by clicking with the Move tool on a pixel on that layer. If you don't have the Move tool selected when you want to switch layers, simply activate the Move tool temporarily by pressing Command (Mac) or Ctrl (Windows) as you click.

A variation on Auto Layer Select is clicking layer content while pressing modifier keys, skipping the context menu entirely. Using any tool, Command-Option-Control-click (Mac) or Ctrl-Alt-right-click (Windows).

On the other hand, we personally find Auto Layer Select somewhat irritating because it's too easy to select the wrong layer. Instead, we prefer to Control-click (Mac) or right-click (Windows) layer content and choose the layer we want to select from the context menu that appears.

These techniques typically work only when you click on a pixel that has an opacity greater than 50 percent. (We say "typically" because it sometimes *does* work if the total visible opacity is less than 50 percent. See "Info

Palette," later in this chapter.) In general, if you make sure you click on reasonably opaque areas of layers, these techniques should work fine.

Creating layer groups. The more layers you have in your document, the more difficult it is to manage them. Fortunately, Photoshop offers *layer groups* in which you can group contiguous layers (layers that are next to each other). Layer groups are so easy to use that they don't require a great deal of explanation. They basically work like (and look like) the folders on your desktop. Here are the basics, though.

▶ To create a layer group, select the layers you want to group and then press Command-G (Mac) or Ctrl-G (Windows), which is the keyboard shortcut for Layer > Group Layers. You can also click the New Layer Group button in the Layers palette (see **Figure 6-29**), but then you have to drag layers into the group yourself.

Figure 6-29

Layer groups

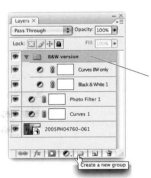

In this example, the "B&W version" layer group contains only layers that produce a black-and-white version of the image. Hiding the layer group leaves the original full-color layers.

▶ To add a layer to a group, just drag it on top of the group. Or, to create a new layer inside the group automatically, select the group or any layer within the group (in the Layers palette) and click the New Layer button. You can remove a layer from a group simply by dragging it out.

▶ You can move layer groups in the same way you move layers: just drag them around in the palette. You can also copy a whole group of layers to a different document by dragging the layer group over.

▶ If you have more than one layer group, it's helpful to color-code them: just double-click on the layer group's name and pick a color in the Group Properties dialog. You should probably name the group, too, while you're there (the default "Group 1" doesn't help identify what's in it). Watch out, though: If you drag a color-coded layer out of the group, it still retains its color-coding!

▶ If you want to move all the layers within a layer group at the same time, select the layer group in the Layers palette. This is easier and faster than linking the layers together or selecting them all.

▶ You can add a layer mask to the layer group (see Chapter 8, "The Digital Darkroom," for more on masks) and it'll apply to every layer in the group. Similarly, locking a group locks every layer within the group.

▶ You can nest one layer group inside another. Just drag one layer group onto another. Or, if you select a layer inside a group first, when you create a new group, it will also be nested. You can nest your layer groups up to five deep.

▶ Layer groups act almost like a single layer, so when you show or hide the group, all the layers in that group appear or disappear.

▶ When you delete a layer group, Photoshop lets you choose to delete the group *and* the layers and sets inside it or just the group itself (leaving the layers and nested sets intact).

Unfortunately, you can't apply a layer effect to a layer group or use a layer group as a clipping mask (see Chapter 8).

Layer groups and blending modes. If you had your coffee this morning, you'll notice that you can change the blending mode of a layer group. Normally, the blending mode is set to Pass Through, which means, "let each layer's blending mode speak for itself." In this mode, layers inside the group look the same as they would if they were outside the group. However, if you change the group's blending mode, a curious thing happens: Photoshop first composites the layers in the group as though they were a single layer (following the blending modes you've specified for each layer), and then it composites that "single layer" with the rest of your image using the layer group's blending mode. In this case, layers may appear very differently whether they're inside or outside that group.

Similarly, when you change the opacity of the group, Photoshop first composites the layers in the group (using their individual Opacity settings) and then applies this global Opacity setting to the result.

Layer Comps Palette

The Layer Comps palette is one of David's favorite features in Photoshop. David loves keeping his options open, and is forever trying to decide among various permutations of reality. For instance, he'll picture in his mind's eye five different ways to drive to the grocery store before committing to one. The Layer Comps palette won't help him with his driving choices, but it's an awesome help when making decisions about how to edit an image in Photoshop.

The Layer Comps palette is like a clever combination of the Layers palette and the History palette: It lets you save the state of your document's layers so you can return to it later. It seems like the Layer Comps feature should be part of the Layers palette, but perhaps Adobe figured the Layers palette was already complex enough. While the snapshots feature of the History palette can perform most of the same tasks as the Layer Comps palette, the History palette is significantly more memory-intensive and—this is important—layer comps can be saved with the document while snapshots disappear when you close the file. Saving a layer comp makes almost no difference to your file size (each comp is only a few K on disk).

Layer comps don't only record visibility. A layer comp doesn't just remember which layers are visible. It also remembers the position of items on each layer, layer effects, and the layer's blending mode (see **Figure 6-30**). To create a layer comp, press the New Layer Comp button in the Layer Comps palette. Now Photoshop displays the New Layer Comp dialog, which lets you name the layer comp (it's easy to lose track of what each layer comp represents), specify which settings Photoshop should remember, and insert a comment about the comp.

Photoshop can remember three kinds of information about your layer comps: Visibility, Position, and Appearance.

▶ By default, layer comps just remember the *visibility* of each layer—that is, which layers and layer groups are visible and which are hidden in the Layers palette.

▶ When you turn on the Position check box, the layer comp remembers where on the layer the pixel data is sitting. For example, let's say you save a layer comp with Position turned on, and then use the Move tool to reposition the image or text on that layer. When you return to the

Figure 6-30
Layer comps

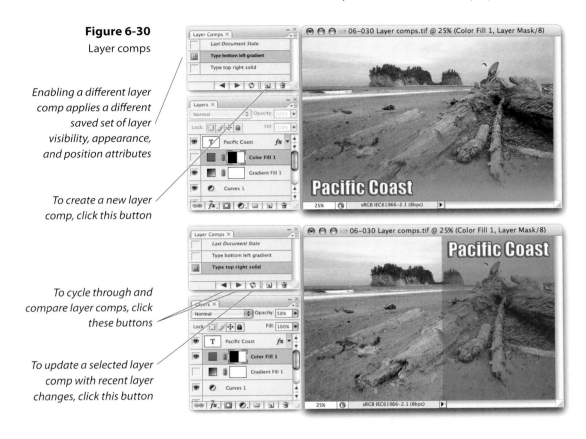

Enabling a different layer comp applies a different saved set of layer visibility, appearance, and position attributes

To create a new layer comp, click this button

To cycle through and compare layer comps, click these buttons

To update a selected layer comp with recent layer changes, click this button

saved layer comp, the image or text reverts back to where it was when you saved the comp.

► The Appearance option tells the program to remember any layer effects and blending modes that you've applied to your layers. For example, let's say you save a layer comp with Appearance turned *off*, then you change the blending modes of one or more layers in the Layers palette. When you return to the saved layer comp, the blending-mode changes remain because you hadn't told the layer comp to retain the appearance of the layers.

For a quick and dirty layer comp with the default name, no comment, and the same attributes as the last comp you made (by default, just the Visibility option), hold down the Option/Alt key while clicking the New Layer Comp button. Remember that, like layers and channels, you can always rename a layer comp by double-clicking on its name in the palette.

If you double-click on the thumbnail (anywhere other than its name), you open the Layer Comp Options dialog.

Quick display of comps. Once you have saved one or more layer comps in the Layer Comps palette, you can return to a comp state by clicking the small square to the left of the comp name. You can also click the left and right arrow icons at the bottom of the Layer Comps palette. Better yet, if you have ten comps but only want to cycle through three of them, select those three (Command- or Ctrl-click on the comps to select more than one) and then use the arrow buttons in the palette. If you use layer comps much, we strongly suggest that you use the Keyboard Shortcuts feature (in the Edit menu) to apply keyboard shortcuts to the Next Layer Comp and Previous Layer Comp features so you don't have to click those silly arrow buttons all the time.

You'll notice a layer comp called Last Document State in the Layer Comp palette. This is just the state of your document before you chose a layer comp. For example, let's say you display a layer comp, then hide some layers and move some text around. Now if you select any layer comp, your changes disappear—but if you click on the Last Document State comp, the changes return.

Updating comps. Need to change the layer comp? You don't have to delete it and start over. Just set up the Photoshop document to reflect what you want the comp to look like, then select the comp in the palette and click the Update Layer Comp button (that's the one that looks like two rotating arrows).

Sending comps to clients. The fact that Photoshop saves layer comps—comments and all—with your files is pretty cool. That means you can save a file as a PSD, TIFF, or PDF file and have someone else open the file in Photoshop and browse through the Layer Comp palette. Even cooler, however, are the three Export Layer Comp scripts in the Scripts submenu (under the File menu): Export Layer Comps to Files, Export Layer Comps to PDF, and Export Layer Comps to WPG. Each of these lets you save all (or the currently selected) layer comps to one or more flattened files on disk. The PDF can even be a slideshow presentation that progresses automatically every few seconds if you want. It took us some time before we figured out what WPG is: It's a Web Photo Gallery of your comps, ready to post on a Web site.

Note that when you run the last two of these scripts (each written in JavaScript, by the way), you'll see each of your comps appear twice. The first time, Photoshop is flattening and saving to disk; the second time, it's opening that flattened version and adding it to the presentation.

Clear comp warnings. If, after making one or more layer comps, you delete or merge a layer, you'll notice that small warning icons appear in the Layer Comps palette. These tell you that Photoshop can no longer return to the layer comp as saved (because the layer no longer exists as it was when you made the comp). You can still choose a layer comp that has a warning icon—it'll still apply to all the layers that still do exist. If you delete a layer and you don't want to see the warning icons anymore, Control-click (or right-click in Windows) on one of the icons and choose Clear All Layer Comp Warnings from the context menu.

Info Palette

In a battle of the palettes, we don't know which Photoshop palette would win the "most important" prize, but we do know which would win in the "most telling" category: the Info palette. We almost never close this palette. It just provides us with too much critical information.

At its most basic task, as a densitometer, it tells us the gray values and RGB or CMYK values in an image. But there's much more. When you're working in RGB, the Info palette shows you how pixels will translate to CMYK or grayscale. When working in Levels or Curves, it displays before-and-after values (see Chapter 7, "Image Adjustment Fundamentals"). Especially note the Proof Color option, which shows the numbers that would result from the conversion you've specified in Proof Setup, which may be different from the one you've specified in Color Settings (see Chapter 4, "Color Settings"). The Proof Color numbers appear in italics—a clue that you're looking at a different set of numbers than the ones you'd get from a mode change.

But wait, there's more! When you rotate a selection, the Info palette displays the selection's angle. And when you scale, it shows percentages. If you've selected a color that is out of the CMYK gamut (depending on your setup; (see Chapter 4, "Color Settings"), a gamut warning appears on the Info palette.

Finding opacity. When you have transparency showing (e.g., on layers that have transparency when no background is showing), the Info palette can give you an opacity (Op) reading. However, while Photoshop would display this automatically in earlier versions, now you have to do a little extra work: You must click on one of the little black Eyedroppers in the Info palette and select Opacity (see **Figure 6-31**).

Figure 6-31
Color and units
display options

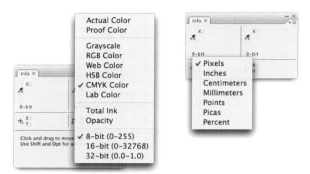

Switch units. While we typically work in pixel measurements, we do, on occasion, need to see "real world" physical measurements such as inches or centimeters. Instead of traversing the menus to open the Units dialog (on the Preferences submenu under the File menu), we find it's usually faster to select from the Info palette menu. Just click on the XY cursor icon (see Figure 6-31). Another option: double-clicking in one of the rulers opens the Units Preferences dialog. You can also do this by Control-clicking (Mac) or right-clicking (Windows) on one of the rulers. If the rulers aren't visible, press Command-R (Mac) or Ctrl-R (Windows).

Expand the display. To display a wealth of data in the Info palette, choose Palette Options from the Info palette menu, turn on check boxes in the Status Information section, and click OK (see **Figure 6-32**).

Color Palettes

The Color Picker and the Color palette both fit into one category, so we almost always group them into one palette on our screens and switch between them as necessary.

Most novice Photoshop users select a foreground or background color by clicking once on the icons in the Tool palette and choosing from the Color dialog. Many pros, however, have abandoned this technique, and

Figure 6-32
Status Information options

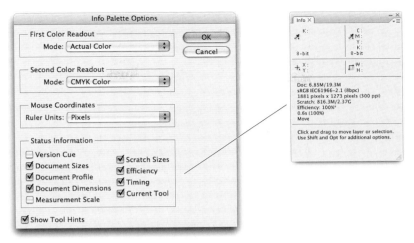

focus instead on these color palettes. Here are a few tips to make this technique more…ah…palettable.

Switching color bars. Instead of clicking on the foreground color swatch in the Tool palette, you might consider typing values into the Color palette. Are the fields labeled "RGB" when you want to type in "CMYK" or something else? Just choose a different mode from the Color palette menu. If you like choosing colors visually rather than numerically, you can use the color bar at the bottom of the palette (no, the Color Bar is not just another place to meet people). While the spectrum of colors that appear here usually covers the RGB gamut, you can switch to a different spectrum by Shift-clicking on the area. Click once, and you switch to CMYK; again, and you get a gradient in grayscale; a third time, and you see a gradient from your foreground color to your background color. Shift-clicking again takes you back to RGB. You can also use the context menu to choose a color space.

Just remember that changing the color spectrum only changes the way you specify the color. The color is stored in the document in the color space of the document itself. For example, if you're working in an RGB document and you specify a color in CMYK, the color is translated into RGB as you apply it to the document.

Editing the color swatches. You've probably ignored all those swatches on the Swatches palette because they never seem to include colors that have anything to do with your images. Don't ignore…explore! You can add, delete, and edit those little color swatches on the Swatches palette.

Table 6-2 shows you how. If you're looking for Web-safe colors or other useful colors, check out the palette menu.

You can't actually edit a color that's already there. Instead, you can click on the swatch (to make it the current foreground color), edit the foreground color, then Shift-click back on the swatch (which replaces it with the current foreground color).

Table 6-2

Editing the
Swatches palette

To do this...	Do this...
Add foreground color	Click any empty area
Delete a color	Command/Alt-click
Replace a color with foreground color	Shift-click (Mac only)

History Palette

There is a school of thought that dictates, "Don't give people what they want, give them what they need." The Photoshop engineering team spends hours listening to and thinking about what people ask for, and then comes back with a feature that goes far beyond what anyone had even thought to request. For example, people long asked Adobe for multiple undos (the ability to sequentially undo steps that you've taken while editing a Photoshop image). The result is the History palette, which goes far beyond a simple undo mechanism into a much more powerful way of working in Photoshop.

The History palette, at its most basic, remembers what you've done to your file and lets you either retrace your steps or revert back to any earlier version of the image. Every time you do something to your image—paint a brushstroke, run a filter, make a selection, and so on—Photoshop saves this change as a *state* in the History palette (see **Figure 6-33**). At any time, you can revert the entire image to any previous state, or—using the History Brush tool or the Fill command, which we'll discuss in a moment—selectively paint back in time.

The only issue with using History is that it can vastly increase the size of your scratch files. It's unlikely that heavy History use will hurt performance significantly, though if Photoshop has to hunt for something in 50 GB of scratch disk space, you may experience a momentary lapse in responsiveness—the bigger danger is that you run out of scratch disk space and find yourself unable to do anything, possibly including saving

Figure 6-33

The History palette

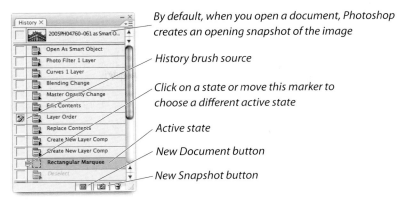

By default, when you open a document, Photoshop creates an opening snapshot of the image

History brush source

Click on a state or move this marker to choose a different active state

Active state

New Document button

New Snapshot button

the file. If you plan on using 1000 history states, make sure you have plenty of scratch disk space!

Turning off History. If you're low on disk space or just want to avoid the History feature's heavy scratch disk overhead, you can reduce the number of history states to just one. While having one history state may be too limiting if you're in the middle of trial-and-error design or image editing, you won't need more than one history state if you're executing basic production steps or running batch actions. To change the number of history states, open the Preferences dialog and click the Performance panel, type a value into the History States option, and click OK.

The default value of 20 history states is a good balance between flexibility and disk space usage.

The History palette has two sections: snapshots and states. Let's take a look at each of these and how you can use them.

Snapshots. The History palette lets you save any number of snapshots—representing a moment in time for your image—so that at any time you can go back to a specific state. There are two main differences between snapshots and states.

▶ Photoshop records almost everything you do to an image as a state. By default, snapshots are only recorded when you first open an image and when you click the New Snapshot button in the History palette.

▶ When the number of states recorded on the History palette exceeds the Maximum Remembered States value (set in the History Options dialog), the oldest states start dropping off the list. Snapshots don't disappear until you close the document.

What's in the snapshot. When you click the New Snapshot button on the History palette (or select New Snapshot from the palette menu), Photoshop saves the whole document (individual layers and all). Depending on how many layers you have and how large your document is, this might require a lot of scratch space. If you Option-click (Mac) or Alt-click (Windows) the button, Photoshop offers two other less-storage-intensive snapshot choices: a version of the image with merged layers, or just of the currently selected layer. (If you find yourself Option/Alt-clicking the button a lot in order to get these options, then turn on the Show New Snapshot Dialog By Default check box in History Options. That way, you don't have to press the Option/Alt key anymore.)

Stepping through states. As we mentioned earlier, Photoshop saves every brushstroke, every selection, every *any*thing you do to your image as a state on the History palette (though the state only remains on the palette until you reach the maximum number of states or you close the document). There are three ways to move among your images's states.

▶ To revert your image to a state, you can click on any state's thumbnail in the History palette.

▶ You can move the active state marker to a different state on the History palette.

▶ To step back to the last state, press Command-Z (Mac) or Ctrl-Z (Windows), which works like a standard undo. But you can also move backward one state at a time by pressing Command-Option-Z (Mac) or Ctrl-Alt-Z (Windows), or move forward one state at a time by pressing Command-Shift-Z (Mac) or Ctrl-Shift-Z (Windows).

In general, when you move to an earlier state, Photoshop grays out every subsequent state on the History palette, indicating that if you do anything now, those grayed-out states will be erased. This is like going back to a fork in the road and choosing the opposite path than the one you took before. Photoshop offers another option: If you turn on the Allow Non-Linear History check box in the History Options dialog, Photoshop doesn't gray out or remove subsequent states when you move back in time (though it still deletes old states when you hit the maximum number of states).

Non-Linear History is like returning to the fork in the road, taking the opposite path, but then having the option to return to any state from the first path. For example, you could run a Gaussian Blur on your image using three different amounts—returning the image to the pre-blurred state in the History palette each time—and then switch among the three states to decide which one you want to use.

The primary problem with Non-Linear History is that it may confuse you more than help you, especially when you're dealing with a number of different forks in the road.

The History Brush. Returning to a previous state returns the entire image to that state. But the History feature lets you selectively return portions of your image to a previous state, too, with the History Brush and the Fill command. Before painting with the History Brush, first select the source state in the History palette (see Figure 6-33). For instance, let's say you sharpen a picture of a face with Unsharp Masking (see Chapter 10) and find that the lips have become oversharp. You can select the History Brush, set the source state to the presharpened state, and brush around the lips (though you'd probably want to reduce the opacity of the History Brush to 20 or 30 percent by pressing 2 or 3 first).

The History Brush tool (press Y) is very similar to the Eraser tool when the Erase to History check box is turned on in the Options bar, but the History Brush lets you paint with modes, such as Multiply and Screen. We used to prefer the History Brush over Erase To History or Fill From History, because they didn't work on high-bit files, but that limitation has disappeared in Photoshop CS3, so now we use whichever gets the job done most easily.

Take a snapshot before an action. If you run an action in the Actions palette that has more steps than your History States preference, you won't be able to undo the action. That's why, before running the action, you should either save a snapshot of your full document or set the source state for the History Brush to the current state. The latter works because the source state in the History palette isn't automatically deleted when the History palette exceeds the maximum number of states you've set.

Fill with History. One last nifty technique that can rescue you from a catastrophic "oops" is the Fill command on the Edit menu (press Shift-F5). This lets you fill any selection (or the entire image, if nothing is selected) with the pixels from the current source state on the History palette. We prefer this to the History Brush or Eraser tools when the area to be reverted is easily selectable. Sometimes when we paint with those tools, we overlook some pixels (it's hard to use a brush to paint every pixel in an area at 100 percent). This is never a problem when you use the Fill command.

You've always been able to press Option-Delete (Mac) or Alt-Delete (Windows) to fill a selection or layer with the foreground color. In version 4, Photoshop added the ability to automatically preserve transparency on the layer when you add the Shift key (slightly faster than having to turn on the Preserve Transparency check box in the Layers palette). Similarly, you can fill with the background color by pressing Command-Delete (add the Shift key to preserve transparency). To fill the layer or selection with the current history source state, press Command-Option-Delete (Mac) or Ctrl-Alt-Backspace (Windows). And, of course, you can add the Shift key to this to fill with Preserve Transparency turned on.

Persistent states. Remember that both snapshots and states are cleared out when you close a document. If you want to save a particular state or snapshot, drag its thumbnail over the Create New Document button on the History palette. Now that state is its own document that you can save to disk. If you want to copy pixels from that document into another image, simply use the Clone Stamp tool (you can set the source point to one document and then paint with it in the other file).

Copying states. Although Photoshop lets you copy states from one document to another simply by dragging them from the History palette onto the other document's window, we can't think of many good reasons to do this. The copied state completely replaces the image that you've dragged it over.

When History stops working. Note that you cannot use the History Brush or the Fill From History feature when your image's pixel dimensions, bit depth, or color mode has changed. Pixel dimensions usually change when you rotate the whole image, use the Cropping tool, or use the Image Size or Canvas Size dialogs.

Purging states. As we said earlier, the History palette takes up a lot of scratch disk space. If you find yourself running out of room on your hard disk, you might try clearing out the History states by either selecting Clear History from the History palette menu or choosing Histories from the Purge submenu (under the Edit menu). The former can be undone in a pinch; the latter cannot. Curiously, neither of these removes your snapshots, so you have to delete those manually if you want to save even more space. Remember that closing your document and reopening it will also remove all snapshots and history states.

History Log. Although there's no way to keep history states and snapshots after you close a document, you can keep a record of what you did, and it's called the History Log. The History Log is text that records your edits, but you can only read it—you can't play it back or reload it. You can use the History Log to track your edits down to the settings you used in dialogs, and you can use that to manually reproduce the edits made to the file.

If you want to keep a History Log, turn on the History Log check box in the General panel of the Preferences dialog (see **Figure 6-34**). You can choose whether you want to save a log with each file (select Metadata) or maintain a central log for all files (Text File). You can also use the Edit Log Items pop-up menu to set the level of detail for the log.

This all seems simple enough, but there are privacy issues you might want to think about. If you increase the History Log's level of detail, the History Log can record minutiae like the folder paths and names of files you open, and the text you enter on text layers. If you choose to store the History Log in metadata, it travels wherever the image travels. For example, if you type "My Stupid Boss" on a text layer because you're just playing around, and then you delete the text, the original text entry is still in the log. If you store the log in the image metadata, and your boss views the file in Adobe Bridge, which can display the metadata, your boss may come across the log entry containing that text. If you or your organization have an interest in restricting certain information, you may not want detailed editing records to travel with the file. You might limit the level of detail or choose not to store the log in file metadata.

If you set up the History Log in a way that's appropriate for your work, it can be a valuable tool in analyzing your processes and techniques.

Setting Preferences

There's a scene in Monty Python's *Life of Brian* in which Brian is trying to persuade his followers to think for themselves. He shouts, "Every one of you is different! You're all individuals!" One person raises his hand and replies, "I'm not."

This is the situation we often find with Photoshop users. Even though each person uses the program differently, they think they need to use it just like everyone else does. Not true. You can customize Photoshop in a number of ways through its Preferences submenu (on the Photoshop menu in Mac OS X, and on the Edit menu in Windows).

We're not going to discuss every preference here—we're just going to take a look at some of the key items. (We also discuss preferences where relevant elsewhere in the book; for example, we explore color preferences more in Chapter 4.)

Return of Preferences. If you make a change in one of the many Preferences dialogs and then, after closing the dialog, you realize you want to change some other preference, you can return to the last Preferences panel you saw by pressing Command-Option-K (Mac) or Ctrl-Alt-K (Windows).

Navigating through Preferences. The Preferences dialog contains many different panels, each of which offers a different set of options (see **Figure 6-34**). Sure, you can select each screen from the pop-up menu at the top of the dialog, or by clicking the Next and Prev buttons. But the fastest way

Figure 6-34
General Preferences

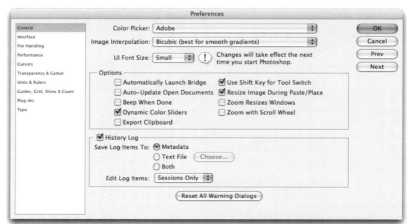

to jump to any of the first nine panels while in the Preferences dialog is to press a number key along with Command (Mac) or Ctrl (Windows). For example, if you want to switch to the fourth Preferences pane (Performance) on a Mac, press Command-4. Instead of clicking Next, you can press Command-N (Mac) or Ctrl-N (Windows); instead of clicking Prev, press Command-P (Mac) or Ctrl-P (Windows).

Propagating your preferences. Any time you make a change to one of the Preferences dialogs, Photoshop remembers your alteration, and when you quit, saves it in the file Adobe Photoshop CS3 Prefs.psp. In Mac OS X, it's in Users\username\Library\Preferences\Adobe Photoshop CS3 Settings. In Windows XP, it's in Documents and Settings\username\Application Data\Adobe\Adobe Photoshop CS3\Adobe Photoshop CS3 Settings. In Windows Vista, it's in Users\Username\AppData\Roaming\Adobe\ Adobe Photoshop CS3\Adobe Photoshop CS3 Settings.

> **Tip:** In Windows, the Preferences folder may be hidden by default. To see it in Windows XP, in a folder window choose Tools > Folder Options, and in the Folder Options dialog, select Show Hidden Files and Folders. To see it in Windows Vista, in a folder window choose Organize > Folder and Search Options, click the View tab, and then select Show Hidden Files and Folders in the Advanced Settings list.

If anything happens to the Adobe Photoshop CS3 Prefs.psp file, all your hard-won preference settings are gone. Because of this, on the Mac, we recommend keeping a backup of that file, or even the whole settings directory (people often back up their images without realizing they should back up this sort of data file, too).

Certain kinds of crashes can corrupt the Photoshop Preferences file. If Photoshop starts acting strange on us, our first step is always to replace the Preferences file with a clean copy (if no copy of the Preferences file is available, then Photoshop will build a new one for you). To reset the Preference files, hold down the Command, Option, and Shift keys (Ctrl, Alt, and Shift keys in Windows) immediately after launching the program—Photoshop will ask if you really want to reset all the preferences.

Conrad doesn't like going all the way back to the default preferences because there are so many performance-altering settings to remember (scratch disks and so on). He prefers to use the built-in ability of both Mac OS X and Windows to create a ZIP archive of the Preferences file in the same folder as the original, so that when something goes wrong, he can trash the bad prefs file and unzip the known good one.

> **Tip:** In Mac OS X, you create a Zip archive by choosing File > Create Archive Of (filename). In Windows, it's File > Send To > Compressed (Zipped) Folder.

If you administer a number of different computers that are running Photoshop, you may want to standardize the preferences on all machines. The answer: Copy the Photoshop Prefs file to each computer. Finally, note that Photoshop doesn't save changes to the preferences until you Quit. If Photoshop crashes, the changes don't get saved.

UI Font Size. If you have a high-resolution monitor, you may want to increase the UI Font Size setting to keep text in the Photoshop user interface from becoming too small to read.

Export Clipboard. When the Export Clipboard check box is on, Photoshop converts whatever is on the Clipboard into your operating system's clipboard format when you switch out of Photoshop. This is helpful—indeed, necessary—if you want to paste a selection into some other program. But if you've got 10 MB on the Clipboard, that conversion is going to take some time. In situations when you're running low on RAM, the operating system may slow down. Since the Clipboard is probably the least reliable mechanism for getting images from Photoshop into some other application, we recommend leaving Export Clipboard off until you really need it.

Resize Image During Paste/Place. When this option is off, if you place or paste a graphic into a Photoshop document and the Photoshop document is much smaller than the incoming graphic, you'll only see the center of the incoming graphic and can't grab its handles unless you zoom out. Turning on this option always scales down an incoming graphic to fit it within the current document. Sounds convenient, so why would you want to turn it off? If you regularly place graphics that need to maintain their original size, you don't want Photoshop to scale them at all—in that case, you should keep this option off.

Use Grayscale Toolbar Icon. By default, the Photoshop icon at the top of the toolbar is blue. If you would rather that your user interface be a neutral gray (a better background for color correction), you'll want to turn on this option (see **Figure 6-35**), in addition to choosing a neutral gray user interface color in your operating system preferences. The screen shots in this book use this preference, combined with the nice, neutral Graphite color scheme in the Appearance system preference in Mac OS X.

Show Menu Colors. This preference makes a difference only if you've used the Edit > Keyboard Shortcuts command to colorize menu commands. For example, if you choose Window > Workspace > What's New in CS3 and you can't figure out why the new commands aren't appearing in blue like they're supposed to, it's because this preference is turned off.

Figure 6-35
Interface Preferences

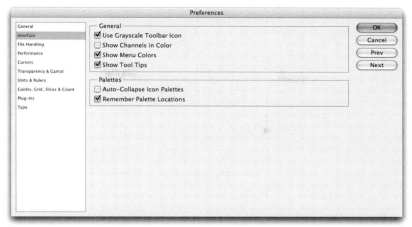

Remember Palette Locations. This does what it says—it remembers which palettes were open, which were closed, and where they were located on the screen the last time you quit. We leave this turned on, but we tend to rely on the Save Workspace feature to manage our palettes instead. Note that if you change your monitor resolution, the palettes return to their default locations anyway.

Image Previews. When you save a document in Photoshop, the program can save little thumbnails of your image as file icons. Image previews increase file size on disk by a small amount, so if you need the smallest possible files, you might set this option (see **Figure 6-36**) to Never Save or Ask When Saving. We always set Image Previews to Ask When Saving, so we can control it on a file-by-file basis.

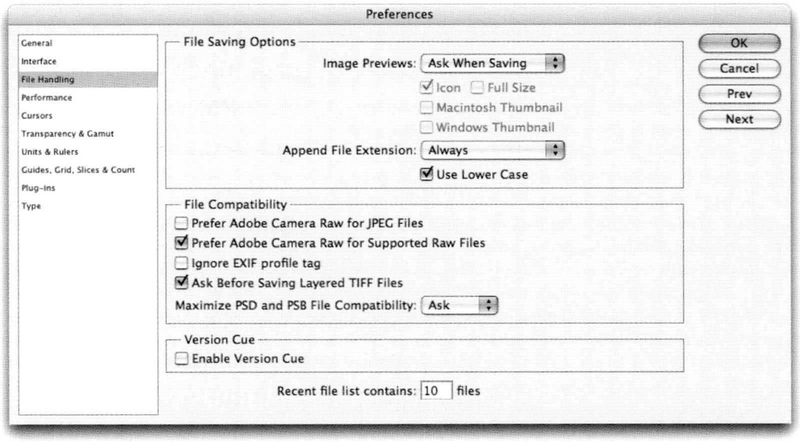

Figure 6-36
File Handling Preferences

Ask Before Saving Layered TIFF Files. Many benighted souls still don't realize that TIFF files are first-class citizens that can store anything a Photoshop (.psd) file can, including Photoshop layers. We discuss this in detail in Chapter 12, but we should point out one thing here: When the Ask Before Saving Layered TIFF Files option is turned on in Preferences (as is by default), Photoshop will always alert you when you try to save a file that was a flat (nonlayered) TIFF but now has layers. For example, if you open a TIFF image and add some type, the text shows up on a type layer. Now if you press Command-S (Mac) or Ctrl-S (Windows) to save the file, Photoshop displays the TIFF Options dialog, in which you can either flatten the layers or keep them.

If you find yourself staring at this dialog too much and you keep thinking to yourself, "If I wanted to flatten the image, I would have done it myself," then go ahead and turn this option off in the Preferences dialog. Then Photoshop won't bother you anymore, and layered documents will always save as layered files.

Ignore EXIF Profile Tag. This option exists because some early digital cameras embedded the wrong profile into their images, and turning on this option decreased the chance that Photoshop would misinterpret such an image's color. If you use a recent camera or shoot in raw format, keep this option turned off.

Maximize PSD and PSB File Compatibility. People have strong opinions about this feature, which was known in earlier versions as Maximize Backwards Compatibility in Photoshop Format, Include Composited Image with Layered Files, or 2.5 Format Compatibility. Many users strongly resent the fact that turning on this option can greatly increase file size, because Photoshop saves a flattened version of your layered image along with the layered version. Because Photoshop can open a file just as easily whether this option is off or on, a lot of people choose to turn it off and save the disk space.

However, there are good reasons why this preference exists, and those reasons are enough for us to set this option to Ask.

▶ Some non-Adobe programs claim to view or open layered Photoshop files, but (of course) they don't contain the entire Photoshop imaging engine. To view Photoshop files, they depend on the flattened compatibility copy that's provided by the Maximize PSD and PSB File

Compatibility option. Without it, you see a placeholder (see **Figure 6-37**). For example, if you save a Photoshop document with this option turned off and then you try to view the document in a non-Adobe application such as Apple Preview, you won't be able to view the contents.

► If you use Photoshop files in other Adobe Creative Suite programs such as Adobe InDesign or Adobe After Effects, you need to leave this option on, for the same reasons we just talked about.

► If you use a digital asset manager, chances are you won't be able to view layered Photoshop files in it unless the files were saved with Maximize PSD and PSB File Compatibility turned on. Adobe Lightroom 1.1 falls into this category.

► Some programs can only understand 8-bit RGB Photoshop files, and they can't handle Photoshop files saved in other color modes or at other bit depths unless Maximize PSD and PSB File Compatibility is turned on.

► Future versions of Photoshop may interpret blending modes slightly differently than they do today due to improvements or bug fixes. If changes occur, and that change affects the look of your file, then you would at least be able to recover the flattened version, if there is one.

Conrad uses Photoshop files in other Creative Suite applications, and on top of that, he uses a couple of different digital asset managers, so he prefers to leave this option set to Always.

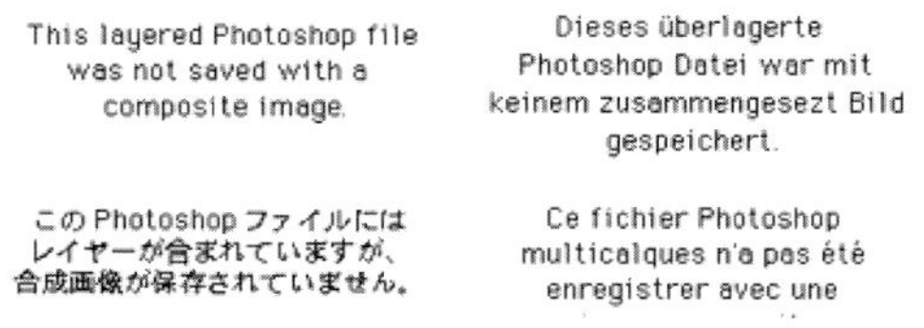

Figure 6-37

The placeholder that may be displayed by other programs when a layered Photoshop file doesn't include a composite version

This layered Photoshop file was not saved with a composite image.

Dieses überlagerte Photoshop Datei war mit keinem zusammengesezt Bild gespeichert.

この Photoshop ファイルには
レイヤーが含まれていますが、
合成画像が保存されていません。

Ce fichier Photoshop multicalques n'a pas été enregistrer avec une

Painting Cursors and Other Cursors. We like to set our Painting Cursors (see **Figure 6-38**) to Normal Brush Tip or Full Size Brush Tip. Both display the diameter of the currently selected brush, but the difference is that Normal only marks the diameter of the areas that are 50 percent opacity or more based on the opacity and hardness of the current brush.

Figure 6-38

Cursor Preferences

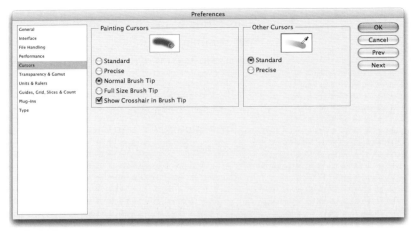

For Other Cursors, we prefer the Precise setting because it helps us position the cursor better than the default cursor icons do. If you set Other Cursors to Standard, you can temporarily display cursors in Precise mode; just press the Caps Lock key.

Gamut Warning. When you turn on View > Gamut Warning (or press Command-Shift-Y on the Mac or Ctrl-Shift-Y in Windows), Photoshop displays all the out-of-gamut pixels in the color you choose here. We recommend you choose a really ugly color (in the Transparency & Gamut Preferences dialog, see **Figure 6-39**) that doesn't appear anywhere in your image, such as a bright lime green. This way, when you switch on Gamut Warning, the out-of-gamut areas are quite obvious.

Figure 6-39

Transparency & Gamut
Preferences

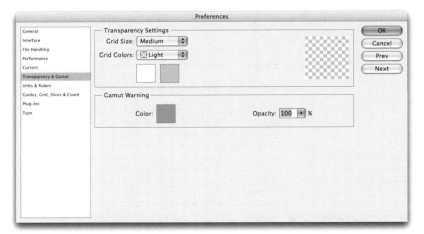

Note, however, that Gamut Warning is of limited use. It tells you which colors are out of gamut, but not how they look. It's generally more informative to set up and use the View > Proof Colors command instead.

Transparency. Transparency is not a color—it's the absence of any color at all, even black or white. Therefore, when you see it on a layer, what should it look like? Typically, Photoshop displays transparency as a grid of white and gray boxes in a checkerboard pattern. The Preferences dialog lets you change the colors of the checkerboard and set the size of the squares. We've never found a reason to do so, but in the event you're creating a design that actually uses a gray checkerboard, you can use this preference to avoid confusing those areas with transparent areas.

When Things Go Worng

It's 11 PM on the night before your big presentation. You've been working on this image for 13 hours, and you're beginning to experience a bad case of "pixel vision." After making a selection, you run a filter, look carefully, and decide that you don't like the effect. But before you can reach Undo, you accidentally click on the document window, deselecting the area.

That's not so bad, is it? Not until you realize that undoing will only undo the deselection, not the filter…and that you haven't saved for half an hour. The mistake remains, and there's no way to get rid of it without losing the last 30 minutes of brain-draining work. Or is there? In this section of the chapter, we take a look at the various ways you can save yourself when something goes terribly wrong.

Undo. The first defense against any offensive mistake is, of course, Undo. You can find this on the Edit menu, but we suggest keeping one hand conveniently on the Command or Ctrl and Z keys (Mac) or Ctrl and Z keys (Windows), ready and waiting for the blunder that is sure to come sooner or later. Note that Photoshop is smart enough not to consider some things undoable. Taking a snapshot, for instance, doesn't count; so you can take a snapshot and then undo whatever you did just before the snapshot. Similarly, you can open the Histogram, hide edges, change foreground or background colors, zoom, scroll, or even duplicate the file, and Photoshop still lets you go back and undo the previous action.

Revert. You'd think this command would be pretty easy to interpret. If you've really messed up something in your image, the best option is often simply to revert the entire file to the last saved version by selecting Revert from the File menu. When you apply the Revert command, you don't lose your undo/History steps—Revert simply becomes another step you can undo. This is useful, because it means you can undo a Revert!

Note that if the only changes you've made are in the Missing Profile or Profile Mismatch dialogs that may appear while opening a file, Photoshop CS3 doesn't enable the Revert command.

History. If you get disoriented after hitting the Undo and Redo shortcuts too many times, or you just want to see the entire list of undo steps available, simply open the History palette and get oriented, then click on the history state on which you want to start over. See "History Palette" earlier in this chapter.

Easter Eggs

It's a tradition in Mac software to include *Easter eggs*—those wacky little undocumented, nonutilitarian features that serve only to amuse the programmer and (they hope) the user. Note that if your friends think you have no sense of humor, you might want to skip this section; it might just annoy you. There are several Easter eggs in Photoshop—the usual ones that are included just for fun, and one important tribute.

Red Pill. A tradition even more venerable than Easter Eggs is code names. Almost all software has a code name that the developers use before the product is christened with a real shipping name. Photoshop code names have been Big Electric Cat (Photoshop 4), Strange Cargo (Photoshop 5), Venus in Furs (Photoshop 6), Liquid Sky (Photoshop 7), Dark Matter (Photoshop CS), and Space Monkey (Photoshop CS2). Most of the code names are favorite pop culture references of the Photoshop team; Google can help you track those down. The code name for Photoshop CS3 was Red Pill. To see the Red Pill splash screen in Photoshop in Mac OS X, hold down the Command key while choosing About Photoshop from the Photoshop menu. In Photoshop for Windows, press Ctrl and choose About Photoshop from the Help menu (see **Figure 6-40**).

Figure 6-40
Alternate Splash Screen

Credits and quotes. If you leave open the standard About Photoshop screen or the Red Pill splash screen, you'll notice that the credits at the bottom of the screen start to scroll by, thanking everyone and their dog for participating in the development process.

The now-legendary Adobe Transient Witticisms demonstrate just how twisted people get when building a new version of Photoshop. Here's how to find them in Photoshop CS3: Wait until the scrolling credits stop scrolling at the end, then, as soon as they've finished, Option-click (Mac) or Alt-click (Windows) in the space between Version 10.0 and the credits.

In Memoriam. On a more somber note, the Photoshop team felt that it was only fitting to remember this book's coauthor, Bruce Fraser, with more than just a line in the splash screen credits. While readers appreciated Bruce's gift for explaining the most technical aspects of Photoshop and digital imaging in clear, down-to-earth language, the Photoshop team valued Bruce just as much for his ability to clearly express the real needs and concerns of Photoshop users. As Bruce passed away before Photoshop CS3 was complete, the Photoshop team included an additional Easter egg in memory of Bruce Fraser.

Viewing the Bruce Fraser memorial Easter egg takes a bit more effort than viewing other hidden splash screens, because you have to process it in Photoshop.

1. Open the alternate Red Pill splash screen as we just described.

2. Take a screen shot and put it on the Clipboard, which you can do in one step. In Mac OS X, press Control-Command-Shift-4 (Mac) and drag a

rectangle around the splash screen. On Windows, press Print Screen (Windows).

3. Close the splash screen.

4. In Photoshop choose File > New (the Preset pop-up menu should say Clipboard), click OK, and choose Edit > Paste.

5. Choose Image > Adjust > Levels, and drag the black Input slider all the way to the right. You should see a portrait of Bruce taken by his friend Jeff Schewe (see **Figure 6-41**).

Figure 6-41
Memorial splash screen for our friend and coauthor, Bruce Fraser

Paw Prints. While the Levels dialog is open on the alternate splash screen, you can check out yet another version of the splash screen. Option-click (Mac) or Alt-click (Windows) the Cancel button; pressing the Option/Alt modifier key changes Cancel to Reset so you can undo your earlier slider change. Choose Red from the Channel pop-up menu, and then slowly drag the white slider to the left. You will first see the face of a cat appear in the red pill; when you drag the white slider all the way to the left, you'll see red cat paw prints and Jeff Tranberry's dedication at the bottom of the splash screen.

Merlin Lives! Finally (at least, this is the last one we know about), there's a little hidden dialog nestled away. When you hold down the Option/Alt key while selecting Palette Options from the palette menus in either the Paths, Layers, or Channels palette, Merlin happily jumps out.

Image Adjustment Fundamentals

Stretching and Squeezing the Bits

Tonal manipulation—adjusting the lightness or darkness of your images—is one of the most powerful and far-reaching capabilities in Photoshop, and at first it may seem like magic. But there's nothing magical about it. Once you understand what's happening as you adjust the controls—it all comes back to those ubiquitous zeros and ones—it starts to look less like magic and more like clever technology. But your increased understanding and productivity should more than make up for any loss in your sense of wonder, and besides, you'll have more time to play.

Tonal manipulation makes the difference between a flat image that lies lifeless on the page and one that pops, drawing you into it. But the role of tonal correction goes far beyond that. When you correct color in an image, you're really manipulating the tone of the individual color channels.

In fact, just about every edit you make in Photoshop involves tonal manipulation. In Chapter 8, "The Digital Darkroom," we'll show you some more esoteric techniques for getting great-looking images, but in this chapter we'll concentrate on the fundamentals—the basic tonal manipulation tools and their effects on pixels. Much of this chapter is devoted to two tools—Levels and Curves—because until you've mastered these, you simply don't know Photoshop! But we also cover the considerable number of other useful commands found on the Adjustments submenu in the Image menu.

Stretching and Squeezing the Bits

Every tonal edit you make causes some data loss. The purpose of this bald statement isn't to scare you, but simply to make you aware that like most things in digital imaging, editing tone and color involves a series of trade-offs. As you stretch and squeeze various parts of the tonal range, the trick is to throw away what you don't need, and to keep what you do need. Teaching you that valuable trick is one of the goals of this book.

When you work with images in Photoshop, they're often made up of one or more 8-bit channels, in which each pixel is represented by a value from 0 (black) to 255 (white). Grayscale images have one such channel, while color images have three (RGB or Lab) or four (CMYK). If you're more adventurous, you may work with *high-bit* images, where each channel uses 16 bits per pixel to represent a value from 0 (black) to 32,768 (white).

You lose a great deal more information in 8-bit/channel files than you do in high-bit ones, simply because you have much less data to start with. Here's a worst-case scenario that you can try yourself.

Tip: Do not use adjustment layers for this exercise.

1. In Photoshop, choose File > New, and choose Default Photoshop Size from the Preset menu. Choose Grayscale from the Color Mode pop-up menu, and click OK.

2. Press D to set the default black foreground and white background colors. Using the Gradient tool (press G to select it), Shift-drag to create a horizontal gradient across the entire width of the image.

3. Choose Image > Adjust > Levels, change the gray Input slider (the middle Input setting) to 2.2, and click OK (see **Figure 7-1**). You'll notice that the midtones are much lighter, but you may already be able to see some banding in the shadows.

4. Open the Levels dialog again (press Command-L in Mac OS X and Ctrl-L in Windows), and change the gray slider value to 0.5. The midtones are back almost to where you started, but you should be able to see that, instead of a smooth gradation, you have some distinct bands in the image (see **Figure 7-2**).

What happened here? With the first midtone adjustment, you lightened the midtones—stretching the shadows and compressing the highlights.

Figure 7-1

Adjusting the gamma

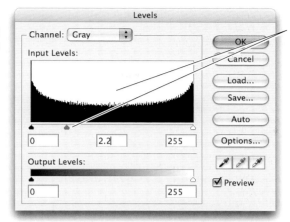

While it's not labeled as such, the gray Input slider applies a gamma correction, which adjusts the midtone values in an image.

With the second midtone adjustment, you darkened the midtones—stretching the highlights and compressing the shadows.

But with all that stretching and squeezing, you lost some levels. Instead of a smooth blend, with pixels occupying every value from 0 to 255, some

Figure 7-2

Data loss due to tonal correction: an 8-bit file

While the visual effect of successive tonal correction moves on images may be subtle, the effect on the data within the image—as expressed in the histogram—is profound.

Histogram for the gray wedge at the right side of the image

Before tonal correction   *After two gamma moves*

of those levels became unpopulated—in fact, if we're counting right, some 76 levels are no longer being used.

If you repeat the pair of midtone adjustments, you'll see that each time you make an adjustment, the banding becomes more obvious as you lose more and more tonal information. Repeating the midtone adjustments half a dozen times produces a file that contains only 55 gray levels instead of 256. And once you've lost that information, there's no way to bring it back.

Now repeat the experiment, but create a 16-bit/channel file instead of an 8-bit one (in the New dialog, choose 16 bit from the menu to the right of the Color Mode pop-up menu). The difference between this result and the 8-bit result is dramatic, as shown in **Figure 7-3**.

This set of adjustments represents, as we noted earlier, a worst-case scenario. No one with any significant Photoshop experience would make edits like this, with one edit attempting to undo the effect of the previous one. (And now that you've read this, you won't either!) In short, whenever

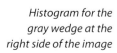

Figure 7-3
Data loss due to
tonal correction:
a 16-bit file

With a high-bit file, you still lose some data, but the effect is much less drastic, as shown by the histogram of the edited image. The lesson is that high-bit files give you much more editing headroom than do 8-bit-per-channel ones.

Histogram for the gray wedge at the right side of the image

Before tonal correction   *After two gamma moves*

you edit tone and color, you have a finite number of levels to play with, so when you push tones up and down, something has to give. See the sidebar, "Difference Is Detail: Tonal-Correction Issues," on the next page.

Data Loss in Perspective

Photography has always been about throwing away everything that can't be reproduced in the photograph. We start with all the tone and color of the real world, with scene contrast ratios that can easily be in the 100,000:1 range. We reduce that to the contrast ratio we can capture on film or silicon, which—if we're exceptionally lucky—may approach 10,000:1. By the time we get to reproducing the image in print, we have perhaps a 500:1 contrast ratio to play with. All tonal and color edits lose data in one of two ways:

▶ When you stretch a tonal range, pixels that formerly had adjacent values may now differ by several levels. When you stretch the data too far, you lose the illusion of a continuous gradation, and you start to see distinct jumps in tone or color.

▶ When you squeeze or compress a tonal range, pixels that formerly had different values are now compressed to the same value. If you compress the range too much, you may lose desirable detail.

This loss of image data may seem scarier than it really is. We simply want to make you aware where and how it happens, so that your editing techniques can protect the data you need and let go of the data you don't need. To get there, we'd like to hammer home the following lessons:

▶ All tonal manipulations incur some data loss.

▶ Once the data is gone, you can't bring it back.

▶ You'll minimize visible data loss when you work with more bits (such as 16-bit/channel images) compared to working with fewer bits (such as 8-bit/channel images).

▶ Data loss from successive tonal manipulations is cumulative. If you can achieve the same result in one move versus five moves, one move will preserve more quality.

▶ Successive edits that counteract each other should always be avoided.

Difference Is Detail: Tonal-Correction Issues

What do we mean when we talk about image information? Very simply, adjacent pixels with different values constitute image detail. If the difference is very slight, you won't be able to see it (especially in shadows); but it's there, waiting to be exploited. You can accentuate those differences—making those adjacent pixels *more* different—to bring out the detail.

The color of noise. Difference isn't always detail, though. Low-cost scanners and digital cameras shot at high speeds introduce spurious differences between pixels. Those differences aren't detail, they're just noise (like the static on the radio that drowns out the traffic report), and they're one of our least favorite things. When making tonal and color corrections, you need to decide what is desirable detail and what's noise, accentuating the detail while minimizing the noise.

Posterization. Noise isn't the only problem to deal with when you're doing tonal correction, though. There's also *posterization*—the stair-stepping of gray levels in distinct, visible jumps rather than smooth gradations (see **Figure 7-4**). Unless you're working with a high-bit image, Photoshop gives you only 256 possible values for a gray pixel.

Posterization manifests itself in two ways. When you start making dark pixels more different, you eventually make them *so* different that the image looks splotchy—covered with patches of distinctly different pixels rather than smooth transitions. But posterization can also wipe out detail and turn smooth gradations into flat blobs.

Lost detail. When you accentuate detail in one part of the tonal range, making slightly different pixels more different (*expanding the range*), you lose detail in other

Preserving Image Quality

There are a number of practices and techniques that you can employ to minimize the tones and colors that you lose when editing images.

Get good data to begin with. Whether you're shooting with a digital camera or scanning prints or film, pay attention to proper exposure. Some problems, such as clipped highlights in the capture data due to overexposure, simply can't be fixed after capture no matter how many bits are in the file. The bigger the corrections you have to make later, the higher the chance of posterization and lost detail. It's better to get the image as close to "right" as you possibly can while the image is in high-bit form. The whole point of high-bit capture is to make the most important decisions while you've got the high-bit data, so that you get the right 8-bit data when you downsample to 8 bits per channel. With digital cameras, it's especially important to avoid underexposure: Because camera sensors are linear capture devices, underexposed images are much more prone to posterization and noise.

Figure 7-4 The effects of posterization

Figure 7-5 Loss of highlights

Before tonal correction

After tonal correction

areas, making slightly different pixels more similar (*compressing the range*).

For instance, when you stretch the shadow values apart to bring out shadow detail, you inevitably squeeze the highlight values together (see **Figure 7-5**). If you make two different pixel values the same, you can't re-separate the original difference later—that detail is gone forever. That's what we mean when we say that information is "lost."

Note: You gain nothing by capturing at a lower bit depth and converting to a higher one, such as capturing in 8-bit mode and editing in 16-bit mode. Converting to a higher bit depth just takes up more disk space and processing power.

Capture high-bit data when possible. Most digital cameras and scanners sold today can capture at least 12 bits per channel. When you shoot in raw mode, a digital camera saves all 12 bits; in JPEG mode, a camera must convert images to 8-bit files.

When you set your digital camera or scanner to its highest bit depth, you are, in effect, telling your capture device to "just give me all the data you can capture" so that you can have the most flexibility in Photoshop. In the 16-bit/channel space, you have much more editing headroom before you run into posterization. Photoshop opens a file of any bit depth between 8 and 16 bits as a 16-bit image.

Don't overdo it. Small tonal moves are much less destructive than big ones. The more you want to change an image, the more compromises you'll have to make to avoid obvious posterization, artifacts due to noise, and loss of highlight and shadow detail.

Use adjustment layers. You can avoid some of the penalties incurred by successive corrections by using an adjustment layer instead of applying the changes directly to the image. Adjustment layers use more RAM and create bigger files, but the increased flexibility makes the trade-off worthwhile—especially when you find yourself needing to back off from previous edits. But since the various tools offered in adjustment layers operate identically to the way they work on flat files, we'll discuss how the features (Curves, Levels, Hue/Saturation, and so on) work on flat files first. For a detailed discussion of adjustment layers, see Chapter 8, "The Digital Darkroom."

Cover yourself. Since the data you lose is irretrievable, leave yourself a way out by working on a copy of the file, by saving your tonal adjustments in progress separately (without applying them to the image by applying your edits using adjustment layers), or by using any combination of the above. Or you can use the History palette to leave yourself an escape route—just remember that History only remembers the number of states you specify in the Preferences dialog, it's only retained until you close the file, and it can consume mind-boggling amounts of scratch disk space.

With all these caveats in mind, let's take a look at the tonal-manipulation tools in Photoshop.

Tonal-Correction Tools

Two Photoshop tools, Levels and Curves, let you address almost all tonal issues, and mastering them is a basic necessity for productive Photoshop work. As you'll find out later in this book, Levels and Curves aren't always necessarily the easiest way to correct tone, but until you've learned what they can do, you just don't know Photoshop.

We should mention at this point that in Photoshop CS3, the Curves dialog is so improved and takes on so many features of the Levels dialog that there is much less of a need to use the Levels dialog. We don't want the Levels dialog to go away because it's still a simpler way to make basic corrections, but with the new Curves dialog, we expect to use Levels a lot less.

Two additional Photoshop features, the Histogram and Info palettes, provide information that can help guide your corrections. They let you analyze both the unedited image and the effect of your tonal manipulations. So before plunging into the Levels and Curves dialogs, both of which are quite deep, let's look at the analytical tools: the Histogram palette and the Info palette.

The Histogram Palette

A *histogram* is a simple bar chart that plots the tonal levels from 0 to 255 along the horizontal axis, and the number of pixels at each level along the vertical axis (see **Figure 7-6**). If there are lots of pixels in shadow areas, the bars are concentrated on the left; the reverse is true with "high-key" images, where most of the information is in the highlights. The height of the bars is arbitrary—they're simply comparative indicators of how many pixels have a given tonal value.

Some of the information offered by the Histogram palette may not seem particularly useful—for most image reproduction tasks, you really don't need to know the median pixel value, or how many pixels in the image are at level 33. But histograms show some useful information at a glance.

Figure 7-6
Histogram palette

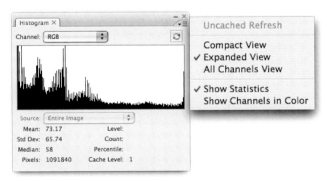

Endpoints

With a quick look at the histogram, you can see if the image has suffered clipping in the highlights or shadows (see **Figure 7-7**). If there's a spike at either end of the histogram, the highlight or shadow values are almost certainly clipped—we say "almost" because there are some images that really do have a very large number of pure white or solid black areas. But they're pretty rare.

Figure 7-7
Highlight and
shadow clipping

Clipped highlights and shadows

Figure 7-8
Limited dynamic range

No blacks or whites

You can also see if the image covers the whole dynamic range (see **Figure 7-8**). If the data stops a long way south of the white point or a long way north of the black point, you'll usually need to stretch the data out so that it occupies the whole dynamic range. There are exceptions, but the vast majority of images need a few pixels that are very close to pure white and a few pixels that are very close to solid black if they're going to have decent contrast on output.

Figure 7-9
A previously manipulated image

The comb-like appearance in the histogram is a sign that the image has already been manipulated (but it looks better than the unedited version in Figure 7-8).

How Much Information Is Present?

The overall appearance of the histogram also gives you a quick, rough-and-ready picture of the integrity of your image data (see **Figure 7-9**). A good capture uses the entire tonal range, and has a histogram with smooth contours. The actual location of the peaks and valleys depends entirely on the image content, but if the histogram shows obvious spikes, you're probably dealing with a noisy capture device. If it has a comb-like appearance, it's likely that the image has already been manipulated—perhaps by your scanning software or camera firmware.

The histogram also shows you where to examine the image for signs that you've gone too far in your tonal manipulations. If you look at the histograms produced by the earlier experiment in applying gamma adjustments to a gradient, you can see at a glance exactly what each successive adjustment did to the image, because spikes and gaps will start to appear throughout the histogram.

Note that a gap of only one level is almost certainly unnoticeable in the image—especially if it's in the shadows or midtones—but once you start to see gaps of three or more levels, you may begin to notice visible posterization in the image. The location of the gap gives you a good idea of where in the tonal range the posterization is happening.

Tip: If you start with high-quality, high-bit data, there are so many levels available that you can worry less about the overall look of the histogram, and instead concentrate on the overall tonal distribution, and whether any important highlight or shadow detail is being clipped.

Histograms Are Generalizations

Once you've edited an image, the histogram may look pretty ugly. This is normal; in fact, it's almost inevitable. The histogram is a guide, not a rule. Histograms are most useful for evaluating images before you start to edit. A histogram can show clipped endpoints and missing levels, but a good-looking histogram isn't necessarily the sign of a good image. And many good-looking images have ugly histograms.

Fixing the histogram doesn't mean you've fixed the image. If you want a nice-looking histogram, the Gaussian Blur filter with a 100-pixel radius will give you one, but there won't be much left of the image! The histogram is just a handy way of looking at the data so that you can see how it relates to the image appearance. The image is what matters. Take what useful information you can from the histogram, but concentrate on the image.

For performance reasons, while you work on an image, the Histogram palette shows you values based on the anti-aliased screen display of your image instead of evaluating the full resolution of your image. This view can hide posterization, giving you an unrealistically rosy picture of your data. Photoshop warns you of this by displaying a warning icon when the histogram is showing you an approximation of your data. To see what's really going on, click the Refresh button in the Histogram palette. (See **Figure 7-10**.)

Figure 7-10
Histogram
warning

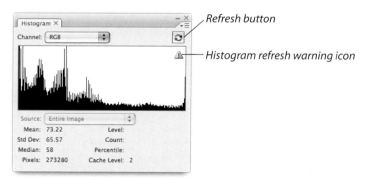

Refresh button

Histogram refresh warning icon

The Info Palette

Like the Histogram palette, the Info palette is purely an informational display. It doesn't let you do anything to the image besides analyze its contents. But where the Histogram palette shows a general picture of the entire file, the Info palette lets you analyze *specific* points in the image.

When you move the cursor across the image, the Info palette displays the pixel value under the cursor and its location in the image. More important, when you have one of the tonal- or color-correction dialogs (such as Levels or Curves) open, the Info palette displays the values for the pixel before and after the transformation (see **Figure 7-11**).

Figure 7-11
Info palette

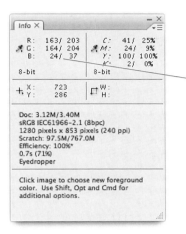

When you're working in one of the Adjust dialogs, such as Levels or Curves, the Info palette shows the pixel value before and after the correction.

Palette Options

Tip: You can use the Info palette to hunt down hidden detail, particularly in deep shadows and bright highlights where it can be hard to see on the monitor. If the numbers change as you move the cursor over an area of the image, tonal differences are lurking—it may be detail waiting to be exploited or it may be noise that you'll need to suppress, but something is hiding in there.

You can control what sorts of information the Info palette displays in one of two ways. You can select Palette Options from the Info palette menu to open the Info Palette Options dialog, or click a tiny black triangle to open a pop-up menu (see **Figure 7-12**). We have several different palette setups that we use for different kinds of work, and we use the Workspace feature, which captures the Info palette settings in addition to all the other palette locations, to load them as needed (see "Palettes and Workspaces" in Chapter 6, "Essential Photoshop Tips and Tricks").

For grayscale, duotone, or multichannel images, we generally set the First Color Readout to RGB and the Second Color Readout to Actual Color. Actual Color automatically displays the color model of the image you're viewing. We just about always display the mouse coordinates as pixels, because it makes it easier for us to return consistently to the same spot in the image.

Figure 7-12
Info Palette Options dialog
and icon pop-up menus

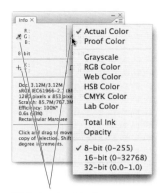

*Open the Info Palette
Options dialog by clicking
the Info palette menu.*

*Click the tiny black arrows
to open pop-up menus for
color readouts.*

Why display RGB values for a grayscale image? Simply for the precision. Grayscale and Total Ink show percentages, on a scale of 100 instead of 255. For outrageous precision, Photoshop can also display 16-bit values—ranging from 0 to 32,768—when you work on high-bit files. (If these numbers make your head explode, you're not alone! We'd really like to be able to see the 8-bit and 16-bit values side by side, at least until we get used to thinking of midtone gray as 16,384.) Photoshop also supports high dynamic range (HDR) images with 32-bit floating-point values per channel, and the Info palette can display those too.

The numbers for R, G, and B are always the same in a grayscale image, so the level just displays them three times. Setting the second readout to Actual Color lets you read the dot percentage, so you can display levels and percentages at the same time. We use different setups for color images, which we cover later in this chapter.

Now let's look at the tools you can use to actually change the image.

Levels

The Levels command opens a tonal-manipulation powerhouse (see **Figure 7-13**). This deceptively simple little dialog lets you identify the shadow and highlight points in the image, limit the highlight and shadow dot percentages, and make dramatic changes to the midtones, while providing real-time feedback via the onscreen image and the Info palette. For more detailed tonal corrections, we use the Curves command; but there are a

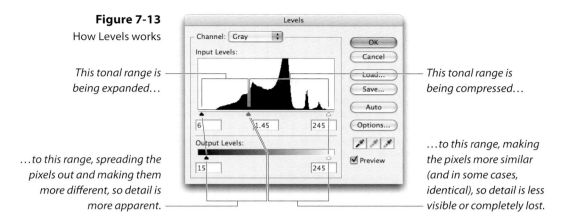

Figure 7-13

How Levels works

This tonal range is being expanded...

This tonal range is being compressed...

...to this range, spreading the pixels out and making them more different, so detail is more apparent.

...to this range, making the pixels more similar (and in some cases, identical), so detail is less visible or completely lost.

couple of things that we can do in more easily in Levels, and for a considerable amount of grayscale work, it's all we need.

The Levels dialog not only displays a histogram of the image, but it also lets you work with the histogram in very useful ways. If you understand what the histogram shows, the Levels controls suddenly become a lot less mysterious.

Input Levels

The three Input Levels sliders let you change the black point, the white point, and the midtone in the image. As you move the sliders, the numbers in the corresponding Input Levels fields change, so if you know what you're doing, you can type in the numbers directly. But we still use the sliders most of the time, because they provide real-time feedback—by changing the image on screen—as we drag them. Here's what they actually do.

Black- and white-point sliders. Moving these sliders in toward the center stretches the dynamic range of the image. When you move the black-point slider away from its default position at 0 (zero) to a higher level, you're telling Photoshop to set all the pixels at that level and lower (those to the left) to level 0 (black), and stretch all the levels to the right of the slider to fill the entire tonal range from 0 to 255. Moving the white-point slider does the same thing to the other end of the tonal range, setting all the pixels at the white-point slider and higher (those to the right of the slider) to level 255 (white), and stretching all the levels to the left of the slider to fill the tonal range from 0 to 255 (see **Figure 7-14**).

Gray slider. The gray slider lets you alter the midtones without changing the highlight and shadow points. When you move the gray slider, you're

Figure 7-14 Black- and white-point tweaks on an 8-bit image

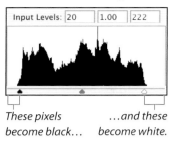

These pixels   …and these
become black…   become white.

Post-correction histogram,
displaying some black- and white-
point clipping

telling Photoshop where you want the midtone gray value (50-percent gray, or level 128) to be. If you move it to the left, the image gets lighter, because you're choosing a value that's darker than 128 and making it 128. As you do so, the shadows get stretched to fill up that part of the tonal range, and the highlights get squeezed together (see **Figure 7-15**).

Conversely, if you move the slider to the right, the image gets darker because you're choosing a lighter value and telling Photoshop to change it to level 128. The highlights get stretched, and the shadow values get squeezed together. David likes to think of this as grabbing a rubber band on both ends and in the middle, and pulling the middle part to the left or right; one side gets stretched out, and the other side gets bunched up.

The number that appears in the slider's edit field is a *gamma* value—the exponent of a power curve equation, if that means anything to you. Values greater than 1 lighten the midtone, values less than 1 darken it, and a value of 1 leaves it unchanged. If you only adjust the midtone slider, you really are applying a pure gamma correction to the image, but if you also move the endpoints, you aren't: instead, you're applying an arbitrary three-point curve correction. If you want a more detailed mathematical understanding of gamma encoding and gamma correction, a good place to start is *http://chriscox.org/gamma/*, written by Photoshop engineer Chris Cox.

Figure 7-15
Gamma tweak

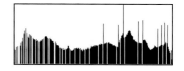

*Adding a gamma adjustment of 1.2 to the image in **Figure 7-14** brings out some shadow detail, though highlight detail is lost, and the histogram displays some additional combing.*

Output Levels

The Output Levels controls let you compress the tonal range of the image into fewer than the entire 256 possible gray levels. In the days before ICC profiles, we used to use these controls to make sure that our highlights didn't blow out and our shadows didn't plug up on press—the sliders let you limit black to a value higher than 0 and white to a value lower than 255. Good ICC profiles tend to make this practice unnecessary, since they take the minimum and maximum printable dot into account.

However, even though grayscale is a first-class citizen in good color-management standing in Photoshop, very few other applications recognize grayscale profiles. When we have grayscale images with no specular highlights (the very bright reflections one sees on polished metal or water), we still use the output sliders in levels to limit our highlight dot, and—in images with very critical shadow detail—our shadow dot. For images with specular highlights, we use Curves instead (we discuss that technique later in this chapter).

We also use the output sliders when we're preparing images for slide-shows that we burn to DVD and play on TV sets, and for producing "ghosted" images. And on those rare occasions when we're forced to deal with old-style legacy CMYK setups that use a single dot-gain value, we may still use the output sliders to make sure that we don't force our highlight or shadow dots into a range that the output process can't print.

Figure 7-16
Output Levels

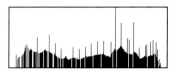

Compressing the tonal range with the Output Levels sliders to the limits of the printing process (we used 12 and 243—about 5 and 95 percent) makes the darkest shadow detail more visible while reducing contrast overall. It also points out the limitations of this targeting approach with images that include specular highlights (or headlights). They become gray.

Black Output Levels. When this slider is at its default setting of 0, pixels in the image at level 0 will remain at level 0. As you increase the value of the slider, it limits the darkest pixels in the image to the level at which it's set, compressing the entire tonal range.

White Output Levels. This behaves the same way as the black Output Levels slider, except that it limits the lightest pixels in the image rather than the darkest ones. Setting the slider to level 240, for instance, will put all the pixels that were at level 255 at 240, and so on (see **Figure 7-16**).

You might think that compressing the tonal range would fill in those gaps in the histogram caused by gamma and endpoint tweaks, and to a limited extent it will; but all that number crunching introduces rounding errors, so you'll still see some levels going unused.

Leave some room when setting limits. Always leave yourself some room to move when you set input and output limits, particularly in the highlights. If you move the white Input slider so that your highlight detail starts at level 254, with your specular highlights at level 255, you run into two problems:

▶ When you compress the tonal range for final optimization, your specular highlights go gray.

▶ When you sharpen, some of the highlight detail blows out to white.

Brightness/Contrast in Photoshop CS3

For many years, everyone who taught or wrote about Photoshop passed along the same piece of advice: Never use the Image > Brightness/Contrast command on images, because you'll push your highlight and shadow data off the edge of the histogram forever, losing those details.

That advice has changed.

In Photoshop CS3, Brightness/Contrast no longer loses highlight and shadow detail by default (see **Figure 7-17**). Brightness now works like the midtone slider in the Levels dialog, and Contrast now works as if you created an S-curve in the Curves dialog.

If, for some odd reason, you want Brightness/Contrast to work the way it used to in Photoshop CS2 and earlier, turn on the Brightness/Contrast dialog's new Use Legacy check box. With Use Legacy turned on, the Brightness/Contrast adjustments are linear. For example, with Use Legacy turned on, the Brightness control simply shifts all the pixel values up or down the tonal range. Let's say you increase Brightness by 10. Photoshop adds 10 to every pixel's value, so value 0 becomes 10, 190 becomes 200, and every pixel with a value of 245 or above becomes 255 (you can't go above 255). This is called "clipping the highlights" (they're all the same value, so there's no highlight detail). Plus, your shadows go flat because you lose all your true blacks. Similarly, with Use Legacy on, the Contrast control stretches the tonal range as you increase the contrast, throwing away information in both the highlights and the shadows, and potentially posterizing the tones in between. When you reduce the contrast, it compresses the tonal range, also losing tonal levels.

The Use Legacy check box can be useful when you're modifying channels and masks (which are usually mostly black or white already). But when you edit images, just keep Use Legacy turned off and Brightness/Contrast will now be safe to use. Still, we prefer to use Curves or Levels, which provide more control.

Figure 7-17 The Brightness/Contrast command in Photoshop CS3

 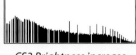  

| *Uncorrected* | *CS3 Brightness increase (Use Legacy turned off)* | *CS2 Brightness increase (Use Legacy on in CS3)* | *CS2 Contrast increase (Use Legacy on in CS3)* |

To avoid these problems, try to keep your significant highlight detail below level 250. Shadow clipping is less critical, but keeping the unoptimized shadow detail in the 5 to 10 range is a safe way to go.

Likewise, unless your image has no true whites or blacks, leave some headroom when you set the output limits. For example, if your press can't hold a dot smaller than 10 percent, don't set the output limit to level 230.

If you're optimizing with the output sliders in Levels, set it to 232 or 233 so you get true whites in the printed piece. If you'll be optimizing later with the Eyedroppers or Curves, set it somewhere around 237 or 240. This lets you fine-tune specular highlights using the Eyedroppers or Curves, but it also brings the image's tonal range into the range that the press can handle. Again, we should emphasize that if you have a good ICC profile for your output, you don't need to compress the dynamic range using the output sliders because the profile will take care of it for you.

Levels Dialog Goodies

There are a few very useful features in the Levels dialog that aren't immediately obvious. But they can be huge time-savers.

Preview. As in other dialogs, use the Preview check box (press P) for a before-and-after comparison of the changes you're making. When it's unchecked, you see the existing image; when checked, you see what the image will look like if you click OK to apply the changes you're making.

Black-point/white-point clipping display. Black-point and white-point clipping is the one feature that keeps us coming back to Levels instead of relying entirely on Curves to make tonal adjustments. It doesn't work in Lab, CMYK, Indexed Color, or Bitmap modes—just Grayscale, RGB, Duotone, and Multichannel—but it's immensely useful.

When you set the black and white points, you typically want to set the white point to the lightest area that contains detail, and the shadow to the darkest point that contains detail. These aren't always easy to see. Hold down the Option or Alt key while moving the black or white Input Levels sliders to see exactly which pixels are being clipped (see **Figure 7-18**).

Auto. Auto Levels and Auto Contrast work identically on grayscale images, though they differ in their handling of color ones. For grayscale, we advise avoiding both unless you want to auto-wreck your images. They automatically move the black and white Input sliders to clip a predetermined amount of data separately on each channel. If you have a large number of images that you know will benefit from a preliminary round of black and white clipping, you *may* want to consider running Auto Levels, but you'll probably want to reduce the default clipping percentages from 0.50 percent to something lower (the minimum is 0.01 percent). To change

Tip: When you Option/Alt-drag Input sliders to view the clipping display, watch out for big clumps of pixels turning on or off. You generally want to set the black and white sliders to a level just outside these clumps, because excluding them removes a lot of detail.

Figure 7-18
The clipping
display in Levels

*Holding down Option or
Alt as you move the left
and right Input sliders
shows which pixels are
being clipped to white or
(in this illustration) black.
The display is really handy
for setting white and black
points, but it's also useful in
many other situations.*

the clipping percentage, click the Options button and enter your desired percentages in the dialog that appears.

Auto Color, however, is one of the more useful features for making quick fixes to *color* images (see "Auto Color," later in this chapter).

Auto-reset. If you hold down the Option key (Mac) or Alt key (Windows), the Cancel button changes to Reset (if you click this, all the settings return to their default states).

Levels in Color

When you work on color images, Levels lets you work on a composite channel (all colors) or on the individual color channels in the image (see **Figure 7-19**).

When you work in the composite (RGB, CMYK, or Lab) channel, Levels works very much the same way it does on grayscale images. It makes the same adjustment to all the color channels, so in theory at least it only affects tone. In practice, it may introduce some color shifts when you make big corrections, so we tend to use Curves more than Levels on color images. But Levels is useful on color images in at least two ways:

Figure 7-19
Levels in color

The image

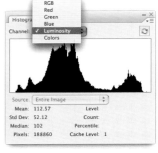

The luminosity histogram

On color images, Levels lets you work on the composite channel or on the individual color channels.

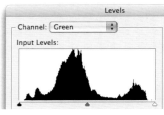

The green channel

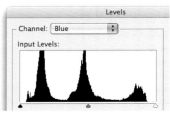

The blue channel

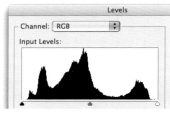

The composite RGB channel

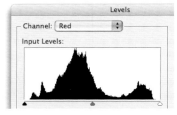

The red channel

▶ As an image-evaluation tool, using both the histograms and clipping display.

▶ When we have a color image that has no problems with color balance, but needs a small midtone adjustment. Often, a move with the gray slider is all that's needed.

We also use the Auto Color feature in Levels to make quick major corrections (see "Auto Color," later in this chapter).

The Levels composite histogram. Like the Histogram palette, Levels displays the histogram for an individual channel when you're viewing a single channel, and offers a Channels menu when you're viewing the composite image. The composite histogram it displays (labeled RGB, CMYK, or Lab, depending on the image's color space) is the same as the default composite histogram in the Histogram palette, but different from the Histogram palette's Luminosity histogram.

In the Luminosity histogram, a level of 255 represents a white pixel. In the RGB and CMYK histograms in Levels, however, a level of 255 *may* represent a white pixel, but it could also represent a fully saturated color pixel—the histogram simply shows the maximum of all the individual color channels. Fortunately, the Levels dialog's clipping display makes this clear (see **Figure 7-20**).

Figure 7-20

Levels color clipping display

White clip at 250

Black clip at 10

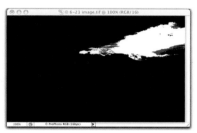

White clip at 230

Black clip at 30

As you Option/Alt-drag the white Input slider, the following colors indicate the channels you're currently clipping:
Black = No channels clipping
Red = Red channel
Green = Green channel
Blue = Blue channel
Cyan = Green and blue channel
Magenta = Red and blue channel
Yellow = Red and green channel
White = All channels

As you Option/Alt-drag the black Input slider, the following colors indicate the channels you're currently clipping:
White = No channels clipping
Cyan = Red channel
Magenta = Green channel
Yellow = Blue channel
Red = Green and blue channel
Green = Red and blue channel
Blue = Red and green channel
Black = All channels

Note that saturation clipping isn't necessarily a problem. It's simply a signal that you should check the values in the unclipped channels to make sure that things are headed in the right direction. If you're trying to clip to white and the unclipped channel is up around 250, or you're trying to clip to black and the unclipped channel is under 10, you don't really have a problem. But if the values in the unclipped channels are far away from white or black clipping, respectively, you may actually be creating very saturated colors that you didn't want.

How Levels works on color images. As the composite histogram implies, any moves you make to the Levels sliders when you're working in the composite channels apply equally to each individual color channel. In other words, you get identical results applying the same move individually to each color channel as you would applying the move once to the composite channel.

However, since the contents of the individual channels are quite different, applying the same moves to each can sometimes have unexpected results. The gray slider and the black and white Output sliders operate straightforwardly, but the black and white Input sliders require caution.

The white Input slider clips the highlights *in each channel* to level 255. This brightens the image overall, and neutral colors stay neutral. But it can have an undesirable effect on non-neutral colors, ranging from over-saturation to pronounced color shifts. The same applies to the black Input slider, although the effects are usually less obvious. The black Input slider clips the values in each channel to level 0, so when you apply it to a non-neutral color, you can end up removing all trace of one primary from the color, which also increases its saturation.

Because of this behavior, we use the black and white Input sliders primarily as image-evaluation tools in conjunction with the Option/Alt-key clipping display. They let you see exactly where your saturated colors are in relation to your neutral highlights and shadows. If the image is free of dangerously saturated colors, you can make small moves with the black and white Input sliders; but be careful of unintentional clipping, and keep a close eye on what's happening to the saturation—it's particularly easy to create out-of-gamut saturated colors in the shadows.

The image shown in **Figure 7-21** is a good candidate for correction using Levels. It has no real color problems, and no dangerously saturated colors, but it's washed-out and flat. The Levels clipping displays reveal that

Figure 7-21
A quick fix with Levels

Original image

Black clip at 10

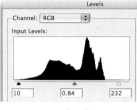

Levels edit

White clip at 232

Edited image

the only data above level 232 is a tiny specular highlight, and clipping the shadows at level 10 introduces a hint of true black. A midtone adjustment with the gamma slider completes the job—three quick moves make an immense difference to the image.

We usually use Levels to make only relatively small corrections like the one in Figure 7-21, because compared to Curves, it's something of a blunt instrument. But some situations call for a sledgehammer rather than a scalpel, and the Auto Color feature in Levels is a case in point.

Auto Color

The Auto Levels feature in the Adjustments submenu (in the Image menu) generally wrecks color images, causing huge color shifts. Its younger sibling, Auto Contrast, while slightly more useful than Auto Levels, still leaves a great deal to be desired. However, the Auto Color feature can be very useful indeed for making major initial corrections, particularly on scans of color negatives or on images that need major adjustments in color balance and contrast.

Figure 7-22 shows a pretty desperate situation—the result of having your bags get lost by the airline and your undeveloped film going through numerous baggage scanners as it chases you around the world!

If you simply use Auto Color's default settings (for example, if you simply chose Auto Color from the Adjust submenu), you'll typically get a less-than-desirable result. With very little help, though, Auto Color can quickly get you a lot closer to where you need to be. Here's how we use it:

▶ We always launch it by opening the Levels dialog and clicking the Options button.

▶ We click the Find Dark and Light Colors button to get Auto Color rather than Auto Contrast, which for some annoying reason is the default.

▶ We enable the Snap Neutral Midtones check box.

▶ We adjust the clipping percentages from the ridiculously high default value of 0.50 percent to a much lower value, typically in the range of 0.00 to 0.05 percent, depending on the image content.

▶ When necessary (that is, more often than not), we click the Midtones swatch to open the Color Picker and adjust the midtone target value.

In the example shown in Figure 7-22, we reduced the default clipping percentages to a lower value to avoid blowing out the highlights in the sky and plugging up the shadows. The default midtone color setting made the image too cold, so we chose an amber warming filter color and adjusted it by dragging the target circle in the Color Picker. The image updates as you change the target values, so the process is quick and interactive.

You can adjust the midtone swatch color by changing the numbers in the Color Picker, or simply by dragging the target indicator in the color swatch. Neither method is better than the other—use whichever you find more convenient.

We don't aim for perfection with Auto Color; rather, we use Auto Color to get the image into the ballpark, and fine-tune the results using the Curves dialog.

Tip: If you plan to use Auto Color in the future, set it up and then turn on the Save as Defaults check box in the Auto Color Correction Options dialog. While correct settings differ among images, turning on Find Dark and Light Colors and Snap Neutral Midtones can save time, leaving you to adjust only the Shadow and Highlight Clip values and the Midtones target color when needed.

Tip: If nothing happens when you adjust the Midtones target color, make sure Snap Neutral Midtones is on.

Figure 7-22
Auto Color

*This image is in need
of serious help!*

Original image

*Auto Color at default
settings produces the cold,
overly contrasty rendering at
right. Reducing the clipping
percentages for Highlights
and Shadows and choosing
a warmer midtone color
produces the much more
pleasing version shown at
bottom right.*

Auto Color default settings

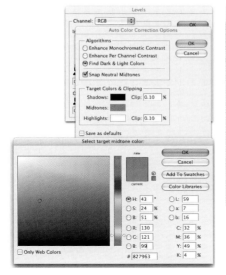

The Auto Color settings at left produced this result.

Curves

We like to think of Levels as an automatic transmission. Accordingly, we think of Curves as a manual transmission: It's indispensable when you're stuck in the snow, but it takes a bit more effort to master. The Curves dialog offers a different way of stretching and squeezing the bits, one that's more powerful than Levels. But it also uses a different way of looking at the data.

Curves displays a graph that plots the relationship between input level and output level (unaltered and altered). Input levels run along the bottom, and output values run along the side. When you first choose the Curves command, the graph displays a straight 45-degree line—for each input level, the output level is identical (see **Figure 7-23**).

Figure 7-23
Curves dialog overview, and compared to Levels

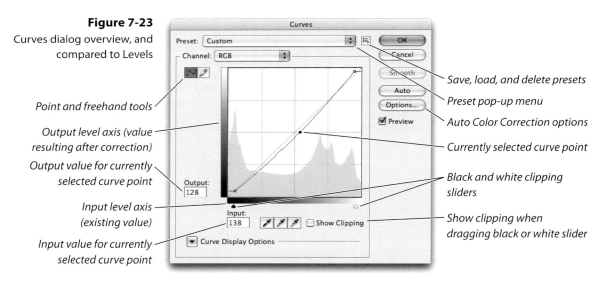

Point and freehand tools

Output level axis (value resulting after correction)

Output value for currently selected curve point

Input level axis (existing value)

Input value for currently selected curve point

Save, load, and delete presets

Preset pop-up menu

Auto Color Correction options

Currently selected curve point

Black and white clipping sliders

Show clipping when dragging black or white slider

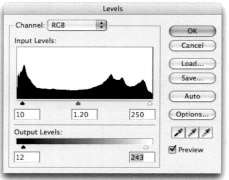

These settings in the Levels dialog create the same result as the settings in the Curves dialog above, because the Curves settings above affect only black clipping, white clipping, and midpoint. If one more point was added to the curve above, the Levels dialog would no longer be able to match it.

Tip: As in other Photoshop CS3 dialogs, you can apply dialog presets using the Preset menu at the top of the dialog, and you can load and save your own custom presets using the button menu to the right of the Preset pop-up menu. The built-in presets are new in CS3, and it's worth taking a look in the Preset pop-up menu to see if any are useful to you.

Tone curves are probably the most useful global image-manipulation tool ever invented; they're indispensable for color correction, but they're also very useful for fine control over grayscale work. You change the relationship between input level and output level by changing the shape of the curve, either by placing points or by drawing a curve freehand (with the pencil tool). We almost always place points on the curve because it's much easier to be precise that way.

Curves versus Levels. Moving the curve midpoint right or left is similar to dragging the middle Input slider in Levels. Setting the other four Levels sliders is equivalent to setting the curve endpoints. Therefore, you can use Curves to produce any result that you can create with Levels. However, it doesn't go the other way—Levels can't do everything Curves can do. With Curves, you can add as many points as you need, so that you can adjust the output value for any input value along the tone curve.

The Curves dialog in Photoshop CS3 adds a histogram and Input/Output sliders with a clipping display. These may seem like minor additions, but they're actually quite monumental. In previous versions, those features were available only in Levels, which meant that we often used both Levels and Curves to get the job done. Now, once you become comfortable with the power of Curves, you may have no reason to use Levels anymore.

Show Clipping. Turn this on to see the pixels that are currently being clipped by the black- or white-point slider at the bottom of the graph area. Show Clipping can show either black clipping or white clipping, but not both at the same time; the clipping you see is for the last slider you touched, or for black if you haven't touched either slider since opening the dialog. Show Clipping works only when Show Amount Of is set to Light.

Customizing the Curve Display Options

Photoshop CS3 throws in a few new ways to customize the Curves dialog. Also, customization options that used to be hidden features are now visible. We welcome this change, although it makes it harder to impress people with secret Photoshop tips at cocktail parties. In the Curves dialog, click Curve Display Options (see **Figure 7-24**) to reveal the options. All of these options are on by default, so if you want to simplify the display, you can turn off any of these options.

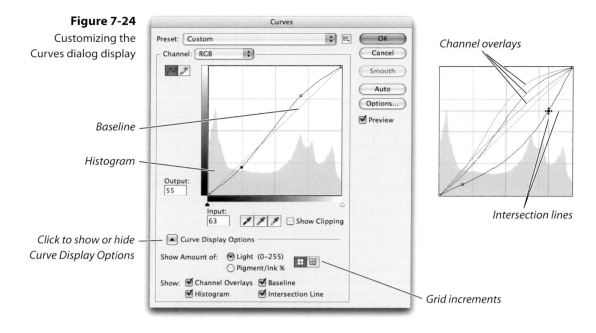

Figure 7-24
Customizing the
Curves dialog display

Channel overlays

Baseline

Histogram

Intersection lines

Click to show or hide
Curve Display Options

Grid increments

Show Amount Of. This option determines the units and graph orientation used to display values on the graph. Users who work with Web, video, and other RGB-based media are used to thinking of tone in terms of levels from 0 to 255. Users accustomed to working with ink on press will want to work with dot percentages. You can switch between them by selecting Light or Pigment/Ink, which flips the graph display. When you select Light, the 0,0 shadow point is at bottom left and the 255,255 highlight point is at top right. When you select Pigment/Ink%, the 0,0 highlight point is at the bottom left and the 100,100 shadow point is at the top right corner. RGB and Lab mode images default to Light; CMYK and Grayscale mode images default to Pigment/Ink.

Tip: Another way to toggle the grid increments is to Option-click (Mac) or Alt-click (Windows) the graph area.

Change Grid increments. You can also change the gridlines of the Curves dialog using the two icons next to the Show Amount Of options. The left icon (the default) displays gridlines in 25-percent increments, but if you select the right icon, the gridlines display in 10-percent increments instead. The 25-percent grid lets prepress folks think in terms of shadow, three-quarter-tone, midtone, quarter-tone, and highlight, while the 10-percent grid provides photographers with a reasonable simulation of the Zone System.

Show Channel Overlays. When you view the composite view (for example, choosing RGB from the Channels pop-up menu), the Curves dialog can display the curves of each channel in each channel's color. However, you can't edit the overlay curves—to do that, choose the name of the channel you want to edit from the Channel pop-up menu.

Show Histogram. The histogram is as useful here as it is in the Levels dialog, so we leave this on.

Show Baseline. This diagonal gray line reminds you of the shape of the unedited state of a curve. We don't find it very useful in its current state; we'd prefer that it show you the shape of the curve at the time you opened the Curves dialog, before you started editing. Maybe in the future it will!

Show Intersection Line. This feature appears only as you drag a curve point. Intersection Line actually consists of two lines that lead from the cursor to all sides of the graph, so that you can see exactly where the curve point values cross the Input and Output axes.

Setting Black and White Points

In Photoshop CS3, setting the black and white points in Curves is simpler and better, and is now consistent with the Levels dialog. At the bottom of the graph area, you'll find the same black and white sliders that you saw earlier in the Levels dialog, and they work the same way. To clip the black or white points, drag the black or white slider toward the center of the graph (see **Figure 7-25**). For instance, to limit the highlight dot to 5 percent, drag the white slider until the Output level displays as 243—or (if

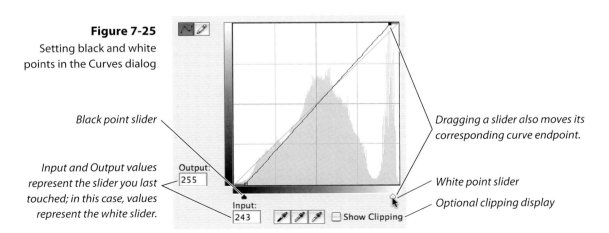

Figure 7-25
Setting black and white points in the Curves dialog

Black point slider

Input and Output values represent the slider you last touched; in this case, values represent the white slider.

Dragging a slider also moves its corresponding curve endpoint.

White point slider

Optional clipping display

Output: 255

Input: 243

Show Clipping

you're displaying Pigment/Ink percentages) 5 percent. Similarly, dragging the black slider to the right so that the info readout reads Input 12, Output 0 clips all the pixels at level 12 or below and makes them all level 0. This is exactly the same as moving the black input slider in Levels from 0 to 12.

The black- and white-point sliders also give you the same interactive clipping preview that you saw in the Levels dialog back in Figure 7-20—to use it, Option-drag (Mac) or Alt-drag (Windows) either slider. If you don't want to hold down keys, you can turn on the Show Clipping check box in the Curve Display Options. We prefer to use the interactive Option/Alt-drag method, because you can view the actual image at any time by releasing the Option/Alt key.

You can still adjust the black and white points by dragging the endpoints of the curve, as you could in previous versions of Photoshop (the endpoints will move the sliders for you), but dragging the points doesn't give you the interactive Option/Alt-drag clipping preview. The Show Clipping check box works whether you drag the endpoints or the sliders.

Editing the Curve

The great power of the Curves command comes from the fact that you aren't limited to placing just one point on the curve. You can actually place as many as 16 curve points, though we rarely need that many. This lets you change the shape of the curve as well as its steepness (remember, steepness is contrast; the steeper an area of the curve, the more definition you're pulling out between pixel values).

For example, an S-shaped curve increases contrast in the midtones, without blowing out the highlights or plugging up the shadows (see **Figure 7-26**). On the other hand, it sacrifices highlight and shadow detail by compressing those regions. We often use a small bump on the highlight end of the curve to stretch the highlights, or on the shadow end of the curve to open up the extreme shadows.

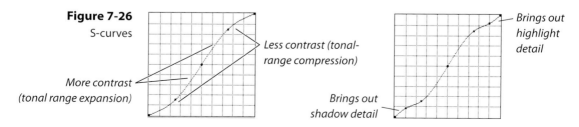

Figure 7-26
S-curves

Less contrast (tonal-range compression)

More contrast (tonal range expansion)

Brings out highlight detail

Brings out shadow detail

Tip: Dragging curve points with the mouse is almost always the least efficient way to proceed. Once you master the various shortcuts we cover here, you'll find that Command/Ctrl-clicking the image to place points and adjusting them using the arrow keys lets you edit precisely and quickly.

Selecting a curve point. Before you can edit a curve (other than dragging the clipping sliders), you need to select a curve point. The most obvious way to do this is to drag a point with the mouse.

You can also select a point with the keyboard. To do this, press Control-Tab (yes, on both Mac and Windows) to cycle through the points on the curve, selecting the next one with each press, or reverse direction by pressing Control-Shift-Tab. If you're editing curve point values numerically, selecting points with the keyboard lets you keep your hands on the keyboard.

The Input/Output levels display. Whenever you move the cursor into the graph area, the Input and Output levels display changes to reflect the cursor's x,y coordinates on the graph. For example, if you place the cursor at Input 128, Output 102 and click, the curve changes its shape to pass through that point, and the readouts become editable fields. The readouts also become editable whenever you select a curve point. All the pixels that were at level 128 change to level 102, and the rest of the midtones are darkened correspondingly (see **Figure 7-27**). You can follow the shape of the curve with the cursor and watch the info readout to determine exactly what's happening to each level.

Figure 7-27
Input/Output levels display

Input and Output values become editable when you select a point or drag a slider.

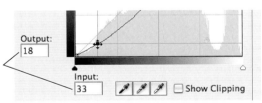

The Eyedropper. When the Curves dialog is open, the cursor automatically switches to the Eyedropper tool when you move it over the image. If you hold down the mouse button, the info display in the Curves dialog shows the input and output levels of the pixel(s) under the Eyedropper, and a hollow white circle shows the location of that point on the curve (see **Figure 7-28**). This makes it very easy to identify the levels in the regions you want to change, and to see just how much you're changing them.

For some reason, the Eyedropper feature doesn't work when you're adjusting the composite (CMYK) channel in a CMYK image, though it does when you're adjusting individual channels.

Tip: You can customize the sample size of the Eyedropper at any time by Ctrl-clicking (Mac) or right-clicking it on an image, even if a dialog is open. In Photoshop CS3, the maximum sample size is 101 by 101 Average—much better for high-resolution images than the 5-by-5-pixel maximum in Photoshop CS2.

Figure 7-28
The Eyedropper in the
Curves dialog

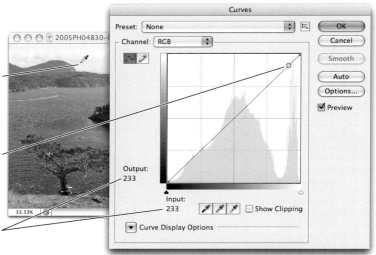

*Move the Eyedropper over the
image; Command-click (Mac)
or Ctrl-click (Windows) to add
a curve point for this value.*

*The circular marker shows the
position on the curve of the
current pixel value.*

*Input and output values are
displayed for the Eyedropper
position (the circle).*

Automatic curve point placement. When you Command-click (Mac) or Ctrl-click (Windows) in the image, Photoshop automatically places a point on the curve for the input value of the pixel on which you clicked. When you're working in the composite channel of a color image, you can place curve points in the individual channels by Command-Shift-clicking (Mac) or Ctrl-Shift-clicking (Windows).

Tip: The numeric field shortcuts that work in other dialogs work in Curves too: Press the up arrow or down arrow keys to change the value by one unit; add the Shift key to change the value by ten units.

Numeric curve entry. For maximum precision, you can specify curve points numerically. We place or select a curve point, press Tab to highlight the Input or Output field as needed, and enter the value we want (see Figure 7-27).

Other Curves command goodies. The Curves dialog contains a few more tricks that we've already covered for other dialogs. Don't forget to use the Preview check box (press P), the Auto and Options buttons (for the Auto Color Correction feature), and the hidden Reset button that takes the place of the Cancel button when you press Option (Mac) or Alt (Windows).

Choosing a Color Mode for Editing

Today, RGB is the color mode in which most images start (when scanned or created with a digital camera), and end (when displayed on the Web, included in an onscreen presentation, used in a digital video project, or sent to an inkjet printer or photo-printing service). It might not even occur to you to work in a color mode other than RGB.

But those other color modes on the Image > Mode menu exist for a reason, and features like Curves and Levels work in more than one of those modes. In particular, CMYK is a natural choice when you are preparing images for press output, and some professionals who spend all day perfecting images for a press may not recommend anything but CMYK.

But don't change modes on a whim. Although Photoshop makes it easy to flip among color modes, each change involves some data loss (as we discussed in Chapter 3, "Color Essentials"), although the amount depends on the quality and bit depth of the image.

Another penalty of changing modes is that some layer features can't be carried across modes. For example, if you create curves in an RGB adjustment layer and convert to Lab mode, the RGB curves simply can't be translated channel to channel and still look the same, because the channels are completely different. It's a similar situation with blend modes. This is why Photoshop asks you if you want to flatten a document when you switch color modes.

Our simple rule. Don't change color modes unless or until you have to, and do as much of your correction as possible in the image's original color mode. The ideal number of color-mode conversions is one or none.

Naturally, there will be times when the simple rule won't be enough. The most common example is when your source images are RGB, but you're going to a CMYK press. In such a case, it's not only a question of if you convert, but when you convert. To answer that question, we have some more guidelines for you.

When to Edit in RGB

If your image comes from an RGB source, such as a desktop scanner or a digital camera, you should do as much of your work as possible in RGB. You have the entire tonal range and color gamut of the original at your disposal, allowing you to take full advantage of the small differences between pixels that you want to emphasize in the image. Compared to CMYK, it's also much easier to repurpose RGB images for different kinds of output, and using three channels instead of four keeps file sizes down.

RGB has less-obvious advantages as well. A number of Photoshop features, such as the clipping display in Levels, are available only in RGB, not in CMYK or Lab. If your final output requires RGB image data, such as a Web page, DVD, or an inkjet printer (see the tip on the next page), you'll probably stay in RGB mode for your entire workflow.

When to Edit in CMYK

Tip: If you order a scan from a color house and you plan to manipulate the image yourself in Photoshop or use the image for different kinds of output, ask the shop to save the image in RGB format. Of course, if your job will ultimately require converting the image to CMYK, you'll now be responsible for performing the final conversion.

If you received your images in CMYK form (such as images from a traditional drum scanner or images from an older edition of that job), it makes no sense to convert them to RGB for correction if they are going to press. You should stay in CMYK. If you find that you have to make major corrections, though, you'll almost certainly get better results by rescanning the image instead of editing it in Photoshop. In high-end prepress shops, it's not unusual to scan an image three times before the client signs off on it.

Certain kinds of fine-tuning, such as black-plate editing, can *only* be done on the separated CMYK file. Similarly, Hue/Saturation changes in CMYK are generally more delicate than in RGB. But if you find you need to make large moves in CMYK after a mode change, it's time to look at your CMYK settings in Color Settings, because the problem probably lies there—a wrong profile, incorrect settings in Custom CMYK, or color management policies that weren't set the way you thought they were (see Chapter 4, "Color Settings"). In that case, it makes more sense to go back to the RGB original and reseparate it using new settings that get you closer to the desired result.

In dire emergencies, such as when you have a CMYK file separated for newsprint and you need to reproduce it on glossy stock, you *may* want to take the desperate step of converting it back to RGB, correcting, and reseparating to CMYK; but in general, treat RGB to CMYK as a strict one-way trip.

Don't Convert to CMYK Too Early

You may encounter people who maintain that if your work is destined for a press, you should work exclusively in CMYK. People who tell you to do everything in CMYK may have excellent traditional prepress skills and a deep understanding of process-color printing, but they probably are not comfortable working in RGB, and may not realize how much image information Photoshop loses during the conversion from RGB to CMYK. As a result, they may convert images to CMYK earlier in the workflow than we'd recommend, then make huge corrections in CMYK, trying to salvage a printable image from what's left. When you prematurely convert to CMYK, you restrict yourself in at least four ways:

▶ You lose a great deal of image information, making quality tonal and color correction much more difficult.

▶ You optimize the image for a particular set of press conditions (paper, press, inks, and so on). If press conditions change, or if you want to print the image under various press conditions, you're in a hole that's difficult to climb out of.

▶ You increase your file size by one-third, slowing most operations by that same amount.

▶ You lose some convenient Photoshop features that work only in RGB, such as some filters and the Levels and Curves clipping displays.

Tip: Some believe that because inkjet printers use CMYK inks, jobs sent to them should be in CMYK. There are two problems with that: First, the inks used in inkjets are not the same as press CMYK inks. Second, inkjet driver software typically expects to receive RGB data and convert it to its specific CMYK inks. If you're printing fine-art photographs on a large-format inkjet, staying in RGB mode should result in optimal quality. On the other hand, if you're preparing a CMYK job for press output and you're using an inkjet to proof it, don't convert that job to RGB.

For the vast majority of Photoshop users, those four reasons mean it's best to work in RGB for as long as possible and convert your image to CMYK only after you're finished with your other corrections and you know the printing conditions. It's useful to keep an eye on the CMYK dot percentages while you work, but you don't need to work in CMYK mode to do that, since the Info palette can display CMYK values for an image in any color mode, as we showed you earlier in this chapter. Using the View > Proof Setup > Custom command (see Chapter 8, "The Digital Darkroom") with your CMYK output profile can also help you visually preview the CMYK results of your RGB edits.

One of the great advantages to doing major corrections in RGB for prepress is that you have a built-in safeguard: It's impossible to violate the ink limits specified by your CMYK profile or Custom CMYK settings, because they'll always be imposed when you convert to CMYK. When you edit CMYK files directly, you have no such constraint—you can build up so much density in the shadows using Levels or Curves that you're calling for 400-percent ink coverage. On a sheetfed press, this will create a mess. On a web press, it will create a potentially life-threatening situation! In any case, it's something to avoid unless you're printing to the rare desktop color printer that can handle 400-percent total ink.

If you work in print, you must learn to edit in CMYK. But it isn't the only game in town.

Converting CMYK to RGB

We can think of two reasons to convert a CMYK image to RGB: You need an image for the Web or multimedia and a CMYK scan is all you have, or you need to repurpose the CMYK image for a larger-gamut output process. In either case, you need to expand the tonal range and color gamut. If you just do a mode change from CMYK to RGB, you'll get a flat, lifeless image with washed-out color, because the tonal range and color gamut of the original were compressed in the initial RGB-to-CMYK conversion, and the mode change reproduces the compressed gamut and squashed tonal range faithfully in RGB.

Instead, use the Convert to Profile command, using perceptual intent, with black point compensation and dither turned on. Then, open Levels and click Auto. If this makes the image *too* saturated, back off the black- and white-point sliders a few levels. You'll find this works surprisingly well (see **Figure 7-29**). That said, this is a last-resort technique. Work on a copy of the file, and watch for color shifts and posterization.

Figure 7-29 Repurposing an image that's been prepared for reproduction on newsprint

The image above left was separated for newsprint. The separation settings resulted in a flat image that would reproduce well in that medium, but that had lost a great deal of its tonal and color range.

For the image above, we started with the newsprint-targeted CMYK file, pulled it back into RGB, made a Levels tweak, then reseparated for this book's wider gamut. The results aren't great, but as we said, it's a last-resort technique.

The image at left was created from the original RGB file and separated using the proper settings for these printing conditions.

CMYK Myths

One of the reasons we wrote this book was to dispel a number of the myths that have cropped up since the advent of desktop prepress (and some others that have been around even longer)—especially those regarding CMYK and RGB issues. We clarify two of those issues here.

CMYK has more colors (false). We've heard experts deride the notion that CMYK contains fewer colors than RGB. "Do the math, stupid," they say. "CMYK has 256^4, or more than 4 *billion* colors." We wish that were the case. CMYK has more than 4 billion color *specifications*, but a large number of them are simply alternate ways of specifying the *same* color using a different balance of black and CMY inks. And many of them (for example, 90C 90M 90Y 100K) are "illegal" specifications that would turn the paper into a soggy mess scattered all over the pressroom floor. When you also take into account the constraints imposed by the black-generation curve and the total ink limit, you end up with far fewer colors than RGB.

CMYK is more accurate (true, sort of). Other experts say, "CMYK may have a narrower gamut, but the data points in CMYK are packed much closer together than they are in RGB, so CMYK specifies colors *more accurately* than RGB."

Here they have a point. You *can* specify smaller differences between colors in CMYK than you can in RGB, because the same number of bits is being used to describe a smaller color gamut. (Whether these smaller color differences are detectable by the human eye is a question we'll leave to someone willing to carry out the empirical research.)

But this is relevant only if your RGB original is being converted to CMYK from high-bit RGB. The CMYK conversion can't be any more accurate than the RGB scan, and even in high-bit mode, your image will suffer from rounding errors. While you can fine-tune your CMYK after conversion, but you're *much* better off doing the heavy lifting on source RGB—preferably high-bit RGB.

When to Edit in Lab

The somewhat obscure Lab color mode is far less popular than RGB or CMYK for editing, but the number of people editing in Lab mode is actually growing due to the special advantages it offers. For example, Lab mode separates luminance (its L channel) from color (its A and B channels), making it far easier to apply tonal corrections and filters (such as sharpening) without introducing hue shifts. This concept appeals to those who tweak the black plate in CMYK. The way that Lab mode puts opposing colors on its two A and B axes also makes it easy to remove color casts or enhance color contrast without wrecking the image or its tonality; we'll cover a few quick fixes later in this chapter.

One of the big reasons that more people aren't working in Lab mode is that going to Lab always adds a conversion step (since original image files are either RGB or CMYK), and we like to keep those conversions to a minimum. Also, Lab mode encompasses such a wide color gamut that editing in Lab usually works better with images containing 16 bits or more per channel, to keep posterization at bay. Also, as we mentioned earlier, if you used adjustment layers and blend modes, you can't retain them when you change modes, and some Photoshop features that are available in RGB mode do not work in Lab mode. If you're able to perform most of your layered editing in Lab mode and don't need to convert your layered working file to another mode, only saving flattened RGB and CMYK copies for final output, mode conversion issues may not come up at all.

Because Lab can be so helpful in situations such as rescuing difficult images, there are times when Lab mode is certainly worth the side trip. If you want to explore the challenging yet powerful world of Lab, look for books by Dan Margulis—a good place to start is *Photoshop Lab Color* (Peachpit Press). Dan's eye-opening techniques have transformed Lab mode from a color scientists' exercise into a surprisingly valuable color-correction tool.

Hands-On Levels and Curves

Tip: The dramatic rise of digital camera raw formats changes our classic order somewhat. In the days of film cameras, you would apply everything in this chapter in Photoshop. Today, if your starting point for an image is a camera raw file, you can do spotting and overall corrections during the raw conversion, using the high-quality tools in Adobe Camera Raw 4 and Adobe Lightroom 1.1. This gives you a polished master raw image. You would then use Photoshop for fine-tuning and localized fixes. You can use the color-correction tools in Camera Raw and Lightroom to apply many of the concepts in this chapter.

Now that you're armed with all the preceding information, let's look at some practical examples of working with Levels and Curves. We'll look at several different scenarios, because we have two different reasons for editing images—see the upcoming sidebar, "Why We Edit."

The classic order for preparing images for print is as follows:

▶ Spotting, retouching, and dust and scratch removal

▶ Global tonal correction

▶ Global color correction

▶ Selective tonal and/or color correction

▶ Optimization (resizing, sharpening, handling out-of-gamut colors, compressing tonal range, converting to CMYK)

We loosely adhere to this, but a great deal depends on the image and on the quality of the image capture. For instance, you often have to lighten an image before you can even consider removing dust and scratches.

And sometimes it's impossible to separate tonal correction and color correction. Changes to the color balance affect tonal values, too, because you're manipulating the tone of the individual color channels. For example, if you add red to neutralize a cyan cast, you'll also brighten the image because you'll be adding light. If you reduce the green to neutralize a green cast, you'll darken the image because you'll be subtracting light.

Image Evaluation

Before we edit an image, we always spend a few moments evaluating the image to see what needs to be done and to spot any potential pitfalls. We check the Histogram palette to get a general sense of the image's dynamic range: If shadows or highlights are clipped, we can't bring back any detail, but we may still be able to make the image look good. If all the data is clumped in the middle, with no true blacks or whites, we'll probably want to expand the tonal range.

We also check the values in bright highlights and dark shadows on the Info palette, in case there's detail lurking there that we can exploit. We're pretty good at identifying color casts by eye, but we still check the Info palette—a magenta cast and a red cast, for example, appear fairly similar, but the prescription for fixing each is quite different.

Fix the biggest problem first. The rule of thumb we've developed over the years is simple: Fix the biggest problem first. This is partly plain common sense. You often have to fix the biggest problem before you can even see what the other problems are. But it's usually also the most effective approach, the one requiring the least work, and the one that degrades the image the least.

Leave yourself an escape route. The great Scot poet Robert Burns pointed out that "the best-laid schemes o' mice and men gang aft agley." He didn't have the benefit of the History palette, or the Undo and Revert commands, but you do. History is a great feature, but it eventually it starts dropping the oldest states, so don't consume them unnecessarily. If a particular move doesn't work, just undo (Command-Z in Mac OS X, or Ctrl-Z in Windows)—you can reload any of the commands in the Adjustments submenu (in the Image menu) with the last-used settings by holding down the Option key (Mac) or Alt key (Windows) while selecting them either from the menu or with a keyboard shortcut. If a whole train of moves has led you down a blind alley, back up in the History palette or revert to the original version.

If you're working on a complex or critical problem, work on a copy of the image. When you apply a move using Levels, Curves, or Hue/Saturation,

Tip: Before you start, zoom to 100 percent (Actual Pixels) or higher and look at every pixel using the Home, Page Up, Page Down, and End keys. (To scroll sideways, press Page Up or Page Down along with the Command key in Mac OS X or the Ctrl key in Windows.) Check for dust or scratches, noise (especially in the blue channel), the strengths and weaknesses visible in each channel, and the tonal range in the histogram. A few minutes spent critically evaluating the image early on can save hours later on.

Why We Edit

When we break it down, we have two different reasons for editing images, though in some situations we may address both reasons with a single round of edits.

▶ We edit to get images into the best shape possible without regard to any specific output process. The goal is to create a "use-neutral" master image.

▶ We edit to optimize the image for a specific output process. The goal is to render the image in the best possible way given the limitations imposed by the output process.

If you're a photographer, you probably hope that the image will have multiple uses, so it makes sense to produce a master version that doesn't make compromises to fit any specific output. If you're working in prepress, on the other hand, it's likely that you only care about the specific output process at the end of your production chain.

Of course, all images that get reproduced eventually require optimization for the reproduction process, so the two approaches are not mutually exclusive.

We always edit our use-neutral color images in an RGB working space, because RGB working spaces are designed to provide an ideal environment for editing. CMYK is inherently use-specific, so we avoid working in CMYK except for final optimizations for known output processes. For grayscale use-neutral edits, we use the Gray Gamma 2.2 working space because it's close to being perceptually uniform.

When we optimize color images for specific outputs, we still prefer to do as much of the work as possible on the RGB image, but we view it through Proof Setup, configured to represent the final output space (see "Customize Proof Condition dialog" in Chapter 4, "Color Settings").

For CMYK output, we may do some required fine-tuning after conversion to CMYK. For RGB output, we've never seen any advantage to working directly in the output space—RGB output spaces are generally nonlinear with poor gray balance, so it's hard to edit in them.

For grayscale optimization, we use a measured dot-gain curve where possible, or failing that, a single dot-gain value. In the latter case, we pay attention to setting endpoints manually since we have no ICC profile to do so for us.

If you only care about a single use of the image, you can combine both sets of edits into a single operation. But in this case too, we recommend doing as much work as possible in RGB viewed through Proof Setup. RGB files are smaller than CMYK because they contain one fewer channel, so your work goes faster. We reserve CMYK editing for small black-channel tweaks and for fine adjustments using Hue/Saturation, which is a much more sensitive tool in CMYK than in RGB.

---

save the image before you apply it. That way, you can always retrace your steps up to the point where things started to go wrong.

Adjustment layers let you avoid many of the pitfalls we've just discussed. You don't need to get your edits right the first time because you can go back and change them at will, without damaging the underlying pixels. You automatically leave yourself an escape route because your edits float above the original image rather than being burned into it.

Sometimes it's impractical to use adjustment layers because of file size and RAM constraints, particularly with high-bit files. Also, to use

Tip: Take advantage of the Image > Duplicate command when you want to experiment with potential solutions without accidentally saving unwanted changes to the original file.

Tip: We tend to display the Histogram palette in Expanded view (choose Expanded View from the Histogram palette menu). For one thing, in Expanded view, you can choose how the histogram measures the image values by using the pop-up menu at the top of the palette.

adjustment layers effectively, you need to know how the various controls operate on a flat file. So even if you plan to use adjustment layers for as much of your editing as possible—and we encourage you to do so—you still need to master the techniques we discuss in this chapter, and the pitfalls they entail. For a much deeper discussion of adjustment layers, see Chapter 8, "The Digital Darkroom."

Evaluation Examples

We show three unedited images in **Figures 7-30** through **7-32** and the conclusions we draw as to what we need to do to them. We'll execute the edits later in this chapter.

The evaluation process only takes a few seconds, and it's time well spent. We may encounter other problems that aren't obvious on the initial

Figure 7-30
A dark, muddy image

 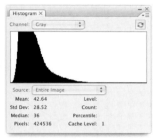

The histogram shows no serious clipping. We may want to finesse the endpoints a little with Levels, but the biggest problem is that the image needs a serious midtone adjustment. We'll start with Levels, then fine-tune the contrast with Curves.

Figure 7-31
A severe color cast

 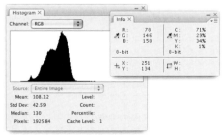

The biggest problem is the color cast. When we check a spot that should be approximately neutral (we used the highlights on the metal wheel in the photo) we find that red is much lower and blue is a little higher than green, indicating a cyan-blue cast. The histogram shows that the image is also quite underexposed. We'll use a single round of Curves adjustments to kill the color cast and fix the contrast.

Figure 7-32

A flat image

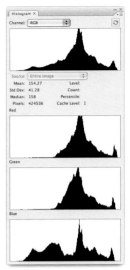

This is a good example of how the RGB histogram can mislead. It shows data all the way down into the shadows, but the image contains nothing resembling black. Most of the "shadow" data is from the yellow-greens, which are close to zero in the blue channel. We'll move the black point and midtone with Levels, and then fine-tune contrast with Curves.

examination, but it's relatively rare that we'll encounter something that causes us to rethink the entire edit.

In the following examples, we'll apply the edits directly to the image, but later you can perform the same edits with adjustment layers. So, now that you're armed with a plan, let's proceed to the edits.

A midpoint fix. Figure 7-33 shows a simple Levels move that makes a huge improvement, and then gets to the finish line when we apply the Curves adjustment shown.

We started by placing points that corresponded to the light, middle, and dark tones on the main tree trunk (points 4, 5, and 6, counting from the shadow [0,0] point), and adjusted them to increase the contrast. This cause both ends of the curve to clip, so the additional points were added to fine-tune the highlight and shadow contrast.

We could have made the entire set of adjustments using Curves, but it's often easier to make basic changes in the simpler Levels dialog. You'll see an example executed completely in the Curves dialog a little later.

We deliberately left a little headroom to accommodate sharpening. As you'll learn in Chapter 10, "Sharpness, Detail, and Noise Reduction," the process of sharpening images is really about adding contrast along edges, so sharpening always adds a little apparent contrast.

Sharpening also drives more pixels towards levels 255 and 0; the significance of this depends on the output process for which you're preparing the image. Individual pixels being driven to black and white usually isn't

Tip: To better understand how curves work, try this exercise. Make an RGB gradient from white to black; somewhere between 512 and 1024 pixels wide works best. Use the Color Sampler tool to place color samplers—we suggest you start at approximately the midtone, quarter tone, and three-quarter tone areas. Then simply watch what happens to the numbers in the Info palette as you manipulate the composite channel (all three RGB values will change equally), and the individual color channels (one value will change while the rest stay the same).

Figure 7-33
A midpoint adjustment
using Levels and Curves

The original image

Black clip at 7   *White clip at 237*

When we check the endpoints
(clipping displays shown at
top right), we see that we can
lighten the image without
losing important detail by
reducing the white Levels
input slider value to 237. We
can also add a little snap to
the shadows by raising the
black Levels input slider value
to 7. Adjusting the gray slider
to 1.69 lightens the midtones.

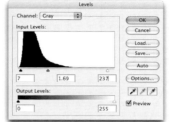

*Levels dialog
adjustments*

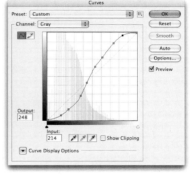

*Curves
dialog
adjustments*

*The image after the Levels
dialog adjustments*

Then in the Curves dialog,
we placed the curve points
by Command/Ctrl-clicking
in the image, and adjusted
them in the Curves dialog by
pressing the arrow keys.

*The image after applying
the curve shown in the
Curves dialog*

*The final,
sharpened version
of the image*

a concern—unless you're printing at resolutions below 100 ppi, you're unlikely to see them on output. For Web work, you may need to be a little more conservative.

Cast away that color. Moving on to color, we'll use Curves to neutralize the nasty color cast in the image from Figure 7-31. Obeying our maxim to fix the biggest problem first, we'll start by tackling the color cast, then, since we're already working in Curves, we'll improve the contrast there.

We use Curves to neutralize the color cast by identifying an area that should be neutral, as shown in **Figure 7-34**. This simple tweak removes the worst of the color cast, allowing us to turn our attention to the tonal issues. **Figure 7-35** shows a tweak to the composite RGB curve that spreads the data across the entire dynamic range. We keep a watchful eye on the Curves histogram as we move the black and white points on the curve. Then we add a couple of points to improve the contrast.

Now we can see that our first approximation at removing the color cast was less than totally successful—the image is pretty green. We return to

Tip: To eliminate a color cast, look for something in the image that should be approximately neutral, then use Curves to make it so. Check the values on a should-be-neutral area with the Info palette, then use Curves to adjust the highest and lowest values to match the middle one. Nine times out of ten, the rest of the color simply falls into place.

Figure 7-34
Killing a color cast
with Curves

When we sample a spot from the highlights on the metal wheel, we see the values shown in the Info palette.

We adjust the red and blue curves to neutralize the point we sampled. In the red curve, we place a point at input value 101 (the value we sampled), and set the output value to 119 (the value we sampled from the green channel). We repeat the process for the blue curve, making a point with input value 138, output value 119, producing the image at right.

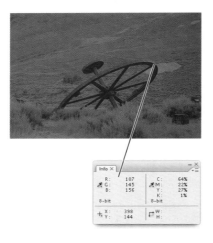

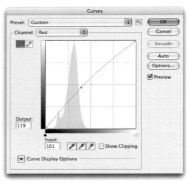

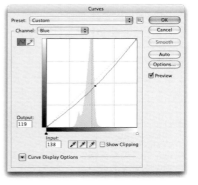

Figure 7-35

Setting endpoints and contrast with Curves

 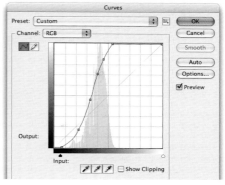

The composite curve adjustment at right spreads the data across the whole dynamic range and increases contrast.

the individual color channels and tweak the existing points with the arrow keys to produce the result shown in **Figure 7-36**.

Note that we made all these edits without closing the Curves dialog, so they're applied as a single pass, avoiding any unnecessary image degradation. In this case, we decided to use Curves for the extra control it offers over contrast. But it's instructive to compare the Curves rendering with alternate results produced by our other favorite technique for killing color casts: Auto Color. **Figure 7-37** shows the results produced by the various Auto options.

Figure 7-36

Fine-tuning the color balance with Curves

The three curve adjustments below produced the final image shown at left. We started with the green curve since the color cast was predominantly green, then we adjusted the red curve, adding a point to put more red into the rusty metal. We finished by tweaking the blue curve to put a little blue back into the image.

Tip: To place a point on all channel curves at once, Command-Shift-click (Mac) or Ctrl-Shirt-Click (Windows) the image while Curves is open. When you view each channel in Curves, you'll find a new point ready for adjustment. You can then Ctrl-Tab (on Mac and Windows) until you select the point, then press the arrow keys to move it, or press Tab to select the point's Input or Output field.

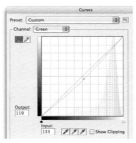 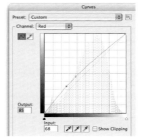 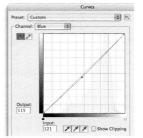

Figure 7-37
Examining Auto Color
options for the wheel image

The original image

*Enhance Monochromatic
Contrast
(same as Image >
Adjustments > Auto Contrast,
but customizable)*

*Enhance Per
Channel Contrast
(same as Image >
Adjustments > Auto Levels,
but customizable)*

*Enhance Per Channel
Contrast with
Snap Neutral Midtones*

*Find Dark and Light Colors
with Snap Neutral Midtones
(same as Image >
Adjustments > Auto Color,
but customizable)*

You need to be comfortable with both techniques to decide which approach makes sense, taking into account both the quality requirements and the time you can afford to spend. Photoshop offers several ways to accomplish any given task, and as we've mentioned, when all you have is a hammer, everything tends to look like a nail. You don't have to learn every single Photoshop feature—we doubt that's possible—but if you master the techniques in this book, you'll have strong Photoshop skills.

Make it pop. In the next example, we'll use only Curves to correct the tone on a color image. **Figure 7-38** shows the original image and the Curves correction. This is an improvement, but we can make matters still better, as shown in **Figure 7-39**.

Figure 7-38
Setting endpoints
and midtone with Levels

We set the black Input slider value to 20, which darkens the shadows and increases the saturation of the yellow-green vegetation by clipping the blue channel to 0.

Then we darkened the midtone by setting the midpoint to 147. We'll fine-tune the contrast with Curves.

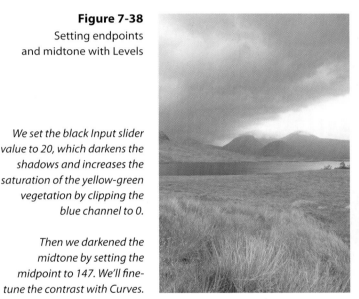

Original image   *After initial Curves adjustment*

*Clipping display
of the black point at 20*

*Curves
adjustment*

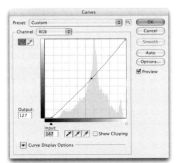

Figure 7-39
Final contrast
with Curves

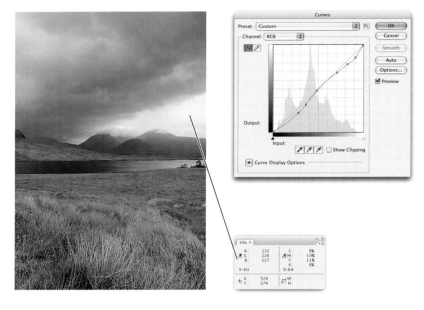

The image after applying the Curve shown at right. The points at the top of the curve bring detail into the bright sky; those on the lower end of the curve add contrast on the hillside.

The remaining problem is that pulling the detail out of the sky turned it red, as we can see from the Info palette. Tweaking the extreme highlight ends of the red and blue curves produces the final version of the image, shown at right.

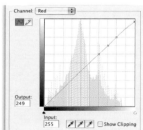

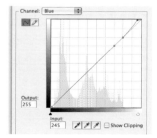

The Eyedroppers

Also common to the Levels and Curves dialogs are the black, white, and gray Eyedropper tools. Back in the days before color management, these were mission-critical tools. Nowadays, we rely on them much less, but they still warrant a mention.

Tip: If you already have a painting tool selected, press the Option key (Mac) or Alt key (Windows) to toggle between it and the Eyedropper tool.

The black and white Eyedroppers let you force the image pixel on which you click to the target value set for the Eyedropper, adjusting all other pixels accordingly. (If you want to know exactly what they do, see the sidebar, "The Math Behind the Eyedroppers" later in this chapter.)

You can click the Eyedropper cursor on any open Photoshop document. When a dialog is open and you position the cursor outside the dialog, you might see the Eyedropper; if you do, that means you can sample that color (from the Swatches palette, for example).

Tip: To sample a color outside of Photoshop (such as a window open in another application), start dragging the Eyedropper from inside a Photoshop document and then release the mouse button only over the color you want to sample outside Photoshop. This is useful in Web and screen design, because it captures only the RGB color values of the color on the display. There is no way for Photoshop to determine the underlying color values in other applications.

Setting minimum and maximum dots. In pre-color-management days, we always used to set our minimum highlight dot with the white Eyedropper, and more often than not we set our maximum shadow dot with the black one. Good ICC output profiles make this practice unnecessary because the profile has a detailed understanding of the tonal behavior of the output device, but we still use the Eyedroppers for unprofiled grayscale output, or in those increasingly rare situations where we're forced to rely on an old-style Custom CMYK setting with a single dot-gain value.

Unlike the Output sliders in Levels, which simply compress the entire tonal range to minimum and maximum values, the Eyedroppers let us set a specific value for minimum highlight and maximum shadow dots. If we want to preserve specular highlights, we can set the white Eyedropper to the minimum printable dot value, then click on a diffuse highlight. This pins the diffuse highlight to the minimum dot, while allowing the brighter specular highlights to blow out to paper white.

Figure 7-40 shows a case in point. We want to hold a dot in the diffuse highlights while allowing the specular highlights to reach paper white. Here we're aiming for a 3 percent dot. Depending on the printing process you're targeting, you may want to set a lower or higher value. To translate Levels to dot percentages, divide the levels value by 2.55, then subtract the result from 100 to get the dot percentage. (The tip at left can also help.) As previously mentioned, we only use this technique when we don't have a good ICC output profile available, as in the following situations:

Tip: The fastest way to load the Eyedroppers with a dot percentage is to use the Color Picker's Brightness field. Subtract the desired dot percentage from 100, then enter the result in the Brightness field.

► Grayscale images

► Custom CMYK with single dot-gain values instead of dot-gain curves

► RGB for non-color-managed, standard-definition television display (we set highlights to 235 and shadows to 15)

Figure 7-40
Setting a highlight
dot with the white
Eyedropper

Original image

*We double-click the white
Eyedropper to open the
Color Picker and set the
target color to Brightness
97 (equivalent to a
3 percent dot).*

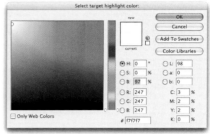

*We click the white Eyedropper
on the brightest pixel value
that we want to hold a
dot on press.*

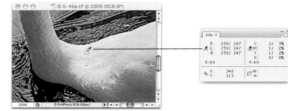

*After the adjustment, the
water droplet holds a dot, but
the specular highlights still go
to paper white.*

The rest of the time, we let the profile handle the minimum dot (though when highlight detail is critical, we check the Info palette numbers).

Killing color casts. We also use the Eyedroppers on occasion as a quick way to eliminate color casts. The black and white Eyedroppers force the pixel on which they're clicked to the target values you set for the tools (the defaults are RGB 255 and RGB 0, respectively), scaling the individual color channels to meet the target value.

This behavior can cause some confusion. While the Eyedroppers appear in two nonlinear editing tools—Levels and Curves—their effect is a linear

The Math Behind the Eyedroppers

For those who want to know exactly what will happen to each value in the image, this is what the two Eyedroppers do.

White Eyedropper. The white Eyedropper simply multiplies all the pixels in the image by *target value ÷ source value*. For example, if we choose a target value of 243 (a 5 percent dot) and click the tool on a pixel with a value of 248, all pixels at level 248 will be turned to level 243. All the other values in the image are multiplied by 243 ÷ 248, or approximately 0.98.

So pixels with an input value of 255 produce an output value of 250, because 255 × 0.98 = 249.85. Pixels with an input value of 128 produce an output value of 125, and so on down the tonal range until you get to level 25, which remains unchanged (because 25 × 0.98 = 24.5, which gets rounded back up to 25).

If you make a much smaller move by choosing a source value of 246 and a target of 243, the multiplier is 0.99, so an input value of 255 produces an output value of 253, 128 produces an output value of 127, and values below 50 remain unchanged.

Note that you can use the white Eyedropper to stretch the highlights (rather than compress them) by choosing a source color that's darker than the target color. This produces a multiplier with a value greater than 1, so the pixel values increase rather than decrease.

Black Eyedropper. The black Eyedropper essentially does the reverse of the white Eyedropper, but the arithmetic is a little more complicated. To limit the effect to the shadows, the algorithm uses the inverse brightnesses of the input value and of the difference between source and target color—the inverse brightness of any value x is 255-x.

If we call the difference between source and target values y, then for each pixel value x, the output value equals:

$$[(255-x) \div (255-y)\,2\,y] + x.$$

If this makes your head hurt, don't worry—the net result is very similar to that produced by the white Eyedropper, only in reverse. The source value is changed to the target value, and all other values in the image change proportionally, with the change becoming progressively smaller as you go toward the highlights.

adjustment. So if you labor mightily in Levels or Curves, then apply the black or white Eyedroppers to the image, they promptly wipe out any adjustments you'd already made. This behavior leads us to use the Eyedroppers only when there's a heavy cast near the shadows or highlights, and we've planned the correction.

The gray Eyedropper. The gray Eyedropper behaves quite differently from the black and white ones. It forces the clicked pixel to the target hue, while attempting to preserve brightness. By default the target is set to RGB 128 gray, since the tool was designed for gray-balancing. Unlike its black and white counterparts, it doesn't undo other edits you've made in Levels or Curves, though it may change their effects.

We still use the gray Eyedropper occasionally for gray-balancing (as in the example shown in **Figure 7-41**), but now we're much more likely to use Auto Color. The results produced by the gray Eyedropper depend critically on where you click in the image, while Auto Color responds in a much more predictable fashion. Instead of clicking around the image with the gray Eyedropper as we hunt for just the right sample pixel that will fix the gray balance, we can drive the color exactly where we want it to go by adjusting the Auto Color midtone target swatch (see Figure 7-22, much earlier in this chapter). In the example shown in Figure 7-41, we were already in the Curves dialog, and the gray Eyedropper was right there, so it made sense to try it, and in this case we obtained a good result.

The Eyedroppers are pretty old technology, and have largely been superseded by newer additions to the Image > Adjustments submenu, but occasionally they're just what you need. So investigate them, learn their behaviors, and use them, but be aware of their limitations.

Figure 7-41 Removing color casts with the Eyedropper tools

The image from Figure 7-32 with the red sky.

If we click the white Eyedropper to neutralize the sky, it wipes out the curves we've already applied and introduces a cyan cast to the clouds.

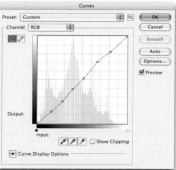

The image with a new tone curve and color-cast correction applied with the gray Eyedropper.

Freehand Curves

We'd be remiss if we didn't mention the freehand (pencil) tool in the Curves dialog, which lets you draw freehand curves rather than bending the curve by placing points. We really have only one use for this, but when we need it, nothing else does the job. We use the freehand tool to handle specular highlights on printing processes where the minimum highlight dot is relatively large, such as laser printer or newsprint output.

Trouble in the transition zone. If you're dealing with newsprint or low-quality printing, the transition zone—that ambiguous area between white paper and the minimum reliable dot—can make your specular highlights messy. Some may drop out, while others may print with a visible dot. The solution is to make a curve that sets your brightest highlight detail to the minimum highlight dot value, and then blows everything brighter than that directly out to white. This is a two-step process.

1. Select the highlight point, then use the numeric fields to set your input point to a value corresponding to your brightest real detail, and an output value corresponding to your minimum printable dot. **Figure 7-42** shows a point that sets the input value at 253 and the output value at 231, corresponding to a 10-percent dot. This sets all the pixels with a value of 253 to 231. But it also sets pixels with values of 253 through 255 to 231, which isn't what you want. You want them to be white.

2. Select the pencil tool, and *very carefully* position it at the top edge of the curve graph until the input value reads 253 and the output value reads 255, then click the mouse button. (See Figure 7-42.) This keeps pixels with an input value of 252 set to an output value of 231, but blows out pixels with a value of 253 through 255 to paper white. Your highlight detail will print with a reliable dot, and your specular highlights will definitely blow out.

If this is something you have to do at all often, click the Save button to save the curve. Don't click the Smooth button, because it will smooth the curve—which in this case is not what you want. You can load the saved curve whenever you need it, or even create an action that you run as a batch to process multiple images.

Figure 7-42
Blowing out
the specular
highlights

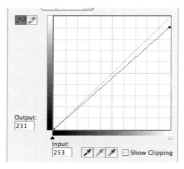

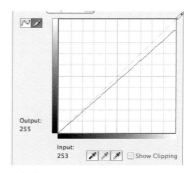

A curve point at Input 253, Output 231 compresses the image to the printable range.

A little touch-up with the pencil tool makes all the white pixels white.

Quick Lab Mode Fixes

The color tools have improved so much in Photoshop CS3 and Camera Raw 4 that you can fix more kinds of problems more easily than you could before. These days, you have much less reason to convert to CMYK or Lab for big moves. But as we mentioned earlier, converting to Lab mode can enable a more direct way to make certain types of corrections:

▶ You want to make major changes in tonality without introducing a color cast or any changes to the color relationships. In this case you can edit just the L channel. (However, you can achieve similar results in RGB mode by editing the master curve or a Curves adjustment layer and applying the Luminosity blend mode to it).

▶ You are having trouble getting rid of a color cast using Auto Color or RGB Curves.

▶ You want to create more contrast between magenta and green.

▶ You want to create more contrast between blue and yellow.

In **Figure 7-43**, we have a sample image that can benefit from a Lab tweak. It's a 16-bit image of a trees along a lake, and we'd like to boost the contrast a bit. The trees along the lake are one mass of similar color, but we think we can create more color contrast there by using Lab mode to enhance the complementary colors in the image.

Figure 7-43
Editing in Lab mode

After adjusting tonal contrast using the L curve, the first color problem to fix is the red cast indicated in the sky by the color sampler, which shows that the A channel is not neutral. Setting the A channel to 0 fixes the cast.

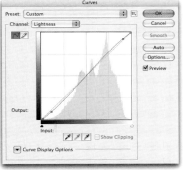

L channel edited for tone only

Color cast   *Cast neutralized*

In the A channel, a center point is added, and a point is added on the red side and moved down to steepen the A curve, to increase magenta/ green color contrast.

Unfortunately the Curves dialog doesn't show you which areas control which colors, so to help you out, we added color gradients to our A and B channel screen shots.

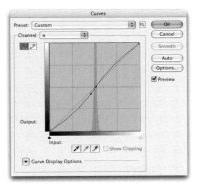

The A channel edited

In the B channel, a center point is added, and points are added on both sides of the center point to boost blue and yellow by different amounts.

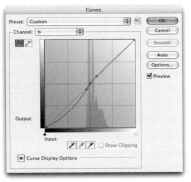

The B channel edited with different adjustments for blue and yellow

Reading Color with the Info Palette

The Info palette is a vital tool for working in color. It lets you read the color values under the cursor, and if you're preparing a job for a press, it can show you the approximate CMYK values that you'll get when you do a mode change to CMYK. We say "approximate" because if you examine the CMYK values for an RGB file, then convert to CMYK and examine the values again, they may differ by a percentage point in one channel (which is a closer match than many production processes can consistently hold).

You can edit images in their native color space while simultaneously monitoring the CMYK values Photoshop will produce when you make color separations. It's the best of both worlds.

When you're working on a non-CMYK file, the CMYK values displayed by the Info palette are governed by the settings in the Color Settings dialog. If those settings represent your target CMYK output conditions, you should have to do little or no work on the CMYK file after you've converted it from RGB to CMYK. See Chapter 4

for strategies for setting up these key preferences.

We prefer working visually—relying on a well-calibrated monitor—rather than going strictly by the numbers, but even the best monitor and the best calibration have inherent limitations. Some things are hard to detect visually. For example, without looking at some kind of printed reference under controlled lighting, it's very difficult to tell from the monitor whether or not a gray is really neutral. But the numbers in the Info palette provide an infallible guide.

Likewise, it's hard to see differences of one or two levels between adjacent pixels, but the Info palette lets you find these differences. Remember, difference is detail.

Overly macho prepress guys will tell you that monitor calibration isn't necessary, and that you can do color correction using a black and white monitor and the Info palette. This is true only if you are intimately familiar with the target values for a specific output device. But that only comes from long experience examining the

values on the Info palette for the key areas of your images.

Info palette setup. For prepress work, we use the same Info palette setup most of the time. We set the first color readout to RGB, the second color readout to CMYK, and the mouse coordinates to pixels. You can set all these options with the Palette Options menu on the Info palette, or you can set individual readouts using the palette's pop-up menus.

Setting Eyedropper options. You can set the size of the sample area from the Sample Size pop-up menu in the Options bar, or by Ctrl-clicking (Mac) or right-clicking an image with the Eyedropper. You can sample as little as a single pixel (Point Sample) or as large as 101-by-101 pixels. David chooses 3-by-3 Average unless he's working with a very high-resolution image, in which case he might increase it. If you leave the Eyedropper set to Point Sample, make sure you don't sample a noise pixel by mistake; zoom in to make sure.

We've noticed that the sky might be too red, and the Info palette confirms our suspicion. We Shift-click a color sampler on the sky so we can track its values later.

Editing the L channel. After choosing Image > Adjustment > Curves, our first move is to edit the L (luminosity) channel, which in Lab mode contains all tonal information. Changes you make to the other two channels don't affect tones at all. Edit the L curve as you would the RGB composite curve, (or the K curve when editing in CMYK). Our change boosts tonal contrast, but the colors are still a bit weak.

Editing the A channel. When we open the a channel curve, the first thing we do is add a point and set it to Input 0, Output 0. This locks down the current color balance in that channel, because (if you review Chapter 2, "Image Essentials") the A channel of Lab mode has magenta on one end, and green on the other end. At the center—Input 0, Output 0—the A channel is neutral.

The Info readout for the color sampler says L 93, A 3, B 0. We aren't concerned with L (luminosity), we're concerned with the A and B numbers; A is slightly red and B is neutral. We press Ctrl-Tab to select the 0,0 midpoint we added, and keeping an eye on the Info palette, we press the right arrow key to nudge the point until the A channel "after" readout (after the slash) reads 0. Now that the Info palette reads 0 for both the A and B channels, we know that point is now perfectly neutral.

Now we'll do what we came here for: bumping up the color contrast. With the Curves dialog still open, we Command-click (Mac) or Ctrl-click (Windows) a green area of a tree to add a curve point, and press the down arrow and right arrow keys to nudge the point away from the center, making the curve steeper (pivoting it around the neutral center point) and boosting the contrast between green and magenta. Not only does this create more variation in the foliage, it boosts magenta in the wooden pier, setting it off against the green.

It's normal for the A and B channel histograms to be narrow and centered—most of the action happens close to the center of Lab, where moderately saturated colors live in the real world. The gamut of Lab mode is so wide that you don't have to get very far from the center to oversaturate your colors. Don't steepen the curve so far that your colors go neon on you. (In the A and B channels, drawing a flat horizontal line across the center would desaturate the colors completely.)

Editing the B channel. We performed the same procedure on the B channel: We added a center pivot point and steepened the curve. However, we also added a point on the yellow side for more control. When we steepened the curve to boost the blue in the water, the yellow in the trees became

---

Tip: If you need an Eyedropper sample bigger than 5-by-5 pixels, make a marquee selection of the required size, choose Average from the Blur submenu (under the Filter menu), and read the result from the Info palette. Just don't forget to undo the filter once you've read the values! (Or use a Smart Filter.)

too vivid, so we used the curve point on the yellow side to pull that side of the curve back in, closer to the baseline.

Lab is worth a try when you need to make large moves, quickly correct a color cast, or set complementary colors against each other, but you may find it easier to make subtle color changes in RGB mode (or for a camera raw image, using the HSL tab in Camera Raw to isolate a color).

Using Color Samplers

When you're evaluating and editing images, tracking pixel color values with the Info palette is critical. When you're comparing or tracking two or more areas in an image, you don't want to have to position the mouse in the same position every time. Fortunately, you don't have to. To leave a marker that stays in one place and continuously reports the underlying color values, just drop a color sampler on the image. You can position as many as four color samplers in an image.

Tip: To delete a color sampler, Option-click (Mac) or Alt-click (Windows) it. If a painting tool is active, you can access the Color Sampler tool and edit color samplers using the same shortcuts you use for the Eyedropper tool, but you must also press Option (Mac) or Alt (Windows).

Color Sampler shortcuts. You can select the Color Sampler tool in the Tools palette, but that usually isn't necessary. If you're using the Eyedropper, you can temporarily switch to the Color Sampler tool by holding down Shift, so that Shift-clicking creates a color sampler. If you're using a painting tool, Option-Shift-click (Mac) or Alt-Shift-click (Windows).

The time when you're most likely to need a color sampler is when you're inside an open dialog such as Levels or Curves, where the Tools palette is inaccessible. But because moving the mouse outside an open adjustment dialog turns the cursor into the Eyedropper, the Color Sampler shortcut works—you can Shift-click to drop a color sampler.

To reposition a color sampler, drag it. If you're using the Eyedropper tool, Shift-drag a color sampler to move it. To delete a color sampler with the Color Sampler tool, Option-click (Mac) or Alt-click (Windows) the color sampler. To delete a color sampler while you're using the Eyedropper tool or a painting tool, Option-Shift-click (Mac) or Alt-Shift-click (Windows) the color sampler.

Hue, Saturation, and Lightness

When we see people trying to make skin tones less red or skies less purple with Curves, we have to roll our eyes and bite our tongues, which is uncomfortable to say the least! The best tool for addressing issues with hue and saturation is, believe it or not, the Hue/Saturation feature.

However, Hue/Saturation is a tad more mysterious than Levels and Curves for at least three reasons:

▶ The relationship between the controls and the numbers that represent the image is much less obvious than it is in Levels and Curves.

▶ Much of the power of Hue/Saturation is hidden—you have to dig to find it.

▶ Unlike Levels and Curves, which are global adjustments (though we'll show you how to turn them into local ones in Chapter 8, "The Digital Darkroom") Hue/Saturation is, at heart, a localized correction tool.

But Hue/Saturation isn't hard to master, and once you've done so, you'll find it's indispensable. The basic Hue/Saturation dialog looks deceptively simple—see **Figure 7-44**.

Figure 7-44
The master panel of the
Hue/Saturation
dialog

Unfortunately, the master panel of Hue/Saturation is of limited use. It does provides one of many ways of converting color images to grayscale (just reduce the Saturation slider all the way down to -100); it lets you produce colorized versions of color images using the Colorize check box; and it lets you produce "postcard" color by boosting saturation with the Saturation slider. The real power is hidden a little deeper, but let's deal with Colorize first.

Colorize

Figure 7-45 shows various treatments of an image with Colorize. The appearance is similar to a duotone, but the images are color images, and editable as such—you can run Hue/Saturation only on color images, while you can create duotones only from grayscale images.

Figure 7-45
Colorize

Original image

You can use Colorize for quick and easy simulations of sepiatones, cyanotypes, selenotypes, bromide prints, and the like, as well as creating images that were impossible to make using traditional darkroom methods.

When the Colorize check box is checked, the Hue slider sets the dominant hue (the number is the hue angle, the same as the Hue field in the Color Picker); the Saturation slider sets the saturation on a scale from 0 to 100, with 0 being grayscale (completely unsaturated) and 100 being fully saturated; and the Lightness slider lets you darken or lighten the image on a scale of –100 to 100, with the default center point at 0. If you experiment, you'll find that the same settings produce different results depending on both the color mode (RGB, CMYK, or Lab), and the specific RGB or CMYK color space.

Tip: Colorize is great for CMYK or RGB output, but if you're trying to make a true multitone image and not simply an RGB or process-color simulation of one, choose Image > Duotone instead of applying Colorize.

The Master Panel Controls

When the Colorize check box is disabled, the Lightness slider's behavior doesn't change, but the Hue and Saturation sliders behaviors do change.

The Hue slider. The Hue slider shifts all the colors in the image by the specified hue angle. Small shifts are sometimes useful, but shifting hue by more than 5 degrees or so usually produces effects that can charitably be described as "creative"—see **Figure 7-46**. The top color bar shows the original color, and the bottom color bar shifts to show the resulting color.

Figure 7-46

Master Hue slider

This color shifts…

…to this color.

6-degree hue shift

180-degree hue shift

This color shifts…

…to this color.

Tip: Avoid using Saturation to create a black-and-white image—if you're concerned about image quality, the new Black & White adjustment layer is far superior. See "The Color of Grayscale" in Chapter 11, "Essential Image Techniques."

Global hue shifts are not usually useful except for creative effects, so we rarely use the Master Hue slider—instead, we adjust the hue of specific color ranges (see the next section, "The Color Panel Controls").

The Saturation slider. As with the Hue slider, the master Saturation slider is more chainsaw than scalpel. Boosting the master Saturation value can work in small doses, but it's easy to drive your color into postcard territory (which is fine if you're in the postcard business).

We're much more likely to adjust the hue and saturation of individual color ranges separately (which we'll show you how to do shortly), because with the Master panel sliders, when we get one color right, we've typically pushed another too far, and yet another not far enough.

The Lightness slider. We never use the Master panel's Lightness slider—it simply shifts all the values, and usually clips either highlights or shadows. We do use the Lightness slider for individual colors, as we describe next.

The Color Panel Controls

The real power of Hue/Saturation is inside the individual color panels. When you open the Edit pop-up menu in the Hue/Saturation dialog, you can choose Reds, Yellows, Greens, Cyans, Blues, or Magentas. At first glance, the controls offered in the individual color panels may seem identical to those in the Master panel—there's a Hue slider, a Saturation slider, and a Lightness slider. These work the same way as the Master panel sliders, only they're constrained to operating on the selected color. What's much less obvious is that the named color ranges are simply starting points that you can adjust to affect exactly the color range you want. The controls operate the same way in all the other color panels; the only difference between the panels is the menu name and the preset range of color they affect.

The not-so-obvious controls are at the bottom of the dialog. In between the two color bars are two inner vertical sliders and two outer triangular sliders. These define the range of color affected by the sliders (see **Figure 7-47**).

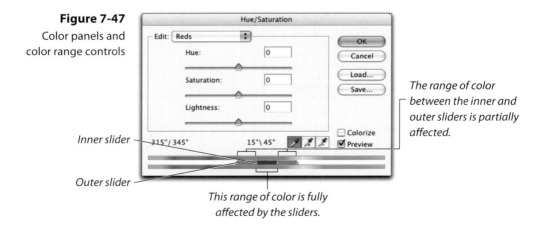

Figure 7-47
Color panels and color range controls

Inner slider

Outer slider

The range of color between the inner and outer sliders is partially affected.

This range of color is fully affected by the sliders.

For additional feedback, the numbers above the color bar show you the hue angles of the four slider positions. You can adjust the range of color that will be fully affected by dragging the dark gray bar between the inner sliders, or by adjusting the inner sliders individually, and you can adjust the "feather"—the range of colors that will be partially affected—by dragging the outer sliders.

You can also adjust the range by selecting the three Eyedropper tools located above the color bars by clicking them in the image. The left Eyedropper centers the range of fully affected colors on the hue of the pixel on which you click; the center Eyedropper (with the plus sign) extends the range of fully selected colors to include the hue of the pixel on which you clicked; and the right Eyedropper (with the minus sign) excludes the hue of the pixel on which you clicked from the fully affected range of colors. The size of the feather doesn't change with the Eyedroppers, but it moves as the fully affected color range expands and contracts. Essentially, the controls provide a color-range selection with a controllable feather.

It's also worth noting that the preset ranges are simply arbitrary labels. There's nothing to prevent you from tweaking six different ranges of reds, or greens, or yellows—though we find we rarely need more than three.

Skin tone adjustments. Hue/Saturation is invaluable for adjusting skin tones. It's a great deal easier to adjust the red-yellow balance of Caucasian skin with the Hue slider than it is to do so with Curves—in Curves you usually have to adjust all three color curves to obtain the correct hue, where the Hue slider lets you get it right in a single move.

Figure 7-48 shows an image of Bruce shot by our friend and colleague Jeff Schewe. As with many digital captures, the skin tones are a bit too red. We'll use Hue/Saturation to make his complexion a little less florid.

Making these kinds of adjustments with Curves is akin to medieval torture! In RGB, you'd have to manipulate at least two curves, and probably all three color curves plus the composite, and you'd probably have to bounce back and forth between the individual curves several times, since each move affects the others. In CMYK, a curve edit is even more complex since you have four color channels plus the composite rather than three.

Hue/Saturation is useful in both RGB and in CMYK, but it lends itself to much finer adjustments in CMYK than in RGB. In RGB, it manipulates light, while in CMYK it manipulates ink percentages. If you have sharp eyes, you will have noticed that we made the edits to this image in RGB with CMYK soft-proofing turned on.

When we're preparing images for a CMYK destination, we always softproof, especially on Hue/Saturation adjustments. But even with good

Tip: We never bother choosing the different Eyedropper tools. The left Eyedropper is always selected by default, and as with other tools, you can temporarily switch to another form of the tool by pressing a modifier key. To use it to expand the color range, simply Shift-click; to eliminate colors from the color range, Option-click (Mac) or Alt-click (Windows).

Tip: The color-range controls don't provide additional visual feedback as to which colors are affected, which can make subtle changes hard to follow. Here's a simple trick: Move the Hue slider all the way to the right or left before you start adjusting the color-range sliders, then set it back to 0 once you've adjusted the range.

Figure 7-48

Using Hue/Saturation to fix
skin tones

*The skin tones
are much too red.*

*We start by targeting the very red areas,
using the Hue slider to make the selected
range obvious.*

*We tame the screaming reds by shifting
the hue slightly and lightening.*

The first adjustment lets us apply a huge tweak to all the skin tones, but we made sure that we excluded the yellow stars on the vest from the color range.

A smaller hue shift with further lightening, accompanied by a saturation boost to counteract the lightening, produces the result shown above.

The effect of the Saturation slider in CMYK is much more subtle than in RGB. We also made a very small hue adjustment.

output profiles and a well-calibrated display, we're likely to make small adjustments after conversion to CMYK, though we try to get as close as possible to the desired result in RGB. When we looked at CMYK proofs, we felt that the skin tone was just a hair too yellow-green, so we made one more correction before calling it final.

The Color Picker's Gamut Warning. The View > Gamut Warning command (press Command-Shift-Y on Mac OS X or Ctrl-Shift-Y in Windows) isn't something we find terribly useful on images. It shows us which RGB or Lab colors are outside the gamut of our CMYK working space, but it doesn't show how far out of gamut they are, nor does it show us where the nearest in-gamut colors lie.

However, if you turn on the Gamut Warning command while you're in the Color Picker, you can see exactly where the gamut boundary lies at different hue angles and lightness—see **Figure 7-49**.

Figure 7-49

Gamut Warning in the Color Picker

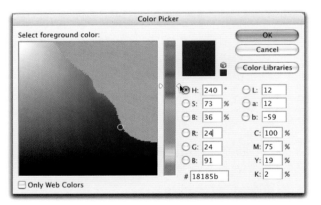

When you turn on the Gamut Warning in the Color Picker, it shows you the gamut boundary for all lightness levels at a single hue angle. To change the hue, click or drag along the vertical spectrum.

Bear in mind that the Gamut Warning always shows you the gamut of your current CMYK working space—see "Choosing a CMYK Working Space" in Chapter 4, "Color Settings"—so make sure that you have the correct CMYK profile loaded before you try to use this tip!

Matching hues. Another common task for which Hue/Saturation is well suited is matching hues across images. The light may change during an event, or you may simply have to force two disparate images to match.

Figure 7-50 shows a typical hue-matching challenge. Bruce stumbled across this wedding procession in La Paz, Bolivia, and had to switch from slide to color negative film halfway through. (The lack of oxygen at the 13,000-foot altitude made it somewhat miraculous that he managed to load *any* kind of film in the camera!)

The red shirts are rendered as a magenta-red by one film stock and as an orange-red by the other. And just to make things a little more challenging, one image is in ProPhoto RGB and the other is in ColorMatch RGB, so the RGB numbers are of little help. Fortunately, the Info palette lets us display Lab values, so we'll use these as a guide—on a well-calibrated system you can make the match by eye, but the numbers always provide a useful reality check, and Lab numbers act as a universal translator, letting you match colors in different color spaces, or even different color modes.

While the Image > Adjustment submenu offers a command labeled "Match Colors," we confess that we've yet to find a way to make it produce predictable results, though it can make for some interesting creative effects. Hue/Saturation is quick and controllable.

Gamut-mapping. One further task for which we rely on Hue/Saturation is gamut-mapping—controlling the rendering of colors present in the source image that are outside the gamut of the output process. In theory, perceptual rendering is supposed to take care of this for you. In practice, though, it sometimes fails. All profile-creation tools make assumptions, almost invariably undocumented, about the source space they attempt to map into the gamut of the device being profiled, and when the source space doesn't match the undocumented assumption, you can wind up with solid blobs of saturated color.

Sometimes the fix is as simple as just desaturating the color while looking at a soft-proofed version of the image. In other cases, you may be able to improve the rendering by adjusting hue and/or lightness too. You have to make the fix before converting to the output space, because after the conversion is done, all you can do is make the blobs more or less saturated—you can't recover the differences that represented detail.

We can't show you the out-of-gamut RGB colors in this book because the CMYK print process we use to print this book won't let us. What we can do is to show you the unadjusted profile conversions of some problem images, the fixes we applied, and the results.

Figure 7-50
Matching hues

The red shirts don't match!

We set the Eyedropper tool to
5-by-5 pixels average, then
placed a color sampler set to
read Lab color in each image,
taking care to choose spots
with the same luminance.

After refining the color range
to focus on the red of the
shirts and hatbands, we
adjusted hue, saturation,
and lightness to get a close
match—we're one level off in
the B channel, which isn't a
visually significant difference.

The red shirts match!

Figure 7-51 shows some problem images. The unadjusted versions are darn close to what we saw in the soft-proofs that alerted us to the potential problems. In all these instances, something—hue, lightness, or saturation—has to give. There's an element of subjectivity in these decisions; we can't get the color we really want, so we have to settle for something else. There's no objectively correct answer as to what that something else is, but in all three cases, we feel that our choices are improvements over the straight, unadjusted profile conversions.

Figure 7-52 shows the adjusted images, along with the Hue/Saturation moves we used to make them. Only one of the examples—the red shirts in the last image—was fixed by a simple desaturation. The other fixes all involved changes to lightness and to hue, and in some cases the hue and lightness moves allowed us to boost saturation rather than decrease it.

Printing blues with CMYK inks is always tricky, because CMYK spaces contain so few of them! In most other color ranges, desaturation is our first line of defense for out-of-gamut colors. However, in the blue regions, lightness moves are often more effective, as shown in the middle image in Figure 7-52.

Other Methods. Levels, Curves, and Hue/Saturation are *the* fundamental tools for adjusting global tone and color (we'll show you to apply them as selective local adjustments in Chapter 8, "The Digital Darkroom"). But several of the other commands on the Adjustments submenu are extremely useful, albeit in fewer situations.

You *must* master Levels, Curves, and Hue/Saturation to consider yourself any kind of Photoshop user. But the more specialized tools—to which the remainder of this chapter is devoted—can save you time and let you produce better-quality work, which is, after all, the object of the whole exercise. Photoshop always offers multiple ways to do just about anything, but one way is usually better or faster than the others.

Figure 7-51
Gamut problems

The red gloves have
plugged up into solid
blobs with no detail.

The more-saturated
greens have turned
into featureless blobs.

The darker blues in the ocean
are washed-out
with poor contrast.

The red shirts and green
sleeve are plugged up with
little or no detail.

Figure 7-52
Gamut fixes

A combined desaturation, hue shift, and darkening puts detail into the gloves.

We improved the problem greens by desaturating, darkening, and shifting slightly towards yellow.

We improved the blues by darkening, boosting saturation, and shifting the hue slightly.

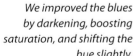

We replaced the unprintable green with a lighter one.

We introduced detail into the shirts by desaturating.

Replace Color

Replace Color (choose Image > Adjustments > Replace Color) is really a shortcut for making a Color Range selection (see "Color Range" in Chapter 9, "Making Selections"), then performing a Hue/Saturation tweak.

Replace Color doesn't let you do anything you couldn't do with Hue/Saturation, but if you only need to adjust a single color, it's sometimes more convenient to use Replace Color. To emphasize the point that Photoshop always offers multiple methods of achieving the same goal, **Figure 7-53** shows how we'd do the correction shown in Figure 7-50 using Replace Color instead of Hue/Saturation.

Figure 7-53
Replace Color

We want to match the red shirts.

We start by making the color-range selection. Typically, we click the Eyedropper in the image to get a starting point, then build up the selection by Shift-clicking. Then we adjust the color, either by the numbers from the Info palette or by eye.

This time we achieved an exact, by-the-numbers match according to the Info palette.

Selective Color

Selective Color (choose Image > Adjustments > Selective Color) mimics the "system color" or "color-in-color" controls found in most traditional prepress drum scanners. We use Selective Color as a fine-tuning tool on images that have already been converted to CMYK, where it's a precision instrument for fine-tuning color. For RGB images, Selective Color doesn't really do anything that can't be done as easily with Hue/Saturation.

Selective Color lets you increase or decrease the percentage of Cyan, Magenta, Yellow, and Black in the nine preset color ranges that appear on the Colors menu (see **Figure 7-54**).

Figure 7-54
Selective Color Options

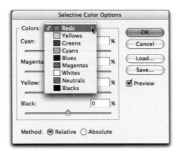

These color ranges are hard-wired—you can't change them. In Absolute mode, Selective Color adds or subtracts the specified percentages of each ink from colors in the center of the color range.

So, for example, if you ask for –20 percent magenta from reds, in Absolute mode, a 100M 100Y red becomes an 80M 100Y red, an 80M 80 Y red becomes 64M 80Y, a 60M 60Y red becomes 48M 60Y, and a 40M 40Y red becomes 32M 40Y. As you move away from the pure-red axis, the percentage by which magenta is reduced lessens in proportion to how far off the red axis the color lies.

Absolute and Relative Methods. If you're using a well-tuned color management system and are creating direct-to-plate output, stick with the Relative method. When using the Relative method, Selective Color looks at how much of the specified ink is present in each pixel in the color range, how close it is to the center of the named color range, and how saturated the color is, so the effect is gentler than Absolute mode on everything except the fully saturated colors corresponding to the named color ranges.

It's hard to predict the final numbers from the numbers you plug in—it's a complex formula—so use the Info palette if you need numeric feedback. **Figure 7-55** shows one of the images from Figure 7-56, before and after fine-tuning with Selective Color.

The before-and-after differences are quite subtle, though they're obvious when pointed out. Relative mode is much more useful than Absolute for making fine adjustments to CMYK images, and these are the kinds of small but useful moves at which Selective Color excels.

The Absolute method was more useful back in the bad old days of the non-color-managed prepress workflow, when we burned film to make plates and a nominal 4 percent dot could reproduce as anything from paper white to around 7 percent. Then, we'd sometimes use Absolute mode on Whites and Neutrals, making small moves to tune the gray balance.

Figure 7-55
Selective Color

Intensifying the light blues
in the ocean

Before Selective Color

After Selective Color

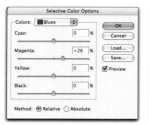

Intensifying the dark blues
in the ocean

Brightening
the reds

Shifting the yellow-greens
slightly away from yellow

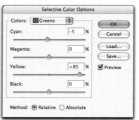

Making the bluer
greens more yellow

Channel Mixer

The Channel Mixer (choose Image > Adjustments > Channel Mixer) does what it says—you can mix the channels, combining content from one or more channels and feeding it into another. For maximum flexibility, the Channel Mixer is typically applied as an adjustment layer.

The Channel Mixer is a useful color-correction tool, but we don't use it as a global correction tool on RGB images. We sometimes use it to make local corrections, typically to bring out highlight or shadow detail that's only present in one channel.

On CMYK files, it's useful for tweaking the black plate in specific color ranges, as we show in **Figure 7-56**. The original separation setup added black into the skin tones, making them muddy. We'd rather fix this by going back to the RGB original and reseparating the image, but that's not always possible. Lightening the black plate in Levels or Curves would destroy the contrast—we only want to change the skin tones—and the Channel Mixer provides an easy means of doing so, with better feedback and finer control than Selective Color. We set the Output Channel to black, subtracted some of the magenta and yellow channels from the black, and boosted the black to preserve the black values in the shadows.

Tip: The Channel Mixer has been a popular way to convert color images to black-and-white images, but in Photoshop CS3 it's much better and easier to use the new Black & White adjustment (see "The Color of Grayscale" in Chapter 11, "Essential Image Techniques").

Figure 7-56 Removing black from skin tones

The image at left has black in the skin tones. We subtracted some yellow and a smaller amount of magenta (the pink background relies on magenta), and boosted the black slightly to produce the result at right.

Photo Filter

The Photo Filter command (choose Image > Adjustments > Photo Filter) is designed to simulate traditional over-the-lens warming and cooling filters, though it actually lets you choose custom colors in addition to the presets. Its effect is similar to a solid color layer set to Color Blend mode.

We find that the default 25-percent intensity is usually about twice what we need, and we often disable the Preserve Luminosity check box because it tends to exaggerate the effect in the highlights. **Figure 7-57** shows some Photo Filter warming and cooling adjustments.

Photo Filter is particularly effective at low intensity settings. We typically use intensities in the 3 to 12 percent range, but we set our examples here a little higher to make the effect obvious in print.

You can also achieve many different creative effects using either the stronger preset colors, or by creating your own filter color—just double-click on the color swatch to open the Color Picker.

Figure 7-57
Warming and cooling with
Photo Filter

The original image

Warming adjustment

Cooling adjustment

Shadow/Highlight

Tip: In Adobe Camera Raw, the Recovery and Fill Light commands are similar to the Shadow/Highlight feature in Photoshop.

The Shadow/Highlight command is unlike all the other commands on the Image > Adjust submenu. All of the other commands treat each pixel the same way, while Shadow/Highlight is an adaptive command that evaluates and adjusts each pixel differently depending on the values of its neighboring pixels. Shadow/Highlight lets you recover detail from nearly blown-out highlights and nearly plugged shadows in a way that Curves or Levels just can't do. Where Levels and Curves shift all pixels at the same level by equal amounts, Shadow/Highlight evaluates local contrast and preserves it by making adaptive, context-sensitive adjustments.

In its default form, the Shadow/Highlight dialog is very simple—frankly, too simple to be of real use. Turn on the More Options check box to reveal the full capabilities of Shadow/Highlight (see **Figure 7-58**).

Figure 7-58
Shadow/Highlight
dialog

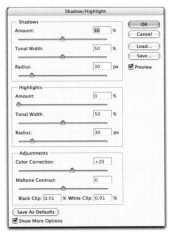

In its simple form, above, Shadow/Highlight offers two Amount sliders that control the strength of the Shadow and Highlight corrections. Click Show More Options to unlock its full power.

In its expanded mode, Shadow/Highlight offers Amount, Tonal Width, and Radius sliders for Shadows and for Highlights; a Color Correction slider (on grayscale images, it's replaced by a Brightness slider); a Midtone Contrast slider; and clipping percentage fields for black and white. The interactions between the controls are fairly complex, so let's look at them in turn.

Amount. The Amount sliders for Shadow and Highlight control the strength of the correction—they're the "volume knobs."

Tonal Width. The Tonal Width sliders dictate how far up the tonal range from black the Shadow correction applies, and how far down the tonal range from white the Highlight correction applies. They let you constrain the correction to the tonal range that needs it.

Radius. The Radius slider dictates the neighborhood that the command evaluates for each pixel, thereby affecting local contrast. A good rule of thumb is to set the Radius to the size of the features you're trying to emphasize. If you set too large or too small a radius, you tend to lose detail rather than emphasizing it. The easiest way to master the Radius slider is to experiment with it.

Tip: If you're working with raw digital camera images with blown highlights, recover those highlights using the Recovery slider in Camera Raw, which has access to all of the image's raw data, rather than using Shadow/Highlight to recover them.

Color Correction. The Color Correction slider is a saturation control, but it operates only on the corrected colors, not on colors that are unchanged by the correction. Increasing its value saturates the corrected colors; reducing it desaturates them. We generally find that the default value of +20 is usually about right, but don't be afraid to experiment.

Brightness. On grayscale images, the Brightness slider replaces the Color Correction slider. It lightens or darkens the image and unlike the Color Correction slider, it affects the entire image, not just the pixels that are affected by the Shadow and Highlight adjustments.

Midtone Contrast. The Midtone Contrast slider adjusts contrast—negative values decrease contrast and positive ones increase it. While its effect is most pronounced on the midtones, it affects the entire image, so use it carefully; if you push it too far, you might just end up undoing most of the effects of the Shadow and Highlight adjustments.

Tip: Use care when using the Shadows Amount slider with underexposed or noisy images. Such images withstand less of a shadow boost before shadow noise appears.

Black Clip/White Clip. The clipping percentages dictate how many of the corrected pixels are mapped to black (0) and white (255), so these controls let you adjust the contrast of the pixels close to black and white. Note that unlike the clipping percentage fields in Levels, these use three decimal places. Use them to fine-tune the contrast near the endpoints—when they're set too low, the image can turn muddy.

Figure 7-59 shows a step-by step Shadow/Highlight correction of an image with blown highlights and plugged shadows. The result would be impossible to obtain with Curves or Levels! Shadow/Highlight is an amazingly flexible tool.

Figure 7-59
Shadow/Highlight
adjustment

The unadjusted image

*At the default settings, Shadow/
Highlight applies a fairly strong shadow
correction with no highlight correction
(above right).*

*But we can push the
adjustments further. We
increased the Shadow
amount while reducing the
Radius, to emphasize the fine
details; added a Highlight
correction to darken the sky;
added a slight boost to the
Color Correction so the image
doesn't turn gray; reduced the
Midtone Contrast to preserve
detail; and added some
punch back to the shadows by
raising the Black Clip value.*

Shadow/Highlight isn't available as an Adjustment layer. It has to calculate the value for each pixel based on surrounding pixels on the same layer, while adjustment layers only compare a pixel with the same pixel on layers behind it. The additional calculations required by Shadow/Highlight would make it agonizingly slower than any other adjustment layer. In Photoshop CS3, you *can* use Shadow Highlight as a Smart Filter, where you have more control over when the lengthy recalculations take place.

Tools We Don't Use

We've covered most of the tools on the Adjustments submenu, but we've left a few out, for the simple reason that we never use them. That said, we feel that a few words of explanation are in order, so here, briefly, are the tools we don't use and our reasons for avoiding them.

Don't feel that you have to do as we do, or even do as we say. If you find any of the following tools useful, you know something we don't, and you can be proud of your hard-won knowledge. But first take a moment to ponder our critiques in case *you* are missing something.

Color Balance

The Color Balance command lets you make separate adjustments for red/cyan, green/magenta, and blue/yellow to three arbitrary tonal ranges labelled Highlights, Midtones, and Shadows. The problem is that these ranges overlap, and are never quite where we need them.

Nowadays, color crossovers are relatively rare—some early '90s desktop flatbed scanners were rather notorious for producing them, but when we see them now they're usually caused by shooting under mixed lighting, and the required corrections are usually selective rather than global. We find that it's easier to tweak the color balance of different tonal ranges using Curves.

Brightness/Contrast

As we noted in the sidebar, "Brightness/Contrast in Photoshop CS3," much earlier in this chapter. While Brightness/Contrast now "works right" in Photoshop CS3 since Adobe updated the feature to avoid highlight and shadow clipping by default, it's still kind of a blunt instrument compared to Levels or Curves. If you actually *want* to blow out your highlights while washing out shadows, or make your highlights more gray while plugging up shadows, the Brightness slider is the perfect tool when you turn on the new Use Legacy check box. The Contrast slider with the Use Legacy check box on is likewise great for simultaneously blowing out highlights and plugging up shadows.

We suspect that the only reason that Brightness/Contrast still appears on the Adjustments submenu is that the Photoshop development team never removes features. There is simply nothing you can do with Brightness/Contrast that you can't do as easily, with more control, using Levels or Curves.

Match Color

Match Color sounds like a great idea. We've just never been able to get it to work with any significant degree of reliability. Match Color can produce some interesting creative effects, particularly when you use a source image with a completely different color palette from the one you're adjusting, but the results depend a great deal on any selection you make in the source image, and if you want to tweak that selection, you have to Cancel out of the Match Color dialog to do so.

We find that we can create color matches a great deal more quickly by using either Hue/Saturation or Replace Color. Match Color is just too fickle and unpredictable for our taste.

Gradient Map

Gradient Map is useful for making custom grayscale conversions and for creating truly wacky color effects. It's low on our list of grayscale conversion methods because it takes a lot of work—you have to edit the gradient to get the results you want, then use Gradient Map to actually get them—and we don't really do wacky color effects, though we have nothing against folks that do.

Exposure

The Exposure command is really designed for working with HDR (High Dynamic Range) images. On those, it's pretty useful—see "HDR Imaging" in Chapter 11, "Essential Image Techniques"—but on 8-bit or 16-bit/channel images, it doesn't do anything useful that you can't do just as easily with the gray Input slider in Levels. Worse, the Exposure and Offset sliders basically replicate the behavior of the Brightness slider in Brightness/Contrast.

Invert, Equalize, Threshold, and Posterize

Tip: You can use a Threshold adjustment layer to mark highlight or shadow levels without keeping the Levels or Curves dialog open.

We often use Invert on masks (when we masked the area we wanted revealed and vice versa), but it's not something we'd ever do to an image. We never use Equalize—it redistributes the tonal values so that the brightest pixels are white, the darkest pixels are black, and the intermediate values are evenly distributed across the tonal range. We've yet to find a use for that, though we try to stay open-minded. These commands are more useful for image analysis or special effects than they are for photographic image processing.

Threshold is useful for turning images into 1-bit black-and-white bitmaps. We use it when we scan line art, but not as an image correction tool. Posterize does something we generally struggle to avoid!

Variations

Variations is a nice tool for learning to distinguish different color casts, but a very blunt instrument indeed for correcting them, and it's limited to 8-bit/channel images. It doesn't do anything that can't be done with a great deal more control and precision using Hue/Saturation. If you're still uncertain of your ability to distinguish a red cast from a magenta one, or a cyan cast from a blue one (and it does take practice), a quick look in Variations can help you make the call, but we don't recommend using it to take whatever remedial action the image needs.

8 The Digital Darkroom

Layers, Masks, Selections, Channels, and More

What would you say if we told you that you could perform color correction, use dodging and burning, build up density in overexposed areas, open up underexposed areas, and more—all with a minimum of image degradation and with an unlimited number of undos? You might just laugh at us. But in this chapter, we'll show you how to do all that.

You can do a lot using the controls we've already covered, but you can go much further, and with more freedom to experiment, when you apply them as adjustment layers rather than simply burning the changes into your image. The controls in adjustment layers behave just as they do in a flat file, but with far more freedom and flexibility. You can change your adjustment settings at any time, and vary their overall strength by changing the adjustment layer's opacity. Even better, you can restrict corrections to specific areas by painting on the layer mask that every adjustment layer has. In effect, you have not just unlimited undo, but selective, partial undo.

The techniques in this chapter can help you get a better image with little or no degradation and unprecedented control. But just as importantly, they're designed to give you maximum flexibility so that you can experiment and play with your images more while still having an escape route back to safe territory if you push things too far. Making mistakes is one of the surest ways to learn lessons—we're living proof—so an environment where you can make mistakes safely is a great learning tool.

Why Use Adjustment Layers?

Whenever you apply a Curves or Levels tweak (or even a Hue/Saturation adjustment) to an image, you're degrading it a little by throwing away some image data, as we showed in Chapter 7. Once that data is gone, you can't get it back. In the digital darkroom, this degradation can be avoided because you can make edits to adjustment layers that you add in front of the image rather than editing the image itself. It's somewhat analogous to working with raw format camera files, where the changes you make are stored alongside the original file without changing it, and take effect only when you export or print a new version of the image. For example, you can apply a Curves adjustment layer, which you can turn off to see the unadjusted, original image.

There are several other reasons we love working in the digital darkroom of Photoshop.

▶ **Changing your mind.** With adjustment layers, you can change an edit at any time without increasing cumulative degradation. This gives you endless freedom to experiment. Because you can fine-tune your edits with no penalty, you're more likely to get the results you want.

▶ **Instant before-and-after.** You can always tell exactly what you're doing when you use adjustment layers. Because all your edits are on layers, you can easily see before-and-after views by hiding the adjustment layer you're editing, and then turning it back on again (by clicking on the eyeball in the left column of the Layers palette).

▶ **Variable-strength edits.** The Opacity slider in the Layers palette acts as a volume control for your edits.

▶ **Applying the same edits to multiple images.** You can drag an adjustment layer to other images, and even script the layer with actions to batch-apply the adjustment layer to a folder full of images.

▶ **Brushable edits.** You can make selective, local edits to a particular area of an adjustment layer. This means you not only have essentially unlimited undo, but also *selective and partial* undo.

▶ **Storing alternative edits in the same file.** Because you can hide an adjustment layer, you can create multiple versions of the same adjustment layer edit and display only the edit you want to use at any particular time. For example, you can store two different Curves adjustment layers that store contrast curves for two different printers, and display only the adjustment layer for the printer you're using at the moment.

▶ **Doing the impossible.** You can use adjustment layers in conjunction with blending modes to do things that are usually extremely difficult, if not impossible—such as building density in highlights or opening up shadows without posterizing the image.

Why Not Use Adjustment Layers?

With all these advantages, why not use adjustment layers for all your edits? Two reasons: file size and file complexity.

Tip: You can minimize the file-size increase caused by adjustment layers by turning off the Maximize Compatibility option (see "Setting Preferences" in Chapter 6, "Essential Photoshop Tips and Tricks"). However, this reduces compatibility with other software you may be using with Photoshop files, such as Adobe InDesign or Adobe Lightroom.

Adjustment layers increase file size. An adjustment layer is an additional component stored with an image, so it uses more RAM and hard drive space, both for scratch space and storage, than simply saving an edit directly into the image itself. Adjustment layers add very little to the RAM requirements because they contain almost no data, but painting on the Layer mask adds pixels that take up space.

Adjustment layers don't enlarge file size as much as you'd think, though. Yes, the first adjustment layer you add to a file usually makes the file roughly twice as large as it was before. But don't be alarmed—any adjustment layers you add after the first one add relatively little to the file size.

Painting on adjustment layer masks does add to an image's file size, because you're adding more pixels to the image.

Adjustment layers add complexity. If you open a file you made a year ago, and it contains 20 layers with names like Curves 13 and Hue/Saturation 5, you may have to spend quite a bit of time remembering what all those layers did! Naming your layers and organizing them into (informatively named) layer groups helps a lot.

All things considered, the advantages of adjustment layers far outweigh the disadvantages. Most people will get better results faster using adjustment layers. We can't live without them.

Adjustment Layer Basics

It's much easier to get understand adjustment layers if you think of them as copies of the base image, particularly when you start using adjustment layers in conjunction with blending modes. Fortunately, using an adjustment layer takes less RAM and disk space than making an actual copy of the base image.

You can't do much harm to your image with adjustment layers because your original image layer stays intact until you flatten the file. However, there's no free lunch. When you flatten the image, the adjustment layers are calculated by their stacking order, so you should still avoid successive edits that go in the opposite direction from one another—don't apply a Curve layer that darkens the image and another that lightens it, for example.

Creating Adjustment Layers

Photoshop offers two different ways to create an adjustment layer:

▶ **The Layer menu.** You can create an adjustment layer by choosing an adjustment layer command from the Layer > New Adjustment Layer submenu (see **Figure 8-1**).

▶ **The Layers palette icon.** You can choose an adjustment layer type by clicking the New Content Layer icon in the Layers palette.

Figure 8-1
Creating an adjustment layer

The New Adjustment Layer submenu

The adjustment layer pop-up menu in the Layers palette

One method isn't better than the other, but using the Layers palette's one-click pop-up menu is easier than navigating to a submenu off the menu bar.

The controls in adjustment layers work exactly as they do in flat files. For example, the Curves dialog looks the same whether you open it as a normal dialog (as we did in Chapter 7) or as an adjustment layer. The difference is that when you add an adjustment layer, you see the adjustment layer appear in the Layers palette, available for further editing in the future (see **Figure 8-2**).

Controlling Adjustment Layers

The big difference between using adjustment layers and editing a flat file is that adjustment layers give you much more freedom to control and refine your edits. There are several ways to do this when using an adjustment layer that don't exist with a flat file. We'll introduce them here and go into more detail with examples a little later.

Tip: Be careful where you double-click in the Layers palette. To edit an adjustment layer, double-click the thumbnail—not the name, mask, link, or empty area. They all edit different things.

Double-click to edit settings. To edit an adjustment layer (changing the curve or choosing other options), double-click the adjustment layer thumbnail in the Layers palette (see **Figure 8-2**). When you do this, Photoshop displays the settings you last used in the adjustment layer's dialog. Double-clicking is a shortcut for choosing Layer > Layer Content Options.

Figure 8-2
Editing an adjustment layer

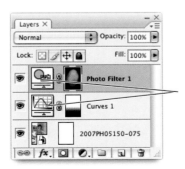

Double-click an adjustment layer thumbnail to change an adjustment layer's settings.

Use Opacity to vary strength. You can control the opacity of the adjustment layer by changing the Opacity slider in the Layers palette. This lets you change the intensity of the overall adjustment. We often make edits that are slightly more extreme than we really want, then back off the opacity of the editing layer to reduce the effect to just where we want it. We find this faster than trying to fine-tune the adjustment in the adjustment layer's dialog.

Isolate edits using multiple adjustment layers. You can use as many adjustment layers as you want, each stacked on top of the next, to make successive edits. This technique is particularly useful when you want one curve to correct the image globally while another curve edits the image in selective places. However, if one adjustment counteracts another, you'll suffer the same amount of image degradation you'd get if you applied the edits successively to flat files. To restrict the effect of an adjustment layer to specific areas, paint in an adjustment layer's mask; see "Selections, Masks, and Channels" later in this chapter.

Adjustment layers apply to all visible layers beneath them. As a result, the stacking order makes a difference since each layer's result depends on the layers underneath it. Sometimes the differences are fairly subtle—you may need to check the numbers in the Info palette to see them—but occasionally the difference can be significant.

Tip: If adjustment layers will be standard practice for you, use the Edit > Keyboard Shortcuts command to add keyboard shortcuts for your favorite adjustment layers. For example, you can reassign the keyboard shortcut for Image > Adjust > Curves to Layer > New Adjustment Layer > Curves.

Tip: When painting on the layer mask, don't forget that you can press X to switch the foreground and background colors. Press the number keys (0–9) to set the opacity of the paintbrush—for instance, typing 0 sets the opacity to 100 percent and typing 9 sets it to 90 percent. For smaller increments, type two digits quickly: typing 05 sets it to 5 percent, typing 45 sets it to 45 percent, and so on.

Edit specific areas using masks. While the Opacity slider applies to the entire adjustment layer, you can vary the opacity of the layer locally by painting on the adjustment layer's layer mask. To paint on the layer mask, click the adjustment layer thumbnail in the Layers palette and paint; the paint automatically goes on the layer mask. Black paint hides the effect of the adjustment layer; white paint reveals it; gray paint applies the effect partially (25 percent black ink applies 75 percent of the adjustment layer's effect). By varying the brush opacity in the Options bar, you can achieve precise control over the adjustment layer's opacity in specific areas.

Note that an additional channel automatically appears in the Channels palette whenever you select an adjustment layer in the Layers palette. This is the channel that you're actually drawing on. You can use all the usual layer-mask tricks, like Shift-clicking on the layer mask (in the Layers palette) to turn the mask on or off and Option-clicking (Mac) or Alt-clicking (Windows) to view or hide the layer mask (see "Selections, Masks, and Channels," later in this chapter).

Save adjustment layers. You can save an adjustment layer separately from an image. We find this most useful when we want to apply the same color- and tonal-correction edits to multiple images.

To save an adjustment layer into either a new or a different document, select an adjustment layer, and then choose Layer > Duplicate Layer. For Destination, you can either choose an open document or enter a name if you want Photoshop to create a new document containing the adjustment layer. When you're done, click OK.

Note that if you send the duplicated adjustment layer to a new document, the new document will have the same document specifications as the original—potentially a disk-space issue if it's very large. If you haven't altered the adjustment layer's mask, you can use the Image > Image Size command to reduce the dimensions of the document you're using to store the adjustment layer—if an adjustment layer doesn't use its layer mask, it's resolution-independent. However, if you've painted in the layer mask, you'll probably want to maintain the document size.

The ability to copy adjustment layers also opens up some new workflow possibilities. Without adjustment layers, you'd want to take care of retouching (dust and scratches, and so on) before editing for tone or color. However, with adjustment layers, the order of these tasks doesn't matter as much. Two people can even work on the same image at the same time—one doing the retouching while the other edits tone and color—then later, you can apply the adjustment layer(s) to the retouched image.

Tip: Another way to copy an adjustment layer between two existing documents is to simply drag it from the Layers palette in one document to another document window. To center a layer or mask precisely when you release the mouse, Shift-drag the layer or mask.

Selections, Masks, and Channels

The ability to restrict the effect of an adjustment layer to specific areas using its layer mask means that it's important to understand how selections, masks, and channels work in Photoshop. While we give this subject the full treatment in Chapter 9, "Making Selections," you'll want to get the basics here, since we'll be referring to masks shortly.

The key to understanding selections, masks, and channels is to realize that deep down, they're all the same thing. No matter what kind of selection you make—whether you draw out a rectangular marquee, draw a path with the Lasso, or use the Quick Selection tool to select a colored area—Photoshop sees the selection as a grayscale channel. If you've ever carefully painted around a window (the kind in the wall of your house), you've probably used masking tape to mask out the areas you didn't want to paint. If you apply the masking tape to the window, you can paint right over it, knowing that the window remains untouched. Selections, masks, and channels are electronic forms of masking tape.

In Photoshop, the masking tape is typically colored black. Let's say you use the Marquee to select a square. Behind the scenes, Photoshop sees this square as a grayscale channel. In this selection channel, the areas that you selected (the parts with no masking tape over them) are white, and the unselected areas (the parts with masking tape over them) are black. As our friend and colleague Katrin Eismann likes to intone, "Black conceals, white reveals."

Photoshop offers three ways of interacting with this selection information, but the relationship between them isn't always obvious.

▶ You can use the selection tools—Marquee, Lasso, Magic Wand, Color Range, and so on, to create a selection.

▶ When you save a selection, Photoshop saves the selection as an *alpha channel*, which is simply a regular grayscale channel stored alongside the color channels. "Alpha channel" is a scary term. Whenever you see it, feel free to mentally substitute "saved selection," because that's all it really means!

▶ To apply the selection information nondestructively to a layer (meaning that you can change or remove the selection), you use it as a *layer mask*—you're attaching the masking tape to just that layer.

We'll show you how to bounce the information back and forth between these three states a little later in this chapter, but first, let's take a look at the information and how it manifests itself in each of these three forms. Selections can be very simple or extremely complex, but no matter how simple or complex they may be, they share the same behaviors.

We'll start with a simple example, a rectangular marquee (see **Figure 8-3**). The rectangular marquee is a very simple bi-level selection—each pixel is either selected or unselected, and the channel that results when the selection is saved contains only black and white pixels. It works like real masking tape—the black pixels in the selection are the masking tape, protecting whatever's underneath, and the white pixels represent the area without masking tape, letting the paint (or the Curve, or Levels) pass through.

Figure 8-3

A basic rectangular selection drawn with the Rectangular Marquee tool

Figure 8-3

A basic rectangular selection drawn with the Rectangular Marquee tool

Feathered and Semitransparent Selections

There's reality, and there's Photoshop. In real life, light never forms solid edges; there's always some transparency along edges. The ability to create feathered (soft-edged) selections and masks is key to making localized corrections blend into the image in a way that seems natural—and it makes Photoshop selections a lot more useful than hard-edged, solid, real-world masking tape.

Figure 8-4 shows a soft-edged selection. We created it by clicking the Refine Edge button in the Options bar while the selection was active, and then applying a 50 pixel Feather. Behind the scenes, rather than creating

Figure 8-4

A selection with an edge feathered using Refine Edge

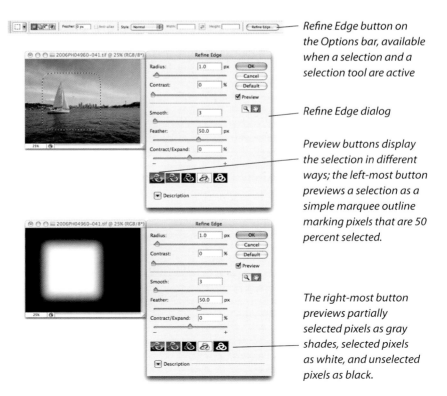

Refine Edge button on the Options bar, available when a selection and a selection tool are active

Refine Edge dialog

Preview buttons display the selection in different ways; the left-most button previews a selection as a simple marquee outline marking pixels that are 50 percent selected.

The right-most button previews partially selected pixels as gray shades, selected pixels as white, and unselected pixels as black.

a simple bi-level channel, the feathered selection creates a channel that contains intermediate grays as well as black and white, which you can see if you click the right-most button at the bottom of the Refine Edge dialog. The gray pixels are partially selected—lighter grays are more selected than darker ones—so any effect applied through the selection affects the fully selected pixels completely and the partially selected pixels in direct proportion to how selected they are, and it doesn't affect the unselected pixels at all.

The ability to partially select pixels is insanely useful in all sorts of situations, many of which we cover in Chapter 9, "Making Selections." For the purposes of this chapter, we'll focus on the role of partially selected pixels in layer masks.

Saving, Reusing, and Converting Selections

Another huge advantage of digital masking tape is that, unlike its real-world equivalent, you can easily copy it, move it, tweak it, or reuse it a year later. When you save a selection as a channel, you can recall it easily, and either reuse it as a selection or apply it as a mask to a layer. Basically, the difference between a mask and a channel is that a mask currently affects its layer, while a channel is stored in the Channels palette without affecting the image in any visible way until you convert it to a selection or mask.

You can very easily bounce between selections, channels, and masks, which, considering they're all the same thing, isn't surprising. The flexibility with which you can turn a selection into a channel or mask and vice versa is one of the major reasons why you should always get into the habit of saving any selection that's even slightly complex. A second reason is that if you fail to do so, you'll find that as soon as the selection becomes unavailable, you'll undoubtedly need it again!

Saving selections as channels. To convert a selection into a channel, click the Save Selection as Channel button at the bottom of the Channels palette (see **Figure 8-5**). The selection appears as a new channel in the Channels palette. That's a shortcut for choosing the Select > Save Selection command and filling out the dialog, which provides more options.

Figure 8-5
Saving a selection
as a channel

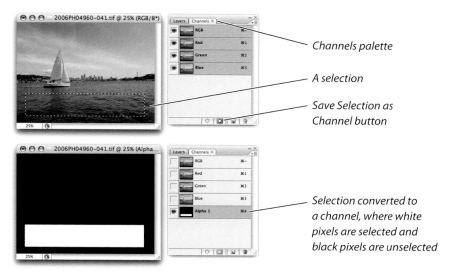

Channels palette

A selection

Save Selection as
Channel button

Selection converted to
a channel, where white
pixels are selected and
black pixels are unselected

Converting channels to selections. To turn a channel into a selection, Command-click (Mac) or Ctrl-click (Windows) the channel in the Channels palette (see **Figure 8-6**). That's a shortcut for selecting the channel and then clicking the Load Channel as Selection button in the Channels palette, or choosing Select > Load Selection.

Figure 8-6
Converting a channel
to a selection

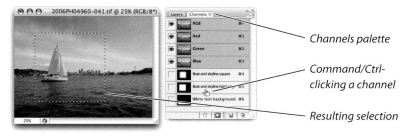

Channels palette

Command/Ctrl-
clicking a channel

Resulting selection

Tip: If a selection is active when you create an adjustment layer, the selection becomes the layer mask for the adjustment layer—very convenient.

Converting selections to masks. Photoshop always adds a layer mask when you create an adjustment layer. Even better, if you have a selection active when you add an adjustment layer, that selection automatically becomes the layer mask for that adjustment layer.

For other types of layers, select a layer and click the Add Layer Mask button at the bottom of the Layers palette (see **Figure 8-7**). The long way to do the same thing is to choose a command from the Layer > Layer Mask submenu (the menu also provides more options).

Figure 8-7

Converting a selection to a layer mask

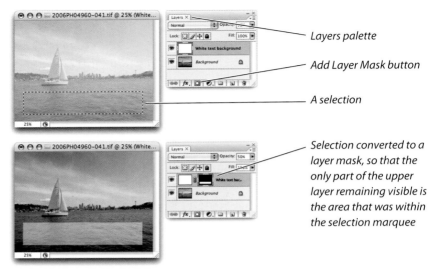

Layers palette

Add Layer Mask button

A selection

Selection converted to a layer mask, so that the only part of the upper layer remaining visible is the area that was within the selection marquee

Adding selections to existing masks. Sometimes we add an adjustment layer without remembering first to load the selection we want to use as a mask. In this case, the procedure is a little trickier.

If the selection is saved as an alpha channel, you can copy it into the mask channel. The trick is that you *must* make the channel and then the mask visible before copying and pasting, otherwise you'll get a new layer instead of the mask you wanted (this still trips us up). Click the alpha channel's thumbnail in the Channels palette to make it visible, choose Edit > Select All, then choose Edit > Copy. Click the Layer mask thumbnail in the Channels palette, click the eyeball to make it visible, and choose Edit > Paste (see **Figure 8-8**). Of course, it all goes much faster if you've memorized the keyboard shortcuts for those Edit menu commands: Command-A for Select All, Command-C for Copy, and Command-V for Paste (Mac), or respectively, Ctrl-A, Ctrl-C, and Ctrl-V (Windows).

Tip: To quickly disable or enable a layer mask, Shift-click on the layer mask thumbnail in the Layers palette. When the mask is disabled, it shows a red X. This is a shortcut for choosing Layer > Layer Mask > Disable.

Figure 8-8

Copying a channel to a layer mask

In the Channels palette, click the alpha channel's thumbnail to select it and make it visible, then Select All and Copy.

Click the layer mask's thumbnail to select it, and click the eyeball to make it visible.

Paste the contents of the alpha channel into the layer mask.

Tip: The Option (Mac) and Alt (Windows) key reverses the selected and unselected areas when you click the Add Layer Mask button in the Layers palette, or the Save Selection as Channel or Load Channel as Selection buttons in the Channels palette.

If a selection is already active, you can use the following method instead. Target the mask channel either by clicking its thumbnail in the Layers palette or by clicking its thumbnail in the Channels palette. Make sure that black is the Background color (press D to set black and white as foreground and background, respectively, then press X to switch them), and hit Delete to fill the selection with black on the Layer mask. This gives you the opposite selection from the one you want. To fix it, deselect the current selection (Command-D on Mac, Ctrl-D in Windows), and then invert the layer mask (Command-I on Mac, Ctrl-I in Windows). It's a little fiddly, but it takes less time to do than to explain.

Painting on the layer mask. We like to apply an adjustment layer and then restrict the effect to the places that need it. With layer masks, you can do exactly that.

Typically, we make edits to a layer so that it affects the entire image (we ignore what's happening in the areas we don't want to change). Then we'll edit the layer mask. Sometimes that means inverting the layer mask to turn it black, hiding the entire edit, and painting with white on the mask to reveal the edit where it's wanted. Sometimes it means painting with black to mask out the areas we want to leave unchanged, we'll use whichever method requires less brushwork. Quite often, we'll use a gradient fill to apply a graduated change across the image, and sometimes we'll even resort to using the selection tools! (Again, see Chapter 9, "Making Selections," for more on selections and masking.)

Tip: If you want an adjustment layer to affect a small area, fill its mask with black and paint in the adjustment with white. Press D to set the default mask colors (white foreground and black background). Press Command-Delete (Mac) or Ctrl-Delete (Windows) to fill the layer with the background color (black). Now you're ready to brush in the adjustment with white. If needed, press X to switch between foreground and background colors.

So with all the aforementioned techniques under our belts, let's look at their application to actual images.

Adjustment Layers in Practice

Figure 8-9 shows an image of a swan that needs a lighting tweak and how adjustment layers can save the day. (This is also a much safer technique than having your assistant chase a swan with a reflector!)

We started by applying a Curves adjustment layer to the entire image, which lightened the head and neck but blew out all the detail on the swan's back. So we chose the Gradient tool and applied a short white-to-black linear gradient to constrain the Curves adjustment to the area in shadow.

Figure 8-9
Masked adjustments

*The original image.
We want to get rid of the
shadow on the swan's
neck and head.*

*We applied the curve, above,
as an adjustment layer,
producing the result shown
at left.*

*We applied a gradient fill
to the layer mask using the
Gradient tool, producing the
result shown at right.*

*A gradient fill on the
layer mask*

*Painting on the layer
mask*

*We duplicated the Curves
layer and reduced the
opacity to 67 percent,
producing the result shown at
near right. Then we painted
black into the duplicate layer's
mask to produce the final
result at far right.*

This gave us a big improvement over the original, but we took it further. We duplicated the Curves layer and reduced the layer opacity to 67 percent. This produced the tonality we wanted on the swan's head and neck, but made the water a little too bright, so we painted the adjustment out with a soft-edged brush and black paint.

The whole process was very quick, with absolutely no time spent making painstaking selections. Painting on the mask with a soft-edged brush is often the quickest and easiest way to constrain local adjustments.

Tip: When you're happy with your adjustment layer edits, you can lower memory requirements by flattening the document (choose Layer > Flatten Image). Just remember that flattening is a one-way trip—once you save and close a flattened file, you can never get the layers back. Instead of flattening everything, you can select a few layers and choose Layer > Merge Layers.

If you want to see *only* the layer mask (as its own grayscale channel), Option-click (Mac) or Alt-click (Windows) on the layer mask's thumbnail in the Layers palette. This is most helpful when touching up areas of the layer mask (it's sometimes hard to see the details in the mask when there's a background image visible).

Copying layer masks. To copy a layer mask, just Option-drag (Mac) or Alt-drag (Windows) the layer mask thumbnail in the Layers palette to the layer to which you want to apply the mask. If you've already been making selections or masks, it's often quicker to start from an existing mask and edit it than it is to start from scratch.

Figure 8-10 shows an image that needs different adjustments for the subject and the sky. The two areas are mutually exclusive, so it's easy to keep each area's adjustments away from the other using a copied, then inverted, layer mask.

Figure 8-10

Copying and then inverting a layer mask

In the original image, the sky needs a different correction than the pyramid. We start by selecting the sky.

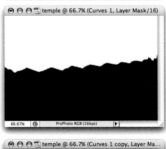

When we add a Curves adjustment layer, the selection automatically becomes the layer mask, so its settings will affect only the sky (the white part of the mask).

Tip: An adjustment layer affects all layers behind it. If you want an adjustment layer to affect just one layer, select the adjustment layer and press Command-Option-G (Mac) or Ctrl-Alt-G (Windows). That's a shortcut for choosing Layer > Create Clipping Mask. You can also Option-click (Mac) or Alt-click (Windows) the dividing line between the two layers.

Because the corrections for the pyramid will occupy all of the area other than the sky, we simply copied the sky's adjustment layer and inverted its mask.

Tip: Remember that, because the mask is simply a channel, you can edit it using all the Photoshop tools you apply to images, including selecting specific areas of the layer mask.

To invert a layer mask, click its thumbnail in the Layers palette and press Command-I (Mac) or Ctrl-I (Windows), which is the shortcut for choosing Image > Adjustments > Invert.

Masking techniques all together. As you become familiar with different masking techniques, learn how to recognize which will isolate your corrections the fastest. **Figure 8-11** shows examples where we used several different masking techniques and why we chose them.

Figure 8-11

Masking techniques

We Command-clicked (Mac) or Ctrl-clicked (Windows) the image to place two curve points, one for the medium sky tones and another for the darker shades in the snowcaps, and tweaked them to increase the contrast. Switching to the green channel, we Command/Ctrl-clicked the magenta part of the sky and added green. The remaining points are anchors.

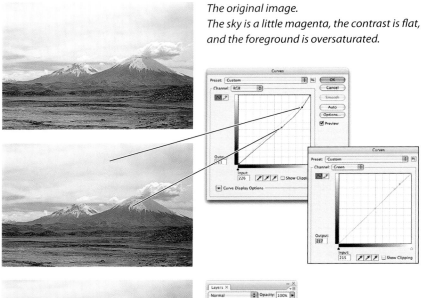

The original image.
The sky is a little magenta, the contrast is flat, and the foreground is oversaturated.

The Curves adjustment improved the sky and mountains, but made the foreground too dark, so we applied a gradient fill to the layer mask, starting above the mountains and ending at their bases.

Our next Curves layer focused on the mountains. We Command/Ctrl-clicked to place two curve points and increased the contrast.

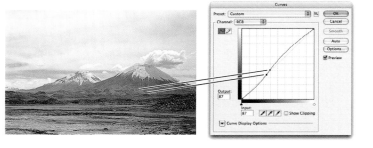

To constrain the Curves adjustment to the mountains, we inverted the layer mask, then painted the adjustment in by painting with white on the mask.

Another Curves layer increased contrast on the ice caps. We liked what it did to the mountains too, but it flattened the sky, made the foreground too contrasty, and made the blue sky too saturated.

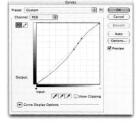

We duplicated the layer mask from our first Curves layer (Sky) to mask the foreground.

To take care of the oversaturated sky, we made a Color Range selection, then filled the selected area on the mask with black.

For our final edit, we put detail back in the sky by making a marquee selection that started at the top of the image and ended just above the blue sky. Then we filled the selected area with a gradient fill.

Image Adjustment with Blending Modes

Applying Levels, Curves, Hue/Saturation, and the other adjustments as adjustment layers offers tremendous flexibility and power, but they aren't always the quickest or easiest ways to fix your images. In some cases, you may find it easier and faster to do the heavy lifting with blending modes, and save Curves for fine-tuning.

Using Layer-Blending Modes

The appealingly simple idea behind editing images with blending modes is that you apply a blending mode to a second copy of a layer and stack the copy on top of the original. Fortunately, you don't have to actually copy the image layer—you can achieve the same result by adding an adjustment layer and then make no changes to it other than changing its blending mode. This is faster and easier than making a duplicate of an image layer, and it saves disk space. Of course, the act of adding an adjustment layer makes it easy to make minor additional tweaks if the result of the blending mode isn't quite perfect; you just edit the curve to cover the rest of the distance. Combining blending modes with the power of adjustment layers opens up a whole new world of possibilities.

Before looking at actual examples, though, it's time to get your head around just what the blending modes do. They're sometimes referred to as "procedural blends" because they all use some arithmetical formula to calculate pixel values based on the values in the overlying (applied) layer and the layers behind it.

Another advantage of using blending modes rather than just stretching and squeezing the bits with Levels and Curves is that blending interpolates tonal values, producing smoother results. We'll show you some examples of how we use blending modes, but we encourage you to experiment—there are plenty of new techniques waiting to be discovered.

If the following explanations make your eyes glaze over, hang on—we've got some examples coming up.

How blending modes think. The biggest question anyone has when using blending modes is, "How do I know which blending mode will do what I want?" To find out, ask yourself the following questions:

▶ **Do I want to alter the light areas of the underlying layers, the dark areas, or both?** Many blending modes have a *neutral color* that doesn't change the layers behind it. For example, for the Lighten, Screen, Color Dodge, and Linear Dodge blending modes, black pixels on the applied layer don't alter the same pixels on the underlying layer, and the farther an applied pixel is from black (that is, the lighter it is), the more it affects the underlying layer.

For other blending modes, white or 50 percent gray are the neutral colors. When 50 percent gray is the neutral color, that means 50 percent gray pixels on the applied layer don't affect underlying pixels at all; and the farther an applied pixel is from 50 percent gray (that is, the closer it is to black or white), the more it affects the underlying layer.

Tip: You can, of course, use a layer's Opacity value to reduce the effect of a blending mode.

▶ **How much additional contrast do I want?** Part of the reason there are so many blending modes is that quite a few of them are merely variations of other blending modes that produce more or less contrast. For example, Hard Light is a higher-contrast version of Soft Light. Certain blending modes, such as Difference, take contrast to the extreme, inverting (creating the negative of) the original layer color. The blending modes that produce lower contrast tend to compare an applied pixel to an underlying pixel and simply keep one or the other, while the blending modes that produce higher contrast tend to mathematically amplify the differences between the applied and underlying layers.

▶ **What do I want to change?** Most blending modes affect any underlying pixel (other than those in the blending mode's neutral color, if it has one), while some blending modes affect only color or tone.

The blending modes are arranged in logical groups, according to the way they answer those three questions.

The Independent modes. Normal and Dissolve both replace the underlying pixels with the pixels of the applied layer when the layer is at 100 percent opacity. At lower opacities, Normal blends the overlying pixels with the underlying ones according to opacity, while Dissolve replaces pixels randomly (see **Figure 8-12**).

Figure 8-12

Blending mode examples

The layers used in the examples that follow. Watch what happens to white, black, 50 percent gray, color, and the semitransparent circle in the lower right corner of the top layer.

Overlying (applied) layer

Underlying (base) layer

Independent modes

Normal *Dissolve*

The Darken modes. The neutral color for the Darken modes is white. White pixels on a layer set to a Darken mode leave the underlying pixels unchanged. Non-white pixels darken the result by varying amounts, depending on each blending mode's math and the difference in value between the applied and underlying pixels (see **Figure 8-13**). Darker Color is a new mode in Photoshop CS3.

Figure 8-13

Darken modes

Darken *Multiply* *Color Burn* *Linear Burn* *Darker Color*

The Lighten modes. The Lighten modes are the inverse of the Darken modes. The neutral color for the Lighten modes is black—black pixels on a layer set to a Lighten mode leave the underlying pixels unchanged. Non-black pixels darken the result by varying amounts, depending on each blending mode's math and the difference in value between the applied and underlying pixels (see **Figure 8-14**). Lighter Color is a new mode in Photoshop CS3.

Figure 8-14

Lighten modes

Lighten *Screen* *Color Dodge* *Linear Dodge* *Lighter Color*

The Contrast modes. The Contrast modes combine corresponding Darken and Lighten modes. The neutral color for the Contrast modes is 50 percent gray—50 percent gray pixels on a layer set to a Contrast mode leave the underlying pixels unchanged. Lighter pixels lighten the result, and darker pixels darken the result by varying amounts, depending on the blending mode and the difference in value between the applied and underlying pixels (see **Figure 8-15**).

Figure 8-15
Contrast modes

Overlay   *Soft Light*   *Hard Light*   *Vivid Light*   *Linear Light*   *Pin Light*

Hard Mix

The odd man out is the Hard Mix blend, which has no neutral color, but it doesn't really fit anywhere else either. It reduces the image to eight colors—red, cyan, green, magenta, blue, yellow, white, or black—based on the mix of the underlying and blend colors, with a strength related to 50 percent gray.

The Comparative modes. The neutral color for the Comparative modes is black. The Comparative modes look at each channel and subtract the underlying color from the overlying color or the overlying color from the underlying color, choosing whichever arrangement returns a result with higher brightness. Blending with white inverts the underlying color values (see **Figure 8-16**).

Figure 8-16
Comparative modes

Difference   *Exclusion*

The HSL modes. While the members of the other groups do basically the same things in different strengths, the members of the HSL group each do something rather different, though they all operate on hue, saturation, and luminosity. Hence it makes sense to discuss them individually (see **Figure 8-17**).

▶ **Hue.** Hue creates a result color with the brightness and saturation of the underlying color and the hue of the overlying color.

▶ **Saturation.** Saturation creates a result color with the brightness and hue of the underlying color and the saturation of the overlying color.

▶ **Color.** Color creates a result color with the luminosity of the underlying color and the hue and saturation of the overlying color.

▶ **Luminosity.** Luminosity is the inverse of Color. It creates a result color with the hue and saturation of the underlying color and the luminosity of the overlying color.

Figure 8-17
HSL modes

Hue   *Saturation*   *Color*   *Luminosity*

Layer-Blending in Practice

Despite the mind-bending variety of blending modes, for the purposes of tonal and color correction, we tend to use just a few of them most of the time. We use Multiply to build density, Screen to reduce it, Soft Light and Hard Light to increase contrast, Color to change color balance without affecting luminosity, and Luminosity to sharpen images without introducing color fringes (we discuss sharpening layers in much greater detail in Chapter 10, "Sharpness, Detail, and Noise Reduction."

The practical examples that follow don't pretend to exhaust the power of blending modes. They're simply examples that we hope will fire your imagination and give you alternative ways of approaching problems.

Building density with Multiply. Multiply mode always creates a result that's darker than both the layer you apply it to and the layer behind that. If you've worked in a darkroom, it's like sandwiching two negatives in an enlarger. Mathematically, Multiply takes two values, multiplies them by each other, and divides by 255.

If a pixel is black in the base image, the result after applying an adjustment layer with Multiply is also black. If a pixel is white in the base image, the adjustment layer has no effect (because white is the neutral color for

Multiply). We use Multiply with Curves adjustment layers to build density, particularly in the highlights and midtones of washed-out images like the one in **Figure 8-18**.

This image represents a scene with a huge dynamic range—a backlit boat against the sun rising over the Ganges. The image has detail in both the brightest part of the sun and in the darkest part of the boat, but the distribution of the midtones is quite wrong—they're much too light, rendering a potentially dramatic image merely pleasant. We can improve it very quickly with a single Curves adjustment layer using the Multiply mode.

We create a new Curves adjustment layer, making no changes to the curve, and set the blending mode to Multiply by choosing it from the blending mode pop-up menu in the Layers palette. This is equivalent to duplicating the Background layer on top of itself and changing the new layer's blending mode to Multiply (see Figure 8-18).

Figure 8-18
Building density
with Multiply

The original image

We added a Curves layer, clicked OK to dismiss the Curves dialog without making any adjustments, and set the blending mode to Multiply.

Adding Contrast with Hard Light. We use Soft Light, Hard Light, and Overlay to build contrast (since the overlying and underlying pixels are identical, Hard Light and Overlay produce exactly the same result). We use Soft Light for smaller contrast boosts and Hard Light or Overlay for stronger ones. All three blending modes preserve white, black, and 50 percent gray, while lightening pixels lighter than 50 percent gray and darkening those that are darker. **Figure 8-19** shows a contrast adjustment with hard light.

Figure 8-19
Increasing contrast
with Hard Light

*We added a second Curves
layer set to Hard Light to
increase contrast.*

*This made the image too
dark, so we reduced the
opacity of the Multiply layer
to 80 percent.*

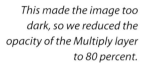

Adjusting color balance with Color. While we sometimes use Photo Filter adjustment layers for warming and cooling effects, we find that a Solid Color layer set to the Color blending mode and low Opacity offers more control, because we can tweak the color by double-clicking on the layer without having to tunnel through the Photo Filter dialog.

We start out by creating a Solid Color layer of approximately the color we want, then we reduce the opacity, typically to around 10 to 20 percent. Then we fine-tune the color to get the result we want—we usually tweak the Hue and Saturation fields of the Color Picker by placing the cursor in them and pressing the up and down arrows on the keyboard.

Figure 8-20 shows the process and the result of adding a Solid Color layer. We started out by picking the approximate color—the image is a little green, so we picked its opposite, magenta—then we used the Color Picker to fine-tune the solid color to get the result we wanted. Now the edited image does a much better job of conveying the oppressive heat, the omnipresent smoke and dust, and the languor of the millennia-old ritual that takes place at dawn on the Ganges.

Figure 8-20

Adjusting color balance
with the Color mode

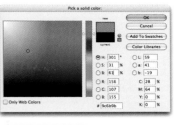

*The image is a little green,
so we added a Solid Color
layer using magenta, set the
blending mode to Color, and
reduced the opacity
to 20 percent.*

*This made the image a
little too blue-purple, so we
nudged the color toward
red by double-clicking the
adjustment in the Layers
palette to open the Color
Picker, then adjusted the Hue
by selecting the Hue field and
pressing the arrow keys.*

Opening shadows with Screen. Screen is literally the inverse of Multiply. The best real-world analogy we've heard comes from Russell Brown of Adobe. Screen is like projecting two slides on the same screen. The result is always lighter than either of the two sources.

If a pixel is white in the base image, the result is white, and if it's black in the base image, the result is also black (black is the neutral color for Screen). Intermediate tones get lighter. We often use Screen to open up dark shadows.

If you're a techno-dweeb like each of us, you probably want to know what Screen does behind the scenes. Photoshop inverts the two numbers (subtracts them from 255) before doing a Multiply calculation (multiplies them by each other and divides by 255); then the program subtracts the result from 255. That's it. Now, don't you feel better knowing that?

Bruce shot the image in **Figure 8-21** from his deck, using a Canon EOS 1Ds, on a typically foggy San Francisco late afternoon. The image holds detail in both highlight and shadow, but the foreground is dark and muddy, an ideal candidate for opening up with Screen blending. We want to preserve the dark sky and hold the detail on the sunlit buildings across the bay, so we'll make the adjustment, then localize it using the layer mask.

Tip: If you're more comfortable thinking in terms of f-stops than in levels or percentages, thank our friend and colleague Jeff Schewe for this insight. You can lighten and darken shadows by 1 stop by applying Screen and Multiply, respectively, at an opacity of 38 percent. For a half-stop adjustment, use 19 percent. For a one-third stop, 13 percent seems to be slightly closer than 12, and for a quarter stop, 9 percent is the magic number. Multiply and Screen always affect the shadows more than the midtones and highlights, so the analogy with f-stops isn't perfect, but it's still useful.

Figure 8-21
Opening shadows
with Screen

The original image

*We added a Curves
adjustment layer set
to Screen mode to
open up the shadows.
We painted black in
the upper part of the
adjustment layer's mask
so that the adjustment
would apply only to the
dark foreground.*

*We wanted to open up the
foreground a little more, so we
duplicated the adjustment layer
and its mask. That effect was too
strong, so we reduced the opacity
of the copied layer to 40 percent.*

Letting the Image Edit Itself

Tip: Get into the habit of giving your layers descriptive names. Instead of accepting default layer names such as "Curves 78" or "Color Fill 15", use names like "Sky color cast" or "Foreground brightness."

We confess to being lazy. One of the ways that laziness manifests itself is that we're always looking for simpler solutions, which in the field of digital imaging can be difficult and occasionally dangerous. But using the Contrast, Darken, and Lighten blending modes to adjust tonality is one of those few solutions that is both simple and safe.

Bruce called this "letting the image edit itself" because rather than having to place curve points and carefully manipulate them, the image content does all the work. If you need more contrast, apply a Soft Light or Hard Light layer. The blending mode takes the contrast that's already in the image and increases it, with no danger of clipping, and no futzing around in the Curves dialog. Likewise, when you need to lighten or darken an image, Screen and Multiply do those things proportionally, again with no danger of clipping. Moreover, the blending modes tend to introduce less hue-shifting than major tonal moves with Curves.

Tip: If a blending mode edit doesn't get you where you want to be fairly quickly, and it's not a masking issue—an edit that needs to be localized to a specific area in the image—it's probably time to go back to conventional corrections, such as Curves.

Each layer affects all the layers underneath it, so we often end up going back to a previous layer to tweak it to take into account the effect of the layers above it. Using the blending modes, we can simply adjust the layer opacity without having to open dialogs, or when we need to make localized changes, we edit the layer masks.

Once you get accustomed to working with the blending modes, you'll find that they're useful for many different kinds of edits. But they may be most powerful when used in combination with conventional correction tools, such as Levels and Curves.

The image shown in **Figure 8-22** is an unadjusted scan from a Kodak Portra 160 NC color negative. Two quick blending mode edits put it into a much better state for the subsequent fine-tuning.

Figure 8-22
Heavy tonal lifting with blending modes

Original image

Two Curves layers, the first (Contrast) set to Hard Light, the second (Lighten) set to Screen, quickly remap the tonal values in this image. Making extreme edits like these with Curves or Levels can introduce hue shifts that may cause problems later.

Next, we shift the color balance—the image has a color cast that's basically cyan, as is common with scans from color negative. So we add red as a solid Color Fill layer, setting it to Color blending mode and 12 percent opacity. Then we go in and fine-tune the color (see **Figure 8-23**).

The Color Fill layer generally moves the color balance in the direction we want, but it's clear that the sky is going to need a localized correction. The blue sky is relatively easy to isolate, but we need to be careful, because the dark areas on the background hills are also blue, so we'll need to take that into account when we make the selection.

Figure 8-23

Fixing color balance with a
Color Fill layer

*We add a red Color Fill layer,
set the mode to Color, and
reduce Opacity to 12 percent.
To tune the color, we double-
click the layer's thumbnail to
open the Color Picker.*

We're also faced with the question of how to edit the sky color. We could use a Hue/Saturation layer or a Curves layer, or we could apply another solid-color layer set to Color blending. They all require approximately the same amount of work, but we opt for a solid-color layer because it's likely to be the easiest of the three to fine-tune afterward.

If we used a Hue/Saturation layer or a Curves layer, we'd almost certainly apply it at 100 percent opacity, so if we needed to make the effect stronger, we'd have to tunnel into the dialogs. Color Fill layers, on the other hand, always use fairly low opacities, so we have an immediately available adjustment to make them weaker or stronger using the layer opacity—we only need to open the dialog to adjust the actual color.

So we make a marquee selection that covers the sky blue areas, then refine it with Color Range. We add a Color Fill layer with a sky-blue color. The layer automatically uses the selection as a layer mask, so we set the blending mode to Color and reduce the opacity until it looks right, as shown in **Figure 8-24**.

There is, however, the danger of falling in love with these techniques to the extent that you make extra work for yourself by overlooking the more conventional techniques—we learned this the hard way!

We want to make the background hills less blue (the dark areas are green vegetation), and we want to increase the saturation and the separation of the red and yellow tones in the foreground. We could do this with careful masking and two or three Color Fill layers, but since we're dealing with separate ranges of color, and we already have a mask that isolates the blue sky from the blue hills, it makes more sense to use a "conventional" Hue/Saturation layer with the blue sky masked out.

Figure 8-24

A local correction with a
Color Fill layer

*We use Color Range to help
select blue sky, then add a
blue Color Fill layer. We set
the blending mode to Color
and reduce the opacity to 12
percent to produce the final
result at right.*

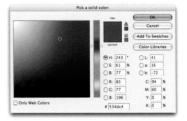

We start by Command-clicking (Mac) or Ctrl-clicking (Windows) the Sky Color layer's layer mask in the Layers palette to load it as a selection, then we press Command-Shift-I (Mac) or Ctrl-Shift-I (Windows) to invert the selection, to select everything except the blue sky. When we add our Hue/Saturation layer, it automatically uses this selection as its layer mask.

We boost the saturation of the foreground yellows and shift the hue of the background hills toward green. We have to darken the green to keep the same tonality, so we reduce the lightness as well as shift the hue—see **Figure 8-25**.

Our next problem is that the clouds are too cyan. They're relatively easy to select, so the simplest fix is a masked Color Fill layer using red to counteract the cyan cast. (Hue/Saturation doesn't work well on colors that are close to neutral, and Curves would require quite a lot of fiddling—we'd need to adjust at least two points on the red curve, and possibly tweak green and blue too.) **Figure 8-26** shows the fix.

Two simple blending mode edits let us adjust the final lightness and contrast. We add a Screen layer and a Soft Light layer, setting the opacities to 7 percent and 62 percent, respectively. The Screen layer at 7 percent opacity provides a very gentle lightening, and the Soft Light layer at 62 percent gives a healthy contrast boost—see **Figure 8-27**.

Figure 8-25

A local correction with a Hue/Saturation layer

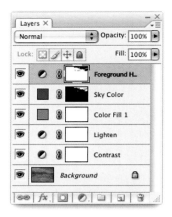

We load the layer mask from our previous edit as a selection, then invert the selection so that the sky is masked rather than revealed. We then add a Hue/Saturation adjustment layer.

We click in the foreground of the image to center the Yellows color range on the foreground yellows and boost the saturation.

Then we switch to the Blues tab, click on the background hills to center the color range, and make a major adjustment to both Hue and Lightness.

Figure 8-26

Warming the clouds with a Color Fill layer

We make a quick Color Range selection of the clouds, then add a red Color Fill layer. We set its blending mode to Color and reduce the opacity to 30 percent.

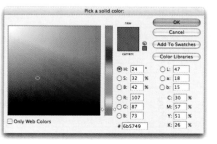

Figure 8-27
Tonal fine-tuning
with blending modes

*Two Curves layers, one set
to Hard Light, the other set
to Screen, quickly remap the
tonal values in this image.*

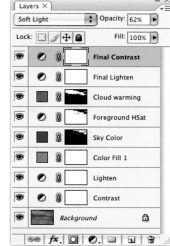

One of the biggest problems in digital imaging is knowing when the image is finished! We can't claim to do better than anyone else in that department, so we have two more edits. The first is to make the foreground a little warmer—we really want it to glow. We could use a Photo Filter layer, but we find Color Fill layers easier to control—there's one fewer dialog to tunnel into if we need to tweak the color.

So we apply an amber warming color as a solid Color Fill layer, set the blending mode to Color, and reduce the layer opacity to 12 percent. This does wonders for the foreground but makes the clouds much too warm. So we select the Background layer, make a quick Color Range selection on the clouds, select the warming layer's layer mask, and fill the selection with black. (We had to target the background layer to make the Color Range selection because Color Range only works on layers that contain pixels, a quirk that has tripped us up more than once!) **Figure 8-28** shows the image with the Color Fill layer applied, before and after masking. We've come a long way since our original image in Figure 8-22.

Figure 8-28
Warming with
a Color Fill layer

We apply a warming color as a Color Fill layer…

…then mask the clouds using Color Range.

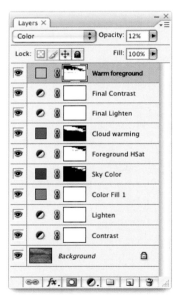

Beyond Adjustment Layers

Using "empty" adjustment layers to blend an image into itself is a very powerful technique, but in some cases you may need to duplicate the image to a new layer, then edit the duplicate pixels themselves.

The image shown in **Figure 8-29** is an old favorite that we've used in the past to demonstrate several different techniques. The big problems are that the main subject is dark, flat, and a little blue.

We can fix most of the problems using blending modes and layer masks as shown in Figure 8-29. We use Screen to lighten, Soft Light to add contrast, and a Solid Color fill, set to Color, mode for warming. All the masks were created using soft, low-to-medium-opacity brushes.

The first layer, set to Screen, lets us paint some virtual fill-flash that lightens the subject. The second layer, set to Soft Light, lets us add contrast to the face with a single dab of the brush. The third layer applies a solid amber fill, set to Color blending with a low opacity, and warms the whole image. The fourth layer, set to Screen, softens the shadows on the left side of the face.

We're left with one remaining problem—the very bright highlight on the hair. If we simply add a masked adjustment layer set to Multiply, we can build density, but the result is also highly oversaturated. However, if we copy the actual pixels to a new layer set to Multiply, we can edit those pixels to produce a much more satisfactory result—see **Figure 8-30**.

In this case, we use the Channel Mixer to exploit the detail in the blue channel by replacing some of the red and green channels with blue, then we use Hue/Saturation to desaturate the pixels. Then, with the highlight fix in place, we apply one more Soft Light layer to get the final contrast.

One thing you'll see in Figure 8-29 is a red overlay on the image. That's an alternate way of viewing a channel or mask—you can see the mask and the image together, which is a great help when you're fine-tuning mask edges. To toggle this view, press the backslash (\) key. The mask will appear as semitransparent red, similar to the QuickMask mode. If you want to customize the layer mask color, double-click the layer mask thumbnail (not the layer content thumbnail).

Figure 8-29 Blending mode corrections

In this original image, we need to lighten, warm, and add contrast to the subject.

1. Screen blending at 100 percent opacity, brush at 20 percent.

2. Soft Light blending at 100 percent, brush at 20 percent opacity.

3. Amber solid color fill, set to Color blending, at 11 percent opacity.

4. Screen blending at 45 percent, brush at 10 percent opacity.

5. Soft Light at 100 percent opacity, brush at 20 percent opacity.

Figure 8-30
A pixel layer
set to Multiply

*We select the hair
highlight, copy it to a new
layer, which we move to
the top of the layer stack,
and set the blending
mode to Multiply.*

*The result is quite
oversaturated, so
we edit the pixels on the
Multiply layer with the
Channel Mixer and
Hue/Saturation.*

*Editing the pixels lets us keep the
Multiply layer at full opacity, so
we get the maximum darkening
effect without oversaturating the
hair color.*

*We finish the image off with a Soft
Light layer at 40 percent opacity
to get the final contrast.*

Advanced Pixel-Blending

Blending pixel layers lets you do things that you simply can't do by adjusting a single image. One situation where we blend pixel layers is when we want to extend the apparent dynamic range of digital captures. Of course, the best way to do this is to take several bracketed exposures and merge them to a 32-bit floating point HDR (High Dynamic Range) image. But that requires planning, a hefty tripod, and a subject that moves little if at all.

It may seem that it's pointless to blend different renderings of a single digital capture. After all, all the data is in the capture, so why not simply edit it to get the results you want? We feel that there are two reasons:

▶ It's extremely difficult to get everything right from a single rendering of the image.

▶ Most cameras capture 12 bits of data. By blending multiple renderings of the 12-bit capture, you can populate more levels in 16-bit space than you can by stretching and squeezing the original 12 bits.

Figure 8-31 shows an "impossible" image produced just this way.

We chose this completely over-the-top example to make it clear just how far you can take this approach, but the techniques are equally applicable to interior shots with bright window light or to any other kind of wide-dynamic-range scene.

Figure 8-31
An impossible image

The sun is just outside the frame at the top of the image. We wouldn't even have attempted this with film!

We started by creating three different renderings of the same camera raw image—one for highlights, one for midtones, and one for shadows—using Camera Raw (see **Figure 8-32**).

In many cases, you can get away with only two renderings, but this is an extreme example. Our first rendering is for the shadows, using significant

Figure 8-32

Three renderings
from Camera Raw

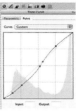

Rendered for shadows

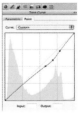

Rendered for midtones

Rendered for highlights

positive Exposure and Brightness adjustments, with fine-tuning applied using the Tone Curve tab in Camera Raw. The second rendering concentrates on the sky and the distant hills. The third rendering makes use of the extended highlight recovery in Camera Raw, with a major negative Exposure correction, further aided by the Curve tab, to squeeze every last drop of highlight detail out of the image. (For much more about Camera Raw, see Chapter 5, "Building a Digital Workflow.")

Combining the Pixel Layers

We always start with the lightest layer and add the darker ones, because it makes the masking much easier. Why? Because a very good starting point is to load the luminosity of the lightest layer as a selection and use it as the layer mask for the darker layer. That way, the shadow detail in the lightest layer gets preserved, while the blown-out areas are replaced by the darker layer.

We start by opening the first rendering in Photoshop. Then we open the second rendering, select all, copy, and paste it into the first rendering, where it appears as a new layer.

Loading the luminosity as a selection. Our next step is to mask the pasted layer. As we just noted, the best starting point for the mask is to load the luminosity of the background layer as a selection, using either of the following methods:

▶ Hide all layers except the background and then Command-click (Mac) or Ctrl-click (Windows) on the RGB channel thumbnail in the Channels palette.

▶ Hide all layers except the background by pressing Command-Option-~(tilde) on the Mac or Ctrl-Alt-~(tilde) in Windows. Mac users take note that OS X 10.4 and later hijacks this useful keyboard shortcut to "Move Focus to Window Drawer," but you can reassign it or turn it off in the System Preferences for Keyboard & Mouse.

A key point in either case is that the selection that gets loaded is the combined luminosity of all visible layers—that's why you have to "solo" the background layer, which you can do quickly by Option-clicking (Mac) or Alt-clicking (Windows) the Background layer's eyeball icon in the layers palette. **Figure 8-33** shows the layers before and after masking.

Figure 8-33
Layer masking

Before layer masking

Option/Alt-click the eyeball to "solo" the Background layer, then…

…Command/Ctrl-click the RGB thumbnail to select Luminosity.

After layer masking

Click the Add Layer Mask icon to create a new layer mask from the selection.

Tip: The term *solo* in this chapter is not a Photoshop term, but a useful concept we took from the pro audio world: When you solo an audio channel, you silence all channels except the one you soloed, so you can hear that one in isolation. For Photoshop, solo is our way of saying "hide all other layers" (or channels) so that you instantly see just one.

With less-challenging images, two layers masked this way may be all you need, but in this case, we need to add a third layer for the highlight detail. We open the third rendering of the image, the one adjusted for highlight detail, and use the Move tool to Shift-drag it into the document we've already been working on, so that it becomes the third, topmost layer. From here, the procedure for adding the third layer and masking it is essentially identical to what we did with the second layer, but this time we need to hide the new layer so that we can select the combined luminosity of the two existing layers.

The resulting image is pretty flat, but all the tones we need are now present. We can improve matters somewhat by tweaking the layer opacities—see **Figure 8-34**.

Figure 8-34
Tweaking the layer opacities

Adjusting the layer opacities as shown in the Layers palettes at far right produces this result.

Producing the final image. To get from here to the result shown back in Figure 8-31, we used masked layers, set to Multiply, to darken, Screen to lighten, and Soft Light to add contrast. We left all the layers at 100 percent opacity and used the layer masks to control them.

On this image, the process was iterative, bouncing back and forth between the layers, and in all honesty it's unlikely that we'd be able to produce absolutely identical results twice in a row, though we'd come pretty close. **Figure 8-35** shows the almost-final image, with layers applied to add contrast (Soft Light), lighten (Screen), and darken (Multiply).

Figure 8-35

Fine-tuning with blending modes

The image adjusted with masked layers set to Soft Light, Screen, and Multiply, respectively

 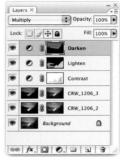

We started by adding a layer set to Soft Light to increase contrast. We left the layer mask white while we added two more layers, one set to Screen and the second to Multiply. On those layers, we inverted the layer mask (target the mask and press Command-I in Mac OS X or Ctrl-I in Windows) to hide the effect, then we painted the lightening and darkening into the image by painting on the masks with a soft-edged brush at opacities between 10 and 20 percent. Then we returned to the Soft Light layer and painted out some of the contrast in the foreground trees.

While we didn't resort to doing so in this case, we'd be remiss if we failed to mention that it's also possible to edit the layer masks using Levels or Curves. To lessen the strength of a layer, you can use the white Output Levels slider in Levels to turn the white (fully revealing) areas of the mask to a light gray, or to let just a little of the effect show through fully masked areas, you can use the black Output Levels slider to turn the black (fully concealing) areas of the mask to a dark gray.

We finished off the image by adding a fully masked Soft Light layer, then painting the additional contrast in with a 5 percent-opacity brush to get the final result shown back in Figure 8-31.

Alternative workflows. In this example, we created three separate DNG files by saving them from Camera Raw with their respective settings, then opened them in Photoshop and copied and pasted to get them all into the same document. But there other useful ways to handle the task of combining multiple renderings of the same raw image.

▶ **Edit and Open in Camera Raw without saving settings.** If the edits needed to produce the different renderings are simple enough, it's probably not worth saving them as separate settings. Instead, you can change how the Open key works in Camera Raw so that it opens a copy of the image without saving the settings. First, open the raw file in Camera Raw hosted by Photoshop, and then Option-click (Mac) or Alt-click (Windows) the Open button. The Open button changes to Open a Copy when you press Option in Mac OS X or Alt in Windows.

   This technique is useful when you want to produce a few different renderings quickly without altering the master settings for a raw file. Once the images are open in Photoshop, the techniques for combining them are the same as in the example we've just covered.

▶ **Place Smart Objects.** Another alternative is to open the raw file as a Smart Object and then place the other versions into that file. If you haven't set up Adobe Camera Raw Workflow Options to open raw files as objects by default, you can press Shift to change the Open Image button to the Open Object button. When you place raw images as Smart Objects, you can edit the settings for each rendering by simply double-clicking the layer thumbnail for the Smart Object—it opens the image up in Camera Raw and lets you edit the settings, which are applied only to that specific Smart Object. However, while you can edit the images in place, the Photoshop document doesn't update until you close the Adobe Camera Raw dialog.

One of the most appealing aspects of layer-based editing is its nondestructive nature—the edits aren't committed until you flatten the file—but sometimes, you can take nondestructive editing so far that you create extremely complex files that are both large and hard to understand. So don't be overly afraid to mix a little destructive editing in with the nondestructive stuff. Remember that you can edit pixel layers directly, and sometimes it's a good idea to do so. If you're nervous about making edits without an escape route, there's one more Photoshop feature that provides a handy fallback position—the History palette.

History and Virtual Layers

Layer-based edits offer great freedom and flexibility, but they have one major disadvantage—they make large files that can also be dauntingly complex. It's often a sobering exercise to return to a layered file you created months or years ago and try to figure out what each layer was supposed to do. Layer-naming helps, but only to a point.

A possible and often quite useful alternative to layers is the History palette. History does a lot more than give you as many as 1000 levels of Undo. When you use History in conjunction with blending modes and the History Brush, you have something that lets you apply very similar effects to those you can achieve with layers and masks.

Virtual Layers

We like to think of History as providing "virtual layers" because it lets us do many of the things we can also do with layers. But let's look at the important ways in which History virtual layers differ from real ones.

Tip: Conrad likes to think of History states as layers in time, as opposed to the layers in space available in the Layers palette.

▶ History is ephemeral. It's only around as long as your file is open. Once you close the file, its history is gone forever, giving a whole new twist to the old adage that those who can't remember history are doomed to repeat it. You can't save the history with the file, so you have to get your edits right before you close. (You can save a History log, either in the file's metadata or in a text file, but the log doesn't let you recreate previous states of the image.)

▶ History is easier to use than layers when you know exactly what you're doing and can get things right on the first (or possibly second) try, but if you're less decisive than that, it quickly becomes more work than using layers to achieve the same effects. On the other hand, layers require some advance planning and organization, and if that doesn't fit your creative personality, you may find History more fluid and natural.

▶ History can be even more demanding on your hardware than adjustment layers. It requires plenty of scratch space, and the faster the disk, the better.

Nevertheless, History is a powerful feature for making quick, effective—dare we say gonzo?—edits.

History Tools

History works using just a handful of tools. The History palette lets you set the source for your History-based edits—the pixels that you'll apply to the image (see **Figure 8-36**).

Figure 8-36
The History palette

Click this column to set the History source.

This icon indicates the current History source.

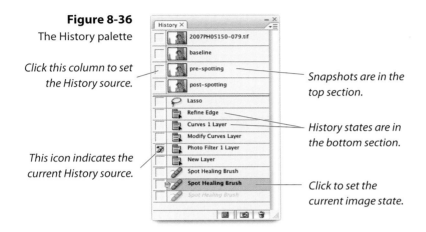

Snapshots are in the top section.

History states are in the bottom section.

Click to set the current image state.

The History palette. The History palette lets you click in the left column to set the History source to a History state or snapshot (the paintbrush icon indicates the current History source), or click on a snapshot or a History state's thumbnail to set the current state of the image.

The three icons at the bottom of the palette let you create a new document from the current History state, create a new snapshot, and delete the current History state, respectively. Snapshots are a convenience feature because they're usually easier to track than History states, and unlike History states, you can name them.

Applying History. You can apply History using either the History Brush tool or by choosing Edit > Fill. Fill is easier to use when you have a selection or you want to affect the entire image. The History Brush is useful for actually brushing in edits. When you use either one, you can immediately use the Fade command (on the Edit menu) to adjust the edit's opacity (and hence its strength).

Figure 8-37 revisits the image from Figure 8-18, but this time we'll make the edits using History instead of layers. No masking is involved, so we simply use Fill from History to make all the edits.

Figure 8-37
Simple History edits

The unedited image

*We set the History source to
the current state.*

*We choose Fill, History,
Multiply, and 83 percent.*

*We set the History source to
the current state.*

*We choose Fill, History,
Overlay, and 100 percent.*

*For the next edit,
the History source is
irrelevant, so we
leave it alone.*

*We set the background color,
then choose Fill, Background
Color, Color, and 20 percent.*

The process is very simple. Our first edit was a layer set to Multiply with
an opacity of 83 percent, so we set the History source to the current image
state (actually, since the image is newly opened, it's already set that way),

and choose Fill from the Edit menu. In the Fill dialog, we choose History from the Use menu, Multiply from the Mode menu, and 83 percent for the opacity.

Our second edit was an Overlay layer set to 100 percent. Again, we set the History source to the current image state—otherwise the Overlay blend would use the original image rather than the image after Multiply, and hence wouldn't match the layered version. Then we choose Fill, and the dialog in choose History, Overlay, and 100 percent.

Our final edit was a solid color layer set to Color blending mode with an opacity of 20 percent. For this, we don't need to use a History state. We simply set the background color (or foreground color, if you prefer) to our desired color (in ProPhoto RGB it was R 156, G 107, B 123), then we choose Fill, and in the dialog, we choose Background Color from the Use menu, Color from the mode menu, and 20 percent opacity.

The result is pixel-for-pixel identical to the layered version we produced earlier in the chapter. We don't have any layers to tweak, but we could, if we wished, fine-tune by continuing to blend the different History states.

Using History to Combine Blending Modes

History also lets you do things that you can't do as easily with layers. One trick we often use is to make a basic setup of three snapshots: one for the original image, a second darkened with Multiply, and a third lightened with Screen. Then we apply the darkened and lightened versions using Soft Light or Hard Light/Overlay to darken or lighten while adding contrast.

Figures 8-38 and **8-39** show a quick set of edits performed entirely with History. We don't necessarily advocate using this approach for all or even most edits, but it's one more useful set of techniques to get under your belt—the more techniques you master, the easier it is to pick the one that will get you the results you want with the minimum of effort in any given situation.

In this case, the unedited image is flat, so we want to pump up the contrast. Specifically, we want to darken the sky, then add contrast to the sagebrush while brightening the highlights. To do so, we first set up a series of snapshots that lighten and darken the image using Screen and Multiply, as shown in Figure 8-38.

Next, we apply the edits. We make a selection of the sky and fill it from the Multiply snapshot. Then we invert the selection, and use the History

Figure 8-38

Setting up Snapshots based on Multiply and Screen

Original image   *After Multiply snapshot fill*   *After Screen snapshot fill*

We set the initial snapshot as source…

Keeping the initial snapshot as the source, we repeat the process using Screen instead of Multiply as the blending mode for the Fill.

…then choose Fill with History, Multiply, and 60 percent opacity, and save the result as a new snapshot.

We create a new snapshot. Now we have a darkened version using Multiply and a lightened version using Screen, in addition to the original image.

brush to paint the Screen snapshot into the sagebrush, using Overlay blending to increase contrast, as shown in **Figure 8-39**.

The trick here, of course, is that you can create a snapshot using one blending mode, then apply it using a different mode either by choosing it in the Fill dialog, or by setting the blending mode for the History Brush.

Optimizing an Image for Print

As with the wet darkroom, the goal when working in the digital darkroom is often to make prints. But the digital darkroom offers a key advantage over its analog counterpart: Thanks to the wonders of color management, it lets you see what will happen in the print before you make it.

The naïve view of color management is that it makes your prints match your monitor. If you've read this far, you've probably realized that this is an

Figure 8-39
Applying the edits

Original image

We make a quick Color Range selection of the sky and save it as a snapshot in case something goes wrong. Then we set the History source to the Multiply snapshot.

With the selection active, we choose Fill from History, using the Multiply layer as source, with Normal blending.

After filling the sky with the Multiply snapshot and painting in the Screen snapshot with the History Brush

We invert the selection, and then we choose the History Brush and set it to a large brush size, 60 percent opacity, and Overlay blending. We set the History source to the Screen snapshot and use it to brush increased contrast into the sagebrush.

impossible goal—printers simply cannot print the range of color a good display can display. Instead, color management tries to reproduce the image as faithfully as the limitations of the output process will allow.

But color management knows nothing about images; it only knows about the color spaces in which images reside. So no output profile, however good, does equal justice to all images. When you convert an image from a working space to the gamut and dynamic range of a composite printer, the profile treats all images identically, using the same gamut and dynamic range compression for all.

Thanks to the soft-proofing features in Photoshop, you can preview exactly how the profile will render your images, allowing you to take the necessary corrective action. If you want great rather than good, you need to optimize images for different output processes, because something always has to give, and each image demands its own compromises.

Adjustment layers provide a very convenient method for targeting images for a specific output process. You can use adjustment layers grouped in layer sets to optimize the same master image for printing to different printers, or to the same printer on different paper stocks. The following technique uses three basic elements.

▶ **A reference image.** Create a duplicate of the image, with Proof Colors turned off, to serve as a reference for the image appearance you're trying to achieve.

▶ **A soft-proof.** Use the Proof Setup command to provide a soft-proof that shows how the output profile will render the image.

▶ **A layer set containing adjustment layers.** Group each set of optimizations for a specific output condition (printer, paper, ink) into a layer set, so that you can turn them on and off conveniently when you print to different devices.

Making the reference image. Choose Image > Duplicate to create a copy of the image in another window. The duplicate will serve as a reference for the appearance you're trying to achieve in the print.

You need to make a duplicate rather than simply open a new view because you'll be editing the master image to optimize it for the print, and the edits would show up in a new view. The duplicate isn't affected by the edits you make to the master file, so it can serve as a reference—a reminder of what you want to achieve in the print.

Setting the soft-proof. Choose View > Proof Setup > Custom to open the Customize Proof Condition dialog. Load the profile for your printer and check Simulate Paper Color to make Photoshop use absolute colorimetric rendering to the monitor (see **Figure 8-40**). All of the soft-proof views (using the different combinations of Paper Color and Black Ink) tell us something useful, but the absolute colorimetric rendering produced by checking Simulate Paper Color is, in theory at least, the most accurate.

However, the first thing you'll notice is that checking Simulate Paper Color makes the image look much worse. Sometimes it seems to die before

Tip: When you turn on the Simulate Paper Color check box, look away from the monitor. Much of the shock you feel when you see absolute colorimetric rendering to the monitor stems from seeing the image change. If you look away, your eyes will adapt to the new white point more easily. It's even easier if you go into Full Screen mode (press F), which hides the palettes that make the image look wrong because they don't change with the image.

Figure 8-40

Setting the soft-proof

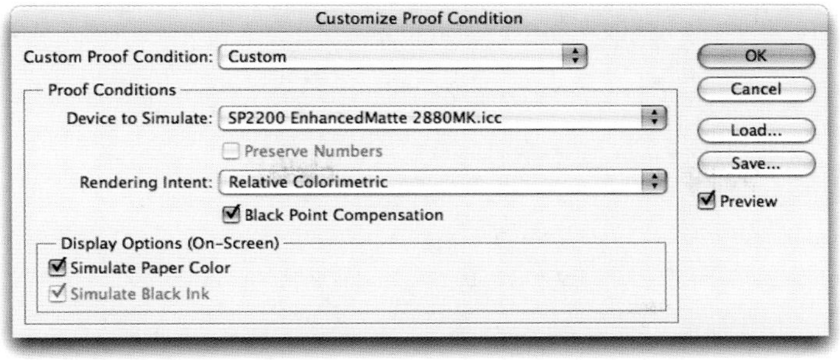

Load the profile for your output device and turn on Simulate Paper Color.

your eyes. At this point, a good many people think the soft-proof must be inherently unreliable and give up on the whole enterprise. What's really going on is that Photoshop is trying to show you the dynamic range compression and gamut compression that will take place upon printing.

The reason the soft-proof looks bad at first glance is that Photoshop can only show you the gamut and dynamic range compression within the confines of your monitor space, and it can only do so by turning things down, so white in the image is always dimmer than your monitor's white.

A second problem is that the vast majority of monitor profiles have a black hole black point (a black with a Lightness of 0 in Lab). Real monitor black typically has a Lightness of 3 or higher, so the soft-proof typically shows black as slightly lighter than it will actually appear on the print.

Typically, in the soft-proof you'll see washed-out shadows, compressed highlights, and an overall color shift caused by the difference between the white of your working space and the white of your paper. Some images are only slightly affected by the conversion to print space, while others will show a dramatic change. As with just about any proofing method we've encountered, you need to learn to interpret the soft-proofs in Photoshop.

A further problem, particularly with vendor-supplied profiles for older printers, is that they weren't built with soft-proofing in mind. They do a good job of converting the source to the output, but they don't do nearly as good a job of "round-tripping"—converting the output back to a viewing profile. That said, all the profiles we've built with current third-party profiling tools make the round-trip very well.

If all this seems discouraging, take heart. Soft-proofing for RGB output may have passed its infancy, but it hasn't yet reached adolescence. And problems with profiles aside, the soft-proofs offered by Photoshop are not, in our experience, any less accurate than those offered by traditional proofing systems. You simply need to learn to "read" them. **Figure 8-41** shows an example.

Figure 8-41

The soft-proof and the reference image

The soft-proof, left, shows a color shift in addition to the reduced dynamic range when compared with the reference image at right.

Tip: If you're spending a lot of time editing an image, take a break. When you stare at an image, an afterimage of opposite colors builds up in your eyes that can distort your color perception. Some popular optical illusions are based on this principle.

Make your edits. We suggest starting out by viewing the soft-proof and the reference image side by side. Once you've edited the soft-proofed image to get it back to where you want it to be, fine-tune your edits while looking at the soft-proofed image in Full Screen view.

Some images need minimal editing; others may require significant reworking. We start by applying adjustment layers to get the soft-proofed image to match the reference (the duplicate) as closely as possible. Then we group these adjustment layers in a layer group named for the print process it addresses. That way, we can easily optimize the master image for different print processes by turning the layer sets on and off without having to create a new file for each print condition. **Figure 8-42** shows the edited and reference images with the individual edits and their accompanying layer sets.

Figure 8-42
The edited image and
the reference image

The Curves adjustment
layer adds contrast using
the RGB curve.

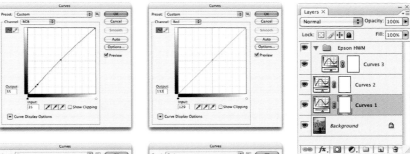

We added small amounts of
red and green, and reduced
blue, to remove the color cast
in the sky and on the building.

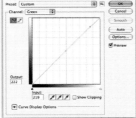

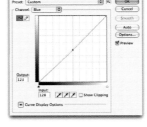

*Our Layers palette
includes an Epson HWM
layer group to be turned
on only when printing to
a specific type of Epson
paper.*

This technique is particularly useful when printing to inkjet printers directly from Photoshop—we can keep a single RGB master file with
built-in optimizations for each print condition, and let Photoshop do the
conversion from RGB working space to printer space at print time. But
it's also valuable when preparing images for CMYK output, which often
involves, if anything, greater compromises. We may do final fine-tuning

on the converted CMYK image, but we make heavy use of soft-proofing to get the RGB image into the best possible state to withstand the conversion before we actually make it.

Once we've edited the soft-proofed image to match the reference image, we use Full Screen view to take a final look at the soft-proofed image prior to printing. (We prefer the gray background, with the menu bar hidden—the black background makes the shadows look too light.) In the majority of cases, we find that no further editing is necessary, but occasionally we'll fine-tune highlight and shadow detail.

The final step is, of course, to print the image. For all the details, see "Imaging from Photoshop" in Chapter 12, "Image Storage and Output."

Making Selections

Getting Just What You Need

You love the painting and retouching tools that Photoshop offers; you love layers; you even love all the options it gives you for saving files. But as soon as someone says "alpha channel" or "mask," your eyes glaze over.

It doesn't have to be this way. Masks, channels, and selections are actually really easy once you get past their bad reputation. Making a good selection is obviously important when silhouetting and compositing images—two of the most common production tasks. But perhaps even more important, selections are also a key ingredient for nondestructive tonal corrections, color corrections, sharpening, and even retouching. We discussed some of these in the previous chapter, and we'll explore them further in later chapters. But before we get there, we must first make you a mask maven and a channel champion!

Note that in this chapter we're only talking about pixel-based selections; we'll discuss sharp-edged vector clipping paths and masks in Chapter 11, "Essential Image Techniques."

Masking-Tape Selections

Back in Chapter 8, "The Digital Darkroom," we introduced a few concepts that are crucial to becoming a selection expert.

▶ Selections, channels, and masks are actually all the same thing in different forms, and you can convert one to another easily.

▶ A channel is a saved selection and looks like a grayscale image where the black parts are fully deselected ("masked out"), the white parts are fully selected, and the gray parts indicate partially selected pixels.

▶ A layer mask is a selection or channel applied to a layer so that the black areas of the mask fully hide the layer and the white areas of the mask are transparent (they show the layer's pixels). If an area in a layer mask (or channel) is 25 percent gray, then that area is 75 percent visible. Remember: "Black conceals, white reveals," and the lighter the gray, the more selected or visible the area.

▶ Smooth transitions between selected (white) and unselected (black) areas are incredibly important for compositing images, painting, correcting areas within an image—in fact, just about everything you'd want to do in Photoshop.

Tips for All Selection Tools

Although there are many ways to make a selection in Photoshop, the selection tools in the Tools palette let you create or fine-tune selections by hand, and for that reason they'll never go out of style. They fall into distinct groups: the Marquee tool group, the Lasso tool group, and the Quick Selection tool group (see **Figure 9-1**).

Of course, the little black triangles at the bottom right corner of each tool button let you know that you can hold down the mouse button to reveal more tools. The Marquee tool group contains other tools for basic selection shapes. The free-form Lasso tool contains the Polygonal Lasso tool that draws straight lines and the Magnetic Lasso tool that draws a selection that follows contrasty edges. And in Photoshop CS3, the Magic

Figure 9-1

Selection tools

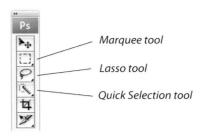

Marquee tool

Lasso tool

Quick Selection tool

Wand is grouped with the new Quick Selection tool, which acts like the Magic Wand but works more like a brush that paints a mask.

The important thing to remember about these selection tools (and, in fact, every selection technique in Photoshop) is that you can freely switch among them as you work. Don't get too hung up on getting one tool to work just the way you want it to; you can always modify the selection using a different technique (this idea of modifying selections is very important, and we'll touch on it throughout the chapter). Here are some pointers that can help you use the selection tools most efficiently:

▶ **You can always move your selection.** One of the most frequent changes you'll make to a selection is moving it without moving its contents. For instance, you might make a rectangular selection, then realize it's not positioned correctly. Don't redraw it! Just click and drag the selection using one of the Marquee or Lasso tools. The selection moves, but the pixels underneath it don't. Or press the arrow keys to move the selection by one pixel. Add the Shift key to move the selection ten pixels for each press of an arrow key.

▶ **You can move a selection while you're drawing it.** One of the coolest and least-known selection features is the ability to move a marquee selection (either rectangular or oval) while you're still dragging out the selection. The trick: hold down the spacebar while you're still holding down the mouse button. This also works when dragging frames and lines in Adobe InDesign and Adobe Illustrator.

▶ **You can add to and subtract from selections.** No matter which selection tool you're using, you can always add to the current selection by holding down the Shift key while selecting. Conversely, you can subtract from the current selection by holding down the Option key (Mac) or Alt key (Windows). Or, if you want the intersection of two selections, hold down the Option/Alt and the Shift keys while selecting

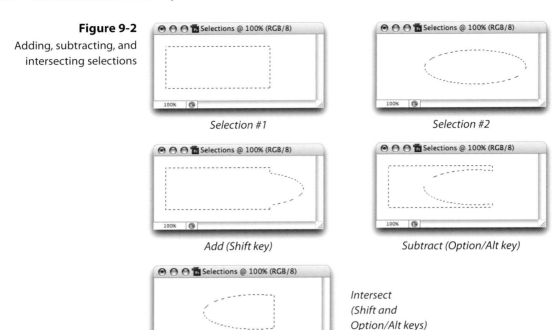

Figure 9-2

Adding, subtracting, and intersecting selections

Selection #1

Selection #2

Add (Shift key)

Subtract (Option/Alt key)

Intersect
(Shift and
Option/Alt keys)

(see **Figure 9-2**). If you don't feel like remembering these keyboard modifiers, you can click on the Add, Subtract, and Intersect buttons on the far-left side of the Options bar instead.

▶ **You can select it again.** It's too easy and natural to charge ahead with edits after selecting an area and later realize you need that last selection back. Fortunately, you can recall it by pressing Command-Shift-D (Mac) or Ctrl-Shift-D (Windows), the shortcut for Select > Reselect.

▶ **You can transform selections.** When you choose Select > Transform Selection, Photoshop places the Free Transform handles around your selection and lets you rotate, resize, skew, move, or distort the selection however you please. When you're done, press Enter or click the check mark button in the Options bar.

Even less obvious is that after you choose Transform Selection, you can pick options from the Edit > Transform submenu, or type transform values into the fields in the Options bar. For example, if you want to mirror your selection, turn on Transform Selection, drag the center point of the transformation rectangle to the place around which you want the selection to flip, then choose Flip Vertical or Flip Horizontal from the Transform sub-menu (see **Figure 9-3**).

Figure 9-3
Transforming a selection

We select the type by Command-clicking (Mac) or Ctrl-clicking (Windows) the type layer thumbnail.

We choose Select > Transform Selection, and then Command-drag (Mac) or Ctrl-drag (Windows) the center top handle to distort the selection. Command/Ctrl-drag works with any handle.

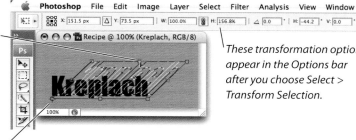

These transformation options appear in the Options bar after you choose Select > Transform Selection.

Before entering transformation values into the Options bar, we dragged the origin point from the center of the transformation box to this location, to set the origin for numerical transformations.

After pressing Enter to apply the transformation, we add a Levels adjustment layer and move the midpoint slider to darken the "shadow."

Marquee

The Marquee tool is the most basic of all the selection tools. It lets you draw a rectangular or oval selection by clicking and dragging. If you hold down the Shift key, the marquee is constrained to a square or a circle, depending on whether you have chosen Rectangle or Ellipse in the Marquee Options bar. (Note that if you've already made a selection, the Shift key adds to the selection instead.) If you hold down the Option key (Mac) or Alt key (Windows), the selection is centered on where you clicked.

Tip: You can cycle through the Rectangular, Elliptical, Single Row, and Single Column selection tools by choosing from the Tools palette, but it's faster to press M once to select the tool, then press Shift-M to cycle through the tools. Option/Alt-clicking the Marquee tool in the Tool palette also cycles through them.

▶ **Pulling out a single line.** If you've ever tried to select a single row of pixels in an image by dragging the marquee, you know that it can drive you batty faster than Mrs. Gulch's chalk-scraping. The Single Row and Single Column selection tools (click and hold the mouse button down on the Marquee tool to get them) are designed for just this purpose. We use them to clean up screen captures or to delete thin borders around an image. They're also useful with video captures, because each pixel row often equals a video scan line.

Tip: To select an area of a specific size, choose Fixed Size from the Style pop-up menu in the Options bar, and then after typing a value, enter the units you want ("in" for inches, "px" for pixels, and so on). Then press Return or Enter.

▶ **Selecting thicker columns and rows.** If you want a column or row that's more than one pixel wide or tall, set the selection style to Fixed Size on the Options bar and type the thickness of the selection into the Height or Width field (note that you have to type a measurement value, like "px" for pixels, or "cm" for centimeters). In the other field, type some number that's obviously larger than the image, like 10,000px. When you click on the image, the row or column is selected at the thickness you want.

▶ **Selecting that two-by-three.** You've laid out a page with a hole for a photo that's 2 by 3 inches. Now you want to make a 2-by-3-inch selection in Photoshop. No problem: Choose Constrained Aspect Ratio from the Style pop-up menu in the Options bar (when you have the Marquee tool selected). Photoshop lets you type in that 2-by-3 ratio.

Lasso

The Lasso tool lets you create a free-form outline of a selection. Wherever you drag the mouse, the selection follows until you finally let go of the mouse button and the selection is automatically closed for you (there's no such thing as an open-ended selection in Photoshop; see **Figure 9-4**).

▶ **Let go of the Lasso.** Two of the most annoying attributes of selecting with the Lasso are that you can't lift the mouse button while drawing, and you can't draw straight lines easily (unless you've got hands as steady as a brain surgeon's). The Option key (Mac) or Alt key (Windows) overcomes both these problems.

When you hold down the Option/Alt key, you can release the mouse button, and the Lasso tool won't automatically close the selection. Instead, as long as the Option/Alt key is held down, Photoshop lets you draw a straight line to wherever you want to go. This solves both problems in a single stroke (as it were).

The folks at Adobe saw that people were using this trick all the time and decided to make it easier on them. Photoshop includes a straight-line Lasso tool that works just the opposite of the normal Lasso tool—when

Figure 9-4
Lasso selections

Beginning the selection   *End of (very rough) selection*   *Closed on mouse release*

you hold down the Option/Alt key, you can draw nonstraight lines. If you press the L key once, Photoshop gives you the Lasso tool; then press Shift-L, and you get the Straight-line Lasso tool. (Of course, the Shift-key trick won't work if you've turned off the Use Shift Key for Tool Switch option in the Preferences dialog.)

In order to close a selection when you're using the Straight-line Lasso tool, you have to either click at the beginning of the selection or double-click anywhere.

▶ **Select outside the canvas.** You may or may not remember at this point in the book that Photoshop saves image data on a layer, even when it extends past the edge of the canvas (out into that gray area that surrounds your picture). Just because it's hidden doesn't mean you can't select it. If you zoom back far enough and enlarge your window enough (or switch to Full Screen mode) so you can see the gray area around the image canvas, you can hold down the Option/Alt key while using the Lasso tool to select into the gray area. (Ordinarily, without the modifier key, the selections stop at the edge of the image.)

Magnetic Lasso. The Magnetic Lasso tool (it, too, is hiding in the Tool palette behind the Lasso tool) lets you draw out selections faster than the regular Lasso tool. The Magnetic Lasso can seem like magic or it can seem like a complete waste of time—it all depends on three things: the image, your technique, and your attitude.

To use the Magnetic Lasso tool, click once along the edge of the object you're trying to select, then drag the mouse along the edge of the selection (you don't have to—and shouldn't—hold down the mouse button while moving the mouse). As you move the mouse, Photoshop "snaps" the selection to the object's edge. When you're done, click on the first point in the selection again (or triple-click to close the path with a final straight line).

So the first rule is: Only use this tool when you're selecting something in your image that has a distinct edge. In fact, the more distinct the better, because the program is really following the contrast between pixels. The lower the contrast, the more the tool gets confused and loses the path.

Here are a few more guidelines that will help your technique:

► **Be picky with your paths.** If you don't like how the selection path looks, you can always move the mouse backward over the path to erase part of it. If Photoshop has already dropped an anchor point along the path (it does this every now and again), you can remove the last point by pressing the Delete key. Then just start moving the mouse again to start the new selection path.

Tip: While the selection marquee animation helps the human eye see a selection on a possibly busy background, it can also be so distracting that you can't see how your edits affect the image. To hide those little ants, press Command-H (Mac) or Ctrl-H (Windows), a shortcut for turning off Select > Extras. The only problem is that you must remember that a selection is active, and where the selection is.

► **Click to drop your own anchor points.** For instance, the Magnetic Lasso tool has trouble following sharp corners; they usually get rounded off. If you click at the vertex of the corner, the path is forced to pass through that point.

► **Vary the Lasso Width as you go.** The Lasso Width (in the Options bar) determines how close to an edge the Magnetic Lasso tool must be to select it. In some respects it determines how sloppy you can be while dragging the tool, but it becomes very important when selecting within tight spots, like the middle of a "V". In general, you should use a large width for smooth areas and a small width for more detailed areas.

Fortunately, you can increase or decrease this setting while you move the mouse by pressing the square bracket keys on your keyboard. (For extra credit, set Other Cursors to Precise in the General Preferences dialog; that way, you can see the size of the Lasso Width.) Also, Shift-[and Shift-] set the Lasso Width to the lowest or highest value (1 or 40). If you use a pressure-sensitive tablet, turn on the Stylus Pressure check box on the Options bar; the pressure then relates directly to Lasso Width.

► **Sometimes you want a straight line.** You can get a straight line with the Magnetic Lasso tool by Option-clicking (Mac) or Alt-clicking (Windows) once to set the beginning of the segment, and then Option/Alt clicking again to set the end of the segment.

▶ **Occasionally, customize your Frequency and Edge Contrast settings.** These settings (on the Options bar) control how often Photoshop drops an anchor point and how much contrast between pixels it's looking for along the edge. In theory, a more detailed edge requires more anchor points (a higher frequency setting), and selecting an object in a low-contrast image requires a lower contrast threshold. To be honest, we're much more likely to switch to a different selection tool or technique before messing with these settings.

▶ **Scrolling while selecting.** It's natural to zoom in close when you're dragging the Magnetic Lasso tool around. Nothing wrong with that. But unless you have an obscenely large monitor, you won't be able to see the whole of the object you're selecting. No problem; the grabber hand works just fine while you're selecting—just hold down the Spacebar and drag the image around. You can also press the + and - (plus and minus) keys to zoom in and out while you make the selection.

The last rule is patience. Nobody ever gets a perfect selection with the Magnetic Lasso tool. It's not designed to make perfect selections; it's designed to make a reasonably good approximation that you can edit. We cover editing selections in "Quick Masks," later in this chapter.

Magic Wand

The last selection tool in the Tool palette is the Magic Wand, so called more for its icon than for its prestidigitation. When you click on an image with the Magic Wand (dragging has no effect), Photoshop selects every neighboring pixel with the same or similar gray level or color. "Neighboring" means that the pixels must be touching on at least one side (see **Figure 9-5**). If you want to select all the similar-toned pixels in the image, whether they're touching or not, turn off the Contiguous check box in the Options bar before clicking.

How similar can the pixels be before Photoshop pulls them into the selection? It's entirely up to you. You can set the Tolerance setting on the Options bar from 0 to 255. In a grayscale image, this tolerance value refers to the number of gray levels from the sample point's gray level. If you click on a pixel with a gray level of 120 and your Tolerance is set to 10, you get any and all neighboring pixels that have values between 110 and 130.

Figure 9-5
Magic Wand
selections

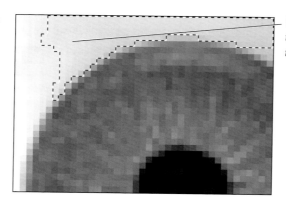

*We clicked here with
the Magic Wand
tolerance set to 18.*

In RGB and CMYK images, however, the Magic Wand's tolerance value is slightly more complex. The tolerance refers to each and every channel value, instead of just the gray level.

For instance, let's say your Tolerance is set to 10 and you click on a pixel with a value of 60R 100G 200B. Photoshop selects all neighbors that have red values from 50 to 70, green values from 90 to 110, and blue values from 190 to 210. All three conditions must be met, or the pixel isn't included in the selection (see "Grow," later in the chapter for more info).

The Magic Wand will probably be less frequently used now that Photoshop has the Quick Selection tool (which we talk about in the next section). This is no doubt because the Magic Wand involves a lot of careful trial-and-error clicking, which may be why some have dubbed this tool the "Tragic Wand." The following techniques can increase your chances of success.

▶ **Select on a channel, not composite.** Because it's often difficult to predict how the Magic Wand tool is going to work in a color image, we typically like to make selections on a single channel of the image. The Magic Wand is more intuitive on this grayscale image, and when you switch back to the composite channel, the selection's flashing border will still be there. You can switch to the composite channel by clicking on the RGB, CMYK, or Lab thumbnail in the Layers palette, or by pressing Command-~ (tilde) in Mac OS X or Ctrl-~ (tilde) in Windows.

▶ **Sample small, sample often.** The Magic Wand tool can be frustrating when it doesn't select everything you want it to. When this happens, novice users often set the tolerance value higher and try again. Instead, try keeping the tolerance low (between 12 and 32) and Shift-click to add more parts, or Option-click (Mac) or Alt-click (Windows) to take parts away.

► **Sample points in the Magic Wand.** Note that when you select a pixel with the Magic Wand, you may not get the pixel value you expect. It all depends on the Sample Size pop-up menu on the Options bar (when you have the Eyedropper tool selected). If you select 3 by 3 Average or 5 by 5 Average in that pop-up menu, Photoshop averages the pixels around the one you click on with the Magic Wand. On the other hand, if you select Point Sample, Photoshop uses exactly the one you click. For more hints on sample points, see the sidebar "Reading Color with the Info Palette" in Chapter 7, "Image Adjustment Fundamentals."

► **Reverse-selecting.** One simple but non-obvious method that we often use to select an area is to select a larger area with the Lasso or Marquee tool and then Option-click (Mac) or Alt-click (Windows) with the Magic Wand tool on the area we don't want selected (see **Figure 9-6**).

Figure 9-6
Reverse-selecting

To select the green leaf, we first draw a marquee around the whole area.

By Option-clicking (Mac) or Alt-clicking (Windows) with the Magic Wand tool twice (once on the background and once on the yellow), our selection is almost complete. Now we can clean up the rough selection with the Lasso tool or in Quick Mask mode.

Quick Selection

The Quick Selection tool is new in Photoshop CS3. If you're more comfortable painting a selection area rather than drawing an outline around a selection area, you may want to try this tool. You drag the Quick Selection tool as if you were painting a mask, but instead of getting painted bits back, you get a selection outline as if you had drawn a lasso selection. In that way, the Quick Selection tool lets you paint a selection (as if you were working with masks or channels) but see a marquee outline (as if you were dragging a Lasso or Marquee tool). Another way to look at this tool is that it lets you select while painting, while saving you the step of converting a mask or channel into a selection.

Tip: When using the Quick Selection tool, keep your left hand camped out by the bottom left corner of the keyboard. When it's there, you're always ready to press Command-Z/Ctrl-Z to undo, or Option/Alt to remove areas from the selection.

Use the Quick Selection tool as if you're painting a mask. Drag it through the area you want to select (see **Figure 9-7**). Like a brush (and unlike the other selection tools), any additional areas you drag with the Quick Selection tool are automatically added to the existing selection—no need to hold Shift to do that. For this reason alone, Magic Wand fans may want give the Quick Selection tool a try. Be careful, though, because if you drag any part of the brush over a color you don't intend to select, whole unwanted areas may be added to the selection. If this happens, simply press Command-Z (Mac) or Ctrl-Z (Windows) to undo, and try again. To remove an area selectively, Option-drag (Mac) or Alt-drag (Windows) the tool. The tool remembers which colors you've included and excluded until you switch tools or switch to Quick Mask mode.

If you're consistently selecting too much, go to the Options bar and make the brush harder and its size smaller. If you're using a pressure-sensitive stylus, apply less pressure for a smaller brush tip, or just turn off Pen Pressure in the Brush pop-up menu and use a small brush size.

Figure 9-7
Quick Selection tool

In this example, we want to select a car and its shadow, but the similar colors inside and outside our desired selection confuse most color-based selection tools. With the Quick Selection tool, we can indicate where our desired edges actually are.

First we try the Magic Wand tool, but one click selects too many similar colors all over the image. The car color is too close to the pavement color, and the Magic Wand can't tell the difference between the car's shadow and other shadows.

We do better by dragging the Quick Selection tool, which easily includes the colors of the red taillight and orange turn lamps in the selection, yet without including the unwanted areas outside the car and its shadow.

We accidentally overshoot the car outline with the brush edge, causing the tool to pick up some unwanted background.

Option-dragging (Mac) or Alt-dragging (Windows) the Quick Selection tool over unwanted areas excludes them.

Tip: If the background contains colors that don't also occur in the subject, Option-drag (Mac) or Alt-drag (Windows) through unwanted background colors. This marks those colors "off limits," so that the tool avoids those colors when you finally drag the tool through the areas you do want to select.

In the Options bar, the Auto-Enhance option tries to guess at making a better selection. If you think it's guessing wrong, turn off Auto-Enhance and fine-tune the edge yourself by clicking Refine Edge. We cover the Refine Edge dialog later in this chapter.

While the Quick Selection tool has gotten a lot of press as a miraculous selection tool, it's really just another weapon in your selection arsenal. Like the Magnetic Lasso, the effectiveness of the Quick Selection tool depends a large part on the amount of contrast along the edges of the area you want to isolate. There are still many situations where another selection method (such as Select > Color Range) may be faster or easier.

Floating Selections

We need to take a quick diversion off the road of making selections and into the world of what happens when you move a selection. Photoshop has traditionally had a feature called floating selections. A floating selection is a temporary layer just above the currently selected layer; as soon as you deselect the floating selection, it "drops down" into the layer, replacing whatever pixels were below it. When you move a selection of pixels within an image, Photoshop acts as though those pixels were on a layer. Unfortunately, while these floating selections act like layers, they don't show up in the Layers palette. For that reason, The Photoshop engineering team has been trying to get rid of floating selections for years, but there are still a few instances where they appear. We prefer to avoid floating selections and instead move pixels to a real layer for accurate positioning.

Tip: To cut out selected pixels and leave a blank spot behind, drag the selection with the Move tool. If you'd rather copy the pixels into a floating selection, you can hold down the Option/Alt key while dragging or press Command/Ctrl-J. Note that floating selections doesn't appear on the Layers palette.

You can manipulate a floating selection as you do a layer. You can change the mode of a floating selection to Multiply, Screen, Overlay, or any of the others, and even change its opacity. But if the floating selection doesn't appear in the Layers palette, how are you to make these changes? After floating the pixels, choose Edit > Fade. (Nonintuitive, but true.) However, as soon as you try to paint on it, or run a filter, or do almost anything else interesting to the floating selection, Photoshop deselects it and drops it back down to the layer below it. That's one reason we would rather just place pixels onto a real layer before messing with them.

Quick Masks

When you select a portion of your image, you see the flashing dotted lines—they're fondly known as *marching ants* to most Photoshop folks. But what are these ants really showing you? In a typical selection, the marching ants outline the boundary of pixels that are selected 50 percent or more. There are often loads of other pixels that are selected 49 percent or less that you can't see at all from the marching ants display. Very frustrating.

Fortunately, Photoshop includes a Quick Mask mode to show you exactly what's selected and how much each pixel is selected. When you enter Quick Mask mode (select the Quick Mask icon in the Tool palette or type Q), you see the underlying selection channel in all its glory. However, because the Quick Mask is overlaying the image, the black areas of the mask are 50 percent opaque red and the white (selected) areas are even more transparent than that (see **Figure 9-8**). The red is supposed to remind you of Rubylith, if you remember the amber-colored acetate we used to cut up to create masks for film.

Figure 9-8
Quick Mask mode

The marching ants show some of the selected areas of the image.

The Quick Mask view shows all of the selected pixels (fully and partially selected).

You can change both the color and the transparency of the Quick Mask in the Quick Mask Options dialog (see **Figure 9-9**)—the fast way to get there is to double-click on the Quick Mask icon in the Tool palette. If the image you're working on has a lot of red in it, you'll probably want to change the Quick Mask color to green or some other contrasting color. Either way, we almost always increase the opacity of the color to about 75 percent so it displays more prominently against the background image.

Note that these changes aren't document-specific. That is, they stick around in Photoshop until you change them.

Figure 9-9
Quick Mask Options dialog

Editing Quick Masks

The powerful thing about Quick Masks isn't just that you can see a selection you've made, but rather that you can edit that selection with precision. When you're working in Quick Mask mode, you can paint using any of the painting or editing tools in Photoshop, though you're limited to painting in grayscale. Painting with black is like adding digital masking tape (it subtracts from your selection), and painting with white (which appears transparent in this mode) adds to the selection.

If the element in your image is any more complicated than a rectangle, you can use Quick Mask to select it quickly and precisely. (We do this for almost every selection we make.) Here's how:

1. Select the area as carefully as you can using any of the selection tools (but don't spend too much time on it).

2. Switch to Quick Mask mode (press Q).

3. Paint or edit using the Brush tool (or any other painting or editing tool) to refine the selection you've made. Remember that partially transparent pixels will be partially selected (we often run a Gaussian Blur filter on the Quick Mask to smooth out sharp edges in the selection).

4. Switch out of Quick Mask mode by pressing Q again. The marching ants update to reflect the changes you've made (see **Figure 9-10**).

Note that if you switch to Quick Mask mode with nothing selected, the Quick Mask will be empty (transparent). This would imply that the whole document is selected, but it doesn't work that way.

Tip: Even when you're in Quick Mask mode, it's difficult to see partially selected pixels (especially those that are less than 50 percent selected). Note that the Info palette shows grayscale values when you're in this mode; those percentage values represent the opacity of the selection at that pixel, which makes partial (feathered) selections possible. It's just another reason always to keep an eye on the Info palette.

Figure 9-10
Editing Quick Masks

Original, quick-and-dirty selection with the Lasso tool

In Quick Mask mode, you can clean up the selection using any tool, including the brushes.

When you leave Quick Mask mode, the selection is updated.

Filtering Quick Masks. The Quick Mask mode is also a great place to apply filters or special effects. Any filter you run affects only the selection, not the entire image (see **Figure 9-11**). For instance, you could make a rectangular selection, switch to Quick Mask mode, and then run the Twirl filter. When you leave Quick Mask mode, you can fill, paint, or adjust the altered selection.

Customizing the color. If you're the kind of person who likes the selected areas to be black (or red, or whatever other color you choose in Quick Mask Options) and the unselected areas to be fully transparent, you can change this in Quick Mask Options. Even faster, you can Option-click (Mac) or Alt-click (Windows) on the Quick Mask icon in the Tool palette. Note that when you do this, the icon actually changes to reflect your choice.

If you do change the way that Quick Mask works, you'll probably want to reverse the way that channels and layer masks work, too (double-click on the channel in the Channels palette). Otherwise, you'll have a hard time remembering whether black means selected or unselected. You might not need to worry about this too much; when a selection is the opposite of what you want, just press Command-Shift-I (Mac) or Ctrl-Shift-I (Windows), the shortcut for Select > Inverse. When you're editing a Quick Mask, channel, or layer mask, you can swap black and white by pressing Command-I (Mac) or Ctrl-I (Windows), the shortcut for Image > Adjustments > Invert.

Figure 9-11
Filtering Quick Masks

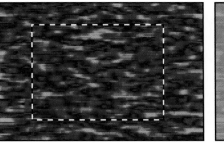

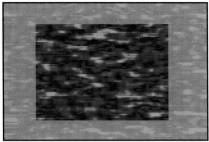

Original selection   *Quick Mask of original selection*

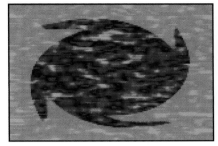

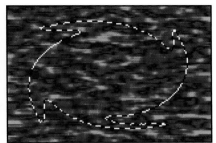

Quick Mask after Twirl filter applied   *Post-Twirl selection*

Anti-Aliasing and Feathering

If you've ever been in a minor car accident and later talked to an insurance adjuster, you've probably been confronted with their idea that you may not be fully blameless or at fault in the accident. And just as you can be 25 percent or 50 percent at fault, you can partially select pixels in Photoshop. One of the most common partial selections is around the edges of a selection. And the two most common ways of partially selecting the edges are anti-aliasing and feathering.

Anti-Aliasing

If you use the Marquee tool to select a rectangle, the edges of the selection are nice and crisp, which is probably how you want them. Crisp edges around an oval or irregular shape, however, are rarely a desired effect. That's because of the stair-stepping required to make a diagonal or curved line out of square pixels. What you really want (usually) is partially selected pixels in the notches between the fully selected pixels. This technique is called *anti-aliasing*.

Every selection in Photoshop is automatically anti-aliased for you, unless you turn this feature off in the selection tool's Options bar. Unfortunately, you can't see the anti-aliased nature of the selection unless you're in Quick Mask mode, because anti-aliased (partially selected) pixels are often less than 50 percent selected. Note that once you've made a selection with Anti-alias turned off on the Options bar, you can't anti-alias it—though there are ways to fake it (see below).

Feathering

Anti-aliasing simply smooths out the edges of a selection, adjusting the amounts that the edge pixels are selected in order to appear smooth. But it's often (too often) the case that you need a larger transition area between what is and isn't selected. That's where feathering comes in. *Feathering* is a way to expand the border around the edges of a selection. The border isn't just extended out; it's also extended in (see **Figure 9-12**).

To understand what feathering does, it's important to understand the concept of the selection channel that we talked about earlier in the chapter. That is, when you make a selection, Photoshop is really "seeing" the selection as a grayscale channel behind the scenes. The black areas are totally unselected, the white areas are fully selected, and the gray areas are partially selected.

Tip: In Mac OS X, the traditional Photoshop keyboard shortcut for Feather is Command-Option-D. Mac OS X took over this shortcut for hiding and showing the Dock. If you want the Feather shortcut to work, either redefine it by choosing Edit > Keyboard Shortcuts in Photoshop, or open the Keyboard Shortcuts tab in Mac OS X System Preferences to redefine or disable the hide/show Dock shortcut.

Figure 9-12
Feathering

Original selection (no feather)

Feather: 5 pixels

Feather: 15 pixels

When you feather a selection, Photoshop is essentially applying a Gaussian Blur to the grayscale selection channel. (We say "essentially" because in some circumstances—like when you set a feather radius of over 120 pixels—you get a slightly different effect; however, there's usually so little difference that it's not worth bothering with. For those technoids out there who really care, Adobe tells us that a Gaussian Blur of the Quick Mask channel is a tiny bit more accurate and "true" than a feather.)

There are several ways to feather a selection:

▶ Before selecting, specify a feather amount in the Options bar.

▶ After selecting, click Refine Edge in the Options bar and adjust the Feather option. (We talk about Refine Edge in the next section.)

▶ After selecting, choose Select > Modify > Feather.

▶ Apply a Gaussian Blur to the selection's Quick Mask.

If you use the Refine Edge dialog, your entire selection is feathered. Sometimes, however, you want to feather only a portion of the selection. Maybe you want a hard edge on one half of the selection and a soft edge on the other. You can do this by switching to Quick Mask mode, selecting what you want feathered with any of the selection tools, and applying a Gaussian Blur to it. When you flip out of Quick Mask mode, the feathering is included in the selection.

Note that if you want a nice, soft feather between what is feathered and what isn't, you first have to feather the selection you make while you're in Quick Mask mode (see **Figure 9-13**).

Tip: You don't need to use whole numbers when feathering. We find we often need a value of only 0.5 or 0.7 to get the a nice, subtle transition we're looking for. It's a great way to anti-alias a hard-edged selection, mask, or channel.

Figure 9-13 Feathering part of a selection

Original image   *Anti-aliased selection*   *After Gaussian Blur*   *Mustache and neck feathered*

Refining a Selection

Software engineering teams sometimes make new features simply by streamlining multistep production chores. The Refine Edge dialog, new in Photoshop CS3, represents this type of new feature. In previous versions of Photoshop, if you applied the Select > Feather command, the only way to actually see the size of the feather was to view the selection as a quick mask or channel. And we have often mentioned how you can tweak a selection edge by converting the selection to a quick mask or a channel, and then using image-editing commands (such as Levels and Gaussian Blur) to alter contrast along the edges of the selection channel. Of course, that meant you had to know which series of operations would get you to the result you wanted.

Tip: Refine Edge isn't just an Options bar button. It's also a command (Select > Refine Edge), so you can also open it by pressing its keyboard shortcut—Command-Option-R (Mac) or Ctrl-Alt-R (Windows).

The Refine Edge dialog takes away much of that brainwork. Now you can simply tell Refine Edge how you want to tune the selection edge, and it's done. Behind the scenes, Refine Edge works with a selection as a channel, so that you don't have to go through those steps yourself. You can even use Refine Edge on a mask or channel.

To use Refine Edge, click the Refine Edge button in the Options bar while a selection tool and a selection are both active (see **Figure 9-14**). You'll see five sliders divided by a line. The Radius and Contrast options above the line set the initial edge, and the other three options below the line take it from there. The best way to use the controls is as they're laid out, in order from top to bottom.

Figure 9-14
Opening the
Refine Edge dialog

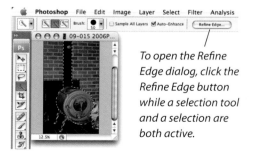

To open the Refine Edge dialog, click the Refine Edge button while a selection tool and a selection are both active.

Tip: Refine Edge should usually be your next step after using tools such as the Quick Selection or Magnetic Lasso. Those tools usually produce an edge that needs to be cleaned up.

Radius. Starting from the initial edge you created, the Radius value determines how far out Refine Edge extends the feathered transition between selected and unselected pixels. A higher Radius value can help when the exact edge is harder to identify, such as the edge of a soft shadow or hair.

Radius is more sophisticated than a standard feather or edge blur, in that it protects existing hues and creates a less artificial-looking transition. For a traditional feather, leave Radius at 0 and use the Feather slider instead (see **Figure 9-15**).

Figure 9-15
Using
Radius and Contrast

*Selection viewed in Refine
Edge at default settings*   *Radius widened to include
more hair variations*   *Contrast increased to
sharpen hair details*

*Original selection edge,
before using Refine Edge*

Contrast. This option determines the sharpness of the feathered transition across the radius you set. A higher value creates a sharper edge.

Smooth. The Smooth slider evens out bumps along the selection edge to help compensate for sloppy selections. However, if your edge follows details like hair, a high Smooth value can obliterate the details. If you have to set such a high Smooth value that you lose details, you may need to click Cancel and improve the precision of your initial selection (see **Figure 9-16**).

Figure 9-16
Adjusting Smooth
and Feather

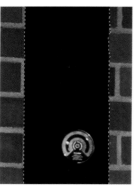

The Quick Selection tool created the bumpy-edged selection above, which we see in Refine Edge below.

Reducing the Feather value in Refine Edge creates a harder edge, which is appropriate for a metal stovepipe. However, the bumps become more obvious.

Increasing the Smooth value flattens the bumps. The selection is above and seen in Refine Edge below.

Feather. The Feather slider is essentially the traditional Feather command in Photoshop (which is still available at Select > Feather). It simply blurs the edge resulting from your Radius, Contrast, and Smooth settings.

Tip: To toggle the Refine Edge selection view off and on, press the X key. Of course, as in other dialogs, the P key toggles the Preview check box.

Contract/Expand. If your selection is a little bit inside or outside of the area you wanted to select, use Contract/Expand to compensate. As the last option in the second group of options, it acts on the results of the four options above it, so if no Contract/Expand value gets you what you want, try adjusting the other sliders (see **Figure 9-17**).

Selection View icons. The five icons along the bottom of the Refine Edge dialog are simply different ways of previewing the selection. They follow the basic principle we set forth earlier in the chapter: A selection can be represented as a marching-ants border, a Quick Mask, or a grayscale image channel. Click an icon to set the view your way, or just press F to toggle through the viewing modes with the keyboard.

Figure 9-17
Contract/Expand

Lowering the Contract/Expand value pulls the selection in from its original edge.

It isn't just for selections. Instead of using Levels and Curves to adjust layer mask edges, the Quick Mask view, and channels, the next time you need to do that, try Refine Edge instead. It's completely functional when a layer mask or channel is selected; it isn't necessary for the layer mask or channel to be visible. Sounds incidental, but this is actually a huge, huge feature—it means you can use Refine Edge to edit a layer mask while seeing its true effect on the final image.

Channels

Back in "Masking-Tape Selections," we told you that selections, masks, and channels are all the same thing down deep: grayscale images. This is not intuitive, nor is it easy to grasp at first. But once you really understand this point, you've taken the first step toward really surfing the Photoshop big waves.

A *channel* is a solitary grayscale image—each pixel described using either 8 bits or 16 bits of data, depending on whether or not it's a high-bit image. You can have up to 56 channels in a document—and that includes the three in an RGB image or four in a CMYK image. (Actually, there are two exceptions: First, images in Bitmap mode can only contain a single 1-bit channel; second, Photoshop allows one additional channel per layer to accommodate layer masks, which we'll talk about later in this chapter.)

But in the eyes of the program, not all channels are created equal. There are three types of channels: alpha, color, and spot-color channels (see

Figure 9-18
The Channels palette

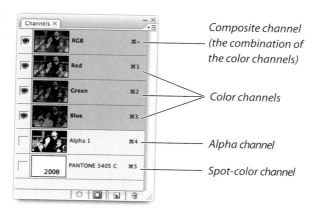

Composite channel (the combination of the color channels)

Color channels

Alpha channel

Spot-color channel

Figure 9-18). We discuss the first two here, and the third in bonus Chapter 13, "Spot Colors and Duotones." For the URL to download this chapter, see "Introduction: Photoshop in the Real World."

Alpha Channels

People get very nervous when they hear the term "alpha channel," because they figure that with such an exotic name, it has to be a complex feature. Not so. An *alpha channel* is simply a grayscale picture. Alpha channels let you save selections, but a solid understanding of these beasts is also crucial to tackling layer masks.

Saving selections. Again, selections and channels are really the same thing down deep (even though they have different outward appearances), so you can turn one into the other very quickly. Earlier in this chapter we discussed how you can see and edit a selection by switching to Quick Mask mode. But Quick Masks are ephemeral things, and aren't much use if you want to hold onto that selection and use it later.

When you turn a selection into an alpha channel, you're saving that selection in the document. Then you can go back later and edit the channel or turn it back into a selection.

As we pointed out in the last chapter, the slow way to save a selection is to choose Select > Save Selection. It's a nice place for beginners because Photoshop provides you with a dialog (see **Figure 9-19**). But pros don't bother with menu selections when they can avoid them. Instead, click the Save Selection icon in the Channels palette. Or, if you want to see the Channel Options dialog first (for instance, if you want to name the channel), Option-click (Mac) or Alt-click (Windows) the icon (see **Figure 9-20**).

Figure 9-19
Save Selection
dialog

Figure 9-20
Saving a selection

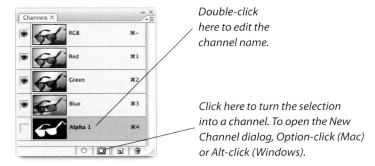

Double-click here to edit the channel name.

Click here to turn the selection into a channel. To open the New Channel dialog, Option-click (Mac) or Alt-click (Windows).

Of course, you can also assign a keyboard shortcut to the New Channel feature if you use it a lot.

Loading selections. Saving a selection as an alpha channel doesn't do you much good unless you can retrieve it. Again, the slowest method is to choose Select > Load Selection (though there are benefits to this method; see "Saving Channels in Other Documents," later in this chapter).

One step better is to Command-click (Mac) or Ctrl-click (Windows) on the channel that you want to turn into a selection. Even better, press the Command and Option (Mac) or Ctrl and Alt (Windows) keys along with the number key of the channel you want. For instance, if you want to load channel six as a selection on a Mac, press Command-Option-6. Note that if you press Command-Option-~ (tilde) (Mac) or Ctrl-Alt-~ (Windows), you load the luminosity mask. This isn't really the "lightness" of the image; rather, it's like getting a grayscale version of your image.

Channels in TIFF files. If you're saving a mess of channels along with the image you're working on, and you want to save the file as a TIFF, you should probably turn on LZW compression in the Save as TIFF dialog. Zip compression is even better, though QuarkXPress and most other programs

Tip: Every time it takes you more than 10 seconds to make a selection in your image, you should be thinking, "Save this selection." We try to save every complex selection as a channel or a path until the end of the project (and sometimes we even archive them, just in case). You never know when you'll need them again, and they don't take up that much space.

can't read Zip-compressed TIFF files yet. However, Adobe InDesign can, and of course you can always reopen Zip-compressed TIFF files in Adobe Photoshop. Whatever the case, use some kind of compression—otherwise, the TIFF will be enormous. Of course, you could save in the native Photoshop format, but we find that a Zip-compressed TIFF file is almost always smaller on disk (see Chapter 12, "Image Storage and Output").

Adding, subtracting, and intersecting Selections. Let's say you have an image with three elements in it. You've spent an hour carefully selecting each of the elements, and you've saved each one in its own channel (see **Figure 9-21**). Now you want to select all three objects at the same time.

Figure 9-21

Adding, subtracting, and intersecting selections

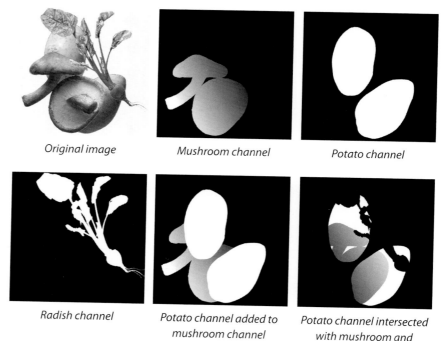

Original image

Mushroom channel

Potato channel

Radish channel

Potato channel added to mushroom channel

Potato channel intersected with mushroom and radish channels

In the good old days, you would have sat around trying to figure out the appropriate channel operations (using Calculations) to get exactly what you wanted. But it's a kinder, gentler Photoshop now. After you load one channel as a selection, you can choose Select > Load Selection to add another channel to the current selection, subtract another channel, or find the intersection between the two selections.

Even easier, use the key-click combinations in **Table 9-1**. Confused? Don't forget to watch the cursor icons; as you hold down the various key combinations, Photoshop indicates what will happen when you click.

Table 9-1

Working with selections

To get this…	…press this:
Add channel to current selection	Command-Shift-click (Mac) Ctrl-Shift-click (Windows)
Subtract channel from selection	Command-Option-click (Mac) Ctrl-Alt-click (Windows)
Intersect current selection and channel	Command-Shift-Option-click (Mac) Ctrl-Shift-Alt-click (Windows)

Moving Channels to Other Documents

As we said earlier, your alpha channels don't all have to be in the same document. In fact, if you've got more than 56 channels, you have to have them in multiple documents. But even if you have fewer than 56, you may want to save off channels in order to reduce the current file's size. Here are a bunch of tips we've found helpful in moving channels back and forth between documents.

Saving channels in other documents. As long as another file is currently open, you can save a selection into it using Save Selection, or you can load a selection (from a channel) from the file using the menu items. You can even save selections into a new document by selecting New from the Document pop-up menu in the Save Selection dialog.

If you have two similar documents open and you've carefully made and saved a selection in one image, you might want to use it in another image. Instead of copying and pasting the selection channel, take a shortcut and use the Load Selection dialog. You can load the selection channel directly by choosing it from the Document and Channel pop-up menus.

The catch here is that both documents have to have exactly the same pixel dimensions (otherwise, Photoshop wouldn't know how to place the selection properly).

If you've already saved your selection into a channel in document A, how can you then get that channel into document B? One method is to select the channel and choose Duplicate Channel from the Channel palette menu (see **Figure 9-22**). Here you can choose to duplicate the channel into a new

Tip: The fastest way to copy a channel between documents is to drag the channel's thumbnail from the Channels palette to the other document. It's less of a drag on the system than copying and pasting. Again, for the channel to align with the new document, the two documents must be the same size.

document or any other open document (as long as the documents have
the same pixel dimensions).

Dragging selections. Photoshop is full of little, subtle features that make
life so much nicer. For instance, you can drag any selection from one
document into another document using one of the selection tools. (The
Move tool actually moves the pixels inside the selection; the selection tools
move the selection itself.)

Normally, the selection "drops" wherever you releaese the mouse button. However, if the two documents have the same pixel dimensions, you
can hold down the Shift key to pin-register the selection (meaning it lands
in the same location as it was in the first document). If the images don't
have the same pixel dimensions, the Shift key centers the selection.

Color Channels

When a color image is in RGB mode (under the Mode menu), the image is
made up of three channels: red, green, and blue. Each of these channels
is exactly the same as an alpha channel, except that they're designated as
color channels. You can edit each color channel separately from the others.
You can independently make a single color channel visible or invisible.
But you can't delete or add a color channel without first changing the
image mode.

The first thumbnail in the Channels palette (above the color channels)
is the composite channel. Actually, this isn't really a channel at all. Rather,
the composite channel is the full-color representation of all the individual
color channels mixed together. It gives you a convenient way to select or
deselect all the color channels at once, and also lets you view the composite color image, even while you're editing a single channel.

Selecting and seeing channels. The tricky thing about working with channels is figuring out which channel(s) you're editing and which channel(s)
you're seeing on the screen. They're not always the same!

Selections from Channels

Why would you go through all the trouble of creating a selection if the selection was already made for you? More often than not, the selection you want is already hidden within the image; you only have to look at the color channels that make up the image (see "Color Channels," in this chapter).

Here's one good way to tease a selection mask out of an image (see **Figure 9-23**). We demonstrate these techniques in more detail in the step-by-step examples at the end of this chapter.

1. Switch through the color channels until you find the one that gives the best contrast between the element you're trying to select and its background.

2. Duplicate that channel by dragging the channel thumbnail onto the New Channel icon in the Channels palette.

3. Use Levels or Curves to adjust the contrast between the elements you want to select and the rest of the image.

4. Clean up the mask manually. We typically use the Lasso tool to select and delete areas, or the Brush tool with one finger on the X key (so you can paint with black, then press X to "erase" with white, and so on).

Using Levels and Curves. The real key to this tip is step number 3: using Levels or Curves. With Levels, concentrate on the three Input sliders to isolate the areas you're after.

In the Curves dialog, use the Eyedropper tool to see where the pixels sit on the curve (click and drag around the image while the Curves dialog is open, and watch the white circle bounce around on the curve). Then use the pencil in the dialog to push those pixels to white or black. The higher the contrast, the easier it is to extract a selection from it.

Some people use the Smooth button after making these sorts of "hard" curve maps. But in this case, we often run a small-value Gaussian Blur after applying the curve, so we just don't bother with smoothing the curve.

Using RGB. It's usually easier to grab selection masks from RGB images than from CMYK images. However, if you're going to switch from CMYK to RGB, make sure you do it on a duplicate of the image, because all that mode-switching damages the image too much.

Figure 9-23 Starting with a channel

Red channel

Green channel

Quick-and-dirty Levels adjustment to blue channel

Fine-tuned version of blue channel

Blue channel (best contrast)

The Channels palette has two columns. The left column contains little eyeball icons that you can turn on and off to show or hide individual channels. Clicking on one of the thumbnails in the right column not only displays that channel, but lets you edit it, too. The channels that are selected for editing are highlighted. The two columns are independent of each other because editing and seeing the channels are not the same thing.

Channel shortcuts. When you're jumping from one channel to another, skip the clicking altogether and press the Command (Mac) or Ctrl (Windows) key along with the number of the channel you want. For instance, in Mac OS X, Command-1 shows the red channel (or whatever the first channel is), and Command-4 shows the fourth channel (the first alpha channel in an RGB image or the black channel in a CMYK image). Sorry, there's no way (that we know of) to select channels above number nine with keystrokes. To select the color composite channel (deselecting all other channels in the process), press Command-~ (tilde) (Mac) or Ctrl-~ (Windows).

You can see as many channels at once as you want by clicking in the channel's eyeball check boxes. To edit more than one channel at a time, Shift-click on the channel thumbnail.

Note that when you display more than one channel at a time, the alpha channels automatically switch from their standard black and white to their channel color (you can specify what color each channel uses in Channel Options—double-click on the channel thumbnail).

The Select Menu

If making selections using lassos and marquees and then saving or loading them were all it took to make selections in Photoshop, life would be simpler, but duller. Fortunately for us, there are many more things you can do with selections, and they all—well, almost all—help immeasurably in the production process.

You can find each additional selection feature under the Select menu: Grow, Similar, Color Range, and Modify. Let's explore each of these and how they can speed up your work.

Grow

Earlier in the chapter, when we were talking about the Magic Wand tool, we discussed the concept of tolerance. This value tells Photoshop how much brighter or darker a pixel (or each color channel that defines a pixel) can be and still be included in the selection.

Let's say you're trying to select an apple using the Magic Wand tool with a tolerance of 24. After clicking once, perhaps only half of the apple is selected; the other half is slightly shaded and falls outside the tolerance range. You could deselect, change the tolerance, and click again. However, it's much faster to choose Select > Grow.

When you choose the Grow command, Photoshop selects additional pixels according to the following criteria:

1. First, it finds the highest and lowest gray values of every channel of every pixel selected—the highest red, green, and blue, and the lowest red, green, and blue of the bunch of already-selected pixels (or the highest cyan, magenta, yellow, and black, and so on).

2. Next, it adds the tolerance value to the highest values and subtracts it from the lowest values in each channel. Therefore, the highest values get a little higher and the lowest values get a little lower (of course, it never goes above 255 or below 0).

3. Finally, Photoshop selects every adjacent pixel that falls between all those values (see **Figure 9-24**).

In other words, Photoshop tries its hardest to spread your selection in every direction, but only in similar colors. However, it doesn't always work the way you'd want. In fact, sometimes it works very oddly indeed.

For instance, if you select a pure red area (made of 255 red and no blue or green), and a pure green area (made of 255 green and no red or blue), then select Grow, Photoshop selects every adjacent pixel that has any red or green in it as long as the blue channel is not out of tolerance's range. That means that it'll pick out dark browns, lime greens, oranges, and so on—even if you set a really small tolerance level (see **Figure 9-25**).

If you switch to a color channel (like red or cyan) before selecting Grow, Photoshop grows the selection based on that channel only. This can be helpful because it's much easier to predict how the Magic Wand and Grow features will work on one channel.

Figure 9-24
The Grow
command

After Magic Wand click   *After Grow*

Figure 9-25
Anomalies with the
Grow command

When the two center squares
are selected, Grow selects all the
bottom squares and none of the
top squares. Why? Because of
slight blue "contamination" in
the top squares.

Many of these colors are selected
unexpectedly with Grow.

Similar

The Grow command only selects contiguous areas of your image. If you're trying to select the same color throughout an image, you may click and drag and grow yourself into a frenzy before you're done. Choosing Select > Similar does the same thing as choosing Select > Grow, but it chooses pixels from throughout the entire image (see **Figure 9-26**).

Note that Similar and Grow are both attached to the settings on the Options bar when you have the Magic Wand selected; Photoshop applies both the Wand's tolerance and its anti-alias values to these commands. We can't think of any reason to turn off anti-aliasing, but it's nice to know you have the option.

Figure 9-26
The Similar
command

Selection made with Magic Wand.
A tolerance setting of 24 manages to avoid
the shadows and green areas.

After Similar is selected. Some
brighter areas of the apples
are still not selected.

Color Range

One of the problems with Similar and Grow is that you rarely know what you're going to end up with. On the other hand, Color Range lets you make color-based selections interactively, and shows you exactly which pixels will be selected. But there's one other advantage of Color Range over the Magic Wand features (we think of Similar and Grow as extensions of the Magic Wand).

The Magic Wand–based features either select a pixel or they don't (the exception is anti-aliasing around the edges of selections, which only partially selects pixels there). Color Range, however, fully selects only a few pixels and partially selects a lot of pixels (see **Figure 9-27**). This can be incredibly helpful when you're trying to tease a good selection mask out of the contents of an image.

There are four areas you should be aware of in the Color Range dialog: selection eyedroppers, the Fuzziness slider, canned sets of colors, and Selection Preview.

Tip: Color Range is always in Sample Merged mode. It sees your image as though all the visible layers were one. To exclude a layer from the selection mask, hide that layer before opening Color Range.

Adding and deleting colors. When you open Color Range, Photoshop creates a selection based on your foreground color. Then you can use the eyedropper tools to add or delete colors in the image (or, better yet, hold down the Shift key to get the Add Color to Mask eyedropper, or the Option/ Alt key to get the Remove Color from Mask eyedropper). Note that you can always scroll or magnify an area in the image. You can even select colors from any other open image.

Tip: To open the Color Range dialog with exactly the same settings you last used, hold down the Option key (Mac) or the Alt key (Windows) when choosing Select > Color Range.

The Fuzziness factor. The Fuzziness slider in the Color Range dialog is *not* the same as the Tolerance field on the Magic Wand Options bar. As we said

Figure 9-27 Magic Wand, Color Range, and Quick Selection compared
While you can make similar selections with the Magic Wand, Color Range, and Quick Selection, each is more efficient in particular situations. Magic Wand is faster for big, consistent areas; Color Range excels for finer details; and Quick Selection is effective at including dissimilar colors in one selection.

The original image. It is photographed on a good, uniform white background, and includes an area of relatively solid color (the reds) that is an obvious target for change.

Three quick Shift-clicks with the Magic Wand yield a very serviceable silhouette mask. A bit of feathering or a Gaussian Blur on the mask (combined with a Levels tweak to adjust the blur) deals with the hard edges.

Because the object is hard-edged to begin with, the Magic Wand's inability to partially select pixels doesn't pose much of a problem in compositing.

A mask created with Color Range (here with few sample points and a high Fuzziness setting) is more appropriate for subtle selections.

A detail of the mask shows that there are partially selected pixels (the gray areas), which create more natural edges for corrections and compositing.

This more-subtle mask is just the ticket for a Hue/Saturation tweak, changing the red areas to blue without an artificial look.

A mask created from the inside out using the Quick Selection tool, which makes it easy to include dissimilar colors within a specified boundary.

We used the mask to darken all of the main shape except for the red areas and the "eye."

earlier, pixels that fall within the tolerance value are either fully selected or not; pixels that fall on the border between the selected and unselected areas may be partially selected, but those are only border pixels. Color Range uses the Fuzziness value to determine not only whether a pixel should be included, but also how selected it should be. We're not going to get into the hard-core math, but **Figure 9-28** should give you a pretty good idea of how fuzziness works.

Sampling vs. Fuzziness. Should you use lots of sample points or a high Fuzziness setting? It depends on the type of image. To select large areas of similar color, tend toward a lower Fuzziness (10 to 15) to avoid selecting stray pixels. For fine detail, you need to use higher Fuzziness settings, because the fine areas are generally more polluted with colors spilling from adjacent pixels. Either way, try adding sample points to increase the selection range before you increase fuzziness.

Canned Colors

Instead of creating a selection mask with the eyedroppers, you can let Photoshop select all the reds, or all the blues, or yellows, or any other primary color, by choosing the color in the Select pop-up menu (see **Figure 9-29**). The greater the difference between the color you choose and the other primaries, the more the pixel is selected. (To get really tweaky for a moment: The percentage the pixel is selected is the percentage difference between the color you choose and the primary color with the next highest value.)

You can also choose from Highlights, Midtones, or Shadows—which we tend to use much more than the preset (what we call "canned") colors in the Select pop-up menu. When you choose one of these, Photoshop decides whether to select a pixel (or how much to select it) based on its Lab luminance value (see **Table 9-2** and Chapter 4, "Color Settings," for more information on Lab mode).

We find selecting Highlights, Midtones, and Shadows most useful when selecting a subset of a color we've already selected (see the tip near the top of this page).

Invert the Color Range selection. Do you often find yourself following up a Color Range selection by choosing Select > Invert? If you are trying to select the opposite of what's selected in the Color Range dialog, you can remove that extra step by turning on the Invert check box in the Color

Tip: Color Range picks up the specified color everywhere it occurs in an image. To tell Color Range to pick up colors only within a particular area, select that area first.

Tip: You can change your Quick Mask options settings while the Color Range dialog is open. Hold down the Option key (Mac) or Alt key (Windows) while selecting Quick Mask from the Selection Preview pop-up menu.

Figure 9-28 Fuzziness versus sample points for Color Range

Four selections created with Color Range. At far right is the result of a Hue/Saturation move on the selection.

Few sample points, low fuzziness

Few sample points, high fuzziness

Many sample points, low fuzziness

Many sample points, high fuzziness

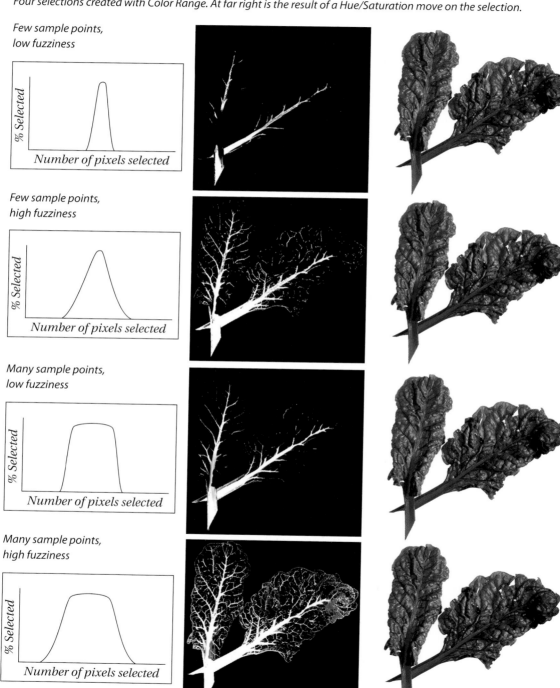

Figure 9-29
Color Range
dialog

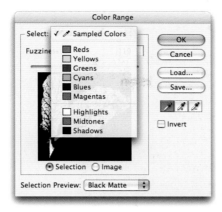

Table 9-2
Ranges for Color Range
(L value in Lab mode)

Select name	Fully selected pixels	Partially selected pixels
Shadows	1–40	40–55
Midtones	55–75	40–55 and 75–85
Highlights	80–100	75–85

Range dialog; Photoshop automatically inverts the selection for you. If you already have a selection made when you invert the Color Range selection, Photoshop deselects the Color Range pixels from your selection.

Selection Preview. The last area to pay attention to in the Color Range dialog is the Selection Preview pop-up menu. When you select anything other than None (the default) from this menu, Photoshop previews the Color Range selection mask.

The first choice, Grayscale, shows you what the selection mask would look like if you saved it as a separate channel. The second and third choices, Black Matte and White Matte, are the equivalent of copying the selected pixels out and pasting them on a black or white background. This is great for seeing how well you're capturing edge pixels. The last choice, Quick Mask, is the same thing as clicking OK and immediately switching into Quick Mask mode.

Because the Selection Preview can slow you down, we recommend turning it on only when you need to, then turning around and switching back to None. It can be really helpful in making sure you're selecting everything you want, but it can also be a drag on productivity.

Tip: Instead of using the Image and Selection radio buttons, press the Command or Control key (either one works on the Mac). This toggles between the Selection Preview and Image Preview much faster than you can click buttons.

Modify

When you think of the most important part of your selection, what do you think of? If you answer, "what's selected," you're wrong. No matter what you have selected in your image, the most important part of the selection is the boundary or edge. This is where the tire hits the road, where the money slaps the table, where the invoice smacks the client. No matter what you do with the selection—whether you copy and paste it, paint within it, or whatever—the quality of your edge determines how effective your effect will be.

When making a precise selection, you often need to make subtle adjustments to the boundaries of the selection. The four menu items on the Modify submenu under the Select menu—Border, Smooth, Expand, and Contract—focus entirely on this task.

Border. Police officers, take note: There's a faster way to get a doughnut than driving down to the local Circle K. Draw a circle using the Marquee tool, then choose Select > Modify > Border. You can even specify how thick you want your doughnut (in pixels, of course). Border transforms the single line (the circle) into two lines (see **Figure 9-30**).

The problem with Border is that it only creates soft-edged borders. If you draw a square and give it a border, you get a soft-edged shape that looks more like an octagon than a square. In many cases, this is exactly what you want and need. But other times it can ruin the mood faster than jackhammers outside the bedroom window. To get a harder edge out of the Border command, switch to Quick Mask mode (press Q), then use the Levels or Curves dialog to adjust the edge of the selection. If the edge of the selection is too jaggy, apply a 0.5-pixel Gaussian Blur to smooth it out. Remember that when you're in Quick Mask mode, you can select the area to which you want to apply the levels or blur.

Creating More Border Options. Here's one other way to make a border with a sharper, more distinct edge.

1. Save your selection as an alpha channel.

2. While the area is still selected, choose Select > Modify > Expand.

3. Save this new selection as an alpha channel.

4. Load the original selection from the alpha channel you saved it in.

Figure 9-30
Border

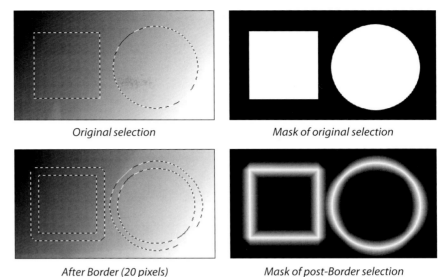

Original selection   *Mask of original selection*

After Border (20 pixels)   *Mask of post-Border selection*

5. Choose Select > Modify > Contract.

6. Mix the two selections (expanded and contracted) together by Command-Option-clicking (Mac) or Ctrl-Alt-clicking (Windows) the other channel.

You can save this selection and delete one or both of the other alpha channels you saved. Note that you don't have to expand *and* contract the selection; this method also lets you choose to only contract or expand.

Note that we also discuss another way to make borders (edge masks) in Chapter 10, "Sharpness, Detail, and Noise Reduction."

Smooth. The problem with making selections with the Lasso tool is that you often get very jaggy selection lines; the corners are too sharp, the curves are too bumpy. You can smooth these out by choosing Select > Modify > Smooth. Like most selection operations in Photoshop, this actually runs a convolution filter over the selection mask—in this case, the Median filter. That is, selecting Smooth is exactly the same thing as switching to Quick Mask mode and choosing the Median filter.

Smooth has little or no effect on straight lines or smooth curves. But it has a drastic effect on corners and jaggy lines (see **Figure 9-31**). Smooth looks at each pixel in your selection, then looks at the pixels surrounding it (the number of pixels it looks at depends on the Radius value you choose in the Smooth dialog). If more than half the pixels around it are selected, then the pixel remains selected. If fewer than half are selected, the pixel becomes deselected.

Figure 9-31
Smooth

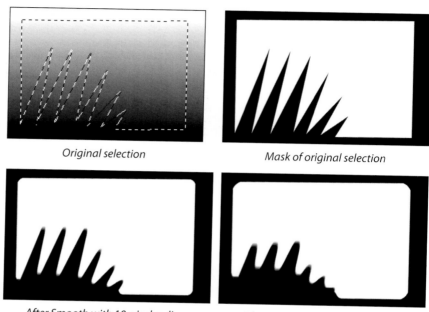

Original selection

Mask of original selection

After Smooth with 10-pixel radius

After Smooth with 16-pixel radius

If you enter a small Radius value, only corner tips and other sharp edges are rounded out. Larger values make sweeping changes. It's rare that we use a radius over 5 or 6, but it depends entirely on what you're doing (and how smooth your hand is!).

Expand and Contract. The Expand and Contract features are two of the most useful selection modifiers. They let you enlarge or reduce the size of the selection. This is just like spreading or choking colors in trapping (if you don't know about trapping, don't worry; it's not relevant here).

Once again, these modifiers are simply applying filters to the black-and-white mask equivalent of your selection. Choosing Expand is the same as applying the Maximum filter to the mask; choosing Contract is the same as applying the Minimum filter (see **Figure 9-32**).

Note that if you enter 5 as the Radius value in the Maximum or Minimum dialog (or in the Expand or Contract dialogs), it's exactly the same as running the filter or selection modifier five times. The Radius value here

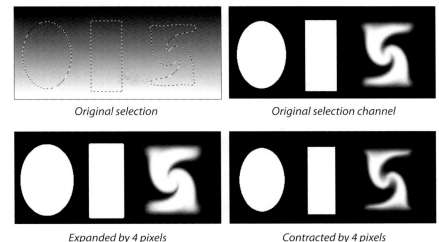

Figure 9-32
Expand and Contract

Original selection   *Original selection channel*

Expanded by 4 pixels   *Contracted by 4 pixels*

is more of an "iteration" value; how many times do you want the filter applied at a 1-pixel radius?

While we frequently find these selection modifiers useful, they aren't very precise. You can only specify the radius in 1-pixel increments. For a lot more control, use the Refine Edge dialog instead.

Selections and Layers

We've talked about making selections; we've talked about saving channels; now it's time to delve into masks—specifically: transparency masks, layer masks, and using layers as a mask. But as you read the following pages, don't forget that masks are just channels, which are 8-bit (or 16-bit) grayscale images. Photoshop also lets you build a hard, vector-edged mask that is *not* based on a channel, called a *vector mask*; we'll discuss this in "Shapes and Vector Masks," in Chapter 11, "Essential Image Techniques."

Transparency Masks

Most of the time when you create a new layer, the background is transparent. When you paint on it or paste in a selection, you're making pixels opaque. Photoshop is always keeping track of how transparent each pixel is—fully transparent, partially transparent, or totally opaque. This information about pixel transparency is called the *transparency mask* (see **Figure 9-33**).

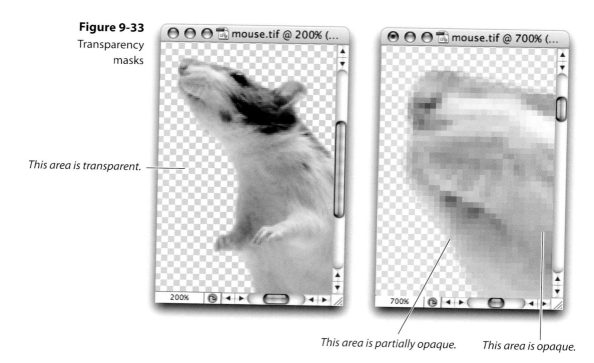

Figure 9-33
Transparency
masks

This area is transparent.

This area is partially opaque.   This area is opaque.

Remember the analogy we made to masking tape earlier in the chapter? The selection/channel/mask (they're all the same) acts like tape over or around your image. In this case, however, the mask doesn't represent how selected a pixel is; it's how transparent (or, conversely, how visible) it is. You can have a pixel that's fully selected but only 10 percent opaque (90 percent transparent).

Layer Masks

It's hard to emphasize in print just how important nondestructive editing is in our workflow. Perhaps you're compositing several images on a background, or you're retouching an image, or you're adjusting the hue and brightness of a photograph. Whatever the case, you know that after hours of sweat and mouse-burn, when you show the result to your art director, she's going to say, "Move this over a little, and we need a little more of this showing here, and you shouldn't have changed the color of this part...."

Fortunately, you can use layer masks to avoid this sort of nightmare in your work. Layer masks are just like transparency masks—they determine how transparent the layer's pixels are—but you can see layer masks and, more importantly, edit them (see **Figure 9-34**). If you had used nondestructive layer masks, instead of erasing or editing your original pixels, you would have smiled at your art director and made the changes quickly and painlessly. Here's how you do it.

Figure 9-34 Layer masks

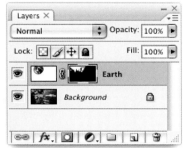

The earth is on a separate layer above the background image of the car.

The layer mask

After the layer mask is applied to the Earth layer

Creating and editing layer masks. To apply a layer mask to a selected layer, choose Layer > Add Layer Mask. When a layer has a mask, it can have only one (or two, if you include layer clipping paths)—the Layers palette displays a thumbnail of the mask (see **Figure 9-35**).

Faster layer masks. While there's no built-in keyboard shortcut to add a layer mask (you can assign one if you want), it is a little faster to click on the Add Layer Mask icon in the Layers palette. If you Option-click (Mac) or Alt-click (Windows) on the Add Layer Mask icon, Photoshop inverts the layer mask (so that it automatically hides everything on the layer).

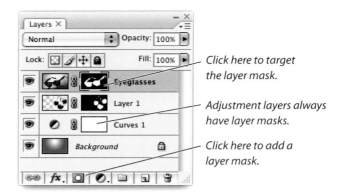

Figure 9-35
Adding a
layer mask

*Click here to target
the layer mask.*

*Adjustment layers always
have layer masks.*

*Click here to add a
layer mask.*

Tip: To fade an effect across a layer (such as an adjustment layer in which you want to affect only the sky), use the Gradient tool to add a gradient to the layer mask. If the gradient isn't quite right, open the Levels or Curves dialog and make adjustments to the layer mask itself. These tonal adjustments to the mask give you almost infinite control over how your effect is applied.

Note that you can make a selection before clicking on the icon. In this case, the program "paints in" the unselected areas with black for you (on the layer mask). This is usually much easier than adding a layer mask, then using the paint tools to paint away areas. Of course, Option-clicking (Mac) or Alt-clicking (Windows) on the icon with a selection paints the selected areas with black, so that whatever was selected "disappears."

At first, it's difficult to tell whether you're editing the layer or the layer mask. But there are two differences: The layer mask thumbnail has a dashed border around it (on a high-resolution screen, the two borders look about the same) and the document title bar says "Layer *x* Mask." We typically glance at the title bar about as often as we look in our car's rear-view mirror; it's a good way to keep a constant eye on what's going on around us.

Editing a mask is as simple as painting with grays. Painting with black on the layer mask is like adding masking tape; it covers up part of the adjoining layer (making those pixels transparent). Painting with white takes away the tape and uncovers the layer's image. Gray, of course, partially covers the image.

Tip: By default, moving a layer also moves its layer mask. To move them independently, turn off the Link icon (click between the layer and layer mask previews in the Layers palette).

Paint it in using masks. Layer masks let you paint in any kind of effect you want. For example, duplicate the Background layer of an image in the Layers palette, apply a filter to the new layer (like Unsharp Mask), then Option/Alt-click on the Add Layer Mask icon to mask out the entire effect. Now you can paint the effect back in using the Brush tool and non-black pixels. If you change your mind, you can paint away the effect with black pixels. This flexibility is addictive, and you'll soon find yourself using this technique over and over, whether it's painting in texture, sharpening or blurring, or whatever.

Getting rid of the mask. As soon as you start editing layer masks, you're going to find that you want to turn the mask on and off so you can get before-and-after views of your work. You can make the mask disappear temporarily by choosing Layer > Layer Mask > Disable. Or do it the fast way: Shift-click on the Layer Mask icon.

If you want to hide the mask with extreme prejudice—that is, if you want to delete it forever—choose Layer > Layer Mask > Delete (or, faster, drag the Layer Mask icon to the Trash icon). Photoshop gives you a last chance to apply the mask to the layer. Note that if you do apply the mask, the masked (hidden) portions of the layer are actually deleted.

All layer masks go away when you merge or flatten layers.

Layer mask shortcuts. When you're working on a layer, you can jump to the layer mask (which is making it active, so all your edits are to the mask rather than the image) by pressing Command-\ (Mac) or Ctrl-\ (Windows). When you're ready to leave the layer mask, press Command-~ (tilde) (Mac) or Ctrl-~ (Windows) to switch back to the composite view.

If you Option-Shift-click (Mac) or Alt-Shift-click (Windows) the Layer Mask icon in the Layers palette (or just press the \ key—that's the back-slash), Photoshop displays the mask *and* the layer, as if you're in Quick Mask mode. If you don't like the color or opacity of the layer mask, you can Option-Shift-double-click (Mac) or Alt-Shift-double-click (Windows) the icon to change the mask's color and opacity. Then, when you're ready to see the effects of your mask editing, Option-Shift-click (Mac) or Alt-Shift-click (Windows) the icon again to "hide" it (or press backslash again). If you want to see only the layer mask (as its own grayscale channel), Option/Alt-click its icon. This is most helpful when touching up areas of the layer mask (it's sometimes hard to see the details in the mask when there's a background image visible).

Layers as Masks

Layers not only have masks, but they can act as masks for other layers. The trick is to use *clipping masks*. Normally, putting one layer above

---

Tip: If you used to press Command-G (Mac) or Ctrl-G (Windows) to create a clipping mask, note that you now need to add the Option key (Mac) or Alt key (Windows). This is because the old shortcut was reassigned to the Layer > Group Layers command for consistency with other applications. If you want it to work the old way, simply redefine the shortcut using Edit > Keyboard Shortcuts.

Tip: The fastest way to load the transparency mask for a layer as a selection is to Command/Ctrl-click on the layer's thumbnail in the Layers palette. For instance, if you want to create a selection from text on a type layer, Command/Ctrl-click on the type layer's thumbnail. This loads the selection, and you're ready to roll.

another obscures the lower layer. When you create a clipping mask, the lower layer acts as a mask for the upper layer, so that the upper layer appears only where the lower layer is visible (see **Figure 9-36**).

Figure 9-36
Using a layers as masks

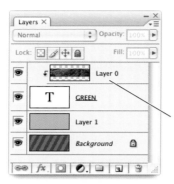

Option-clicking (Mac) or Alt-clicking (Windows) between the layer thumbnails causes Layer 0 to use the underlying layer as a mask, so that the grass shows through the type. Layer 0 becomes indented in the Layers palette, indicating that it is using a clipping mask.

To create a clipping mask, first position the content layer immediately above the mask layer in the Layers palette (you can't do this with more than two layers), and then do one of the following.

▶ Option-click (Mac) or Alt-click (Windows) between their thumbnails in the Layers palette.

▶ Press Command-Option-G (Mac) or Ctrl-Alt-G (Windows), which is a shortcut for Layer > Create Clipping Mask.

It's possible to have multiple layers indented above the clipping mask, in case you want one clipping mask to affect multiple layers.

Masking Layer Groups

A layer group can have a mask, and that's handy for creating nested masks. Select the layers, group them by pressing Command-G (Mac) or Ctrl-G (Windows), which is the shortcut for choosing Layer > Group Layers, and then add a mask to that layer group (see **Figure 9-37**).

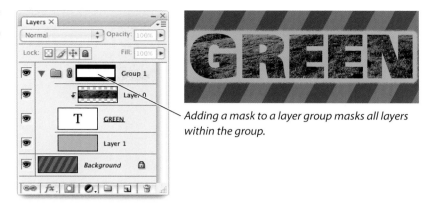

Figure 9-37
Masking a layer group

Adding a mask to a layer group masks all layers within the group.

Step-by-Step Selections

If there's one thing that makes silhouettes difficult, it's the edge detail. In most cases (especially when you're trying to select fine details), some of the color from the image background spills over into the image you want, which causes an obvious fringe when you drop the silhouetted image onto a different background (even white). While the addition of Refine Edge goes a long way toward automating these processes, we sometimes find it more effective to use the old-school manual methods of massaging selections with the full range of image-processing capabilities in Photoshop.

Pulling Selections from Channels

Trying to build a selection mask for the tree in **Figure 9-38** with the basic selection tools would drive you to distraction faster than having to watch *Barney and Friends* reruns with your four-year-old. Instead, we found the essence of a great selection hiding in the color channels of the image. While you can often pull a selection mask from a single channel, in this case we made duplicates of both the blue and green channels. Then, using Levels, we pushed the tree to black and the background to white. After combining the two channels, it took only a little touch-up to complete the mask.

Removing Spill with Preserve Transparency

Edge spill is insidious, and—as you saw in the last example—it can be a disaster when compositing images. Here's one more method for removing spill that we like a lot. If you place the pixels on a transparent layer, you can make use of the Preserve Transparency feature in the Layers palette to "paint away" the edge spill.

Figure 9-38 Creating subtle masks from multiple channels

The original. Our goal: to select the tree and make it more green.

The blue channel has the best contrast between sky and tree.

The green channel has the best contrast between tree and grass.

We copy the blue channel, and force the sky to white and the tree to black with the Levels dialog.

A similar move on the green channel creates a mask for the lower part of the tree.

We delete the "garbage" areas from each mask with the Brush and Lasso. To edit the channels better, we make the mask and the color channels visible at the same time.

We use Calculate (Add) to merge the two channels into one, providing the final mask.

After loading the selection mask, we use Curves to brighten and saturate the greens in the tree, and we pull back the reds and blues slightly.

Tip: Two filters can help you create selections by enhancing edges: Find Edges and High Pass. We typically duplicate the image we're working on, then use one or more filters on the copy to extract the selection we want. Find Edges can bring out edges that are hard to see onscreen. The trick to using High Pass is to use very small values in the High Pass dialog, usually less than one or two pixels. Then, you can use the Levels or Curves dialog to enhance the edges by increasing the contrast of the image.

In the example in **Figure 9-39**, the color from the blue sky is much too noticeable around the composited trees. So we place the trees on a layer and build a selection that encompasses just their edges. This step is really just a convenience—it makes our job of painting out the edge spill easier. With Preserve Transparency turned on, we select the Clone Stamp tool and clone interior colors over the blue edge pixels. In some areas, we also use Curves to pull the blue out (because our border selection is feathered, these moves affect only the pixels we're after).

This is a trick you can use with all sorts of variations. If the edge color is relatively flat, you might be able to use the Brush tool (we usually add a little noise after painting in order to match the background texture); this is also an area where it behooves you to test out different Apply modes (Lighten, Multiply, and so on).

Enhancing Edges with Adjustment Layers

Adjustment layers are almost always used for tonal or color adjustments (we talk about adjustment layers in quite some detail in Chapter 8, "The Digital Darkroom)." But here's a method that Greg Vander Houwen showed us that uses adjustment layers to help make selections. This is particularly useful when you're trying to select a foreground image out of a background, and the two are too similar in color (see **Figure 9-40**).

First, add an adjustment layer above the image. You can make a radical adjustment in this layer and know that you're not actually hurting your original image data. Boost the contrast between the foreground and background so that you can make a better selection.

Using Plug-Ins for Complex Masks

After working with the Photoshop selection tools for a while, you begin to know instinctively when you're up against a difficult task. For instance, trying to create a selection mask for a woman in a gauzy dress, with her long, wispy hair blowing in the wind, could be a nightmare. And if you have to perform 20 of these in a day…well…'nuf said. It's time to plunk down some cash for one of the several masking programs on the market—for instance, Mask Pro from OnOne Software or KnockOut from Corel.

We're not saying that these plug-ins are perfect. In fact, far from it. But they can often get you 90 percent of the way to a great selection in 10 percent of the time it would take you with Photoshop itself.

Figure 9-39 Painting out edge spill using layers, a border mask, and Preserve Transparency

The original image

A mask created using Color Range

The trees are copied onto a layer above the sunset image. The blue spill ruins the compositing effect.

A close-up of the composited image shows the blue edge spill from the original sky.

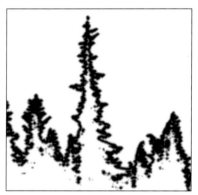

We create a border mask by using Border on the transparency mask, then running a Gaussian Blur.

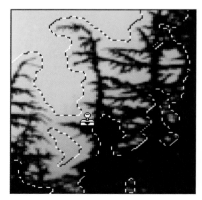

With the border mask selection loaded and Preserve Transparency turned on, we use the Clone Stamp tool to paint dark interior pixels over the blue pixels.

The final image after the blue edge spill has been removed

A close-up of the final image

Figure 9-40 Using adjustment layers to emphasize elements and build masks

The original image

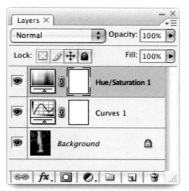

We add two adjustment layers: a Curves layer that drastically increases the image contrast, and a Hue/Saturation layer that desaturates the image slightly.

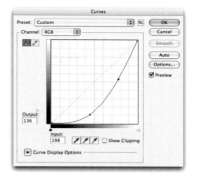

The Curves dialog of the Curves adjustment layer. Note that the shadows have been completely blown out to black. The curve has also been tweaked on the red, blue, and green channels.

After these extreme adjustment layers are applied, the image looks almost unrecognizable.

We duplicate one of the channels of this "extreme" image and clean it up for our water mask. Now we can throw away the adjustment layers (they've done their job).

Finally, we load our new mask into the layer mask of a new, more subtle Hue/Saturation adjustment layer. This way, the effect only affects the water.

10

Sharpness, Detail, and Noise Reduction

Getting an Edge on Your Image

The human visual system depends to a great degree on recognizing edges. Our eyes pass information to our brain, where every detail is quickly broken down into "edge" or "not edge." (Thousands of years of evolution have developed our brains to ignore most of what's going on in our field of vision and instead focus immediately on moving edges that might turn out to be a hungry tiger.) An image may have great contrast and color balance, but without good edge definition, we simply see it as less lifelike.

No matter how good your camera or scanner and how crisp your original may be, you always lose some sharpness when an image is digitized. Images from scanners and digital cameras always need a considerable amount of sharpening, though high-end scanners may sharpen as part of the scanning process. Even a high-resolution digital camera back mounted on a finely focused view camera produces images that will benefit from sharpening. You *cannot* solve the problem of blurry scans by scanning at a higher resolution. It just doesn't work that way.

Your images also lose sharpness in the output process. Halftoned images (almost anything on a printing press) and dithered ones (such as those printed on inkjet or other desktop printers) are by far the worst offenders. But even continuous-tone devices such as film recorders and dye-sublimation printers lose a little sharpness.

Detail and Noise

In addition to detail, images contain *noise*—digital captures have camera noise, film scans have film grain that may be exacerbated by scanner noise. We only want to sharpen the detail, not the noise. However, because it's hard for software to tell the difference between noise and detail, all noise-reduction solutions have to walk the fine line between increasing edge detail and decreasing noise.

In Photoshop itself, we generally apply noise-reduction techniques only on very noisy images—scans of color negatives and digital captures at ISO 800 and up are prime candidates. When working with digital raw captures, we often make use of the noise reduction in Adobe Camera Raw. Otherwise, we prefer to concentrate on sharpening the available detail but not the noisy areas, partly because we don't want to soften the image unnecessarily with noise reduction, and partly to avoid another workflow step.

When we do perform noise reduction—either the Reduce Noise filter in Photoshop or a third-party plug-in such as Noise Ninja, Grain Surgery, or Neat Image—we always do so before sharpening, for the simple reason that it works better than doing so afterward (why sharpen noise?). We'll cover noise reduction further later on in this chapter.

Lens Defects

Lenses introduce their own quirks to the mix. Some lenses are simply sharper than others. (The Lens Blur mode in the Smart Sharpen filter specifically addresses lens softness.) A second lens problem, which we encounter a great deal more with digital capture than we did with film, is chromatic aberration, where the lens fails to deliver the red, green, and blue wavelengths to the same plane of focus, producing color fringing. It's a particular problem towards the wide end of wide-angle zooms.

We suspect that we see chromatic aberration in digital capture more than in film simply because digital is much less forgiving to lenses. Film grain and interlayer scattering of the light tend to mask chromatic aberration where digital capture reveals it quite brutally—shooting film and digital with the same lens tend to bear this out. The Lens Correction filter can address chromatic aberration in Photoshop, but if you have a raw, JPEG, or TIFF file, you may prefer the slightly more interactive chromatic aberration correction controls in Adobe Camera Raw (see Chapter 5, "Building a Digital Workflow.")

We'll cover noise reduction and lens corrections in the course of this chapter, but while only some images need noise reduction or lens fixes, *every* image needs sharpening, so that's where we'll start.

Sharpening

To counteract the blurries in both the input and output stages, you need to sharpen your images. Photoshop offers several sharpening tools, but Unsharp Mask and Smart Sharpen are the only ones that really work as production tools. The Sharpening tool and the other sharpening filters may be useful for creative effects (and even then, we prefer other approaches), but they'll wreck your images very quickly if you use them to compensate for softness introduced during either acquisition or output.

Smart Sharpen is a newer, more powerful sharpening filter than Unsharp Mask. However, if you want to understand sharpening, the place to start is the Unsharp Mask filter. It's easier to understand and executes more quickly than Smart Sharpen.

Unsharp Masking

Unsharp masking (often abbreviated as USM) may sound like the last thing you'd want to do if you're trying to make an image appear sharper, but the term actually makes some sense; it has its origins in a traditional film-based technique for enhancing photographic sharpness.

The things we see as edges are areas of high contrast between adjacent pixels. The higher the contrast, the sharper the edges appear. So to increase sharpness, you need to increase the contrast along the edges.

In the traditional process, the photographic negative is sandwiched in the enlarger along with a slightly out-of-focus duplicate negative—an unsharp mask—and the exposure time for printing is approximately doubled. Because the unsharp mask is slightly out of focus and the exposure time has been increased, the light side of the edges prints lighter and the dark side of the edges prints darker, creating a "halo" around objects in the image (see **Figure 10-1**).

As you'll see throughout this chapter, this halo effect is both the secret of good sharpening and its Achilles' heel depending on the size and intensity of the halo and where it appears in the image. Photoshop lets you control the halo very precisely, but there's no single magic setting that works for all images; so you need to know not only how the controls work, but also what you're trying to achieve in the image.

Figure 10-1
Edge transitions and
sharpening

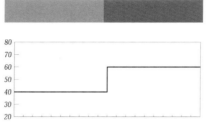

This image and graph depicts an edge transition—from 40 to 60 percent. Each tick mark across the bottom of the graph represents a column of pixels.

After sharpening, the transition is accentuated—it's darker on the dark side, and lighter on the light side, creating a halo around the edge.

The effect on images ranges from subtle to impressive to destructive. This image is somewhat oversharpened to make the effect clear.

Unsharpened

Sharpened

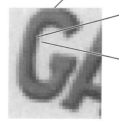

These samples are darker after sharpening.

These samples are lighter after sharpening.

The net result is a sharper-looking image.

How the Unsharp Mask Filter Works

The Unsharp Mask filter operates pixel by pixel, which explains why it can sometimes take so long. It compares each pixel to its neighbors, looking for a certain amount of contrast between adjacent pixels, which it assumes is an edge. It then increases the contrast between those pixels according to the parameters you set. This creates a halo that, at normal viewing distances, increases apparent sharpness.

But Photoshop can't actually detect edges—it just looks at contrast differences (zeros and ones again). So unsharp masking can also have the undesired effect of exaggerating texture in flat areas and skin tones, and emphasizing any noise introduced by the scanner in the shadow areas.

You need to walk a fine line, sharpening only where your image needs it. The filter itself has few controls to adjust what gets sharpened (see **Figure 10-2**). So, we much prefer running sharpening through a mask. But to do so, you still need to understand the settings you can control in the Unsharp Mask filter, what they do, and how they interact.

Figure 10-2
The Unsharp
Mask filter

Amount

We think of Amount as the volume control—it adjusts the intensity of the sharpening halo (see **Figure 10-3**). High Amount settings—you can enter up to 500 percent—produce intense halos with many pixels driven to pure white or solid black); low Amount settings produce less intense ones. Amount has no effect on the width of the halos—just on their contrast.

Figure 10-3
Varying the USM
Amount setting

Image resolution: 266 ppi
Radius: 0.5
Threshold: 0

Amount: 65   *Amount: 175*   *Amount: 350*

As you increase the Amount setting, the blips around big tonal shifts (edges) can be pushed all the way to white and black. At that point, increasing Amount has no effect—you can't get more white than white! Worse, the all-white halos often stand out as artifacts and can look really dumb.

We almost always start out by setting Amount much higher than we'll eventually want it—between 400 and 500—until we set the Radius. Then we adjust downward from there, depending on the image (see "Working the Controls," later in this chapter).

Radius

Radius is the first thing to consider when sharpening; it sets the width of the halo the filter creates around edges (see **Figure 10-4**). The wider the halo, the more obvious the sharpening effect. Choosing the correct Radius value is probably the most important choice in avoiding an unnaturally oversharpened look, and there are several factors to take into account when you choose, starting with the content of the image itself, the output method, and the intended size of the reproduction (see the sidebar "Image Detail and Sharpening Radius," later in this chapter).

Note that a Radius value of 1.0 does not result in a single-pixel radius. In fact, the halo is often between 4 and 6 pixels wide for the whole light and dark cycle—two or three pixels on each side of the tonal shift. However, it varies in width depending on the content of the image.

Tip: If sharpening looks too strong after closing the Unsharp Mask dialog, choose Edit > Fade and lower the Opacity value (see "Filters and Effects" in Chapter 11, "Essential Image Techniques.")

Figure 10-4
Varying the USM
Radius setting

Image resolution: 266 ppi
Amount: 250
Threshold: 0

Radius: 0.4   Radius: 0.9   Radius: 1.6

Threshold

Unsharp Mask only evaluates contrast differences: it doesn't know whether those differences represent real edges you want to sharpen or areas of texture (or, even worse, scanner noise) that you don't want to sharpen. The Threshold control lets you specify how far apart two pixels' tonal values have to be (on a scale of 0 to 255) before the filter affects them (see **Figure 10-5**). For example, if Threshold is set to 3, and two adjacent pixels have values of 122 and 124 (a difference of two), they're unaffected.

You can use Threshold to make the filter ignore the relatively slight differences between pixels in smooth, low-contrast areas while still creating a halo around details that have high-contrast edges. And, to some extent at least, you can use it to avoid exaggerating noisy pixels in shadow areas.

Low Threshold values (0 to 4) result in a sharper-looking image overall (because fewer areas are excluded). High values (above 10) result in less sharpening, but often produce unnatural-looking transitions between the sharpened and unsharpened areas. We typically start out with a zero Threshold value, and then increase it only if necessary.

Tip: If your computer is on the slow side, try turning off the Preview check box to avoid the time-consuming full-screen redraw of the preview. You can still use the preview inside the Unsharp Mask dialog to check the results. Remember, pressing the mouse button inside the dialog preview toggles between the before and after states.

Figure 10-5
Varying the USM Threshold setting

Image resolution: 266 ppi
Amount: 350
Radius: 0.7

Threshold: 0   Threshold: 6   Threshold: 12

Everything's Relative

One of the most important concepts to understand about sharpening is that the three values you can set in the Unsharp Mask dialog are interrelated. For instance, as you increase the Radius setting, you generally need to decrease Amount to keep the apparent sharpness constant. Similarly, at higher Radius settings, you can use much higher Threshold values; this smooths out unwanted sharpening of fine texture while still applying a good deal of sharpness to well-defined edges.

Working the Controls

When we're trying to determine the right sharpening settings for an image, we start by setting the Radius. We usually start out with exaggerated Amount and Threshold settings (400 percent and 0), then we experiment with the Radius value. The exaggerated Amount and Threshold make it easy to see what's happening as we adjust the Radius (see **Figure 10-6**).

Figure 10-6 Radius versus Amount versus Threshold

Very different USM settings can combine to provide equivalent apparent sharpness. We've sharpened this 225 ppi image with four different settings for Amount, Radius, and Threshold.

230 / 0.6 / 12   *390 / 0.6 / 33*   *79 / 4 / 19*   *300 / 5 / 113*

As you increase the Radius, the apparent sharpness also increases—often to an undesirable extent. This is where the aesthetic considerations come in. Some people like more sharpening than others. We find highly sharpened images more disturbing than slightly soft ones, but that's a matter of taste. It's up to you to decide how much sharpening you want.

However much sharpening you decide to apply, you'll find that as you increase the Radius setting, you need to decrease the Amount to keep the apparent sharpness constant. You can work these controls in opposition to achieve a wide range of sharpening effects.

Tip: To start over with any filter, press Command-Z (Mac) or Ctrl-Z (Windows) to undo, then press Command-Option-F (Mac) or Ctrl-Alt-F (Windows) to reopen the filter dialog with the last-used settings.

Threshold is the third part of the equation. You can think of it as a selective smoothing function. At small (less than 1 pixel) Radius settings, a Threshold value as low as 15 or so will probably wipe out most of the sharpening effect. At higher Radius settings, you can use much higher Threshold values to smooth out unwanted sharpening of fine texture while still applying a good deal of sharpness to well-defined edges.

There are dangers lurking here, though. As you use higher Amount and Threshold settings, you run an increased risk of driving pixels to solid black or solid white. The solid black ones aren't usually too much of a problem, but the blown-out white ones can appear as noticeable artifacts, especially when they're large due to higher Radius settings.

With higher Threshold settings, you get dramatic, unnatural sharpening of high-contrast edges while leaving smaller details soft. This makes the image look quite disturbing because it's hard for the eye to reconcile the sharp edges and the soft detail. The image looks like there's something wrong with the focus.

In short, the three parameters provided by Unsharp Mask give you a lot of control over the sharpening effect, but it takes a while to get your head around the way they interact.

A Practical Sharpening Workflow

If we got a nickel for each time we'd been asked what sharpening settings someone should use, we'd probably be sipping wine on a tropical island rather than writing books on Photoshop. Of course, we couldn't really come up with a short answer any less lame than "it depends."

The longer answer, of course, involves explaining the various factors on which it depends, which we'll now proceed to do. First, a necessary disclaimer: PixelGenius, a company Bruce co-founded, publishes a sharpening plug-in called PhotoKit Sharpener. While we'd be pleased as punch if you considered purchasing PhotoKit Sharpener, you should know that a lot of what it does is based on the information in this chapter. The plug-in just does it a lot faster than you can do it manually.

To understand how to sharpen, we first have to understand why we're doing it at all. It turns out that there are basically three reasons why an image might need to be sharpened. Each of those reasons imposes its own demands, and often, these demands contradict one another. Fortunately, the reasons break down nicely into three stages that are easy to handle separately and in sequence during a production workflow.

Tip: For a deeper dive into the multistage sharpening workflow, pick up a copy of Bruce's book *Real World Image Sharpening in Photoshop CS2.*

Sharpening the capture. Whenever you turn photons into pixels, you lose some sharpness, because no matter how high the resolution of your capture devices, they sample a fixed grid of pixels, turning the continuous gradations of tone and color that exist in the real world into discrete pixels. Each capture device imposes its own noise pattern on the image, whether it's from digital camera sensor noise or film grain.

You need to sharpen the image content to restore what was lost in the conversion to pixels, but you don't want to also sharpen—and hence emphasize—the noise and grain. The goal of capture sharpening is to take into account the source of the image, compensating only for the amount of sharpness lost to a specific digital camera or scanner sensor.

Tip: If noise reduction is required, we'll do it before sharpening, by running the Despeckle filter through a mask, running Reduce Noise on its own merged layer, or if it's a digital camera raw file, we may employ the noise reduction in Adobe Camera Raw 4.1 or Lightroom. When extreme noise reduction is required, we'll apply a mask to the noise reduction layer to protect the edges.

Sharpening the image content. People often sharpen for creative reasons: to tell a story, to make a point, to emphasize an area of interest, or to sell a product. To do this successfully, you need to match your sharpening to the content of the image. A busy, high-frequency image with lots of tiny details, like a forest full of trees, has much narrower edges than a close subject with soft detail, like a head shot or a pumpkin (see Figure 10-7).

When sharpening image content, you want to emphasize the edges without overemphasizing textures—like skin tones—and without introducing spurious texture into flat areas, like skies. The point of creative sharpening is to take the image content into account, reproducing its details as effectively as possible.

Sharpening the output. When you print, you lose sharpness again. In most cases, individual pixels aren't translated into individual dots of ink or dye, and even in those cases where they are (such as when printing to photographic printers like the Durst Lambda or Fujifilm Pictrography) the printed "pixels" tend to be round rather than square. In either case, the output loses some sharpness. Because you want to make the print as sharp as the output device can render it, effective sharpening must take into account the output process.

The chances are exceedingly slim that you can satisfy all these different sharpening criteria with a single round of Unsharp Mask applied globally to the image. Of course, if one pass of Unsharp Mask is all you have time for in your workflow, it's better than not sharpening at all. But for the highest quality (and flexibility when an image is expected to be repurposed), we recommend using a two- or three-stage approach to sharpening which we'll lay out soon. Rather than try to satisfy all the criteria simultaneously, this workflow approach to sharpening addresses them separately.

Of course, if approached carelessly, this workflow can create ugly images. Just hitting the image with three rounds of Unsharp Mask using different radii is a recipe for certain disaster. Instead, retaining optimum quality requires finesse and some fairly advanced sharpening techniques.

We'll admit that taking a workflow approach to sharpening is a fairly radical idea, but the more we use it, the more we find that it makes sense. We've done a great deal of testing—Bruce reckoned that he sharpened about 5000 images to build and fine-tune PhotoKit Sharpener—but plenty of work remains to be done. We look at individual sharpening techniques in detail later in this chapter, but here's the 30,000-foot overview.

Capture Sharpening

Our first sharpening pass aims to compensate for the shortcomings of the capture in a way that's sensitive to the image content. We create a sharpening layer, apply an edge mask, sharpen with a radius that matches the image content, then constrain the tonal range to the midtones using the Blend If sliders in the Layer Style dialog. We use the edge mask so that only the high-contrast edges get sharpened. We use the Blend If sliders to focus the sharpening on the midtones, protecting highlights and shadows so that they don't get driven to solid black and solid white.

With very grainy or noisy originals such as high-ISO digital capture or fast color negative, you may first want to apply some noise reduction using the Reduce Noise filter or a third-party noise reduction plug-in. If you're working with raw digital camera files, you can use the sharpening sliders in Adobe Camera Raw 4.1 or Lightroom 1.1—their sharpening features were specifically designed for the capture sharpening stage, so that you only need to use Photoshop for creative and output sharpening.

This first round of sharpening must be done very gently indeed; otherwise the result is likely to be a hideously oversharpened mess. Remember, it's only the first stage of sharpening, where you essentially perfect the capture. Don't try to solve all of an image's sharpening issues at this stage, because all you need to do here is set a solid baseline of overall sharpness that you'll build on during the next two stages.

Creative Sharpening

In the creative sharpening pass, we concentrate on the sharpening needs of the image content itself. If we find ourselves wanting to apply different amounts of sharpening to various parts of an image, this is the time to do it. We apply creative sharpening after we've fine-tuned the tone and color both globally and locally, because changes to contrast and color can easily affect the perceived sharpness.

Image Detail and Sharpening Radius

You can achieve the same apparent sharpness with many different combinations of the Amount, Radius, and Threshold settings, but the difference between good and bad sharpening lies largely in matching the Radius setting to the image content.

To set the Radius value properly, look closely at the image. How big, in pixels, are the details that you want to sharpen? You need to match the size and intensity of the sharpening halo to the size of the details in the image.

High-frequency images contain a lot of detail, with sharp transitions between tonal values, while *low-frequency* images have smoother transitions and fewer small details. Whether a given image is high frequency or low frequency depends on the content of the image and on its pixel density. High-frequency images, where the edges of objects are

reproduced using only one or two pixels, need a smaller Radius setting than low-frequency images, where the edges may be a dozen or so pixels wide.

An image containing fine detail, such as a picture of trees, is likely to have many more high-frequency transitions than a head shot, for example. But if you scan the trees at a high enough resolution, even the edges on the tiniest leaves will be reproduced several pixels wide in the scan. So it isn't *just* the content that dictates the sharpening, it's the relationship between content and resolution.

Unpleasant settings. Too large a radius is the prime cause of oversharpened images. Moreover, an overly large radius can actually wipe out the detail it's supposed to be accentuating. Too small a radius can result in too little apparent sharpening. This might

in turn seduce you into cranking up the Amount setting so far that you create spurious specular highlights and overemphasize textures such as skin in undesirable ways. With very extreme settings, you can change the overall image contrast—which in most cases isn't what you want.

Figure 10-7 shows two images that need very different sharpening settings. The trees contain fine details that need a low Radius setting and a fairly high Amount setting to bring them out. If we apply the same sharpening to the pumpkin, it fails to bring out the necessary detail, while threatening to create unpleasant mottling.

Conversely, sharpening settings that work well on the pumpkin don't work at all well on the trees. The larger Radius sharpens the larger elements well, but the more delicate elements in the trees are lost. It creates a very confused

For creative sharpening, you can build "sharpening brushes" to paint your sharpening just where you want it, such as the eyes of a portrait. One way to do this is to create a new merged layer, setting the layer's blending mode to Luminosity (to avoid color-fringing), applying a global Unsharp Mask to the layer, then adding a layer mask set to Hide All. As you paint on the layer mask, Photoshop adds or removes the sharpening.

Creative sharpening effects are really only limited by your imagination. For example, one way to make an object appear sharper is to blur its surroundings—you can create "smoothing brushes" using the same techniques as sharpening brushes, but substituting a blur for the sharpen.

Figure 10-7 Unsharp Mask settings for high- and low-frequency images

Settings that work for one image can be ineffective or destructive on another. Resolution: 266 ppi

| *Unsharpened* | *High-frequency settings:* | *Low-frequency settings:* |
| | *Amount 275, Radius 0.6, Threshold 3* | *Amount 200, Radius 2, Threshold 9* |

appearance, where the same element in the image appears sharp in some places and soft in others.

A good strategy is to get the Radius setting correct first. You can then achieve the degree of sharpness you want by tweaking the Amount setting. Finally, adjust the Threshold setting to suppress noise and to avoid oversharpening patterns, film grain, and the like.

After capture and creative sharpening, we end up with an idealized image—corrected and enhanced as far as possible without being shackled to one specific purpose, size, or output device. You can still repurpose it (our mothers always taught us to keep our options open as long as possible), and responds well to resizing and final output sharpening.

Output Sharpening

Since the image-specific and source-specific concerns were already addressed in the capture and creative sharpening phases, output sharpening can concentrate solely on the requirements of the output process.

We apply output sharpening globally, by using a sharpening layer with no layer mask. For halftone and inkjet outputs, we often use the Hard Light/High Pass sharpening technique. Output sharpening *must* be done at final output resolution. If you think it's likely the image will be resized after it leaves your hands, we advise omitting the output sharpening step; anyone who resizes the image will probably resharpen it anyway, and if you've done a reasonably good job in the capture and creative phases, the final result will still be sharp.

The key difference between output sharpening and the earlier phases is that more often than not we produce a result that looks downright scary on the monitor. Keep in mind the physical size of the sharpening halo on output. Light and dark contours that are 3 pixels wide may look hideous on the monitor; but if you're printing at 300 ppi, they'll translate into contours (light and dark parts of the sharpening halo) that are only $\frac{1}{100}$ of an inch wide, so they won't be obvious on the final print.

Note that you can only sharpen the image's pixels—Photoshop has no control over how those pixels are rendered to ink on paper (or any other output process). So the key factor in output sharpening is the relationship between the pixels and the resulting hard copy. Hence output sharpening must be done at the final size and resolution, often as the last step before converting an RGB file to CMYK and saving the file to disk. Note that unlike capture and creative sharpening, output sharpening is something we always apply globally. Here are a few other considerations:

> ► A rule of thumb that has served us well is to aim for a sharpening halo of approximately $\frac{1}{50}$- to $\frac{1}{100}$-inch (0.5 to 0.25 mm) in width, the thinking being that at normal viewing distances, a halo this size falls below the threshold of human visual acuity, so you don't see the halo as a separate feature, you just get the illusion of sharpness that it produces.
>
>   For output sharpening, a good starting point for the Unsharp Mask filter's Radius setting is image resolution ÷ 200. (Remember: we're talking about final image resolution, after it has been placed on a page and scaled to fit.) Thus, for a 300-ppi image, you'd use a Radius of 1.5 (300 ÷ 200). For a 200-ppi image, you'd use a Radius setting of 1. This is a suggested starting point, not gospel. As you gain experience, you'll find situations where the rule has to be bent. When sharpening using methods that don't involve Unsharp Mask, you'll have to look closely and do some math yourself.

Tip: To keep output-specific edits, such as output sharpening, from accidentally being saved with your layered master image, choose Image > Duplicate (with the Duplicate Merged Layers Only option enabled) to create a flattened duplicate document. You can then apply output-specific optimizations to the copy, such as the appropriate sharpening settings for the printer you're about to use.

▶ On very large prints, you may have to use a slightly larger sharpening halo—if the resolution is less than 100 ppi, the halo will be larger than $\frac{1}{50}$-inch because it takes at least two pixels (one light, one dark) to create the halo. But large prints are generally viewed from further away, so the longer viewing distance tends to compensate for the larger halo.

▶ Of course, there's really no way to get an accurate onscreen representation of how a sharpened halftone output will look—the continuous-tone monitor display is simply too different from the halftone. An image well-sharpened for halftone output will typically look "crunchy" on screen. And the monitor resolution and view percentage can help or hinder your appraisal of an image's sharpness. See the sidebar "Sharpening and the Display" for more on the subject.

Attempting to show the apparent onscreen sharpness in print is a very uncertain endeavor. What we've attempted to do in **Figure 10-8** is to show the image pixels at 200 percent through the various phases of sharpening, along with the final printed image at print size, in the hope that doing so will give you some idea of the relationship between what happens to the pixels themselves and the influence on the final printed result.

Obviously, the onscreen appearance at Actual Pixels view will vary dramatically over different display types and resolutions, but as you zoom in, the differences between display types become much less significant. We hope that the figure at least demonstrates the dramatic differences in halos created by the capture and creative sharpening phases, and those created by the final output sharpening. To help understand what you're seeing, we've also noted the sharpening settings we used for each step of the sharpening process, from capture to final output.

Output sharpening is the only phase that easily lends itself to a formula, because once the image has been sized and the output process chosen, the physical size of the pixels, and hence of the sharpening halos, is a known quantity. For the capture and creative phases of the sharpening workflow, common sense, good taste, and in the long run, experience are the best guides! The techniques that follow are ones that we use every day in our sharpening workflow, and as we describe them, we'll tell you how we use them. But we don't claim to have solved every conceivable sharpening problem, so feel free to pick and choose, and to adapt them to your own work.

Figure 10-8 The sharpening workflow

The first pass: Capture sharpening applied on a layer (with an edge layer mask) set to the Luminosity blending mode at 66 percent opacity. Unsharp Mask applied at Amount 100, Radius 0.8, Threshold 0.

The unsharpened image pixels at 200 percent view

Capture sharpening at 200 percent view

Creative sharpening applied on a layer set to Overlay at 50 percent opacity, Unsharp Mask applied at Amount 500, Radius 0.6, Threshold 0, then High Pass filter applied at Radius 5. Sharpening brushed in with a brush at 33 percent opacity.

Creative sharpening at 200 percent view

We downsampled the image from its native 3072-by-2048 pixels to 488-by-732 pixels using Bicubic Sharper interpolation in the Image Size dialog. Final output sharpening was applied to a layer set to Luminosity at 66 percent opacity, with Unsharp Mask set to Amount 187, Radius 1.3, Threshold 0 to produce to the result at right. A detail is shown below.

Downsampled to print size, then sharpened for output, at 200 percent view

The final image

Sharpening Techniques

We use a host of techniques in the sharpening workflow—some obvious, others less so. Some attempt to avoid accentuating dust and scratches, noise, and film grain by sharpening through a mask. Others seek to make sharpening nondestructive and editable after the fact by applying the sharpening on a layer, and still others use localized sharpening applied with a brush to pick out specific details in the image. In practice, we often mix these techniques into a single sharpening move, and we'll provide some examples. However, it's easier to digest the various techniques separately, so that's how we'll present them.

Tip: Some people like to sharpen images by converting them to Lab and sharpening only the Lightness channel. You can get an almost identical result by sharpening the RGB file, then choosing Edit > Fade, and set the Mode to Luminosity. It's faster, and you don't lose layers through a mode change.

Sharpening with Layers

We prefer to do most of our sharpening on layers, for much the same reasons we prefer using adjustment layers to burning Curves or Levels directly into an image—it's nondestructive, it affords us control after the fact, and it allows us to use masking when we need to. In the first stage of the sharpening workflow, layer-based sharpening also provides an easy way to concentrate the sharpening in the midtones through the Blend If sliders in the Layer Options dialog.

Figure 10-9 shows the steps for creating a sharpening layer on a flat file or on a layered one. The layer is set to Luminosity mode to avoid any color shifts or color fringes—it produces essentially the same result as converting the image to Lab and sharpening the Lightness channel. You can then run the Unsharp Mask filter globally on the layer or apply Unsharp Mask through an edge mask.

Figure 10-9
Setting up
a sharpening layer

On a flat file, duplicate the Background layer and set the duplicate to Luminosity mode.

On a layered file, create a new layer, then merge the visible layers into the new one by pressing Command-Option-Shift-E (Mac) or Ctrl-Alt-Shift-E (Windows), or hold down Option (Mac) or Alt (Windows) while choosing Layers > Merge Visible. Then set the new layer to the Luminosity blending mode.

Sharpening and the Display

Back in the days when all our monitors were CRTs, we thought we had a good idea of how to judge sharpness from the screen. But the vast differences in apparent sharpness between LCD and CRT monitors, and the research we've undertaken in applying output sharpening, have caused us to reevaluate that position.

LCD monitors are much, much sharper than CRTs at any given display resolution. Moreover, an image will appear quite different in terms of sharpening at a lower display resolution than it will at a higher one.

So where color management lets us compensate for a huge range of different display behaviors, we have no such solution for sharpening.

What we do have is a new set of very general rules of thumb. Use these with caution: You need to learn the relationship between what you see on your particular display at your preferred resolution and the resulting output (just as you had to do with color in the days before color management). With that caveat in mind, here are some very general guidelines.

Zoom percentage. We believe it's a good idea to look at the Actual Pixels view to see what's happening to the actual image pixels, but unless your output is to a monitor, Actual Pixels view may give a fairly misleading impression of the actual sharpness on output.

For halftone output, bear in mind that each halftone dot may be comprised of four image pixels. Viewing at 25 percent or 50 percent view may give a truer impression of halftone sharpness. Avoid the "odd" zoom percentages—33.3, 66.6, and so on, because Photoshop applies fairly heavy anti-aliasing to those views. For inkjet output, the key factor is the resolution you're sending to the printer. Look at the even-division zoom percentage that comes closest to reproducing the image at actual print size on the display.

How sharp is sharp? For the first two passes of sharpening—capture and localized creative—our general rule of thumb is to apply sharpening that looks good on a CRT display, or very slightly over-sharpened on an LCD.

For output sharpening, you can really push the sharpening far beyond what looks acceptable on the monitor at Actual Pixels view, particularly when you print at higher resolutions (like 350 ppi for a 175-lpi halftone or 360 ppi for an inkjet print).

The key here is to bear in mind the actual size of the pixels on output. At 360 ppi, each pixel is only $\frac{1}{360}$ of an inch, so to produce a $\frac{1}{50}$ of an inch halo, you'd need a dark contour approximately 3.6 pixels wide ($\frac{1}{100}$ of an inch) and a light contour the same size.

Sharpening with Smart Filters

Photoshop CS3 brings a new way to keep sharpening separate from the original layer: Smart Filters, which extend the Smart Object feature that first appeared in Photoshop CS2. With Smart Filters, you enjoy a freedom of choice with filters that's similar to what you have with adjustment layers. Unlike Undo steps and the Fade command, you can edit the settings of a Smart Filter at any time without altering the original layer, even after you close and reopen a document.

You can apply a filter as a Smart Filter only to a Smart Object; if you're working with a file from Adobe Camera Raw that you opened as an object, you're ready to go. With any other layer, you must first select the layer and choose Filter > Convert for Smart Filters (which is actually the same as

Tip: A stack of Smart Filters can have only one mask for all of the filters in the stack. If you need to use a separate mask for each filter, you may have to stick with duplicating the image layer.

Figure 10-10
Using Smart Sharpen as a
Smart Filter

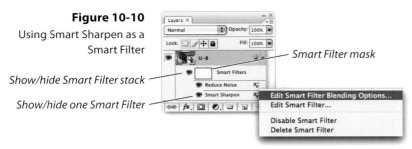

Show/hide Smart Filter stack

Show/hide one Smart Filter

Smart Filter mask

In the Layers palette, all Smart Filters for a layer are listed under a single Smart Filter heading indented within that layer. To control the blending mode and opacity, Ctrl-click (Mac) or right-click the empty area of a Smart Filter and choose Edit Smart Filter Blending Options.

For Smart Filters, use the Blending Options dialog instead of the Fade command or the Layers palette blending controls.

Tip: When evaluating what a layer looks like with Smart Filters off, avoid hiding or showing individual Smart Filters whenever possible, because it forces Photoshop to re-render the entire filter stack. It's dramatically faster to click the eye icon next to a layer's Smart Filters heading in the Layers palette, which hides and shows all Smart Filters, because then all Photoshop has to do is hide or show the cached image for the entire layer stack.

choosing Layer > Smart Object > Convert to Smart Object). As long as a layer is a Smart Object, applying any available filter from the Filter menu creates a Smart Filter, shown in the Layers palette under a Smart Filters heading indented under the layer that uses them (see **Figure 10-10**). Not all filters are available as Smart Filters, but many of our favorite production filters are, including Unsharp Mask and Smart Sharpen. To edit a Smart Filter, just double-click it in the Layers palette.

One subtle aspect of Smart Filters you need to get is how to fade them. You can't use the Layers palette blending mode or Opacity controls to edit a Smart Filter independently of its layer or the layer's other Smart Filters, and the Edit > Fade command isn't available either. What do you do? Ctrl-click (Mac) or right-click the Smart Filter thumbnail and choose Edit Smart Filter Blending Options, where you see a Mode pop-up menu, an Opacity value, and a preview (see Figure 10-10).

Given the ways that Smart Filters preserve your options indefinitely, it sure sounds like Smart Filters could be editing nirvana. Unfortunately, it isn't. Smart Filters suffer from the same gotchas that afflict Smart Objects: They place huge demands on the CPU and on disk space, slowing down operations and creating very large files. For this reason, Conrad sometimes talks about Smart Objects as "editing with credit cards." That is, Smart Objects give you a lot of very desirable power and flexibility, but overusing them can create an ongoing burden that can cost more than you expected.

We ran a quick test to see whether Unsharp Mask applied to a duplicate layer would take up more or less disk space than Unsharp Mask applied to the original layer as a Smart Filter. We found that a 13.7 MB TIFF file became a 36.2MB TIFF file after duplicating the original layer, running Unsharp Mask on the duplicate layer, and creating and painting on a layer mask for the duplicate layer. We took an unaltered copy of the original file and applied the same filter settings and mask, but this time as a Smart Filter, and ended up with a file size of 49.8 MB. The difference in RAM usage was similarly dramatic.

The trade-off is clear. If you've got the CPU, the RAM, and the disk space, Smart Filters can totally revolutionize your workflow, but on a machine with mediocre performance or limited available disk space, the old-school techniques will help preserve your sanity.

Edge Masking

Edge masks are an indispensable tool for both sharpening and noise reduction. When sharpening, we use an edge mask to concentrate the effects of the sharpen on the edges, so that flat areas such as skies, and textured areas such as skin tones, don't get oversharpened. For noise reduction, we use the same kind of mask, but inverted, so that the edges are protected from the noise reduction.

Figure 10-11 shows the steps for building an edge mask. The first step is to create a channel that has good contrast between the edges and the non-edges. Sometimes one of the existing color channels will work—simply duplicate the channel to serve as the basis for the edge mask—but often you can achieve better results by using Channel Mixer or Calculations to create the channel. See "The Color of Grayscale" in Chapter 11, "Essential Image Techniques," for a slew of methods for creating a grayscale version of an image.

Once you have a grayscale version of the image, run the Find Edges filter to locate the edges, then use a combination of blurring and contrast adjustments to control the relationship of the edges and non-edges. Once you've created the edge mask, you can load it as a selection through which you apply the sharpening, or you can add it to the sharpening layer as a layer mask. Each approach has advantages and disadvantages.

Edge mask as selection. To load the edge mask as a selection, Command-click (Mac) or Ctrl-click (Windows) on the channel's thumbnail in the Channels palette. We suggest hiding the selection's marching ants by pressing Command-H (Mac) or Ctrl-H (Windows), the shortcut for the View >

Figure 10-11 Building an edge mask

Add a new channel, either by duplicating an existing color channel, or by using the channel mixer to create a grayscale version of the image. Then run the Find Edges filter to isolate the edges.

The raw image

The new channel

The new channel after Find Edges

A Gaussian Blur softens the transitions and blurs the noise.

Inverting the image creates white edges where we want sharpening.

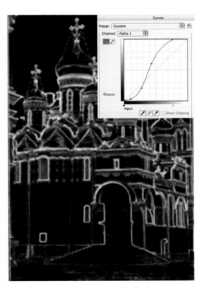

A Curves move controls the contrast between edges and non-edges.

Extras command. Then, with the sharpening layer targeted, you can run Unsharp Mask. The white areas in the edge mask get fully sharpened, the black areas are fully protected from sharpening, and the gray areas receive sharpening proportional to the gray value.

The disadvantage is that you have no control over the transition between sharpened and unsharpened areas once you've applied the sharpening.

Edge mask as layer mask. Instead of sharpening through the mask as a selection, you can sharpen the layer globally, then add the edge mask as a layer mask: Load the edge mask as a selection, target the sharpening layer, and then click the Add Layer Mask icon in the layers palette (see Chapter 9, "Making Selections").

Once you've added the layer mask, you can tweak the contrast of the layer mask with Levels or Curves to fine-tune the relationship between the sharpened and unsharpened areas. The downside to using the edge mask as a layer mask (rather than just sharpening the selection) is simply that it creates a larger file. **Figure 10-12** shows the steps for applying the edge mask as a selection or as a layer mask.

Figure 10-12
Applying the edge mask

To apply the edge mask as a selection, Command-click (Mac) or Ctrl-click (Windows) the edge mask channel's thumbnail.

After the mask is loaded as a selection, use it to create a layer mask. In the Layers palette, click the sharpening layer, and then click the Add Layer Mask icon.

Edge mask for noise reduction. You can use approximately the same edge-masking technique to apply noise reduction instead of sharpening. Invert the mask (or omit the inverting step when creating the mask), leaving the edges black (so that they're protected from the noise reduction), and the non-edges white (so that they receive the full benefit of noise reduction). It's usually a good idea to use a slightly different blur, as well as different contrast, on the noise mask than on the edge mask—if you simply invert them, you can exaggerate the transition between the edges and non-edges in both the noise reduction and sharpening layers. Making the masks slightly different helps a great deal.

We find that the Despeckle filter does a great job of minimizing film grain and digital noise, but we generally apply it separately to each color channel, because typically one channel will need more applications than another. With film or print scans, the blue channel is almost invariably the noisiest, so we may run Despeckle once on the red channel, twice on the green channel, and three or more times on the blue channel. On digital images captured as JPEG, we look at each channel to determine where the noise lies and Despeckle accordingly. With digital raw images, unless they're extremely noisy, we rely on the noise-reduction features in Camera Raw. Note that in Adobe Camera Raw 4.1, the Mask slider in the Detail tab creates an edge mask for the image; see "The Detail Tab" in Chapter 5, "Building a Digital Workflow."

If the noise is primarily in luminosity, as it is with transparency film, we prefer to carry out noise reduction on a layer that's set to Luminosity blending. Using separate layers for sharpening and noise reduction offers more control, but at the cost of a larger file size.

We also use masks with the new Reduce Noise filter, especially on higher-resolution film scans, where the filter seems to want to preserve the grain as well as the detail. The ability to edit the layer mask adds a level of post-filtering control that we often find useful.

Controlling the Tonal Range

One of the keys to a successful multipass sharpening workflow is to concentrate the first round of sharpening on the midtones while protecting the extreme highlights and shadows. It's so much easier to do this using a sharpening layer that we don't even try to use a nonlayered sharpen. The trick to controlling the tonal range is to use the Blend If sliders in the Layer Style dialog—choose Layer > Layer Style > Blending Options, or double-click the layer's thumbnail in the Layers palette (see Figure 10-13).

The Blend If sliders let you control which tonal values in the overlying (sharpening) layer get applied to the underlying layer (and, conversely, which tonal values in the underlying, unsharpened layers are affected by the sharpening layer). Bruce talked about the overlying layer as a ton of bricks suspended over a basket of eggs (the underlying layers). The top Blend If slider controls which bricks fall, and the bottom Blend If slider dictates which eggs receive the impact.

Figure 10-13 Controlling the tonal range

The Blend If sliders let us focus sharpening on the midtones.

Unsharpened   Before blending tweak   After blending tweak

Here, the top sliders fully apply tonal values between level 65 and 200, and gradually feather values from 65–20 and 200–245.

The bottom sliders protect the underlying values below 20 and above 245, and feather the adjustment to values from 20–40 and 230–245.

The result is that the contrast of the dark and light sharpening halos is reduced, allowing headroom for subsequent creative or output sharpening.

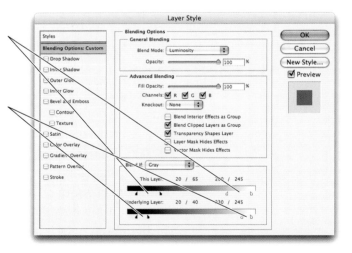

Figure 10-13 shows some typical settings for the Blend If sliders for initial midtone sharpening. Depending on the image source (film or digital) and the amount of noise present, you may find that the shadow values need to be set higher or lower, but the basic principle is to set the bottom sliders to protect extreme highlights and shadows, and the top sliders to apply most of the sharpening in the midtones.

Sharpening Brushes

For localized creative sharpening, nothing beats painting with a brush. We have two methods that we use to make a sharpening brush: one using a layer, the other using History. Layer-based brushes offer more control because you can control the local opacity of the layer mask by brushing with different opacities, and you can control the strength of the entire sharpening layer by varying the opacity of the layer itself. However, layers increase your file size. Using the History brush is less controllable (because your only control is through the brush opacity itself) but doesn't increase file size.

Layer-based sharpening brush. To create a layer-based sharpening brush, first make a sharpening layer as we showed earlier in **Figure 10-8**. It's usually a good idea to apply slightly more sharpening to the layer than you ultimately desire, because that way you have more control after the fact. Next, add a layer mask set to Hide All. To brush in the sharpening, make sure that the layer mask is targeted, then choose the Brush tool, set the foreground color to white, and simply brush the sharpening in as desired. We prefer to use a brush set to substantially less than 100 percent opacity, because it gives you some headroom to increase sharpening by increasing opacity. **Figure 10-14** shows the results of a sharpening brush.

History Brush sharpening. If you're too lazy to create masks, you're in a RAM-limited situation, or if you just want more interactivity than a mask offers, you can use the History Brush to paint sharpening into the image. This is a particularly handy technique with a pressure-sensitive stylus. By setting the pressure-sensitivity of the stylus to Opacity, you can achieve fine control over both the strength of the sharpening and where it's applied. The basic technique is a simple three-step process:

1. Apply the Unsharp Mask filter.

2. Set the History state to the step before you applied Unsharp Mask, and the source for the History brush to the Unsharp Mask step.

3. Paint the sharpening into the image as desired.

Or, if you prefer, you can *reduce* the sharpening with the History Brush by leaving the History state at the Unsharp Mask step, and then loading the step before it as the History Brush source. We typically choose the method that will require least brushwork on the image at hand.

Figure 10-14 A layer-based sharpening brush

The unsharpened image

*The unmasked sharpening layer
(before choosing Hide All)*

*The sharpening, brushed
in locally on the mask*

The unmasked sharpening layer

The brushed layer mask

The unsharpened image in **Figure 10-15** is quite soft. If we apply enough sharpening to pick up the texture in the fabric, it leaves the skin crunchy, which is bad at the best of times, but particularly so on babies!

In this case, it's much less work to set the History Brush source to the unsharpened state and brush out the crunchies than it would be to brush them in. A few quick strokes with a soft, low-opacity History Brush produce the much more pleasing rendition shown in Figure 10-15.

Luminosity Sharpening with History. Earlier you saw that you can apply luminosity sharpening by choosing Edit > Fade after running the Unsharp Mask filter (and by setting the blending mode in the Fade dialog to Luminosity). If you're brushing sharpening in rather than out, you can do the same thing by setting the blending mode for the History Brush to Luminosity using the Mode pop-up menu in the Options bar (see **Figure 10-16**).

Figure 10-15

Sharpening with the History brush to avoid crunchy skin

 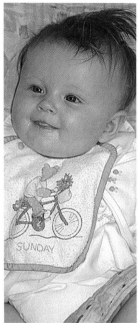 

Unsharpened image *Sharpened globally* *After painting skin with History brush set as below*

Taking the globally sharpened image as the starting point, we set the source for the History Brush to the unsharpened state and brushed out the crunchies.

Figure 10-16

Luminosity sharpening with History

You can run Unsharp Mask, then choose Edit > Fade Unsharp Mask, and set the blending mode to Luminosity…

Selected History state (highlighted)

History Brush source

…or you can run Unsharp Mask, set the History state to the unsharpened image and set the History Brush source to the sharpened image (left), and then set the blending mode for the History Brush to Luminosity in the Options bar (below).

High-Pass Sharpening

Unsharp Mask is the Swiss Army knife of sharpening tools, but it's not the only way to sharpen images. One technique that we often use, particularly when sharpening for output, is to make a duplicate layer using the techniques we described earlier in this chapter under "Sharpening with Layers." But rather than setting the blending mode to Luminosity and running Unsharp Mask, we use one of the contrast-increasing blending modes such as Soft Light or Hard Light, then we run the High Pass filter on the layer.

The High Pass filter (in the Other submenu, under the Filter menu) is a simple way to create an edge mask, but in this case we don't use it that way. Instead, we apply the High Pass filter directly to the duplicate layer and set the layer's blending mode to Soft Light or Hard Light. This increases the contrast around edges only, effectively sharpening the image.

As with the other layer-based sharpening techniques, you can use a whole bag of tricks to refine the sharpening—like blurring noise in the mask, or painting on the layer itself with 50 percent gray (the neutral color for both the Hard Light and Soft Light blending modes) to erase the sharpening in local areas. You can apply a layer mask to confine the sharpening to a specific area, and you can stack multiple sharpening layers to apply selective sharpening to different areas of the image.

The critical parameter in using this technique is the Radius setting for the High Pass filter. If it's too small, you'll get little or no sharpening. If it's too big, grain and noise will appear in the image as if by some evil magic. However, for optimum output sharpening, we often need to produce a result that appears very ugly onscreen (see the sidebar, "Sharpening and the Display," earlier in this chapter). **Figure 10-17** shows the application of this technique and the resulting image—it looks fine in print, but the onscreen appearance is downright scary! When you look at the actual pixels onscreen, bear in mind the size at which they'll reproduce in print—a 6-pixel-wide halo with three pixels in the light contour and three in the dark contour, will produce an "ideal" sharpening halo when you print at 300 ppi, even if it looks hideous on screen. The only way to really judge print sharpness is to make a print.

Figure 10-17 Sharpening with High Pass/Hard Light

We create a sharpening layer by duplicating the original image, set its Layers palette blending mode to Hard Light (top), and then run the High Pass filter (bottom).

The filtered layer set to Hard Light creates an unsharp mask very similar to a photographic unsharp mask. You can vary the character of the sharpening by using different Radius settings in High Pass, and you can vary the strength of the sharpening by adjusting the layer's opacity.

On soft subjects and skin tones, Hard Light can give too strong a sharpening effect. On these types of image, or in any case where we want a more gentle sharpening effect, we often use Soft Light instead of Hard Light to avoid oversharpening the skin texture, as shown in **Figure 10-18**. You can switch between Hard Light and Soft Light after running the High Pass filter to see which rendering you prefer.

Sharpening in Photoshop vs. Camera Raw

When we originally wrote about many of the techniques in this chapter, such as High Pass sharpening and edge masks, Photoshop was pretty much the only place in town where you'd consider doing them. Today, far more images are being captured by digital cameras, and for many of them, the first stop after the camera isn't Photoshop, but intermediate processing software such as Adobe Camera Raw, Adobe Lightroom, or Apple Aperture,

Figure 10-18 Sharpening with High Pass/Soft Light

Starting with the unsharpened image, left, we create a sharpening layer and set the blending mode to Soft Light; then we run the High Pass filter to produce the result shown below.

Setting the blending mode before running the High Pass filter lets us see the effect of different Radius settings on the image—the proxy window in the High Pass filter only shows the duplicate layer on which the filter is operating.

The image is now acceptably sharp with no exaggerated noise pixels, but the eyes could benefit from a little extra sparkle.

We quickly use the Lasso tool with Feather set to around 5 pixels to select the eyes. Then we target the Background layer and press Command-J (Mac) or Ctrl-J (Windows) to copy the selected eyes to a new layer, which we set to Hard Light. We then run High Pass on the new layer to produce the result shown at left.

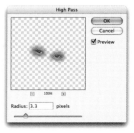

all of which have their own sharpening controls. Camera Raw 4.1 and Lightroom 1.1 go so far as to include a competent implementation of edge masking and the ability to process digital camera raw files, JPEG files, and TIFF files. (Apple Aperture is outside the scope of this book.)

As the feature sets of Camera Raw and Lightroom have expanded so dramatically, where and how do they fit into the sharpening workflow? Should you do any sharpening in those programs, or leave it to Photoshop?

Camera Raw 4.1 and Lightroom 1.1 are not yet ready to replace all three stages of the sharpening workflow, but they're more than good enough to take care of the first stage, capture sharpening. The biggest benefit of using Camera Raw and Lightroom for capture sharpening is ease of use. If you feel at all intimidated by our multistep descriptions of manipulating layers, channels, masks, and blending modes, you owe it to yourself to study the Camera Raw and Lightroom sharpening controls, which automate and condense stacks of layers and channels into four simple and well-engineered sliders. (If we sound a bit enthusiastic about Camera Raw and Lightroom sharpening, it's because Bruce helped design how those controls work.) We describe Camera Raw 4.1 sharpening in Chapter 5, "Building a Digital Workflow;" the controls in Lightroom 1.1 operate the same way.

One of the few remaining reasons to perform capture sharpening of digital camera images in Photoshop is if you want more control over the sharpening parameters than the four sliders in Camera Raw can provide. For example, you may want to tune the sharpening mask more than you can using the Mask slider in Camera Raw. Another reason would be if you are still using Camera Raw 3 or earlier, because we routinely skipped the more rudimentary sharpening controls in those earlier versions.

After you apply the proper capture sharpening to your digital camera images in Camera Raw and Lightroom, you can open them in Photoshop to apply creative sharpening and output sharpening. Neither Camera Raw 4.1 nor Lightroom 1.1 has any provision for localized creative sharpening; their controls are all or nothing. Lightroom has a limited output sharpening feature in its Print module, in the form of the Print Sharpening option. Until Adobe sees fit to beef up Camera Raw and Lightroom's creative and output sharpening capabilities, you'll continue to perform those stages in Photoshop.

Tip: If you don't want to apply Camera Raw sharpening to your images as you convert them, open the Camera Raw preferences and choose Preview Images Only from the Apply Sharpening To pop-up menu.

Noise Reduction

Any attempt at reducing noise will also soften the image. Despite the noise-reduction features in Photoshop, dedicated third-party plug-ins such as PictureCode's Noise Ninja, ABSoft's Neat Image, and Visual Infinity's Grain Surgery remain healthy because they do tend to be more effective. We've been known to use all of these in various situations, but since this is a Photoshop book, we've always felt bound to develop Photoshop noise-reduction techniques that don't rely on third-party add-ons.

Until the Reduce Noise filter appeared in Photoshop CS2, we generally relied on the Despeckle filter, applied separately to individual channels multiple times through an edge mask. We wish we could say that the Reduce Noise filter renders such kludges unnecessary, but unfortunately we encounter two major problems with Reduce Noise:

▶ The Preserve Detail feature really doesn't know the difference between detail and digital noise or film grain, so we still need to use masks.

▶ If you're using a machine that isn't well optimized for Photoshop (such as a notebook computer with a single-core CPU), Reduce Noise can be frustratingly slow, especially when you turn on the Preview check box to preview the entire image.

However, even with these problems, when we encounter *really* noisy images, we will use Reduce Noise rather than Despeckle.

Light Noise Reduction with Despeckle

When all we need is relatively light noise reduction, we still resort to the Despeckle filter. A typical case is noisy skies from a transparency scanner. We generally run Despeckle first on the red channel, then we run it a few more times on the green channel, and run it even more times on the blue channel, which tends to be the noisiest.

Figure 10-19 shows an image shot on Kodak Ektachrome 100 Plus Professional transparency film and scanned on an Imacon Flextight 848. The sky is quite a bit grainier than we'd like, so we tried both methods (Despeckle and Reduce Noise). Both filters required masking, so we made a quick Color Range selection of the sky and used it as a mask for the noise-reduction layer.

The Despeckle'd result has some slight mottling, but it's relatively clean and responds well to subsequent sharpening. The version that uses Reduce

Figure 10-19 Despeckle or Reduce Noise?

The image above has had noise reduction and final sharpening applied. The red box shows the area of detail we're examining for noise reduction.

The detail at Actual Pixels view before noise reduction

Even at the extreme settings we used, the version with Reduce Noise contains artifacts that are emphasized by subsequent sharpening that the Despeckle version lacks.

Despeckle at 400 percent

Reduce Noise at 400 percent

Noise reduced by Despeckle, four times on the red channel, six times on the green, ten times on the blue

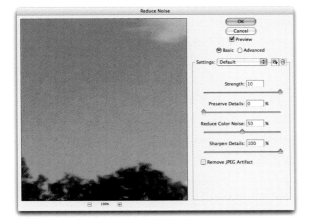

Noise reduced by Reduce Noise, settings shown at left

Noise—even when cranked all the way up—retains characteristic "wormy" dark artifacts that get much worse with output sharpening, as shown in the 400 percent blowups in **Figure 10-19**. Reducing the strength of Reduce Noise actually creates worse results, and moving the Preserve Detail control away from 0 makes it preserve the noise we're trying to eliminate.

Moreover, even though we ran Despeckle 20 times in all, it still took less time than setting, previewing, and running the Reduce Noise filter, and we could easily see what happened each time we ran Despeckle, while with Reduce Noise, we have to wait each time we move a control for the proxy to be updated, which, even on fast machines, typically takes several seconds. So for moderate luminance noise, like the example shown in **Figure 10-19**, we'll continue to use Despeckle with a mask.

The Reduce Noise Filter

We don't, however, mean to suggest that Reduce Noise is useless—far from it. But you *do* have to be careful, tune the subsequent sharpening to the noise reduction to avoid exaggerating the characteristic artifacts that Reduce Noise produces, and (in some cases) you may want to mask edges and important textural detail so that Reduce Noise doesn't destroy them. **Figure 10-20** shows the Reduce Noise dialog.

In Basic mode, Reduce Noise offers four slider controls and a check box for reducing JPEG artifacts. The four sliders operate as follows.

Strength. The Strength slider controls the strength of the luminance noise-reduction effect—it's not an overall strength control. Permissible values range from 0 to 10. (At 0, you can still apply color noise reduction or use the Advanced options on the individual channels.)

Preserve Details. The Preserve Details slider (permissible values are from 0 to 100 percent) attempts to do what it says—preserve details. Unfortunately, on anything except very low-resolution files, it also seems to preserve the noise you're presumably trying to eliminate. We find that the useful range is between 1 and 5—beyond that, it's difficult to get rid of the noise (See **Figure 10-20**).

The Preserve Details and Sharpen Details controls seem designed to sharpen and reduce noise in one fell swoop. On Web-resolution images, this works reasonably well. But if you plan on sharpening later, you need to keep the Preserve Details slider at a very low (or 0) value.

Figure 10-20 Preserve Details

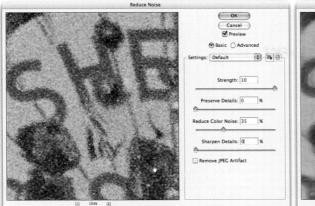

The unadjusted image

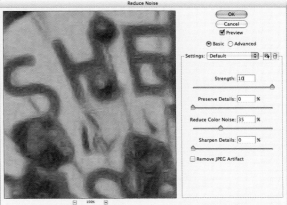

Preserve Details at 0

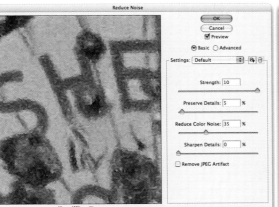

Preserve Details at 5

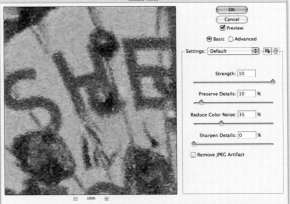

Preserve Details at 10

Reduce Color Noise. The Reduce Color Noise slider (permissible values are from 0 to 100 percent) reduces color noise independently of luminance noise. Transparency film has little or no color noise, negative film typically has more, while digital captures often have color noise reduced in the raw converter or the camera. At very high settings, Reduce Color Noise can lose saturation, but settings of 35 to 50 percent work well (see **Figure 10-21**).

Sharpen Details. While the Sharpen Details slider works independently of Preserve Details, its effect depends very much on that slider's value (whose effect depends—as we said just above—on the image resolution). Feel free to try reducing noise *and* sharpening with Reduce Noise, but we sug-

Figure 10-21 Reduce Color Noise

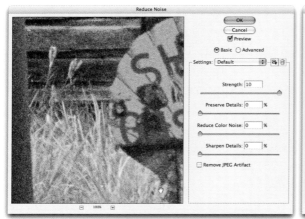

The unadjusted image

Reduce Color Noise at 0

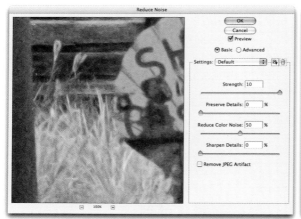

Reduce Color Noise at 50 percent

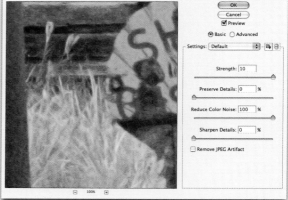

Reduce Color Noise at 100 percent

gest you only attempt to do so on low-resolution images—the significant lack of speed with which the filter updates the proxy on higher-resolution images doesn't really invite experimentation!

If you plan on sharpening the image after running Reduce Noise, we recommend leaving Sharpen Details at 0. Otherwise, you'll wind up with artifacts that are almost impossible to deal with.

Remove JPEG Artifact. The Remove JPEG Artifact check box attempts to remove the characteristic 8-by-8-pixel artifacts caused by heavy JPEG compression. Sadly, we haven't enjoyed much success with it.

Tip: When you're in the Advanced mode of the Reduce Noise dialog, you can use the same channel display shortcuts available in the Channels palette. For example, press Command-2 (Mac) or Ctrl-2 (Windows) to display only the Green channel.

Advanced Mode. In Advanced Mode, Reduce Noise lets you set values for Strength and Preserve Details for each channel individually. You can use this to apply noise reduction only to the noisiest channel, which is usually blue. Advanced Mode settings apply in addition to the settings you make in the main panel of the dialog. Piling all of these settings on top of each other can take a while to render, so on a slower or older machine, you may be better off running Despeckle through a mask.

Using Reduce Noise

We use Reduce Noise on very noisy images as a precursor to sharpening. But we prefer to run it on a layer made by merging the visible layers, usually through a light edge mask (that is, a mask with no solid blacks, that de-emphasizes rather than fully protects the edges). Since we only use Reduce Noise on extremely noisy images, we tend toward extreme settings.

The degree to which we feel comfortable reducing noise depends in part on the eventual use of the image. While we like the idea of creating "use-neutral" master images (which is one of the goals of the sharpening workflow), we also recognize that there's a limit to the size at which images, and in particular noisy images, can be reproduced. With noisy 35 mm images, for example, we may scan at 6300 ppi, perform noise reduction and sharpening, then downsample to 4000 ppi to create a smaller but cleaner master image. **Figure 10-22** shows a noisy 35 mm color negative scan that lends itself well to this approach.

Reducing Noise with Image Stacks

Tip: For best results with noise reduction using Image Stacks, try to shoot five or more images of the subject. The optimal number of frames depends on the anticipated level of noise, so it's always a bit of a guess.

The Image Stacks feature in Adobe Photoshop CS3 Extended was designed primarily as a tool for scientific image analysis, but it turns out to be useful for noise reduction. Don't confuse Image Stacks with the Stacks feature in Adobe Bridge—this is completely different. In Photoshop Extended, you process Image Stacks using the Stack Mode commands on the Layer > Smart Objects submenu. You can apply Stack Mode commands only to a Smart Object containing multiple images.

In our example (see **Figure 10-23**), we shot six handheld images under a fluorescent lamp using a Canon PowerShot S60 point-and-shoot camera in Raw mode. To achieve a decent shutter speed in such low indoor light, we set the camera to ISO 200, which happens to be a recipe for noise on that particular pocket camera. We applied no noise reduction while processing the images using Adobe Camera Raw.

Figure 10-22 Reduce Noise in action

The image above has had noise reduction and final sharpening applied. The detail views show actual pixels before noise reduction, right; after noise reduction, below left; and after capture sharpening, below right.

To reduce the noise, we ran Reduce Noise using these settings: Strength 7, Preserve Details 0 percent, Reduce Color Noise 35 percent, and Sharpen Details 0 percent.

In Photoshop, we choose File > Scripts > Load Images Into Stack, click Browse, and select our six images. We turn on the two check boxes at the bottom of the dialog, Attempt To Automatically Align Source Images (because our handheld shots are not perfectly lined up) and Create Smart Object After Loading Layers (required to create an Image Stack). Finally, click OK and stand back as Photoshop aligns the images and gathers them into a Smart Object. In the finished Smart Object, it's obvious how much noise is in this low-light scene, but we're about to take care of that.

We select the Smart Object in the Layers palette, and then choose Layer > Smart Objects > Stack Mode > Mean. As you may remember from math class, mean means average—Photoshop averages the color value of each pixel across the six images. This smooths out the noise in the image, as you can see in Figure 10-23.

Figure 10-23
Reducing Noise
with Image Stacks

The six original images   *Load Layers dialog with images loaded*

Stack Mode icon
indicates that a Stack Mode
command is applied

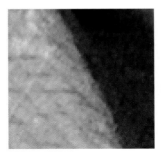

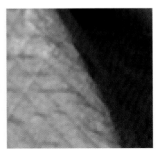

*The Smart Object
containing the six
images as an
Image Stack*

*Noisy detail before applying
Mean command*

*Detail after applying Mean
command to Image Stack*

This technique may seem like a godsend for high-noise, low-light situations, and sometimes it is. But keep in mind that you can use it only when you're able to take several frames of a still subject. If the subject moves at all, it may not be sharp after the frames are averaged—this technique won't work well for sports or theater. You also can't cheat by duplicating a single image—the noise won't average out, because it will be in the same place in all the duplicates. Where this technique doesn't work, you must fall back on the Reduce Noise or Despeckle filters.

Smart Sharpen

The Smart Sharpen filter is a fascinating piece of work. Unfortunately, it shares with Reduce Noise a significant lack of speed on slower machines, both in execution and, worse, in updating the proxy image when you change settings. For high-resolution images, it's most useful if you have the latest fast hardware.

If you need to make low-resolution images look good on screen, Smart Sharpen is great. If the idea of making sharpening masks fills you with terror, Smart Sharpen does a fairly good job of differentiating edges from non-edges. It's quite useful for capture sharpening, though on the whole we still prefer our tried-and-true techniques. On the other hand, it's a very slow and difficult way to do output sharpening. Smart Sharpen is also more effective on digital camera images than it is with scans.

Smart Sharpen Remove Modes

Smart Sharpen is really three sharpening filters in one. You select which one you want to use by choosing an option from the Remove menu (see **Figure 10-24**).

Tip: If your machine isn't fast enough to use Smart Sharpen for rapid production work, you can obtain very similar results running Unsharp mask on masked layers set to Luminosity mode. When we automate the process with actions, it's quite a bit faster than Smart Sharpen.

Gaussian Blur. The Gaussian Blur mode is the Unsharp Mask filter with a different user interface. If you turn on the More Accurate option, the result is a good deal gentler than Unsharp Mask at the same amount and radius, but it's basically the same type of sharpening. The reason you have a choice of not using More Accurate is that takes a lot more time to process.

Lens Blur. In Lens Blur mode, Smart Sharpen is a whole different animal than Unsharp Mask. Lens Blur uses much more sophisticated algorithms than Unsharp Mask (or Smart Sharpen in Gaussian Blur mode) to detect edges and detail, and hence typically produces better sharpening with less-obvious sharpening halos.

Motion Blur. In Motion Blur mode, Smart Sharpen tries to undo the effects of blurring caused by either camera or subject movement. If the movement is truly unidirectional, it does a surprisingly good job, but camera shake rarely happens in just one direction, and subject movement is often quite complex, so don't expect blurred subjects to be rendered razor-sharp by the filter. We typically apply Smart Sharpen's Motion Blur on small areas of images—few images benefit from global application.

Advanced Mode

When you click the Advanced radio button, two additional tabs, labeled Shadow and Highlight, become available. They offer controls very similar to those offered by the Shadow/Highlight command found in the Adjust submenu (under the Image menu)—see "Shadow/Highlight" in Chapter 7, "Image Adjustment Fundamentals."

Each tab provides three sliders for Fade Amount, Tonal Width, and Radius. They let you reduce the strength of the shadow and highlight sharpening contours, allowing stronger sharpening of the midtones.

▶ Fade Amount controls the strength of the fade from 0 to 100 percent.

▶ Tonal Width controls how far up from the shadows or down from the highlights the adjustment extends into the tonal range.

▶ Radius controls the size of the neighborhood used to decide whether a pixel is in the shadows or the highlights. A useful rule of thumb is to set the Radius in the Shadow and Highlight tabs to double the Radius setting in the main panel.

Thus far, our use of Smart Sharpen is confined to the Lens Blur and Motion Blur modes, and we always use the Advanced setting with the More Accurate option turned on.

Smart Sharpen in Action

As with the Unsharp Mask filter, the key parameter is Radius. While you can obtain some interesting contrast effects with very high Radius settings (just as you can with Unsharp Mask), you typically need to match the Radius to the image content to obtain good sharpening. But as you'll see, you need very different Radius settings for the Lens Blur and Motion Blur modes.

We start out by setting the Amount all the way up to 500 percent in Basic mode, while we find the correct Radius setting (see Figure 10-24).

At a Radius setting of 1, the high-resolution image in Figure 10-24 barely looks different from the unsharpened version, even with the Amount cranked all the way up. At a Radius setting of 5, we see sharpening starting to happen, but it's emphasizing the film grain and the artifacts left by Reduce Noise rather than sharpening the image details. A Radius of 10 matches the image content nicely, though the Amount is obviously now far too high.

Figure 10-24 Setting the Radius

The unadjusted image

Radius at 1

Radius at 5

Radius at 10

We proceed by bringing the Amount down to 50 percent, then we switch to Advanced mode and further soften the Shadow and Highlight contours (see **Figure 10-25**).

In practice, finding the right settings for all three tabs in Smart Sharpen is an iterative process—after adjusting the Shadow and Highlight tabs, we may go back and tweak the Amount in the main panel, then revisit the Shadow and Highlight tabs once again.

Smart Sharpen is also effective at much smaller Radius settings, depending on the image. The image shown in **Figure 10-26** requires a very different Radius setting than the previous example because of its finer details, but the process is essentially the same.

As before, we started by setting the Radius in the main panel with the Amount set to 500 percent. This time, we kept the Amount setting and used the Advanced panels to reduce the contrast on the sharpening halos.

Tip: To sharpen a small area of a large image more quickly than using a mask, select the small area, press Command-J (Mac) or Ctrl-J (Windows) to duplicate the selection as a new layer, and run the filter on the new small layer. This is faster than running the filter on an entire image, especially if the layer is large.

Figure 10-25

Setting the Amount and
Advanced settings

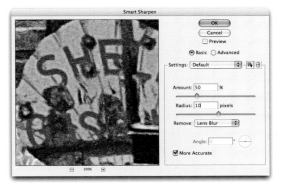

*Reducing the Amount to
50 percent eliminates the
unnatural-looking halos, but
the effect is still stronger than
we want.*

*Switching to Advanced
mode, we soften the Shadow
contour. We set the Radius
to 20, which is double the
sharpening radius, then set
the Tonal Width to 50 percent
and the Fade Amount to 20
percent, producing the result
shown at left.*

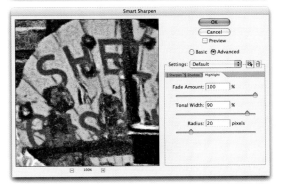

*We finish sharpening by
setting the Highlight tab. We
use the same Radius setting as
we did for Shadows, but this
time we choose much higher
settings for Fade Amount and
Tonal Width, to produce the
result shown at left.*

When we use Smart Sharpen to remove Motion Blur, the process is only slightly different. Radius is still very much a key parameter, but so is the setting of the angle. **Figure 10-27** shows an image at various stages of the application of Smart Sharpen set to remove Motion Blur.

Making the filter settings is only part of the process. After running the filter, we applied a solid black layer mask, then we painted the filter effect into the image where we wanted it. Few, if any, images benefit from global application of Smart Sharpen in Motion Blur mode.

Figure 10-26

Small-radius sharpening

Clockwise: The sharpened image, the unsharpened image, the sharpening applied in the main panel, the Shadow adjustment, and the Highlight adjustment.

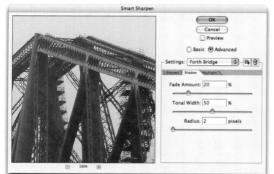

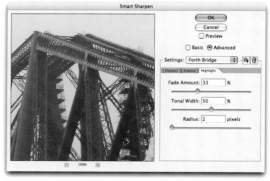

One final note: If you have sharp eyes, you may have noticed that many of the screen shots of Smart Sharpen use a named setting. It's great that Smart Sharpen lets you save settings, but in practice, the mechanism doesn't seem to be at all reliable. If you load a saved setting, change it, and simply run the filter without renaming the saved setting, the new settings overwrite the old ones, so the next time you call up your carefully constructed saved setting, it doesn't contain the values you expect. We suspect that this isn't the intended behavior!

Figure 10-27 Removing Motion Blur

*Setting overall sharpening and
tuning the Motion Blur angle*

The image before removing motion blur

Fading the shadow contours

*Smart Sharpen settings applied to entire image—the
Remove Motion Blur setting enhances the details on the fish*

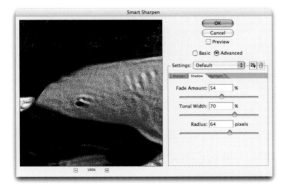

Fading the highlight contours

*Smart Sharpen settings masked, then painted on fish—the
water looks more natural when left unsharpened*

Lens Correction

The Lens Correction filter lets you address barrel and pincushion distortion, chromatic aberration, vignetting, and perspective errors (see **Figure 10-28**). While the Lens Correction filter (yes, this feature appears in the Filter menu, too) doesn't reduce noise or sharpen, it does have an impact on detail, especially when it's used to correct chromatic aberration, and also to a lesser extent when you use it to correct perspective.

In our testing, it's become clear that Lens Correction should be run before you do any sharpening—you definitely don't want to sharpen the color fringes caused by chromatic aberration, but even seemingly harmless perspective and distortion corrections are better performed before sharpening than afterward. The relationship to noise reduction is less clear: If pressed, we probably have a slight preference for doing noise reduction before running the Lens Correction filter, but if you prefer doing the lens corrections first, we won't quibble.

Figure 10-28
The Lens Correction filter

Tool palette

Zoom controls

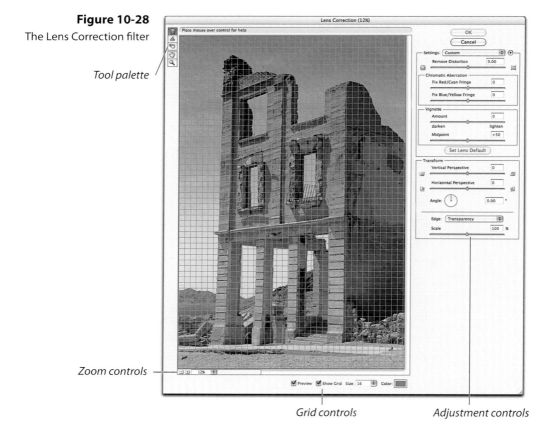

Grid controls

Adjustment controls

Lens Filter Controls

The Lens Filter controls are arranged in five groups: the tool palette, the zoom controls, the grid controls, the main control buttons and Settings menu, and the actual filter adjustment controls.

Tool palette. The Tool palette contains five tools. The Remove Distortion tool is a rather blunt instrument—we can make much finer adjustments using the slider control—but we use the Straighten tool to set horizontals or verticals to rotate and straighten the image because it's often easier than typing in an angle. The Move Grid tool lets us adjust the position of the alignment grid, which is particularly useful when adjusting distortion or perspective. But we never choose the Zoom and Hand tools from the palette, preferring to use the keyboard shortcuts—Option (Mac) or Alt (Windows) to zoom out, Command (Mac) or Ctrl (Windows) to zoom in, and the spacebar to scroll.

Zoom controls. You can change the preview zoom by pressing the zoom in (+) or zoom out (-) buttons, or by choosing a zoom percentage from the Zoom menu. In addition, Command-0 (zero) in Mac OS X or Ctrl-0 (zero) in Windows enlarges the filter dialog to fill the screen, then zooms the image to fill the preview area, while Command-Option-0 (zero) in Mac OS X or Ctrl-Alt-0 (zero) in Windows displays the image at 100 percent view.

Grid controls. The grid controls let you show and hide the grid and control its size and color. Also in this cluster is the Preview check box, which lets you toggle between previewing the adjusted and unadjusted image.

Main control buttons. The OK button commits the changes and returns you to Photoshop. The Cancel button cancels the changes and dismisses the filter, returning you to Photoshop. When you press Option (Mac) or Alt (Windows), the Cancel button changes to Reset. Clicking the Reset button resets all the controls to their initial values, undoing any changes you've made, but leaving the filter dialog open.

The Settings menu lets you choose saved settings that were saved in the filter's Settings folder, while the unlabeled menu immediately to its right lets you load settings saved anywhere on disk, save new settings, or delete settings.

The remainder of the dialog is devoted to the image preview, and to the filter's meat and potatoes, the adjustments themselves. These are arranged in two groups—Settings and Transform.

Setting lens defaults. The first group contains the Remove Distortion, Chromatic Aberration, and Vignette corrections, which (for digital captures, at least) you can save as defaults for a specific camera, lens, and focal length by clicking the Lens Default button. Then, when the filter detects other images shot with the same camera, lens, and focal length by reading the image metadata, the Lens Default setting becomes available in the Settings menu, and choosing it applies those settings.

The Transform settings can't be saved as part of the lens default because they depend on the angle between the camera and subject, and hence are image-dependent. You don't have to save Lens Default settings (and unless the image contains the necessary metadata, which means either a digital capture or a very assiduous photographer, you can't), but they can be a huge time-saver. Let's look at the individual adjustments in turn.

Remove Distortion. The Remove Distortion slider lets you remove pincushion or barrel distortions, which bow straight lines inward and outward, respectively. **Figure 10-29** shows an image before and after correction for moderate barrel distortion.

The grid is useful for checking barrel distortion, since it makes it easier to detect bowing of straight lines. You can drag the Remove Distortion tool toward or away from the center of the image to correct barrel and pincushion distortion, respectively, but we find it's easier to use the slider. The up and down arrow keys change the value by increments of 0.1; add Shift to change it in increments of 1.

Chromatic Aberration. The Chromatic Aberration sliders work by changing the size of the red (for red/cyan fringing) and blue (for blue/yellow fringing) channel relative to the green channel. With digital raw images, we prefer to fix chromatic aberration in Camera Raw, because it's earlier in the workflow. However, sometimes we need to make different corrections on different parts of the image (with the help of masks), so we'll apply Chromatic Aberration correction in Photoshop instead. **Figure 10-30** shows a detail of an image before and after chromatic aberration correction.

Chromatic aberration is less common on film scans, though it happens with wide-angle zooms at the short end, But digital capture is brutal at showing the lens flaws that film masks. We see significant chromatic aberration on digital captures with zooms shorter than 24 mm. You can go crazy trying to eliminate it entirely, but if you can render it unobjectionable at 200 percent view, you're unlikely to notice it in the final image.

Figure 10-29
Remove Distortion

The image before we correct for barrel distortion. The wall of the building on the left is bowed slightly outward.

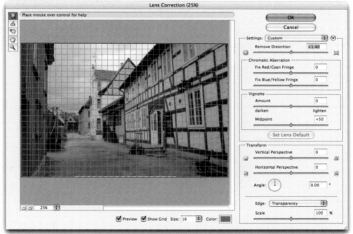

After correction, the wall is straight (though not quite vertical).

Vignette. Vignetting, where the lens illuminates the sensor or film plane unevenly, causing darkening in the corners, is most commonly seen when shooting at wide apertures. The Vignette Amount slider controls the amount of lightening or darkening, while the Vignette Midpoint slider controls how far from the corners the correction extends; lower values affect more of the image, higher ones confine the correction closer to the corners. **Figure 10-31** shows a vignetting correction.

The Remove Distortion, Chromatic Aberration, and Vignette corrections can be saved for a particular camera, lens, and focal length combination. If you plan to do this, test the settings on more than one image—even then, you're likely to have to fine-tune the results for each image.

Figure 10-30
Chromatic Aberration
correction

*The uncorrected image s
hows color-fringing along
high-contrast edges.*

*After correction, the color
fringing is greatly reduced, if
not entirely eliminated.*

The Transform controls. The Transform controls are image specific. They can reduce the perspective errors caused by tilting the camera, and while they do an impressive job, they don't turn an SLR into a view camera. But they do provide a reasonable substitute for 35 mm tilt/shift lenses. **Figure 10-32** shows the image before and after perspective corrections.

Edge. When you make Distortion and perspective corrections, you lose some of the image. The Edge menu lets you deal with the corrected edges, but the Edge Extension option rarely does anything useful, so we usually stick with Transparency. If we need to preserve the aspect ratio, we use the Scale slider to fill the image area, eliminating any empty areas resulting

Figure 10-31
Vignetting correction

*The uncorrected
image shows slight
vignetting in the corners.*

*After correction, the
vignetting is eliminated.*

from the lens correction. When we want to keep as much of the image as possible, we crop in Photoshop instead.

Figure 10-32 shows the unadjusted image and the image after lens corrections, noise reduction, and sharpening.

Avoiding the Crunchies

The ability to sharpen your images is a powerful tool. Used well, it can give your images the extra snap that makes them jump off the page. Used badly, it gives images the coarse, crunchy look we see in all too many Sunday newspaper color supplements. In overdoses, it can make images

Figure 10-32
Perspective correction

After correction, the perspective errors are greatly reduced. Compare to the second image in Figure 10-31.

Original image

Image after applying lens corrections, noise reduction, and sharpening

look artificial or even blurry. With that in mind, we leave you with two final pieces of advice.

First, it's better to err on the side of caution. Despite what we've said about output sharpening, an image that's too soft will generally be less disturbing than one that's been oversharpened.

Second, always leave yourself an escape route using layers or Smart Filters, since sharpening mistakes that are permanently saved into the image are difficult or impossible to reverse. Sharpening skill is definitely one of those things that improves with experience, and a considerable part of that experience can be gained from revisiting your earlier efforts and figuring out what went wrong. If you save an unsharpened copy or use layers to do your sharpening, you can always go back and refine your sharpening to get closer to the result you want.

Essential Image Techniques

Pushing Pixels into Place

The vast majority of Photoshop users stare at the program many hours a day, doing the same sort of image manipulation over and over again. Retouch the background of this photo; convert this color image to grayscale; add a drop shadow behind this car; silhouette this pineapple; put a new background behind this amazing kitchen aid; incorporate this logo into that image.

In this chapter we offer a whole mess of tips and tricks to make your images fly a little faster, and perhaps even make them a little more fun to manipulate, too. The chapter is split up into a hodgepodge of common Photoshop issues: retouching, grayscale conversions, working with vector graphics and text, and so on. Read 'em and reap!

Taking Care of the Basics

Two of the most important techniques in image editing are, in many respects, the simplest to accomplish:

▶ Look at every pixel.

▶ Build base camps.

Look at every pixel. Try to get in the habit of returning to 100 percent (Actual Pixels) view frequently so you can get a sense of what's going on in your image and check for sensor dust, skin imperfections, or film scratches in scans. You usually don't need to zoom in further than 200 percent.

When the image is larger than the screen, you can get around using keyboard shortcuts. Press Home to start at the top left corner, then press Page Down to move down until you reach the bottom. Press Command-Page Down (Mac) or Ctrl-Page Down (Windows) to move one screen to the right, then press Page Up to move up a screen. To move to the right, press Command-Page Up (Mac) or Ctrl-Page Up (Windows). The End key zips you to the bottom right corner. When pressing Page Up or Page Down, add the Shift key to scroll a small amount instead of a whole page.

Build base camps. Our friend and colleague Greg Vander Houwen (you've probably read about him elsewhere in this tome) turned us on to the mountaineering phrase "base camp." The concept is simple: While you're working on an image, don't just save every now and again; instead, create an environment that you can return to at any time. That means taking snapshots in the History palette or—better yet—using Save As at strategic moments in your image manipulation. Take advantage of all the places in Photoshop where you can save settings and alternative versions, such as adjustment layers, layer comps, layer groups, and the Load and Save buttons in dialogs.

The Color of Grayscale

Photoshop is a wonderful tool for handling color, but we don't live by color alone. Grayscale images have a magic all their own, and many photographers—even those who print exclusively in grayscale—find that they can produce much better grayscale images from color captures than they can from black-and-white captures, whether they're shooting with film or digital cameras.

We could have ended this topic right here by simply telling you to choose Image > Mode > Grayscale to convert color to grayscale. However, the reason this section doesn't end here is that the Grayscale command always converts the same way, without adapting to the image. It isn't likely to give you the optimum level of contrast and tonal range—the two most important qualities of a black-and-white image. Instead, we recommend that you customize the conversion.

Start from color. Although many digital cameras and scanners let you capture images in grayscale, you can often get better results by starting from a color image and converting to grayscale in Photoshop. The key is understanding that some hues are darker than others at the same level of saturation (for example, the most-saturated yellow is much lighter than the most-saturated red). Whenever you have an image in which color helps define the subject, you'll want to try one of the techniques that lets you customize the conversion to grayscale, so that the existing color relationship is translated into a similar tonal relationship.

The Black and White dialog

In Photoshop CS3, the wonderful new Black and White dialog lets you control how colors translate into tones in a way similar to how film photographers place colored filters in front of their lenses to control contrast in the resulting black-and-white image. You'll probably find Black and White to be easier and more intuitive than older Photoshop grayscale conversion techniques.

Tip: If you use the Black and White dialog as an adjustment layer, you can keep both color and black-and-white versions in the same document. When the layer is on, it's your tuned black-and-white conversion. When the layer is off, the image is in color.

The Black and White dialog is available as an adjustment layer, and that's how we recommend that you use it. As with any other adjustment layer, you use Black and White by clicking the Create New Fill or Adjustment Layer button and choosing Black and White from the pop-up menu at the bottom of the Layers palette. You can also choose Layer > New Adjustment Layer > Black and White. In the Black and White dialog (**Figure 11-1**), each of the color sliders determines how dark each color appears in the grayscale image. For example, to deepen a blue sky, drag the Blues slider to the left to darken the blues in the grayscale image. By altering the relationships of colors to tones in the Black and White dialog, you can often arrive at more satisfying grayscale conversions in less time than if you had simply converted to grayscale and adjusted tones using curves, masks, and blending modes. You may still need to use those tools, but probably just for fine-tuning and special cases. If you are after a certain look, try the Preset pop-up menu at the top of the dialog—it includes settings that emulate effects traditionally produced using color filters with black-and-white film, along with an infrared simulation. You can use the Tint sliders to apply color effects such as sepiatones.

Tip: Clicking Auto is a good first step in the Black and White dialog. It adapts to the colors in an image, giving you a good starting point.

If you're working with a raw digital camera file, you may prefer to perform the grayscale conversion using the HSL/Grayscale tab in Adobe Camera Raw (see Chapter 5, "Building a Digital Workflow"), because it's earlier

Figure 11-1
The Black and White dialog

Original image

Storing alternate conversions in the Layers palette

After clicking Auto in the Black and White dialog

After adjusting the Black and White dialog sliders to darken the blue sky and maintain grass contrast

Tip: Not sure which slider to drag in the Black and White dialog, especially since you can't see the colors in the image? No problem: Move the mouse over the image (the cursor becomes an eyedropper) and click the area you want to adjust. Photoshop automatically selects the slider value that affects the part of the image you clicked.

in the workflow and doesn't require saving a much larger Photoshop file and adjustment layer. On the other hand, if you want the original raw file to maintain its color conversion settings, or if the image needs additional edits that can be done only in Photoshop, you may prefer to perform the grayscale conversion in Photoshop using Black and White. The controls are similar in both places; the main difference is that in Photoshop, you can choose saved conversions from the Preset menu.

Instant Grayscale Images

The following techniques can be useful when you just want a quick grayscale and don't want to face a dialog full of sliders.

The Grayscale command. As we mentioned earlier, you can simply choose Image > Mode > Grayscale. When you do so, Photoshop weights the red, green, and blue channels differently using a standard formula that purports to account for the varying sensitivity of the eye to different colors.

Desaturate. The Image > Adjustment > Desaturate command produces the same result as reducing the Saturation setting in the Hue/Saturation dialog to 0, producing a different result than the Grayscale command. Note that the Desaturate command affects only the selected layer, so it can be useful when you want to convert just one layer to grayscale while leaving the rest of the document in color.

Load the luminance mask. One of David's favorite methods for squeezing a grayscale image out of a color photograph is to Command-click (Mac) or Ctrl-click (Windows) on the composite color channel (the RGB or the CMYK thumbnail in the Channels palette), which loads the file's luminance map. You can then choose Select > Save Selection to save the selection to a new document. This produces a different result than the previous techniques and also usually looks better than choosing the Grayscale command.

Finding Hidden Grayscale Images in Channels

In Chapter 9, "Making Selections," we showed you how every color image is made up of multiple grayscale channels that can help you isolate the structure of an image. Each of an image's channels typically looks completely different than the other channels, so if you're trying to get a grayscale image out of a color image, just looking at the individual channels gives you a nice head start. Looking at each channel can help you see which sliders to adjust in the Black and White dialog, or you may decide to simply grab one of those channels. You can copy and paste it, or use Duplicate Channel from the Channel palette menu to save it into a new document. Or you can quickly delete the other two channels: first display the channel you want, and then choose Image > Mode > Grayscale.

RGB and Lab images have three channels each, and CMYK images have four channels. For Lab images you can try taking just the L channel, which carries all luminance information. For CMYK images, the K channel is the one you want.

The Channel Mixer. If you look at all of the channels in various color modes and you still don't see the grayscale you want, you can try recombining the channels using the Channel Mixer (see **Figure 11-2**). You'll find Channel Mixer on the same adjustment layer menus as the Black and White command you saw earlier in this chapter. You mix channels by percentage, and the result is a single channel (you can choose which channel the result will end up on in the Output Channel pop-up menu).

Figure 11-2

Channel Mixer dialog

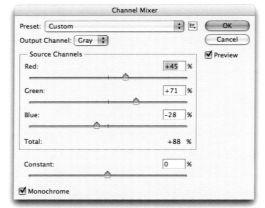

When you enable the Monochrome check box at the bottom of the Channel Mixer dialog, the Output Channel becomes Gray, letting you mix proportions of the image's channels into a single grayscale channel.

Tip: The Channel Mixer works fine with CMYK images, but it's much harder to maintain the images' tone. We prefer working from an RGB image when building grayscale images with the Channel Mixer, even if it means converting from CMYK to RGB first.

When using the Channel Mixer to convert a color image to grayscale, remember two things: First, the percentages in the dialog should always add up to 100 percent to maintain the same overall tone of the image (though there may be situations where you don't *want* to maintain the overall tone of the image). Second, turn on the Monochrome check box to ensure that the result is neutral gray.

Before Photoshop CS3, the Channel Mixer was probably the most popular way to manually control the color-to-grayscale conversion. In Photoshop CS3, most Channel Mixer aficionados will probably move on to the easier and more flexible Black and White dialog.

Tip: Want to know more about Calculations and other channel manipulations? Check out *The Photoshop Channels Book* by Scott Kelby (Peachpit Press).

Building gray from color with Calculations. Like the Channel Mixer, choosing Image > Calculations lets you mix and match a new grayscale image from the existing channels, but with much more power and flexibility (see **Figure 11-3**)—as long as you need only two channel sources. The options in the Blending pop-up menu are the same as the ones in the Layers palette, and the Opacity field serves the same function as the Layers palette's Opacity slider. By keeping the Preview check box on, getting feedback on your changes is about as fast as using layers.

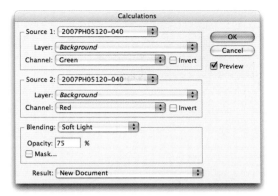

Figure 11-3

The Calculations
dialog

Line Art

Line art—those black-and-white images (or *bitmapped images*, in Photoshop terminology) with no halftoning, dithering, or anything else—is seemingly as simple as can be. Each pixel is either on or off, black or white, and you aren't concerned with levels of gray or halftones. Scanning, manipulating, and printing these things should be easy. And it is—at least compared to the vagaries that surround grayscale and color images. We've found that many people's line-art images have jaggy edges, fine lines that break up, and dense patterns that clog up. You can improve your reproductions of line art with a little additional effort.

Scan as Grayscale

It's *essential* that you scan in Grayscale mode to take advantage of the techniques covered here. If you scan in Bitmap mode (line art or 1-bit), you're stuck with the black pixels you get. In Grayscale mode, you can sharpen, adjust the black/white threshold to control line widths, and increase your effective line-art resolution; each of these techniques helps create a beautiful reproduction.

So avoid the temptation to scan line art *as* line art, and scan it as grayscale instead. Sure, your files will be eight times as large, but it's only temporary. When you complete the sharpening and threshold techniques that follow, you'll convert the grayscale image to a 1-bit black-and-white image, and the file size will drop.

Resolution

When you're printing to an imagesetter, you need very high image resolution to match the quality of photographically reproduced line art. That
means 800 ppi minimum image resolution. You *can* see the difference
between 800- and 1200-ppi line art (see **Figure 11-4**), so you may want
to opt for the higher resolution if your printing method can hold it. On
the other hand, if you're printing on newsprint, the spread of the ink as it
hits the paper will likely blur any jaggies, so a lower resolution of 800 ppi
should be fine.

Of course, you never need image resolution higher than your output
resolution. If you're printing your final artwork on a 600-dpi laser printer,
for instance, you don't need more than 600-ppi image resolution. The
additional data just gets thrown away.

Sharpening

Nothing will do more for the quality of your line-art images than sharp-
ening the grayscale scan (see **Figure 11-5**). We recommend running the
Unsharp Mask filter twice with these settings: Amount 500, Radius 1,
Threshold 5. However, if the second pass makes the image look terrible

Figure 11-4
Line-art resolution

Grayscale scan

144 ppi

800 ppi

1,200 ppi

Figure 11-5
Line art with and
without sharpening

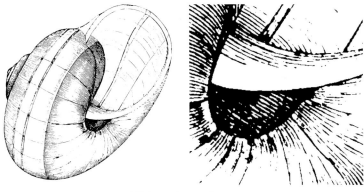

Without sharpening

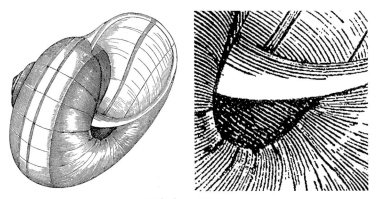

With sharpening

(as it often does if you're scanning poorly printed originals), undo it and stick with just one pass of the Unsharp Mask (which you might be able to do with the scanner software itself).

Threshold

Tip: For simple line-art images that don't include very detailed and dense shadow areas, set Threshold to 2. For densely detailed shadows, try values up to about 55. Find a good middle value; back off if fine lines break up or if dense areas clog up.

When you scan line art in Grayscale mode, lines are captured as a collection of pixels with different values (see **Figure 11-6**). But although you scanned in grayscale, you ultimately want a straight black-and-white image. The way you get there is by choosing Image > Adjust > Threshold. The Threshold command turns gray pixels above a certain value to black and pushes all other pixels to white. By adjusting the break point where pixels go to black or white in the Threshold dialog, you can control the widths of lines in your scanned-as-grayscale line-art image.

Figure 11-6
Line art scanned
as grayscale

Scanned as line art

400 percent

Scanned as grayscale

400 percent

*Scanned as grayscale with sharpening and
threshold adjustment applied*

400 percent

The Final Conversion

When you're ready to produce the final line-art image, choose Image >
Mode > Bitmap (see **Figure 11-7**) to drop the image to a one-bit-per-pixel
black-and-white image.

Figure 11-7
Bitmap dialog

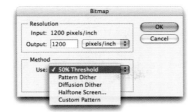

When converting a grayscale scan to line art, enter the desired line-art resolution for the Output resolution, and choose 50% Threshold from the Use pop-up menu.

Reproducing Screened Images

The problem with scanning photos already printed on a press is that they've already been halftoned. That is, the grays or colors of the image are simulated with little dots, and while our eyes are easily fooled, scanners are not. If you scan these images in Grayscale or Color mode, an imagesetter rescreens them, applying another halftone screen on top of the first. The conflict between the original halftone screen and the output screen results in a real mess (see **Figure 11-8**). The other problem is that in the original screening, a lot of the image detail is lost; the coarser the screen, the less detail remains.

> **Tip:** Since there isn't much detail in screened images, try to reproduce them at a smaller size than the original. Because the image is smaller, less detail is needed.

There are two basic approaches to working with screened images:

▶ **Line art.** Reproduce the image as black-and-white line art. This only works well with low-frequency images, under about 85 lpi. Note that you can't resize the image in a page-layout program later without making the image fall apart or creating moiré patterns. If your halftone was printed at 100 lpi or higher, it's probably better to convert it into a grayscale image using the techniques from the previous section.

> **Tip:** Many copyright violations in digital imaging occur when people scan pictures from magazines or books without thinking about rights issues. Make sure you've secured the right to reproduce the images you use.

▶ **Grayscale.** Scan in grayscale or color, then use filters to remove the halftone pattern while maintaining detail. The essential concept is "blur, then sharpen."

Frequency Considerations

One of the first things to consider when working with rescreens is the printed images' screen frequency (the dot size and spacing). Our techniques vary depending on whether we're working with low-, mid-, or high-frequency halftones.

The original halftoned image   *A halftoned halftone*

Low-frequency halftones. Low-frequency images contain little detail; scanning as grayscale is almost always futile. If the line-art techniques aren't working for you, however, you can try using the methods for medium-frequency images described in the next section.

Medium-frequency halftones. Capturing medium-frequency halftones—80 lpi to 120 lpi—is perhaps the hardest of all. These halftone spots are too small to re-create in line art, but they're too large and coarse to blend together as a grayscale image without blurring the image unacceptably (see "High-frequency halftones," later in this chapter). You know a halftone falls into this category if you can see the halftone dots when the paper is 6 inches away from your face, but you can't see them (at least, not clearly) when the paper is 2 feet away.

There are six techniques that we commonly use when scanning midfrequency halftones (there are other techniques, but we usually find these ones effective). All five attempt to capture grayscale information and remove the moiré patterns that typically occur (see **Figure 11-9**).

> ▶ **Median, Despeckle, and Dust and Scratches.** The Median and Dust and Scratches filters are probably the most effective methods for removing dot patterning, but they can also blur the images. Often you can retrieve some of the edges with Unsharp Mask, but sometimes you have to apply the filters so much that the image is damaged. Nonetheless, even a 1-pixel Dust and Scratches filter can smooth out many of

Tip: If you scan an image and you see horrible moiré patterns at 33 percent view, don't panic. Zoom in to Actual Pixels (100 percent) view to see the actual pixel structure. At magnifications below Actual Pixels, a moiré pattern can also result from the interference of the halftone pattern with the grid of screen pixels.

the problem areas in an image. Try Despeckle first, and if it doesn't work well enough (or it damages the image in ways you don't like), undo it and try Median.

► **Downsampling.** Downsampling using Bicubic Sharper interpolation (see Chapter 2, "Image Essentials") can often remove patterning, because Photoshop groups together a number of pixels and takes their average gray value. The problem, of course, is that you can also lose detail. Your goal is to downsample just enough to average out the halftone dot pattern, but not so much that you lose details in the image.

► **Upsampling.** After you downsample, you might need to upsample again to regain image resolution. You will never get lost details back, of course, but sometimes sharpening the higher-resolution image can make it appear as though you did.

► **Rotating.** When you rotate an image in Photoshop, the program has to do some heavy-duty calculation work, and those calculations typically soften the image somewhat, breaking up the halftone pattern. If you have a very slight patterning effect after scanning a pre-halftoned image, try rotating the entire image 10 or 20 degrees, and then rotate back by the same amount. This can average out some patterns.

Figure 11-9 Moiré patterns can result from rescreening mid-frequency halftones.

A 400-ppi scan of the screened image printed with a 75-lpi screen   *After using the Despeckle, Median, and Unsharp Mask filters (75 lpi)*   *After downsampling (133 lpi)*

Once you've managed to break up the halftone pattern, you'll need to go after the image with the Unsharp Mask filter to give the impression of sharpness for the detail that remains. Since the image will probably be fairly blurry, you'll have to make the more extreme sharpening moves that we suggest in Chapter 10, "Sharpness, Detail, and Noise Reduction," while being careful not to bring back the halftone pattern.

High-frequency halftones. Scanning pre-halftoned images with high screen frequencies—over 133 lpi—is often easier, because the dot patterns blur into gray levels while maintaining detail. You often need to use the techniques listed above, but you don't have to work as hard at salvaging the image. In fact, we often find that just scanning at the full optical resolution of the scanner and downsampling to the resolution you need is enough to get rid of patterning. Or, try placing the artwork at an angle on the scanner, then downsampling and rotating in Photoshop (the Crop tool lets you do both at once).

HDR Imaging

If 16 bits per channel just isn't enough, Photoshop supports HDR (High Dynamic Range) imaging, which uses 32-bit/channel floating-point data to record unlimited dynamic range. Photoshop supports established HDR formats such as Industrial Light and Magic's OpenEXR and the Radiance format used by the open-source Radiance ray-tracing and rendering engine, in addition to Portable Bitmap Format (PBM), Large Document Format (.psb), Photoshop (.psd), and TIFF. The last three formats allow profile embedding, but be aware that color-managing HDR data is an uncertain endeavor at best.

Thus far, HDR imaging has largely been confined to the movie industry and synthetic imaging produced by ray-tracing applications. Its applicability to "normal" photography is unclear, mainly because we lack any output methods that can handle the dynamic range—not even our monitors can do that. For most people, the most interesting aspect of Photoshop HDR support is that it allows you to create HDR images from bracketed exposures shot with normal cameras.

Merge to HDR

You can create HDR documents using Merge to HDR with bracketed exposures in Camera Raw format or from bracketed exposures shot as JPEG. You can also merge processed files saved in any of the formats Photoshop supports that allow EXIF metadata, but these only work if you haven't made any edits to the file, so using anything other than Camera Raw or camera-generated JPEGs just creates extra work.

Merge to HDR uses the EXIF metadata to determine the exposures and blend them accordingly. If you apply edits to Camera Raw files, they're simply ignored by Merge to HDR: If you apply edits to JPEGs (or to any of the other formats), you'll get really nasty results.

Tip: It may occur to you to use your camera's auto-bracketing feature to bracket for HDR. Check your camera specs first—many cameras can't bracket in the wide increments (one stop or greater) that are more appropriate for HDR work. You may have to bracket manually.

Shooting for HDR. We find that we get the best results when we bracket by one-third of a stop, though this may be overkill. Bracketing by one stop, using enough exposures to cover the entire dynamic range you're trying to capture, often works well. A heavy tripod, mirror lockup, and a static scene all help. Any objects in the scene that move will result in ghost fragments of the moving objects as they vary across frames, and such objects can be as seemingly innocuous as fluttering leaves.

Using Merge to HDR. The process of creating an HDR document is quite simple. You start by shooting a series of bracketed exposures that cover the dynamic range you're trying to capture. (Don't vary the aperture; that will vary your depth of focus, which you don't want to do.) The easiest way to merge the images to an HDR document is to select them in Bridge, then choose Tools > Photoshop > Merge to HDR. Or, if you want to do things the hard way, you can choose File > Automate > Merge to HDR. If you do the latter, you'll see a dialog (see **Figure 11-10**) where you choose the source images. The Attempt to Automatically Align Source Images check box benefits from the greatly improved layer alignment code in Photoshop CS3, but don't expect miracles—we find that a solid tripod remains essential.

Figure 11-10
Merge to HDR
file selection dialog

When you launch Merge to HDR from Bridge, or when you click OK in the Merge to HDR dialog, you get the dialog shown in **Figure 11-11** (also, somewhat confusingly, named Merge to HDR). The purpose of this dialog is to double-check the shots you're bringing into the merged HDR document (displayed in the filmstrip along the left side), and to preview the image that would result from the files you've selected in the filmstrip. To exclude an image from the merge, turn off its check box—handy if something in the scene has moved to the extent that it causes artifacts.

Figure 11-11
Merge to HDR
preview dialog

Click a check box to include or exclude an image from the conversion.

The histogram represents only the images included at left. Drag the preview slider to shift the 8-bit preview to the higher and lower tonal ranges of the 32-bit image.

Tip: If you used 32-bit HDR imaging in Photoshop CS2, you'll find that more editing features are available in 32-bit mode in Photoshop CS3.

Because an HDR image has far more dynamic range than a monitor can display, you can set a white point for the image preview by dragging the slider under the histogram. The preview slider only affects the 8 bit/channel preview on screen. The preview has no effect on the data in the HDR document itself—don't worry, it's all still there. When you click OK, Photoshop closes the dialog and produces the merged HDR document.

Editing the merged HDR document. Some, but not all, Photoshop features are available for a 32-bit HDR document. The available features are focused on basic image correction, such as Levels, Photo Filter, Smart Sharpen, Unsharp Mask, and the healing and cloning tools. In Photoshop Extended, painting and layers are also available. Don't try to do everything

Tip: Remember…highlights and shadows in a 32-bit image aren't necessarily clipped just because they look that way onscreen. Always drag the 32-bit preview slider to check the results of your edits on tonal levels darker or lighter than your monitor can show at any moment. The 32-bit preview slider works when a dialog is open; take advantage of that.

here—your goal is simply to create a great 32-bit source file that you'll downsample later. We find we get significantly better results sharpening the HDR image than we do sharpening after we've downsampled to 16 or 8 bits per channel.

In the 32-bit merged HDR document, the preview slider you saw in the Merge to HDR preview dialog now appears in the status bar at the bottom of the document window. When you make an adjustment that affects the entire image, drag this slider to see how the adjustment affects different parts of the tonal range (see **Figure 11-12**). Again, the preview slider only shifts the preview's tonal range—it doesn't alter the image itself. If you actually do want to alter the tones in a 32-bit image, use one of the available adjustment commands, such as Exposure or Levels.

Figure 11-12
Previewing an HDR edit

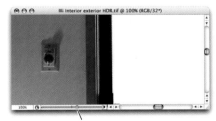
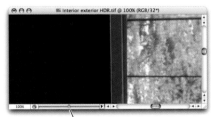

This image was just sharpened. We first drag the 32-bit preview slider at the bottom of the image to check sharpening in a darker area of the image…

…and then we drag the slider to the left to check a lighter area of the image.

We haven't mentioned the Exposure command until this point in the book because it's primarily intended for use with 32-bit images. It's similar to Levels in that you can use its controls to adjust highlights, midtones, and shadows, but the difference is that it operates in a gamma 1.0 (linear) color space. (All other adjustments in Photoshop operate using the gamma correction of the document's color space.) There are only three sliders in the Exposure dialog: Exposure controls highlights, Offset sets the shadow level, and Gamma Correction sets the midtones (see **Figure 11-13**).

Figure 11-13
Exposure dialog

Downsampling HDR Images

To do just about anything else with an HDR image, including print it, you need to downsample to 16-Bits/Channel or 8-Bits/Channel mode by choosing a command from the Image > Mode submenu. If you are working with a layered file and you want to have control over how the 32-bit tones map to the lower bit depth, first choose Layer > Flatten Image, so that when you choose Image > Mode > 8-Bits/Channel or 16-Bits/Channel, the HDR Conversion dialog appears (see **Figure 11-14**). It offers four ways to convert to a lower bit depth. Note that while you can display the Toning Curve and Histogram at the bottom of the dialog in all four methods, the controls are enabled only when you choose Local Adaptation.

Exposure and Gamma. The default method, Exposure and Gamma, offers two slider controls. Exposure sets the white point, so drag it until you like where the highlights clip. Gamma sets the midtone, so drag Gamma after setting Exposure.

Highlight Compression. There are no options for Highlight Compression—it simply does what it says. The biggest change to the image is that the highlight end of the tonal range is compressed to fit the luminance values into the 16-bit or 8-bit version.

Equalize Histogram. As with Highlight Compression, there are no options for Equalize Histogram.

Local Adaptation. Local Adaptation offers the most control, but at default settings, it often produces the least encouraging results. Nevertheless, persistence is rewarded. Local Adaptation is loosely akin to the Shadow/Highlight command in Photoshop. The Radius setting adjusts the size of the neighborhood the algorithm uses to calculate the local adaptation, while the Threshold setting tells it how far apart two pixels' tonal values must be before they're no longer part of the same brightness region. The Threshold setting essentially sets the local contrast, while the Radius setting controls the size of the local pixel neighborhood to which that contrast applies. Images with finer details will generally require a smaller Radius value.

For further control, Local Adaptation also offers the Toning Curve and Histogram. The Toning Curve differs from Photoshop Curves in a couple of ways. First, the red tick marks on the horizontal scale represent 1 EV

Figure 11-14

Converting a 32-bit HDR
image to 16-bit

*The Toning Curve and Histogram are
functional only when you choose the
Local Adaptation method.*

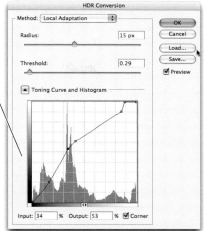

*We first try the Exposure and Gamma
method, but with just two sliders to cover
such a wide range of tones, it's hard to
avoid clipping and flat contrast.*

*Using the Local Adaptation method with a
customized Toning Curve, we're better able
to maintain detail all the way from the
shadows to the highlights.*

(Exposure Value) increments—approximately one f-stop (remember that
you're dealing with an unbounded dynamic range). The second difference
is that you can place corner points on the curve (click the Corner check
box to turn the selected curve point into a corner point), thereby creating
a sharp tonal break. This can be useful for placing a diffuse highlight and
ensuring that the specular highlights blow out.

As with the Curves dialog, you can click in the image to see where on
the curve the pixels under the cursor lie, but in the HDR Conversion dialog, you can't place points by Command-clicking (Mac) or Ctrl-clicking
(Windows) in the image.

Retouching

It's useful to make the distinction between "dust-busting" (removing specks of dirt, dust, mold, hair, and so on) and "retouching" (actually changing the content of an image). In many cases, the tools and techniques overlap, but dust-busting and retouching typically happen at different times—we prefer to do dust-busting early in the workflow, and whenever possible, do it once (since it's about as much fun as getting a root canal). In this section, we'll relay a few key pointers that we've learned over the years about both dust-busting and retouching images, in the hope that they'll make you more efficient in whatever work you're undertaking.

Dust-busting

While dust tends to be a bigger problem with film scans than with digital captures, the latter are by no means immune. For digital SLRs, dust can land on the sensor when you change the lens. We generally dust-bust early in the editing process. We usually apply noise reduction and correct overall tone and color before dust-busting.

Tip: If you discover that a certain dust spot occurs in exactly the same position on a number of frames, consider using the Retouch tool in Adobe Camera Raw 4. Once you retouch a spot in Camera Raw, you can use the Synchronize command to apply the same correction to any number of other raw, TIFF, or JPEG images. Another way to sync the correction is by using the Copy Camera Raw Settings and Paste Settings commands in Bridge.

Painting corrections on a separate layer. However you retouch your image—with the Clone Stamp tool, the Healing Brush, painting, copying pixels from other portions of the image, and so on—it's good to paint the corrections on a separate layer. When your edits are on a separate layer, it's easy to erase a change, and it's easy to see before-and-after views by turning the layer's visibility off and on. Conrad normally adds such a layer and names it "Patcher."

By default, a retouching tool paints on the layer you're correcting. However, when you're painting corrections on a separate layer, you need a way to tell the correction tool to base its correction on the image layer, since your retouching layer starts out blank. To achieve this, some tools, such as the Clone Stamp tool, provide a Sample pop-up menu in the Options bar, so that you can also make the tool sample from the current layer and layers below, or from all layers. Other tools, such as the Spot Healing Brush tool, provide only the option to sample all layers. We showed this in "Brush Tips" in Chapter 6, "Essential Photoshop Tips and Tricks."

Figure 11-15
Painting with the
Healing Brush

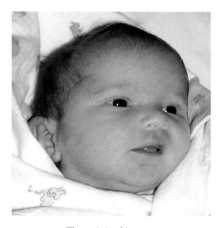 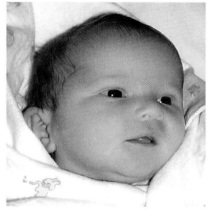

*The original image.
Infants often have splotches and
scratches that pass in a day or two.*

*Here, the red marks and
other distractions have been
removed with the Healing Brush.*

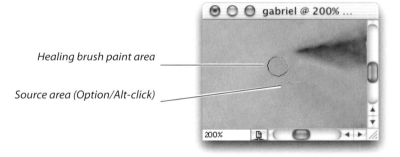

*The lip, caught by
the camera at a bad
moment, was selected with
a feathered edge and fixed
with the Liquify command.*

Healing brush paint area

Source area (Option/Alt-click)

The Healing Brushes and the Patch Tool

Photoshop introduced two new tools that should make even the most hardened retoucher crack a smile: the Healing Brush and the Patch tool. The Healing Brush (press J) is quite a marvel of modern science; you first pick a spot on your image you want to clone. Like the Clone Stamp tool, you Option-click (Mac) or Alt-click (Windows) to pick the source. You then paint in the area you want to change (see **Figure 11-15**). While the mouse button is pressed, the screen looks as though you were using the Clone Stamp tool. However, when you let go of the mouse button, Photoshop uses a complicated algorithm to blend the image of the source layer with the tone and texture of the area you're painting. The result is a clone that blends in better than the Clone Stamp tool ever could.

The more automatic Spot Healing Brush does away with the pesky requirement to choose a source point—instead, it automatically samples

Tip: The Clone Stamp tool doesn't work particularly well with soft-edged brushes because the edges get too blurry. When either brush is selected, you can select Replace from the Mode pop-up menu in the Options bar. This makes those brushes act just like the Clone Stamp tool, but it works much better if you have a hankerin' to use a soft-edged brush.

Figure 11-16

Using the Spot Healing Brush

Dust spot   Scratch   Hair

The red outline in the image above shows the area seen in detail, right.

the surrounding area. **Figure 11-16** shows an image with its fair share of flaws—the typical dust, hair, and scratches that often bedevil film.

The Spot Healing Brush handles the dust spot in **Figure 11-17** flawlessly just by clicking—we used a small brush just big enough to cover the spot. For the hair, we simply painted over it by dragging the Spot Healing Brush, again using a brush just wide enough to cover the flaw. The scratch proved slightly more problematic: Often, we can fix scratches like this by clicking the Spot Healing Brush at one end of the scratch, holding down the Shift key, and clicking at the other end of the scratch to paint in a straight line with the Spot Healing Brush. This worked everywhere except where the scratch crosses the horizon (see Figure 11-17).

In a situation like this, our first instinct is often to hit Undo, but since the repair was good everywhere except on the horizon, a better starting point is to use the History Brush to paint out only the part of the repair that didn't work. So, we set the History Brush Source to the step before the scratch-healing, then clicked with a History Brush sized to cover the artifact. In this case, we made the repair by zooming to 300 percent view, then painting with a very small (3-pixel) Spot Healing Brush.

The Patch tool is like a combination of the Healing Brush and the Lasso tool. Drag the Patch tool around an area you want to fix the same way you would make a selection with the Lasso tool. Then click inside this selection and drag it to the part of your image that you want to copy. When you let

Tip: To create straight-line segments with the Patch tool, Option-click (Mac) or Alt-click (Windows), just as you can with the Lasso too.

Figure 11-17
Spot Healing Brush results

The dust spot disappears with a single click.

The scratch is a challenge. Painting in a straight line causes an artifact where the scratch crosses the horizon.

The hair disappears with a single brushstroke.

Tip: While the Healing Brush and the Patch tool are designed to maintain the original texture of the image (such as film grain), the other retouching tools tend to destroy texture, and hence make the result appear unnatural. You can sometimes simulate lost texture by running the Add Noise or Grain filter on the affected area at a low setting, but it's generally better to keep a close eye on what's happening to your texture as you retouch.

go of the mouse button, Photoshop clones that source area over the area you first selected, and then performs its "healing" algorithm to blend in the source properly (see **Figure 11-18**).

We find that the Patch tool rarely makes a perfect fix, and the results usually need to be cleaned up with the Healing Brush or Clone Stamp tool. But using it and then cleaning up the details is still significantly faster than not using the Patch tool at all.

Snapshot patterns. Sometimes it's nice to paint a texture or a pattern with one of the brush tools. For instance, instead of adding noise to a selection, you might want to paint noise selectively. The most flexible way to do this is to create a layer by Option-clicking (Mac) or Alt-clicking (Windows) on the New Layer button in the Layers palette (which brings up the New Layer dialog). Choose Overlay from the Mode pop-up menu and turn on the Fill with Overlay-Neutral Color check box. Now run the Grain filter or Add Noise filter to this layer and add a layer mask. When you paint on the layer mask with black and white pixels, you paint the effect on and off.

A myriad of small spots. Mildew, dust, bugs, corrosives, abrasive surfaces, or even a mediocre scanner can cause hundreds or thousands of tiny white or black spots in an image. And after sharpening, these spots pop out at you like stars on the new moon. If you're like us, you're already cringing at the thought of spot-healing all those dots out.

Figure 11-18
Quick fixes with
the Patch tool

 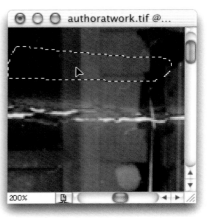

The original photograph has scratches
and folds.

After dragging out a selection
with the Patch tool, drag it on top
of an area you want to copy (above).
Here, we hold down the Shift key to
constrain the drag vertically, ensuring
the door frame will align properly when
we let go (below).

The Patch tool fixes most of the
heinous problems quickly, but the
image still requires help, especially
in the newly created anomalies in the
window panes.

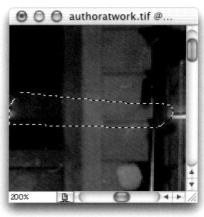

We use the Healing Brush to fix the details,
including despotting.

Here's a technique that can stamp out thousands of dust spots in a single move. You still may have to use the Healing Brush tool to get rid of a few artifacts and some of the larger spots, but most of your work will already be done (see **Figure 11-19**).

1.   Select the area with the spots, and feather the selection.

2.   Copy the selection to a new layer by pressing Command-J (Mac) or Ctrl-J (Windows).

3.   If you're trying to remove white spots, set the blending mode in the Layers palette to Darken. For black spots, set the mode to Lighten.

Figure 11-19
Getting rid of spots

The unretouched image

Setting the blending mode

Tip: When you're retouching a selected or masked area of an image, feathering the selection or mask by a pixel or two can help blend the correction with the background. If retouching causes texture to be lost, undo and try again using a lower feather amount.

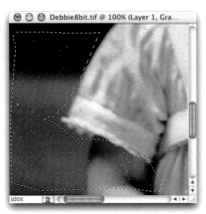

The dust spots copied to a new layer, and moved 4 pixels up and to the left

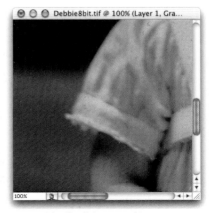

The final despotted image

4. Use the Command (Mac) or Ctrl (Windows) and arrow keys to move the new layer left, right, up, or down by a few pixels—just enough so you see the dust spots disappear (if the spots are tiny, a one- or two-pixel move does the trick).

5. You can see a before-and-after difference by turning the visibility of the new layer on and off.

6. If you want, you can merge the new layer back into the original. However, we often leave these as separate layers, so that we don't damage the original image before we have to.

At first, this seems like it takes a lot more work, but with experience, you'll find that you can make the right selections very quickly, and the dust spots simply disappear. Note that instead of using the Lighten or Darken blending mode, you can also use the Blend If sliders as we describe in "Blending Layers with the Blend If Sliders," later in this chapter. Layer blending takes more time, but offers more control.

Dust and Scratches

Tip: If your scanner has an hardware-based dust and scratch removal feature such as Digital ICE, which detects actual dust and scratches at scan time, it will be significantly more effective than the Dust and Scratches filter in Photoshop.

While the Dust and Scratches filter promises great things ("Wow, a filter that dust-busts my image!"), you should be aware that this tool can do significant harm to the rest of your image, too. The Dust and Scratches filter is basically the same as the Median filter, but with a threshold feature (so you have some control over what gets "Median-ized"). That means that it removes all small details in your document, including film grain or other image details that might be important.

If, in fact, you're trying to smooth out a grainy image while dust-busting, Dust and Scratches might be just the ticket. In that case, make sure you set the Radius value as low as possible and the Threshold value as high as possible. (It'll take some trial and error to get it right, so that the dust and scratches are gone but the image isn't too blurry.) Then, resharpen the image with Unsharp Mask to return some edge contrast.

The Clone Stamp Tool

The Clone Stamp tool lets you copy pixels from anyplace in your image (or even another image) and then paint them someplace else: Option-click (Mac) or Alt-click (Windows) to pick up a source point, and then paint away elsewhere to copy those pixels. Remember that you can control the opacity and blending mode of the tool using the Options bar or with keystrokes (see Chapter 6, "Essential Photoshop Tips and Tricks").

Keep jumping around. The single biggest mistake people make when using the Clone Stamp tool to clone from one area to another is dragging the mouse in a painting fashion. You should almost never paint when cloning. Instead, dab here and there with a number of clicks.

One exception to this rule is when the area you're cloning is relatively flat and has little texture or detail (like the blurry background behind a portrait). The second exception we make is when we're using the Clone Stamp tool with a blending mode like Darken, Lighten, Soft Light, and so on—and then only when the effect is subtle and doesn't create an obvious clone.

A second mistake people make is continuing to clone from the same area. Keep changing the source point that you're cloning (the point on which you Option/Alt-click). For example, if you're erasing some specks of

Tip: Don't let the boundaries of your image's window restrict you. If you want to clone from another open document, go right ahead and do it. You don't even have to switch documents, as long as you have a large enough monitor.

Figure 11-20
Changing the
source point

The annoying tree branches in the above left image can be removed by cloning with the Clone Stamp. But simply selecting a source point and painting with the Clone Stamp produces the "hall of mirrors" effect seen in the image above right. Dabbing with the Clone Stamp and choosing a new source point each time produces the more convincing result shown at left.

dust on someone's face, don't just clone from one side of the specks. Erase one speck from pixel information to the left; erase the second speck from the right, and so on. That way, you avoid creating repeating patterns, and you make the retouch less obvious (see **Figure 11-20**).

There are times, of course, when both of these pieces of advice should be chucked out the window. For example, if you're rebuilding a straight line by cloning another parallel line in the image, you'd be hard-pressed to clone it by any other method than painting in the whole line. The following tip provides a way to do so relatively painlessly.

Stroking paths. If you're trying to get rid of long scratches in an image, or to clone out those power lines that are always much more noticeable in a

Figure 11-21
Stroking a path with the
Clone Stamp tool

Getting rid of the power lines by hand would take forever.

We draw a path along the power line. Then, with the Clone Stamp tool set to a small, soft-edged brush, we carefully click a source point slightly offset from one end of the path.

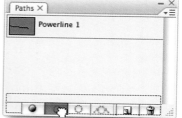

We Shift-click on the path in the Paths palette to hide the path, then drag the path over the Stroke Path with Brush button at the bottom of the palette.

Repeating the process for the remaining power lines cleans up the image. The critical steps are setting the correct brush size and source point. In some cases, it's best to split the path into sections, choosing a different source for each one.

photograph than they were in reality, you can use the Pen tool to define a path, then use the Clone Stamp tool to stroke the path, obliterating the offending pixels in one fell swoop (see **Figure 11-21**).

1. Draw the path using the Pen tool, keeping it as close to the center of the scratch (or power line, or whatever) as possible. It's a good idea to save it (double-click on Work Path in the Paths palette and name it).

2. Select the Clone Stamp tool and click the Aligned button in the Options bar. To remove a light-colored scratch, set the mode to Darken; to remove a dark power line, set the mode to Lighten.

3. Choose a soft brush a little wider than the widest point of the scratch.

Tip: Having trouble precisely aligning the source point? Try using the preview overlay in the Clone Source palette, which we talk about next.

4. Option-click (Mac) or Alt-click (Windows) beside the start of the path to set the source point for the cloning operation, just as you would if you were going to clone-stamp the scratch by hand.

5. Shift-click on the path in the Paths palette to hide it, then drag the path over the Stroke button at the bottom of the palette. Presto, the scratch is gone.

Using the Clone Source Palette

New in Photoshop CS3, the Clone Source palette removes many of the hassles associated with the Clone Stamp or Healing Brush tool. In previous versions of Photoshop, if the destination wasn't perfectly aligned with the source point due to rotation or distortion in the subject, you had to compensate by frequently changing the source point of the Clone Stamp tool. The Clone Source palette helps you position and angle the source point precisely, before you start cloning. On top of that, the Clone Source palette can remember up to five source points, so that if you have to go back and redo or refine a previous area, you don't have to tediously re-establish where it was. These features save so much time that you'll never want to use previous versions' Clone Stamp tool again.

Tip: Not sure if you're about to wipe out a Clone Source button you're already using? Hold the mouse over the Clone Source button to see its tool tip. If it's in use, the tool tip displays the clone source's document. If it isn't in use, the tool tip says "Clone source: not in use."

Open the Clone Source palette by choosing Window > Clone Source, or click the Clone Source icon in the dock, if it's visible (see **Figure 11-22**).

Setting multiple clone sources. The five icons across the top of the Clone Source palette represent the five source points you can save. The selected Clone Source button is the one that remembers where you've Option-

Figure 11-22
Clone Source palette

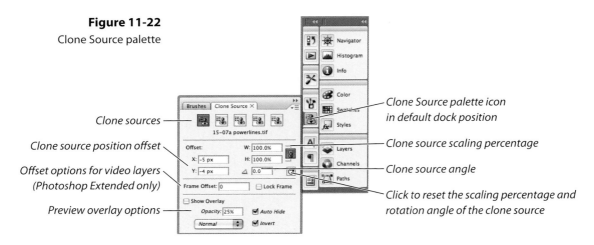

Clone sources

Clone source position offset

Offset options for video layers
(Photoshop Extended only)

Preview overlay options

Clone Source palette icon
in default dock position

Clone source scaling percentage

Clone source angle

Click to reset the scaling percentage and
rotation angle of the clone source

clicked/Alt-clicked, so if you want the Clone Source palette to remember a different source point, select a different Clone Source button first. Of course, all you have to do to switch to a different clone source is to click the Clone Source button you used to save it—kind of like saving and recalling radio stations using the radio buttons on a car stereo. Keep in mind that a clone source can be in a different open document, so your five saved clone sources can come from various open documents.

Setting the clone source offset. Use the Offset section of the Clone Source palette to make the clone source do your bidding. The X and Y fields describe how far away you Option-clicked/Alt-clicked the clone source, or you can enter values here (to change the unit of measure there, right-click, or Ctrl-click in Mac OS X). The keys W and H control the scaling percentage of the width and height of the clone source, respectively, and the angle field lets you rotate the clone source in degrees.

Using the preview overlay. The preview overlay shows you where the cloned pixels will land when you click or drag. One way to show it is to turn on the Show Overlay check box in the Clone Source palette; when you do this, you'll see a semitransparent copy of the image that moves with the cursor (see **Figure 11-23**), telling you where you'll be painting the cloned source pixels when you click or drag. As soon as you click or drag, the overlay goes away, because you've positioned it. (If the Auto-Hide check box is on, the overlay remains visible as you paint.) If you Option-click/Alt-click a new source point, the overlay appears again until you click or

Tip: You can nudge the position, scale, or angle of the Clone Source overlay using the usual arrow key shortcuts in the Clone Source palette fields. Click in a field and press the up arrow or down arrow keys, and optionally add the Shift key for larger nudge increments.

Figure 11-23
Clone source
preview overlay

*In the original image, we
Option/Alt-clicked the
clone source point where
these four tiles meet.*

*We dragged the overlay to
another tile intersection to
preview the alignment of
the clone to the original.*

*Thanks to the preview
overlay, the cloned pixels
align perfectly when we
brush them in.*

drag to set the new source. If you chose to leave Show Overlay off, you can press Option-Shift (Mac) or Alt-Shift (Windows) to display the overlay.

If you don't quite manage to align the overlay correctly the first time, there's no need to start over. Just Option-Shift-drag (Mac) or Alt-Shift-drag (Windows) to reposition the overlay; the overlay will be visible only when you drag. To numerically position, scale, or rotate the overlay, enter values into the Offset section of the Clone Source palette. To reflect the clone you're painting, click the link icon to turn it off, and enter a negative value into the W or H fields. An undistorted reflection is represented by -100 percent.

> **Note:** In Photoshop Extended, the Clone Source palette includes the Frame Offset and Lock Frame options, used when cloning between video frames (Photoshop video layers are outside the scope of this book).

Removing Red-Eye

A common retouching task is removing red-eye—that devilish effect that appears when a camera flash reflects off the retina. Ideally, you'll avoid red-eye by using off-camera flash, but if your (or someone else's) photograph already has red-eye, you'll have to remove the red. The Red-Eye tool (sharing a Tool-palette slot with the Healing Brushes and the Patch tool) is by far the easiest way of doing so, but sometimes it removes the eye color too, so we still resort to the following techniques when necessary.

> **Tip:** You can also use the Red-Eye Removal tool in Camera Raw if you're retouching a camera raw, TIFF, or JPEG image.

Hue/Saturation. Select the offending pupils with an oval marquee, feather the selection by a few pixels, copy the selection to a new layer (Command-J in Mac OS X, Ctrl-J in Windows), and then use Hue/Saturation to shift the color, brightness, and saturation. Every image requires different values, but we usually start with Hue at +40 (for brown eyes) or -120 (for blue eyes), Saturation at -75, and a Lightness value of -50. The key is to remove the glaring color while still maintaining the specular highlights and color that make the eye look alive.

Color Replacement tool. The Color Replacement tool now shares a slot with the Brush in the Tool palette. It lets you change the color of pixels to the foreground color but leave the pixels' saturation and brightness alone. In other words, it changes the color but retains the detail. We haven't found it useful for large areas, but it's quite good at fixing things like red-eye. Hold down the Option key (Mac) or Alt key (Windows) and click on the darkest part of the eye (or some other dark area nearby), then let go of the Option/Alt key, adjust the brush size to slightly smaller than the pupil, and draw over the red portions. You may need to increase the Tolerance level in the Options bar to 35 or 40 percent.

Perspective Retouching

The Vanishing Point filter makes editing in perspective orders of magnitude easier than it used to be. Vanishing Point is a very deep plug-in, and if you plan to use it a lot, we strongly recommend reading about Vanishing Point in the online Photoshop Help file, and mastering the considerable number of keyboard shortcuts. Perspective cloning isn't something we do a lot, so we'll barely scratch the surface here, but we hope to at least give you an idea of the process and a hint of its power.

To open Vanishing Point, choose Filter > Vanishing Point, or press Command-Option-V (Mac) or Ctrl-Alt-V (Windows).

Defining the planes. The first step in using Vanishing Point is to define a perspective plane by clicking on four points, and then enlarge the plane to cover the area you want to affect, as shown in **Figure 11-24**. Watch the color and size of the grid when dragging its corners or sides: Red means the grid is not a valid perspective; yellow is pretty close, and blue is good. But in general it's better to see a grid of bigger squares than smaller rectangles. Sometimes moving the grid corners by a pixel or two will make a big difference in the quality of the perspective.

Performing the cloning. Once you've defined the plane, you can use the Marquee or Clone Stamp tool to clone regions in the image or paste elements from other images. In this simple example, we used the marquee to select the light fixture, then Option/Alt-dragged it to create duplicates. Note that the selection created by the marquee automatically conforms to the perspective plane (see **Figure 11-25**).

In this simple example, we used a single perspective plane. Once you've defined the basic plane, you can create additional hinged planes

Tip: Create a new layer for Vanishing Point to keep your Vanishing Point edits separate from the original layer.

Tip: Take care of lens distortions first. Vanishing Point calculates mathematically perfect planes, so if your lens shows any barrel or pincushion distortion, the cloned results may be a little off. We recommend running the Lens Correction filter before running Vanishing Point.

Figure 11-24
Defining a
perspective plane

Figure 11-24
Defining a
perspective plane

*The Create Plane tool
lets you click to define
the corners of a
perspective plane.*

*New in Photoshop CS3 is a
pop-up menu containing
commands for viewing,
rendering, and exporting the
perspective grid.*

*The Edit Plane tool
lets you scale the plane by
dragging the edge and
corner handles.*

by Command-dragging (Mac) or Ctrl-dragging (Windows) a side (not corner) handle on the edge of a plane. In Photoshop CS3, after you extend a
hinged plane, you can adjust its angle by Option-dragging (Mac) or Alt-
dragging (Windows) one of its side handles or by editing the Angle field at
the top of the Vanishing Point dialog. And while we generally find that it's
easier to fine-tune the result on a layer after we've run Vanishing Point, the
Transform tool in Vanishing Point lets you transform floating selections.

For more complex cloning operations, we use Vanishing Point's Stamp
tool, which works just like the Clone Stamp tool. We could have achieved
the same result in **Figure 11-25** by using the Clone Stamp tool instead of
the technique shown in the figure.

In Photoshop CS3, Vanishing Point adds a round pop-up menu button,
just to the right of the Tool palette. The menu contains commands for

adjusting the view, rendering the grid data as a Photoshop layer, and exporting the grid as 3D data (Photoshop Extended only).

Figure 11-25
Cloning with the marquee

We select the area we want to clone with the marquee, which automatically conforms to the perspective grid.

We Option/Alt-drag the selection to create duplicates in perspective.

Compositing Images

The number one problem in making selections and compositing images together is *edge spill*, where some of the background color gets picked up as a distracting fringe along the edges of your selection. Photoshop provides several tools for intelligently removing edge spill instead of crudely cutting out the background pixels. The Blend If sliders provide an easy way to isolate areas by their gray level. The Extract feature is designed to search out edges, erase pixels, and—most important—perform edge-color decontamination, where Photoshop distills out background colors while leaving the foreground colors. The Magic Eraser and Background Eraser tools erase to transparency, but because they aren't very flexible we prefer the other methods.

Compositing images can also mean assembling multiple images along their common areas or edges, such as building a panorama. For this type of compositing, Photoshop CS3 brings major improvements in the form of the Auto-Align Layers, Auto-Blend Layers, and Photomerge features.

Blending Layers with the Blend If Sliders

One of our favorite compositing techniques doesn't involve making selections or using Extract. It involves the little-known and less-understood Blend If feature in the Layer Style dialog. If your image stands out well from its background on any one channel, layer blending is often the fastest way to composite it into a different background (see **Figure 11-26**).

Figure 11-26

Compositing an image with layer-blending

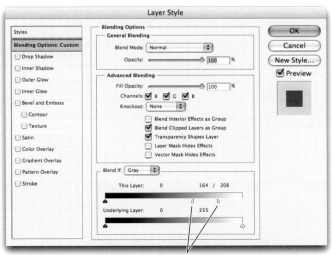

We Option/Alt-drag one half of a Blend If slider to split it from the other half of the slider, feathering the blend at the specified values.

When you set the right This Layer slider in the Layer Style dialog to 20 percent gray, you're telling Photoshop *not* to include any pixels in the layer that are lighter than 20 percent. The problem: this creates a hard edge, so you get a jaggy composite. The solution: Option-drag (Mac) or Alt-drag (Windows) any Blend If slider to break it into two half-sliders. This provides a smooth blend between what is included and what is not.

Extract: Quick 'n' Dirty Masking

Separating objects from backgrounds is such a common, yet challenging, task that people often buy a plug-in for it. The good news is that Adobe created the Extract feature to save you the trouble. The bad news is that you'll probably still want to go buy one.

Tip: We recommend running Extract on a duplicate layer, because it actually changes and deletes pixels instead of creating a mask or selection. Alternatively, create a History snapshot. In any case, leave yourself an escape route.

Don't get us wrong: The Extract feature is reasonably good at what it does, but what it does is not nearly as powerful as most people want. Nonetheless, Extract is what we've got for now—assuming that you don't have another plug-in, such as OnOne's Mask Pro—and so Extract is what we're going to talk about.

When to use Extract. There is a temptation to use Extract for any and every selection. Don't. Remember that Color Range or any of the other selection tools may provide a better, faster result. It depends entirely on the image and what you mean to do with it. Extract works best with images that display significant contrast between foreground object and background color, and where the edges aren't too detailed. For instance, your best friend photographed against a bright-blue sky would work well. On the other hand, you're going to have more trouble with an image of the typical blond model, hair shimmering against golden sand.

Tip: If you're comfortable creating a good initial edge selection outside of the Extract dialog (see Chapter 9, "Making Selections"), choose Select > Modify > Border to create a wide outline and save the selection as a channel. In the Extract dialog, you can choose the saved selection from the Channel pop-up menu instead of having to draw one using the Edge Highlighter tool.

The best reason to use Extract is its edge-color decontamination. If you're just trying to make a selection and you're not planning on compositing an object on top of some other background (one with a very different tonal or color range than its original), then you'll probably find more peace of mind with another selection method.

Step-by-step extraction. Once you've identified an appropriate image, open the Extract dialog by choosing Extract from the Filter menu (in earlier versions, it was in the Image menu). Better yet, just press Command-Option-X (Mac) or Ctrl-Alt-X (Windows) to open the Extract dialog (see **Figure 11-27**).

Figure 11-27

The Extract dialog

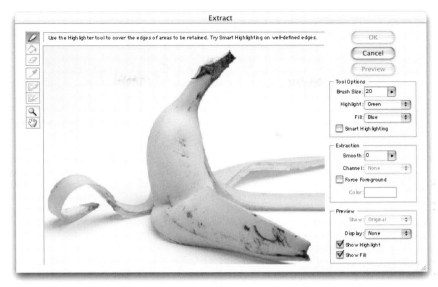

Tip: Shift-click to draw faster edges with the Edge Highlighter tool. We don't have particularly steady hands, so when it comes to drawing out the edge of the image with the Edge Highlighter tool, we tend to click once on the edge, then Shift-click someplace else. Photoshop draws a straight line between the two points. These straight lines are often perfect for tracing the edge of an image.

1. Use the Edge Highlighter tool to paint a line along the edge of the foreground object (the thing you're trying to extract). The Edge Highlighter should already be highlighted; if it's not, press B to select it. If you make a mistake, you can erase the "paint" with the Eraser tool (press E).

    When painting, you can press the bracket keys—[and]—to change the size of the highlighter brush. This is important because the brush size has a direct effect on the way Photoshop extracts the image. In general, you want a smaller brush around hard, defined edges, and a larger brush around soft, hairy, difficult edges. Note that you need to completely cover the edge transition with the highlighter, but you want the smallest brush you can get away with (see **Figure 11-28**). You also want to target the transition area and stay away from the foreground object (the part you want opaque) as much as possible.

2. Now select the Fill tool (press G) from the Extract dialog and click on the foreground object (inside the line you just drew). This tells Photoshop which side of the line is the stuff you want to keep. If the Fill tool fills past the boundaries of your highlighter line, then there's a break in the line somewhere. In that case, select the Edge Highlighter tool again, fill in the break, and then re-click with the Fill tool.

3. Once you've marked the edge (with the Edge Highlighter) and marked the inside of the object (with the Fill tool), you must click the Preview button to see the result. If you don't like what you see, you can tweak

Figure 11-28
Extracting the
foreground object

 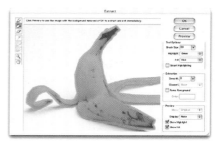

*First, use the highlighter tool to define the
edge of the object. Use as small a brush
as you can while still overlapping the
transition pixels.*

*Click inside the object to tell Extract what
to save.*

*After you click Preview, you can change
the matte color (here it's green) to see the
image over different colors.*

the highlighter edge, but first turn on the Show Highlight check box
and set the View pop-up menu to Original.

4. Finally, when you have the effect you want, you can click OK. Photoshop
deletes the background pixels, leaves the inside pixels, and "decon-
taminates" the pixels covered by the highlighter. The result is hardly
ever perfect, so you must typically use the History Brush, the Clone
Stamp tool, or any number of other methods to tune the image.

Auto-Align Layers and Auto-Blend Layers

We think Auto-Align Layers and Auto-Blend Layers are two of the coolest
features in Photoshop CS3. They not only automate the onerous task of
aligning images, but they do it quickly and well.

Auto-Align Layers. This feature aligns selected layers intelligently and reliably by looking for common areas in an image. Auto-Align Layers comes in
handy any time you need to perfectly register two images, especially when

Note: Auto-Align Layers works only with raster layers; you'll need to rasterize other types of layers before applying Auto-Align Layers. For example, if an image is a Smart Object, select it and choose Layer > Smart Objects > Rasterize.

you want to combine them. For example, you may have two or three nearly identical handheld photos of a group, and one of your subjects blinks in each photo. Just apply Auto-Align Layers and paint in some masks, and you can easily produce a photo in which everyone's eyes are open. Because that example is widely demonstrated, we have another example: Two photos with a common overlapping side. We select them in Bridge and press Return or Enter to pop them open in Photoshop.

Auto-Align Layers only aligns layers within a single image, so we use the Move tool to drag one image into the other image window, without worrying where we drop it (see **Figure 11-29**). Now we select both layers in the Layers palette, and choose Edit > Auto-Align Layers.

In the Auto-Align Layers dialog, we try a Projection option and click OK. If we don't like it, we undo, choose the command again, and try another

Figure 11-29
Using Auto-Align Layers

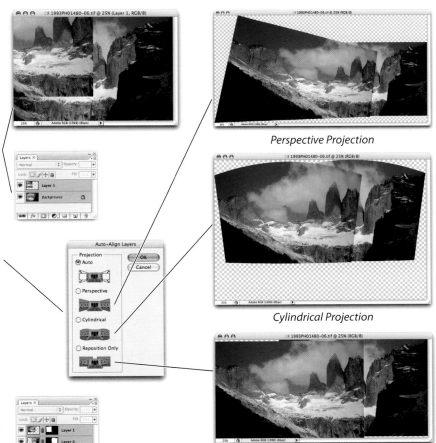

We first drag one image into another to create one image with two layers, and select the layers in the Layers palette.

We choose Edit > Auto-Align Layers, and we try the Projection options in the Auto-Align Layers dialog. We show the results of each option along the right column. When you select Auto, Photoshop chooses one of the other options depending on the images.

After auto-aligning layers, the layers are still separate, along with new layer masks added by Photoshop. You can edit the layer masks.

Perspective Projection

Cylindrical Projection

Reposition Only (no projection)

option. The Auto option just picks one of the other three. For our images, it looks like a toss-up between Cylindrical and Reposition Only, but upon closer inspection, there is an edge mismatch in Reposition Only that is resolved with the Cylindrical option, so we go with Cylindrical. There is still a visible seam due to exposure and contrast differences—we'll take care of that by applying Auto-Blend Layers a little later on. If there were a third photo, Perspective would have created a better result, because Perspective takes the center image and makes it the reference image for applying perspective projection to the left and right images. You can use any number of images you want, but more images take longer to analyze and process.

Auto-Blend Layers. Often, getting layers aligned is only half the battle. Exposure differences and lens vignetting can leave visible seams across images that are quite time-consuming to remove by hand (using masks, curves, and cloning tools). Auto-Blend Layers automates seam removal, and is even easier than Auto-Align Layers because there are no options: Select the layers in the Layers palette, and choose Edit > Auto Blend Layers (see **Figure 11-30**). If you weren't very happy with the automatic layer-blending in Photoshop CS2, take a second look; blending in Photoshop CS3 is much improved.

Tip: While Auto-Align Layers, Auto-Blend Layers, and Photomerge are far more forgiving than the panorama features in Photoshop CS2, you'll still maximize your chance of a successful panorama if you capture each frame using the same exposure settings and the same lighting, using a tripod to keep the camera level.

Figure 11-30
Using Auto-Blend Layers, and the final image

Applying Auto-Blend Layers removes the visible seam caused by the exposure differences between layers.

The final image after cropping, applying curves, and sharpening.

Photomerge

You might have noticed that the example we used for Auto-Align Layers and Auto-Blend Layers is a two-image panorama. While you could use those features to build panoramas, it's easier to save a step by using the Photomerge feature. As usual, the easiest way to run Photomerge is to select images in Bridge and choose Tools > Photoshop > Photomerge. If you're starting from Photoshop, choose File > Automate > Photomerge

Figure 11-31
Photomerge

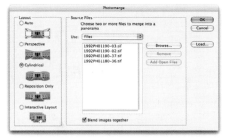

In Bridge, we select four sloppily photographed scans of color negatives.

The Photomerge dialog combines the Auto-Align Layers dialog with a file selector.

Thanks to Auto-Align Layers, Photomerge can detect any common edges—one of the images is vertical, attached to the others by all edges except its bottom. Also, the first photo selected in Bridge is not actually part of this scene, and Photomerge correctly omits it from the panorama.

The odd shape was interesting, but we decide to crop the corrected and sharpened image.

and select files using the Source Files options in the Photomerge dialog (see **Figure 11-31**).

Because Photomerge is essentially a combination of Auto-Align Layers and Auto-Blend Layers, you've seen the rest of the options in the Photomerge dialog. The Layout options are the same as the ones in the Auto-Align Layers dialog, and the Blend Images Together check box applies Auto-Blend Layers. Unlike the Auto-Align Layers command, you don't have to convert multiple files into a single layered file before you can begin—Photomerge streamlines that for you.

Auto-Align Layers (and by extension, Photomerge) doesn't just align variations of a single scene or frames of a horizontal panorama. It is fully capable of two-dimensional stitching, intelligent enough to find common edges along any sides of the selected images. For example, you can shoot a scene as a set of tiled images, eight across and eight down, and Photomerge can snap it all together, even if you shoot each image at a different angle.

If you're looking for the manual vanishing point and positioning controls that Photomerge contained in Photoshop CS2, stop looking: They're gone. Those controls were there only because Photomerge couldn't always figure out what to do with the images. Photomerge is so much more intelligent in Photoshop CS3 that the manual controls are no longer needed.

Tip: When you must align layers completely by hand, let opacity or a blending mode help you. Lowering the opacity lets you see if you're aligning to underlying layers. Changing the blending mode to Difference, Darken, or Lighten helps emphasize overlapping layers that are in register.

Vectors vs. Pixels

So far, we've talked about pixel editing, because that's the reason Photoshop exists at all. But you can also create and edit vector-based paths, as you can in a drawing program like Adobe Illustrator CS3.

What good are vector paths and drawing tools in Photoshop? Vectors are infinitely modifiable, resolution independent, and can easily be converted to bitmapped images at the drop of a hat. Here are some of the ways you can take advantage of vector paths in Photoshop:

▶ Draw smooth lines a lot faster than trying to paint them

▶ Copy and paste paths between Photoshop and Adobe Illustrator

▶ Convert among paths, selections, masks, and channels

▶ Create vector masks, called *shapes*

▶ Draw shapes that remain smooth vectors all the way to output

▶ Convert text to shapes (so you can edit the outlines)

▶ Save EPS or TIFF images with a vector mask called a *clipping path*

▶ Maintain vector paths as a Smart Object layer

Photoshop also has very powerful tools for handling text (which by default are vectors), including placing text along a path. We cover the text features later in this chapter.

Tip: If you think you'll be drawing paths often, the best way to train is to use any of the many drawing tutorials designed for Adobe Illustrator. We can suggest *Real World Illustrator CS3* by Mordy Golding, and the *Adobe Illustrator CS3 Wow! Book* by Sharon Steuer, both from Peachpit Press.

Strengths and weaknesses. Curiously, the primary strength and weakness of paths stem from the same attribute: Paths have no connection to the pixels below them; they live on a separate mathematical plane in Photoshop, forever floating above those lowly bitmapped images.

The strength of this is that you can create, edit, and save paths without regard for the resolution of the image or even for the image itself. You can create a path in the shape of a logo (or better yet, import the path from Illustrator or FreeHand) and drop it into any image. Then you can save it as a path in Photoshop, ask the program to rasterize the path (turn it into a bitmapped image), drop it down into the pixel layers, convert the path to a selection, or just leave it as a path so that it prints with sharp edges (as high resolution as the PostScript device you print on).

The weakness of paths used as selections or masks is that they can't capture the subtlety and nuance found in most bitmapped images. A path can't, for instance, have any partially selected pixels or blurry parts; you can only achieve hard-edged selections (see **Figure 11-32**).

Figure 11-32
Paths versus channels

 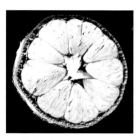 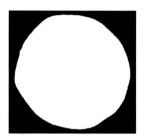

The original image *Selection masks can partially select pixels (here only selecting orange).* *Paths are good at clean, sharp outlines, but they can't select image detail.*

Creating and Editing Paths

If you've used an advanced drawing program such as Adobe Illustrator, you're already familiar with drawing and editing paths in Photoshop (see **Figure 11-33**).

The Paths palette displays all the paths in your document and gives you some control over what to do with them. To draw a path, you must select one of the Pen tools or Shape tools in the Tools palette. There are seven Pen tools and six Shape tools, but we tend to use only two or three of the Pen tools, using modifier keys to get to the rest.

In the same way that a channel has no visible effect on a document until you apply it as a selection or mask, it's important to understand that just because you can see a path doesn't mean it currently has a visible effect on a document. When you select a path in the Paths palette, you can see it in the document, but the path can't visibly change the document until you convert it to a selection, vector mask, or clipping path. A shape or a vector mask are paths that are visible because they act as a mask on a layer; we talk about those in "Shapes and Vector Masks" later on.

Pen tool. The Pen tool (press P) is our primary tool for drawing paths, because it's the most precise. Without modifier keys, you can draw straight-line paths by clicking, or curved paths by clicking and dragging. You can also easily access any of the other tools. For instance, if you move this tool over a point on a line, it automatically changes to the Delete Anchor

Figure 11-33
Paths

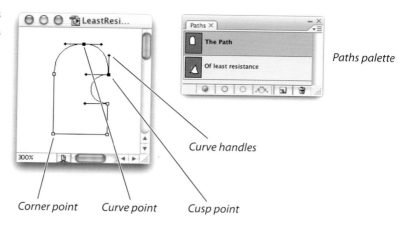

Paths palette

Curve handles

Corner point   Curve point   Cusp point

Point tool. If you move the Pen tool over a segment, it lets you add a point (click or click and drag). If you're forever adding or deleting points when you don't mean to, just turn off the Auto Add/Delete check box on the Options bar.

Freeform Pen tool. David got into this business because he can't draw worth beans, but if you've got a steady hand and a sure heart—and a graphics tablet wouldn't hurt, either—you might find yourself wanting to draw paths with the Freeform Pen tool. When you release the mouse button, Photoshop converts your loose path to a smooth path full of corner, curve, and cusp points. (Exactly how closely Photoshop follows your lead is up to the Curve Fit setting on the Options bar.)

Selection tools. As in Illustrator and InDesign, Photoshop has both a Selection tool and a Direct Selection tool. You can press A (for "arrow") to jump to the selection tool in the Tools palette, and then press Shift-A if you want the other selection tool. These tools let you select a point or points on the path. For example, you can select points on a curve with the Direct Select tool by clicking on them or by dragging a marquee around them. To select all the points on a curve, click the curve with the Selection tool or Option-click (Mac) or Alt-click (Windows) the path with the Direct Select tool; you can also Command-Option-click (Mac) or Ctrl-Alt-click (Windows) the Pen tool on a curve.

Once you've selected a point or a path, you can move it. As in most other programs, if you hold down the Shift key, Photoshop only lets you move the points in 90- or 45-degree angles. If you hold down the Option/Alt key when you click and drag, Photoshop moves a copy of the entire path.

Tip: You can move selected paths or points one pixel at a time using the arrow keys—but only when the Pen or one of the Selection tools is selected in the Tool palette. Or, if you hold down the Shift key, the arrow keys move the path ten image pixels (not screen pixels). At 100 percent view, image pixels and screen pixels are the same thing, of course.

Convert Point tool. When you're working with the Pen tool, you can create a sharp corner by clicking or a rounded corner by dragging. When you have two round corners on either side of a corner point, that corner point is called a *cusp* point. But what if you change your mind and want to make a corner into a curve, or a curve into a cusp?

The Convert Point tool lets you add or remove curve *handles* (those levers that stick out from the sides of curve or cusp points). If you click once on a point that has curve handles, the curve handles disappear (they get sucked all the way into the point), and the point becomes a corner. If you click and drag with the Convert Point tool, you can pull those handles out of the point, making the corner a curve.

Similarly, you can make a cusp by clicking and dragging on one of the control handles on either side of the point. If you select the Pen tool, you can get the Convert Point tool by holding down the Option/Alt key.

Tip: As in Illustrator, you can drag a path segment with the Selection tool; you don't first have to select the points on the ends of the segment. If it's a curved segment, Photoshop adjusts the curve handles on either side of it automatically. If it's a straight-line segment (hence there are no curve handles to adjust), Photoshop moves the points on either side of the segment.

Cusp points. Many folks tell us that they make all points cusp points while drawing paths. Here's how: To create the first point of the path, just click and drag to set the angle of the first curve. All subsequent points on the path are created by clicking, dragging to set the angle of the previous curve, and then Option-dragging (Mac) or Alt-dragging (Windows) from the point to set the launch angle of the next curve. Finally, to close the path (if you want it closed), Option/Alt-click if you want the final segment to be a straight line. If you want the final segment to be a curve, Option-drag (Mac) or Alt-drag (Windows) the first point of the path. While it takes some getting used to and takes a bit more work, this technique gives you much more control over the angle and curve of each segment in the path because each point is independent of the ones on either side.

Magnetic Pen tool. Once the engineers at Adobe figured out how to make the Magnetic Lasso tool, it was a snap for them to add the functionality to the Pen tool, too. Thus, the Magnetic Pen tool was born. (Well, it's not really a separate tool; you get it by turning on the check box labeled Magnetic on the Options bar.) The Magnetic Lasso and the Magnetic Pen work so similarly that it's hardly worth discussing twice; instead go read that section in Chapter 9, "Making Selections." Their similarity extends to producing a result that you will almost certainly have to finesse; the magnetic tools are not known for their precision.

Paths vs. Shapes vs. Pixels. When you use the Pen tools, you need to specify in the Options bar whether you want the Pen tools to create a path or a vector shape. When you select one of the Shape tools, you can choose path, vectors, or pixels (see **Figure 11-34**).

Figure 11-34
The Options bar for the Path and Shape tools

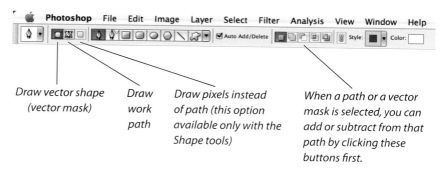

Draw vector shape (vector mask)

Draw work path

Draw pixels instead of path (this option available only with the Shape tools)

When a path or a vector mask is selected, you can add or subtract from that path by clicking these buttons first.

Connecting paths. Want to connect two paths? It's not too hard to do.

1. Use the Path Selection tool to select one of the path's endpoints.

2. Switch to the Pen tool.

3. If you want that point to be a cusp, Option-drag (Mac) or Alt-drag (Windows) a handle out of the point.

4. Click and drag on the other path's endpoint. Alternatively, Option-drag (Mac) or Alt-drag (Windows) to make it a cusp point.

Paths to Selections

Once you have a path, you can convert it into a selection, rasterize it (turn it into pixels), or fill it with a color or adjustment. Let's look at converting to selections first. When a path is selected in the Paths palette, you can convert it into a selection in one of four ways:

▶ Select Make Selection from the Paths palette menu (or drag the path's thumbnail on top of this button).

▶ Click on the Convert Path to Selection button (see **Figure 11-35**).

▶ Command-click (Mac) or Ctrl-click (Windows) on the path's thumbnail in the Paths palette.

▶ Press Command-Enter (Mac) or Ctrl-Enter (Windows).

Tip: The Edit > Free Transform command works on paths, as do the many commands in the Transform submenu (under the Edit menu). You don't have to transform the entire path, either. You can transform just selected points, segments, or subpaths (to select a subpath, Option/Alt-click with the Selection tool).

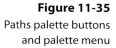

Figure 11-35
Paths palette buttons
and palette menu

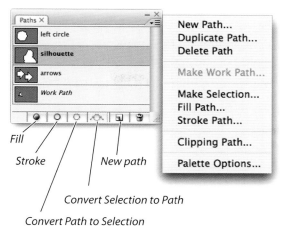

Fill

Stroke   *New path*

Convert Selection to Path

Convert Path to Selection

Tip: When a path is selected in the Paths palette or a vector mask is selected in the Layers palette, Photoshop displays the path as a gray line. When you have a non-painting tool selected in the Tool palette (like the selection tools or the Move tool), you can deselect and hide the path by pressing the Enter key.

If you hold down the Option key (Mac) or Alt key (Windows) while dragging a path on top of, or clicking on, the Convert Path to Selection button, Photoshop displays the Make Selection dialog. This dialog lets you add, subtract, or intersect selections with selections you've already made (if there is no selection, these options are grayed out). It also lets you feather and anti-alias the selections. The default for selections (if you don't go in and change this dialog) is to include anti-aliasing, but not feathering.

Alternatively, you can use these keyboard shortcuts instead of the Make Selection dialog to add, subtract, or intersect paths:

▶ Command-Shift-Enter (Mac) or Ctrl-Shift-Enter (Windows) adds the path's selection to the current selection (if there is one).

▶ Command-Option-Enter (Mac or Ctrl-Alt-Enter (Windows) subtracts the selection.

▶ Command-Shift-Option-Enter (Mac) or Ctrl-Shift-Alt-Enter (Windows) intersects the two selections.

Each of these works when clicking on the Make Selection icon or dragging the thumbnail over the icon, too, but the Enter key is faster.

Selections to Paths

Tip: If you make a selection before filling or stroking your path, Photoshop fills or strokes only within that selection. This has tripped up more than one advanced user, but if you're aware of the feature, it can really come in handy.

To turn a selection into a path, choose Make Work Path from the Paths palette menu. When you ask Photoshop to do this, you're basically asking it to turn a soft-edged selection into a hard-edged one. Therefore, the program has to make some decisions about where the edges of the selection are.

Fortunately, the program gives you a choice about how hard it should work at this: the Tolerance field in the Make Work Path dialog. The higher the value you enter, the shabbier the path's representation of the original selection. Values above 2 or 3 typically make nice abstract designs, but aren't otherwise very useful.

There's one more way to convert a selection into a new path: Click on the New Path icon in the Paths palette. Note that this uses whatever Tolerance value you last specified in the Make Work Path dialog, unless you hold down the Option (Mac) or Alt (Windows) key while clicking on the icon, in which case it brings up the dialog.

Rasterizing Paths

As we said back in Chapter 2, "Image Essentials," rasterizing is the process of turning a vector object into pixels. Photoshop lets you rasterize paths in two ways: You can fill the path area and you can stroke the path.

Filling. To fill the path area with the foreground color, drag the path's thumbnail to the Fill Path icon or click on the Fill Path icon in the Paths palette. Or, better yet, Option-click (Mac) or Alt-click (Windows) the icon, and the Fill Path dialog appears (this is the same dialog you get if you choose Fill Path from the Paths palette menu). The dialog gives you options for fill color, opacity, mode, and so on.

Stroking. Stroking the path works just the same as filling: You can drag the path's thumbnail to the Stroke Path button or click on the Stroke Path button in the Paths palette. You can change the tool it uses to stroke by Option-clicking (Mac) or Alt-clicking (Windows) the Stroke Path icon, or select Stroke Path from the Paths palette menu.

Clipping Paths

When you're putting together a publication like a catalog, where you place pictures of objects over a color, tint, or photo, you want the object to look like it's seamlessly placed on the background. If you don't have a way to hide the placed image's own background, it will appear on the layout with its own background as a big ugly rectangle (see **Figure 11-36**). A common production task is getting that image into a page-layout program without an unnaturally harsh edge along its silhouette.

The latest versions of page-layout workhorses Adobe InDesign and QuarkXPress can use the layer transparency or alpha channels in an image

Tip: When a painting tool is selected in the Tool palette and a path is selected, pressing Enter strokes the path with that tool using the current brush size and blending mode.

Tip: When you're drawing paths around objects to silhouette them in Photoshop, make sure you draw the path very slightly inside the object's border—perhaps one or two pixels inside the edge. This usually avoids most of the spillover from the background color. If spillover is a significant problem with an image, you should be thinking about building a Photoshop composite instead of using a clipping path.

Figure 11-36
The effect of
a clipping path

to hide the image's background. The great thing about layer transparency and alpha channels is that they can be soft-edged, so that drop shadows and hair can blend smoothly into the background. InDesign can read the transparency in TIFF, PDF, or native Photoshop files, so you may not need to construct clipping paths at all.

However, not everyone has the latest versions of the tools they use. In some cases, such as in older versions of XPress, the tools don't support Photoshop layer transparency or grayscale alpha channels. You might need to resort to using clipping paths.

Making paths. If you need a clipping path, head for the Paths palette. Remember that Bézier paths are generally smoother than raster (bitmap) data, because they're always imaged at the resolution of your output device, whereas bitmapped images print at whatever resolution they're set to, or at the coarseness of your halftone screen. Any path saved with the image can be designated as a clipping path in the Paths palette.

Tip: If a clipping path prints slowly or causes a PostScript "limitcheck" printing error, raise the PostScript flatness value in the Clipping Path dialog. Try a value between 3 and 5; at higher values curves may start to look like corners.

1. Choose Clipping Path from the Paths palette menu (see Figure 11-35).

2. Select the path that you want as a clipping path (see **Figure 11-37**).

3. If needed, enter a flatness value (see the tip at left).

4. Click OK. The name of the path (in the Paths palette) should now be in outline style, indicating it's a clipping path.

5. Save the image as a TIFF or EPS file, and then import it into your page-layout program of choice.

TIFF vs. EPS. Photoshop is able to save clipping paths in either TIFF or EPS files, and InDesign and XPress can read them. Because we tend to use TIFF files, this is great news. Remember that clipping paths don't really delete

Figure 11-37

Setting up a clipping path

*Setting a flatness value
for the clipping path*

*In the Paths palette, the
designated clipping path
appears in outline type.*

the data they hide; the entire image gets sent to the printer along with the instructions on how to clip it down.

Pick your clipping path. Not only can InDesign and XPress use a clipping path in your Photoshop TIFF image, they can see use any other path saved with the file, too. You can control the clipping path behavior of TIFFs in QuarkXPress on the Clipping tab of the Modify dialog. In InDesign, select Object > Clipping Path. This is useful for two reasons:

▶ You don't have to specify that a path be a clipping path in Photoshop. Save the TIFF file with any path, and InDesign or XPress can use it.

▶ If you have more than one path saved with your TIFF file, you can choose which path you want to use from within InDesign or XPress. This is great if you won't decide which portions of a picture you want to use until you see it alongside the rest of your page layout.

Shapes and Vector Masks

Photoshop lets you create *vector masks*—that is, vector paths that define the boundary of a layer, as though someone had snipped around that layer with a pair of scissors. Basically, these are exactly the same as layer masks, except that instead of an 8- or 16-bit channel defining a layer's transparency, Photoshop uses a sharp-edged line. What's cool is that the line always matches the resolution of your PostScript printer—just like text from InDesign or XPress might look blocky on screen but is perfectly smooth from a laser printer or imagesetter.

You may hear people talking about the Shapes feature in Photoshop, but in reality, the Shape tool is just a way to create a vector mask quickly.

Tip: While a major reason for the existence of vector masks is to provide a layer mask that prints at the native resolution of a PostScript output device, vector masks (shapes) are also useful because they are so easy to edit. For example, if you use a vector shape for a button on a Web page, you can resize it at any time without worrying about unsightly scaling artifacts.

Tip: Because a shape is a solid color adjustment layer with a vector mask, you can easily change the shape's fill by double-clicking the layer thumbnail. To totally change the layer type, choose a new one from the Layer > Change Layer Content submenu. For example, you can change the shape fill to a gradient or a pattern.

Drawing something with the Shape tool is the same thing as creating a Solid Color adjustment layer, adding a vector mask, and drawing on it. What we say about vector masks also applies to shapes.

Making a vector mask. There are several ways to make a vector mask (see **Figure 11-38**):

▶ **Shape tool.** When you draw any shape with the Shape tool (press U to select this tool, then choose a shape from the Options bar), Photoshop automatically creates a Solid Color layer with a vector mask. If you want to create a working path (in the Paths palette) instead, you can click on the Working Path button in the Options bar. Note that you can set various options—Opacity, Layer Style, and so on—in the Options bar before drawing the shape, but if you forget to set them, you can always apply them afterward in the Layers and Styles palettes.

▶ **Adjustment layer.** If you add an adjustment layer while a path is selected in the Paths palette (if it's visible on screen, it's selected), Photoshop automatically uses that path as a vector mask for the new layer. (We discuss adjustment layers in Chapter 8, "The Digital Darkroom.")

▶ **Add a vector mask.** You can add a vector mask to any layer (except the Background layer) by selecting either Reveal All or Hide All from the Add Vector mask submenu (under the Layer menu). But that's slow; instead, just Command-click (Mac) or Ctrl-click (Windows) on the Add Layer Mask button in the Layers palette. To add a vector mask that hides everything by default, add the Option (Mac) or Alt (Windows) key to the shortcut. If a path is already selected in the Paths palette, Photoshop automatically assigns it to the vector mask; otherwise, you can just start drawing a path with the Pen tool.

Adding and subtracting paths. If you use the Shape tool while a vector mask is selected in the Paths palette (if it's visible on screen), then Photoshop adds your shape to that vector mask. Before you draw the shape, you can tell the program how you want this new path to interact with the path that's already there by clicking on the Add, Subtract, Intersect, or Exclude Intersection button in the Options bar (see **Figure 11-38**). If you forget to select one, don't fret: Command-click (Mac) or Ctrl-Click (Windows) with the Shape tool on the shape you just drew (to select all its points), and *then* click the button in the Options bar.

Figure 11-38
Working with vector masks

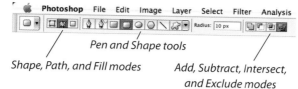

*The Shape tool always creates
or adds to a vector mask.*

*Options bar for a Pen or
Shape tool*

Pen and Shape tools

Shape, Path, and Fill modes

*Add, Subtract, Intersect,
and Exclude modes*

*To create the vector mask for
the Flower layer, we selected
the "flower outline" path
in the Paths palette and
Command/Ctrl-clicked the
Add Layer Mask button
in the Layers palette.*

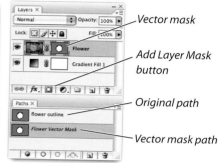

Vector mask

*Add Layer Mask
button*

Original path

Vector mask path

*The background of the Flower layer
is hidden by a vector mask, revealing
the gradient layer underneath.*

*Selecting the Flower layer's vector
mask displays the mask path in
the Paths palette.*

Tip: To invert a vector mask
or path, select the path by
Command/Ctrl-clicking it with
the Shape tool or Option/Alt-
clicking it with the Selection
tool, then click on either the
Add or Subtract button in the
Options bar (if one doesn't invert
the path, the other will).

Making vectors and pixels interact. Putting vector artwork on a layer on top of pixels is no great feat; if that's all you want to do, you can do the same thing in Illustrator, FreeHand, QuarkXPress, InDesign, or whatever. The real value to Photoshop vector masks is in how pixels can blend together and still retain a sharp edge. For example, you can use the Shape tool to draw a solid black oval on top of your background layer, and then change the opacity of that layer to 50 percent. Now you can see the background image through your semitransparent black oval. Of course, the vector artwork isn't really blending with the pixels beneath it. Rather, Photoshop is mixing the pixels on one layer with the pixels on another layer and then using the vector mask to define the edge between the two layers.

If you zoom in to magnify the edge of the oval, it appears as though the edge is anti-aliased with the background; however, when you print from Photoshop (or save the image as an EPS and print it from a page-layout program), you'll see that the edge is sharp (see **Figure 11-39**). Remember that what Photoshop is showing you onscreen is what the image would look like if you flattened it (losing the vector paths).

Figure 11-39
Vectors fool the eye

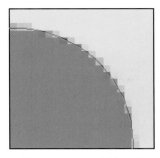 

The vector-based "shape" looks like this onscreen.   *When you print to a PostScript printer, it's much sharper.*

Tip: You can disable a vector mask (turning it off, so the whole layer is visible) the same way you turn off a regular layer mask: Shift-click on the vector mask's thumbnail in the Layers palette. That's a shortcut for Layer > Disable Vector mask.

Any layer can have a vector mask (even text layers), and you can change the opacity, blending mode, or layer effect of a clipped layer just the way you would ordinarily. So, if you want your shape layer to have a drop shadow, use the Overlay mode, and have a 75 percent opacity, you can change all that in the Layers palette.

Blending vectors and a layout. How do those folks at Sports Illustrated do those covers anyway? You know the type: a photo of some sports star partially over and partially under the title of the magazine, where the pixels have to anti-alias into the text. What used to be difficult is easy in current versions of Photoshop and InDesign. In Photoshop, you can put the text on one layer over the image layer. Then select a portion of the image that you want to appear over the type, make it a new layer (press Command-J on Mac or Ctrl-J in Windows) and move it in above the type layer in the Layers palette (see **Figure 11-40**).

Tip: If you can't see the intended PostScript, EPS, or PDF file in the Open or Place dialog, it probably means that the file type, creator, or suffix is missing. Your best bet is to try changing the file's name so that it ends in ".eps" or ".pdf". If this still doesn't work, the file may have become corrupted.

Maintaining vectors. If you've used vector masks and you want to retain those sharp edges when you print your image from your page-layout application, you should probably save your file as either a Photoshop PDF or an EPS file. If you are using a spot color, use the DCS 2.0 format. Note that while the EPS format saves and prints the layers and clipping paths properly, when you reopen your EPS file in Photoshop, it automatically gets flattened. Very annoying. So, make sure you save the EPS as a copy, and archive your layered Photoshop file just in case you need to go back to edit it. PDF files don't have this problem, and PDF is more current.

Importing Vectors: Open vs. Place

Many people don't realize that Photoshop has a built-in PostScript RIP that can read virtually any PostScript, EPS, PDF file and convert it to pixels.

Figure 11-40
Weaving vector and
pixel graphics

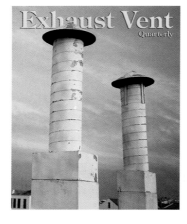

*This is what we're after:
Vector text behind the tower,
but in front of the sky.*

*We select the area that we want in front of the
type, and press Command/Ctrl-J to make it into
its own layer. (All other layers are hidden here.)*

*In the Layers palette, we drag
the new layer (Layer 1) in front
of everything else, and we
also add a layer mask to it.*

*Finally, we paint white and black in the new
layer's mask to hide or reveal areas as needed.*

Tip: When colorizing a black-
and-white EPS file (like a
logo), the Colorize feature in
the Hue/Saturation dialog
doesn't colorize pixels that are
completely black or white. We
solve this by adding a Solid Color
adjustment layer above the
logo's layer in the Layers palette,
Option/Alt-clicking between the
two layers to create a clipping
mask, and then setting the
adjustment layer's mode to
Screen. To edit the color, just
double-click the Solid Color
adjustment layer.

Your client gave you their logo in a PDF and you need to use it in Photo-shop? No problem! There are two ways to import EPS and PDF files: Open and Place.

Open. When you open an EPS or PDF file via the Open dialog, Photoshop recognizes it as such and gives you additional options. The additional options you get with an EPS or PDF file let you specify the resolution and size of the final bitmapped image. When you click OK, Photoshop makes a new document and rasterizes the EPS or PDF (turns it into a bitmapped image). Any areas of the EPS or PDF that don't have a fill specified come in transparent.

Place. When you select Place rather than Open, Photoshop drops the EPS or PDF file into your current document and then lets you scale and rotate it to fit your needs (you can scale it by dragging a handle, rotate it by drag-ging outside the rectangle, and move it by dragging inside the rectangle). Hold down the Shift key while dragging a handle to constrain the width/height ratio (so it stays proportional).

When you have finished scaling the image, press Return or Enter. Photoshop doesn't rasterize the image into pixels until you do this, so scaling won't degrade the final image. (Note that you can always press the Escape key to cancel the Place command.) Like Paste, Place almost always creates a new layer for your incoming image (although it won't if you place an EPS or PDF on a spot-color channel, for instance). Note that your new layer is automatically imported as a Smart Object, which we talk about next.

Smart Objects

Tip: If you import a digital camera raw file as a Smart Object, you can always edit the raw conversion by double-clicking the Smart Object. If you convert a raw file to a Photoshop document normally, the conversion settings are permanent and irreversible.

Simpler graphics programs (and most earlier versions of Photoshop) always rasterized placed or pasted graphics at the resolution of the current document—they were converted to pixels. If the original image had more pixels before it was imported and you scaled up the image, you'd find that many of the original pixels were gone, never to return.

Photoshop CS3 (and CS2) is smarter than that. You can import a file as a *Smart Object* layer, which is a layer with special abilities. You can transform it (moving, scaling, warping, skewing, and so on) and it will maintain all of its original quality and resolution, even if you scale it down to 10 pixels tall and back up to 1000 pixels tall. The way this works is that a Smart Object contains the complete imported file, and doesn't actually rasterize it to a specific resolution until you output or flatten the Photoshop document. We think of this as *deferred rendering*, because rendering is when you commit to a specific resolution. Smart Objects are also the basis for the new Smart Filters feature in Photoshop CS3.

Tip: When you duplicate a Smart Object layer in the Layers palette or using the Layer > New Layer Via Copy command, the copy actually points back to the same embedded document. If you edit the Smart Object, all instances update—great for maintaining batch layouts such as a page full of identical business cards. Note that this behavior doesn't happen if you choose the Layer > Smart Object > New Smart Object Via Copy command.

Creating a Smart Object. You can make a Smart Object layer by placing an external file—either a vector file (such as a PDF, EPS, or AI) or an image file (including TIFF, JPEG, or a raw digital camera file). Here are some other ways you can make Smart Objects:

▶ In Photoshop, choose File > Open as Smart Object. Use this when you want to use a file as a Smart Object without importing it into another existing document. Another way to do this is to select an image in Adobe Bridge, and then choose File > Place > In Photoshop.

▶ In Photoshop, choose File > Place. The difference between this method and the previous ones is that this way requires that you have a Photoshop document open, so do this when you want to add a file as a Smart Object to the document you're already working on.

▶ Paste an object from Adobe Illustrator. Photoshop offers you the option to automatically convert the vector data to a Smart Object (see **Figure 11-41**).

Figure 11-41
Pasting Illustrator or FreeHand paths

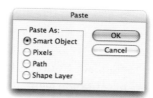

▶ Select one or more layers in the Layers palette, and then choose Layer > Smart Objects > Convert to Smart Object. In the Layers palette, the selected layers become one layer with a Smart Object badge. That Smart Object layer is actually a new Photoshop document containing the selected layers, embedded into the current document—you'll see this additional document when you edit the Smart Object.

Smart Object layers look and act the same as normal layers in the Layers palette, with one small difference: A small badge appears in the corner of the Smart Object layer's preview thumbnail (see **Figure 11-42**).

Tip: As with many other features, we find it easier to use Smart Object menu items using the context menus available for a Smart Object in the Layers palette, rather than hunting for them in the Layer > Smart Objects submenu. Be sure to right-click or Ctrl-click (Mac) on the layer name, not the thumbnail, or you won't see all the Smart Object commands.

Editing Smart Objects. Once you create a Smart Object layer, you can transform it like any other layer (use the Move tool to drag it around, use Free Transform to scale or skew it, and so on). You can also adjust its blending mode, opacity, or layer style in the Layers palette. However, if you double-click on the layer's preview thumbnail in the palette (or take the long way and choose Edit Contents from the Smart Objects submenu), Photoshop opens the Smart Object in its own window, ready for you to edit. If it was a raw image, Photoshop launches Camera Raw (see Chapter 5, "Building a Digital Workflow"). Or, if it's vector data from Illustrator, Photoshop will launch Illustrator and open the file there.

Unlike placed files in layout programs, files placed in Photoshop do not link back to the original file you placed from disk, because Photoshop embeds all imported files into the Photoshop document itself. When you edit a Smart Object, Photoshop opens a temporary, invisible file. After you make edits to the file, save it and close it. (And if necessary, switch back to Photoshop.) Like magic, you'll see the Smart Object update as Photoshop replaces the embedded Smart Object data with the new file.

Figure 11-42
Smart Objects in
the Layers palette

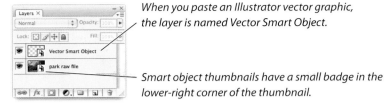

*When you paste an Illustrator vector graphic,
the layer is named Vector Smart Object.*

*Smart object thumbnails have a small badge in the
lower-right corner of the thumbnail.*

Replacing Smart Objects. You can replace a Smart Object with another Smart Object by choosing Replace Contents from the Smart Objects submenu, then choosing the new file you want. For instance, you might want to switch one image with another. When you replace an image, any scaling, warping, or effects you applied to the first image are maintained.

Exporting Smart Objects. Because a Smart Object is just a file embedded in your Photoshop document, you can unembed it—saving it out to disk as a separate file. To do this, select the Smart Object layer in the Layer palette, then choose Layer > Smart Objects > Export Contents. You don't have a lot of control over the format of the export: Image Smart Objects are saved as a PSB file (Photoshop Large Document; yes, we know the name doesn't match the extension), and vector objects are saved as PDF files.

Tip: Keep your eye on the lower-right corner handle of a text block. When there's too much text to fit the frame, Photoshop places a little + sign there.

Rasterizing Smart Objects. When Photoshop embeds the Smart Object in your document, the file size grows accordingly. That is, if you place a Camera Raw file, your document (and the RAM it needs) grows the size of the raw image data, plus the normal amount the file would grow when you add an additional layer. If you know you no longer need to edit the Smart Object data, you might consider converting it to a normal layer (discarding the embedded data) at its current size, resolution, and so on. To do this, choose Layer > Smart Objects > Convert to Layer. Alternately, you can choose Layer > Rasterize > Smart Object.

Text and Typography

Photoshop gained typographic prowess late in its career; in fact, for a long time it was downright painful to get good-looking type out of it. But that's all changed now. It's like the folks on the Photoshop team took a look at the typography in InDesign and suddenly said, "Hey, *we* can do that!" Photoshop lets you tweak kerning, leading, color, hyphenation, and more to your heart's content. You can set beautiful type in Photoshop…but that doesn't mean you should.

People who want to overlay text on top of pictures often ask us, "Should we use the Type tool in Photoshop, or the features in our page-layout or illustration program?" The answer, as always, is "it depends."

▶ If the text is integrated into your image—you want to apply a wacky filter to it, you want it to sit partially behind part of your image, or something like that—instead of being a separate element overlaying the image, there's a good chance that you'll need to create it in Photoshop. But check the capabilities of your layout program; for example, Adobe InDesign CS3 can produce many popular text effects.

▶ If you want sharp vector (as opposed to anti-aliased) text, you need to be very careful about what file format you use when saving. In many cases (such as if you save as TIFF), the text gets rasterized—if you're working with a 225-ppi image, any text you add to that image in Photoshop is similarly 225 ppi. That's high enough for most images, but it looks crummy for hard-edged type. (See Chapter 12, "Image Storage and Output," for more information about saving files with text layers.)

▶ The text controls in Photoshop are cool, but they're not exactly speedy. In general, the more text you have, the more you should set it in some other program. While Photoshop now provides a high level of typographical sophistication (for an image editor), programs like InDesign are still far better optimized for speedy typographical refinement.

So, if you're setting more than a few words, you should probably set them in a good page-layout program. But if you're hell-bent on using Photoshop to lay out text, we'll help you do so more efficiently.

Making text blocks. Most people who have used Photoshop for years use the Type tool by simply clicking on their image. That works, but if you're going to type more than one line of text, the click-and-type procedure is a pain because you have to manually break lines by hitting Return. Instead, drag out a text frame with the Type tool before typing. Photoshop automatically wraps the text to fit that frame, and you can always reshape the frame by dragging its corner or edge handles, or rotate the text block by dragging outside of the frame.

Tip: If you want to create a new text block near or on top of another bit of text, you might have trouble because Photoshop will think you're trying to select the existing text. No problem: Shift-click or Shift-drag with any Type tool to force Photoshop to create a new text layer.

When you're done creating or editing text, you can apply text changes and deselect the text frame by pressing Enter on the numeric keypad, Command-Return (Mac), or Ctrl-Enter on the main keyboard (Windows). If you press Return (Mac) or Enter above the Shift key (Windows), you'll type a return character instead. If you want to discard your latest text editing changes, press Esc instead.

Editing type layers. Once you have created some text on a type layer, there are several ways to edit it:

▶ Double-click on the type layer's thumbnail icon in the Layers palette. (Double-clicking on the name lets you edit the layer name, and double-clicking outside the layer name opens the Layer Style dialog.)

▶ Click the text with the Type tool. You know your cursor is in the right place when the Type tool's cursor changes to an I-beam cursor. However, if you click in the wrong place, Photoshop will create a new type layer; in this case, press the Escape key to cancel the new layer.

▶ Best yet, when you have both the Type tool selected in the Tool palette and the type layer selected in the Layers palette, you can choose Edit Type from the context menu.

As long as one or more type layers are selected in the Layers palette and the Type tool is selected, you can use the Options bar, the Character palette, or the Paragraph palette to apply formatting to the entire text block, without having to select the text characters themselves.

Tip: Do you need a text block exactly 144 points wide? No problem: Just Option-click (Mac) or Alt-click (Windows) with any of the Type tools, and a dialog will appear where you can enter an exact size.

Rendering type layers. Because text layers are vector-based (like Shapes, you can't paint or run filters on them or do anything else that relies on pixel editing. If you need to do something like that, you have to render them (turn them into pixels) by selecting Layers > Type > Rasterize. For maximum quality, it's best to do all your transformations (rotating, scaling, positioning, skewing), and layer effects (drop shadows and so on) that you need before rendering the type layer.

Making text masks. There are two tools in the Tool palette that create text masks rather than text (that is, as you type, Photoshop makes a selection in the shape of text rather than text itself). However, when it comes to making selections in the shape of text, we would rather create a normal type layer and then Command-click (Mac) or Ctrl-click (Windows) on it in the Layers palette. By actually creating a type layer, we can preview it in the image before clicking OK, we can edit the text later, or we can use the type someplace else (even in another image). If we had simply used a Type Selection tool, we'd have nothing but an ephemeral group of marching ants.

Check your spells. No, the Check Spelling feature won't help you with your spells if you end up at Hogwarts School of Magic, but it might help if your Photoshop document has a lot of text in it. To check the spelling of a single word, select the word with the Type tool and choose Edit > Check Spelling. If no word is selected, Photoshop checks the spelling of every text layer in your file.

We find this feature especially helpful with foreign words, which we often have no idea how to spell correctly. Photoshop ships with a number of different language dictionaries, such as Spanish and Swedish. However, in order for the Check Spelling feature to work correctly with foreign words, you must first select the words and choose the appropriate language from the Language pop-up menu in the Character palette.

Find and replace text. If you use Photoshop to create advertisements or other materials more appropriate for page-layout applications, note that Photoshop has a Find And Replace Text feature that lets you search for simple text strings. This feature isn't nearly as powerful as those in other programs (for instance, there's no way to search for text formatting or special characters such as tabs). But if you're trying to find a word or phrase that has gone missing, it does the trick.

Text on a path. Need to run text along a path? Simply draw a path with the Pen tool (see "Creating and Editing Paths," earlier in this chapter) and then click on it with the Type tool. Note that the Type tool's cursor icon changes when it's on top of a path, and when you click and then start typing, the text begins from the point you clicked. To adjust the starting and ending points for the text on the path, switch to the Path Selection tool (press A); as you hover the cursor over the start point or endpoint, the cursor changes to a vertical line with a thick black arrow. If you click and drag with this cursor, you adjust where the text begins or ends on the line.

The direction in which you draw your path determines how Photoshop draws the text. If you draw a path from left to right, the text flows on the top of the line; if you draw from right to left, the text flows from right to left—upside down. To flip the text over, use the Path Selection tool and drag the beginning or ending endpoint to the other side of the line.

Photoshop doesn't offer a lot of control over how the text flows along the line, but you can rotate the text so that it flows "vertically" along the line by clicking the Change Text Orientation button on the far left of the Options bar (see **Figure 11-43**).

Text Formatting

Placing text in your image is all very well and good, but you won't win design awards until you've figured out how to format your text. (Well, there might be a few other steps before you win awards, too. We make no guarantees.) There are two types of formatting: Character (which can apply to one or more characters) and Paragraph (which always applies to one or more paragraphs). You can find these settings in the Options bar when the Type tool is selected in the Tool palette or in the Character and Paragraph palettes (see Figure 11-43).

Leading. Leading (pronounced "ledding") determines the amount of space between lines in a paragraph. In Photoshop, leading is considered a character attribute—this will seem natural if you use InDesign, as David and Conrad do. However, this may throw you off if you're used to QuarkX-Press, where leading is a paragraph attribute. If you want the leading to be consistent throughout a paragraph, make sure you select every character in the paragraph (easily accomplished by triple-clicking a paragraph with the Type tool) *before* you set the leading in the Character palette.

Tip: The highlighting that appears when you select text can make it hard to see what you're doing. Press Command/Ctrl-H to hide the text selection highlight. The text remains selected, but you can see your changes more easily. Just remember to press the shortcut again when you're done; otherwise, the lack of selection feedback may confuse you.

Kerning and tracking. Kerning determines the amount of space between each character. Tracking is the same thing, but over a range of text (which is why some folks call it "range kerning"). Photoshop lets you do both in the Character palette—if your cursor is placed between two characters, you can kern them; if you've selected more than one character, then you can track them. (Or, if the type layer is selected in the Layers palette but no text is selected, then tracking applies to every character on that layer.) Note that the kerning and tracking values in Photoshop are based on $^1/_{1000}$ em (one em in a 24-point font is 24 points wide; in a 50-point font, it's 50 points wide, and so on).

The default kerning value for text is Metrics—these are the kerning pairs built into the font. But we almost always select the type layer (with no text selected on it) and change the kerning to Optical in the Character

Figure 11-43

Formatting text

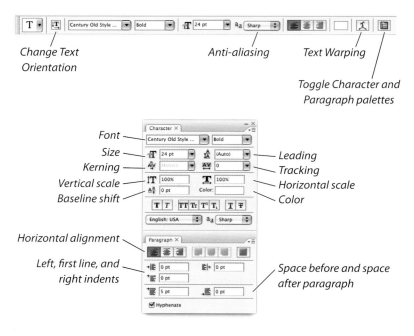

palette, which tells Photoshop to use its very cool method of analyzing the shape of each character and adjusting the kerning accordingly. If it's small text, this sometimes makes it look really ugly, so we change it back to Metrics, or even possibly change it to 0 (zero).

Anti-alias settings. While some people recommend turning off anti-aliasing for very small text, we find that anti-aliasing almost always helps onscreen readability, so we generally leave it on. The problem is that in small text sizes, anti-aliasing sometimes leaves fonts looking a bit anemic. Fortunately, Photoshop lets you change the anti-aliasing style. We usually set the Anti-alias pop-up menu (in the Options bar or the context menu when the Type tool is selected) to Crisp or Smooth (there's too little difference between the two to notice most of the time). However, when working with small text, we sometimes use the Strong option. It's entirely a judgment call—if Strong is too bold, then we'll switch back to Smooth.

Fractional widths. Text characters rarely fit perfectly on a 72-dpi grid—for instance, a letter "A" might be 18.1 pixels wide, and thus they're called fractional widths. When the Fractional Widths feature is turned on in the Character palette menu, Photoshop rounds the character widths to the nearest pixel, which usually results in some characters moving slightly closer together. In large point sizes, this is usually a good thing, but in small text sizes, the characters often run into each other and it looks dorky. Fractional Widths affects the entire text block, not just selected characters.

Other character styles. Photoshop offers a number of other character styles to help make your award-winning text. Here are a few others you should know about:

> **Tip:** If you want to change the color of selected text and the color you want to use is already the foreground or background color, use the Fill Foreground or Fill Background shortcuts that work with layers. Option/Alt-Delete fills with the foreground color, and Command/Ctrl-Delete fills with the background color.

▶ **Scaling and moving.** You can scale individual characters (or all the words on a text layer) vertically or horizontally in the Character palette, though we find that many designers overuse this and create really far-out, stretched typefaces that are simply unreadable. Use with discretion. The Character palette also offers a Baseline Shift feature, which you can use if you want to move individual characters up or down (like in a math equation, the little ® symbol, and so on).

▶ **Case and caps.** Want to make your text REALLY SCREAM? Then turn on All Caps in the Character palette menu. (Personally, we find All Caps rather annoying to look at.) There are other features in this menu, too: Small Caps, Superscript, and Subscript. Each of these applies to selected text unless no text is selected on a type layer. You can turn them off again by reselecting them from the palette menu. Note that unless you're using OpenType fonts, the Small Caps feature fakes the small caps (if you have an Expert font that contains the real small caps, you'll get better quality using that instead).

▶ **Faux styles.** Want Hobo Bold? Or Zapf Dingbats Italic? Sorry, those fonts don't contain those variations, so Photoshop won't let you select them. But Photoshop is ready and willing to fake them. When you turn on Faux Italic in the Character palette menu, Photoshop obliques (skews) the font slightly. Faux Bold makes the font heavier. However, because they aren't real font styles, you can't embed Faux Bold fonts in PDF files and expect them to remain vector type. Use faux styles as a last resort—it's better to use fonts containing actual variations.

Keyboard shortcuts. Photoshop provides a long list of keyboard shortcuts for text formatting (see **Table 11-1**). Many of them will be familiar if you've used InDesign or Illustrator, and they save you time in Photoshop, too.

Table 11-1 Type tool keyboard shortcuts

To do this…	…press this in Mac OS X	…or press this in Windows
Show/Hide selection indicators	Command-H	Ctrl-H
Move right one word	Command-Right arrow	Ctrl-Right arrow
Move left one word	Command-Left arrow	Ctrl-Left arrow
Select right one word	Command-Shift-Right arrow	Ctrl-Shift-Right arrow
Select left one word	Command-Shift-Left arrow	Ctrl-Shift-Left arrow
Move to next paragraph	Command-Down arrow	Ctrl-Down arrow
Move to previous paragraph	Command-Up arrow	Ctrl-Up arrow
Increase size 2 pts	Command-Shift-. (period)	Ctrl-Shift-. (period)
Decrease size 2 pts	Command-Shift-, (comma)	Ctrl-Shift-, (comma)
Increase leading 2 pts	Option-Down arrow	Alt-Down arrow
Increase leading 10 pts	Command-Option-Down arrow	Ctrl-Alt-Down arrow
Decrease leading 2 pts	Option-Up arrow	Alt-Up arrow
Decrease leading 10 pts	Command-Option-Up arrow	Ctrl-Alt-Up arrow
Increase kerning $2/100$ em	Option-Right arrow	Alt-Right arrow
Increase kerning $1/10$ em	Command-Option-Right arrow	Ctrl-Alt-Right arrow
Decrease kerning $2/100$ em	Option-Left arrow	Alt-Left arrow
Decrease kerning $1/10$ em	Command-Option-Left arrow	Ctrl-Alt-Left arrow
Increase baseline shift 2 pts	Option-Shift-Up arrow	Alt-Shift-Up arrow
Increase baseline shift 10 pts	Command-Option-Shift-Up arrow	Ctrl-Alt-Shift-Up arrow
Decrease baseline shift 2 pts	Option-Shift-Down arrow	Alt-Shift-Down arrow
Decrease baseline shift 10 pts	Command-Option-Shift-Down arrow	Ctrl-Alt-Shift-Down arrow

Hyphenation and justification. Hyphenation and justification (usually just called "H&J") are two methods of making text fit into a given space by controlling the amount of space between letters and words, and by breaking certain words at line endings with hyphens. Photoshop can also stretch text in order to help it fit a particular column width. If any one of these methods is used in excess, the results are awful. So it's important to find a good balance among them.

The H&J settings are only relevant when you have a paragraph or more of text—that is, when you've created a text frame, rather than just clicked and typed (see "Converting Point Type to Paragraph Type," later in this chapter). And the H&Js are always paragraph-wide formats; you can't apply them to a single character or line within a paragraph. Let's look at the several features in Photoshop that relate to H&Js:

▶ **Hyphenation.** By default, Photoshop hyphenates words that fall near the end of a line of text if it thinks it will make the imaginary line down the right side of the text (sometimes called "the rag") look better. If you don't want a paragraph to have any hyphenated words, then turn off the Hyphenate check box in the Paragraph palette.

You have a significant amount of control over what sort of words get hyphenated in the Hyphenation dialog (choose Hyphenation from the Paragraph palette menu; see **Figure 11-44**). Alas, there is no way to save these settings so you can later apply them to other paragraphs. If you want a whole text block, to have the same hyphenation settings (rather than just the currently selected paragraph), then make sure the cursor isn't in the text block, but that the text layer is selected in the Layers palette when you make the change.

▶ **No Break.** Sometimes Photoshop will hyphenate a word you don't want hyphenated. No problem: Select the word in the text block and choose No Break from the Character palette menu.

▶ **Justification.** The paragraphs in this book are *justified*, meaning that the right margin is carefully aligned in a straight line (this is sometimes called "flush left and right"). As we said earlier, this is pulled off by adding or removing space between characters and words. Photoshop offers one other control: stretching or compressing text. You can justify a paragraph by selecting it and clicking one of the Justified Text buttons in the Paragraph palette. (There are four, each of which handles the last line of the paragraph differently.)

Figure 11-44
Hyphenation and
Justification dialogs

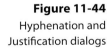

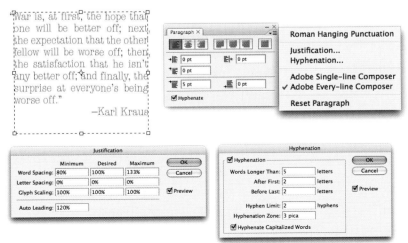

If you don't like the way Photoshop justifies your text, you can alter its built-in settings by choosing Justification from the Paragraph palette menu. Most typographers agree that justified text should have little character spacing, a reasonable amount of word spacing, and no character ("glyph") scaling. However, in a pinch, you may need to bump up the character spacing and glyph scaling by 1 or 2 percent; just be careful that it doesn't make the text look too unnatural.

▶ **Composer.** Adobe InDesign shook the publishing world by packaging an old idea into new software: calculating the justification settings based on all lines text in a paragraph together, rather than setting each line individually (like QuarkXPress and PageMaker have always done). Photoshop uses the same type engine, enabled by selecting Adobe Every-line Composer from the Paragraph palette menu. This almost always gives you tighter, better-looking paragraphs with more consistent spacing. We turn this on and leave it on.

▶ **Hanging punctuation.** Photoshop hangs small punctuation—such as periods, hyphens, quotation marks, commas, and so on—outside the text block, because the human eye tends to ignore these little extrusions and the text usually looks better, especially in justified text. If you don't like it, you can turn it off in the Paragraph palette menu.

Ultimately, while it's cool that Adobe included all these typography features in Photoshop, we do find it a little absurd because it's so rare that you would ever want to set more than a few lines of text in Photoshop. The one exception is creating images for a PDF workflow. In fact, unless you save your files in PDF, the text will either be rasterized (anti-aliased into the background pixels) or it'll take forever to print the file, and you'll also end up with enormous EPS files.

Converting point type to paragraph type. As we said earlier, you can create text in Photoshop by either clicking or dragging with the Type tool. If you drag, you get *paragraph type*, which is a text block with text handles whose text can reflow. If you click, you get *point type*, which is text that starts at a point. With point type, all line breaks have to be made by hand, and you can't apply justification or hyphenation. You can change paragraph type to point type (and vice versa) by making sure no text or text blocks are selected (clicking on the text layer in the Layers palette will do this), then choosing Convert To Point Text or Convert To Paragraph

Text from the Type submenu (under the Layer menu). You can also select this from the context-sensitive menu you get when right-clicking or Ctrl-clicking (Mac) with the Type tool.

Filters and Effects

Sure, you can paint and retouch and composite within Photoshop, but you know as well as we do that the most fun comes from playing with filters. But when you're up against a deadline for a picky client, productivity with filters becomes more important than fun. Here are some techniques we've found to be useful.

Float before filtering. One's natural inclination is to make a selection, then choose a filter from one of the Filter submenus. We suggest adding a step: copy the selection to a new layer first (press Command-J in Mac OS X or Ctrl-J in Windows). Doing so gives you much more flexibility in how the filter is applied. For instance, once the filter is applied on the new layer, you can move it, change its blending mode, run an additional filter, soften the effect by lowering the layer's opacity, and so on. Best of all, you don't damage your original pixels until you're sure you've got the effect exactly right. If you don't like what you've done, you can undo, or just delete the entire layer. Similarly, if you're going to run a filter on a whole layer, consider duplicating the layer first. It's safer and much more flexible.

Filter shortcuts. Like many other features of Photoshop, you can speed your work with keyboard shortcuts. You can tell Photoshop to run a filter again by pressing Command-F (Mac) or Ctrl-F (Windows). However, this doesn't let you change the dialog settings. If you want to follow this advice, press Command-Option-F (Mac) or Ctrl-Alt-F (Windows); this opens the dialog for the last filter you ran so you can change the settings.

Fading filter effects. Most folks figure that once they run a filter, the choice is to either move forward or select Undo. But the Fade feature (in the Edit menu) allows you to take a middle path by reducing the opacity of a filter, or even changing the blending mode, immediately after running it. (As soon as you do anything else—even make a selection—the Fade feature is no longer available.) You can get to the Fade dialog quickly by pressing Command-Shift-F (Mac) or Ctrl-Shift-F (Windows).

The Fade feature works not only with filters, but also with any of the features in the Adjustments submenu (under the Image menu) and almost every paintstroke. For example, you can run Hue/Saturation on an image, then reduce the intensity of the effect with Fade. However, we use this much less than we used to, because adjustment layers are more powerful (see Chapter 8, "The Digital Darkroom").

Tip: Katrin Eismann taught us that running a filter on a layer mask can produce cool effects. Try running filters on a layer mask filled with white, black, or 50 percent gray.

Build textures on neutral layers. Instead of burning filter effects directly into an image, you can filter a neutral-colored layer. Using filters in conjunction with neutral layers gives you much more freedom to change your mind later. When you choose Layer > New Layer or Option-click (Mac) or Alt-click (Windows) the Create a New Layer button in the Layers palette, many blending modes enable the Fill with Neutral Color check box. For instance, if you set the layer to Screen mode, the check box says Fill With Screen-Neutral Color (Black). The exact wording of that check box changes depending on the mode you select.

Now, when you apply a filter to that layer, the parts that get changed are no longer "neutral." They change the appearance of the pixels below. Then you can run filters on this layer and they will begin to affect the image below (see **Figure 11-45**). Of course, this primarily works with filters that add texture to an image, like the Texturizer filter. It typically won't have any effect at all with the Distort filter or an artistic filter.

You can now play with the filter without affecting the actual image by taking advantage of the neutral color. If you want to make a texture less prominent, paint with the neutral color on the neutral-colored layer. If the neutral color is 50 percent gray, anywhere you paint using that color will remove the texture. For example, you could paint the neutral color with a brush set to 10 percent to gradually fade a texture in some areas of a image. You can also try out different filters by running them on your neutral-colored layer, and again, the original underlying image is never disturbed. You can combine this technique with layer masks depending on what you need.

Smart Filters

Smart Filters represent a powerful new way to use filters in Photoshop CS3. Like many of the newer features in Photoshop, Smart Filters help you keep your options open, because Smart Filters make it possible for you

Figure 11-45

Filtering a neutral-colored layer

 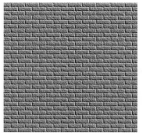 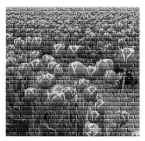

Original image   *Texturizer filter applied to a neutral layer*   *Background image and neutral layer visible at the same time*

New Layer

Name: Bricks

☐ Use Previous Layer to Create Clipping Mask

Color: ☐ None

Mode: Overlay   Opacity: 100 ▶ %

☑ Fill with Overlay-neutral color (50% gray)

OK

Cancel

The Fill With check box appears for blending modes that have a neutral color.

to change filter settings at any time in the future, even if you closed and reopened the document. Not even the History palette can do that.

We covered Smart Filters pretty extensively back in "Sharpening with Smart Filters" in Chapter 10, "Sharpness, Detail, and Noise Reduction." As we mentioned back there, because Smart Filters are based on Smart Objects, they can dramatically increase the file size and RAM requirements of a Photoshop document, and can also slow it down. Despite that, it's nice to have Smart Filters as an option when you need them.

Before you can apply a Smart Filter to a layer, the layer must be a Smart Object. If you placed or opened a graphic as a Smart Object, you've already got that covered. If you intend to apply Smart Filters before you even get a graphic into Photoshop, remember that there are now more ways to import graphics as Smart Objects, such as selecting a file and choosing File > Place > In Photoshop (when in Bridge CS3), or clicking the Open As Object button in Camera Raw 4 (if you don't see it, press Shift).

If a layer isn't already a Smart Object, you don't have to navigate the Layer menu to turn it into one. Just choose Filter > Convert for Smart Filters, which is simply another way to convert a layer to a Smart Object.

Once a layer is a Smart Object, you'll notice that many commands on the Filter menu are not available for Smart Objects. However, choosing any command on the Filter menu that's available applies that command as a Smart Filter. There are actually a couple more important commands

Tip: When you transform a Smart Object using the Edit menu, it doesn't show up in the Layers palette, but the next time you choose the same transform command, you'll be able to edit the transformation settings you last applied to that layer.

that you can use as Smart Filters that are not on the Filter menu: Image > Adjust > Shadow/Highlight and some of the commands on the Edit > Transform submenu. These are commands that users have wanted to be able to use in a nondestructive way, but that aren't practical or possible to implement as adjustment layers. Smart Filters have given Photoshop a way to give these important commands nondestructive editing capabilities (see **Figure 11-46**).

You can create Smart Objects inside Smart Objects if you really need to, but nesting Smart Objects can really accelerate the file bloat that happens with Smart Objects.

Figure 11-46
Smart Filters in
the Layers palette

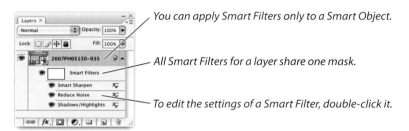

You can apply Smart Filters only to a Smart Object.

All Smart Filters for a layer share one mask.

To edit the settings of a Smart Filter, double-click it.

The Nondestructive Workflow

At this point in the book, you've probably noticed that we are the kind of people who like to work nondestructively whenever possible, using tools like adjustment layers and masks to keep our options open as long as possible. With Smart Filters and the enhancements to Smart Objects, particularly when it comes to raw camera images, Photoshop CS3 makes it possible to keep a wide range of edits in a reversible state, so that you can back out of them at any time. We've alluded to bits and pieces of this workflow in various parts of the book, but we thought we should put it all together here for you. Here are all of the typical image-editing steps using the nondestructive editing features in Photoshop CS3 (see **Figure 11-47**).

Using these techniques, you can, at any time, strip away every last edit and return to the original base image, or adjust the intensity of any edit whenever you like. It's an astounding degree of flexibility, but again, pushing nondestructive editing this far can eat up your hard drive space and RAM in a hurry. To mitigate this, you can head for a middle ground where you rasterize some layers into pixels when you're happy with them.

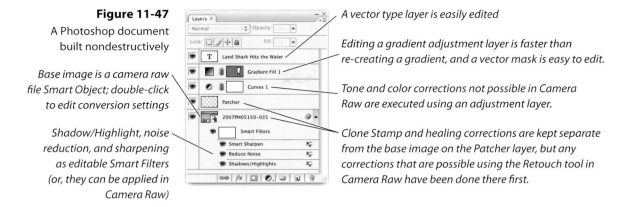

Figure 11-47
A Photoshop document
built nondestructively

A vector type layer is easily edited

Editing a gradient adjustment layer is faster than
re-creating a gradient, and a vector mask is easy to edit.

Base image is a camera raw
file Smart Object; double-click
to edit conversion settings

Tone and color corrections not possible in Camera
Raw are executed using an adjustment layer.

Shadow/Highlight, noise
reduction, and sharpening
as editable Smart Filters
(or, they can be applied in
Camera Raw)

Clone Stamp and healing corrections are kept separate
from the base image on the Patcher layer, but any
corrections that are possible using the Retouch tool in
Camera Raw have been done there first.

Actions, Automate, and Scripting

The trick to being really productive and efficient with computer technology is to be lazy. Yes, it's a paradox, but it's true; the lazier you are, the more likely you are to find the really efficient ways of doing things so you can get out of work faster and go to the beach. If you have an overzealous work ethic, you probably don't mind repeating the same mind-numbing tasks 400 times, but you also don't exploit the power of your computer.

Photoshop offers four automation features: actions, Automate, Variables, and scripting. Actions live in the Actions palette and let you repeat a series of steps, similar to the macros you may have used in office programs. Photoshop ships with a number of premade actions, and you can easily build your own (we'll show you how). Automate refers to the built-in tools in the Automate submenu (under the File menu). Variables is a way to create a template image that changes depending on data imported from a spreadsheet or a database. Scripting is a way to automate Photoshop from behind the scenes using AppleScript, JavaScript, or Visual Basic. We'll look at each of these techniques in turn.

Actions

In the last chapter, we discussed the basics of building actions—particularly actions that help in the processing of raw files. But Photoshop also comes with a number of premade actions that are not only useful, but educational, too, because you can look at them to see how they produce their magic. (You can load additional sets of actions by selecting Load Actions from the Actions palette menu, or by choosing the presets that appear at the bottom the palette menu.)

The key is that you can only make an action for something you can do blindly, with no feedback from the program, and with little or no brain activity. For example, you can't record an action that says, "If the pixels in the upper-left corner of the image are sort of reddish, then do such-and-such." Photoshop would have to be able to see and respond. No can do.

However, you can easily create an action that runs a particular set of Curves, adds a text layer, adds a layer effect, sharpens the background layer, and so on, because all these things are methodical.

Tip: You can export all the actions visible in the Actions palette as a text file that you can open in a word processor. This is a great way to study how someone else's actions are put together. To do the export, select any action set in the Actions palette, and then hold down Command and Option (Mac) or Ctrl and Alt (Windows) as you select Save Action from the Actions palette menu.

Action limitations. Before you get too heady with your newfound actions power, you should know that Photoshop doesn't let you record everything you might want. While Photoshop can record blending modes, opacity, shapes, brush selections, and even pixel selections, you still cannot record paintstrokes (like those made with the Brush, Airbrush, and Clone tools), zooms, window switching, and scrolls. And there are many features that aren't necessarily recordable, but that you can force into an action (see "Editing actions," later in this chapter). Last but not least, the whole Actions mechanism has a logic unto itself. If an operation isn't recordable by keyboard shortcut, it may be recordable by choosing the menu command instead, or vice versa.

Planning Your Actions

Besides the limits of what you can and cannot record in the Actions palette, there are a few more things to keep in mind.

Difficulty. While recording and playing simple actions (those with only two or three steps) may be easy, trying to build complicated actions can be damaging to your head (and the wall you're banging it against).

Modularity. Rather than trying to make one big action that does everything you want, break it down into smaller steps that you can debug individually, then chain together to reuse in more complex actions.

Think it through. You should always think the action through completely before you start recording it. You might even write down each step on paper, and then record it after you're pretty sure everything will work out the way you think.

Generic actions. Try to make your actions as generic as possible. That means they should be able to run on any image at any time. Or, barring that, provide the user with a message at the beginning of the action noting what kind of image is required (as well as other requirements, such as "needs text on a layer" or "must have something selected"). This is a good idea even if you're the only one using your actions, because (believe us) after you've made a bunch of actions, you'll forget which action requires what (see "Talk to Your Users," later in this chapter).

There are a number of things to think about when making your actions generic. The following list is a good place to start:

▶ Never assume image mode. The image may be in RGB, CMYK, Grayscale, or even Indexed Color mode. This is very important when running filters, because some filters don't run in certain modes. You may want to add a step that converts to your intended mode.

▶ Don't assume the image has layers (or doesn't have layers). Also, don't assume that if the image does have layers, the background layer is selected (or even that there is a layer called Background). If you need the lowest layer selected, press Option-Shift-[(Mac) or Alt-Shift-[(Windows). You may want to add a step that flattens an image.

▶ Avoid using commands that pick layers by name, unless the Action has already created and named the layer. For example, if you record clicking on a layer in the Layers palette, Photoshop records the click by layer name, not position. Instead, record pressing Option-[or Option-] (Mac) or Alt-[or Alt-] (Windows) to target the next layer down or the next layer up, respectively. Command-[and Command-] (Mac) or Ctrl-[and Ctrl-] (Windows) move layers up or down, respectively.

▶ If you're saving and loading channels, you'll almost certainly have to name the channels. Make sure you give them names that are unlikely to already be present in the image. *Do* name them, though, rather than leaving them set to the default names like "#4". If a document has two channels with the same name when you run an action, Photoshop always uses the first channel with that name.

Cleanup. It's a good idea to make your actions clean up after themselves. In other words, if your action creates three extra channels along the way to building some other cool effect, the action should also probably delete them before ending. If the action hasn't cleaned up after itself and you run it a second time, those channels (or layers, or whatever) are still hanging around and will probably trip up the action.

Get more info. This section offers a quick overview of actions, but if you have Web access, check out one or more of the actions-oriented sites like *http://share.studio.adobe.com*. You can also find more links from a site such as *www.photoshopnews.com*.

Actions Basics

Making an action is pretty straightforward:

1. Open the Actions palette (see **Figure 11-48**).

2. Click the New Action button (or select New Action from the Action palette menu). Give the action a name (and a keyboard shortcut, if you want). If you have more than one set (see "Sets," later in this chapter), choose which set this new action will be part of. When you click OK, Adobe Photoshop begins recording automatically.

3. Perform the steps that you want the action to do.

4. Click the Stop button in the Actions palette (or select Stop Recording from the Actions palette menu).

Then, to run the action, select the action's thumbnail in the Actions palette and click the Run button. Better yet, just Command-double-click (Mac) or Ctrl-double-click (Windows) on the action. If the action is relatively simple, it may perform perfectly the first time. But in most of the actions we make, we find that something goes wrong somewhere along the line, usually due to our performing a step that Photoshop can't record into an action (see "Troubleshooting Actions," later in this section).

Save your work first. If you run an action and then decide that you don't like what it did, you're in trouble because you cannot undo a full action, only the last step of an action. If the action used only a few steps, you might be able to use the History palette to return to a pre-action state, but this isn't always possible either, particularly if you ran the action as a batch process on multiple files. To guarantee an undo option, we're in the habit of saving a snapshot of our document in the History palette before running any action. That way, if something goes wrong or we don't like

Tip: When you run an action for the first time, run it on a folder of test files. There's nothing worse than ruining a folder of original images because of a glitch in an untested action. Don't run an action on production files until you've tested and debugged it.

Figure 11-48
The Actions palette

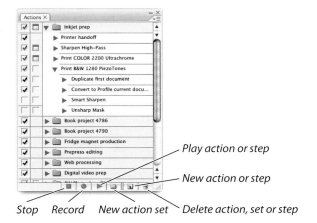

Play action or step

New action or step

Stop   Record   New action set   Delete action, set or step

the effect, we can revert back to this snapshot. Another option is to simply save your document first, and then use the Revert command (in the File menu) to undo the action. Of course, neither of these techniques works with actions that save and close the file—we recommend always making actions that use Save As rather than saving over the original.

Tip: You can change the Actions palette into a palette full of buttons by choosing Button Mode in the palette menu. When it's in Button mode, you only have to click once on a button to run it. Switch out of Button mode to create new actions or edit existing ones.

Sets. Photoshop lets you create sets of actions, a godsend to anyone who works with dozens of actions. Sets are pretty self-explanatory.

▶ To create a new action set, choose New Set from the Action palette menu (or by clicking the New Set button in the palette). You can delete a set by selecting it and choosing Delete from the same palette menu, or by clicking the Delete button in the palette.

▶ To move actions between sets, drag them.

▶ To rename a set, double-click its thumbnail in the Actions palette.

▶ To show or hide the actions within a set, click the triangle to the left of the set's name.

▶ You can also save sets (see "Saving actions," a bit later).

▶ To play all the actions in a set (in order), select the set and click the Play button in the Actions palette.

Editing actions. Once you've built an action, you can edit it (in fact, you'll almost certainly want to edit it unless it worked perfectly the first time). If you want to record additional steps somewhere in the middle of the action (or at the end of the action), select a step in the action and click the Record button. When you're done recording actions, click the Stop button. All the new actions fall after the step you first selected.

If you want to add a step that cannot be recorded for some reason (perhaps it's an item in the View menu), you can select Insert Menu Item from the Action palette menu. This lets you choose any one feature from the menus, and then inserts it into the action (after whatever step is currently selected).

To change the parameters of a step, double-click on it in the Actions palette. For example, if a step applies a curve to the image (using the Curves dialog), but you want to change the curve, double-click on the step and choose a different curve. Note that when you do this, you may actually change the current image; just press Command-Z (Mac) or Ctrl-Z (Windows) to undo the change (to the image, not to the action).

Annoyingly, some steps cannot be rerecorded. For instance, a step that sets the foreground color to red should be able to change so that it sets it to blue…but it can't. Instead, you have to record a new step, then delete the original.

If you want to change the action's name, its thumbnail or button color, or its keyboard shortcut, just double-click on the action's name.

Stop where you are. Normally, Photoshop won't display any of the usual dialogs when you run an action. For instance, if you include a Numeric Transform step in an action, Photoshop just performs the transform without displaying the dialog. But you can force Photoshop to display the dialog, stop, and wait for the user to input different settings before continuing. To do so, click once in the second column of the Actions palette, next to the step. A black icon indicating a dialog appears next to the step, and a red icon appears next to the action's name.

Don't click on a red dialog icon! If you do, it turns black *and* Photoshop adds a black "stop here" icon next to every step in the action that can have one. There's no Undo here, so the only way to reset the little black icons to their original state is to turn them on or off one at a time. (You can, however, turn off *all* of them by clicking the black icon next to the action's name.)

Note that if you insert a step using the Insert Menu Item command, Photoshop always opens the appropriate dialog and doesn't even offer you the chance to turn this icon on or off (because steps inserted in this way are meant to simulate the user actually selecting the item).

Tip: To duplicate a step, Option-drag (Mac) or Alt-drag (Windows) duplicates. For instance, if you want to use the same Numeric Transform step in two actions, you can Option/Alt-drag that step from one action to the proper place in the second action.

Tip: if you record loading a Curves file (or a Levels or Hue/Saturation file, or any other adjustment) from disk, Photoshop records the name of the file rather than the curve itself. Instead, record loading the setting in the dialog, then change the settings just a tiny bit before clicking OK. As long as there is a difference, Photoshop records the settings in the dialog rather than the file's name. You can always go back and change the settings back to the way you want them.

Talk to your users. You can insert a command at any point in your action that stops the action and displays a dialog with a message in it. This message might be a warning like, "Make sure you have saved your image first," or instructions such as, "You should have a selection made on a layer above the background." To add a message, select Insert Stop from the Actions palette menu. Photoshop asks you what message you want to show and whether the message dialog should allow people to continue with the action (see **Figure 11-49**).

Figure 11-49

Adding a message

If your message is a warning, you should turn on the Allow Continue option, but if you're communicating instructions, you may want to leave this check box off. When Allow Continue is turned off, Photoshop stops the action entirely. After the user clicks the OK button in the message dialog, Photoshop automatically selects the next step in the Actions palette, so the user can continue running the action by clicking the Run button again (this works even if the Actions palette is in Button mode).

Saving actions. After you've created the world's most amazing action, you may want to share it with someone else. You can get actions out of your Actions palette and onto your hard drive by selecting Save Actions from the Actions palette menu. Unfortunately, you cannot save a single action; the Save Actions feature only saves sets of actions. Fortunately, the workaround isn't too painful.

1. Create a new set (click on the New Set button at the bottom of the Actions palette) and name it something logical.

2. Either move the action you want to save by dragging it, or duplicate it by Option-dragging (Mac) or Alt-dragging (Windows) it into the new action set.

3. Select the new action set and choose Save Actions from the Actions palette menu.

Of course, you can load sets of actions just as easily with the Load Actions and Replace Actions features in the Actions palette menu. Watch out for Replace Actions and its cousin Clear Actions; these replace or clear *all* the actions in the palette, not just the selected one.

Troubleshooting Actions

Sometime, somewhere, something will go wrong when you're building actions. That's where troubleshooting comes in. When troubleshooting (or debugging, as it's often called), the most important thing to keep in mind is that there *must* be a logical solution to the problem. (This isn't always true, but it's good to keep a positive attitude…)

Dummy files. After building an action, don't immediately test it on some mission-critical image. Rather, try it on a dummy image. Even better, try it on several dummy images, each in a different mode (RGB, CMYK, Grayscale, Indexed Color), some with layers, some without, some with selections made, others without, and so on. If it doesn't work right on any one of these, you can decide whether to work at making it work or to add a message at the beginning of the action that says "don't try it on such-and-such type of images" (see "Talk to your users," earlier in this section).

Tip: By its nature, the History palette is a record of the steps that an action performed. You may need to increase the number of History steps so that it can hold all of the steps that a particular action executes.

Step-by-step. You can force Photoshop to pause between each step and redraw the screen by selecting Step-By-Step in the Playback Options dialog (choose Playback Options from the Actions palette menu). This is often useful, but the best troubleshooting technique in the Actions palette (in fact, probably the only troubleshooting technique) is to select the first item in the action and click the Run button while holding down the Command key (Mac) or Ctrl key (Windows). This plays only the first step. Now go check out all the relevant palettes. Is the Channels palette the way you expect it? What about the Layers palette? What are the foreground and background colors?

When you're convinced that all is well, Command-click (Mac) or Ctrl-click (Windows) the Run button again to check the second step in the action, and so on until you've tested the entire action. If at any time you find the palettes or colors set up improperly, now is the time to replace the last step or double-click on it to change its settings. If something is really messed up, you can fall back on your History snapshot, or revert.

Automated Workflows

Earlier we said that actions cannot perform any task that requires brain activity. However, Photoshop contains somewhat smarter automation features in two places: the Automate submenu (under the File menu) and the Tools menu in Bridge. These menus are also home to the Batch feature, which lets you run an action on an entire folder of images.

We don't cover every Automate command here. We talked about Photomerge earlier in this chapter, looked at the oft-infuriating Batch command in Chapter 5, "Building a Digital Workflow," and we cover Web Photo Gallery in Chapter 12, "Image Storage and Output."

Tip: A droplet contains action steps as they were when you saved the droplet. If you update the action that the droplet's based on, don't forget to update the droplet too!

Making droplets. We're not sure why the Make Droplet feature is hiding in the File > Automate submenu instead of the Actions palette, but that's where you can find this really awesome feature. You can use Make Droplet to save any Photoshop action to disk as a file. Then, when you want to process an image (or a folder full of images) with that action, you can simply drag the image (or folder) on top of the droplet file.

Bonus tip: If you work in both Mac OS X and Windows, you can copy droplets from one platform to the other. On the PC you simply have to make sure the droplet has an *.exe* extension. When you bring a PC droplet to the Mac, you have to initialize it once by dragging it on top of the Photoshop application icon.

Picture Package. Picture Package is a boon to any photographer tired of duplicating, rotating, and scaling photos to fit pictures on one page. You can use Picture Package to lay out different versions of the same picture (like school photos, where you want so many wallet-sized prints, and so on). Or you can use it to lay out different images together on one page. The interface is simple enough to understand quickly (see **Figure 11-50**), though there are a few things to watch out for:

Tip: If you want different images than the ones you see in the Picture Package dialog, just drag and drop the photos you want directly into the placeholders. You can drag from the desktop or from applications such as Bridge, Lightroom, and iPhoto.

▶ Make sure you pay attention to the final resolution and final image mode setting. If you're planning to print your page, make sure the resolution is appropriate for printing—at least 150 dpi, and ideally between 200 and 300 dpi for most types of printers.

▶ If you want all the images on the page to be the same, just select File from the Use pop-up menu and then click the Choose button to select your file. If you want different images, you can click on one or more of the preview images in the lower-right area of the dialog.

Figure 11-50
Picture Package

▶ Photoshop lets you choose a label to add to the images. However, the choices are pretty slim. For instance, the label is always added on top of the image (there's no way to put it in a margin), the fonts are limited, and there are no options for styles (like drop shadows or glow around the label to make it stand out better).

▶ If you choose more than one image (either by selecting Folder from the Use pop-up menu or by selecting more than one image in Bridge and setting the Use pop-up menu to Selected Images in Bridge), Picture Package doesn't lay them out on the same page; it prepares one page for each image. Unfortunately, there doesn't appear to be any way to preview more than one page at a time, so we generally avoid selecting more than one image when using this feature.

Customizing package pages. Photoshop offers about 20 different Picture Package layouts, but in case you just gotta be you, you're welcome to create your own layouts, too. Photoshop sports a nifty layout editor. Select a template from the Layout pop-up menu to use as a starting point, and then click the Edit Layout button in the lower-right corner of the Picture Package dialog.

The Edit Layout dialog (see **Figure 11-51**) works like a basic drawing program: First choose a page size that corresponds to your printed paper size in the Layout area. Then, click on a box (a "zone") to move it or change its size. You can remove a zone by clicking the Delete Zone button or add

Figure 11-51

Customizing Picture Package

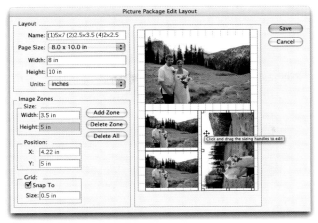

one by clicking Add Zone. Unless you're really going wacky and wild, do yourself and everyone around you a favor and turn on the Snap To check box so that as you drag or resize a zone it snaps to a grid line; the grid is based on the value in the Size field.

When you're done, give your layout a name and click Save. Photoshop knows just where to save these files (in the Photoshop > Presets > Layouts folder), so you just need to name your file (probably something similar to your layout name) and click Save. The layout name is what appears in the Layout pop-up menu; the filename is just the on-disk filename.

Contact Sheet II. Contact Sheet builds pages of thumbnails from a folder full of images. Careful, though; Photoshop doesn't know what to make of long filenames, and usually truncates them.

Crop and Straighten Photos. The Automate features are designed to save you from mind-numbing grunt work, and the Crop and Straighten Photos feature fits that bill exactly. If you throw four photos on a flatbed scanner, you can either scan four times (adjusting the scanning area each time) or scan once, duplicate the resulting file three times, and crop each one as a unique image. Now you've got another choice: Scan once and choose Automate > Crop and Straighten Photos. This feature does the work for you by analyzing the image, duplicating it, cropping it, and rotating each one so that it sits straight. If you decide you only want a couple of the images on the page, draw selection marquees around the ones you want, and Photoshop will focus on them.

Obviously, the more clear the boundaries are between the images, the better the feature works. Crop and Straighten Photos usually works quite well, but we've found we sometimes still need to do a little cropping cleanup on some images—especially old photos that don't have clearly defined boundaries or in contact sheets with black borders. On rare occasions, Photoshop breaks an image into two or more pieces if the colors in the image have areas that are too similar to the color around the images. In that case, make a selection around the image and then hold down Option (Mac) or Alt (Windows) while choosing Automate > Contact Sheet II.

Scripting Photoshop

If actions and variables got you all excited about automating Photoshop, you're going to love scripting. Scripting is a way for one application (or your system) to talk to another application behind the scenes. For instance, in Mac OS X 10.3 or later, you can attach a script to a folder, so that as soon as you drop an image into the folder, your system launches Photoshop, performs several operations on it, saves the file, and then closes it again; it's all handled automatically.

Scripting is one of the coolest features in Photoshop, and it works on both the Mac and Windows platforms, but almost no one knows about it because Adobe doesn't advertise it well.

Scripting vs. actions. There are four basic differences between actions (which are also called macros) and scripts. First, actions are entirely dependent on the user interface—the menus, dialogs, keyboard shortcuts, and so on. Scripts, however, let you sneak in the backdoor of the program and control it from behind the scenes, almost like a puppeteer pulling the strings of a marionette. Second, scripts have *flow control*, a programming term that means you can set up decision trees and loops, like "keep doing this until such-and-such happens." Third, scripts often contain variables, so you can save a value (like the color of a pixel) for later use.

Last, scripting lets you control more than one program at time. For example, if you use QuarkXPress (which is also scriptable on the Mac) or InDesign (which is scriptable on both Mac and Windows), you could write a script that would automatically "see" how you've rotated, sized, and cropped images within your picture boxes. It could then open the images in Photoshop, perform those manipulations on the original images, resave them, and reimport them into the page-layout program.

Hiring a scripter. Even though scripting is extremely powerful, it's just a fact of life that most people don't want to learn the ins and outs of scripting. Fortunately, there are a number of scripters for hire. You can find a good scripters on Adobe's scripting forum: *www.adobe.com/support/forums*. If you're looking for a scripter for the Mac, there are also consultants listed at *www.apple.com/applescript/resources*.

Scripting languages. You can script Photoshop using several languages. On Mac OS X, you can use AppleScript or JavaScript. On Windows, you can use JavaScript, Visual Basic, or any other language that is COM-aware, such as VBScript, Perl, or Python. Only JavaScript scripts can be used cross-platform. That would seem to make it the best option for scripting, but unfortunately, only a few other applications are JavaScript-aware—notably, Adobe applications such as Adobe InDesign and Adobe Bridge.

First steps in scripting. We don't pretend that we can actually teach you how to script Photoshop in this book. Although we believe that almost anyone can learn how to write scripts (especially using AppleScript, which is much easier than other forms of scripting), scripting is still a form of computer programming and as such, it takes time and patience to learn. So where can you learn it?

Tip: Photoshop CS3 installs the Adobe ExtendScript Toolkit into the Adobe Utilities folder in your Utilities folder. You can use ExtendScript Toolkit to debug JavaScripts that you write for Adobe applications.

▶ **Scripting Guide folder.** When you install Photoshop CS3, you get a folder called Scripting Guide that's inside the Photoshop CS3 application folder. There are PDF reference guides for scripting Photoshop in the supported languages, and the Scripting Guide itself—a reference to the scripting model. The Utilities subfolder contains the Scripting Listener plug-in, which can log what you do in Photoshop as JavaScript.

▶ **Books.** Several good books have been published on scripting. Most are general, such as *AppleScript: The Definitive Guide* by Matt Neuburg (O'Reilly), the *AppleScript for Applications (Visual QuickStart Guide)* by Ethan Wilde (Peachpit Press), and *Visual Basic 6 (Visual QuickStart Guide)* by Harold Davis (Peachpit Press). While these don't discuss Photoshop scripting, they'll get you up to speed so that Adobe's own documentation makes more sense. Also, consider Sal Soghoian's book *AppleScript 1-2-3* (Peachpit Press)—Sal knows everything there is to know about scripting.

▶ **Examples.** The best way to learn how to script Photoshop is by looking at and deconstructing other people's scripts. If you can find a script that already does what you want, then use it. If the script isn't quite right, then edit it to make it work for you. Adobe has provided a number of scripts to play with, including scripts that add text, warp it, and then convert the text to a selection. You can open AppleScripts in Script Editor (the free AppleScript editor that comes with the Mac), and Windows scripts in any Visual Basic editor in Windows to see how they work or edit them to suit your needs. JavaScripts are just text, so you can use any text editor to read or write them.

You can find even more scripts on Web sites, such as Adobe Exchange at *www.adobe.com/cfusion/exchange.*

▶ **Scripting dictionary.** On the Mac, all scriptable applications have a built-in scripting dictionary that outlines the various things that can be scripted in that program. One way to see this information is to open the AppleScript Editor utility and choose File > Open Dictionary. The dictionary can be helpful as a quick reference when you want to know what AppleScript commands are supported by a program.

▶ **The Web.** The World Wide Web is, naturally, one of the best sources for AppleScript, Visual Basic, and JavaScript information. There are a number of great sites out there that offer both tutorials on scripting and scripts that you can download, use, and learn from. If you want AppleScript information, start at Apple's own scripting site: *www.apple.com/applescript.* Another excellent place to learn about scripting is the Photoshop Scripting user forum on the Adobe web site at *www.adobeforums.com,* or at *www.ps-scripts.com/.*

Running scripts. Even if you never write scripts, you're missing out if you don't know how to run them. The example scripts that Adobe provides are extremely helpful. AppleScript and Visual Basic scripts must be run from outside of Photoshop, from a program like Script Editor.

JavaScript scripts are even more flexible: The easiest way to run a Java-Script from within Photoshop is to place it in the Adobe Photoshop CS3\ Presets\Scripts folder. Photoshop lists these files on the File > Scripts submenu. If your script doesn't live in that folder, you can tell Photoshop where to find it by choosing File > Scripts > Browse. Here's a brief description of the JavaScripts in the File > Scripts submenu:

▶ **Export Layers to Files.** This script saves each layer in your document as a separate, flattened file on disk. You get to choose what file format to save in.

Tip: Russell Brown always stays one step ahead of Photoshop; he didn't stop with his Image Processor script. To download Russell's latest and greatest Photoshop scripts and tutorials, go to russellbrown.com and click Photoshop Tips and Techniques.

▶ **Image Processor.** Originally created by Russell Brown (if you look up "inimitable" in the dictionary, his picture should really be there), Image Processor lets you save multiple versions of your images—a high-resolution TIFF and a Web-resolution JPEG, for example—while also allowing you to apply an action in the process.

▶ **Export Layer Comps to Files.** When you have created one or more layer comps in the Layer Comps palette, this script saves each one as a flattened image. You can choose the file format and output options.

▶ **Export Layer Comps to PDF.** This script saves your layer comps in a single PDF file, one comp per page. We find this is a great way to send multiple comps to a client.

▶ **Export Layer Comps to WPG.** If you want to post your layer comps on a Web site, choose Export Layer Comps to WPG. *WPG* stands for Web Photo Gallery. We cover these galleries in more detail in Chapter 12, "Image Storage and Output."

Photoshop Extended includes three additional scripts: Load Files into Stack (we talked about one use for this in "Reducing Noise with Image Stacks" in Chapter 10, "Sharpness, Detail, and Noise Reduction"), Load Multiple DICOM Files (for analyzing medical images), and Statistics (for analyzing image stacks).

Running Scripts on Events. You can set up Photoshop so that it runs a script or action when certain application events occur, such as opening Photoshop, saving, or printing. To tie a script to an event, choose File > Scripts > Script Events Manager and turn on the Enable Events to Run Scripts/Actions check box (see **Figure 11-52**).

Next, choose an event from the Photoshop Event pop-up menu, such as Open Document, Save Document, or Start Application. (You can also add your own events if you understand the Photoshop scripting model well enough.) Now choose a script or action at the bottom of the dialog (the action must already be loaded into the Actions palette).

When you click Done, Photoshop starts "listening" for your event to take place. When the event happens, the action or script is triggered. For example, you might have a script that opens a set of files each time you launch Photoshop and an action that creates a thumbnail and saves it as a JPEG each time you open a document. In our example in Figure 11-52,

Figure 11-52

Run a script on an event

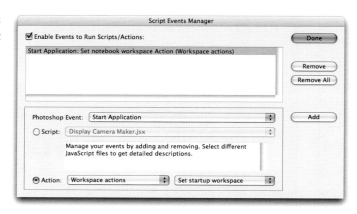

Conrad uses the Start Application event to run an action that applies the workspace for his notebook computer, so that no matter how chaotic the palettes become while he works, Photoshop always starts up with the palettes reset to his preferred arrangement. Just remember that if you're troubleshooting a problem or letting someone else use your computer, you may want to turn off the check box at the top of the Scripting Events dialog, in case you used it to significantly alter the behavior of Photoshop.

Image Storage and Output

The Right File for the Right Job

We've filled the last few hundred pages with techniques for making great-looking images in Photoshop. What we haven't done yet is look at how to get these images *out* of Photoshop. Perhaps you'll be printing your image directly from Photoshop. Or perhaps you're saving the file to be used in a page-layout application, such as InDesign or QuarkXPress, or on a Web page. How you save your image or how you print it is determined by what you want to do with it next.

In this chapter we're going to explore two key subjects: how to save your images to disk and how to create printed or online output. Along the way, we'll also discuss some of the concepts you'll need to be familiar with in order to make good decisions in Photoshop, including halftoning methods, metadata, clipping paths, and transparency.

Storing Images

When Photoshop writes an image to disk, it really just saves a bunch of zeros and ones. But the zeros and ones that one program writes to disk may not be readable by another program. The same data can be written to disk in a variety of ways, called *file formats*. Different file formats may be as different as two languages (like Spanish versus Chinese), or as similar as two dialects of the same language (like American English versus British English).

The world would be a simpler place if everyone (and all software) spoke the same language, but that's not going to happen. Fortunately, programs such as Photoshop, QuarkXPress, and InDesign can read and sometimes even write in multiple file formats. The important thing, then, is not for us to understand exactly what makes one different from the others, but rather what each file format's strengths and weaknesses are, so that we can use them intelligently.

In the first part of this chapter, we'll take an in-depth look at each of the many file formats that Photoshop understands. Note that we won't cover camera raw formats or DNG here, because Photoshop can't write these files—it can only read them using Adobe Camera Raw. We talk about those formats in Chapter 5, "Building a Digital Workflow."

However, before we get to our discussion of file formats and compression, it's useful to talk about the options you have in the Save As dialog: Format, Save, Color, and Image Previews settings.

Save As Dialog

Most descriptions of the Save As dialog options (see **Figure 12-1**) cover the options item by item, but that's a shortsighted way of looking at them. To really understand the Save options, think about the big picture.

When you choose File > Save As in just about any program, two things happen: The program writes out an entirely new copy of the document, and that new document is what you work with after you click Save. If you specify a filename that's the same as the filename of the document you're working on, you replace it with your new version.

However, the traditional Save As approach doesn't necessarily work well for Photoshop. In older versions of Photoshop, many users started with a layered file, used Save As to create a flattened version by turning off the Layers check box, and absentmindedly found themselves saving the flattened version over the layered version—a monumental loss if you wanted to be able to keep working with those layers.

Recent versions of Photoshop try to protect you from that type of data loss through the As A Copy option. When it's on, As A Copy fundamentally changes what you'll get from the Save As dialog. Instead of saving over the original, As A Copy creates a separate, new document.

Tip: Think the list in the Format pop-up menu is too long? In the Photoshop application folder, you'll find the Plug-Ins\File Formats folder. Move any format plug-in out of the Plug-Ins folder, and it won't show up in the menu any more. (Photoshop will still find it if it's anywhere inside the Plug-Ins folder.

Figure 12-1
The Save As dialog

In the Save As dialog, you control how Photoshop saves a document. The Mac dialog is on the left, and the Windows dialog is on the right. Turning off a Save option check box turns on the As A Copy check box. Preview, thumbnail, and case options are enabled by the Preferences dialog, in the File Handling pane (see Figure 12-2).

On top of that, when Photoshop finishes saving as a copy, the document you return to is not the copy you saved—you return to the document that you were working on before you saved, because it's the one that's still full-featured. If you don't realize you're not working with the copy you just saved, you may end up very confused.

As A Copy will turn itself on if you choose Save As and then you turn off check boxes for any of the options in the Save section, because you're telling Photoshop to discard data.

But As A Copy can also turn itself on if you don't touch those Save check boxes. If you simply try to save to a format that can't hold the features you've used in the document, As A Copy turns on, and you have to choose a more-capable format.

The bottom line: If As A Copy comes on, know that you're about to save a less-capable file separately from the document you've been working on. And if you don't want As A Copy to come on, then don't change the state of the Save or Color check boxes, and choose a format that can preserve the checked features. Now that we've gotten that out of the way, let's look over the options in the Save As dialog.

Tip: If the Save As dialog appears when you are just doing a simple Save (using the Save command), it means you've added a feature to the document that you can't store in the document's current format. This often happens if you start from a JPEG, add a layer, and then save. Go ahead and save the file in a more capable format, such as TIFF or PSD.

Format Menu

The Format pop-up menu lists all of the formats that can handle the document you're saving. You can't always see the formats you want, but when that happens, there are a couple of good reasons. If your Photoshop document uses features like color spaces or bit depths that are pretty far from the mainstream, such as 16-bit Lab color or 32-bit HDR, the list of file formats will be pretty short. If formats seem to be missing from the Format pop-up menu, try choosing Image > Duplicate, and on the Image > Mode submenu choose both RGB and 8 Bits/Channel. This will enable the widest range of file formats in the Format pop-up menu.

Save Options

Tip: If the Annotations check box is on, you might want to see what those annotations are, in case they're private notes that aren't intended for clients or other recipients.

The check boxes in the Save section are available only if you're saving a file that includes those features and you've chosen a file format that supports them. You already know about alpha channels and layers—we talked about those earlier. Annotations are the text or audio notes that you create using the Notes tool, and Spot Colors are channels that you've specifically designated for spot color inks (see Chapter 13, "Spot Colors and Duotones," our bonus chapter that's available online. For the URL, see the Introduction).

We're not sure why you'd want to delete spot colors when you save your file, but if you wanted to, this is where you would do it. We think the Spot Colors check box is most useful as an indicator: When it's grayed out, you can be sure that the file format you've chosen cannot handle spot colors. What we'd like is the ability to automatically merge the spot-color channels into our RGB or CMYK image (for when we want to send a proof to a client)—but this feature doesn't do that.

Color Options

The color options in the Save As dialog let you control whether or not you embed an ICC profile in the image, and, for some file formats, these options let you make a color conversion during the save.

Use Proof Setup. This option is only available for EPS and PDF formats, and for EPS DCS when Proof Setup is set to a CMYK profile. When turned on, it tells Photoshop to convert the image from its current space to the Proof Setup space, using the target profile and rendering intent specified there (see "Soft-Proofing Controls" in Chapter 4, "Color Settings"). When you turn on Use Proof Setup, the profile listed under the Embed Color Profile option changes to the one specified in Proof Setup. We don't use this option much—it's not intuitive, and we only use it in those rare cases where we're already in the Save As dialog and realize that we forgot to convert the image to the correct output space.

Embed Color Profile. The easiest way to get accurate color when you move your image from one machine to another is by sending information about the image's color space with it (see Chapter 4, "Color Settings"). You could write down the color space information on a piece of paper and mail it to the image's recipient, or you could just turn on Embed Color Profile (it's on by default unless you set your Color Management Policy to Off), which embeds the color information in the file itself. That said, there are two instances when you might consider turning off this check box.

▶ You might not want to include the color profile when you need to send a file to an organization that doesn't support color management. They may get nervous upon seeing an embedded profile, and screw up your image in one way or another.

▶ CMYK profiles are notoriously large (they may add between 700 K and 3 MB to the file size). If your file will be further edited on another machine, it's important to include the profile. However, if you've got a tiny 100 K CMYK file that you want to send in an email to a friend for her newsletter, it's ridiculous to add the profile to it. All the color images in this book use the same profile, so we did not save the profile in the images; instead, we brought the untagged images into Adobe InDesign and set the default *document* profile, which works just as well. Of course, if we had to send one of these images to a friend for further editing, they'd be lost unless we sent them our color profile, too.

Image Preview Options

When you use Save As, by default Photoshop can create miniature preview images within your file if you choose Ask When Saving from the Image Previews pop-up menu in the File Handling pane of the Preferences dialog (see **Figure 12-2**). From then on, the Save As dialog offers you Preview choices: in Windows, you get a Thumbnail check box; on the Mac, you get three check boxes, one each for saving an icon, a thumbnail, and a full-size preview (see Figure 12-1). We don't bother with these, because today's operating systems and professional imaging programs like Bridge and Lightroom tend to create their own previews. But if you do want to use them, here's what they are:

Figure 12-2

File Handling pane of the
Preferences dialog

Image Previews options

File extension default setting

Layered TIFF alert setting

*Maximize PSD and PSB
Compatibility default setting*

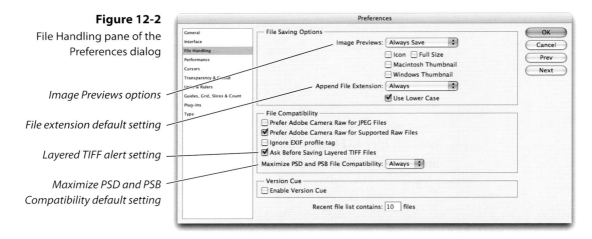

Icon. The first preview, Icon, acts as a desktop picture, so you can see (with a little imagination) what the image is when you're staring at the file on your desktop. It doesn't seem to work reliably in Windows.

Thumbnail. The second preview, Thumbnail, is provided for the Open dialogs of QuickTime-savvy applications. We leave this off because many programs create a thumbnail on the fly, whether you save one or not.

Full Size. You only see this on Photoshop in Mac OS X when Ask When Saving is turned on in File Handling preferences. It adds a 24-bit PICT resource that is the physical output size of the image, downsampled to 72 pixels per inch. You don't need this for an EPS file, because that format can include its own full-size preview.

Opening Images

You might think you know how to open images, especially if you've been doing it in other programs all this time. But Photoshop has a few useful power options in case a file isn't opening quite the way you expect.

If a file doesn't open in Photoshop when you double-click it, try dragging it to the Photoshop program icon. If that doesn't work, try choosing File > Open in Photoshop and locating the file.

If you see the file in the Open dialog but it isn't selectable, try choosing the file's format from the Enable pop-up menu. If that doesn't work, try choosing All Documents from the Enable pop-up menu. This can help if you receive an image created on a different platform that's missing the right file extension. The Enable pop-up menu can also help if you're opening a document that contains more than one format and you want to dictate how it opens.

If you want to open multiple images, you can select more than one image in the Open dialog, or you can drag multiple images from the desktop or Bridge to Photoshop. You can also select multiple images in Bridge and just press the Return (Mac) or Enter key.

Creating Output for Prepress

In the prepress world, most people don't print directly from Photoshop—at least for their final output. Instead, they print from separation programs, presentation programs, or page-layout programs. In this section, we're going to focus on the latter item: page-layout programs, such as Adobe InDesign and QuarkXPress.

Our assumption here is that if you're printing from a page-layout program, you're probably printing to a PostScript imagesetter or platesetter, resulting in paper, film, or plates with black-and-white halftoned images. We summarize the recommended file formats for prepress in **Table 12-1**. You'll find more-detailed information about these formats in "File Formats," later in this chapter.

Table 12-1
File formats for print

File format	Notes
Photoshop	Preserves transparency, layers, clipping paths, and layers in InDesign and XPress
TIFF	Preserves transparency and clipping paths
Photoshop PDF	Preserves vector type and graphics
EPS/DCS	Preserves vector type, graphics, and clipping paths; not color-managed; increasingly being replaced by PDF

Adobe InDesign and QuarkXPress

It appears that Adobe InDesign is taking the desktop publishing crown away from QuarkXPress, which reigned in the last gasp of the twentieth century. No matter which page-layout tool you use, it's crucial that you consider how your images will transport from Photoshop to the printed page. There are some basic rules you should follow.

File formats. When it comes to printing from page-layout programs, always use TIFF, PDF, DCS, or EPS. With the latest versions of InDesign or XPress, you can also use the native Photoshop (PSD) format. We tend to use the TIFF format for almost all of our files, though we'll occasionally use EPS or DCS for specialized effects, such as duotones or custom screening. If your image has vector artwork (like text layers) in it, you should use EPS or (preferably) PDF.

Placing layered Photoshop files in InDesign. There are advantages to placing layered Photoshop files into your InDesign layouts. One advantage is speed: You can drag a Photoshop document into an InDesign layout as soon as it's ready, instead of going through another step to create a flattened copy. Also, you can use the Object > Object Layer Options command in InDesign to control which Photoshop layers or layer comps are visible. If you're using layers to create variations on an image, you only need to place the layered original into InDesign once, duplicate it on the layout, and change which layers are visible in InDesign (see **Figure 12-3**).

Tip: If you use the same layered Photoshop file multiple times in InDesign with different layer settings, make sure you choose Keep Layer Visibility Overrides from the When Updating Link pop-up menu in the Object Layer Options dialog in InDesign. If the images are set to Use Photoshop's Layer Visibility and you update the Photoshop file, all your variations become the same (taking on the last layer visibility settings in Photoshop).

Figure 12-3
Controlling Photoshop document layers in InDesign

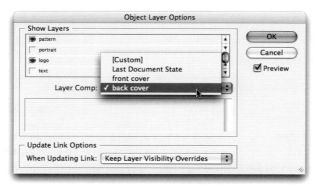

This workflow is not without its costs. Because you aren't locking down the image in a flattened file, there are all sorts of opportunities for things to go haywire. For example, a production person down the line may activate the wrong layer or layer comp. Also, layered Photoshop files take up more disk space, so the final package you deliver to your printer may take longer to transmit or require another DVD. But if you and your production team can stay on top of all that, go ahead and take advantage of the flexibility.

TIFF vs. EPS for Prepress

As we travel around the world doing seminars and conferences, we are forever hearing people say "My service bureau told me to only use EPS files," or "I was told I'd get better images if I used TIFFs," or "Don't EPS files print better?"

While the confusion is understandable, we want to make a few points about TIFF and EPS that will, we hope, clear the air a tad.

For most images, TIFFs and EPSs contain *exactly the same image data*. The way in which it's written (encoded) may be somewhat different, but that doesn't change the image one iota.

The key differences between TIFF and EPS are not what these formats are or how they're written, but what other programs can do to them and what Photoshop features they can contain.

Encapsulated data. The philosophy behind EPS (Encapsulated PostScript) files is that they're self-contained capsules of information. Other programs aren't expected to go in and change the data.

EPS files were designed to be imported into other programs so that all those programs have to do is send the EPS down to the printer, trusting that the PostScript code inside would image correctly. EPS files depend on a PostScript interpreter, so if you're using a non-PostScript desktop inkjet, you may have trouble printing an EPS from a program like QuarkXPress.

Open TIFF format. TIFF files were designed so that they could be exchanged among image editors, so they are much more open to being edited. Programs such as InDesign and QuarkXPress take advantage of this by incorporating features that let you make changes to the TIFF image. On pages, for instance, you can apply a color to a grayscale TIFF image. When you print, the program alters the image data while sending it to the printer without changing the saved image file.

Downsampling and cropping. Adobe InDesign and QuarkXPress have the ability to downsample TIFF data at print time, sending only the data that's needed and thus potentially speeding up the print job.

Two common examples are sending a high-resolution image to a low-resolution printer and cropping. In either case, sending down all of an image's data wastes time in transmission and printer processing. If an image is a TIFF, InDesign and XPress can send only the amount of data required, but they can't do that with an EPS file—they can only send down the entire file.

Previews and separations. One of the biggest hassles of TIFF images, however, is that they can take a long time to import on slow machines, because the page-layout program has to read the entire file in order to create a screen preview for the image. EPS files can import quickly because Photoshop has already created a preview image.

Color management. It isn't very practical to color-manage EPS files, but embedding profiles in TIFF files was worked out long ago and is reliable.

Workflow considerations. The output characteristics of TIFF files are set and can be changed by the program that outputs them, but EPS files can contain non-editable transfer functions, duotones, and halftone screening information. Whether that's a feature or not depends on how you work.

As for us, when we have a choice, we almost always use TIFF files; we prefer them for their flexibility, and we do a *lot* of page proofing with large grayscale images, so the downsampling at print time helps a lot. However, if we need fast importing of large files or a duotone image, we switch to EPS. But don't listen to us. The most important reason why you should use one over the other is not "my consultant/service bureau/guru told me so," but because of your own workflow. The sorts of images you work with, the kind of network and printers you have, and your proofing needs all play a part in your decision.

CMYK vs. RGB. The choice between importing RGB or CMYK images involves two decisions—when do you want to do your separations, and what program do you want to do them in? You can preseparate all your images with Photoshop (or another program), or you can place RGB images in InDesign or XPress and rely on their color management systems to do the separations for you.

Preseparating has a lot going for it. Images land on pages ready to print; the page-layout program just sends the channels down, with no processing necessary at print time. Note that CMYK EPS files are not color managed in the page-layout program, though CMYK TIFF files may be. That is, if the page-layout program's CMS is turned on, your CMYK values may be altered at print time. To ensure that the image data stays the same, choose an output (target) profile that matches the image (source) profile.

Placing unseparated RGB files has advantages as well, though. You can use the page-layout program's color management system to produce better proofs using color printers, and you don't have to target the images until the last minute, when you know all your press conditions and are ready to pull final seps (separations). However, when it comes right down to it, we separate almost all our images in Photoshop first. (But we archive the RGB files, just in case we need to reseparate to some other target.)

Rotating, scaling, cropping, et cetera. While you can perform all kinds of wonderful transformations in today's page-layout programs, each rotated, scaled, skewed, and flipped image adds processing overhead. If you want to keep your page-layout workflow as simple and efficient as possible, transform and crop images before you import them into layouts.

Now, this advice is not absolute. If you're on a deadline, staying in your page-layout program and making minor image adjustments can save a lot of time, and if your prepress service provider has up-to-date imagesetters, image adjustments in the layout might not slow down the job so much.

It also matters how essential and extensive the changes are. By "essential," we mean something basic, like correcting a crooked horizon. If it's likely that the correction will need to be made every time the image is used, then correct the original and never worry about it again. But if it's more of a one-time design variation, it may be better to do it to the image only on the layout for that particular job.

Extreme cropping is a more clear-cut case. When you take an 8-megapixel digital SLR frame, crop it down to around 5 megapixels, and send it on to InDesign, InDesign receives 5 megapixels. But if you crop the image in InDesign, InDesign will import and manage 8 megapixels, which can turn out to be an ongoing performance drag on your system and on printers. InDesign and XPress can be configured to print only the cropped portion, so this won't necessarily slow down output. Still, if you're going to crop out a lot of an image, do it in Photoshop.

Halftone, Contone, and Hybrid Screening

We all live in an illusion: When we see a leaf, our eye makes us think we see a continuous range of colors and tones, continuous lines, and continuous shapes. That's an illusion, because the eye simply doesn't work that way. Without going too far into visual physiology, suffice it to say that the eye works much like an incredibly high-resolution digital camera.

It turns out that because the brain is already so good at fooling us into thinking that we're seeing detail where there is none, or continuous colors where there aren't any, we can fool it even more. The process of imaging data is inherently one of fooling ourselves, and some methods are better than others. The two primary methods of imaging are halftone and contone. Let's take a closer look at each of them.

Halftone

Tip: Want to play around with halftones? Start with a photo or a gradient, convert it to grayscale, choose Image > Mode > Bitmap, choose Halftone Screen from the Method pop-up menu, and click OK. In the Halftone screen dialog, try the different halftone methods and angles; the effects are easier to see if you specify a low screen frequency. Unfortunately, there's no preview feature in the Halftone dialog, so you have to click OK to see the results.

Printing presses, platesetters, inkjet printers, and laser printers all share one thing: they only print on or off, black or white. They can't print shades of gray. To print 15 different colors, you'd have to run the paper through the machine 15 times with different-colored inks, or toners, or whatever. However, lithographers figured out in the late nineteenth century that they could create a tint of a colored ink by breaking the color down into a whole bunch of little spots. Our brain plays along with the game and tells us that we really are seeing the shade of gray, not just spots (see **Figure 12-4**). These spots make up the *halftone* of the image.

There are a number of ways to halftone an image, but the most common is to combine printer dots—those tiny square marks that platesetters or laser printers make, sometimes as small as $\frac{1}{3,600}$ of an inch—together into larger spots (see **Figure 12-5**). The darker the gray level, the larger the spot—the more dots are turned on. Each spot sits on a giant grid, so the center of each spot is always the same distance from its neighbors. (The

Figure 12-4
Halftoning

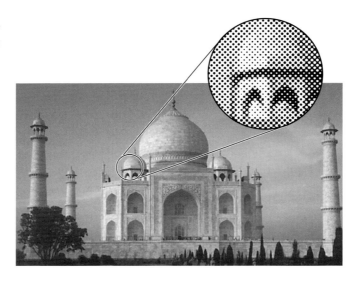

Figure 12-5
A representation of
digital halftone
cells (spots)

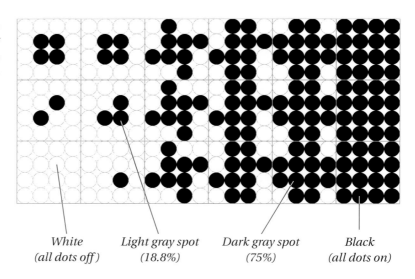

*White
(all dots off)*

*Light gray spot
(18.8%)*

*Dark gray spot
(75%)*

*Black
(all dots on)*

Figure 12-6
Tint percentages

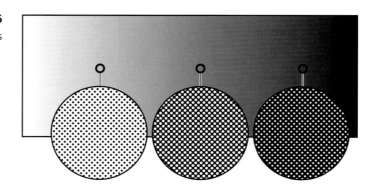

spots don't really get closer or farther from each other, just bigger and smaller; see **Figure 12-6**.)

You can print multicolor images by overlaying multiple color halftones (typically cyan, magenta, yellow, and black). Again, our eyes fool us into thinking we're seeing thousands of colors when we're only seeing four.

David and Conrad coauthored a book with Glenn Fleishman and Steve Roth called *Real World Scanning and Halftones* (3rd edition, Peachpit Press). That book covers halftoning in much more detail than we can get into here. However, we should at least cover the basics. Every halftone has three components, or attributes: screen frequency, screen angle, and spot shape.

Screen frequency. The more halftone spots you cram together within an inch, the tighter the grid, the smaller the spots, and so on. The number of halftone spots per inch is called *halftone screen frequency,* specified in lines per inch, or *lpi* (though we're really talking about "rows of spots per inch," not actual lines). Higher frequencies (small spots, tightly packed, like those in glossy magazines) look smoother. However, because of limits in digital halftoning, higher lpi values reproduce fewer levels of gray at a given output resolution and produce much more dot gain on a printing press, so tints clog up and go muddy more quickly (see "Image Differences," later in this chapter).

Lower screen frequencies (as in newspapers) are rough-looking, but they're easier to print, and you can achieve many levels of gray at lower output resolutions.

Screen angle. Halftone grids are not like bitmapped images; you can rotate them to any angle you want. (In a bitmapped image, the pixels are always in a horizontal/vertical orientation.) Halftones of grayscale images are typically printed at a 45-degree angle because the spots are least noticeable at this angle. However, color images are more complex.

When you overlap halftone grids, as in color printing, you may get distracting moiré ("mwah-RAY") patterns that ruin the illusion. In order to minimize these patterns, it's important to use specific angles. The greater the angle difference between overlapping screens (you can't get them any farther apart than 45 degrees), the smaller the moiré pattern. With four-color process printing, the screens are typically printed 30 degrees apart at 15, 45, and 75 degrees (yellow, the lightest ink, is generally printed at 0 degrees—15 degrees offset from cyan).

Spot shape. The last attribute of halftones is the shape of each spot. The spot may be circular, square, a straight line, or even little pinwheels (see **Figure 12-7**). The standard PostScript spot shape is a round black spot in the highlights, square at 50 percent, and an inverted circle (white on black) in the shadows. Changing the shape of the spot is rarely necessary. However, if, for example, you're producing cosmetics catalogs, or need to solve tonal shift problems printing on newsprint at coarse screen frequencies, controlling the halftone spot shape can definitely improve the quality of your job.

Figure 12-7
Spot shape

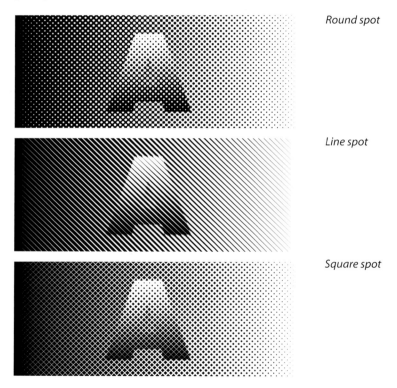

Round spot

Line spot

Square spot

Contone Output

With binary devices such as platesetters and printers, you need to use a halftone to fool the eye into seeing shades of gray because you can't create color or gray pixels. With a continuous-tone device, usually called *contone*, you *can* vary the color or gray shade of each pixel. Compared to halftoning, in contone images the pixels touch each other with no visible space between marks. Also, each pixel is a specific color made by building up varying densities of primary colors in the same spot.

A CRT monitor is an example of a contone imaging device, because the color of each pixel is made by mixing together varying amounts of red, green, and blue.

A dye-sublimation printer is another type of contone device. It overlays varying amounts of ink to build a color. Dye-subs are typically 300-dpi devices, but the lack of halftoning or white space between pixels makes images look surprisingly photorealistic. Because of the lack of resolution, hard-edged objects such as type or line art may appear fuzzy or jaggy, but the soft edges and blends found in natural images may be indistinguishable from chemically printed photographs.

Hybrid Color Screening

There is one more method of simulating a "real-world," continuous-tone image: using tiny spots to simulate tints and colors, but making those spots so small and so diffuse that the image appears contone. The three primary examples of this sort of imaging are: high-resolution inkjet; color laser; and stochastic screening, either on a conventional press or on a direct-digital press such as the HP Indigo E-Print or the Agfa Chromapress.

Inkjet. In inkjet technology, the printer sprays a fine mist of colored inks onto paper. The amount of each ink is varied, much like a contone printer, but it results in tiny spots on paper, often with paper white showing through, more like halftones. While older, low-resolution inkjets couldn't be mistaken for contone imaging devices, prints from current high-resolution inkjets are so smooth that for all practical purposes, they can be considered contone devices. This holds true for both large-format inkjets like the Epson Stylus Pro 9880 and their desktop-size siblings. They use tiny droplet sizes of four, six, or more inks, deployed with very sophisticated error-diffusion screening, to produce results that are indistinguishable to the naked eye from a true continuous-tone print.

With inkjet printers, you're expected to send down the image data and let the printer driver handle the details, so you can't control ink percentages like you can on a press, unless you also use CMYK RIP software. Ultimately, CMYK RIPs are sometimes useful for inkjets used as proofing devices; but in our experience, if your goal is to produce final photorealistic output, you're better off feeding RGB data to the printer. That said, we have obtained stunning results with some of the RGB RIPs designed for photographic output on inkjets, such as Colorbyte Software's ImagePrint.

Tip: When we need to print from a PostScript-dependent program to a printer that doesn't contain a PostScript RIP, we create an Acrobat PDF file of our document. Then we print the file from Acrobat (which acts like a PostScript RIP) to the inkjet. However, Adobe Creative Suite applications print beautifully through most inkjets' raster drivers, so we just print from the native application file rather than messing around with this PDF work-around.

Stochastic screening. Earlier in this chapter we discussed how halftones are formed by clumping together groups of printer dots into a regularly spaced grid of spots. However, we oversimplified; this is actually only one way to make a halftone. Remember, a halftone is just a way to simulate tints or colors with tiny spots. Another method of halftoning is a diffusion dither (see **Figure 12-8**).

Figure 12-8
Diffusion dither
as halftone

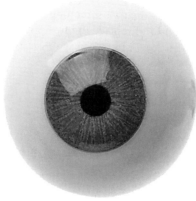

Grayscale image screened by PostScript at 133 lpi

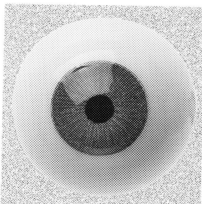

1000-dpi, 40-lpi halftone from Photoshop

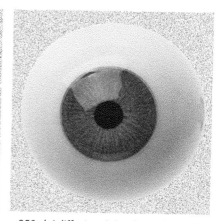

250-dpi diffusion dither from Photoshop

Diffusion dithers can create near-contone quality. Various vendors have created proprietary dithering techniques, usually called *stochastic screening*, that let you reproduce contone-like images from a printing press. Note that proprietary stochastic screening is a type of "frequency modulated" (FM) screen, more sophisticated than Photoshop diffusion dithering.

Stochastic screening can be an attractive option when you need to avoid the moiré patterns that can be caused by halftoning, or print with

Overriding Screen Settings

When you send a grayscale or color bitmapped image to a PostScript printer, the computer inside the printer converts the image into a halftone. That means that the printer sets the halftone screen frequency, angle, and spot shape. Sometimes you might want to override the printer's default settings to use your own halftone screening information. Unfortu-

nately, while most programs offer you ways to do this, many printers just ignore the application's halftoning instructions.

Instead, platesetters and image-setters usually use screening "filters" that catch all screening instructions and replace the frequency/angle combinations with similar (or not) built-in settings. This is particularly important if

you're trying to achieve a special-ized spot shape. However, in most cases, you'd want to use a custom halftone spot shape for special effects at somewhat low halftone frequencies. In these cases, we recommend people simply create the halftone in Photoshop rather than relying on the output device.

more than four inks, or need more detail at a given resolution. One of the reasons you see stochastic screening on far more desktop printers than presses is that it's harder to control dot gain on a press, and the size of the stochastic dot also limits the amount of highlight detail you can reproduce. You can use software to create stochastic screens, but it's more likely that you'll work with a prepress service provider who can hook into the screening algorithms built into platesetters such as Agfa's CrystalRaster or Linotype-Hell's Diamond Screening.

Color laser printer. Most color laser printers use some kind of diffusion dither to simulate a very high screen frequency. It's almost always best to let the laser printer do the screening using its own proprietary algorithms, rather than doing it ourselves. Controlling color on these devices isn't easy—where possible, we prefer to send a calibrated RGB image through a color management system (see Chapter 4, "Color Settings").

Image Differences

Now that we've explored the various imaging methods, we should recap and highlight some of the different techniques you can use in building images suitable for output on halftone and contone devices. We say "recap," because we've mentioned most (if not all) of these in previous chapters, though never in one place.

Resolution. The first and foremost difference between contone and halftone imaging is the required image resolution. It's quite a bit harder to work out the resolution needed for halftone output than it is for contone, so we'll deal with halftone output first.

▶ **Resolution requirements for halftone output.** For halftones, the halftone screen frequency matters much more than the resolution. You never need an image resolution above two times ($2\times$) the halftone screen frequency (and often you can get almost-equivalent results with as little as $1.2\times$ or $1.4\times$). Even if you're printing on a 2400-dpi imagesetter, your image resolution can (and should) be much lower. For instance, printing at 150 lpi, you never need more than a 300-ppi image, and usually no higher than 225 ppi (we generally use the 1.5 multiplier; see Chapter 2, "Image Essentials").

▶ **Resolution requirements for contone output.** The resolution needed for a contone output device is easy to figure, but it can sometimes be hard to deliver. Your output resolution should simply match the resolution of the output device. If you're printing to a 300-dpi dye-sub printer, your image resolution should be 300 ppi at the printed dimensions. The appropriate resolution for stochastic screening is less clear, but in general, you rarely need images over 300-ppi.

▶ **Resolution requirements for inkjet output.** The necessary resolution for today's photorealistic inkjets is to some extent a guessing game. In part, it depends on the paper stock—matte papers generally require less resolution than glossy ones. Anecdotal evidence suggests that a resolution around 240 ppi is sufficient for most images, but if you're really picky, you may want to determine the ideal resolution for a particular paper stock yourself using good old trial and error. It's certainly possible to send too much data to an inkjet printer, not only increasing print times unconscionably but also degrading the image: You do *not* want to send a 1440-ppi image to a 1440-dpi inkjet!

Synthetic targets composed of black and white line pairs show an improvement when they're printed at an integral divisor of the printer resolution, such as 360 ppi on a 1440-dpi inkjet, but it's uncertain how applicable this is to images with more natural content. For real-world photography, 240 to 360 ppi provides sufficient quality for most images. While in theory you could print the highest-quality image on an inkjet at 480 ppi, you'd see the difference only if you shot with a sufficiently sharp lens, with zero motion blur and no errors in sharpening.

Tonal and color correction. We talk a great deal about compressing tonal range ("targeting") for halftone output in Chapter 7, "Image Adjustment Fundamentals," so we won't go into it here. Contone output needs less tonal and gamut compression than halftone output, because contone devices generally have a greater dynamic range and a wider gamut than do halftone devices. Keep a watchful eye on shadows and saturated colors—the most challenging tonal levels and colors to reproduce. Using the Proof Setup command with a good output profile can help a great deal.

Sharpening. As we noted back in Chapter 10, "Sharpness, Detail, and Noise Reduction," contone images need less sharpening than halftone images do. But that doesn't mean they don't need any at all. Halftones, again because of their coarse screens and significant dot gain, mask details and edges in an image; sharpening can help compensate for both the blurriness of the scan and the blurriness of the halftone. And, halftones being what they are, you have a lot of room to play with sharpening before the picture becomes oversharpened (most people actually end up undersharpening).

In contone images, however, there's a real risk of oversharpening. Not only should you use a lower Amount setting for unsharp masking, but also a smaller radius. Where a radius less than 1 is often lost in a halftone image, it's usually appropriate in contone images. In this context, inkjet printers tend to behave more like contone devices.

Image mode. This last item, image mode, isn't really dependent on what output method you're using. However, because we still see people confused about image mode, we thought we'd throw in a recap here, too.

If you're printing to a color contone device that outputs to film, or if the image is only seen on a color screen, you should leave your image in RGB mode. Contone and hybrid devices that print on paper use CMYK inks or toners, but in most cases you'll get better results sending RGB and letting Photoshop or the printer handle the conversion. If you have a good profile for the output device, you can preview the output using Proof Setup and convert the image from your RGB editing space to the device's space at print time (we discuss this in the next section). If you're printing separations, though, you need to send a CMYK file.

Printing from Photoshop

As in almost every other Mac or Windows program, there are two menu items (and accompanying dialogs) tied to imaging: Page Setup and Print, both found under the File menu. Because Mac OS X and Windows XP currently don't allow applications to add features to the Print and Page Setup dialogs, Adobe added the Print with Preview command to Photoshop CS2. It was such a useful idea that in Photoshop CS3, Adobe simply replaced the Print dialog with the former Print with Preview dialog. Most of the options you need to change when you're printing from Photoshop can be accessed easily in the Print dialog (see **Figure 12-9**). If you use them correctly, you can avoid a lot of wasted paper.

Print dialog

Tip: In Mac OS X, you'll probably see a Printer pop-up menu in the Page Setup dialog. If you see this, choose your printer here too—even if you've already chosen your printer in the Print dialog. If the wrong printer is chosen in Page Setup, the wrong paper sizes may be listed.

The Print dialog lets you control the position, scaling, and color management of your image on the paper, which you can preview using the proxy image superimposed on a preview of the paper size. In Photoshop CS2, the proxy image wasn't color-managed, but in Photoshop CS3, it is. In addition, turning on the Match Print Colors check box applies your current Proof Setup to the proxy.

Printer and Page Setup. These options are not just here as a convenience. The only way that Photoshop knows how big it can print a document is

Figure 12-9
Print dialog
and its Output options

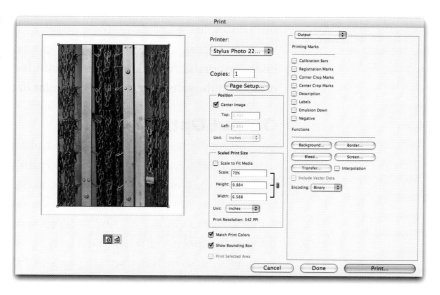

Tip: If clicking the Center Image check box doesn't center the image, the margins provided by the printer driver are asymmetrical. Open Page Setup and choose an option or paper size that provides equal or minimum margins, if available.

from the paper sizes provided by the printer driver you've chosen. For accurate positioning and scaling, it's important for you to set the printer, paper type, and options correctly. To do this, first choose your printer from the Printer pop-up menu, which lists the printer drivers installed on your computer. Then click Page Setup and ensure that all of the options are set correctly. Note that Page Setup is not provided by Photoshop—all Page Setup options are put there by the printer driver. Photoshop simply gives you access to Page Setup because it needs that information in order to calculate the available margins. This fact causes much confusion that's hard to avoid, since printer driver and program options are typically walled off from each other in both Mac OS X and Windows.

Scaling and positioning. You might just want to fit the image on the paper and center it. If so, leave Center Image and Scale to Fit Media checked. If you want to customize the image size, turn off Scale to Fit Media. If you want to customize its position, turn off Center Image. To be able to scale and position by dragging, Show Bounding Box must be turned on. You can't change the aspect ratio of the image in this dialog.

The initial size that's displayed when you open the Print dialog is based on the dimensions specified in the Image Size dialog. When you change the scaling, be aware that you aren't creating any new pixels—the scaling options are just like changing the size or resolution in Image Size with the Resample Image check box turned off.

Tip: We recommend you always apply scaling in the Print dialog, and leave the scaling in Page Setup at 100 percent. The Print dialog doesn't know about scaling applied in Page Setup; so if you apply scaling there, the preview and dimensions in the Print dialog will be incorrect.

Print Selected Area. To print just a small portion of an image, you don't have to duplicate and crop the image. Simply draw a selection marquee around the area you want to print, then turn on the Print Selected Area check box in the Print dialog. This check box is unavailable if no selection exists or if the selection is nonrectangular or feathered.

Output Options

The Output Options tell Photoshop how to print the document. A couple of these items (screens and transfer curves) also apply when you save files in various file formats. Some features in the dialog are determined by which printer driver is selected. Because these are standard system-level features, we're going to skip them and get right to the good stuff: the Photoshop-specific items. Some Output options apply only to prepress-oriented PostScript printing, which is why Photoshop alerts you with the dialog shown in **Figure 12-10** if you print to a non-PostScript printer.

However, if you are primarily outputting to desktop printers, turn on the Don't Show Again check box and forget about this warning, since the features mentioned in the alert won't affect you.

Figure 12-10

The non-PostScript printer alert

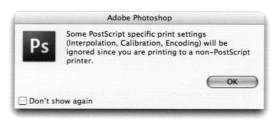

Tip: The diamond spot shape, perfected by Peter Fink, is better in almost every instance than the standard round spot because it greatly reduces the optical tonal jump that is sometimes visible in the mid-to-three-quarter tones—the 50 to 75 percent gray areas. We've also been told that the diamond spot is much better for silkscreening.

Screen. This is a PostScript-only option. When you click the Screen button, Photoshop brings up the Halftone Screens dialog, where you can specify the halftone screen angle, frequency, and spot shape for your image (see **Figure 12-11**). When the Use Printer's Default Screens check box is turned on (it is unless you go and change it), Photoshop won't tell the printer anything about how the image should be screened. Leave this check box on unless you want to take responsibility for setting your own halftone screens. Photoshop gives you a wide array of possibilities for setting the halftone screen. However, most platesetters and imagesetters override the screen values (see "Overriding Screen Settings," earlier in this chapter).

▶ **Frequency and Angle.** The Frequency and Angle settings are self-explanatory.

▶ **Shape.** When the Use Same Shape For All Inks check box is on, the Shape pop-up menu applies to each process color. We'd only change this for special low-frequency effects.

Tip: If you're not comfortable thinking of transfer curves as numbers, do what David does: He tries out his transfer curves in the Curves dialog first. When he gets a curve just the way he wants it, he saves the curve to disk (using the Save button in the Curves dialog), then goes to the Transfer Functions dialog and loads it.

▶ **Use Accurate Screens.** When you turn on the Use Accurate Screens check box, Photoshop includes the PostScript code to activate Accurate Screens in your PostScript RIP. However, if your RIP doesn't have Accurate Screens technology, or if it uses some other screening technology, such as Balanced Screens or HQS, just leave this off.

▶ **Auto.** If you don't know what frequency/angle combinations to type in, check with your RIP vendor. If they don't know, you're probably in trouble. However, as a last resort, you could try clicking the Auto button and telling Photoshop approximately what screen frequency you want and the resolution of the printer you're using.

Figure 12-11

Halftone Screens
dialog

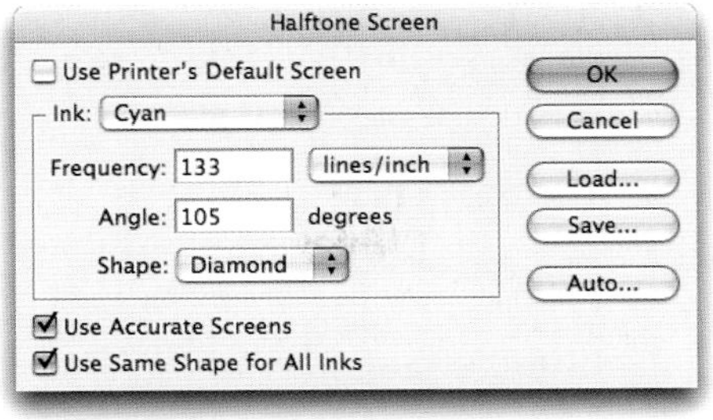

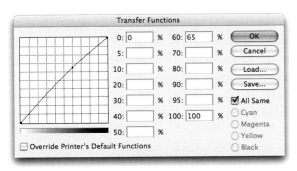

Note that you can include these screen settings in EPS files (see "Encapsulated PostScript (EPS)" later in this chapter).

Transfer. A transfer curve is like taking a curve that you made in the Curves dialog and downloading it to your printer. It won't change the saved image data, but when you print with the transfer curve, it modifies the printed gray levels. This option also works on non-PostScript printers.

It's rare to use a transfer curve these days; they've mostly been replaced by printer profiles. If you do use them, click the Transfer button to open the Transfer dialog (see **Figure 12-12**). You can save a transfer curve with an image in any format that Photoshop supports, but the curve is only recognized when you print directly from Photoshop. To print images with transfer curves from a page-layout application, you need to use EPS files, but there's no obvious signal to tell anyone working with the image that it contains a transfer curve, except that the values in the file aren't the same as those that print. The only way to tell is to open the image in Photoshop and check to see if there's a transfer curve specified. If you do use a transfer curve, make sure that whomever is responsible for printing the file knows it's lurking there!

Tip: The Override Printer's Default Functions check box appears at the bottom of the Transfer Functions dialog. Don't turn this on unless you really know what you're doing with transfer functions. If you're printing through a linearized RIP, turning this check box on will override the linearization, and could give you nasty results.

Figure 12-12

Transfer Functions
dialog

Tip: If you typically make prints with a white border, you can make your highlights appear much snappier if you lay down a small amount of ink in the border. This works because our eyes tend to assume that the paper-white border is white. When you print a very light gray or yellow tone in the border, the eye still interprets this as paper white, so any specular highlights that use the actual paper white appear brighter than they really are.

Background. Background—and the next 11 features—are only relevant when you're printing from Photoshop; you cannot save them in an EPS format (or any other format, for that matter) and expect them to carry over to other programs, like you can with Screen and Transfer.

When you print your image from Photoshop to a color printer, the area surrounding the image is typically left white (or clear if you're printing on film). The Background feature lets you change the color that surrounds the image using the standard Photoshop Color Picker. The background color that you pick acts like a matte frame around the image to the edges of the printable area.

Border. If you add a border, Photoshop centers the frame on the edge of the image when you print; that is, half the frame overlaps the image, and half the frame overlaps the background. The border's always black.

Bleed. Setting a Bleed value adjusts where Photoshop places the corner crop marks. This is useful for the increasingly rare act of manual stripping. Note that if you specify a 0.125-inch bleed, Photoshop sets the crop marks in 0.125 inches from the image boundary, not outside of it: It effectively says, "cut off the edges of this image."

Interpolation. This PostScript-only item usually does absolutely nothing. In theory, this feature tells your printer to upsample low-resolution images at print time so they'll print more smoothly. We've heard various claims that some PostScript Level 2 or greater printers are actually capable of doing this, but we've yet to see evidence of it. But thanks, Adobe, for giving us the choice!

Calibration Bars. This is a PostScript-only option. When you turn on the Calibration Bars check box in the Print dialog, Photoshop prints one (for grayscale images) or several (for color images) series of rectangles around the image (see **Figure 12-13**). Beneath the image is a ten-step gray wedge; to the left is the same gray wedge, but on each color plate; to the right is a series of colors: Yellow, yellow and magenta, magenta, magenta and cyan, cyan, cyan and yellow; cyan, magenta, and yellow; and black. Each color is 100 percent (solid).

Registration Marks. If you're outputting separations, you need to add registration marks so that the printer can align the four colors properly.

Figure 12-13
Printer marks

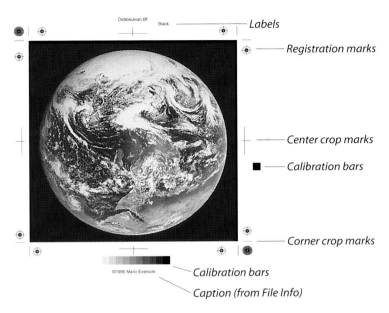

Labels

Registration marks

Center crop marks

Calibration bars

Corner crop marks

Calibration bars

Caption (from File Info)

Turning on the Registration Marks check box adds ten registration marks (eight bull's-eyes and two pinpoint types).

Corner Crop Marks. These specify where the edges of the image are. This is useful if you need to use a straightedge to trim a print down to the size you want. It's essential if the image has a clear white background (like a silhouette); without crop marks, it's impossible to tell where the image boundaries are.

Center Crop Marks. If you need to specify the centerpoint of your image, turn on the Center Crop Marks check box.

Description. David loves the ability of Photoshop to save a description with a file because of the File Info metadata tie-in to InDesign, but it's also helpful when printing a whole mess of images that you need to peruse, file, or send to someone. When you turn on the Description check box in the Print dialog, the program prints whatever caption you have saved in File Info (under the File menu) beneath the image. If you haven't saved a description, this feature doesn't do anything.

You might even include your name or copyright information in the Description field of the File Info dialog, even though there are other fields for this. At least your name prints out with your images.

Newspaper publishers and stock-photo agencies can make much more elaborate use of the File Info feature, including credit lines, handling instructions, and keywords for database searches.

Labels. When you're printing color separations, turning on the Labels check box is a must. This feature adds the file name above the image on each separation, and also adds the color plate name (cyan, magenta, yellow, black, or whatever other channel you're printing). If you're printing a spot color in addition to process colors, it's even more vital that you label the spot separation.

Negative and Emulsion Down. When it comes to the Negative and Emulsion Down options, our advice is to ignore them unless you're a prepress service provider printing to an imagesetter, and even then, these options are usually better set in the imagesetter RIP itself. For the record, Emulsion Down is a PostScript-only option, while Negative applies to non-PostScript printers too.

Encoding. Binary is more compact and therefore takes less time to send over a network, but because ASCII is more compatible, it's often preferable on networks that are administered using DOS or Unix machines. Start by using binary; if it doesn't work, try ASCII85, which is somewhat more compact than ASCII and almost always works.

JPEG is much smaller (and therefore faster) than either binary or ASCII, but uses slightly lossy compression, the effects of which may not be visible (see "Lossy Compression" later in this chapter). JPEG encoding only works when printing to PostScript Level 2 or 3 printers, because they know how to decompress JPEG.

Color Management Options

The Color Management options inside the Print dialog let you tell Photoshop to do one of three things: perform a color conversion on the data that gets sent to the printer, pass the image data and the profile that describes it to the printer driver for printer driver color management, or simply send the pixels to the printer (see **Figure 12-14**).

Unlike the Output options, the Color Management options apply to any color output device, from a desktop inkjet printer to a platesetter.

Document versus Proof. By default, the Print option is always set to Document, which is either the space represented by the profile embedded in

Figure 12-14

Color Management options in the Print dialog

the image or, in the case of untagged images, by the current working space you've set for the document's color mode in the Color Settings dialog (see Chapter 4, "Color Settings").

The other option, Proof, tells Photoshop to convert the image from the document space to the profile specified in Proof Setup, using the rendering intent set in Proof Setup, before handing off the data to the printer. We use this feature when we're trying to make a desktop printer simulate final printed output when we haven't yet converted the file to the final output space. If, for example, we have a ProPhoto RGB image destined for press output, and we want to simulate the press on an inkjet printer, we set Proof Setup to simulate the press by choosing the press profile there, then click the Proof button in the Print dialog.

When we do so, the Proof Setup Preset menu and the Simulate Paper Color and Simulate Black Ink check boxes become enabled, and the Rendering Intent menu becomes disabled. See "Proof Setup Preset," slightly later in this chapter.

Color Handling. The Color Handling pop-up menu allows you to specify whether or not Photoshop will apply a color conversion before sending the data to the printer. There are four options:

Tip: Don't downsample high-bit files before printing from Photoshop. It's both unnecessary and unwise to downsample jobs to 8 bits per channel prior to printing. Photoshop is smart enough to downsample the data and convert the color space before sending it to the printer.

▶ **Printer Manages Colors.** This option tells Photoshop to send the data to the printer in its current document space with that space's profile embedded. This option is designed for use with printers or printer drivers that perform their own color management.

We almost never use this option. It's for devices using true PostScript color management (very rare), or when we print to an inkjet through a RIP that has been configured to translate the color correctly.

▶ **Photoshop Manages Colors.** This sends the data to the printer using the color space of the Printer Profile in the next menu. We nearly always print this way because Photoshop performs all the necessary color conversions better than almost any other program or print driver. When you use this method, though, you must make sure that any color management options in the non-Photoshop section of your printer's driver are turned off; otherwise you'll get a double conversion, with results that range from unacceptable to ghastly.

If you choose Photoshop Manages Colors in the Color Handling pop-up menu, you can pick any ICC profile from the Printer Profile menu to tell Photoshop to convert the image to that profile's space before handing it off to the printer. When you choose a profile, you are also given the opportunity to choose the rendering intent used for the conversion. This is usually the easiest, and sometimes the only, way to use custom rather than vendor-supplied profiles with inkjet printers.

▶ **No Color Management.** We use No Color Management only when we're printing a calibration target and only care about the numbers in the file, not the colors they represent, or when we're printing an image that's already been converted to the intended output space.

▶ **Separations.** To print each color on its own plate (rather than a composite color image), select Separations from the Color Handling pop-up menu. This option is available only when you're printing an image that's already in CMYK or Duotone mode.

Proof Setup Preset. When you choose Proof as the source space, the Proof Setup Preset menu becomes enabled and the Rendering Intent menu becomes disabled. You can choose any saved Proof Setup preset from this menu—if you've applied a Proof Setup to the document, it defaults to that setup. When you print, Photoshop first converts the documents colors from the source space to the Proof Setup space using the rendering intent specified in Proof Setup. It then converts the Proof Setup colors to the printer space specified by Printer Profile. The rendering intent is controlled by the two check boxes, Simulate Paper Color and Simulate Black Ink, as follows:

▶ When both check boxes are turned off, Photoshop converts the Proof Setup colors to the printer space using Relative Colorimetric rendering with Black Point Compensation, so the Proof Setup paper white is translated to the printer's paper white, and the Proof Setup black is rendered as the blackest black the printer can reproduce.

▶ When Simulate Black Ink is turned on, Photoshop converts the Proof Setup colors to the printer space using Relative Colorimetric rendering *without* Black Point Compensation: The Proof Setup paper white is still translated to the printer's paper white, but the Proof Setup black is rendered as the actual shade of black that the final output being simulated will produce.

▶ When Simulate Paper Color is turned on, Simulate Black Ink is turned on and dimmed. Photoshop converts the Proof Setup colors to the printer space using Absolute Colorimetric rendering: The Proof Setup paper white and ink black are reproduced exactly. If you're simulating newsprint, for example, the paper white areas will print with some black and yellow to simulate the yellow-gray newsprint stock, and the blacks will print as relatively washed-out newsprint blacks.

Preparing Images for an Online Service

In the past, most people either printed a Photoshop document from Photoshop or printed it from a layout program. With the rise of digital photography, another world of output has emerged: the online photo service. The big difference with online photo services is that they do not represent a single, easily targeted form of output. They encompass onscreen display of images on the Web, as well as printing on photographic paper, or even on products you can order, such as mugs and T-shirts. This means that an image needs to be saved in a way that looks good onscreen and can print reliably to photographic printers (we won't worry too much about reproduction quality on mugs).

Tip: Stock-photo agencies could be thought of as a type of online photo service. However, agencies can have different image requirements, which you should research and understand before you upload files to them.

Types of online services. Photo services range from consumer-oriented services, where the most important feature is simplicity, to services designed for photographic professionals, fine-art photographers, and serious amateurs. Consumer photo services are now a commodity—your local drugstore probably offers in-store printing and free online galleries from files you upload through your Web browser. Most services expect you to upload JPEG files in the sRGB color space, even though most of their photo printers aren't actually printing in the sRGB color space. You should aim for image resolutions of 240 to 300 ppi at the dimensions of the largest print you ever want to order.

Bridge CS3 contains a built-in link to a consumer photo service. Choose Tools > Photoshop > Online Photo Printing to connect to the Kodak Easy-Share printing service. (You may first need to choose Automatically Check for Services the first time you try this.)

Online services that are geared toward professionals offer more flexibility. They may support color spaces other than sRGB, such as AdobeRGB (1998) and ProPhoto RGB. To assist you in soft-proofing, they may have a custom ICC profile that represents their photo printers, and they may make them available for free download. You can add such a profile to the other profiles on your system and then use it in the Proof Setup command in Photoshop, so that you can work in your color space while tuning for their printer's color space. The online gallery component of professionally oriented online services often provides more flexibility and security, such as customizable gallery appearance, private and password-protected galleries, long-term archiving, and the ability to let you take a cut of print sales.

Saving JPEGs for online services. Some services may restrict uploads to JPEG format only. Because JPEG is a lossy format, there is the question of how much compression to apply. If you're determined to preserve every last bit of quality in your images, you could use maximum JPEG compression. In Photoshop, JPEG quality is represented on a scale of 1 to 12, where 12 is maximum (as in the Save As dialog) or on a scale of 1 to 100, where 100 is maximum (as in the Save For Web & Devices dialog). However, you may find it more reasonable to save your JPEG files a step or two below maximum quality. The reason is that the difference in quality among the near-maximum levels is hard to detect, but the differences in file size are significant. If you have 500 images to upload from an event, you'll probably find that JPEG quality level 10 is indistinguishable from JPEG 12, but

Tip: If you want to save full image metadata (including EXIF data and keywords) with a JPEG file that you intend to send to an online service, create the JPEG file using the Save As command. If you want to strip the metadata, create the JPEG file using the Save For Web & Devices command.

the JPEG 10 versions upload much more quickly and consume much less disk space. For JPEG images that are intended to be online masters, we don't advocate dropping below JPEG 10.

Creating Images for the Web

Just as there are techniques for optimizing an image for paper, there are methods you can use to ensure good quality onscreen (as well as tips for preparing your onscreen image efficiently).

If you're upgrading from Photoshop CS2, one of the things you'll notice is that Adobe ImageReady is no longer included with Photoshop; many of its features have been moved into Photoshop. For Web capabilities beyond what Photoshop CS3 can do on its own, Adobe now offers Fireworks, acquired as part of its purchase of the former Macromedia. But you'll only need to go beyond Photoshop if you're getting pretty deep into Web graphics. If you're a photographer wanting to put images on the Web, Photoshop CS3 gives you plenty of options.

Tone

At default Mac OS X and Windows display settings, an image displays lighter in Mac OS X than in Windows. The most significant difference is that Mac monitor gamma defaults to gamma 1.8, while Windows monitors default to gamma 2.2. There are several strategies for dealing with this mismatch, all involving compromises that we'll discuss. Because the destination monitor is essentially unknown, your images are going to look much better (or worse) on some systems than on others. It's simply impossible to produce images that will look good to every Web user. The best you can do is to aim for a point that will look OK on uncalibrated monitors (which is most monitors), and reasonably good on calibrated monitors. We suggest you choose one of the following alternatives:

▶ **Convert to sRGB.** Back in Chapter 4, "Color Settings," we discussed the sRGB color space, developed by several industry giants to describe the general characteristics of the "typical" Windows monitor. Given the marketing muscle behind sRGB, it's probably the most sensible choice for your Web images. Note that this does not mean you have to edit in sRGB; just convert a copy when you're done editing. This capability is built into the Save For Web & Devices dialog in Photoshop CS3 (see "Saving Images for the Web or Mobile Devices" a little later on).

Tip: If you're a Mac user who wants to more precisely anticipate how Windows users see your images, specify gamma 2.2 the next time you calibrate your monitor. The reasons for setting the Mac to gamma 1.8 are as old as the Mac itself, and thanks to modern color management, those reasons are not really relevant today. Changing monitor gamma won't change the gamma of your Photoshop working space or your files.

▶ **Prepare two sets of images.** We know some photographers who care so much about color that they've prepared two sets of their images—one at gamma 1.8 and one at gamma 2.2. Then they code their Web sites so that Mac users see the gamma 1.8 version while Windows users see the gamma 2.2 version. It's a good theory, except it takes a lot more work, and more professional Mac users are now calibrating to gamma 2.2 anyway.

▶ **Embed the profile.** The best solution to the color mismatch problem is to embed an ICC profile in each image, either in the Save As dialog or by using the Edit > Assign Profile command. This approach relies on two conditions: that every person looking at your images has created a custom profile of their monitor, and that his or her browser supports embedded profiles. But let's get real: The vast majority of Web browsers in use today are not color-managed, and of those that are (such as Safari), they're being viewed mostly on monitors which are not calibrated. If you upload a file in a relatively large color space such as AdobeRGB (1998) or ProPhoto RGB with an embedded profile, in a non-color-managed browser it will actually look much worse than an image uploaded in sRGB, only because sRGB happens to be closer to (but still can't exactly match) most uncalibrated monitor gamuts.

Embedding an RGB working space profile usually only adds about 0.5 K to a JPEG image, so file size is only a consideration if you need to upload the smallest possible files.

Note that Photoshop does not embed profiles in GIF files because they're always in Indexed Color mode rather than RGB. If you must color-manage a GIF file, the Web page *http://www.color.org/wpaper2.xalter* suggests a way to do it.

Given this unresolvable conundrum, the easiest way out for now appears to be to convert to sRGB before uploading to the Web. If you have a color-savvy client who runs color-managed browsers on calibrated monitors, populating their in-house Web pages with larger-gamut images containing embedded profiles may be a reasonable option in that specific case.

Color

Not only can you rarely predict tonal shifts in images for the screen, you can't assume anything about color. As we've mentioned, it's pretty likely that your audience's monitors are not calibrated. If you expect your images to be viewed on mobile devices, the quality of the display may vary greatly, possibly displaying a limited range of colors. While monitor calibration is something you can barely hope for on desktop machines, it isn't helpful at all on mobile devices.

When preserving color quality, it's usually more important to retain the contrast between colors than the particular colors themselves. Image details that result from subtle changes in color (like the gentle folds in a red silk scarf) are often lost in translation unless you anticipate and compensate before exporting the image.

Desktop and notebook computers. Try looking at your image on a variety of Mac and Windows systems. If it's only practical to test on the system you happen to own, you can also choose Windows RGB or Macintosh RGB from View > Proof Setup to approximate how the images look different on each platform. To see the pure, unproofed view again, turn off the View > Proof Colors command (toggle that command by pressing Command-Y in Mac OS X or Ctrl-Y in Windows).

Mobile devices. If you're asked to optimize your images for use in content for cell phones or other mobile devices, you can use Adobe Device Central dialog, which emulates many handheld devices. We cover that later in this chapter.

These methods aren't perfect, but they should give you an idea of how the image may look on different systems.

Should you use Web-safe colors? A generation of Web designers was taught that Web graphics should be saved using a Web-safe color palette. The problem is that "Web-safe" really should be "Save for 8 bit/channel monitors," because this is only relevant when viewing images on a display set to 8bit/channel color (256 colors). Now, that was rather high-end for video cards made in the 1990s, but today, even cell phones and iPods support at least 16 bit/channel color, while computer displays support at least 24 bit/channel color. You may still be concerned about Web-safe color if you are working with an organization with very old equipment. Otherwise, don't concern yourself with Web-safe color, especially for photos.

Resolution

One of the wonderful advantages of working on images for screen display is that resolution is measured in pixels, and you need a lot fewer pixels to display an image on a monitor than you do to print it. This makes for very small images (relative to prepress sizes, at least). An 800-by-600-pixel image (rather large for a Web page) saved at JPEG Medium quality weighs in at just 52 K, while an image at roughly the same viewing size saved as an 8-bit Zip-compressed TIFF for print could occupy 4.5 MB, largely because the print version is set to a much higher resolution, such as 300 pixels per inch. The smaller file sizes of onscreen graphics mean faster processing times and lower RAM requirements.

You'll notice we didn't specify the resolution of the Web image. That's because it doesn't matter. On the Web, the only dimensions that matter are the pixel dimensions. If you put an 800-by-600-pixel image on a Web page, it doesn't matter whether the image was set to 72 ppi or 2400 ppi—the browser will always run that image 800 monitor pixels across. Of course, because monitors have different pixel densities that are adjustable, you simply cannot assume the resolution of your Web audience's monitor. All you can assume is that the same Web graphic will look larger on lower-resolution monitors (such as a 17-inch monitor set to 1024 by 768 pixels) and smaller on monitors set to higher resolutions (such as a 1680-by-1050-pixel notebook monitor). This is also why we don't repeat the age-old myth that graphics are 72 ppi in Mac OS X or 96 ppi in Windows—that hasn't been true for a very long time. Go ahead, we dare you: Draw a line 72 or 96 pixels across on your monitor, and hold a real-world ruler up to the screen. Chances are, your onscreen line won't match up to one inch on your real-world ruler. Your true monitor resolution is simply the number of horizontal or vertical pixels of your monitor divided by its physical display height or width in inches, and of course, that number will be different on someone else's monitor. So, for the Web and other onscreen media, pay attention to pixel dimensions, not pixels per inch.

Saving Images for the Web or Mobile Devices

Making images for the Web is a study in compromise: You can have either great-looking images or pictures that download quickly—pick one. The problem is that you need to see all the options to make an informed decision about how much to degrade your image in the name of small file sizes. The solution is the Save For Web & Devices feature.

Save For Web & Devices lets you see exactly what will happen to your images when you convert them to an online format. Better yet, it can display two or four versions at a time and let you tweak each of them until you get just the effect you want. To open this dialog, choose File > Save For Web & Devices or press Command-Option-Shift-S (Mac) or Ctrl-Alt-Shift-S (Windows). We summarize online file formats in **Table 12-2**, and talk about them in more detail in "File Formats," later in this chapter.

Table 12-2

Popular file formats for viewing onscreen

File format	Notes
JPEG	The standard for photographic images on the Web
GIF	Limited colors, supports 1-bit transparency
PNG	Supports true alpha-channel transparency

Save For Web & Devices dialog

Here are the basic steps you should follow after you open the Save for Web & Devices dialog (see **Figure 12-15**).

1. Switch to the 2-Up or 4-Up tab of the window. We like 4-Up except when we're almost sure of what settings we're going to use.

2. Leave the first panel set to Original (so you have something with which to compare your tests). Click on each of the other images and choose for it a preset configuration from the Settings pop-up menu. For a good spectrum of results, David usually starts with these three: JPEG Medium, GIF 64 Dither, and GIF 32 No Dither.

3. Visually check each image's quality and size, and approximate download time (shown under each image).

Figure 12-15

Save for Web & Devices dialog

The colors of the original image look weak because the image's ProPhoto RGB gamut is too wide for average monitors. The colors in the three Web-optimized views have been adjusted for the Web by the Convert to sRGB command, in the pop-up menu at the right side of the dialog.

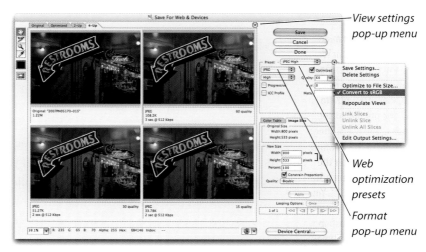

View settings pop-up menu

Web optimization presets

Format pop-up menu

4. Pick the one that is closest to what you're trying to achieve, and tweak the settings to minimize the size while maintaining quality. Below we cover each of the settings and how they work.

5. When you're ready, click OK (make sure the proper image is highlighted; whichever one is highlighted is the one that gets saved to disk).

The problem is that there are many settings in the dialog to tweak, many of them obscure. We'll cover the ones that are most relevant to our interests—reproducing photographic images at an efficient file size.

Tip: In Photoshop CS3, you no longer have to remember to convert an image to sRGB before opening Save For Web & Devices. Just click the round button next to the Settings pop-up menu, and turn on the Convert To sRGB command. The dialog still contains the ICC Profile check box, which determines whether the profile is embedded.

Presets. The Presets pop-up menu lets you recall saved settings. There's nothing magic about the settings that are already built-in; they're only there to get you started. If you don't like the built-in settings, you can delete them by choosing Delete Settings from the pop-up menu to the right of the Settings pop-up menu. If you want to add your own group of settings to the list, choose Save Settings instead; make sure the settings are saved in the Optimized Settings folder (inside your Photoshop Presets folder), with an .irs filename extension.

Format. If you prefer to arrange the settings manually, you should start by choosing GIF, JPEG, PNG, or WBMP from the Format pop-up menu. We discuss these formats in some detail in the last chapter and below.

Checking File Size. The file size that Photoshop displays in the lower-left corner of the document window doesn't take into account any form of

Tip: When you have in mind specific file sizes for your Web graphics, Photoshop can figure out the compression settings for you. Choose Optimize to File Size from the unlabeled pop-out menu next to the Settings pop-up menu. In the Optimize To File Size dialog, enter the file size you want, select a Start With option, and click OK. You probably don't want to simply accept whatever Photoshop gives you: Even the best images still require some tweaking.

Tip: If you're starting with a very large image, such as a 10-megapixel digital SLR photo, it's faster to resample it using the Image Size dialog rather than the Image Size tab in the Save For Web & Devices dialog.

Tip: Commands controlling the viewing area are also available on a context menu if you right-click or Ctrl-click (Mac) on a view.

compression that might be applied. The file size you see in the Save for Web & Devices dialog is more accurate, but it's still not perfect. The only way to find an image's true (postcompression) file size is to save it to disk and switch out of Photoshop. On Mac OS X, select the file and choose File > Get Info. In Windows, right-click the file and choose Properties. If the file size is displayed as "27 K on disk (22,045 bytes used)," pay attention only to the second number. The first value actually varies depending on the block size of your hard disk formatting. If your disk uses 32 K blocks, a 2 K file will occupy 32 K on disk, and a 33 K file will use 64 K of disk space. The second number shows the actual amount of data someone would have to download to see the image, and it's usually smaller than the disk space number.

The following features are all located in the unlabeled view settings pop-up menu (see **Figure 12-16**). Like the View menu in Photoshop, these settings do not affect the image data. They only affect how you're viewing the image so that you can preview it under different scenarios.

Image Size. Do you need your final Web graphic to be smaller than the high-resolution version you have? Use the Image Size dialog to down-sample the image before using Save For Web & Devices, or use the Image Size tab in the Save For Web & Devices dialog. Both do exactly the same thing, although the Image Size dialog provides more options.

Browser Dither. You don't need to worry about this option (located in the unlabeled pop-out menu at the top right of the Save For Web & Devices dialog viewing area) unless you're preparing images for an audience that has 8 bit/channel displays. It simulates how Web browsers dither on those monitors.

Display profiles. As we pointed out earlier, Mac OS X and Windows display images slightly differently by default. You can preview how the image will look under different viewing conditions by choosing one (such as Standard Windows Color) from the third section of the unlabeled pop-up menu at the top right corner of the viewing area.

Some users mistakenly believe that this menu assigns a profile or converts the image to a profile. Neither is true. The commands on the View Settings pop-up menu only change how you preview the effects of your settings, in the same way as the Proof Setup commands in Photoshop.

Figure 12-16
View Settings pop-up menu

Figure 12-16
View Settings pop-up menu

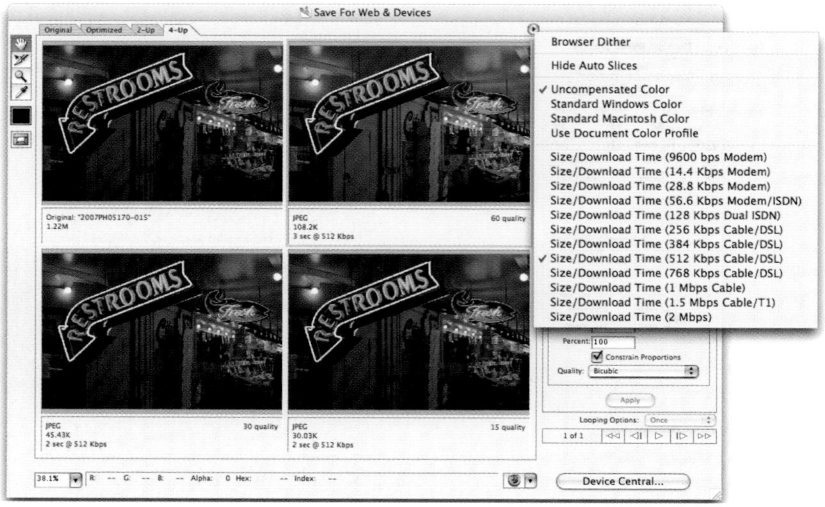

Each view in the Save For Web & Devices dialog can have its own view settings. Simply click to select a view before you open the View Settings pop-up menu.

Tip: You may think that fast broadband Internet speeds mean small file size is not the priority that is used to be. However, remember that the new frontier of the Internet is mobile, handheld devices, where not all networks are fast, and users may be charged per kilobyte. If your Photoshop images will be viewed by this audience, they'll still appreciate small file sizes.

Download time. Each image in the Save for Web & Devices dialog lists the approximate time it would take to download the image. Of course, it's just an estimate, but it can be a useful reality check. To change the setting for any view of the image, click the view and choose a new speed from the bottom half of the menu you get when you click the pop-up menu button at the top right corner of the viewing area.

Other options. We've decided to concentrate on photographic images in this book, so we aren't covering the Color Table option, since it's used for controlling the colors in GIF images, which are not optimal for photographic reproduction. We're also not covering the slicing and HTML export options (since those are mostly geared toward Web designers who for some reason aren't using Adobe Dreamweaver instead) or the looping option and Animation palette for creating animated GIF graphics.

Adobe Device Central

Tip: To see which graphics file formats a mobile device supports, in Device Central select a device on the left side, click the Device Profiles tab, and then click the Bitmap heading.

Cell phones and handheld devices represent millions of multimedia-capable devices with photographic-quality displays, which, of course, become platforms for personal and commercial image content. To preview an image for a mobile device, choose File > Save For Web & Devices (see **Figure 12-17**), set up the conversion specifications you want to test, and then click the Device Central button at the bottom of the Save for Web & Devices dialog. In the Adobe Device Central dialog, click the Emulator tab, and then on the left side of the dialog, double-click the name of device on which you want to preview the image.

Figure 12-17
Previewing a photo in
Adobe Device Central

Zoomify

Tip: The degree of detail at the maximum Zoomify zoom level depends on the size of the image you feed into Zoomify, so if you want to limit the amount of detail, use the Image > Image Size command to downsample your image before you open the Zoomify Export dialog.

New in Photoshop CS3 is the Zoomify feature. It's a way of displaying high-resolution photos online without letting people download the entire image, and without having it take over the entire screen.

The principle is simple. Zoomify creates a Flash-based viewer window at the size of your choice, so you can fit it on your Web page. Inside this window is your image (**Figure 12-18**). To zoom in to see details, click the image; this enlarges the image without making the window bigger. To move around in the zoomed image, just drag the image. You can also navigate using the controls at the bottom of the Zoomify object that ends up on your Web page. It's similar to how Google Maps works. Your audience will need to have Flash installed for their Web browser, but most browsers include it these days.

Figure 12-18
Zoomify on a Web page

Zoomify zoomed all the way out   *Zooming in reveals full-resolution detail*

To create a Zoomify object, start with an 8 bit/channel image, and then choose File > Export > Zoomify to open the Zoomify export dialog (**Figure 12-19**), which contains some straightforward options for file export location, quality, and size of the viewer. Zoomify chops up the image into many small tiles, and uses its Flash application to reassemble them on the fly; the Image Tile Options control how much compression is applied.

After you've specified the options and clicked OK, you need to copy the table code from the HTML document produced by Zoomify, and paste it into the code for your Web page. In the folder Zoomify creates, you can see the image tiles that were generated.

Figure 12-19

Creating a Zoomify object using the settings that created Figure 12-18

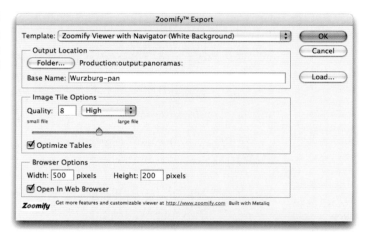

Web Photo Gallery

The Web Photo Gallery, found in the Automate submenu (under the File menu), is like the other automated features: It performs a task that you could do by hand, but it would be so painful and boring that you might fall out of your chair from the sheer monotony of the chore. In a nutshell, the Web Photo Gallery creates a Web page full of image thumbnails (see **Figure 12-20**). If you click on one of the thumbnails, it automatically links to a larger version of the picture. That's about it.

With the increasing popularity of online photo services that provide ready-made galleries with all kinds of features, such as online print ordering and keyword searching, you may prefer not to make your own galleries and simply upload a bunch of photos to a service. The Web Photo Gallery feature is more useful if you want to upload photos to a Web site that you're managing yourself, but all it will do is display the photos.

Figure 12-20

Web Photo Gallery dialog and resulting Web page

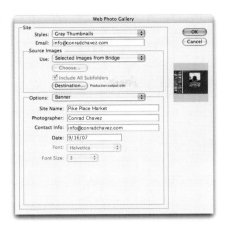

Customize your galleries. You don't like the galleries that Photoshop creates? Not jazzy enough for you? No problem: You can always edit the HTML files in Dreamweaver, GoLive, or some other editor later. However, if you're going to be making a lot of galleries, it would be more efficient to edit the built-in templates instead.

1. Find the Web Photo Gallery folder that contains the templates. It's inside the Presets folder, in the Photoshop application folder.

2. Copy one of the template folders and name the duplicate folder as you would like it to appear in the Web Photo Gallery dialog.

3. Edit the files inside this folder using a text editor. You can edit them to some degree with a Web page editor, but because these files are templates rather than real Web pages, it's safer to make your changes in the actual HTML code. This is because the template works by replacing certain codes with the settings you make in Photoshop. For instance, the %%BGCOLOR%% code in the template automatically gets stripped out and replaced with the background color you chose in the Web Photo Gallery dialog. You want to preserve these codes so that the options in the dialog work. If you always want the same background color, though, you can remove this code from the template and type in your own color.

Now, when you open the Web Photo Gallery dialog, your new template should appear in the Styles pop-up menu. Obviously, making templates requires some knowledge of HTML, but it's surprisingly easy once you get the hang of it.

Tip: Whenever you use an automated Web gallery generator, remember to feed it images that are already sharpened and color-corrected for the Web. For example, if you work in Adobe RGB (1998) or ProPhoto RGB and you forget to convert the images to sRGB color, their colors will look flat on the Web.

File Formats

Photoshop can save or export files to a very long list of formats. In this section, we'll guide you through them and the mind-numbing range of options you will encounter with some formats.

Photoshop

The Photoshop file format—otherwise known as Photoshop native format, or by its filename extension, PSD—used to be the only way to save everything that Photoshop is capable of producing: multiple layers, adjustment and type layers, layer effects, paths, multiple channels, clipping paths, screening and transfer settings, and so on. (Note that Undo states, histories, and snapshots are not saved in any file format.) The PSD file format is less necessary because almost anything you can save in a Photoshop file, you can now also save in either a TIFF or a Photoshop PDF file. It's important to note, however, that other applications may not be able to read those formats properly. For instance, you can now save spot colors in a TIFF file, but no other programs currently handle those spot colors properly.

Saving a composite. By default, Photoshop pretty much insists on saving a flattened composite version of the image in every PSD file because it "maximizes file compatibility." As a result, those of us who have become accustomed to using PSD to save files that consist only of a Background layer and some adjustment layers get a rude shock when we find out how large our Photoshop files are on disk.

You can prevent Photoshop from saving flattened composites in two ways, each tied to the Maximize PSD And PSB File Compatibility pop-up menu in the File Handling panel of the Preferences dialog. By default, this pop-up menu is set to Ask, which means that whenever you try to save a PSD file with layers, you get to choose whether or not you want to "maximize file compatibility." Plus, you get a scary-looking warning (see **Figure 12-21**). The warning is there for two reasons:

▶ Several other applications claim to be able to read Photoshop files, and while a few can actually read layered files, most just read the flattened composite. Adobe Illustrator, Adobe InDesign, and QuarkXPress 6.5 will all attempt to read Photoshop files even if the composite is not

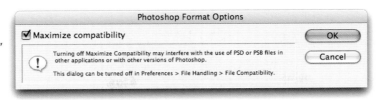

present, so if you're using one of these, you can usually proceed without the composite—if your layered files are relatively straightforward.
However, if your layers use any of the new blending modes such as Pin
Light or Vivid Light, the layers will very likely not be read correctly, so
it's safer to include the composite. Plus, while InDesign and Illustrator
can read 8-bit layered PSD files without a composite, they can't handle
16-bit PSD files without one.

▶ Future versions of Photoshop may change the layer-blending algorithms, which means that when you opened a layered document, it
would look slightly different than it does now. Adobe reasons that with
the flattened composite, you'll still be able to retrieve the correct image
appearance in future versions. Of course, if you someday open the
composite rather than the layered document, you lose all your layers,
so the advantage over saving a flattened copy is questionable.

Our advice? The more you use Photoshop native files in other programs,
including photo organizers such as Lightroom, the more you want this
option to be on, to avoid workflow headaches. If you usually use Photoshop files only within Photoshop, you'll save disk space by turning this
off. The way to stop this dialog from being annoying is to open the File
Handling pane of the Preferences dialog, and choose Always or Never from
the Maximize PSD And PSB File Compatibility pop-up menu, depending
on your workflow. You'll only be nagged if that pop-up menu is set to Ask,
which really means "ask every time."

Duotones. Because TIFF and PDF do almost everything that the native
Photoshop file format does (and often do it better), we almost never use
PSD files anymore. The exception is when using multitone images. Adobe
InDesign CS and later can import PSD files saved in Duotone mode, and
these files are more flexible than PDF, EPS, or DCS files. (See our online
bonus chapter, Chapter 13, "Spot Colors and Duotones," for more on spot
colors and these file formats.)

Photoshop 2.0 format. This is an example of the Photoshop team's philosophy of not removing features. This feature is present only for compatibility reasons. It's available only in Mac OS X.

TIFF

The Tagged Image File Format (TIFF, pronounced just as it reads) is the industry-standard bitmapped file format. Nearly every program that works with pixel-based images can handle TIFF files—either placing, printing, correcting, or editing the pixels. A Photoshop TIFF can be any dimension and resolution (at least we haven't heard of any limits). You can save it in Grayscale, RGB, CMYK, or Lab color mode with 8 or 16 bits per channel, as 8-bit RGB indexed color, or as a (1-bit) black and white bitmap. Before you get totally carried away, though, bear in mind that TIFF files have a permanent, hard-coded file-size limit of 4 GB.

TIFF was once a very straightforward format—the only information it contained beyond the actual pixels themselves was the output size and resolution. But now, Photoshop can save TIFF files that contain just about everything you can put in a native Photoshop file, including vector data, clipping paths, transparency, spot-color channels, annotations, and adjustment layers. The only exception is that you can't save a duotone as a TIFF. But beware: Just because you can save something in a TIFF doesn't mean a program like InDesign or QuarkXPress can open or print it; you'll see examples below.

Spot channels. Even though you can save spot channels in a TIFF, we know of no application other than Photoshop that can print them properly from a TIFF. And even though you can save your vector data (type and layer clipping paths) in a TIFF, it will print as a raster (pixels) image from any application other than Photoshop, not a vector image. So you need to be careful.

Ask Before Saving Layered TIFF Files. When you add layers to a TIFF that started out flat and try to save it, this option forces you to look at the TIFF Options dialog (which we discuss below).

When you save a layered TIFF, Photoshop always includes a flattened composite of the image. As with Photoshop native format, saving layers increases file size significantly. Applications such as QuarkXPress and InDesign import the flattened image, but if you later open the TIFF in Photoshop, it reads the layers.

When you save a TIFF, Photoshop lets you choose from among various options in the TIFF Options dialog (see **Figure 12-22**).

Figure 12-22

Saving TIFF files

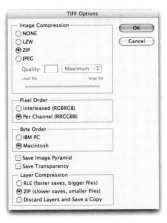

Compression. Photoshop lets you save the composite (flattened) information in TIFF files with LZW or ZIP (lossless), or JPEG (lossy) compression. LZW may still give a few antediluvian applications some problems, but is generally well-supported. However, LZW doesn't work well on high-bit files—it actually makes them bigger rather than smaller. The only program (besides Photoshop) we know of that can read TIFF files with ZIP or JPEG compression is Adobe InDesign.

If you save your TIFF with ZIP or JPEG compression, you do get a warning that these compression options "are not supported in older TIFF readers"—which really means that they're not supported by any application *except* InDesign, Photoshop, and recent versions of other Adobe programs such as Acrobat. We hope support widens, because ZIP compression is lossless and highly efficient. With layered TIFFs, you have the option of applying ZIP compression only to the layers while leaving the flattened composite uncompressed. We use this option a lot, because compressing the layers makes for a much smaller file, and the uncompressed flattened composite is still readable by other applications.

LZW compression is relatively inefficient—and useless on high-bit files—so we generally avoid it (David still uses LZW compression on screen shots, but when pressed, will admit he does so largely out of habit). We use ZIP compression on flattened images destined for InDesign: If we don't know the final destination, we leave our flattened TIFFs uncompressed.

Pixel Order. Photoshop CS2 introduced a new TIFF option—Pixel Order—which lets you choose between Interleaved (known in Neolithic times as "chunky") or Per Channel (also known as "planar"). The difference has to do with how each channel of an image is saved: Interleaved saves a pixel's red channel value, then its green channel value, and then its blue channel value—repeating this cycle for each pixel in the image. That's how every version of Photoshop before CS2 saved TIFFs. Per Channel saves the entire red channel, followed by the green channel, and finally the blue channel.

Most older programs simply can't read Per Channel TIFFs, so we typically just stick with Interleaved. But if you're trying to make your file as small as possible, Per Channel pixel order with ZIP compression produces the smallest file on high-bit images, and Interleaved pixel order with ZIP compression does the same on 8-bit ones.

Byte Order. For some reason, Mac OS X and Windows have different versions of TIFF. It has something to do with the file's byte order and the processing methods of Motorola versus Intel CPUs. These days, no matter what brand of CPU you have in your computer, most programs understand how to read either order: If you find one that isn't, that program is either old or poorly written.

Image Pyramid. This option is completely irrelevant for prepress work and was designed looking forward to a time when TIFFs might be used on the Web. The Image Pyramid is basically the contents of the Image Cache, covered in Chapter 6, "Essential Photoshop Tips and Tricks." Since the necessary browser support essentially never materialized, we don't see any reason to turn on the check box.

Transparency. When your image has transparency (the file is not flattened and has no Background layer), you can save the image transparency in the TIFF file by turning on the Save Transparency check box. Programs that understand transparency (such as InDesign), can read the transparency in these TIFF files. Older programs import the file as though it had been flattened.

Layer Compression. Photoshop also always compresses the layers in a layered TIFF files using either RLE or ZIP. If we're saving layered TIFFs for placement in a page-layout application, we almost always leave the composite data uncompressed, but we choose ZIP compression on the layers (as we noted earlier). ZIP takes a bit longer to save, but it's a much more efficient compression algorithm than RLE, so it results in significantly smaller files.

Tip: You can save even more space by applying ZIP compression to both the layers and the background of a TIFF file, but only a few graphics programs, such as Photoshop and InDesign, will be able to read a TIFF file saved that way.

Compatibility. TIFF is, in many ways, the ideal bitmapped file format, but it has become increasingly flexible over the years, and that flexibility comes at the price of compatibility. Photoshop can easily save TIFFs that are either unreadable by other applications or may not print as expected from other applications. Photoshop can read anything it can save in a TIFF, so TIFF is great as a work file format for Photoshop. But as we've shown, other applications may not know what to do with all the features Photoshop can save in a TIFF image. What to do? We offer this rule of thumb: Assume that anything using or opening a Photoshop TIFF will read the flattened composite and ignore everything else, and assume that the only widely supported compression option for the flattened composite is LZW.

Encapsulated PostScript (EPS)

As we said back in Chapter 2, "Image Essentials," Encapsulated PostScript (EPS) is really an object-oriented file format, but Photoshop can save pixel-based and vector (like text) image data in the EPS format. There are two things you should remember about EPS:

▶ The primary use of EPS files is in page-layout software for printed output. They aren't really useful for Web, video, or other types of output.

▶ EPS is a twentieth-century file format that's being replaced by PDF. Old, second-millennium software like Adobe PageMaker or QuarkXPress 4 handles EPS files better than PDF files, but for modern software (like InDesign CS3), PDF is the vector file format of choice, and is even the native file format of Illustrator.

When you save an image as EPS, Photoshop lets you set the file's preview style and encoding, and it gives you a choice as to whether you want to include halftone screening, transfer curves, PostScript Color Management, and vector data (see **Figure 12-23**). Let's look at each of these.

Preview. EPS files typically have two parts: the high-resolution PostScript data and a low-resolution screen preview. When you import an EPS file into a page-layout program (or a word processor or whatever), the computer usually displays the low-res image on the screen, and when you print

Figure 12-23

EPS file options

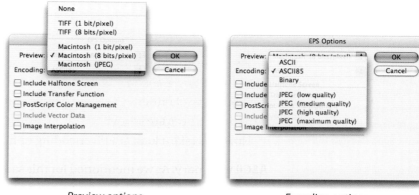

Preview options   Encoding options

the page to a PostScript printer, the computer usually uses the high-res PostScript code. (However, some more-intelligent programs like InDesign can actually read and display the complete contents of an EPS file, because they can render PostScript to the screen.)

On the Mac, Photoshop lets you save EPS files with five preview options. As we mentioned earlier, don't bother with the Thumbnail and Full Size preview options in the Save As dialog, because the EPS preview options do the same thing while giving you more control.

▶ **TIFF.** In Windows, Photoshop only offers 1-bit or 8-bit pixel TIFF from the Preview pop-up menu; we always choose 8-bit. On the Mac, the only time you should select one of these is when your image needs to be imported into a page-layout program on a PC. If you choose one of the PICT formats, the preview is lost when the file is moved to the PC (an EPS without a preview just looks like a gray box on pages, though it prints correctly). Some programs on the Mac, such as InDesign and XPress, can import PC EPS files with the preview image intact; but no programs that we know of on the PC can read Mac PICT previews. (However, InDesign on either platform can generate a preview on the fly for an EPS file that has lost its preview.)

▶ **PICT.** Files that will stay on the Mac should be saved with a PICT preview. Photoshop gives you three choices: 1-bit, 8-bit, and JPEG. When you save an EPS file with a Macintosh JPEG preview, Photoshop has to take the time to build a JPEG preview. However, we gladly take the minor performance hit to get the benefits. JPEG previews are better looking, and take up less space on disk, than their 8-bit brethren. (A JPEG preview for a 300-dpi tabloid-size image is only about 90 K.)

If you're concerned about disk space, you may choose to have no preview (None) or a black-and-white preview (1-bit, either TIFF or PICT). Personally, we'd rather suffer thumbscrews than use either of these when hard drive prices are so low.

Now let's take a look at EPS encoding options.

ASCII vs. Binary. As we mentioned for this same option in the Print dialog, Binary is faster, and ASCII is more compatible; use ASCII only if you're having problems with Binary.

JPEG compression. Instead of saving the EPS file with binary or ASCII encoding, you can choose some level of JPEG compression.

> **Note:** Sorry, there's no way to save an EPS file with lossless compression from Photoshop, even though PostScript Level 2 and 3 interpreters can decompress several lossless compression methods.

There are two downsides to creating JPEG EPS files, though. The first is that you can *only* print them on a printer that has PostScript Level 2 or PostScript 3. Other types of printers may not be able to decompress JPEG images that exist inside an EPS file.

The second problem with JPEG EPS files is a show-stopper: They may not separate properly when printed from QuarkXPress. If you run into this, what you'll find is that the entire image comes out on the black plate. If for some reason you must use JPEG in this way, save the image as a JPEG-compressed DCS file instead.

Halftone screens and transfer functions. If you want to save halftone-screening or transfer-curve information in the image, you must save it as an EPS file. You can set the halftone screens and transfer functions in the Print dialog. Then, when saving the EPS, turn on the Include Halftone Screen check box.

Saving halftone screens in an EPS file is useful whenever you want to set specific screen frequencies and angles for an image and preserve them, such as when saving duotone, tritone, or quadtone images. Note that you can't use InDesign or XPress to override EPS halftone settings.

PostScript Color Management. It's unlikely that you'll turn this on. It includes an ICC profile in the EPS file. If you've got a PostScript output device that knows about profiles, it can handle it, but otherwise the profile will be ignored. If you really need color management, we suggest using TIFF, PSD, JPEG, or PDF instead.

Include Vector Data. If your image includes vector data—vector text or vector clipping paths that haven't been rasterized into pixels—then you must turn on the Include Vector Data check box. If you turn it off, all that vector data gets rasterized upon saving.

Note that this is a one-way street: Photoshop can export EPS files with vector data, but it cannot retain vectors when importing EPS files—it'll rasterize them. Just another reason to use PDF instead of this ol' format when possible.

Image Interpolation. As we noted for this feature in the Print dialog, this feature is of limited use and you probably won't be turning it on.

DCS

DCS (Desktop Color Separation) is a special form of the EPS file format. However, it's weird (and important) enough that Adobe added it as two separate file formats in the Save As dialog: Photoshop DCS 1.0 and Photoshop DCS 2.0.

Originally, DCS was designed to separate the high-resolution image data from a low-resolution "preview" version. The DCS 1.0 format always results in five files: four with high-resolution data for each color plate (cyan, magenta, yellow, and black), and one—called the *master file*—is what you import into a page-layout program. The master file contains three things: a low-resolution screen preview of the image, a low-resolution composite CMYK version, and pointers to the other four files.

Tip: If you don't see Photoshop DCS listed in the Format pop-up menu of the Save As dialog, you may need to convert your image to CMYK. DCS isn't available for other color modes.

There are two problems with DCS 1.0. First, some people don't like to keep track of five files for each image (though to be fair, many other people think this is nifty because they can leave the high-resolution data on a server and just use the master file on their own systems). Second, there is no way to include spot colors.

Ultimately, we know of no good reason to use DCS 1.0, so we'll focus on version 2.0, which does everything that 1.0 does, and more.

Of the various options in the DCS 2.0 Format dialog (see **Figure 12-24**), most of them are equivalent to the ones in the EPS Options dialog (which we discussed in the last section). For instance, Preview lets you determine the quality and kind of RGB screen preview; Encoding determines the format of the data within the file; and so on. In the DCS pop-up menu, you can choose whether you want one single file or multiple files on disk, and what sort of composite image you want.

Figure 12-24
Saving Desktop Color
Separation (DCS) files

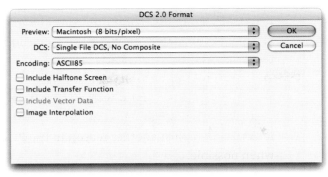

DCS composites. Many people confuse a DCS composite image with the preview image. This is understandable, because they're nearly identical. Both are low-resolution (72 ppi) representations of the original image; and both can be used instead of the high-res image for proofing.

The real difference is in their uses. The preview image is always in RGB mode and is designed for screen use only. The composite image is saved in CMYK mode (it's the same as downsampling the high-res CMYK image to 72 ppi using Nearest Neighbor interpolation), and is meant for sending to a low-resolution color printer for use as a comp or a proof.

For color-proofing devices that require color separations, you can force XPress to send the high-resolution data with a third-party XTension. Adobe InDesign CS2 and later can do this automatically. Honestly, though, we tend to think it's better to proof images before you save them as DCS files; once they're encapsulated like this, it's hard to get any really accurate proofs from them.

Multifile or single file. Whether you tell Photoshop to write a single file or multiple files is up to you and your workflow. Probably the best reason to use multiple files is if you need or want to keep your high-resolution data in a separate place (like on a server or at your imaging bureau). This is especially helpful with very large files.

On the other hand, keeping track of so many files can be a pain, and the links to the high-res images can be broken if you rename or move those files. Fixing broken pointers is often easy: Just open the master file in a text editor and edit the filenames in the lines that begin with "%%PlateFile".

However, don't fear if you lose the master file entirely; you can always reassemble the separate DCS files in Photoshop, like so:

Tip: If your DCS file includes spot colors, your page-layout software must also have colors named exactly the same way (yes, InDesign, and XPress import these names automatically when you import a DCS 2.0 file).

1. Open each of the high-res images in Photoshop. They're all EPS files, and they're all in Grayscale mode. Of course, opening these files will rasterize any vector data. Make sure that each file is flattened.

2. When all four of the files are open, select Merge Channels from the Channels palette's pop-out menu.

3. Make sure the mode is set to CMYK and the Channels field is set to 4 (see **Figure 12-25**); click OK.

Figure 12-25

Merging channels
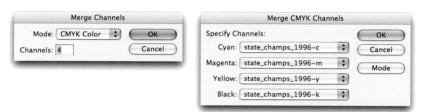

4. Photoshop is pretty good at guessing which file should be set to which color channel in the Merge CMYK Channels dialog, but if it guesses wrong, set the pop-up menus to the proper files.

When you click OK, Photoshop merges the four grayscale files into a single, high-resolution CMYK file. You can now create the five DCS files again, if you want. (Note that if you have spot colors in your DCS files, you'll have to add the additional channels manually, after you merge the CMYK channels.)

PDF (Portable Document Format)

We like to use PDF whenever an image contains a significant amount of vector data (like text) that we want to maintain as sharp-edged vectors in the final output. While text is rasterized in TIFFs (making the edges pixelated) and converted to outlines in EPS files (making them slow to print if there's a lot of text), PDF files handle text beautifully. Best of all, you can embed a font into your PDF file, so it will display and print correctly wherever it goes.

PDF is also an excellent format for sending proofs or samples to clients. Not only can you include password protection, but you can create multipage (multi-image) documents very easily by choosing File > Automate > PDF Presentation.

Round-tripping. When you save an image in the Photoshop PDF format, you're offered a whole mess o' options (see **Figure 12-26**). Some of these options actually override the options you chose in the Save As dialog. For example, the Layers check box in the Save As dialog normally determines whether Photoshop will place the layered data in the PDF file, too. However, Photoshop actually ignores that check box and instead pays attention to the Preserve Photoshop Editing Capabilities check box (in the Save Adobe PDF dialog). When you turn on Preserve Photoshop Editing Capabilities, you can keep all of the Photoshop features you used. If you turn off this option and reopen the file in Photoshop, it rasterizes the whole thing, even if you had saved your vector data.

Figure 12-26

Saving a PDF file

In this example, a Photoshop document is an ad being sent to a newspaper that requires ads to conform to the PDF/X-1a standard. Because the Preserve Photoshop Editing Capabilities check box is not part of the PDF/X-1a specification, it's disabled. The ad designer would retain a complete layered copy of the ad in Photoshop format.

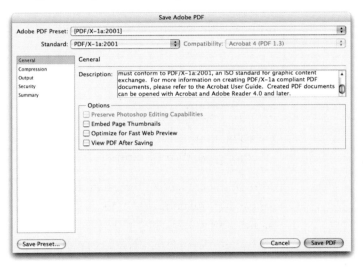

Tip: If you're sending PDF files to a standardized workflow, you may simply need to choose one of the Adobe PDF Presets at the top of the Save Adobe PDF dialog. The company receiving your PDF files may also provide PDF presets for you to install. If either is true, just choose the right preset instead of editing all the settings.

PDF Options. The other options in the Save Adobe PDF dialog are virtually identical to the PDF options from Acrobat Distiller or Adobe InDesign or any of the other Creative Suite applications. This includes the Adobe PDF Preset pop-up menu at the top of the dialog, which lets you choose a preset even if it was created in one of the other Creative Suite applications.

Most important, the options you choose may degrade the image in the PDF, but as long as the Preserve Photoshop Editing Capabilities check box is turned on, these options won't affect the behind-the-scenes PSD data that Photoshop saves with the PDF. For example, if you choose a low-resolution, low-quality JPEG compression in the PDF, the PDF image degrades, but the layered data does not. So when you open it in Photoshop and resave as PDF, you don't recompress (and further degrade) your data.

CompuServe GIF

The Graphics Interchange Format (commonly known as GIF), was once the "house-brand" image file format of the CompuServe online information service. That's why this file format is listed as "CompuServe GIF" in the Save As dialog, even though GIF images have long since broken free of CompuServe's corporate walls and are now a Web standard.

GIF files are designed for onscreen viewing, especially for images where file size is more important than quality, and for screens that only display 8-bit color (256 colors). Photoshop GIF files are always 8-bit indexed color images, making them acceptable for onscreen viewing, but totally unreasonable for printing. GIFs are automatically compressed using lossless LZW compression (see "Compressing Images," later in this chapter). But we never save a GIF file with the Save As dialog; rather, we use the Save For Web & Devices dialog.

JPEG

Tip: JPEG is best used as an output format only. Avoid repeatedly editing and saving a JPEG file, or quality will degrade.

Earlier in this chapter we talked about JPEG as a compression method within another file format—like JPEG DCS—but these days, when most people say "JPEG," they're referring to the JPEG file format itself. Most JPEG images are found on the Web or coming out of digital cameras. The only problem with using the JPEG format for printing is that it's lossy (see "Compressing Images," later in this chapter). We recommend only using JPEG files in a prepress workflow if it's essential that you drastically limit your file sizes.

Tip: If JPEG is not available in the Format pop-up menu in the Save As dialog, make sure your image is in 8-bits-channel mode.

You might have noticed that you can save JPEG files in both the Save As dialog and in the Save For Web & Devices dialog. What's the difference? In the Save For Web & Devices dialog, it's assumed that you want the smallest file possible, so there are no options for features such as embedded previews, and by default, metadata isn't included. If you want to include full metadata and more features, create JPEGs using Save As. If you want smaller files, create JPEGs using Save For Web & Devices.

By the way, don't confuse JPEG with JPEG 2000, which is a newer, more capable format that unfortunately has not caught on. If you do want to use JPEG 2000, no problem—it's one of the extra plug-ins available on your Photoshop installation CD (see "Uninstalled File Format Plug-ins," later in this chapter).

PNG

For a while, it looked like GIF would take over the Internet. Then, in early 1995, CompuServe and Unisys shocked the world by demanding that developers whose software wrote or read GIF files pay a royalty fee for the right to use GIF. Legally, they were entitled; but no one had to pay before, and it jarred the electronic publishing community enough that a group of dedicated individuals came up with a new Web graphics file format.

The result of their work is the PNG format (pronounced "ping"). It officially stands for Portable Network Graphic, though it unofficially stands for "PNG's Not GIF". Not only is it a free format that any developer can use, but it does much more than GIF does.

For instance, PNG can support both 8-bit indexed color and full 24-bit color. Where GIF can include 1-bit transparency (where each pixel is either transparent or not), PNG has full 8-bit transparency with alpha channels, so a graphic could be partially opaque in some areas. PNG also includes some limited ability to handle color management on the Internet by recording monitor gamma and chromaticity. There are many other features, too (among which is the significant bonus of having a relatively unambiguous pronunciation).

Unfortunately, PNG has never been widely accepted by users or Web browsers, and the patents on GIF (which were based on GIF's LZW compression scheme) expired back in 2004. Our prediction is that PNG will slowly fade away over the next couple of years.

Photoshop Raw

The Photoshop Raw option is a way to read or write image data that doesn't appear to be in a Photoshop-supported format. Sometimes these files are simply images that are missing file information that identifies them as images. Don't confuse this with the Camera Raw format, which Photoshop can read but not write (see Chapter 5, "Building a Digital Workflow," for more on Camera Raw.) If you're trying to import from or export to some strange computer system, you may have to rely on Photoshop Raw because that system might not know from TIFF, EPS, or any other normal, everyday file format. This is becoming less of a problem as most mainframe systems (especially the imaging systems that are used for scientific or medical imaging) learn to read the newer, better file formats we've been discussing until now.

The Photoshop Raw option relies on the basics of bitmapped images (see **Figure 12-27**):

▶ All bitmapped images are rectangular grids of pixels.

▶ Some bitmapped images have header information at the beginning of the data.

▶ Color data is usually either interleaved (such as alternating red, green, blue, red, green, blue, and so on) or noninterleaved (such as all the red information, then all the green, and finally all the blue).

Note that Photoshop can only read data using the Raw data format if it's saved as binary data; hexadecimal is out.

Figure 12-27
Opening Raw data

Make Photoshop guess for Raw data. Okay, someone gives you a file and you find you can't open it using any of the Photoshop standard file format options. You decide to take a leap and attempt the Raw format. But when you ask your so-called friend about the file's vital signs—"What are the pixel dimensions? Interleaved or noninterleaved color? Is there a header?"—he just stares at you blankly.

Fortunately, Photoshop can do a little guessing for you. If you click the Guess button in the Open as Raw dialog when the Width and Height fields are blank, Photoshop figures out a likely height/width combination for the image. If it's a color image, you need to know if it's RGB (three channels) or CMYK (four channels).

If there's a header and your friend doesn't know how big it is (in bytes), then it's probably a lost cause. On the other hand, if your friend knows the pixel dimensions but not the header, you can click the Guess button while the Header field is blank.

WBMP

Photoshop pictures go everywhere these days, as big as billboards and as small as little icons on cell phone screens. If you're trying to make pictures for cell phones and wireless PDAs, we've got just the file format for you: WBMP (Wireless Bitmap). You can save files that are already in Bitmap mode as WBMP format from the Save As dialog, or any file as WBMP from the Save for Web & Devices dialog.

BMP

Tip: Some older Mac plug-ins, such as the PhotoCD plug-in, don't work on Intel Macs. To run them, you must switch Photoshop to Rosetta mode. Quit Photoshop, and then in the Finder, select the Photoshop application icon and choose File > Get Info. Turn on the Open in Rosetta check box, and start Photoshop. This will run Photoshop more slowly, because it won't be running natively on Intel CPUs as long as Open in Rosetta is on. We recommend that you convert PhotoCD images to a format like TIFF, because Kodak no longer updates PhotoCD software.

Windows Bitmap (BMP, pronounced by saying the letters) is the bitmap format native to Windows Paint. It's rarely encountered outside of Windows and OS/2 Presentation Manager, and is hardly a professional's file format. You can store a 1-, 4-, 8-, or 24-bit image of various dimensions and resolutions, but we still prefer TIFF, given its strong support by desktop-publishing applications and compatibility across different computer systems. If you're creating wallpaper for your Windows desktop, this is the format for you!

Uninstalled File Format Plug-Ins

As we noted back in the Preface, this book only covers a fraction of the potential uses of Photoshop—those centered around print production. People use this program for so many different things that we couldn't hope to cover them all here. In the last two sections, we discussed each of the file formats that are relevant for professionals who are putting images on paper, film, or the Web. You, however, might be doing something interesting, different, or just plain odd. Don't worry; Photoshop can probably still accommodate you. While we won't cover all of the more obscure or just plain obsolete formats in the Save As or Export commands, we'll tell you where they are in case you need them.

On your Photoshop or Creative Suite install disk, look in the folder Goodies\Optional Plug-ins\File Formats. In there, you'll find file format plug-ins such as Alias, ElectricImage, and even good old MacPaint. To install them, open up your Photoshop application folder (the one that's already installed on your computer), go to Plug-ins/File Formats, and drop the plug-ins in the File Formats folder.

The reason the plug-ins aren't installed is because they're provided as a convenience, but they didn't go through the same rigorous testing as the components that were installed. They're the same as what shipped before.

Compressing Images

Bitmapped images are pigs when it comes to hard disk space. In this day and age, when you can buy a 500 GB hard disk as cheaply as a pair of shoes, saving space on disk isn't nearly as important an issue as trying to transfer that data. Whether you have a modestly fast connection to the Web on your handheld device or a T1 line in your office, moving massive files around is somewhat painful.

Our aim, then, is to stretch out the scarce resources we have on hand, and keep files that we need to move around reasonably small. And we've got three methods to accomplish this goal: work with smaller images (no, seriously!), archive our images when we're not using them, and work with compressed file formats.

Lossless Compression

Let's take the example of a 1-bit (black-and-white) bitmap, 100 pixels wide and tall. Without any compression, the computer stores the value (zero or one) for each one of the 10,000 pixels in the image. This is like staring into your sock drawer and saying, "I've got one blue sock and one blue sock and one black sock and one black sock," and so on. We can compress our description in half by saying, "I've got one blue pair and one black pair."

Run Length Encoding. Similarly, we can group the zeros and ones together by counting up common values in a row (see **Figure 12-28**). For instance, we could say, "There are 34 zeros, then 3 ones, then 55 zeros," and so on. This is called Run Length Encoding (RLE), and it's used by fax machines. We call it "lossless" because there is no loss of data when you compress or decompress the file—what goes in comes out exactly the same.

Figure 12-28

Run Length Encoding
lossless compression

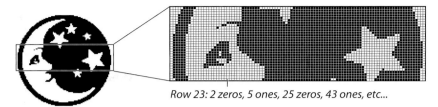

Row 23: 2 zeros, 5 ones, 25 zeros, 43 ones, etc...

LZW, Huffman, and Zip. There are other forms of lossless compression. For instance, RLE compresses simple images (ones that have large solid-colored areas) down to almost nothing, but it can't compress more complex images (like most grayscale images) very much. LZW (Lempel-Ziv-Welch, though you really don't need to know that) and Huffman encoding work by tokenizing common strings of data.

In plain English, that means that instead of just looking for a string of the same color, these methods look for trends. If RLE sees "010101," it can't do any compression. But LZW and Huffman are smart enough algorithms to spot the pattern of alternating characters, and thereby compress that information. Zip is a considerably smarter version of LZW (smarter means it compresses better, but it may take slightly longer to do so).

Lossy Compression

The table of contents at the front of most books is a way of compressing information. If you ripped the table of contents out of this book and mailed it to someone else, they would be able to "unpack" it and read what's in this book. But they wouldn't actually be seeing the words you're reading now. Instead, they'd read an "average" of each chapter. The more detailed chapters have more headings, so your friend would see more detail in them than he or she would in a simple-headed chapter like this one.

Bitmapped images can be similarly outlined (compressed), transmitted to someone else, and unpacked. And similarly, when you look at the unpacked version, you don't get all the detail from the original image. For example, if 9 pixels in a 3-by-3 square are similar, you could replace them all with a single averaged value. That's a nine-to-one compression. But the original data, the variances in those 9 pixels, is lost forever.

This sort of compression is called "lossy" compression because you lose data when compressing it. By losing some information, you can increase the compression immensely. Where a ZIP-compressed TIFF might be 40 percent of the original size, a lossy-compressed file can be 2 percent or less of the original file size.

Levels of JPEG compression. Lossy compression schemes typically give you a choice of how tight you pack the data. With low compression, you get larger files and higher quality. High compression yields lower quality and smaller files. How much quality do you lose? It depends on the level of the compression, the resolution of the image, and the content of the image.

The primary method is JPEG. Different programs implement JPEG differently, and with varying results. Note that JPEG is both a compression method and a file format in its own right, which is why a PDF can contain a JPEG-compressed image.

JPEG warnings. Images with hard edges, high contrast, and angular areas are most susceptible to artifacts from JPEG compression. Similarly, text (rasterized, not vector) almost always looks terrible after JPEG compression because it has such hard edges. On the other hand, compressing natural, scanned images using JPEG—especially those that are already somewhat grainy or impressionistic—probably won't hurt them much at all, especially if you use the Maximum or High quality setting.

You should only use JPEG for final output, after you've finished all editing and correction. Tone or color correction on a JPEG image exaggerates the compression artifacts, and so does sharpening.

To Compress or Not to Compress

Over the years, we've found only a few universal truths. One of those is: "Fast, Cheap, or Good; you can have any two of the three." Compression is certainly no exception. Compressing files can be a great way to save hard drive space (read: "save money") and sometimes to cut down on printing times (read: "save more money"). But compressing and decompressing files also takes time (read: "lose the money that you just saved").

Complicating this is that the more disks you have, the more time you have to spend managing them. In the end, you need to decide whether you'll get more value out of the space you saved by compressing files and not having to buy and manage more disks, or from the time you'd save from not spending so much waiting for the CPU to finish compressing or decompressing the hundreds of images you edit. It kind of comes down to whether you have more money or time.

Index